C0-AYI-493

# RE ORIENT

## Change in Asian Societies

AAT VERVOORN

Second Edition

OXFORD
UNIVERSITY PRESS

OXFORD
UNIVERSITY PRESS

253 Normanby Road, South Melbourne, Victoria 3205, Australia

Oxford University Press is a department of the University of Oxford. It furthers the University's objective of excellence in research, scholarship, and education by publishing worldwide in

Oxford New York

Auckland Bangkok Buenos Aires Cape Town Chennai Dar es Salaam Delhi Hong Kong Istanbul Karachi Kolkata Kuala Lumpur Madrid Melbourne Mexico City Mumbai Nairobi São Paulo Shanghai Taipei Tokyo Toronto



First published 1998
Second edition published 2002
Reprinted 2004



National Library of Australia
Cataloguing-in-Publication data:

Vervoorn, Aat, 1945–.
Re Orient: change in Asian Societies.

New ed.
Bibliography.
Includes index.
ISBN 0 19 551333 9.

1. Asia—Economic conditions. 2. Asia—Social conditions. 3. Asia, Southeastern—Economic conditions. 4. Asia, Southeastern—Social conditions. 5. East Asia—Economic conditions. I. Title.

306.095

Typeset by Cannon Typesetting
Printed through Bookpac Production Services, Singapore

# CONTENTS


| | | |
|---|---|---|
| | List of Tables | iv |
| | Acknowledgments | v |
| | Introduction | 1 |
| **1** | Globalisation and Insulation in Asia | 17 |
| **2** | State, Society, Individual | 37 |
| **3** | Human Rights | 64 |
| **4** | Ethnic Minorities | 82 |
| **5** | Economic and Social Development | 111 |
| **6** | Patterns of Population Change | 146 |
| **7** | Environmental Impact | 173 |
| **8** | Family Matters | 203 |
| **9** | The World of Work | 226 |
| **10** | Media, Communication, Censorship | 255 |
| **11** | Using and Creating Knowledge | 276 |
| | Conclusion | 299 |
| | Notes | 302 |
| | Bibliography | 331 |
| | Index | 357 |

# LIST OF TABLES


3.1 Asian countries party to selected international human rights conventions 69

4.1 Ethnic minorities in selected Asian countries 86

4.2 Populations of China's nationalities 102

5.1 External debt of selected Asian countries 115

5.2 Human Development Index 2001 123

5.3 Improvement in human development, selected Asian countries 125

5.4 Average wage for women working in non-agricultural sectors as a percentage of that for men 130

6.1 Population of selected Asian countries 147

7.1 Air pollution in Asian Cities 187

7.2 Rate of deforestation in Asian countries 189

9.1 Labour force, by gender and sector 232

9.2 Government expenditure on education 237

9.3 Population and projected growth rates of cities with 10 million inhabitants 241

9.4 Estimated number of migrant workers in selected Asian countries 245

9.5 Migrant worker remittances in relation to GDP and value of merchandise exports 247

9.6 Child workers in Asian countries 251

11.1 Educational participation by women 291

# ACKNOWLEDGMENTS

Writing a book that endeavours to describe and analyse the major changes taking place in contemporary Asian societies is an ambitious undertaking. Revising one in the attempt to keep pace with those changes is apt to seem quixotic: it is impossible to write fast enough to keep up. Two things have given me courage to complete the task. One was the very favourable reaction of readers to the first edition. The other was the realisation that, despite the complexity and often breathtaking speed with which events unfolded, they tended to confirm rather than call into question the interpretive framework I had established. Although effort was required to update the historical record, there was no need to rebuild the intellectual scaffolding.

The issues with which the study deals have been the focus of my teaching and research at the Australian National University over the last decade. Inevitably, it draws heavily on my own experience of, and reading about, contemporary Asian societies. But I also owe much to my students. One of the best aspects of university teaching is that it continually brings one into the company of so many enthusiastic, intelligent, idealistic, and good-humoured people, who offer so much in return for what they receive. I thank them for the insights and experiences they have shared.

To my colleagues, past and present, of the Faculty of Asian Studies I am also grateful for their support and friendship. On the many occasions when I have turned to them for information and enlightenment regarding aspects of the numerous histories and cultures of Asian societies about which they know so much more than me, I have never been disappointed.

A substantial part of the original manuscript was written while I was on study leave in the Research School of Pacific and Asian Studies of ANU's Institute of Advanced Studies. During work on this new edition no less than on the original, its staff have been unfailingly generous with their help and advice. Keith Mitchell, of the school's cartography section, prepared the excellent maps and diagrams.

For illustrations, I have been fortunate to have been given access to the photographic collections of friends and former students. Jason Brown has allowed me to use his photographs of the former US Embassy in Tehran on p. 34, the sadhu and Hindu temple on p. 50, the parrot seller and sheep sellers on p. 228, and Iranian school children on p. 295. Lishia Corr I thank for permission to use her pictures of the poppy grower on p. 26, minorities of China on pp. 104–5, kindergarten children on p. 170, Mosuo women on p. 220, the wedding couple on p. 224, and peanut sellers on p. 228. To Helen Leake I owe the illustrations of Khmer Rouge regulations on p. 20, minorities of Thailand on pp. 85, 92, and 98–9, and Angkor Wat on p. 188. Shakira Hussein provided the photographs of Afghan refugee children on pp. 23, 252, and 289; Heidi Hutchinson the photographs of sisters on p. 159, the Japanese couple on p. 165, the rickshaw boy on p. 230, and Qingdao on p. 240. To John Powers I owe the picture of the trekking guide on p. 229 and to Ian Wilson that of the street vendor on p. 253.

The Bangladesh government has kindly given permission to reproduce from its publication *Bangladesh: The Green Mosaic* (revised edition, October 1996) the photographs of jute workers, rice planters, and the fish market on pp. 120, 148, and 194. The photographs of the Tokyo scene on p. 240 and Acros Fukuoka are reproduced by permission of the editors of *Pacific Friend*, Tokyo. That of the amusement park on p. 29 is reproduced by permission of the Korean Overseas Information Service. HEK Communications, Seoul, has allowed me to reproduce the picture of shipbuilding on p. 137. I thank Reuters Australia for permission to use the image of the Tian'anmen incident on p. 268 and China Pictorial Publications, Beijing, for use of the picture of the rocket on p. 273. I also thank the *Atjeh Times* for providing the image of exercise of power on p. 67. Unfortunately, its website was subsequently closed and the organisation has been unreachable. All other photographs are by the author.

The cartoon of the pregnant earth on p. 151 featured in the 3 September 1994 issue of *The Economist*, and is reproduced by permission of Chris Riddell.

Every effort has been made to trace the original source of material used in this book. Where the attempt has been unsuccessful, the author and publishers would be pleased to hear from copyright holders to rectify any errors or omissions.

The data used to construct many of the tables was obtained from reports of United Nations Development Program and the World Bank, and is used by permission of Oxford University Press, New York. Table 4.2 is based on data from C. Mackerras, *China's Minorities*, and appears by permission of Oxford University Press, Oxford. Table 9.4 is from P. Athukorala and C. Manning, *Structural Change and International Migration in East Asia*, and is reproduced by permission of Oxford University Press, Melbourne. Table 9.3 appears by permission of the United Nations Population Division, and Table 9.5, from the Asian Development Bank's *Asian Development Outlook 1996 and 1997*, by permission of Oxford University Press, Hong Kong. Table 9.6 has been reproduced by permission of the *Far Eastern Economic Review*.

# Introduction

This book has two aims: to describe the major issues facing societies in Asia around the turn of the twentieth century, and to use contemporary Asian societies as an exercise in thinking about societies in general. The first could be seen as an attempt to answer factual questions such as 'What is happening in Asian countries now?' and 'What do we need to know in order to understand contemporary Asian societies?' The second could be regarded as a philosophical scrutiny of questions such as 'How do societies work?' and 'How can we make sense of the experience of members of contemporary societies in Asia and elsewhere?'

To the extent that there are such things as facts, the first of these tasks is straightforward enough. It involves presenting, in an accessible way, an outline of the major trends and problems being experienced by Asian societies, without oversimplifying the issues or masking the immense variety that exists between and within them. Although the focus is contemporary experience, this does not mean that the time period with which the book is concerned is narrow. Complex social and political issues, and ways to address them, cannot be understood by just examining the present, or even the recent past. A society's history lives on in its cultural patterns and institutions, and continues to shape the lives even of those who try to free themselves of its influence.

It is tempting, especially for Westerners, to assume that contemporary Asian societies can be understood without a knowledge of their social, economic and political traditions. 'Modern' or 'contemporary' Asia, it is sometimes asserted, begins with Western influences anyway, and one needs to know no more about local traditions than that they are an obstacle to progress, that is, to Westernisation. Were this true, it would be gratifying for those Westerners who like to see themselves as the vanguard of civilisation, and make international understanding much easier (we could no longer call it cross-cultural understanding). As we will see in what follows, however, nothing could be further from the truth.

Therefore in this study of contemporary Asia the past is not ignored. Neither is the future. The trends and problems examined are issues that will continue to be of pressing concern in the decades to come. They include globalisation; demographic change and population growth; ethnicity and political self-determination; economic development and inequality; gender relations; and environmental degradation and resource depletion. Even with the best will in the world, unprecedented international cooperation, and a great deal of luck, solutions for the problems these matters generate will come neither easily nor quickly.

Unfortunately 'the facts' on their own tend to be a sparse and uncommunicative lot that tell us very little. They need some sort of interpretive framework if they are to be at all helpful, and this is more important than the facts themselves. Theories, methods of interpretation, strategies for understanding, and philosophical approaches—call them what we will—date as facts do, but if they are worth anything they will show greater resistance to historical wear and tear. One way of describing what follows would be 'contemporary Asian perspectives on how societies work'. The book will have succeeded if, long after particular bits of information about Vietnam or Sri Lanka or wherever have become obsolete or forgotten, readers continue to find its philosophical framework useful.

## The idea of Asia

A claim to be studying or writing about Asia carries with it an obligation to explain what Asia is, or where it begins and ends. Those who feel they know something about Asia tend to take some persuading that the term is helpful, or that using it can be justified. I have some sympathy with this view. The main historical purpose of the name 'Asia' has been to designate the region and civilisations that lie to the east of Europe, as distinct from the civilisation (usually equated with Christianity) to which educated Europeans saw themselves as belonging. It did not necessarily point to any characteristics common to things Asian beyond this quality of difference. To this extent at least I propose to follow precedent: one purpose of this study, it could be said, is to bury the term, or at least the claim that the terms 'Asia' and 'Asian' can designate readily identifiable, coherent categories of characteristics, societies or individuals.

Claims that there are characteristics distinctively Asian are made with varying degrees of sophistication. At one end of the spectrum there is the crude racism reflected in crime reports in Western countries where suspects are described as being of Asian appearance, and Asians are blamed for rising crime rates, as if all the people east of Suez look the same and share a common propensity to break the law.

'Asian' as a term of abuse became well established in the nineteenth century when, in the heady days of imperialism and colonial expansion, Europeans were convinced of their superiority to all things in the Orient. Asia came to be equated with characteristics such as backwardness, laziness, superstition, despotism, and organisational incompetence. In reaction to this, self-appointed spokesmen for Asia began to identify positive qualities that were distinctively Asian. In this light Asians were seen as polite, restrained, spiritual, where Europeans were crude, aggressive, materialistic. In recent years some senior politicians and businessmen from Asian countries have made much of the attachment of Asian people to community and family values, and their respect for authority, discipline and social cohesion. This has been contrasted with Western individualism, selfishness, social disintegration, lawlessness and so on. Explanations of the rapid economic development of countries such as Japan, South Korea, Singapore, and Taiwan, and predictions that East Asia will catch up with and surpass the USA and Europe in economic power and wealth, have often been couched in terms of these different values.

Rather more sophisticated is the account given by Rhoads Murphey at the beginning of his excellent introductory textbook on the region, *A History of Asia.* Murphey restricts his discussion to 'monsoon Asia' (which ranges from Pakistan to Japan) and, in addition to common climatic features, claims to identify common cultural patterns that distinguish the societies of the region from those elsewhere: 'There is a broad range of institutions, ideas, values, conditions, and solutions which have long been distinctively Asian ... different at least in degree from those elsewhere, and evolving in Asia in distinctive ways.'

These include, among many others, the basic importance of the extended family and kin network and its multiple roles; the respect for and importance attached to learning, for its own sake and as the path to worldly success; the veneration of age and its real or fancied wisdom and authority; the traditional subjugation and submissive roles of women, at least in the public sphere (although South-East Asia is a qualified exception); the hierarchical structuring of society; the awareness of and importance attached to the traditional past; the primacy of group welfare over individual interest; and many more distinctively Asian cultural traits common to all parts of monsoon Asia.[1]

The characteristics listed do not seem to me to be particularly Asian at all. Especially if we shift our attention away from the dominant example of China, they do not appear to be more relevant to Asia than to ancient or medieval Europe, or to many of the pre-modern societies in other parts of the world. There are literally hundreds of different cultures in the Asian region, but it is impossible to support the claim that even the half-dozen or so dominant ones share features that distinguish them from those elsewhere. The variability of Asian cultures is a theme that recurs throughout the following chapters.

We have to reject the temptation to identify certain social or cultural characteristics as being specifically Asian. There is no characteristic Asian mentality, no specifically Asian form of despotism, no Asian mode of production or of development. There are no specifically Asian values. When I use the term 'Asia' I am simply referring to a geo-cultural region, that is, a loosely delineated part of the world's surface containing a number of different countries and cultures. 'Asia' is just a shorthand way of saying 'Afghanistan, Bangladesh, Cambodia, China' and so on. Being in geographic proximity to each other, some of these countries inevitably share elements of historical experience, and also exhibit a certain degree of cultural interpenetration. The extent to which they are alike should not be exaggerated, but neither can their interaction through the centuries be ignored. While much of the discussion of contemporary experience that follows is in terms of globalisation and unprecedented levels of international interaction, it does not involve a claim that such interaction is new. Cross-cultural influences have always been strong in the Asian region, spurred by trade, religious proselytising, and political conquest.[2] Yet this most certainly has not resulted in cultural homogenisation of all the societies within it.

Even in geographic terms, defining Asia as an entity has its problems. The term conventionally refers to the Eurasian landmass east of the Ural Mountains and the Mediterranean Sea, together with the large clusters of islands to the east of it: Japan, the Philippines and Indonesia. The island of New Guinea, due to accidents of colonial history, lies half in and half out of Asia. It appears that the western half, Irian Jaya or West Papua, is part of Indonesia, despite the fact that culturally it belongs with the other half of the island, the nation state of Papua New Guinea, which fits more comfortably with that part of the Pacific known as Melanesia than with Asia. Australia has not generally been regarded as part of Asia, though it may make sense for Australians to debate whether or not they should see themselves that way, either because of growing cultural and economic links with Asian countries or because of the changing ethnic composition of its population.

At the other end of Asia, the situation of Turkey is rather similar. Few would dispute that ethnically, politically, and economically the region now known as Turkey has had stronger links with Asia than with Europe, ancient Greek colonisation of coastal regions and Christian influences in the Byzantine period notwithstanding. Economically, however, Turkey is now integrated with Europe and is eager to join the European Union, that is, to formally become part of Europe.

Because Asia is a vast territory, culturally as well as geographically, it is impossible in the space of one book to discuss adequately all the countries it covers, let alone all the different ethnic or cultural groups to be found there. I do not pretend to present an adequate treatment of every Asian country, or to pay equal attention to the ones I do discuss. Much of the time, like Rhoads Murphey, I concentrate on monsoon Asia, from Pakistan to Japan. However, countries of West and Central Asia—especially Iran—are discussed at various points. My main concern has been to focus on countries that illustrate, in a vivid and informative way, the themes about which I write. The amount of space countries get is roughly proportional to their population. I did not plan it that way, but it does not seem inappropriate.

If terms like 'Asia' and 'Europe' are to some extent imprecise, it is partly due to the fact that their meaning continues to evolve. Many observers argue, for example, that a common identity is emerging in East and South-East Asia as a result of the rapid changes being experienced by most of the countries in the region, including unprecedented rates of industrialisation and economic growth, demographic transition, multilateral treaties and regional cooperation, and a shared resistance to Western dominance. Europe as an entity is gaining new meaning as a result of the integration processes at work there, and indeed the opposition to those processes.[3] It could be argued that the imprecision of labels like 'Asia' and 'Europe' is sometimes a virtue. Social, cultural and political change is ongoing; boundaries continue to shift. Some boundaries are political, some are cultural, and often political and cultural boundaries do not coincide. The term 'Asia' is useful in part because it refers to a large, rather amorphous entity, the constituent parts of which are hard to pin down but continue to influence each other. Its imprecision may help us to widen our focus, to think in terms of an ill-defined domain in which various peoples have been continuously on the move, competing for space, fighting, sharing inventions, trading, intermarrying, and adapting to changing circumstances and needs.

What is unique about the Asian region is the large number of societies there with a long history of high cultural achievement, or that are (to use another value-laden phrase) centres of civilisation. What this means is that they are large-scale, highly differentiated societies that over many centuries have had what are commonly regarded as advanced cultures with sophisticated traditions of statecraft, intellectual and artistic achievement, and technological and material development. Above all, they have been literate. It is their history of advanced culture—accessible through written records—that for many makes the study of major Asian societies particularly rewarding. These are societies whose cultural roots run at least as deep as those of Europe and whose political, social and intellectual achievements are no less sophisticated, yet often embody strikingly different values and presuppositions. Those values and presuppositions often challenge cultural assumptions of the West that appear to Westerners to be both natural and inevitable.

It continues to be common among Western practitioners of the humanities and social sciences, unfortunately, to ignore such challenges. Yet the study of contemporary Asian societies and their historical background, as well as being important for hard-headed reasons—such as improving economic and political relations—also provides invaluable opportunities for deepening our understanding of human society by putting it on a sounder comparative basis. It may be argued that the reason Asia should be studied is not that it represents a cohesive civilisational bloc, but rather that it does not: Asia represents a rich set of variations on the theme of civilisation, showing that there are many ways of satisfying human needs. There is no need to claim that it deserves serious attention because these variations together add up to a symphony.

## Issues and disciplines

The basic approach taken here, as already indicated, is thematic or issue-based. One reason for this is that it offers a way of covering much of Asia within the scope of one book. Another is that the issues are important in themselves, not only as far as Asia is concerned, but also in regard to the world as a whole. They are issues that ultimately cannot be understood, except by consideration in the context of a range of social and political systems. And while it may be argued that a particular society can be understood only by soaking oneself in it, I personally find at least as persuasive the view that adequate understanding only comes when a number of societies are compared. Only then do we start to see that what at first appears natural and inevitable may in fact be merely customary, even arbitrary.

The main reason for focusing on pressing issues, it must be said unapologetically, is that it makes the book relevant. While academics often claim that it is necessary for them to remain detached from social and political concerns in order to safeguard their independence and integrity, it could be argued that a greater threat to intellectual probity is posed by academic insistence on complete detachment than by any pressure to provide instant answers or ready solutions. Practical knowledge and disinterested understanding are not mutually exclusive. Were utility and intellectual commitment really insurmountable barriers to objectivity or intellectual rigour, it would be time to forget the whole business.

This book aims to be practical, therefore, to reach some understanding of matters that affect a large proportion of the world's population, and to consider possible responses to them. If sometimes there are no obvious answers or solutions, we should at least try to critically assess the sorts of responses that are proposed, and to identify some of the elements that a satisfactory response will need to include. Thinking about society in a vacuum does not necessarily lead to greater depth or sophistication. Devising practical responses to social and economic problems that are complex and interlocking, with roots going deep into history, is not something that lends itself to superficial or ready-made responses.

While this study focuses on issues, it does not approach them from the perspective of a particular academic discipline. It is consciously interdisciplinary, wandering across the boundaries to borrow ideas and insights wherever they lie. This may be uncomfortable for those readers who respect such boundaries and believe that only work thoroughly grounded in the theory of a particular discipline deserves to be taken seriously. These concerns are legitimate enough, and the approach adopted here requires some sort of explanation.

At an interview for an academic position not long ago I found myself emphasising that I had research experience in quite a number of disciplines: history, literature, law, sociology, public policy, philosophy ... I also emphasised that I tended to adopt an interdisciplinary approach when teaching. This had the effect of alarming rather than impressing some members of the selection committee, prompting one to ask with apparent distaste and frustration, 'Yes, but in the end, what do you see yourself as?' It was hard to think of a reply that I found convincing, let alone one that would satisfy the committee. 'A philosopher?' I ventured, with a vague hope that the committee would be able to remove the question mark for me.

If the following discussion proceeds from the theoretical framework of a particular discipline, therefore, it is more likely to be philosophy than anything else. However, one of the effects of the philosophical training I received was to make me sceptical of philosophy as an academic discipline. Philosophy is too important to be left in the hands of professional philosophers. Some would argue that this would be like leaving sex to professionals: any gain in technical competence would be completely negated by the resulting loss of fertility. The issues examined in this study and the approaches taken are not the sort of thing usually encountered in philosophy courses, though perhaps some of what is nowadays labelled as applied philosophy would come close.

If belonging to a discipline is one requirement of academic respectability, being proficient in theory is another. The two requirements are usually seen as going together: belonging to a discipline means being familiar with its theoretical foundations and making them part of one's self-identity. My problem is that the rather haphazard career I have followed through assorted corners of a number of disciplines has left me suspicious of the idea of discipline boundaries, and in particular the notion that it is having its own distinctive theoretical framework that makes a discipline separate from another. Discipline boundaries are akin to political boundaries, in Asia and elsewhere: while in some ways they matter, there is nothing inevitable about them and they may in fact blind us to alternative ways of understanding reality.

As a strategy for a division of intellectual labour, discipline boundaries have an obvious attraction.[4] When there is so much information to process and so many books to read, it is a relief to be able to say, for example, 'I'm an anthropologist and don't have to read stuff by sociologists, economists, and historians'. Unfortunately this is often quite untrue, and what makes matters worse is that anthropologists who talk only to anthropologists, philosophers who talk only to philosophers, or economists who talk only to other economists tend to become unintelligible to the rest of the human race. 'Theory' is partly responsible for this. While sometimes theory or technical language is necessary for developing new insights or methods of interpretation, all too often it becomes a way of camouflaging assumptions, of invoking sets of shared premises not seen as needing justification, and of assuming solid foundations where none in fact exist.

## The problem of knowledge

This brings us face to face with some fundamental problems that cannot be put aside. Since they will keep surfacing in the course of what follows it is best to confront them squarely at the outset. They are epistemological problems, that is, problems relating to the nature of human knowledge and understanding. Although these things may seem abstruse to those who just want a practical understanding of what is happening in contemporary Asia, the fact is that they are unavoidable, and their practical consequences are far-reaching.

To encounter the societies of contemporary Asia, whether through work or study, or just as a tourist, is to experience cultures based on very different ways of making sense of human experience, societies based on rules and institutions very unlike our own. This is true of Japanese in India or Filipinos in Persian Gulf states no less than Americans in Thailand or French people in China. It requires us to ask questions such as the following. Are the beliefs and values that guide the lives of these people correct or appropriate, despite the fact that they are very different from those of our own? What criteria are there for choosing between systems of belief or ways of understanding? Is it necessary to choose at all, or is it just a question of fitting in with local customs and beliefs? How we answer such questions directly affects the way we interact with those around us, as well as changing the way we see and understand the world.

Systems of knowledge, no matter where they come from, include criteria for judging what is knowledge (what is 'true') and what is not. Various sorts of criteria are used, and often a number of different sorts are used in conjunction with each other. Not infrequently these include the identification of fundamental knowledge that is beyond question and on which all that is known depends or from which it can be derived. These might be, for example, indisputable principles or axioms such as the basic principles of mathematics, or religious experiences thought to reveal direct knowledge of God. The identification of foundations of knowledge that are beyond dispute, however, raises massive problems.[5] For example, basic axioms of mathematics are true by definition or logic, but cannot serve as a basis for knowledge of the world based on experience. Knowledge based on religious experience runs into the problem that believers of different faiths claim to derive very dissimilar rules and principles from their experience of God. How can we judge which is right?

Those who regard knowledge as being derived from everyday experience—that is, empirical or scientific knowledge—encounter other problems. Knowledge may be based on particular observations or experiences, but we need some sorts of rules for generalisation or methods of interpretation if we are to get beyond those particulars. This is where theory comes in. What is clear is that despite the official ideology of egalitarianism in the scientific enterprise, with my observations counting as much as yours when it comes to establishing or demolishing theories, that is not how things work in practice. The quest for scientific knowledge is no less subject to power relations than other areas of human activity. Some individuals have greater influence and control than others over which ideas are accepted and which are not, for example, those who are in positions of authority in educational institutions, or those who control channels of scholarly communication.

We could push the analogy and say that science too has its prophets and holy men, those through whose lips God speaks and whose utterances have no need for further verification. Naturally we like to think that anyone who achieves a position of authority and influence in the generation of scientific knowledge does so by demonstrating outstanding ability, impartiality, commitment to truth, and so on. We like to think too that all members of the scientific community have equal voice and equal opportunity to rise to positions of authority and influence. But we all know that this is an idealisation. Yet *somehow* community agreement plays an important role in determining what is knowledge and what is not. The fact that the community in question is often a specialist one composed of experts who are to some extent self-selected complicates rather than simplifies the issue.

In scientific theory too we encounter the search for bedrock, for a solid foundation that will stand up to the digging and poking of sceptics. Sometimes we are told that the bedrock cannot actually be uncovered and observed directly, that its existence can only be inferred (that is, that its existence is theoretically necessary). Analysts of human affairs have looked for the ultimate foundation of explanation and understanding in quite dissimilar things. Marx interpreted all human behaviour in terms of economics or material self-interest. Darwin—or, more precisely, Darwinians—looked to the principle of natural selection for all-encompassing explanations. Nietzsche saw everything as a function of the desire for power. Freud identified sexual drive or libido as the fount of all human action and achievement. Einstein replaced Newton's laws with relativity theory and then spent his remaining years trying to develop a unified theory that, at least in physical terms, would explain 'everything'. Physical scientists since then have continued his quest, while in the human sciences, we are told, Grand Theory has staged a triumphant return.[6]

In the social sciences the quest to reach bedrock often takes the form of showing that all human behaviour can be reduced to a certain kind of motivation, or is to be interpreted in terms of the operation of a particular kind of factor. Marx, Nietzsche, and Freud all used this strategy. It may be observed that many social scientists today, no matter what their intellectual affiliation, are satisfied only when behaviour is explained in terms of economic interests. The assertion that human behaviour is economically motivated is so widely accepted that it seldom requires justification. Typical in this regard is the premise of a recent study of the evolution of human society: history is the record of 'materialist man', its driving force 'an overwhelming desire to maximize material advantage.'[7] At the same time, many intellectuals from developing countries are inclined to explain everything—all social problems, anyway—in terms of the harmful effects of colonialism.

## Building bridges, constructing rafts

There are two models for generating knowledge: one is bridge-building; the other is constructing rafts. Bridges are built by sinking piles into solid bedrock, through mud and silt, to support the structure that is to span the water. The problem is that sinking piles becomes increasingly difficult as the water gets deeper, the silt thicker, and solid rock harder to find. The temptation is to start sinking theoretical piles and to assume that they will reach solid rock because the structure requires it.

Rafts cannot do everything that bridges do, but they have other advantages, and when the water is deep they may be the only option. Rafts are not solid edifices fixed for all time, so raft-builders have no need to hunt for bedrock. Rafts are impermanent structures that have served their purpose when we reach the other shore, where they can be pulled to bits and used to construct a cart or glider or whatever else is needed for the next stage of the journey. What matters in a raft is that it be large enough to be stable, and have sufficient strength and flexibility to withstand the forces of current, wave, and wind. Crossing the waters on a raft may be unnerving for those who have been brought up on the idea that only a bridge will do, but once they grow accustomed to it the whole business turns out to be much less stressful than it first seemed.

According to the bridge-builders of knowledge we cannot achieve anything if we fail to construct solid foundations of incontrovertible theory or fact. Raft-builders, on the other hand, point out that all we need to hold a raft together is the shared meanings and purposes of those on board. Knowledge is developed by members of social groups, in accordance with socially agreed procedures and criteria. Not surprisingly, these will reflect authority and power relationships within the group, as well as its underlying interests, needs and technological requirements. Because shared meanings and purposes come from shared experience, a common history, knowledge—and what counts as knowledge—is culturally determined. Further, the procedures and criteria for generating knowledge may change over time as the epistemological understanding of the group evolves.

The analogy of epistemological or cultural rafts inevitably throws up the question of what is sometimes called the incommensurability of knowledge systems or world views. Is it possible for different ways of understanding to be rendered fully in each other's terms, or is knowledge untranslatable across epistemological and cultural boundaries? Can the occupants of different rafts talk to each other, or are they doomed forever to mutual incomprehension?

It is tempting to answer both yes and no. Sometimes it seems extremely difficult, if not impossible, to grasp or to communicate fully all the shades of meaning contained in a set of concepts, a ritual, or social symbol. Yet we must not allow ourselves to be persuaded by those who make a living out of explicating (and not infrequently mystifying) 'the Other', that cross-cultural understanding is more problematic than it really is. Cross-cultural understanding seems hardest when we try to do it in a vacuum, when we sit down to compare world views or systems of ideas. Part of the problem is a tendency to think in terms of texts, as if all the meaning has to be communicated by words, when most of the cues in everyday communication come from the context in which we live and work, where much of the meaning remains implicit. When we share common activities, when we do things together, cross-cultural understanding usually seems much less of a problem.

The fact is that people from different cultures communicate regularly and, on the whole, without too much difficulty, and this has been the case throughout human history. Which is not to say that problems in communication do not occur, or that some cultural gaps are not harder to cross than others. But at least at the level of the individual, as opposed to the polity or state, cross-cultural understanding is a fact of everyday life. Failure of communication is probably just as common because of variations within 'the same' culture as between 'different' cultures. The reason is that everyone seems to have much the same needs, interests, and concerns, despite the fact that those needs, interests and concerns may be articulated and satisfied in quite dissimilar ways. Throughout history people from different cultures have communicated, traded, cooperated, and fought with each other. It appears that even the fighting, as often as not, has arisen from mutual understanding rather than incomprehension. The fact that cross-cultural communication and interaction are everyday occurrences shows that cultural boundaries are not nearly as sharp as is often claimed, and there is good reason to be suspicious of those who declare them inviolable. Moving from raft to raft often does not require much more than goodwill, tact, and a little imagination. You are welcome on my raft if I may visit yours.

## Basic human needs

The claim that human needs and interests tend to be much the same everywhere needs further discussion because it has implications for the approach taken in this study. The idea of basic, universal human needs is one that became topical in the late 1970s and, since the late 1980s, has attracted renewed attention.[8] United Nations agencies put a lot of energy into developing and applying the concept, seeing it as a way of articulating the responsibilities of governments in respect of their citizens and working towards the achievement of certain universal minimum living standards or quality of life. As might be expected, there has been a lot of debate over what the basic human needs actually *are*, especially once the question of physical necessities has been left behind. Building on earlier work, one study identifies six distinct categories—survival needs, societal needs, cultural and psychic needs, welfare needs, adaptive needs and progress needs—and under these headings lists a total of fifty-three different items. 'Humanness', the author comments, 'demands a little more than physical survival', and he believes that his list of basic requirements is not at all 'over-optimistic'.[9]

One of the most persuasive writers to make use of the concept of basic human needs is Barrington Moore Jnr, who in his study of the nature of social justice and injustice argues that all societies are expected to satisfy certain minimum needs to which all members of society have a claim. Some members of society may lay claim to a lot more than this minimum because they occupy positions of authority, status, and so on. But where the minimum is not obtained by all, the system of mutual obligation that holds society together is seen as having broken down. A sense of injustice arises and authority may no longer be accepted as legitimate.[10]

If Moore's list of basic needs appears shorter, it is partly because he chooses to leave it incomplete. He lists the physical need for air, food, water, shelter, and sexual gratification. In regard to psychological needs, he mentions love and respect from other human beings, but then alludes to 'a wide range of favourable responses whose absence can be in some way damaging'. He makes specific mention only of the craving for distinction, the need to escape boredom, and the need for socially acceptable ways of channelling aggressive impulses. He then goes on to say, however, that if any society is to be able to satisfy these basic requirements of all its members, there are certain social imperatives or social needs that must apply. These relate to the way societies are structured in terms of authority, division of labour, and the distribution of goods and services, and to moral codes that inform behaviour when the social structure does or does not satisfy the needs of individuals.

Does this concept of shared needs imply that beneath the imprint of particular cultures on the outlook and behaviour of individuals there is a basic human nature, a set of irreducible characteristics that all humans have in common—the bedrock of humanity, so to speak? Are what we thought were rafts turning into bits of a universal bridge?

Surely the concept of basic human needs may be useful without insisting that a complete and timeless list of such needs (a universal human nature) be spelt out. It is enough that we accept the idea of a universally agreed list as an ideal, while recognising that, given the culturally diverse ways in which needs are manifested and satisfied, there will always be strong debate over what such a list should include.

We also have to recognise that our understanding of needs is subject to changing knowledge and changing expectations. Not only does our knowledge of human physiology and psychology and the nature of society change, but our identification of needs is influenced by wants, aspirations, and expectations that are culturally transmitted.[11] It may be that what was once an aspiration of a social minority in one culture becomes in time a universal expectation, that is, comes to be regarded as a basic human need. Therefore it is right that there should be ongoing debate over what the basic human needs are. There will always be a temptation to smuggle in what is peculiar to our own culture while watching closely for attempts by others to do the same. However, there will also be large areas of agreement that can be identified without a lot of trouble. In part it is a question of how general is the terminology used to articulate needs. The more specific we try to be, the more difficult it becomes to reach agreement.

There are two main reasons for introducing the idea of basic needs at this point. One is to place the emphasis on human sameness rather than difference, to stress that cross-cultural understanding and communication are possible. Cultures are not rafts caught forever in whirlpools of their own making. The other is to highlight the links between basic needs and knowledge. If it is accepted that human beings have a range of needs that are equally fundamental, then it follows that all those needs must carry equal weight as far as explanations of human behaviour are concerned. That is to say, a satisfactory explanation of actions and social events will not be one that reduces everything to a bedrock of, say, economic or psychoanalytical facts, but rather will show how the various basic needs of individuals interact in complex ways to shape their behaviour and the social institutions they establish.

## The study

In this study it is impossible to avoid using a certain amount of terminology that, while conventional and therefore useful, may cause offence in some quarters. I can only plead innocent of malicious intent and try to justify it on the grounds of simplicity. For example, if I write about Myanmar rather than Burma, it is because that is now the country's official title rather than because I hold a particular position on its political situation. The province of Indonesia formerly known as Irian Jaya has officially been referred to since 2000 as West Papua; however, its political status remains unchanged. That on 1 July 1997 Hong Kong ceased to be a separate political entity does not make it less appropriate to write about it as one. If I sometimes discuss Taiwan as if it were an independent country rather than a province of China, this is because it functions independently. I am not making a political point. (Usually my political position is clear enough anyway.) As far as the issue of *developed* versus *developing* countries is concerned, I find the terms irritating and vague, but difficult to lay aside. I take them to mean something like 'the member nations of the Organisation for Economic Cooperation and Development' and 'the rest'. The alternative expressions *First World* and *Third World* are equally clumsy, with the further drawback of being anachronistic now that the Second (communist) World is largely defunct. Nevertheless now and again I use them, more for the sake of stylistic variation than anything else. The terms *North* and *South* I find impossible to use, living as I do in a 'southern' country that, according to most criteria, is a developed nation.

The study begins with a little historical background and discussion of a simple framework in which the wide range of material presented may more easily be understood: two opposing trends that I call globalisation and insulation. This also provides an opportunity to introduce the range of issues to be covered and how they relate to each other. This is followed in Chapter 2 by consideration of some of the key concepts relating to how societies work, and the way they apply to contemporary Asian societies in particular: concepts such as culture, religion, ethnicity, social organisation, authority, morality, and the state.

Detailed treatment of specific issues begins in Chapter 3 with the topic of human rights, an often controversial subject in relation to Asian nations and their links with the West. Ethnic minorities—particularly indigenous minorities—and the problems facing them are the subject of Chapter 4. Focusing on the various nation states of Asia and the differences between them carries the risk of disregarding the differences within them, which in most cases are considerable. The issues facing minorities in many ways resemble those faced by nation states in the global community, and consideration of them gives greater insight into the complexities of socio-political life in contemporary Asia.

The next three chapters are closely related. Chapter 5 deals with economic and social development, which for many is what makes contemporary Asia so interesting. The rapid economic changes occurring throughout the region are compelling Western nations and developing nations in other parts of the world to take notice. The associated social changes are no less astonishing. One particularly important area of change, population, is the subject of Chapter 6. The impact of economic development, population growth, and urbanisation on the natural environment in Asia is considered in Chapter 7.

Chapters 8 and 9 examine aspects of change at a more personal level. The first deals with changes in family structures and functions, the way households adapt in order to try to meet the needs of family members. The second deals with changing patterns of work, that is, the sorts of things people do to make a living. In a sense, therefore, it treats from the perspective of the individual aspects of the economic changes discussed in Chapter 5.

The last two chapters deal with information, the changing ways in which it is generated and communicated within the global community, and the manner in which this affects Asian societies. Chapter 10 focuses on the role of mass media and how new technology changes access to information and government attempts to control it. Chapter 11 deals with the generation of scientific knowledge and technology, and the implications of the world dominance of the Western system of scientific knowledge for Asian countries. It also considers the extent to which knowledge can ever be freed from its cultural and historical context.

**Figure 1.1** East Asia

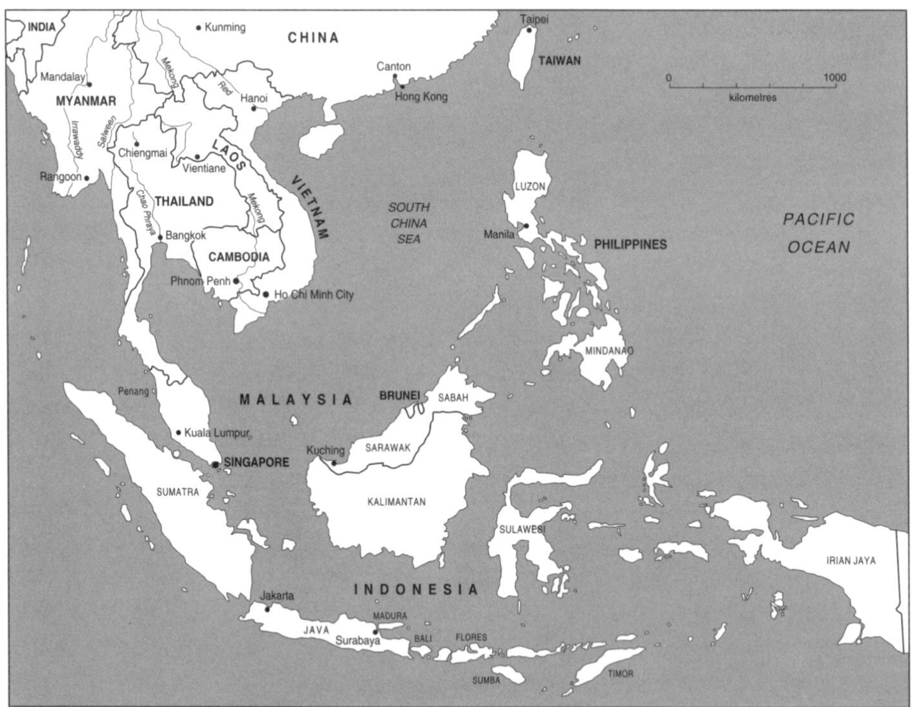


**Figure 1.2** South-East Asia

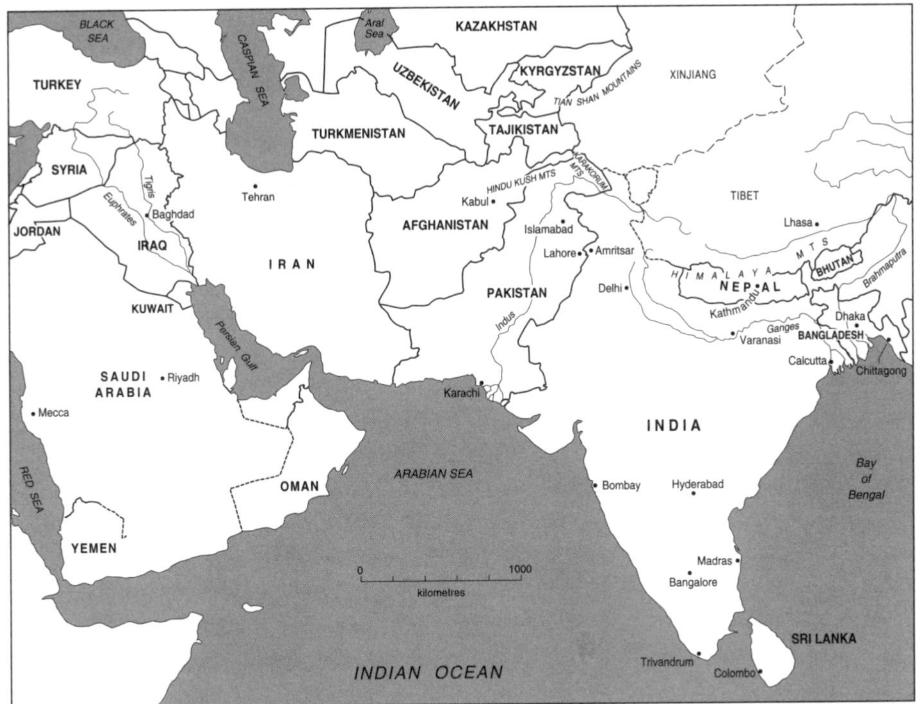


**Figure 1.3** South and West Asia

CHAPTER ONE

# Globalisation and Insulation in Asia

## Globalisation and insulation

Many of the dominant trends shaping the societies of contemporary Asia are similar to those influential in other parts of the world. The word that comes closest to summing up those trends is 'globalisation'. By the beginning of the twenty-first century, this term was suffering from overload, being made to carry a wide array of meanings in numerous fields, from international relations to cultural criticism, and pressed into technical service in most of them.[1] Here it is used simply to refer to the way in which individual and community affairs are being caught up in those of larger and larger entities, so that ultimately interaction occurs on an international or global scale. Influences, concerns and problems are less likely to be local or regional than they used to be. Increasingly, it is at the national and international levels that life is being shaped. For good or ill, it is difficult now to remain unaffected by or indifferent to the forces at work in the wider world.

However, globalisation is only half the story. To understand contemporary Asia we also have to consider the way in which individuals and governments react *against* globalisation. The opposite process or series of tendencies is no less important, and may be referred to as insulation. The basic meaning of the word is to make into an island or become island-like, and by extension may refer to the process or tendency by which individuals and groups separate themselves off, make or conceive themselves as separate or distinctive. Insulation involves setting oneself apart from others, whereas globalisation involves being linked to others on an ever-increasing scale. Whether globalisation is something individuals do or have done to them may be debated. As far as ordinary people are concerned, it would be safe to say that 'being globalised' is something about which they do not have much choice. In fact, insulation may be understood in part as a strategy for regaining control over personal or local affairs lost through globalisation.

In the chapters that follow I describe the main aspects of globalisation and insulation as they affect Asian societies, and reflect on the complex problems generated. Before doing so, I shall discuss briefly what these broad trends include and note some points critical for understanding them.

## Contexts of globalisation

First, however, it is necessary to consider briefly the historical and political context in which globalisation and insulation are occurring.[2] For it may be rightly objected that looking for understanding of the diverse societies of contemporary Asia in the trends they share with each other and the rest of the world does not seem entirely convincing. There must be something that distinguishes them from each other. National or local issues may be at least as significant as global forces in shaping societies, and we have to make sure they do not disappear from view.

A fitting symbol of globalisation is the United Nations (UN), which in 1995 celebrated, discreetly and to less than universal acclaim, its fiftieth anniversary. So the second half of the twentieth century could be called the age of globalisation, beginning with the founding of the UN and the end of the Second World War, and leading to the present world order. It is a useful idea not only for the purpose of historical periodisation: it helps also to reveal the pervasiveness of Western assumptions in historical and social understanding.

It is conventional in the West to treat 1945 as the beginning of the contemporary era, the date when a new world order came into being: a time of peace and international cooperation, despite the tensions of the cold war, when economic development and the pursuit of human rights became dominant world concerns. But for most of Asia 1945 does not have that sort of significance. Even the date of the signing of the UN charter is revealing. When national representatives gathered in San Francisco on 26 June 1945 formally to commit their governments to becoming part of the organisation, the war in Europe had ended, but in Asia the fighting was not over. This, together with the fact that few representatives of Asian governments were in San Francisco to sign the charter, highlights the extent to which the push to establish the new world body came from the United States and Europe. As the most powerful nation in the world at the time, the United States naturally saw itself as playing a leading role in UN affairs.

Asian countries had too many other worries to be concerned with issues of world order. For most, 1945 did not mark the beginning of a time of peace and stability. The number of countries that found themselves at peace was small. For some, what was to follow was more catastrophic than the war against Japan. Since 1945 military action within and across national borders has been so pervasive and persistent that in many places times of peace and stability have been all too brief. It is not surprising then that political, social, and economic advancement has tended to be a recent achievement.

This does not apply to Japan, which had stability forced upon it after the war by an Allied occupation that lasted until 1952. Fundamental political and social reforms were carried out with US 'guidance' but also through popular support. The remains of the militarist regime were dismantled and a Western-style system of democratic government was established. Much of the 1947 Japanese Constitution was strikingly similar to the US Constitution, and the new legal code was couched in terms of US notions of laws and rights. Given the strong US interest in human rights concepts in the late 1940s, it is not surprising that the new Japanese legal system harmonises well with principles of international human rights law. By early 1952 the new order was well established in Japan, and with it the foundation for social and economic development.

China's experience was very different, and had big consequences for the rest of Asia. Whereas 1945 marked the end of eight years of war against Japan, the civil war and revolution that followed ended only in 1949. While the People's Republic of China (PRC) was established on 1 October 1949, it was not until 1971 that the communist regime was recognised as the legitimate government of China and the PRC was admitted to the UN. Upheavals such as the Great Leap Forward (1958), the terrible famine of the Three Hard Years (1959–61), and the Cultural Revolution (1966–76) strained to the limit the country's social and economic resources. Social and political stability cannot be said to have been achieved in China until 1978, when Deng Xiaoping became leader and the revolutionary extremism of Mao and his supporters was put to rest.

Even so, many problems remain unresolved. The biggest is Taiwan. The losers of the Chinese civil war, the Kuomintang regime of Chiang Kai-shek, retreated in 1949 to the island province of Taiwan, which with US support has managed to elude Chinese communist control. In recent years the people and politicians of Taiwan, content with Taiwan's economic success and reconciled to the futility of continuing to claim that the Kuomintang is the legitimate government of China, have begun to assert Taiwan's political independence. The election in 2000 of Chen Shui-bian as president was symptomatic of these changing attitudes, for as well as belonging to a political party long in opposition to the Kuomintang, Chen regards himself as Taiwanese rather than Chinese, and has expressed a clear preference for independence from China. This has been resented by the authorities in Beijing, who see regaining control of Taiwan as a major step in the process of restoring Chinese territorial integrity—this process having begun in 1997 with Hong Kong's incorporation as a special autonomous region into the People's Republic.

Tibet is a very different sort of problem. Since China's invasion in 1950–51 the government has continued to assert that, historically, Tibet has been part of the motherland and therefore sovereignty over the region legitimately lies with the Chinese state. This has failed to convince the international community, which has been sympathetic to Tibetan opposition while offering little in the way of direct support.

Communist victory in China meant support for communist insurrection, both real and imagined, in other countries of the region. It also resulted in US action to stem the red tide. Two of the nations that suffered most from being caught up in this battle of giants were Korea and Vietnam.

In 1945 the Koreans briefly had hopes of peace and independence following forty years of Japanese colonialism. This was not to be. Even before the war ended the United States and the USSR had agreed in principle to divide Korea into two spheres of influence at the 38th parallel. It was only a matter of time before tensions erupted into open warfare. The conflict began in 1950 and ended in 1953, but both the division and the tension remain. Officially the two parties are still at war. Since 1960 South Korea has achieved social stability and remarkable economic growth, and since the late 1980s has enjoyed increasing political liberalisation. Yet politically the situation remains fragile (despite some gestures of conciliation and cooperation during 2000 and 2001), especially regarding the question of reunification. The United States continues to maintain a military presence in South Korea.

Vietnam's colonial master was not Japan, but France. The Japanese defeat in Vietnam marked the beginning of another war, which was to go on for thirty years. It was a war seen as anti-colonial, civil, anti-communist, and revolutionary, according to the viewpoint of the combatants: the Vietnamese, the French, the United States, and its allies. If communist victory in 1975 ended the fighting in Vietnam, it also brought with it the massive problems of reconstructing a bankrupt, ruined country in the face of economic and political isolation. It was not until February 1994 that the United States lifted its trade embargo against Vietnam. Nor did the communist victory mean that Vietnamese soldiers could lay down their arms. In December 1978 the Vietnamese army invaded Cambodia, thereby becoming involved in civil strife that left millions of Cambodians dead. Only two months later fighting also broke out between China and Vietnam. Not until September 1989 were the last Vietnamese troops withdrawn from Cambodia. At the close of the twentieth century, Cambodia itself finally seemed to have achieved some measure of peace and stability.

In other places, communism contributed to tension and instability on a lesser scale. These included the Malay peninsula, where between 1943 and 1957 communists from the Chinese ethnic minority resisted both the Japanese and the British colonial government. A history of tension between the Chinese minority and Malays was one factor that led the predominantly Chinese island of Singapore to leave the Malaysian federation in 1965 to become a separate state.

In Indonesia communism was merely one of many serious issues faced in the postwar period. Although the Indonesians initially welcomed the Japanese as liberators from European colonial oppression, they soon learned that Asian colonialism was no less exploitative. In 1945 the Indonesians, like the Vietnamese and the Koreans, had

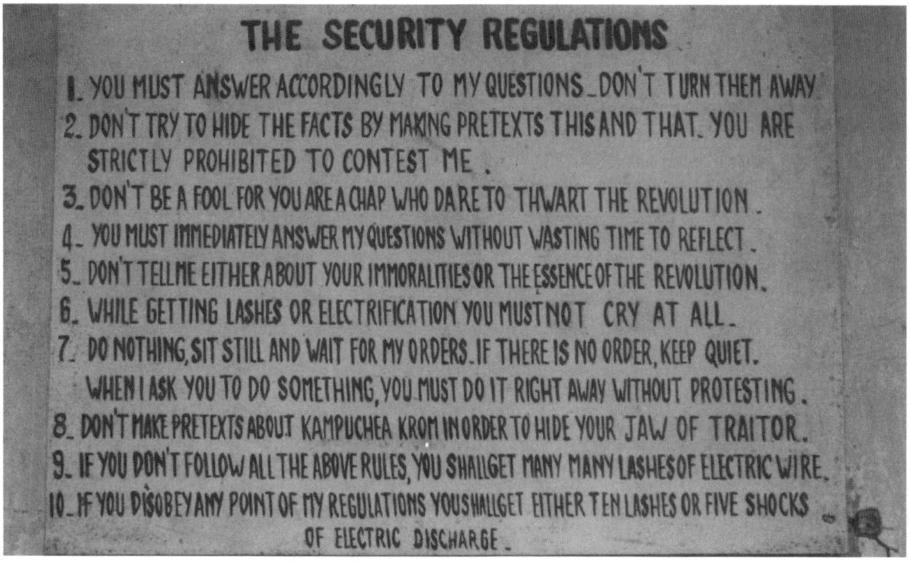

Khmer Rouge interrogation centre regulations, Phnom Penh, Cambodia. In the late 1970s, under the Khmer Rouge, state violation of human rights was extreme.

brief hopes of independence and peace, but things turned out otherwise. When the Japanese retreated there was conflict between Indonesian communists and those who had collaborated with the Japanese. The bitter disputes were set aside when the Dutch came back looking to re-establish themselves as colonial masters. By 1948 much of Indonesia was again under Dutch control, yet by the end of 1949 the Dutch had to accept Indonesian independence. UN opposition to Dutch actions in Indonesia was an important factor. After independence internal tensions remained. Communism was a force in Indonesia until 1965, when an alleged communist coup attempt was quashed and hundreds of thousands of communist 'suspects' were killed or imprisoned. Throughout the Suharto period, survivors and their families continued to be subject to close scrutiny and control.

Not all the tensions and uprisings experienced by Asian countries after 1945 related to communism. Longstanding inter-ethnic conflicts were no less important, but frequently they were perceived or presented as conflicts between capitalism and communism. This allowed one side to turn to the United States for arms and support, the other side to the USSR and China. It appears that many of the alleged communists and sympathisers suppressed in Indonesia in 1965, for example, were simply ethnic Chinese who, following the victory of communism in the People's Republic, automatically became suspect. The economic crisis and President Suharto's resignation in 1998 saw a rise in ethnic tension and the renewed expression by some groups of a desire for independence.

In Myanmar (Burma), on the other hand, inter-ethnic conflicts have always been recognised for what they are. Burma too had been a British colony before the war and, when the Japanese were defeated, Britain moved to reassert its control. It encountered popular resistance, however, which rallied around Aung San (the father of Aung San Suu Kyi, leader of the National League for Democracy). Despite Aung San's assassination in 1947, Burma became independent in January 1948. As elsewhere, the disappearance of the imperialist power coincided with an outbreak of the ethnic conflicts it had manipulated and exacerbated, in this case between the lowland Burman majority and minorities of the mountain regions such as the Karen, Kachin and Shan. The prolonging of these conflicts over a period of more than fifty years has been a major factor in the militarisation and brutalisation of Myanmar society, which has yet to experience harmony or stability.

Ethnic and religious conflict has also had a big impact on the postwar history of the Indian subcontinent. During the Second World War there was still hope on the part of the British leadership that Britain would be able, when the time came, to reassert its control there. However, after the war, the new British government did not stand in the way of what now appeared inevitable, and set about organising free elections in India. But a unified independent India was not to be. While conflict between Hindus and Muslims never degenerated into full-scale civil war, it soon became clear that partition was unavoidable, and in 1947 India and Pakistan came into being as separate nations. Yet this still did not end sectarian violence. Despite the large-scale population transfers that accompanied partition, a very big Muslim minority (107 million according to the 1991 census) remains in India. In 1948 Mohandas Gandhi was assassinated by Hindu extremists who accused him of being too tolerant of Muslims.

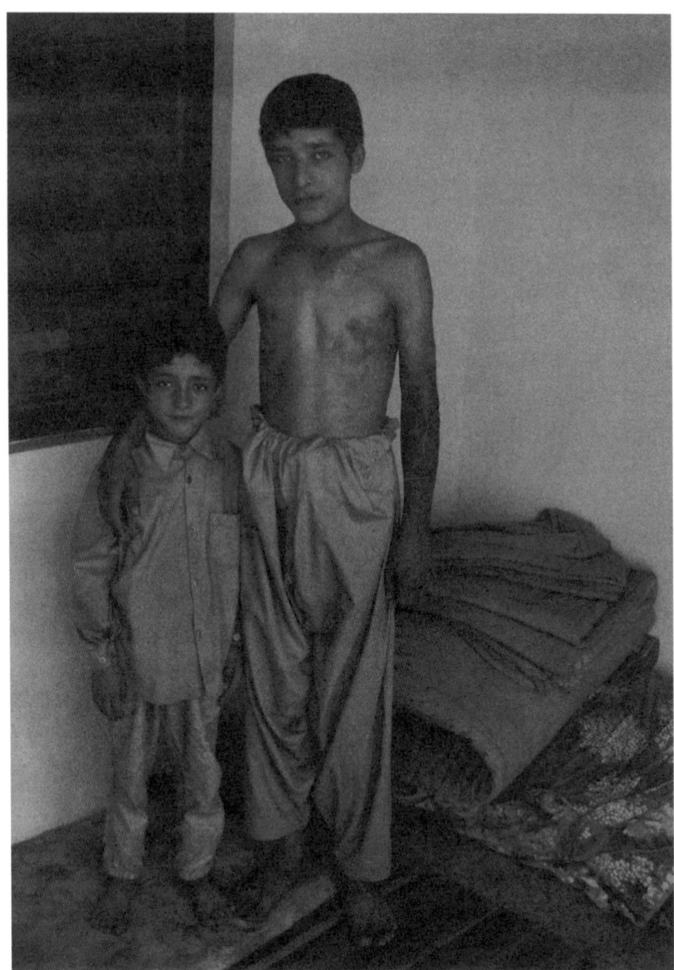

Afghan brothers, refugee camp, Peshawar, Pakistan. Traumatised by events in their war-torn country, they have become elective mutes, not uttering a word since their arrival.

India and Pakistan continue to dispute the status of the Muslim-dominated northern state of Kashmir. Sikh extremists fighting for an independent Sikh state in 1984 assassinated the Indian prime minister, Indira Gandhi, triggering a violent backlash in which hundreds died. In December 1992 the worst violence since partition occurred following the destruction of the Babri Masjid (Mosque) by a Hindu mob: some 1700 were killed and 5500 injured. Mohandas Gandhi's ghost must have experienced a sad sense of *déjà vu* on learning that the widely given reason for Hindu unrest was dissatisfaction with the government's policies favouring minorities.

Pakistan was created in two halves separated by thousands of kilometres of Indian territory. It was only a matter of time before it fell apart. Tensions between East and West Pakistan led in 1971 to a civil war that cost up to 3 million lives. India sided with the East, and the result was a humiliating defeat for the West Pakistani forces and

Sri Lanka's former prime minister Solomon Bandaranaike is cleaned up for the fiftieth anniversary of independence, Colombo, 1998. The Bank of Ceylon tower in the background was damaged in 1996 by a Tamil separatist bomb. Sinhalese nationalist policies introduced by Bandaranaike were a major factor in increasing tensions from the 1950s between the Sinhalese and the Tamil minority.

creation of the new nation of Bangladesh. Since then Bangladesh has struggled in the face of natural disasters, political conflict and a lack of economic resources to establish a stable and democratic society able to meet the needs of its people. Pakistan, though better endowed with resources, has found it even harder to establish a stable democratic system. For many, the 1979 execution of the first democratically elected prime minister, Zulfikar Ali Bhutto, by military ruler General Zia ul Haq sums up Pakistan's political experience since independence. Elected governments ruled for ten years from 1989, but they continued to be plagued by corruption and inefficiency, and failed to solve the serious problems facing the nation. In 1999 there was another military coup, with General Pervez Musharraf taking the office of president.

These examples come from what we are calling 'monsoon Asia'. In West and Central Asia social and political upheavals have been no less common. Until 1979 Iran was reasonably stable under the increasingly repressive regime of Mohammed Reza Shah. Although his strong political and economic leanings to the West brought support from that direction, they did not increase his popularity with his own people. Economic and social policies in the 1960s and 1970s did little to improve the situation of the mass of the population, which became more and more dissatisfied with state-driven secularisation and Westernisation. The crisis came in January 1979 when the Shah fled Iran and Ayatollah Khomeini returned from exile to establish an Islamic revolutionary government. In September 1980 Iran was invaded by Iraq, which commenced a brutal war that was to drag on for eight years and result in a million casualties.

The war, the Islamic revolution and Iran's international isolation led to serious economic problems, so that, by 1988, the per capita GDP was only half what it had been ten years earlier. Despite an easing of the government's revolutionary fervour, Iran's social and economic problems remain severe. In Iraq, despite the human and material cost of the war with Iran, President Saddam Hussein invested heavily in new arms and, only two years later, in August 1990, invaded Kuwait. This was widely condemned by the international community and triggered the Gulf War in January of the following year. The subsequent trade embargo, imposed by the UN Security Council in response to Iraq's failure to keep to the conditions of the peace agreement, has crippled the country and brought severe hardship to its people.

This brief survey of some of the difficulties encountered by Asian countries since the Second World War is enough to demonstrate the very dissimilar situations they have faced. It is clear, then, that if we describe the dominant trends Asian countries have been experiencing over the last few decades in terms of globalisation and reactions against it, it does not mean that the experience of each country has been the same. If we consider the factors underlying the difficulties just outlined—bearing in mind that only the most obvious and spectacular examples have been mentioned—the diversity of the predicaments Asian countries have experienced is obvious. Some, such as India, Pakistan, Indonesia, and Vietnam, have experienced acute difficulties in the process of decolonisation. Others, such as Thailand, China, and Japan, were never colonised but nevertheless have had massive problems to overcome. And while some, including South Korea and Malaysia, have moved from disorder to stability and prosperity, others, such as Afghanistan and Sri Lanka, have slipped deeper into civil and political strife.

## Aspects of globalisation

It is in relation to a political and economic world order that the concept of globalisation is best known. The UN is a familiar organisation, even if what it does is not always transparent. Its fundamental purpose, as spelt out in its charter, is to achieve international cooperation for the peace, security, and well-being of all nations. Its activities have been wide-ranging, and have included peace-keeping missions, famine relief, promotion of public health and family planning, setting and enforcing international human rights standards, promotion of literacy and education, encouragement of economic development, and protection of the environment. Some of its activities have been much more successful than others.

Essential to the concept of the UN is the principle that what happens within the boundaries of any given nation is not necessarily the concern of only its people and government. Other nations may have a legitimate interest. It may be that the government of the country is failing to treat its people according to internationally agreed standards, or that it is acting in ways that could be harmful to the international community. This principle entails a modification of what has been for a long time regarded as a cardinal rule of international relations: that national sovereignty is absolute.[3] If the idea of an international community is to be meaningful, it must allow action to protect or further community interests. Defining the limits of permissible international involvement in affairs that a particular state may see as internal or domestic, however, is not easy.

The UN is not the only body involved in the development of a global political order, despite the fact that it is by far the most conspicuous. It is a mistake, in fact, to assume that only world bodies are involved in the process of globalisation. Regional and bilateral links between nations are at least as important. Such links have also multiplied, in both number and scope.

Closely related to political globalisation but separate from it is the development of international law and the creation of mechanisms to implement it. The law is one area in which it is common to describe the general trend as one of international convergence, as the legal systems of nations increasingly become alike in content and mode of operation.[4] In this regard the UN and other international organisations have been very influential. Some of these organisations, such as the International Labour Organisation (established in 1919), pre-date the UN. However, most were established through UN initiatives. The International Court of Justice, the major international legal institution, dates from 1945, the same year as the UN itself. The scope of international law has grown rapidly. One field deserving particular mention is that of human rights.

## Human rights

Human rights have been a central concern of the UN from the beginning. According to its charter, the UN aims 'to achieve international co-operation ... in promoting and encouraging respect for human rights and the fundamental freedoms for all' (Article 1). Member states pledge to work to establish 'universal respect for, and observance of, human rights and fundamental freedoms for all without distinction as to race, sex, language, or religion' (Articles 55 and 56). In theory, therefore, on becoming members of the UN states undertake to further the human rights of their own people and those of other nations.

A Human Rights Commission was established quickly by the UN and early in 1947 began drafting an international bill of human rights. The result, the Universal Declaration of Human Rights, was adopted in 1948. Two covenants designed to give the provisions of the Declaration legal force—the International Covenant on Economic, Social and Cultural Rights and the International Covenant on Civil and Political Rights—were subsequently adopted and came into effect from 1976. However, these three instruments represent only a small part of international human rights legislation. In 2001 the list of international human rights instruments compiled by the Office of the United Nations High Commissioner for Human Rights contained more than a hundred items.[5]

A significant number of Asian countries to date have not ratified the major human rights conventions. While being a signatory to the relevant declarations and treaties does not always indicate a serious intention to implement their provisions, it does increase the legal obligation of parties to do so. Legal experts argue, moreover, that because international human rights instruments have been ratified by a large section of the international community, their provisions are acquiring the status of international customary law and so are becoming binding even on states that are not signatories. In any case, despite the misgivings various Asian states may have regarding existing human rights law, as recently as 1993, at human rights conferences in Bangkok and Vienna, all those represented have publicly asserted their commitment to upholding and protecting human rights.

## Economics

On the economic front, expressions such as 'global economy' and 'world market' have become clichés. Social scientists of all persuasions discuss the world economic system, some with bitter distaste and others with cheerful optimism. To accept the view that economic interaction between nations is greater than ever before, and that nations are now more economically interdependent than at any other point in human history, we do not have to accept either the argument that this is to the economic benefit of all peoples, or that the world system has been created by rich and powerful nations in order to make exploitation of weaker ones easier. No matter how we interpret the forces shaping it or who we think controls it, it does make sense to think of the web of overlapping economic links between nations as a world system.[6] There are very few countries that remain outside the system.

The internationalisation of economic activity depends on many factors. Industrialisation is necessary to produce goods in the quantity and quality needed for international trade. Efficient and affordable transport and communications networks have to exist. Trade barriers have to be kept to a minimum. International financial systems are necessary for convenient movement of capital and credit. Governments and private

Niche marketing in the global economy: an opium-producer in northern Laos.

enterprise have been active in developing components of the world economic system. While it is natural in this context to think of multinational corporations such as Mitsubishi and Hyundai manufacturing and marketing identical products in a host of countries, or global initiatives such as the General Agreement on Tariffs and Trade and creation of the World Trade Organisation, we must not lose sight of the fact that international operations and initiatives presuppose well-integrated local and regional economies and infrastructures. In other words, the linking up and integration that occurs within national borders is just as essential for globalisation as that which takes place across them. This applies to other aspects of globalisation as well.

Closely connected with economic globalisation is economic development. As already mentioned, this has been a major area of UN activity. The essential idea is that poor, underdeveloped countries should share the benefits of the knowledge and technology of the more advanced countries, and with their help develop the modern industries, infrastructure, health care, education, and administrative systems needed to secure and enhance the well-being of their people. So dominant has this concept of development been in UN policy and action that many supporters and critics of development alike refer to the period from approximately 1950 as the age of development.

If much of the thinking on development has come from UN agencies, much of the funding for projects in Third World countries has come from the World Bank and the International Monetary Fund (IMF).[7] Whether successful or unsuccessful in terms of improving the living standards of most of the people of Third World countries, development has greatly strengthened economic links between developed nations and the Third World. Critics argue that incorporation of developing countries into the world system has been the main aim all along. They point to the crippling foreign debts many developing countries have as a result of the ambitious development projects sold them by their rich advisers. Those debts represent a major aspect of world economic relations.

## Population trends

Global population trends are widely seen as bound up with economic and social development.[8] The United Nations Development Program, for example, uses increasing life expectancy as a measure of human or social development. On the face of it, there are strong reasons for doing so. In some Asian countries, such as China, life expectancy has almost doubled since the first half of the twentieth century, and there can be no doubt that this is linked to the improvements in economic productivity and social services that have occurred over the same period. Demographers claim to identify a pattern of demographic transition that many see as characteristic of developing countries around the world. First, the population increases as death rates fall. As the population grows it gets younger because birth rates continue to be high despite the fact that infant and child mortality rates have fallen. Then, as industrialisation proceeds, family structures change and values associated with having children change. In due course birth rates begin to fall too. The population ages again and demographic equilibrium is re-established. In reality, patterns of population change over the past few decades have not been as tidy or uniform as has been suggested. Yet they certainly have been consistent enough to talk of demographic aspects of the globalisation process.

## The environment

Related to both economic development and demographic change are environmental issues. Again, these tend to fall into a pattern clear enough to warrant their being seen as aspects of the process of globalisation. Population growth, increased consumption of resources and greater pollution have all contributed to environmental damage. Many environmental problems are international or global in nature. Global warming, sea and air pollution, ozone depletion: these problems do not respect political boundaries. China's air pollution causes acid rain in Korea and Japan. Deforestation in Sarawak and Kalimantan has implications for the rest of the world in terms of biodiversity and climate change. If many environmental problems are international in nature, feasible solutions are also likely to be international in scope. Yet the assertion that environmental problems require international responses is seen in many quarters as a threat to local control or national sovereignty in much the same way that international human rights law is seen as a threat.

## The family

Family structure and functions—or, more precisely, household structure and functions—are another area in which global changes are often described in terms of convergence to a single pattern. The pattern entails movement away from complex households with three or more generations living under one roof, performing a wide range of functions, to simple households (nuclear families) that consist only of one married couple and their unmarried children, and have lost many traditional functions to the state or private sector agencies. Whether there is a convergent trend in household structure and functions is debatable. Nevertheless there is no doubt that far-reaching demographic changes, coupled with the transformation of economic life and the role of the state, are having a strong impact on the nature of the family in developing Asian countries.

## Communications and information technology

It was in connection with the impact of electronic mass media that the expression 'global village' was coined in the 1960s. Since then, communications technology has become much more powerful and sophisticated. The rapid development of information technology—particularly the Internet in the 1990s—has also contributed to what may with some justice be called a communications revolution, a revolution that has made it possible to receive and transmit information almost instantaneously at any point on the earth's surface. In technological terms, it could be argued, the global village is close to being a reality. The sophistication of media and communications technology, and its increasing power for good and ill, has encouraged preoccupation with the idea of global culture and the question of who controls the media that shape it.

If some welcome the capacity of the technology to help enlighten and advance backward corners of the world, or to help establish national cohesion where none existed before, others fear it as an instrument by which powerful nations are able to impose their views and ways of understanding on the rest of the world. Cultural imperialism, or electronic colonialism as it is also called, can render the older forms

The Global Village Amusement Park, Seoul, Korea. The kitsch occidentalist facade is an Asian equivalent of orientalism.

of imperialism and colonialism based on military strength unnecessary.[9] Whether we regard the power of mass media—and communications and information technology—with hope or mistrust, it is a potent force for cultural convergence and globalisation. Although the mass media tend to dominate discussion of cultural convergence, the issues of concern clearly have to do with much more than electronic communication. Often 'culture' in this context carries a meaning along the lines of 'the arts and entertainment', high culture and popular culture, *terza rima* and 'Temptation Island'. The emphasis tends to be on areas of activity that strongly influence the way we understand or think about the world, yet stand apart from practical affairs or economic life. On the one hand, such an emphasis runs the risk of understating the extent to which culture even in this narrow sense may be influenced by economic and other 'practical' considerations, while on the other it carries the even greater danger of narrowing our concern to certain types of communication. What should be the main focus is the control of communication *per se*, whether it relies on electronic media, the printed word, or face-to-face interaction. The basic questions relate to how information flows are affected by technological, economic and political change. Expressing the problem in terms of access to and control of information makes it easier to see its links with what is frequently treated as separate issue: the creation and control of knowledge.

## Science and technology

One aspect of the globalisation process that receives close attention is what is commonly referred to as the internationalisation of science and technology, or technoglobalism. These expressions come from Organisation for Economic

Cooperation and Development (OECD) science and technology policy documents, and therefore carry a fairly specific meaning.[10] I prefer to describe the general topic of concern as simply the globalisation of knowledge. While in some ways this may be subsumed under the heading of cultural globalisation, in others it is more fundamental and powerful in its workings, and must be considered separately. What has occurred is an international standardisation of knowledge and its application according to models derived from dominant interpretations of Western science and technology. As long as everyone agrees on the same models and methodologies, everyone is able, in theory, to participate equally in the advancement of knowledge and share in its benefits. Science and technology, according to this view, are becoming more and more international as research and development rely increasingly on collaboration across national boundaries.

In this as in other things, however, globalisation does not necessarily proceed on a basis of equality between nations. Western science and technology have developed in a cultural matrix and are supported by institutions that are quite alien, some argue, to Asian societies. When it is a question of becoming part of that system, therefore, and making use of it, members of Asian societies may have to make difficult decisions. While there may be potential benefits from doing so, it also means taking up Western assumptions, techniques and methods of organisation relating to the production of knowledge at the expense of indigenous knowledge systems and bodies of expertise. This may result in cultural upheaval and social fragmentation as Western-educated elites become isolated from more tradition-oriented sections of society.

The term 'Western science and technology' is regarded by some as highly misleading. Critics point to the fact that nations such as Japan, South Korea, China and India play a big role in the generation of this supposedly Western knowledge. However, this does not change the fact that their capacity to do so has depended on incorporation of a knowledge system that evolved largely in the West, a process that has brought about profound social and institutional change. The globalisation of Western science and technology, after all, involves more than just the physical sciences and engineering. It also extends to fields such as the social sciences, medicine, agriculture, management, public administration, and law. In other words, it affects the understanding and organisation of most areas of social, economic and political life.

## Reactions to globalisation

If we consider the various aspects of globalisation already mentioned, we find that there is no significant aspect of life in contemporary Asian societies that has not been affected strongly by this trend.

In the lives of individuals, or the existence of communities and nations, the various aspects of the process of globalisation interact; they are not experienced as separate elements easily distinguished. How individuals, communities or nations react to a particular aspect of the process, therefore, will be influenced by their experience of other elements. Thai villagers experience economic development, for example, along with their experience of television, family planning programs, public education, Buddhist reform movements, Thai nationalism, and US and Indian movies. Individual experience of all these things varies, and individuals will have quite different opinions regarding whether or not what is happening to them is a good thing. There is little point in asking, therefore, whether something as all-embracing as globalisation is good or bad.

Nevertheless a number of basic points about the process of globalisation cannot be ignored, and strongly influence the way people think about and react to the phenomenon. Most basic of all is the fact that becoming part of a larger system—be it political, social or economic—inevitably entails some loss of independence and control. By definition, parts of a system to some extent depend on each other. Dependence and loss of control will be most severe where the parts of the system are unequal in power or influence. Whatever else may be said about the global system that has developed in the last four or five decades, it cannot be said to be based on equality. Rich developed nations control most aspects of the system, and while other nations may have some say in the extent to which they participate, they cannot choose the conditions under which they will do so.

It is hardly surprising, then, that we encounter very diverse descriptions and judgments of the globalisation process. Some see it positively and describe it in terms such as development, modernisation, progress. Others see it negatively and use words such as Westernisation, imperialism, neocolonialism. However, even those who regard it favourably cannot ignore the fact that the more one community or nation is linked to the rest of the world, and the less self-sufficient it becomes, the more diminished is its autonomy and control over its affairs. This explains much of the process that is contrary to globalisation: the process of insulation.

## Aspects of insulation

Insulation is a matter of putting distance between oneself and others, becoming island-like. That distance will not always be physical, though in the case of ethnic minorities, for example, or social elites, it may be. In political and social contexts this is likely to include emphasis on having special characteristics and needs not shared by others, requiring special attention or treatment. A term used in discussion of the world economic system, 'delinking', has similar connotations, but lacks the symmetry of the insulation/globalisation dichotomy; another alternative is 'localisation', which has recently entered the vocabulary of the World Bank.[11] As emphasised at the beginning of this chapter, insulation has to do with maintaining or re-establishing control over one's own affairs. There may be costs associated with separateness, yet those costs may seem small in comparison with loss of autonomy and control.

It is in the political context that the idea of insulation is most familiar, because of a sharp increase in the number of ethnic groups striving for political independence or greater autonomy from the nation state that has absorbed them. 'Ethnogenesis' is the term applied to the creation of new nation states along ethnic lines. The most spectacular example has been the fragmentation of the former Soviet Union, leading to a large number of new nation states in Eastern Europe and Central Asia. The wars in the former Yugoslavia have been a terrible demonstration of the ferocity with which ethnic insulation may be pursued.

Consideration of some Asian examples demonstrates just how varied assertions of ethnic distinctiveness may be.[12] The long struggle of the ethnic minorities in Myanmar has for much of the time had political independence as its main objective. In the early 1990s, however, an alliance of minorities and democracy activists sought to establish a federation of ethnic states within a united Burma. A section of the Hindu Tamil minority of northern Sri Lanka has been fighting for political secession. Similarly, Tibetans have been campaigning for political independence from China, but in their case this would entail a return to what most regard as the political arrangement that existed until the 1950s. In 1999 the people of East Timor were able to gain independence from Indonesia as a result of a vote on self-determination agreed to by Indonesian President Habibie. However, East Timor had been annexed by Indonesia in 1975, following the withdrawal of the former colonial power Portugal. It is likely that East Timor's secession will strengthen not only independence movements elsewhere in Indonesia, but also the determination of the Indonesian authorities to curtail such movements. In another fairly recent territorial addition to Indonesia, Irian Jaya—or West Papua, as it is otherwise known, and as it is referred to throughout this text—it appears there are difficult times ahead.

But does insulation along ethnic lines necessarily include a demand for political independence? Frequently all that is wanted is more autonomy, a greater recognition by the state of the distinctive identity and needs of the minority in question and a greater say in the management of its affairs. This applies to many Tamils in Sri Lanka, for example, and many of the ethnic minorities in China, India and Vietnam: they would like more control over their own affairs, but for a host of reasons do not see political independence as a realistic option. The Dalai Lama, the Tibetan religious and political leader in exile, has been more cautious than many of his countrymen in recent years, campaigning for regional autonomy under Chinese rule rather than secession from the People's Republic.

The question of regional or local autonomy leads to the issue of insulation in regard to economic and social development. Many critics of development as an economic and social objective argue that it is fundamentally misconceived because it tends to be seen as a single path along which all nations travel. There are not different sorts of development, only different stations along the road to it.[13] Western nations and Japan have moved furthest along this road, naturally, and other nations can only follow in their steps. In reaction to this, critics emphasise the need for each community or nation to pursue its own path, to explore alternatives, and to do what is appropriate in its particular social and economic circumstances. The fact that certain economic strategies have worked for the United States or Japan does not mean that they will work for everyone else. There are no universal rules or solutions because economic and social problems are different in each case, the outcome of combinations of dissimilar circumstances.

One of the more regrettable consequences of the end of the cold war has been the widespread loss of conviction that there is any realistic alternative to capitalism as an economic system. The USSR no longer exists, while China and Vietnam, and to a lesser extent Laos, are turning to the market economy to overcome economic and social problems. North Korea has been forced to call on capitalist neighbours to prevent its people starving. There are no socialist economies to inspire alternative lines of economic development. This makes the task of economic insulation now much harder than in the 1960s and 1970s, say, when China was an inspiration for many Third World countries. In recent years calls for alternative paths of economic and social development have tended not to come from national governments but from individuals, communities, ethnic minorities, non-government organisations, and provincial governments. An example from the last-mentioned category is the Indian state of Kerala. Kerala has given priority to securing the basic needs of its whole population rather than Western-style industrialisation and economic growth, and some see its strategy as a workable alternative to competition in the world economic system.

A particularly powerful form of insulation widely used is religious insulation, that is, the assertion of separateness or distinctiveness on the basis of religion. Historically, this has often involved a claim of being a chosen people, selected by God to carry out his purpose and favoured by him in this world and the next. It is a claim that has by no means been absent from recent acts of religious insulation. It has been made, for example, by various radical or fundamentalist Muslim groups seeking to establish a truly Islamic society in opposition to the secular or Westernised states under which they live. The strongest recent manifestation of religious insulation at a national level has undoubtedly been the Iranian Revolution, after which Iran took up a position that even according to Islamic criteria was very distinctive, and the clergy-dominated government set about purging the nation of the noxious influence of the West. It was a reaction against half a century of Westernisation under Reza Shah Pahlavi (ruled 1926–41) and his son Mohammed Reza Shah (ruled 1949–79), who made determined efforts to undermine Islam in Iran.

At a personal no less than a national level, religion may be a way of emphasising distinctiveness or creating a separate identity. This may be seen particularly in the formation of new religions or cults. Japan and South Korea have witnessed the emergence of many such religious movements, and studies of their membership have reached conclusions similar to those elsewhere. Some argue that people attracted to the new religions tend to feel socially isolated or overwhelmed by the changes going on around them; they tend to be those looking for greater control over the circumstances of their lives, who feel that their particular needs are not being met by existing institutions.

In India, taking on a new religious identity may be done in quite dramatic fashion, in the context of mass conversions involving hundreds or even thousands of *dalits* ('the oppressed') or Untouchables. In order to separate themselves from the Hindu society in which they have experienced severe discrimination and hardship, many *dalits* have converted en masse to Buddhism, Islam or Christianity. The most famous instance was in 1956, when the charismatic leader of the *dalits*, Dr B. R. Ambedkar, converted to Buddhism together with more than 3 million of his followers.[14]

If religion may be used as a means of insulation, the same applies to culture more generally. That is hardly news, of course, since insulation along ethnic lines often amounts to much the same thing. Nevertheless it is a point worth pondering because it is easy to lose sight of the fact that insulation in terms of 'culture' is not necessarily limited to ethnic minorities. It is done by all sorts of social groups developing their own subcultures. It is also done frequently at the level of the nation state, in the context of a search for a national identity or national characteristics. As far as individual citizens go, this may amount to focusing on similarities rather than differences, but there is nothing paradoxical about it. National identity becomes an issue only in the context of increased contact with the outside world, when it becomes necessary to clarify distinctions where before there may have been no need or awareness of them.

Cultural insulation may be pursued in a variety of ways. One of the most familiar is censorship. By controlling the inward flow of information a state or a people may try to preserve cultural distinctiveness. Another type of strategy involves reinforcing those aspects of indigenous culture most incompatible with the external influences causing concern. This often entails going back to customs or institutions that have fallen into disuse, or even inventing a new past. Elaboration of national histories or mythologies is standard practice in the development of group identities that are intended to strengthen social cohesion and keep the outside world at bay. Perhaps the

Opposing the global reach of a superpower: the former US embassy, Tehran, Iran.

most spectacular example of this approach, as well as the most absurd, was the suggestion (apparently serious) that the entire country of Cambodia be turned into a Khmer theme park. The past would literally become the present and provide a response to Cambodia's acute social and economic problems.[15]

Issues of national identity have certainly not arisen only in response to postwar globalisation. Yet it seems true to say that in recent decades national identity has become a dominant preoccupation in much of Asia. Japan, Korea, and Thailand are good examples. In China the question has a longer history, as indicated by the following comments made by writer and social critic Lu Xun (1881–1936) in 1918 in response to calls to preserve China's national characteristics:

> What do we mean by 'national characteristics'? The words appear to denote something peculiar to one country, not found in any other. In other words, something distinctive. But distinctive things are not necessarily good, so why must they be preserved?
>
> Take the case of a man with a wen on his face or a carbuncle on his forehead, which certainly mark him off from other people and make him something special, and can therefore be considered to be his 'characteristics'. I think it would be better to remove these 'characteristics' and be like everyone else ...
>
> A friend of mine has said most aptly: 'If we want to preserve our national characteristics, we must first make sure that they can preserve us'.
>
> Certainly self-preservation comes first. All we ask is whether a thing has the power to preserve us, not whether it is a characteristic or not.[16]

The final sort of insulation that must be mentioned here is what for want of a better term I will call epistemological insulation. Despite the large number of syllables used to designate it, the idea is quite straightforward. The internationalisation of the scientific and technological systems originating in the West has in some quarters intensified a response that has long been around in a variety of forms: a rejection of the claim that 'Western' scientific knowledge can in fact achieve complete objectivity or complete independence of the social context in which it is generated. More positively, the response has tended to attribute value to local or indigenous knowledge systems, and to insist that Western science should complement rather than displace such systems.

It has been pointed out that the theoretical and methodological problems thrown up by the idea of reconciling or combining different knowledge systems are considerable.[17] Here it is enough to emphasise that the view that Western science and indigenous knowledge somehow need to be fitted together has not been arrived at by dogma or intuition. This conclusion has been reached independently by many people involved in projects in developing Asian countries and other parts of the world. The fact is that when it is a question of applying knowledge, or even just understanding what is going on, universal 'laws' often just do not work. The knowledge of local people, even when dependent upon quite divergent systems of interpretation, frequently turns out to be indispensable for success.

An eloquent statement of these concerns is provided by the Indian environmentalist Vandana Shiva. She argues that the widespread replacement in India of naturally diverse native forests with monoculture plantations of exotic species for commercial exploitation is a symptom of a deeper malady. Monocultures are transferred to the ground only after they have colonised the mind. The replacement of the natural richness and biodiversity of indigenous forests occurs when local knowledge and understanding of the forests, derived from varied community interaction with and use of the forests, have been replaced by a narrow 'scientific' understanding dominated by economic interests. Shiva argues: 'Modern scientific knowledge is a particular cultural system with a particular relationship to power. It has, however, been projected as above and beyond culture and politics. Its relationship with the project of economic development has been invisible; and therefore it has become an effective legitimiser for the homogenisation of the world and the erosion of its ecological and cultural richness.'[18]

This is a controversial position that many would regard as denying the possibility of real knowledge altogether. In particular, it could be interpreted as claiming that Western science is the embodiment of a single type of concern or consciousness, sometimes referred to as technological instrumentalism or rationalism. Such claims do not do justice to the complexity of knowledge systems. But the issues raised here leave no doubt about the need to consider seriously the way knowledge is created in different cultural settings, and how globalisation affects our understanding of it.

## In an unequal world

Observed from a distance, the trends of globalisation and insulation as described may seem to acquire, like the principles of *yin* and *yang*, a metaphysical significance and inevitability. I make no such claims on their behalf. Globalisation and insulation are simply useful concepts for finding order in broad sweeps of social, cultural and economic change. Their usefulness may be enhanced by reiterating here a few main points.

Globalisation or the linking up of sociocultural and political entities to form larger ones occurs within nation states as well as between them. Because of the large amount of territory this study attempts to cover, it will not always be possible to give change at the local or regional level the attention it deserves. But this does not make it any less significant. Regardless of whether globalisation is considered internationally or intranationally, however, the single most important point is that it rarely involves equals. Some social groups, some nations, are able to dictate the form global links will take and impose their interests on others. While those in a weaker position may sometimes be able to choose whether or not to be part of the globalisation process, they have little say over the terms of their involvement.

Insulation is a difficult option, even where it is feasible. In the lives of individuals and nations the many aspects of globalisation interact and it is hard to isolate the influence of a single element. To deny that good may come from interaction with the wider world would be as silly as to deny that it may be harmful. A decision to forgo all the possible benefits would require social discipline of a sort rarely encountered. The only realistic general principle can be that a people should have as much control as possible over the ways in which it interacts with the surrounding world.

## CHAPTER TWO

# State, Society, Individual

## Static concepts, fluid reality

The points made in the previous chapter are innocent enough. Nations experience globalisation differently, according to their cultural traditions and historical circumstances. How they react to a given aspect of globalisation depends on their experience of the others. The power relations that characterise global links trigger the countervailing tendency of insulation. Both globalisation and insulation operate within nations as well as between them. This latter point should alert us to the fact that generalisations and stereotypes based on national differences will not take us very far. To understand what is happening in Asian countries we have to consider the differences within as well as between them. We have to get beyond the illusion of solidity and stability that concepts such as nation, state and culture nourish, to grasp something of the variability and fluidity of experience. Nation, state, society, culture: while these terms denote entities that endure over long periods, this does not mean that they are unchanging or homogeneous. It is better to think of them as processes rather than entities. A river exists in time, but its streams and banks continue to shift about.

Before examining in detail the forces of globalisation and insulation at work in contemporary Asian societies, therefore, it is necessary to sluice away the apparent solidity of some of the main concepts with which we have to work. It is also necessary to consider how the elements of those processes we call nation, state, society, and culture interact to produce the complex and fluid reality we experience.

## States, nations, ethnic groups

The UN, that symbol of globalisation, is a body whose members are called 'nations' and which are represented for the purposes of the organisation by 'states'. State representatives vested with authority speak on behalf of the nations in question. Taking this as our cue, we can take the term 'state' to refer simply to those persons and institutions with the highest authority in a society or nation, with a responsibility for government and the maintenance of social order, including the enactment and application of laws. A state may be a democratically elected government (as in India, Japan, and the Philippines), an authoritarian government whose authority is based on a secular ideology (for example, the Marxist governments of China, North Korea, and Vietnam), a theocracy whose authority derives from religion (as in Iran), or a military regime whose authority is based on its claim to serve the interests of the nation (as in the case of Myanmar and Pakistan). The systems of administration and ways of wielding power of status vary widely, but all claim that their power is somehow legitimate, and all receive at least enough tacit support from the people to maintain their position.

One of the assumptions of the UN as an organisation has been that states and nations are coextensive with each other, that a state represents or has authority over one and only one nation. This is the essential idea expressed by the term 'nation state' and the definition of national identity in terms of allegiance to a particular state. For very good reasons, the UN has tended to ignore the fact that the term 'nation' has two common meanings: as well as nation state, a nation is conceived in terms of a people or ethnic group. If in what follows I use the term nation only in reference to nation states, it is in order to avoid possible confusion rather than from fear of destabilising the existing world order.

A nation in the sense of a people is a social group that shares a common identity. Nationalism in this sense is self-identification in terms of belonging to a nation. Members of a nation, people or ethnic group tend to have, or see themselves as having, certain attributes in common, including a shared history or mythology; the same language; a common religion or culture; a homeland or motherland; a shared destiny or purpose; a single system of government and law; and political sovereignty. The list varies and not all items apply to all peoples. Sometimes religion is subsumed under the heading 'culture', sometimes not. Some peoples do not have a distinct language of their own. Others do not have their own territory or control over their own affairs. While a nation in the sense of a people or ethnic group can exist without a territory of its own, a nation state cannot. A nation state must have a territory and a system of government and law, as well as a people, a point implicit in the concept of the political and legal jurisdiction of a state.

In a small number of cases—Korea is the best Asian example—the borders of the nation state coincide with lines of ethnic division, so that the country in question is ethnically homogeneous. In most cases, however, they do not. Some peoples, such as the Kurds of West Asia, the Kazakhs of Central Asia, and the Hmong of South-East Asia, are spread across the boundaries of three or four or even more nation states. Some nation states have large numbers of different ethnic groups or peoples living within their borders. Indonesia has more than three hundred distinct peoples or ethnic groups and India more than two hundred, while China, the Philippines, and Vietnam each have more than fifty. Such ethnic diversity makes generalising about the countries in question a dangerous pastime.

Recent writers on nation states and nationalism emphasise their unnaturalness. Nations, we are told, are 'artifacts of men's convictions and loyalties and solidarities', 'imagined communities' whose members 'will never know most of their fellow-members, meet them, or even hear of them, yet in the minds of each lives the image of their communion'. Nationalism 'invents' nations where they do not exist.[1] The artificial nature of nations was highlighted by the large number of new nation states that emerged during the period of decolonisation after the Second World War. The political changes of the time demonstrated the uncanny power of lines fixed on maps by accidents of history to shape the emotions and lives of individuals. People are prepared to fight with those who live outside those arbitrary lines and die if necessary to preserve them.

Yet those who draw attention to the artificiality of nations usually do so in order to praise rather than to denigrate them. For nation states are seen as the constructs of reason; they rise above the primitive emotions and loyalties of family, tribe and religion, and owe their existence to rational pursuit of the common interest of all citizens. They are regarded as a product of the European Enlightenment, embodying the sorts of socio-political changes introduced by the American and French revolutions. The nation state is regarded as a superior arrangement to the extent that it is democratic, with ordinary citizens able to participate in the political process, and to the extent that it is secular, that is, based on the dictates of reason rather than religious dogma. Nationalism as an emotion is interpreted as a widening of moral concern and social responsibility beyond the limited sphere of propinquity, and therefore a superior type of political sentiment. 'Globalism', according to this account, could be regarded as the next, and presumably the last, progression in sentiment. This is precisely what is claimed by those enthusiastic about aspects of globalisation, whether free trade or global ecology.

This approach to the concept of the nation state is misleading in at least two ways. First, it implies that other forms of group identification and allegiance—especially ethnicity—are more solid and natural, embodying primitive forces that reason should dominate but which all too often break out and reassert themselves. The breakup of nation states and the brutality unleashed thereby, as in the former Yugoslavia, are seen as proof of the continuing potency of those forces. But the fact is that ethnic identity is no more natural or fixed than national identity. While it is true that nationalism and national identity can be fabricated, altered and manipulated, the same is true of ethnic identity. Despite the fact that ethnic identities are typically established over longer timespans, they are no less susceptible to change. Second, this way of looking at the concept of the nation state exaggerates the difference between it and other earlier forms of political organisation, and underestimates the continuity of institutions and ways of doing things where there is a transition from one political form to another. In the case of Asian states with long political traditions, this is particularly important when it comes to understanding their present political cultures.

The fluidity of ethnic identity is discussed further in Chapter 4. It is an issue that has been studied by anthropologists, who have found, for example, that members of numerous ethnic groups in South-East Asia adjust their identity in response to changing circumstances.[2] That individuals may shift across ethnic boundaries, and ethnic identities themselves may change or evolve, does not mean that such identities lack substance or are intrinsically ephemeral. It just means that the foundations of ethnicity—especially culture—are not static. However, the point is not merely that individuals change their ethnic identity, but also that group identities themselves change over time and new group identities are created. Perhaps the best modern Asian example of an ethnic identity being created is that of the Sikhs of India. Sikh identity can be traced to a precise beginning in the religious teachings of Guru Nanak (1469–1538). Around this new religious doctrine a distinct identity developed, in time leading, for example, to the mythologising of Sikh links with the Punjab in north-western India and the quest to establish a Sikh homeland there. (The issue of Sikh identity is discussed further in Chapter 4.)

In terms of solidity, therefore, there may not be much difference between national and ethnic identity. Despite the fact that most ethnic identities have histories longer than that of the relatively recent concept of the nation state and the identities it has generated, ethnic identities are fabricated too, and continue to be adapted to changing circumstances, including the emergence of a world order constructed in terms of nation states. Nor can it be assumed that one form of identity necessarily supplants another. Individuals may, and often do, have multiple identities.

It is true that national identity may be broader and more inclusive than ethnic identity, since one nation may comprise a number of distinct ethnic groups, and in this sense nationalism could be seen as progressive. Yet cross-cultural identities of this sort are not new. The great religious traditions have generated them too. The fifteenth-century Muslim traveller Ibn Battuta could roam from Morocco to East Africa, Mecca to southern Russia, and to India and China, yet everywhere be accepted as a member of the great community (*umma*) that was, and remains, the foundation of Islamic identity.[3] For most of their history, educated Chinese were not greatly concerned about race or ethnicity. They defined civilisation in terms of adherence to the teachings of the sages—what in the West is known as Confucianism—and accepted those of non-Han Chinese background on common terms as long as they followed the same norms. There is more than one reason, therefore, for regarding nationalism as a modern religion.

It would take considerable courage, if not stubbornness, to argue that the broader, more inclusive identities supported by nationalism are somehow more reasonable or enlightened than those based on, say, Islam, Buddhism or Confucianism. Inclusive identities based on religion have not always succeeded in preventing parochial or sectarian strife, but the record of national identities in this regard is no better. There is no justification for assuming that nationalism is the expression of a more 'advanced' way of thinking than religion.

## Culture

The question of the construction and reconstruction of national and ethnic identities has very much to do with sharing a common culture and interests. Continuities and discontinuities between nation states and earlier forms of political organisation can be understood in terms of the evolution of the political culture of groups. It is useful, therefore, to consider briefly the concept of culture itself.

The root meaning of 'culture' is that of cultivation or improvement. The term was transferred from agriculture, the growing of crops, to the cultivation of the mind through the study of the arts and humanities. Culture, in this sense of high culture, was considered to be what distinguished humanity from the world of brutes; culture and nature were seen as opposing spheres. The distinction was taken up by anthropologists when they appropriated the term to refer not just to the arts and humanities, but to everything that is the product of human thought and activity rather than nature.

Culture is what makes it possible for social groups to function and for individuals to develop. Human beings are social animals who 'complete or finish [them]selves through culture'.[4] A group's culture consists of accumulated patterns of thought and action that are not instinctive, that have to be learnt and deliberately passed on from one generation to the next. Cultures evolve over time, and while, by definition, they have continuity, they must be understood as an ongoing process of change and adaptation. A society's cultural heritage may be regarded as the historical record of its efforts to survive in a changing environment. A group's culture is what marks it off from other groups and provides the basis for group and individual identity. Individuals are accepted as members of society by virtue of their knowledge of its culture, by their ability to follow its rules and respect its values.[5]

One of the problems that discussion of culture in general throws up is that it makes it seem as if all culture is beyond criticism, that it is good by definition. After all, the root meaning of the word is improvement, the cultivation or refinement of a state of nature through human effort. Yet if we use the word with something like its anthropological meaning of the accumulated beliefs, ways of doing things and institutions of a society, then we have to allow at least the possibility that some parts of a given culture may be bad, undesirable or (from the perspective of cultures as adaptive systems) dysfunctional. This may be the judgment of not only members of other societies—*that* is common enough and usually amounts to no more than ill-informed prejudice—but also of members of the society in question. Customs, ideas, and institutions may outlive the circumstances that gave rise to them, with the result that they become obstacles to the satisfaction of needs rather than the means of their fulfilment.

Cultural change is rarely 'managed' in a conscious way, and where it is this is usually done unilaterally by the state. A conscious civil process of cultural change requires a host of structures and institutions for the formulation, discussion and evaluation of alternatives, for popular involvement in changes that affect all members of society. There are strong grounds for holding that the management of change—that is, making change timely, orderly and constructive rather than unpredictable, violent, and chaotic—is the single most important problem facing all contemporary societies.

The other basic point to be made here regarding the concept of culture is that although we talk about members of a social group sharing a culture, this does not mean that all individuals in the group think and act in the same way. While this may seem elementary, explanations offered by social scientists often break down at precisely this point: they assume that a certain type of behaviour is explained if they can relate it to broad influences such as, say, Islam, Confucianism or Hinduism. A culture accounts for the differences between members of a society as well as the similarities. This is a fundamental problem in cross-cultural study, particularly when a number of different cultures are being considered. Our attention focuses so strongly on the differences between them that we ignore the fact that it is largely the pattern of differences *within* them that makes them distinctive. How the individual sees the world depends on the particular place in it he or she occupies, and to identify that place as 'Buddhism' or

'Japan' is not very helpful. In the 1960s a series of scholarly works was produced with titles like *The Indian Mind*, *The Chinese Mind*, and *The Japanese Mind*. They were serious publications containing articles by leading indigenous as well as Western scholars. They show that national stereotypes are not necessarily unsophisticated, and that they can appeal to cultural insiders as well as those looking on from outside. Not surprisingly, the Indian/Japanese/Chinese mind turned out to be rather like the minds of the authors, with little suggestion that individuals might vary according to gender, class, caste or ethnic background, let alone personality and experience.[6]

The anthropologist Ward Goodenough draws a useful analogy between knowledge of a culture and knowledge of a language. He points out that while mastery of a language entails applying general linguistic rules and being able to reproduce combinations of sounds in the way that others do, the linguistic competence of each individual is slightly idiosyncratic, somewhat different from that of all other speakers of that language. What matters is not that everyone has precisely the same competence, but that there is enough commonality for them to be able to communicate. Ability to communicate effectively is the functional definition of linguistic mastery. Similarly, it does not matter that no two individuals have precisely the same understanding of their culture. All that is necessary for them to function as members of their society is that their understanding be sufficiently like that of others to enable them to interact successfully, to master the rules and expectations that govern the behaviour of those with whom they come into contact.[7]

## How societies work

'The first principle of civilisation', according to Friedrich Nietzsche (1844–1900), is that 'any custom is better than no custom'. A society can function only in so far as there are rules or guidelines to channel behaviour. For humans to interact, live together and cooperate, they must be reasonably sure what the consequences of any action will be before it is performed. A society without rules would be impossible because the consequences of human behaviour would be unpredictable. There has to be a shared understanding of what sort of response or reaction is appropriate in a given situation. A society's culture embodies or expresses these shared rules and understandings.

The rules that form the basis of society—its customs, mores, norms, laws—help to make social interaction possible by making the future predictable. Only if the future is predictable are humans able to gain some measure of control over it. Our lives are shaped by our expectations, for it is in our expectations that our sense of what will be and what should be come together. Rules establish not only our ability to predict and participate in society, but also our understanding of what is fair or right. Rules give content to the principle of reciprocity that forms the core of social interaction: the expectation that if one person performs a given action, certain appropriate responses by others will follow as a matter of course.

When rules are not followed and social interaction is unpredictable, frustration, insecurity, and anxiety result. These are psychologically damaging. To make the future predictable, and so to be in a position to control it, individuals and social groups are often willing to forgo a great deal, to put up with a lot of inequality and deprivation. The sense of justice may be understood largely in terms of a satisfied expectation that the rules, whatever equal or unequal treatment they may prescribe, will be followed. Conversely, the sense of injustice may be understood largely in terms of disappointed expectations. But expectations do not stay still, they move about, and with them our understanding of how we should treat each other, the forms that reciprocal action should take. So the rules are constantly being revised, with many forces competing for influence. Justice entails a sense of what the rules should be as well as an expectation that they will be observed.[8]

One of the functions of religions the world over has always been to give a sense of purpose and predictability to the life of the individual, to provide reasons for what would otherwise seem random and intolerable. Religions spell out consequences of actions even beyond death, and invoke the power and omniscience of divine beings to render the future predictable. Islam and Christianity both have conceptions of an afterlife in which the consequences of earthly existence are reckoned up. Hinduism and Buddhism both make use of the concepts of *karma* (action or causation) and *samsara* (rebirth) to extend understanding of the consequences of action beyond this life.

The assumptions of Hinduism as a religion amount to what is perhaps the most far-reaching attempt to do away with the unpredictability of human life, by establishing a system of causality that fills all time and space. The doctrine of karma applies strict causality to all human and natural events, in accordance with a cosmic order that is at once both moral and natural. The inevitability of consequences that follow all actions brings certitude with it. The doctrine of samsara extends that strict causation and certitude backward and forward throughout time. Suffering and joy in this life may appear arbitrary or unjust, but may be understood as the outcomes of actions in previous lives, following them as surely as night follows day.

Not all the rules that guide and shape the lives of individuals carry equal weight, in the sense that disregarding them brings strong moral disapproval or legal sanctions. Yet even behavioural codes that do not have the status of moral law and are less formally enforced may be just as important for social harmony or individual well-being. For example, rules governing interaction between parents and their children shape the character and behaviour of children as they develop. This is a matter that received a good deal of attention in the Confucian clan rules traditionally compiled by elite Chinese families. In Indonesia, Thailand or Japan, rules that fall under the heading of manners or etiquette may be elaborate and are regarded as much more than expressions of politeness.

Modes of address, rules about touching others, rules of precedence, gift-giving and style of dress may all help to define the individual's position in society. Sensitive observance of the nuances reveals a person's character and social awareness. Sumptuary laws—regulations designed to reinforce social distinctions by controlling consumption patterns, such as the clothing members of particular social groups may wear, the sorts of houses they may live in, the sorts of transport they are entitled to use—were a feature of most pre-modern Asian societies. One of the reasons for the wide variety in textile design in the traditional societies of what is now Indonesia was that individuals relied heavily on their clothing to give others the information about their social standing that custom forbade them to communicate verbally. While sumptuary codes may have disappeared from most Asian societies, informal distinctions in consumption may still be very significant.[9]

Although the idea of rules is useful for understanding in a rudimentary way how societies work, it can mislead by making everything seem more straightforward, unambiguous and (worst of all) more passive than it really is. It suggests that there are no choices to be made, that individuals do not have space to manoeuvre or negotiate, to bend and adapt rules in the process of applying them. We talk about rules because we need to identify patterns in social behaviour, but the patterns do not stay still; they move about and are constantly being reconstructed. Therefore if we use the concept of rules, it is best to think of them as rules of thumb, as general principles or rough guidelines for behaviour that call for interpretation and perhaps even ingenuity in their application. To be regarded as mature and socially aware in any society, it is rarely enough to demonstrate an ability or willingness to follow rules; exercising judgment or imagination is also necessary.

## Where do rules come from?

How people regard a given set of rules or principles, and their reasons for heeding them or not, is influenced to a large extent by where the rules come from. If they are persuaded, for example, that rules are the result of divine decree, then they are unlikely to question their authority. Even where a rule seriously disadvantages them relative to other members of their society, they accept what they believe is God's will and therefore beyond human control.

Nevertheless, for social rules to be heeded they have to offer at least a possibility of satisfying the basic needs of the majority of the group. But this need not mean that the social majority will have much say in deciding the rules. Everything points to the fact that, even in relatively egalitarian societies, those with high status and authority have a disproportionate amount of influence when it comes to rule-making. Nor is the influence of high-ranking social groups simply the result of their ability to command obedience. Nietzsche pointed out that in a large number of languages the moral terms 'good' and 'bad' can be traced back to social class distinctions. Etymologically, an action was good not because of its results but because it was carried out by a good or well-born person; an action was bad not because of its results but because it was performed by a base or plebeian person.

This does not mean that those of high birth behaved in ways we would now call moral, but it does imply that the behavioural ideals of the social elite were influential in shaping the moral rules of the society. Supporting evidence for this interpretation comes from the philosophy of Confucius. One of the key terms he used was *junzi*. It is conventionally translated as 'gentleman' and refers to someone in earnest about living up to moral ideals. In Confucius' day it literally meant 'the son of a lord', that is, a nobleman, but Confucius used it to advance the idea that nobility was a matter of moral and intellectual refinement rather than hereditary rank. The English word 'noble' has acquired the same double meaning.[10]

A rather different example of the influence of the social elite on rules and customs generally is the old Chinese custom of footbinding. Binding the feet of little girls to keep them small and enhance their sexual attractiveness or erotic power is a custom that appears to have originated at the imperial court during the eleventh century. It is said that a concubine endowed by nature with particularly small feet was lucky enough to establish herself as the emperor's favourite. Within a short time a fashion for small feet had spread among women of the social elite, and in time it extended to the lower levels of society as well. As a custom it was particularly nasty. At an early age a girl's toes were bent back under the soles of her feet and wrapped so tightly that normal development of the bones was arrested. The pain was enormous; severe hygiene and health problems were common; to walk normally was out of the question. Although being unable to walk was not necessarily a problem for upper-class ladies who were carried everywhere in sedan chairs, the implications for those who had to do housework or labour in the fields were more serious. Yet this did not prevent peasant or worker families from binding the feet of their girls. Those who wanted to rise socially and economically bound their daughters' feet if they could. It conferred status and helped to attract a better class of husband, connection with whom would help to raise the social and economic standing of the whole family.[11]

This example is useful because it does not involve compulsion. The social elite did not force those below them to adopt footbinding or use it as a strategy for improving their position. It might be argued that poor people would only adopt such a custom if they saw no other avenues for social or economic advancement, but the evidence suggests that many who adopted it—for example, well-to-do families from every level of society—did have a choice. All that was compelling was the power of fashion, as those below felt obliged to imitate their social betters.

The argument that social elites play a dominant part in setting the rules by which society operates has found expression in what is known as the dominant ideology thesis. According to the thesis, the ruling class determines most of the rules and values that shape society and thereby manages to protect its own privileged position. It does this by persuading the lower social classes to accept its view of the world, despite the fact that this perpetuates their own subordinate position. It is a neo-Marxist idea intended to show that all history is, as Marx said, a history of class struggle, though the struggle is not always overt. The dominant ideology thesis has been strongly criticised, on the one hand because it exaggerates the extent to which lower social groups do accept the elite view of the world and their place in it, and on the other because it understates the extent to which unequal social arrangements may involve genuine cooperation arising from a shared sense of reciprocity or mutual obligation.[12]

While there is little doubt that the rules shaping society do owe a lot to the influence of elites, they will be adopted by the lower social classes only if those rules make sense of their day-to-day experience: there are limits to what people can be persuaded to believe. Even if the world view they share with the ruling class reinforces their subordinate position, it may be acceptable if it provides reasons for their situation and helps to make the future predictable. Acceptance of the world view of the elite need not be total or uncritical; it is much more likely to be selective in accordance with some hard-headed, practical criteria.

## Religion and society

Is religion the source or foundation of the rules by which societies operate? Certainly the major religions have tended to see themselves as providing the ultimate reasons for the way things are and the way they ought to be. However, it is easy to make too much of the explanatory functions of religion, to pay too much attention to religious belief and not enough to religious communities, institutions, and the attitudes and behaviour they require.

One of the most common and influential views of religion in secularised Western societies regards it as pseudo-science, an attempt to explain the world that is irredeemably superstitious and irrational, based on dogma rather than empirical evidence. Religion (*any* religion) is essentially a primitive mode of thought from which Western societies, fortunately, have been able to liberate themselves. Herein lies their superiority. If Asian nations want to develop or modernise, then they too must adopt the modern way of thinking. Without scientific understanding there can be no modern civilisation. Modernisation is thought of largely in terms of secularisation, the winding back of religious influence.

Until quite recently it was not uncommon for Western intellectuals to claim that people from other races or cultures had a mentality or logic different from their own. It was as if the brains of 'primitive people' were wired up in a different way and they would therefore never be able to catch up. Perhaps the most miraculous aspect of what has taken place in East Asia over the last forty or fifty years is that it has put a stop to this nonsense. Nevertheless many of the leaders of Asian countries bent on modernisation have equated religious influence with backwardness, and have done their best to encourage secularisation. This applies to Reza Shah Pahlavi and Mohammed Reza Shah in Iran between 1926 and 1979, Jawaharlal Nehru and his daughter Indira Gandhi in India after 1947, and the communist leaders of China and Vietnam from the late 1940s.

Yet in developed countries modernisation has not meant the extinction of religion at all. In the United States, widely regarded as the quintessential modern society, levels of individual religious involvement remain high and new religious cults continue to thrive. Similarly, in Japan and South Korea, the most developed countries in Asia, religion remains influential in the lives of large sections of the population, with both established and new cults attracting supporters. This indicates that religion cannot be understood simply as an irrational and outmoded way of thinking at odds with modernisation. Some aspects of modernisation may in fact encourage religiosity.

The continuing influence and attraction of religion in contemporary societies becomes easier to understand when we widen our focus from the issue of belief to other aspects of religion, which may turn out to be more significant. These include religious attitudes to experience, membership of the religious community, and the institutions that embody and sustain religion. These considerations make it harder to overlook the fact that religion is a part of society and therefore subject to change and competing influences like any other section of it, and that the differences between religious systems *do* matter. A society usually explains as much about its dominant religion as the religion explains about the society.

The major religious traditions of Asia—Hinduism, Buddhism, Confucianism, and Islam—differ in fundamental ways.[13] Islam is strictly monotheistic while Hinduism has many gods, whose status and patterns of worship vary from place to place, so much so that many scholars argue that Hinduism is really many distinct religions. On the other hand, it is widely held that Buddhism and Confucianism are not really religions at all, because neither requires belief in divine powers or beings that control human affairs and may be influenced through appropriate religious behaviour. The original teachings of the Buddha (Siddhartha Gautama, 563–483 BCE) made no reference to gods or the supernatural, and in the Theravada ('Teaching of the Elders') tradition of Buddhism the psychological and philosophical focus of the original teachings has been maintained, at least in elite versions. In popular Theravada Buddhism, however, admixtures of local animistic cults abound, while in Mahayana Buddhism ('The Greater Vehicle to Salvation') the historical Buddha came to be regarded as one manifestation of an eternal Buddha principle, various incarnations of which may be worshipped more or less independently. Accordingly, in Tibet, China, Mongolia, Korea, and Japan, where Mahayana teachings have been predominant, 'the divine' has been an intrinsic part of religious belief.

Confucianism is very much concerned with the matters of this world rather than the next and is essentially non-theistic. Confucius (551–479 BCE) himself cautioned against too much interest in spiritual matters, and later Confucian philosophers such as Xunzi (third century BCE) gave very rationalistic interpretations of religious practices. Nevertheless, what is commonly called ancestor worship has been central to Confucianism through the centuries, and the Confucian establishment was on the whole quite tolerant of folk religions.

Islam, like Buddhism and Confucianism, is clearly associated with the influence of a historical individual: Muhammad (570–632). But Islam is not regarded by believers as his creation. Rather, Islam is the true religion that has been known since earliest times, but fell into confusion under the influence of Jews and Christians. God is merciful and revealed the sacred word to Muhammad his messenger. The Koran is the final and definitive statement of God. Similarly it may be argued that Confucianism did not start with Confucius. For Confucius taught his followers to value tradition, to internalise the true spirit of their cultural inheritance, which necessarily included practices and values established long before his time. In this sense reverence for one's forebears, or ancestor worship, has been central to Confucianism without being a Confucian practice.

Hinduism differs from the other three major religious traditions in that its origins are not closely related to a historical individual. Such unity as exists between its many gods and cults comes from the Veda, a collection of Sanskrit texts dating from around 1500–900 BCE. One of the arguments for the view that Hinduism should not be seen as a single religion is that its name derives from a Persian word for the Indian subcontinent, and was used by Muslim conquerors to refer to all the indigenous (that is, non-Islamic) cults of the region.

The most significant differences between the four religious traditions and their impact on society relate, however, to their key supporting institutions. The most powerful institution of Confucianism has always been the family. It is within the

Although the influence of Confucius remains strong in East Asia, his home town, Qufu, Shandong, is now a tourist destination rather than a site of imperial sacrifices in his honour. His grave (left) attracts many tour groups (right).

family that essential precepts and understandings have been passed on, and this has largely happened independently of the rise or demise of the main state institutions of Confucianism, that is, the ruler and the imperial examination system. It is the familial basis of Confucianism that has given it its remarkable resilience and durability, its capacity to survive long periods of political upheaval and fragmentation.

Hinduism is somewhat similar to Confucianism in this regard. Its key institution, the caste system, is also family-based. Caste membership is determined by family descent. Just as in Confucianism members of one family do not pray to ancestors of another, so too in Hinduism the members of one caste do not carry out the rituals of another. The individual does not become Hindu or Confucian by conversion or belief, but by birth. In this sense, being Hindu or Confucian is not a matter of choice: one cannot choose whether or not to be born into a caste or to have ancestors.

Buddhism and Islam are different from these two religions. In their case, the key institution is the religious community, a social entity held together by shared beliefs. In Buddhism it is the *sangha* or monastic community, which consists of those who have turned from ordinary society to live in accordance with Buddhist teachings. In Islam it is the *umma* or Islamic community as a whole, in which all who believe in God and submit to him are equal, regardless of their origins, and have the same right to devote themselves to study his word. The primacy of personal belief in Buddhism and Islam helps to explain why these religions have a history of proselytising or

Jesus Christ confers benediction on passers-by from a church roof in predominantly Hindu Trivandrum, Kerala, India. Across the street an Islamic mosque offers alternative spiritual support.

missionary activity. Conversion of members of other religions has been a way of acquiring religious merit as well as spreading the word. Although Hinduism and Confucianism have also spread beyond their place of origin, in comparison with Buddhism and Islam they have certainly been stay-at-home religions.

Yet all religious beliefs are like influenza viruses. By this I do not mean that religion is an illness for which a cure has yet to be found, but rather that religious ideas have an apparently infinite capacity to change their shape, and are usually transmitted from one person to another attached to physical objects rather than in a 'disembodied' state. In other words, religious ideas have tended to circulate less by individual conversion than by association with more tangible products of the civilisation of which they are part: things like fine textiles and ceramics, metal wares, writing systems, government institutions, and administrative techniques. Religious principles and ideals have been

Sadhu (holy man), Dharamasala, Himachal Pradesh, India (top left); temple entrance, Pushkar, Rajasthan, India (top right); Temple of the Tooth, Kandy, Sri Lanka's holiest Buddhist site.

taken over with sought-after material goods and practical skills, as well as for their own merit, and in the process have undergone many changes to fit them to local customs and beliefs. In this way Confucianism has influenced East Asia and Hinduism much of South-East Asia. Buddhism and Islam have been spread by merchants no less than by missionaries.

Religious conversion frequently operates from the top down. Rulers adopt the new system of ideas and then it is taken up by those under their control and influence. As a rule it has been socio-political elites that have had most foreign contact and have stood to gain most from the goods and skills with which the religious ideas go into circulation. New ways of legitimating political power have tended to be part of religious innovation, and where these have coincided with improved systems of government the advantages of conversion are particularly clear. For those lower down the social hierarchy conversion has often occurred through emulation or in response to pressure.

However, on the whole religious innovation happens within a given tradition rather than in terms of movement from one major religion to a completely different one. This means that, if anything, it is more likely to occur 'spontaneously' from within society than to be imposed from the top. New interpretations of particular doctrines and practices often arise unintentionally, in the process of fitting them to local circumstances and understanding. In this way, for example, local animistic beliefs and 'superstitions' have been incorporated into more rigorously intellectual Buddhist teachings at the village level in South-East Asian countries, leading scholars to distinguish between the 'great tradition' and 'little traditions' of Buddhism. Similarly, the Muslim Sufi tradition, which emphasises religious experience and devotional practice rather than interpretation of the written word, has made it easy for local attitudes and practices to be incorporated.[14]

But religious innovation may also be intentional, involving a conscious reinterpretation of central doctrines and practices, challenging the existing authorities, and seeking a new social and religious order based on new rules. While political leaders and intellectuals from some Asian countries have claimed that their religion inculcates respect for authority, that the people want authoritarian government because it is part of their religious view of life, the fact is that, in Asian countries as elsewhere, religion has been used to challenge or overthrow state authority as often as to uphold or reinforce it. Hundreds of the rebellions recorded have claimed some sort of religious justification. Political rebellion and proclamation of a new cult tend to go together. The new religion provides both the authority to assume political power ('God chose me/God made me do it') and guidelines or rules for exercising that power. It is useful to remember that major religions such as Christianity and Islam began not just with claims to religious revelation, but also with challenges to existing political authority.[15]

As a source of authority, therefore, religion may prove to be a two-edged sword. It can be used to bolster the status quo or to legitimate rebellion. It is the double-edged nature of religious authority that has prompted political leaders in many Asian countries, from Indonesia and Malaysia to India and Bangladesh, to demonstrate respect for the dominant religion while at the same time taking care to limit its political influence.

Religions offer an account of experience that claims to be complete and comprehensive, providing instructions for the regulation of social and private life, and reasons for their authoritativeness. Whether the rules derive from the religious rationale or vice versa may be debated. What matters is that in a society where religion is influential, religious reasons will be identified for whatever it is that individuals do or want to do, regardless of whether it accords with the core values of their religion. Hence the anti-Chinese rioting that broke out in Java early in 1997 was given a religious justification by those involved. Public discussion of the economic resentment and frustration at the heart of the conflict was suppressed by the Indonesian government.

In India, caste violence that is largely motivated economically is likewise explained in religious terms by the people from dominant castes responsible: the lower castes are disregarding their religious duties and therefore must be punished. Those who disregard conventions relating to gender distinctions are also likely to be criticised in religious terms, even when the religious authority invoked cannot offer clear guidance on the matters in dispute. In 1994, religious conservatives in Bangladesh called for the execution of the female writer Taslima Nasreen, alleging that she had declared that the Koran should be revised. It appears, however, that the hostility towards her had been aroused largely by her provocative writing on sexuality and gender issues, and her publicly expressed concern at discrimination experienced by Hindus in Bangladesh. In a religious society, religious arguments are the most persuasive, and people develop considerable ingenuity in constructing them, just as in a secular society they learn to construct arguments that claim to be scientific.[16]

## Difference and inequality

A culture has to account for the differences between members of a society as well as the similarities. All societies require their members to learn to categorise those with whom they come into contact and to determine the types of interaction appropriate to each case. This is particularly true of large-scale societies characterised by a high degree of social and economic differentiation, and is one reason why cross-cultural understanding is often difficult: it involves learning to draw social distinctions and recognise nuances of behaviour initially invisible to outsiders, and knowing how to respond to them. Although responding appropriately to social distinctions need not entail perceptions of social inequality, in practice it usually does. Major social categories, including caste, class, gender, age, and ethnicity, give rise to extensive patterns of inequality. Since what is appropriate is determined largely by members of the more powerful social groups, which stand to benefit most from such inequalities being maintained, this is not surprising.

To any non-Japanese, the distinction drawn between Burakumin and other Japanese is undetectable. Burakumin are ethnic Japanese who look and speak like other Japanese, and at least as far as outsiders are concerned have no discernible behavioural characteristics setting them apart. The only way they can be identified is in terms of the occupations of their ancestors and where they live. During the Tokugawa period (1603–1867) their forebears held occupations that according to the ideas of the time were unclean or degrading: they were butchers, tanners, executioners, actors, jugglers or beggars. These people were required to live in particular locations in towns and cities, where their descendants still live. Despite the fact that discrimination on the basis of Buraku status has long been outlawed by the Japanese government, Burakumin continue to experience severe social and economic sanctions. Commercially produced Buraku residential lists enable educational institutions to screen potential students, and employers to check the background of job applicants. It is said that one of the many things flattened by the Great Hanshin Earthquake of January 1995 was the popular illusion that Japanese society is middle class from top to bottom. Houses of the rich came through the earthquake relatively unscathed, but not so those of the poor. In Kobe after the earthquake it was unnecessary to consult Buraku lists; it was obvious where they lived because those were the districts that had been levelled.[17]

Social distinctions based on occupation are common to all societies, but the extent to which behaviour towards an individual is influenced by how his or her forebears earned a living varies widely. While occupational distinctions form part of most systems of social class, the concept of social class is usually understood to imply that movement between classes is possible. Caste, on the other hand, excludes social mobility. The Burakumin case is one in which ancestral occupation amounts to caste identity, from which there is no escape regardless of individual ability or achievement. The Indian caste system is the best-known example of this type of social structure. The consequences of the caste system for social, economic and political life in India are profound. Its defenders argue that the inequalities associated with it are of a ritual or religious nature only, that they should not be interpreted in economic or social terms because all occupations are equally necessary for the functioning of society. Many devout Hindus argue that it is possible to be sensitive to caste distinctions while remaining free from caste prejudice.[18]

It is true that not all social distinctions translate into unequal treatment. *Different* does not always imply *unequal*. Distinctions on the basis of age are a part of every social system, and it is difficult to argue that age should not affect how we interact with others. In most Asian societies great importance is attached to respectful and considerate treatment of members of older generations.

Gender distinctions are like caste distinctions in more ways than one. Like caste, gender is difficult to change. Like caste distinctions, gender-based roles, rights and rewards are often presented as 'different but equal'. Male and female, the argument goes, are unlike physiologically and psychologically, and in the social roles they fill. But both are necessary, so the fact that they are different should not be seen as implying that they are unequal. Male and female complement each other. In East Asia this is often explained by drawing on the classical Chinese cosmological principles of *yin* and *yang*, female and male respectively. The cosmos is generated from the interaction of these complementary principles. Existence depends on both principles equally, so there can be no question of one becoming like the other or one being more important than the other. We cannot live without day or night, hot or cold, dry or wet, male or female.[19]

It is true that difference does not always mean unequal, and few in any society would expect or want men and women to behave or be treated in exactly the same way. Yet it is a simple fact that almost invariably gender differences are associated with far-reaching inequalities that, again like caste inequalities, are so deeply rooted that they are difficult to change. Gender inequalities in the South Asia region are widely regarded as severe, although there are in fact wide variations in the range and degree of discrimination experienced by women.

Nepal is one of the few countries in the world where the life expectancy at birth is shorter for women than for men. In Bangladesh and northern India girls are severely disadvantaged in terms of nutrition and health care, as well as education and employment, with the result that mortality rates for girls are much higher than for boys. One study found that in some parts of the relatively wealthy Punjab region, a second or subsequent girl born in a family had less than a fifty-fifty chance of reaching adulthood. While in southern India and in Sri Lanka the situation of women is much better, they still experience widespread social and economic inequality.[20]

In East Asia as in South Asia, societies are predominantly patrilineal and patriarchal. While in China, Korea, Japan and Vietnam these social patterns pre-dated Confucianism, Neo-confucian teachings from around the thirteenth century certainly helped to reinforce gender inequalities in all four countries. However, the pattern of gender relations cannot be explained in terms of these influences alone.

Class distinctions in Korea have always been more rigid than those in China, yet in regard to gender some distinctions have been less so. Among the lower social classes, for example, it appears that women always had a relatively wide choice of occupation, and this may have helped women in contemporary Korean society to move into a range of jobs. Nevertheless female workers in Korea are still concentrated in what are commonly seen as female occupations: textile and garment manufacturing, nursing, office work, domestic service, and unpaid farm labour. Moreover women get paid much less than men for the work they do. The average wage for women is just over half that for men (see Table 5.4, p. 130). In present-day Korea there is a lot of interest in rediscovering Korean identity and cultural roots, freed of Chinese and Japanese influences. Many regard relative gender equality as a feature of Korean culture, and find evidence in the status and influence of shamanistic religion, traditionally an area of female expertise. Nevertheless women remain subordinate. So strong is the preference for a male child to continue the patrilineal family line that many couples use foetal sex determination and abortion to ensure that their baby will be male rather than female. In South Korea as in China, Taiwan, and India, the proportion of female births fell markedly from the mid-1980s when new technologies for foetal sex determination became widely available.[21]

Like social distinctions drawn in terms of class and gender, ethnic distinctions are mostly associated with discrimination or inequality. In some countries, such as China, Japan, and Indonesia, all ethnic groups are deemed equal in official government policy and the law, but in reality most experience inequalities.

In Japan, for example, the largest ethnic minority is that of the ethnic Koreans (approximately a million people, or 0.8 per cent of the population). In 1952 the peace treaty between Japan and the Allies came into effect and Japan formally renounced all claims in respect of its former colony Korea. At the same time, it stripped all Koreans living in Japan of the Japanese nationality they held under colonial arrangements, thereby reducing them to the status of aliens. Since then these people and their descendants have struggled to obtain legal and social standing, and still experience widespread discrimination in employment, housing, education, and participation in government service and political life.[22]

Indigenous minorities in most countries tend to be worse off than members of the dominant society on measures of individual and social well-being. Nor is disadvantage restricted to minority indigenous groups. In Malaysia, the Malays or *bumiputra* (sons of the soil) are numerically dominant, but in terms of wealth, education, and health are not as well off as the Chinese and Indian minorities. While they have improved their situation relative to the other groups over the last thirty years, they still do not enjoy equality in this sense.[23] In other countries, including China and India, policies to improve the situation of minorities have proved attractive enough for some members of the dominant society to adopt indigenous minority identities.

## Law and morality

The idea that society operates in terms of what may loosely be called rules inevitably focuses attention on the state as the source and enforcer of the formally articulated set of rules that we call the legal system. It is commonly assumed that people follow rules out of fear of the consequences if they do not, and that child-rearing parents establish obedience to rules by means of punishment for those who break them. Yet this is not correct in regard to the operation of legal systems, or, generally speaking, to methods of child-rearing. While legal systems around the world impose punishment on lawbreakers, the fact that the great majority of people rarely, if ever, break the law is not because they fear punishment. Laws cannot lift themselves into legality, nor is it organisationally or socially possible to enforce all laws everywhere at all times. Social order is maintained even though only a small proportion of people ever come into direct contact with the legal system. The law works to the extent that it is supported by the morality of ordinary people. If most people obey the law it is not because they are afraid of punishment, but because they believe not to do so would be wrong. While child-rearing normally includes systems of punishment, their main objective is to get children to internalise the rules, to develop a sense of right and wrong.

This internalisation of rules—or, putting it less crudely, the development of moral understanding and sensitivity—does not end with childhood. All the great religions and philosophical systems of the world include strategies for developing the individual's moral commitment and understanding until principled action becomes preferred or even automatic behaviour. This is true of Hinduism and Buddhism, Confucianism and Daoism, Islam and Christianity. All aim to get the individual to see the world and human affairs in a certain way, and then to modify his or her behaviour until it flows spontaneously from the principles inculcated.

Quite varied concepts are used to describe this process. Some describe it in terms of discovering God or the Holy within and acting in accordance with divine will. Others express it in terms of acquiring an understanding of philosophical truths and learning to put those truths into practice. All, however, aim for something more than minimum standards of behaviour. They are concerned with the realisation of ideals, the achievement of levels of conduct that go beyond what is obligatory or expected. Neither the setting of ideals nor their realisation can be understood except in terms of a moral and social sense that has left rules far behind, when a vision of what could be has become stronger even than the sense of what *should* be. In the end, the proportion of idealists in any society is likely to be small; or, more precisely, the proportion of people who act from idealistic motives most of the time will be small. Motives for following rules for most tend to be a mixture of idealism, self-interest and submission to authority. But this does not mean that the majority have so little moral sense that they cannot admire those who are able to live up to ideals.

Nothing throws the links between law and morality into sharper relief than civil disobedience. Civil disobedience may be defined as a public act that deliberately contravenes some law or measure endorsed by public authority, and is performed in protest against that authority. It entails a recognition of the need to justify the act of disobedience and accept any penalty that may result from failure to provide an adequate justification.[24]

An act of civil disobedience can be justified only on moral grounds and, since civil disobedience usually involves breaking the law, justification tends to take the form of demonstrating a moral obligation to break the law. Civil disobedience, or the justification of it, therefore involves a claim that the individual's obligation to obey the law or authority is less than absolute. In other words, there are times when other moral considerations are judged to be more compelling than the general obligation to comply with the directions of a properly constituted authority.

Sometimes civil disobedience questions only the legitimacy of a particular action or policy of the state. This was the case in protests against suppression of Buddhism and the civil war in Vietnam, which included self-immolation by Buddhist monks and nuns. It continues to be a feature of environmental protest in countries such as India, Japan, and Malaysia.[25] At other times, however, civil disobedience may arise from a judgment that the authority itself has no moral foundation and therefore lacks legitimacy. This was the view held by Gandhi and his followers regarding British colonial authority in India, by the millions of Iranians who in 1977 and 1978 protested against the regime of Mohammed Reza Shah, and the Filipinos whose protests helped to bring about the downfall of President Ferdinand Marcos in 1986. In Gandhi's words, civil disobedience arises not from 'want of respect for lawful authority, but in obedience to the higher law of our being, the voice of conscience'.[26]

No matter how lofty the ideals such dissidents claim to uphold, their questioning of authority causes acute anxiety on the part of many. The view that the individual's obligation could in any way be conditional causes consternation among ordinary citizens as well as those in positions of authority. By definition the law must be enforceable, they say. Obeying it or not cannot be left up to the individual. Some believe that any sort of disobedience represents the thin end of the wedge and undermines legal authority. Even harsh or unjust laws have to be obeyed, it is argued, because not to do so is to subvert the principle of rule by law.

While the reasoning is understandable enough, it must be rejected, for three reasons. First, as already pointed out, people who heed the law do so because of their moral sense or conscience rather than legal sanctions. And laws are not timeless. They change, and the idea of law reform is meaningless unless we can refer to ideals or moral principles that are in some sense higher than actual laws as they exist at any given time.

The second reason for rejecting the claim that the law or authority must always be obeyed is that there is no historical evidence to show that unquestioning submission makes authority strong. In fact there is a lot of evidence that authority based upon absolute obedience is brittle. Authoritarian government is likely to be unstable because it relies on coercion rather than the moral sense of the people. It is sometimes claimed by those in positions of authority in newly industrialised East Asian countries that respect for authority and obedience are basic 'Asian' values, and that this is why these Asian societies are orderly, disciplined, and rapidly becoming rich. Yet a look at the history and culture of the countries in question shows that unquestioning obedience to authority was rarely admired, and that rulers who accepted—or even invited—conscientious criticism from their subjects tended to be held in higher regard than those who did not tolerate it. More fundamentally, and this is the third reason for rejecting the claim that the law and authority must always be obeyed, in all the major traditions of Asia, submission to authority has always been conceived as conditional on those in positions of authority discharging their side of the reciprocal obligations that hold society together. This is discussed further in Chapter 3.

It might be objected that claiming the law and morality to be distinct from each other, and civil disobedience permissible, is an expression of a peculiarly Western assumption: that the state is secular, and that the source of morality lies elsewhere and hence provides an outside reference point from which the state or its actions may be criticised. But what if the state is the source of morality, the embodiment of religious and moral order? Certainly many states, including communist states, make such claims, and regard criticism and disobedience as tantamount to treason. This makes criticism and civil disobedience delicate undertakings. It does not necessarily mean, however, that the claims such states make are true, or that the religious or moral systems they claim to embody provide no criteria for distinguishing truth from falsehood. Nor does it alter the fact that the authority they wield is conditional on states actually discharging the obligations laid on them by the religious or moral ideals they claim to uphold.

## Changing political and legal cultures

Earlier I suggested that it would be a mistake to look on the emergence of the nation state as a new beginning as far as political culture is concerned. As is clear from the preceding discussion, the relationships between political institutions, the law, morality and custom are so complex that, for good or ill, it is impossible to have a completely new beginning. Even revolutionary change imposed from the top must be reconciled with customary values and ways of doing things if it is to be accepted as legitimate and have a lasting effect. The political cultures of nation states such as Iran, India, China, and Korea represent the accretion of thousands of years of nation-building and statecraft. Their influence is so pervasive and subtle that often it is unconscious. The historical experience and the lessons they incorporate are not to be put aside lightly.

At the same time, the emergence of the world system of nation states since 1945, and the multilateral treaties and institutions supporting it, have resulted in profound changes in the way the functions of the state are conceived and how they are carried out. Unprecedented levels of international contact and interaction have brought about a degree of convergence in political and legal cultures. Nowhere is that convergence more visible than in relation to what are regarded as the proper functions and responsibilities of the state, and the formal articulation of the role of state and citizens in a written constitution.

Public health is one area that in recent decades has come to be seen as a proper sphere of government responsibility in Asian countries, partly as the result of improved knowledge of health issues and the technological and organisational capacity needed to address them. Another area of new state activity in most Asian countries has been mass education. While in China and other countries that adopted Confucian institutions the state has long attached importance to formal education, and the official examination system was public in the sense that, at least in theory, it was open to everyone, education remained an elite affair. Japan led the way in Asia in the development of mass education, following the Meiji restoration in 1868, but in most other countries it has been addressed seriously only since 1945. Much of the motivation behind a state's provision of mass education has related to its needing an educated workforce to advance economic development.

Economic development itself is an area of state activity that has grown rapidly. While rulers have tended always to take an active interest in generating wealth, this has usually been for the sake of personal and family interests. Contemporary states are obliged to show at least some interest in national economic well-being, though there is much debate over what the state's role should be in economic development. Japan and South Korea have until recently been seen as outstanding success stories of state economic management, with their example being followed by 'a second wave' of industrialising Asian countries such as Malaysia and Thailand. Although many neoclassical economists argue that these countries have succeeded *despite* government attempts at economic management rather than because of them, a completely hands-off approach makes little sense in theory or in practice.

The natural environment has also come to be seen as a major area of state responsibility. This may be regarded as a consequence of the increasing environmental damage resulting from population growth, industrialisation, and rising levels of consumption. A hands-off approach by the state to economic management may appear to have some plausibility, but few would argue this way in relation to protection of the environment. Environmental protection and rehabilitation tend to be seen as costs rather than benefits, at least in the short term, and commercial enterprises are thus seldom motivated to pursue such activities. It is no coincidence that environmental protection has gone further in Japan than in any other country in Asia, for Japan is also the richest country. But on top of this, Japan has been able to transfer to other nations of the region some of the environmental costs of its industrialisation and consumption. The environmental problems facing relatively poor and densely populated countries such as Bangladesh, India, China, Indonesia, and Vietnam are acute, and need strong action by the state to combat them.

One reason for increased state action on behalf of such things as education, public health and a clean and safe environment is a growing international acceptance of the idea that all people have a right to them. This is linked to another area of state responsibility that has emerged: the advancement and protection of human rights. While there is dispute over what the term should cover, even states suspicious of the doctrine of human rights as a form of neocolonialism accept the underlying concept that the state has a responsibility to ensure that the basic human needs of all individuals are met. Those needs include physical and psychological well-being, and the right to participate in social, cultural, and political life.

The existence of large areas of agreement regarding the proper role of the state does not mean that there are not areas of disagreement. The nature and extent of government activity in the economic sphere, already mentioned, is one. Another is family planning or fertility control, which has become a state concern as a consequence of rapid population growth in most Asian countries. Some argue that fertility declined in Western countries without state-organised family planning programs, and that therefore there is no need for them in developing countries. They say that decisions about the number of children couples have and when they have them are private matters in which the state has no business to interfere. Others are critical only where states resort to coercive measures in fertility control, as has happened in China and India, where enforced abortion and sterilisation have been widespread.

Social security is a third major area of disagreement regarding appropriate levels of government responsibility. That support for the elderly, the sick and the unemployed has traditionally been provided by the family and the community is a reason given by governments of nations as diverse as Japan, Thailand, and Indonesia for resisting calls to direct more public resources to social security. While this is a way of minimising government expenditure and perhaps even of retaining traditional customs and values, changes such as increased population mobility, urbanisation, and a shift away from family-based economic production, coupled with rapid ageing of populations and the social dislocation resulting from industrialisation and economic development, have greatly reduced the viability of traditional mechanisms of family and community support.

On all these fronts the role of the state is changing, and to some extent converging. However, this does not mean that the ideas themselves are new. It could be argued that in many respects the shifts occurring represent a return to traditional wisdom. Active concern for the welfare of the people and for environmental protection have been basic elements in most of the political traditions of Asian societies. The same may be said of the pre-modern traditions of European countries. It was only following the emergence of the concept of the secular state in the eighteenth century, for example, that the idea of state responsibility for the natural world had to be reinvented. In the political philosophies of Renaissance Europe, as in classical Chinese, Hindu, and Islamic conceptions of the state, the ruler was the link between the human world and the natural order, with no distinction drawn between them as far as state responsibility for their welfare was concerned. Dereliction of duty by the ruler, or a failure in the administration of the realm, was seen to disturb the natural no less than the human order.

Although the concept of human rights developed in the European philosophical tradition, the underlying idea that the ruler or state has a responsibility for the well-being of the people is to be found in all the major traditions of Asia, together with the principle that any claim to political legitimacy is conditional on that responsibility being properly discharged. In theory, at least, political authority was never absolute. Early Hindu and Buddhist texts spell out the conditional nature of the ruler's authority and his obligation to govern in accordance with *dharma* or law, the correct order of things. The ancient Chinese concept of the Mandate of Heaven similarly emphasised that political authority was subject to the proper exercise of that authority. Should a ruler fail to discharge his responsibilities, social and natural disorder would result and the mandate to rule would pass to someone else. 'Heaven's Mandate is not constant', ancient texts warn.[27]

Yet whatever the similarities between ancient and contemporary political concepts, many of their practical implications are quite different. Taking responsibility for the well-being of nature in ancient China entailed actions different from what it entails now. The people of present-day Thailand have much the same needs as those of Siam five hundred years ago, but ensuring that those needs are met in contemporary society necessarily requires different sorts of action on the part of the state. Early Buddhist and Chinese concepts of political authority may have stressed that a ruler's right to the throne was conditional on the meeting of his responsibilities towards his subjects, but they did not provide effective mechanisms for redress where that did not happen. The idea of human rights legislation is to provide the necessary mechanisms, well short of revolution.

## Constitutionalism

If the concept of reciprocal obligations as the foundation of social and political order has been part of all cultural traditions, the idea of articulating them in legal documents is a relatively new one associated with the emergence of the secular nation state. Constitutionalism may be conceived as the formal definition, in law, of the responsibilities and legitimate powers of the state. A constitution provides the foundation on which government and rule of law are based, setting out the scope of the government's powers, the mechanisms through which they may properly be exercised, and the limitations placed upon them.

Constitutionalism does not presuppose any particular system of government, such as representative democracy, or a legal system based on the concept of the rights of the individual. Nor does constitutionalism require the existence of a single document—*the* Constitution—as opposed to a series of other documents that between them set out the basic principles of the exercise of government power. What the existence of a constitution does imply is acceptance of the idea that the exercise of government power is legitimate only if it is subject to constraints derived from the mutual obligations of state and people and formally committed to writing. Constitutionalism cannot do away with the possibility that the government of the day may ignore the legal restraints on its power, but it does make it difficult for the state then to claim it is acting legitimately. In itself the idea of rule by law is not a recent innovation. In the third and fourth centuries BCE, for example, Chinese philosophers of the Legalist School argued that the empire must be governed in accordance with laws to which everyone, from the ruler down, is subject.[28] However, the crucial step is to link the principle of rule of law to limits in state power. What is needed is the separation of legal authority from the executive powers of the state, for only that can provide safeguards against the misuse of power.

These ideas have spread very quickly as part of the global convergence of political and legal thinking that has occurred since 1945. Before 1945 not one Asian nation had a constitution. By 1950 four nations had proclaimed one: Indonesia in 1945, while still fighting for independence from the Dutch; Japan, under US occupation, and China, under Kuomintang rule, both in 1947; and India in 1949. Between 1970 and 1991 all the other major countries of Asia acquired a constitution.[29]

Still, it would be easy to make too much of the practical consequences of the adoption of constitutions, and also of the amount of cultural convergence it entails. This becomes clear when we consider particular examples. The Iranian constitution of 1979, the 1982 constitution of the People's Republic of China, and that of Thailand adopted in 1991 are very different from each other. In terms of its content the Iranian document, which emerged from a wave of Islamic resurgence and Iranian nationalism, cannot be regarded as evidence of convergence. On the contrary, it is an assertion of distinctiveness and autonomy. Yet, in terms of the political norms underlying it, it does represent a convergence. It addresses an expectation that a legitimate government will bind itself in a written contract with the people. This is a principle that, in the light of their fifty-year experience of the Pahlavi regime, the Iranian people have every reason to hold dear. Nevertheless it could be interpreted as a symptom of the Westernisation disease of which their leaders complained.[30]

## The threat of the state

While the trend for the state to be a positive force in the pursuit of social, economic, and environmental well-being is welcome, it carries dangers with it. Extension of the functions and concerns of the state brings with it more intrusion and interference in the lives of individuals and communities. There was relatively little danger when the pre-modern state claimed responsibility for everything under the sun—sometimes even *including* the sun—because it did not have the means to act on many of the responsibilities it claimed. The modern state is different. Increased workforce literacy and education, technological advances, and new administrative and organisational systems make it possible for the modern state to extend its information-gathering and interference to all aspects of society and the natural world. At the same time, the increased scale of bureaucratic organisation and the centralisation of functions associated with the nation state make government power more remote from the lives and influence of ordinary individuals.

Max Weber (1864–1920) recognised the costs as well as the benefits of a shift from tradition-oriented communities in which structures and authority are personalised to nation states where authority is legally defined and rules impersonally applied. He was apprehensive of a future in which the state would continue to grow in scale and complexity, centralised and remote, constrained by its narrow instrumentalist rationality and entangled by its own bureaucratic procedures. In such a situation, as likely in a capitalist as in a communist political setting, individual participation becomes increasingly hollow as the relationship with authority becomes more and more attentuated.[31]

The extension of state power and influence may be seen everywhere in contemporary Asia, but particularly in large nation states, such as China and Indonesia, where governments have aimed at direct control down to the village level even in remote districts. In those countries as in most other pre-modern societies, authority and control at the village level had always been left in the hands of locally dominant families with powerful patrons further up the social pyramid. From 1949 in China, the Communist Party moved systematically to weaken the influence of dominant clans and replace them with formal councils and committees. In Indonesia in 1980 a new Village Law came into operation. This formally defined villages on a nationwide basis and made village head a government position, answerable to the state rather than the local community. While communities could nominate candidates, government authorities vetted the nominations to ensure that all nominees are suitable.[32]

## Civil society

Mistrust of the scale and pervasiveness of the modern state, coupled with an emphasis on individual social sense and conscience as the true basis of social order, naturally leads to the view that the machinery of government should be kept to a minimum. It is a view that has long and respectable roots in both East and West. Its most articulate spokesmen in China have been Daoist philosophers. The best ruler, says the early Daoist text *Daode jing*, is one of whose presence his subjects are unaware, one who rules through non-action. Confucianism too, when disengaged from direct imperial involvement, emphasised government by moral influence rather than rule of law. In India its most eloquent modern spokesman has been Gandhi, whose influence continues to be strong among Indian intellectuals.[33]

In seventeenth- and eighteenth-century Europe the concept of civil society originally meant something like 'political society' or 'society ordered by means of state institutions', that is to say, civil in the sense of civilised or refined, as opposed to the rude state of nature. In time its meaning shifted, so that in the work of philosophers such as Kant and Hegel it came to refer to the public sphere established and guaranteed by the state, within which the individual could act freely in accordance with reason, human affections and needs, pursuing his or her ends as a member of the community. Marx, in turn, rejected the distinction between civil society and state. As far as he was concerned, everything was political, and what hope there was for the future lay in acting in accordance with that reality. Society will always be subject to political and economic forces.

In the last decade the concept of civil society has undergone a renaissance closely related to the decline of Marxism as a political and social force. In Eastern Europe, the former Soviet Union and China, the 'defeat' of communism has encouraged wide discussion and high hopes regarding civil society, often without much agreement over what the term means.

To those eager to claim that the West won the cold war, the concept of civil society offered yet another way of demonstrating that Western society (there is no plural) is the most advanced in the world, the model to which all others aspire. It was assumed that when other nations manage to shrug off authoritarian regimes they would become, in effect, Western societies. Modernisation, or more specifically Westernisation, was seen as a precondition for any society becoming truly civil. This view ignores the fact that civil society is regarded by many to be under threat in the Western countries held up as a model, and that many countries in Asia and elsewhere have rich traditions that certainly approximate what is now called civil society: wide-ranging social and economic structures and institutions, involving a high degree of free association, embodying diverse ideologies and pursuing different ends, without fear of state oppression or control. It may be argued that the concept of civil society is intrinsically pluralistic and that it is therefore natural to assume that all civil societies will to some extent differ from each other. All they need have in common, some would argue, is government by rule of law, with their freedoms and institutions defined and protected accordingly. Yet, in this context, law should not be defined narrowly. Any definition would have to be able to accommodate a variety of arrangements from non-Western legal traditions.[34]

One of the strengths of the concept of civil society is the way it focuses attention on the fact that the state, with its legal and institutional structures, is built on the shifting sand of social rules, values and purposes, and whatever legitimacy it may claim has to be expressed in those terms. It enables us to give due consideration to the fact that social order depends, in the end, on the social sense and conscience of individuals, who may from time to time change their mind about what is right, what the state may do or not do, and where the limits of government control should be set.

We cannot lose sight, however, of the fact that the concept of civil society assumes that the state is secular, that its role is or should be separate from religion. The civil society is based on a fragmented view of human affairs in which a separation of powers is primary. Such a view is not an attractive proposition for those who want to believe, or want others to believe, that their government has been appointed by God (or *is* God), because it has a monopoly on truth, or because it is destiny itself, the unfolding of historical inevitability. Nor is it attractive to those who aspire to a more integrated approach to human affairs, who feel that secularism is shallow, and that religious and moral world views cannot just be added to social arrangements as an afterthought.

CHAPTER THREE

# Human Rights

## The complexity of human rights

Nothing highlights the conflicting pressures and trends associated with globalisation more strongly than the controversies surrounding human rights. The issues are fundamental to society and the operation of political systems, the emotions they generate are intense, and the scope for disagreement is enormous. Not only do the issues deserve close examination in their own right, but they also act like spotlights on the varied ways in which human beings relate to each other. Because human rights are a diverse category it is possible to come away with quite dissimilar impressions, depending on which spotlights we decide to use.

Governments are particularly adept at manipulating lighting to obtain the effects they want. For example, those of developed countries tend to focus on the civil and political rights of individuals, and try to apply political and economic pressure to developing countries that violate such rights. The governments of developing countries, on the other hand, emphasise social and economic rights. They argue that unless a society has political stability and economic development it is impossible for individuals to enjoy any civil and political rights at all, and they denounce developed nations for their hypocrisy in putting obstacles on the path to development. But such positions often reflect genuine differences in understanding human rights, as well as the need to respond to different circumstances. It would be a mistake to dismiss them as expressions of political cynicism.

The issues in dispute do not come down to disagreements between East and West, or between North and South. In all nations many intellectuals and non-government organisations disagree with their government's official position on human rights. They argue over what a full list of human rights should include, which rights should have priority, and how the various rights may best be protected. Over time international support for human rights has continued to increase, as the growing list of human rights conventions and the number of signatories show. At the beginning of 1996 there were seventy-two international human rights conventions. Yet at the same time it appears to have become harder rather than easier to reach international agreement on the proper scope of human rights and the best ways to protect them.

Since adoption of the Universal Declaration of Human Rights (UDHR) by the fledgling United Nations in 1948, political realities and legal ideals have become more complicated. The composition of the UN itself has changed as the number of ex-colonial and Third World member states has increased. This has made it harder for Western nations to dominate proceedings. Some of the more recent conventions bear witness to that changing composition and the greater range of attitudes on human rights issues it has introduced. For example, there is more of an emphasis than in earlier documents on group rights as opposed to individual rights.

While matters pertaining to civil and political rights have continued to dominate the UN agenda, there has been a greater willingness to address issues involving economic, social and cultural rights, particularly those arising from unequal relations between nation states. Moves to make equitable economic and social development (a particular concern of Third World countries) an integral part of human rights action have led to an emphasis on the indivisibility of human rights. The Proclamation of Tehran (1968), for example, asserted that 'the full realization of civil and political rights without the enjoyment of economic, social and cultural rights is impossible'. This was followed in 1986 by the Declaration on the Right to Development, which states, *inter alia*, that: 'The right to development is an inalienable human right by virtue of which every human person and all peoples are entitled to participate in, contribute to, and enjoy economic, social, cultural and political development, in which all human rights and fundamental freedoms can be fully realized.' There is also a growing awareness of the need to move beyond the often simplistic distinction between individual and group rights that vitiates much of the debate.[1]

It is not the purpose of this chapter to survey human rights violations in Asian countries. That is done well enough by the United Nations Commission on Human Rights and organisations such as Amnesty International and Human Rights Watch.[2] Nor is it intended to give Asian nations a human rights score and rank their performance on a single international scale of political and social enlightenment. Rather, this chapter tries to address some of the problems associated with applying a concept of universal human rights across nations that vary enormously in social and economic circumstances as well as political and cultural traditions. This requires taking those differences seriously, without assuming that moral and legal relativism is the only feasible response.

Severe and unambiguous human rights violations do not free us from an obligation to consider all aspects of the situation in question. Violation of human rights in Myanmar has been routine under the series of military regimes in power there since 1962. This has included martial law and political suppression, secret trials, extrajudicial killings and disappearances, torture and coercion by the state, indefinite detention without charges being brought, strict censorship, forced labour, and religious persecution. In the late 1980s growing dissatisfaction with the 'Burmese way to socialism' resulted in student-led protests in Rangoon that were bloodily suppressed. In response to public pressure, the military government finally agreed to democratic elections in May 1990. The National League for Democracy, led by Aung San Suu Kyi, the daughter of Burma's national independence hero Aung San, scored a massive victory. The military regime ignored the election result, reassumed power and placed

Aung San Suu Kyi under house arrest. Despite her release in July 1995, her political activity has remained severely constrained. In the meantime, the regime has been able to overcome much of the resistance it faced from both ethnic minorities in the mountain regions and the urban opposition groups that had joined them there. A political campaign of divide and rule, backed by strong military action, meant that by early 1995 the only armed opposition remaining comprised a few thousand Karen along the Thai border.

After more than fifty years of conflict, it looks as if the fight of the Karen and other ethnic minorities for political independence is effectively over. To outsiders the solution to Myanmar's human rights problems may seem simple: just a matter of its rulers becoming more enlightened in their attitudes and granting the people self-determination and democracy. Certainly government reform must be central to any moves to improve the lives of the people of Myanmar. Yet it is necessary to understand how the harshness of military rule in Myanmar came about if the problems are to be solved. While the plight of the minorities may sound like a strong argument for self-determination, the armed ethnic conflict and the threat of political disintegration that have persisted for more than half a century have provided much of the rationale for the army's claim to power and the ruthless way it has been wielded. Greater efforts by all parties for a peaceful resolution of the ethnic conflicts may in turn have made it possible to achieve more in the way of political and social reform. Less preoccupation with political unity may make it easier to devote more attention to meeting basic needs and protecting human rights.

Even where military rule is as brutal and repressive as in Myanmar, it cannot be dismissed as a symptom of moral breakdown or barbarism. In a country where government and civil institutions are weak or non-existent, the army is often seen—or, more to the point, sees itself—as the only organisation capable of coherent and sustained action at the national level, and therefore able to hold the country together. Anarchy and social disintegration are usually feared more than authoritarian rule. Sometimes, however, the military may foment unrest in order to promote its role as the guardian of national order and cohesion. There is little doubt that this happened in Indonesia during the troubled years of 1998 to 2000. Moreover, it is all too easy for the military to present any opposition to its power as a threat to national security, and the resultant suppression of public life makes it impossible for civil institutions capable of replacing military rule to emerge.[3]

The sorts of human rights problems that occur in the area of labour organisation and conditions are no less complex. These are issues that caused headaches for the Indonesian government in the last decade of the Suharto regime. For a large proportion of the Indonesian labour force, working conditions contravened many of the provisions of the International Labour Organisation conventions, which set out internationally agreed minimum requirements. Many Indonesian workers did not receive the legal minimum wage, sick leave or paid holidays, and had to work in dangerous or unhealthy conditions. The right to organise was severely limited, with the only officially recognised union under government control and the army able to intervene in labour disputes. The US government had some success in pressing for greater labour rights in Indonesia in accordance with international conventions when it threatened to end Indonesia's preferred status under its Generalized System of Preferences (which allows many exports from developing countries to enter the US market duty-free). The acute economic difficulties experienced in the wake of the Asian financial crisis and the 'conditionalities' imposed by the IMF for emergency funding mean that, even with government commitment, it may take some time to improve significantly the pay and conditions of Indonesian workers.[4]

In the global economic system, the options for late-developing countries wanting to compete with developed countries are few. Those trying to industrialise by attracting overseas investment and technology can do little more than offer cheap natural resources (if they have them), cheap labour, government subsidies, and minimal environmental controls. Labour exploitation played a large part in the industrialisation of the West in the nineteenth century, Japan in the early twentieth century, and Korea in the 1960s and 1970s. Not surprisingly, then, attempts to impose minimum labour rights and conditions on late-developing countries in Asia have prompted claims that by doing so developed countries are trying to protect their own economic advantage. It is a charge with some plausibility.

These issues are considered further in Chapter 9. Here the point is that government action, whether on the part of developing or developed countries, can only go some of the way towards stopping labour exploitation. Such human rights violations occur largely at the hands of private employers, whether these be local employers or multinational corporations attracted to the developing country by cheap labour. Changes in public attitudes are needed to make labour-market reforms effective, and such changes are not easy to bring about. Where legislative changes are introduced there may not be the resources or the institutional framework needed to enforce

Indonesian authorities exercising power, Aceh, North Sumatra.

them. Labour reform may require government action, but economic realities may impose conflicting demands on a conscientious government. Were developed countries prepared to translate their concern for human rights into more supportive economic relationships with developing countries, it would certainly make it easier for many economic and social rights to be secured. This does not mean, however, that it would necessarily happen.

Yet even labour organisation and employment conditions, which are usually subject to some degree of state regulation, are relatively straightforward in terms of human rights protection compared with the general area of discrimination. Article 2 of the Universal Declaration expounds the right to be free of discrimination based on distinctions such as race, colour, sex, language, religion, property, birth and status. While introducing anti-discrimination legislation is simple enough, by itself it will do little. What is needed is a social climate in which discrimination is considered offensive and unacceptable, and that is more likely to be achieved through moral education than legal sanctions. The issue of discrimination drives home the point that ultimately human rights are a question of how individuals treat each other, in the village or neighbourhood, at school or in the workplace. These are the places, as the first president of the UN Human Rights Commission, Eleanor Roosevelt, pointed out, 'where every man, woman and child seeks justice, equal opportunity, equal dignity without discrimination. Unless these rights have a meaning there they have little meaning anywhere.'[5]

## Universal by definition?

Human rights are defined as rights that 'derive from the inherent dignity of the human person'. They are rights that are universal, shared by everyone equally, regardless of social class, gender, ethnicity or personal characteristics of any kind. Since human rights are the entitlement of all people simply by virtue of their being human, they are also inalienable, and cannot be diminished or impaired even when they are violated.

By definition, then, human rights apply to all individuals no matter what their cultural background or under what political arrangements they find themselves. Delegates to the World Conference on Human Rights in Vienna in June 1993 reconfirmed that the Universal Declaration of Human Rights 'constitutes a common standard of achievement for all peoples and all nations', and that in accordance with the UN charter all states are obligated to work for the achievement of that standard. In the words of the declaration formally adopted by the conference: 'All human rights are universal, indivisible and interdependent and interrelated ... While the significance of national and regional particularities and various historical, cultural and religious backgrounds must be borne in mind, it is the duty of States, regardless of their political, economic and cultural systems, to promote and protect all human rights and fundamental freedoms.'

That all the states represented at Vienna, including those of Asia, supported the Declaration does not mean there has been an end to disagreement over what, in practice, promoting and protecting human rights and fundamental freedoms should entail.

Although the majority of Asian states have ratified the major human rights conventions—including the International Covenant on Civil and Political Rights and the International Covenant on Economic, Social and Cultural Rights (see Table 3.1)—there remains a good deal of ambivalence regarding the scope and implementation of such conventions.[6] Some of the concerns were expressed at the Asian regional meeting in the lead-up to the Vienna Conference, in Bangkok in April 1993, and were restated in Vienna. While the representatives of Asian states reaffirmed 'the universality, objectivity and non-selectivity of all human rights', many also expressed concern at attempts to use human rights as a 'conditionality for extending development assistance', as a way of applying political pressure, or as a pretext for compromising the sovereignty of other nations. The Bangkok Declaration cautioned that 'while human rights are universal in nature, they must be considered in the context of a dynamic and evolving process of norm-setting, bearing in mind the significance of national and regional particularities and various historical, cultural and religious traditions'.

**Table 3.1** Asian countries party to selected international human rights conventions, as at 16 February 2000

| | *International Covenant on Elimination of All Forms of Racial Discrimination 1965* | *International Covenant on Civil and Political Rights 1966* | *International Covenant on Economic, Social and Cultural Rights 1966* | *Convention on the Elimination of All Forms of Discrimination Against Women 1979* | *Convention Against Torture and Other Cruel, Inhuman or Degrading Treatment or Punishment 1984* | *Convention on the Rights of the Child 1989* |
|---|---|---|---|---|---|---|
| Afghanistan | • | • | • | | • | • |
| Bangladesh | • | • | | • | • | • |
| Cambodia | • | • | • | • | • | • |
| China | • | ○ | ○ | • | • | • |
| India | • | • | • | • | | • |
| Indonesia | • | | | • | • | • |
| Iran | • | • | • | | | • |
| Iraq | • | • | • | • | | • |
| Japan | • | • | • | • | • | • |
| Laos | • | | | • | | • |
| Malaysia | • | • | • | • | • | • |
| Mongolia | • | • | • | • | | • |
| Myanmar | | | | • | | • |
| Nepal | • | • | • | • | • | • |
| North Korea | | • | • | | | • |
| Pakistan | • | | | • | | • |
| Philippines | • | • | • | • | • | • |
| Singapore | | | | • | | • |
| South Korea | • | • | • | • | • | • |
| Sri Lanka | • | • | • | • | • | • |
| Thailand | | • | • | • | | • |
| Vietnam | • | • | • | • | | • |

Note: • indicates 'ratification, accession, approval, notification or succession, acceptance or definitive signature'
○ indicates signature not yet followed by ratification

Source: United Nations Human Development Program, *Human Development Report 2000*, Oxford University Press, New York, 2000, 48–51.

Against a background of colonialism and imperialism, and the use of human rights agendas to advance national interests, the concern expressed over interference in internal affairs and loss of national sovereignty is understandable. The Chinese delegate in Vienna expressed this particularly strongly: 'As a people that used to suffer tremendously from aggression by big powers but now enjoys independence, the Chinese have come to realize fully that state sovereignty is the basis for the realization of citizens' human rights. If the sovereignty of the state is not safeguarded, the human rights of its citizens are out of the question ...'[7]

What the Chinese statement ignores is that the main function of human rights law is to protect citizens from oppression and neglect by their own state rather than by others. Moreover, underlying the concept of international human rights legislation, and indeed the UN charter, is the idea that national sovereignty cannot be regarded as absolute. The Japanese delegate in Vienna made this point directly, commenting that human rights 'are universal values common to all mankind' and that human rights within a given domestic jurisdiction may be 'a matter of legitimate concern of the international community'. Human rights legislation aims to set limits on the power of the state to infringe the human rights of its citizens, and this is hard to bring into effect without international pressure. A treaty such as the International Covenant on Civil and Political Rights establishes channels by which such pressure may be brought to bear, which is one reason some Asian states have been reluctant to sign.

The Bangkok statement that human rights must be considered in the context of an evolving process of norm-setting, taking into account local circumstances and traditions, lends itself to many interpretations, as joint statements argued over at international conferences often do. It is not surprising that there were substantial differences in the positions expressed by Asian countries in Vienna. Nevertheless, certain themes recurred. There was a strong emphasis on the indivisible link between economic, social and cultural rights, and civil and political rights. Much mention was made of the right to development, in response to the perceived Western tendency to allege violations of civil and political rights in Asian countries while using Western economic power to deny such countries economic rights.

There was also an emphasis on the group rights of family, community and nation, in contradistinction to the rights of the individual; the need for individual liberty to be balanced with social duty; and the need for state authority as a precondition for all rights. The Malaysian delegate warned that 'Excessive individual freedom leads to a decay in moral values and weakens the social fabric of nations', a sentiment echoed in the Singapore delegate's warning against anarchy: 'Good government is essential for the realization of all rights. Development and good government require a balance between the rights of the individual and those of the community to which every individual must belong and through which individuals must realize their rights.'

Many of the sentiments expressed by Asian governments in Bangkok and Vienna called into question the concept of a 'common standard' of human rights. The Chinese delegate stated that 'one should not and cannot think of the human rights standard and model of certain countries as the only proper ones and demand all other countries to comply with them'. The Indonesian delegate, while rejecting the idea of alternative concepts of human rights, called for 'greater recognition of the immense complexity of the issue of human rights due to the wide diversity in history, culture, value systems, geography and phases of development among the nations of the world', which often result in 'different perceptions ... regarding the relations between man and society, man and his fellow man and regarding the rights of the community as against the rights of the individual'. The Singapore delegate too emphasised the need for diversity of approach, while recognising that tolerance of diversity could be used as a shield by dictators. 'Order and justice are obtained in diverse ways in different countries at different times', he declared, pointing out that there is debate within and between Western countries about the scope of human rights, and that such debate is regarded as evidence of healthy democracy and freedom. There may be a hard core of rights that are truly universal, but most are 'essentially contested concepts' subject to conflicting interpretations. Truly universal rights may include little more than the non-derogatable rights of the International Covenant on Civil and Political Rights and the right to development.

Underlying many of these statements is the view that the Universal Declaration of Human Rights and the covenants derived from it are essentially Western documents containing the cultural assumptions of those most influential in framing them. Some of those assumptions appear to contradict the basic values and ideals of peoples of other nations, and are not seen by them as appropriate. The peoples of many Asian nations are conscious of being heirs of 'ancient and highly developed cultures' with sophisticated social understanding and institutions. It cannot just be assumed that the values of such cultures are wrong and that Western values represent the most highly evolved or advanced social ideal. Unless we are prepared to accept, as was asserted quite confidently in the not too distant past, that non-Western societies are backward, there must be room for discussion, disagreement, and perhaps for divergent approaches to safeguarding human rights. It is necessary to consider the claim that the universality of human rights conventions is limited by the Western cultural assumptions they embody, and that other societies have different values equally worthy of consideration, and in particular the frequently made assertion that there are specifically Asian values that must be protected.

## Cultural assumptions of human rights

The Universal Declaration of Human Rights of 1948 was an attempt at a comprehensive statement of the conditions necessary for a life of material security, dignity and psychological well-being. Inevitably it drew on the philosophical and political traditions of which it was part, especially the European Enlightenment, with its ideals of a secular social order based on reason, and the great eighteenth-century declarations of rights and freedoms that articulated those ideals. But it is also true that the attempt at comprehensiveness led to incorporation into it of elements of the late 1940s vision of the good life, a vision that was strongly influenced by Western and especially US conceptions, despite the fact that a Chinese and a Lebanese were influential members of the drafting committee.

Many of the rights set out in the Universal Declaration presuppose particular socio-political institutions and structures, so that in the end it appears that the only people able to enjoy them fully would be those living in the United States or a country with similar institutions and levels of affluence. For example, the will of the people that is the basis of government authority 'shall be expressed in periodic and genuine elections which shall be by universal and equal suffrage and shall be held by secret vote or by equivalent free voting procedures'. All individuals have a right to education, with their parents able to choose the type of education they will receive. They have a right to free choice of employment and protection against unemployment, to just and favourable working conditions (including paid holidays), and to social security. These provisions reflect basic human needs for political participation and material security, but go beyond this to specify the ways in which these needs are to be satisfied.

It is not surprising, therefore, to find some Western philosophers and legal experts, who would disagree with the Singapore government on other issues, sharing its opinion that the list of human rights should be much shorter than it is and subject to ongoing discussion and debate, becoming part of an 'evolving process of norm-setting', to use a phrase from the Bangkok Declaration. Steven Lukes concludes that 'the list of human rights should be kept both reasonably short and reasonably abstract', for only then will it be possible to secure agreement 'across the broad spectrum of contemporary political life'. Jack Donnelly observes that the list of human rights 'has evolved and expanded, and will continue to do so' as new social and political factors come into play. Eugene Kamenka notes that although the concept of human rights is no longer tied to belief in God or natural law in a classical sense, 'it still seeks or claims a form of endorsement that transcends or pretends to transcend specific historical institutions and traditions, legal systems, governments, or national and even regional communities'. This makes it easy to understand why universal endorsement for specific rights is difficult to obtain.[8]

The culture-specific nature of many aspects of the Universal Declaration of Human Rights and the two covenants derived from it becomes clear when we consider the conflicts that can arise when particular provisions are applied in a cross-cultural context. Some of the conflicts are relatively straightforward. For example, Article 21 of the Declaration states that everyone has the right of equal access to public service in his country. This is a problem in the context of the Indian caste system, since caste distinctions are drawn largely in terms of the type of work individuals do, and promoting this right would require a basic modification of the caste system. The Indian government has reserved places in government and the civil service for *dalits* to counteract some of the discrimination they receive, but there is no likelihood of all castes being treated equally. The limited steps taken have aroused deep resentment, which often spills over into violence.

Relatively straightforward too, but difficult enough, are problems such as those thrown up by Article 5 concerning the right to freedom from cruel, inhuman and degrading treatment, which was prompted largely by European experiences under fascism. It runs up against the fact that ideas about what is cruel, inhuman or degrading are shaped to some extent by custom and familiarity. The legal systems of other societies always appear to arouse indignation at the cruelty of the punishments they inflict. Western photographers in nineteenth-century China had a horrified fascination with punishments such as caning and garrotting, in much the same way as twentieth-century Western journalists have with Islamic punishments such as stoning and beheading. Many non-Western peoples regard as barbarous the Western preference for the extended psychological cruelty of imprisonment over the brief pain of physical punishment. A Papuan commented on the new system of legal punishment that was part of modernisation in his country:

> We used to kill only very bad people, but now one may get into prison simply for stealing or even fighting. One dies if shot by an arrow, but in jail one has to suffer before death. One has to stay in one place and has to work when one does not like it. Jail is really the worst thing. Human beings should not act like that. It is most immoral.[9]

On questions of punishment within societies there is wide disagreement, but between them there is even more. Divergent rationales for punishment are one reason, while different conceptions of what is cruel, inhuman and degrading complicate matters still further. In 1993 the caning of an American youth for vandalism in Singapore, along with local youths found guilty of the same offence, received extensive publicity in the West. There were headlines expressing disgust at 'barbarism' and 'state-sponsored torture', and the president of the United States took a personal interest in the case. Its potency as an example of Asiatic cruelty was muted by the large number of Americans who felt that the youth got what he deserved, and the fact that, in any case, the statute under which the caning was meted out was a relic of Singapore's days as a British colony.[10]

Much more troublesome in a cross-cultural context, however, are the conflicts that can arise between particular human rights, especially those relating to religious and cultural traditions on the one hand, and individual liberty and equality on the other. These conflicts are likely to occur where it is the community rather than the state that threatens human rights, when it is social pressure that is the problem rather than political power. Human rights relating to the family can be particularly problematical in this regard. 'The family is the natural and fundamental unit of society', says the Universal Declaration, 'and is entitled to protection by society and the state'. This includes taking steps to ensure that marriage occurs only between willing couples and that there is equality within marriage. Yet in many cultures the norm is for marriages to be arranged by families rather than individuals, with only limited concern for the preferences of the prospective bride and groom. In many cultures, too, ensuring equality within marriage would be seen as undermining rather than protecting 'the family'. 'The family' cannot be assumed to be a nuclear family resulting from the free decision of a couple to marry. Where 'the family' is understood to include more than a husband and wife and their children, many other relatives may have a legitimate interest in a marriage and its outcomes.

These considerations apply also to the wider and more diffuse issue of gender inequality, of which inequality within marriage is only a part. Despite the fact that discrimination on the basis of sex is rejected in the Universal Declaration and the Convention on the Elimination of All Forms of Discrimination Against Women (1979), gender inequality is widely presented as an aspect of religious belief and practice, and therefore defensible in human rights terms. The right to freedom of religious belief and practice has been used as an argument for the continuation of a wide range of customs, including circumcision of girls and boys, adolescent initiation rites, child marriage, inequality before the law, and unequal rights of inheritance and ownership of property.[11]

It is true, then, that many of the provisions of the Universal Declaration are culture-specific in the sense that they assume institutions and types of social and economic arrangement not present in many societies. Even ideas that seem at first glance to be straightforward, such as that of cruel, inhuman and degrading treatment, may turn out to be complicated by cultural differences. At the very least, many of the rights set out in the Universal Declaration need to be interpreted in reference to a specific cultural context if they are to be applied, and conflicts with other human rights minimised. There is a big difference between abstract formulation of human rights and putting them into practice in diverse cultural contexts. If we think in terms of the latter, the number of human rights that are truly universal may indeed be smaller than at first appears. Nor can it be assumed that the list in the Universal Declaration or any other document will be fixed for all time. The scope and implementation of human rights should always remain the subject of international discussion and debate, on a basis of equality and with all due cultural and historical sensitivity.

## Western values, Asian values

The matters just considered in no way diminish the value of the concept of human rights, nor do they mean that human rights are whatever any state or nation chooses to make them.

The concept of human rights is a product of European philosophical and political traditions. The fact that classical spokesmen for human rights such as John Locke and Jean-Jacques Rousseau could not lift themselves entirely out of their intellectual and historical context, or that the Universal Declaration reflects the time and place of its composition, is no reason to claim that the concept and agenda of human rights can have no universal validity. The position adopted by some Asian intellectuals and political leaders, that concepts originating outside one's own cultural tradition should be rejected, is a strange one, as Aung San Suu Kyi has pointed out: 'If ideas and beliefs are to be denied validity outside the geographical and cultural bounds of their origin, Buddhism would be confined to north India, Christianity to a narrow tract in the Middle East and Islam to Arabia.'[12]

It is a line of argument made all the more puzzling by the fact that those who use it are untroubled about adopting numerous other aspects of Western culture, such as Marxism or the latest industrial and household technologies, which have brought about more fundamental changes than the concept of human rights is ever likely to. Besides, it may be argued that the concept of human rights is quite similar to some of the basic concepts of the major religious and cultural traditions of Asia, and that cultures are neither static nor completely unique, and can accommodate change seen as desirable. Nor does it seem that ordinary members of Asian societies are particularly troubled by the alien origins of the concept, any more than are some governments, including those of Japan, the Philippines, and South Korea.

Some of those who reject human rights because they are alien claim to speak on behalf of 'Asian values', and assert the need to defend them against Western encroachment. A contrast is drawn between Asian communitarian values on the one hand and Western individualism on the other. The communitarian orientation of Asian societies is said to translate into a sense of duty and social responsibility, discipline and respect for authority, social order and harmony. Western individualism translates into selfishness and self-indulgence, social irresponsibility, a lack of respect for authority, and anarchy. Hence the Malaysian delegate to the Vienna conference warned against the moral and social decay that comes from excessive individualism, while the Singapore delegate spoke of authoritative government as a precondition for the enjoyment of any rights at all. 'The East Asian miracle' and 'the decline of the West' are explained in terms of this contrasting set of values.

The contrast is wildly overstated, however, and ignores the variety of values and ideals in both Eastern and Western traditions. The best way to start addressing this problem is by focusing on the concept of human rights itself.

Human rights are not intended to be a solution to every problem that may arise. Neither should they be seen as representing the only mechanism for regulating social and political relations. To a large extent, the complaint that there has been too much concern with individual rights and not enough with the rights of the community and the nation misses the point of human rights, which is to provide safeguards for the individual. The aim of human rights law is to ensure that all individuals are equally able to enjoy the benefits of society, and that the interests of particular individuals or groups are not sacrificed against their will for the sake of the state. Human rights are a way of ensuring that society works the way it should at the individual level.

There are many other mechanisms for protecting the rights of the community or society. Much of the law and many state institutions have the express purpose of fostering the public good, and the role of human rights has to be seen in conjunction with that of other aspects of the state system. It is true, as observed by Vietnam's Vice-Minister of Foreign Affairs, that 'human rights cannot be summed up merely as individual rights', that they also encompass the collective rights of communities and nations to self-determination, the sovereign use of national resources, the right to development, and the right to equality of status among nations.[13] Yet the fact remains that at root human rights are concerned with the well-being of the individual. They present the socio-political and legal system from the perspective of the individual, but since the welfare of the individual is bound up with the welfare of the community and nation, reference to these things must be included in a human rights framework.

In the language of the social contract, human rights spell out what all individuals are entitled to expect from their agreement with the state, and provide a guarantee that the state will keep its side of the bargain. The primary purpose of human rights legislation is to ensure that the state uses its powers to promote and protect human rights rather than violate them. The Chinese government is correct in saying that loss of sovereignty by a state can result in violation of the human rights of its people, but a state fully in control of its own affairs may pose no less of a threat. Where foreign interference does put human rights at risk, there are mechanisms other than human rights legislation to remedy the situation. The Malaysian and Singapore governments rightly emphasise the need for a sense of social obligation and duty on the part of individuals, and respect for authority. But there is no reason to assume that the individual focus of human rights puts these things at risk, especially since exercise of the individual rights and freedoms set out in the Universal Declaration is subject to limitations 'for the purpose of securing due recognition and respect for the rights and freedoms of others and of meeting the just requirements of morality, public order and the general welfare in a democratic society' (Article 29).

Nevertheless, even when allowance is made for the fact that human rights are only one of many instruments for regulating society, and cannot be expected to provide a full statement of the individual's responsibilities towards the state and society, the question of the relative emphasis on individual and community values in different societies remains. What is clear is that there is no neat divide between Western and Asian countries on this issue.

In the West there is a wide range of opinion regarding how much weight should be attached to individual autonomy, whether in relation to religious authority, the state, or traditional morality in the community. It cannot be assumed that a champion of individualism in one sphere will necessarily favour it in another. Political liberals, for example, are often social conservatives. As observed by the Indonesian Minister of Foreign Affairs at the Vienna Conference, some Western intellectual and social traditions passionately espouse individual liberty, while others argue just as passionately the need for strong, lawful authority.

A similar range of opinion exists in Asian societies. As in the West, attitudes are influenced by factors such as education, place of residence, social class, and extent of religious influence. Here too it is unwarranted to assume that importance (or lack of it) attached to authority in the sphere of personal morality invariably translates into a similar attitude regarding political authority. In particular, there is reason to be suspicious when it is those in political power who tell us that respect for authority is an Asian value, in a situation where there is little opportunity for the people to say precisely how much 'strong, lawful authority' they want. The Bangkok Declaration agreed on by representatives of Asian states was strongly criticised by non-government organisation representatives from the same countries, who saw it as evidence of 'the continued attempt by many Governments of the Asia-Pacific Region to avoid their human rights obligations, to put the state before the people and to avoid acknowledging their obligations to account for their failure in the promotion and protection of human rights'.

States asserting that their people prefer 'strong, lawful authority' have a particular obligation to show that the people do in fact have the opportunity to influence the way things are done. The Singapore government, for example, would appear to be right in saying that its people support its strong line on issues such as pornography, drugs, and homosexuality. Rather less convincing is its claim that the Singapore political system is completely open, with all views allowed full expression, and that the government is fully answerable to the people.

It has been argued by intellectuals from a range of cultural backgrounds that, while the concept of human rights is of Western origin, most cultures contain similar concepts and it is therefore not alien at all. The Dalai Lama argues that the Buddhist ideal of universal compassion presupposes that others have the same needs and concerns as ourselves, and aspire, like us, to happiness. He finds it easy to reconcile the basic tenets of his religion with the concept of human rights. Aung San Suu Kyi, when arguing that human rights are not foreign, draws on early Buddhist ideas that the ruler is chosen by the people, and that his authority is limited and conditional upon just rule in accordance with the law and for the sake of the well-being of the people.[14]

Many Muslim writers assert that human rights are central to Islamic teachings. They produce lists of moral rules or principles the Koran says must be universally upheld, principles that are regarded as forming the basis of Shari'a or Islamic law. These are held to confer, for example, rights to personal safety, respect for personal reputation, equality, brotherhood, and justice. Typical is the statement by the Pakistani activist Abul A'la Mawdudi, that 'Islam has laid down some universal rights for humanity as a whole, which are to be observed and respected under all circumstances ... fundamental rights for every man by virtue of his status as a human being'.[15]

Chinese writers refer to the concept of the Mandate of Heaven, according to which a ruler comes to power because of his virtue, caring for the people as if they were his own children. But the Mandate passes to another as soon as he fails to carry out his responsibilities properly. More positive links between human rights and traditional Chinese values are identified by those who focus on the ethical and social ideals developed by Confucius. It is argued, for example, that although 'the term "human rights" did not appear in the *Analects*, many of the values advocated therein are quite similar'. Particularly important in this regard are the concepts of benevolence or human-heartedness, tolerance, justice, and moral government. However, attempts to derive human rights from Confucian principles are likely to result in rights that are different in scope and emphasis from the list that had become internationally familiar by the end of the twentieth century.[16]

The sorts of concepts mentioned show that the idea of mutual obligation or social contract forms the foundation of social justice and political legitimacy everywhere. It certainly also lies at the heart of the concept of human rights. The concept of rights itself, as many have argued, cannot be understood except in terms of a reciprocity of duties or obligations between individuals. One person's rights imply obligations on the part of others. But the language of rights also implies that the duties or obligations they entail cannot be set aside, that they are binding in a way that moral principles are not. 'The distinction between duty and obligation, the right thing to do, and entitlement, i.e., rights, is crucial.'[17] To talk about 'rights' is to say that the individual has a legitimate expectation of being treated in certain ways by others, and legal rights can be enforced by law.

This is what is missing from concepts relating to mutual obligation in Asian and other traditions, and is why the concept of human rights is valuable. Traditional concepts and theories contained the principle of limiting state power and making authority conditional on the state discharging its obligations towards the people, but lacked any mechanism for enforcing those principles. Although it was possible—if dangerous—to tell the ruler he was failing to do his duty, it was impossible to *make* him do it. According to the old Chinese doctrine of the Mandate of Heaven, revolution is justified, but revolution is a drastic measure and the outcome may be no better than what it aims to replace.

Human rights legislation is a way of ensuring that the state fully discharges its obligations without resorting to extreme measures. As stated in the preamble to the Universal Declaration of Human Rights, it is a way of ensuring that 'man is not compelled to have recourse, as a last resort, to rebellion against tyranny and oppression'. It is a mechanism that will work, if at all, as part of a global political system. Domestic human rights legislation, like any other domestic legal initiative, cannot be enforced against the wishes or the inertia of the state. It is true that the effectiveness of international pressure is limited, and that sometimes pressure may be used for the wrong reasons. But this makes it all the more necessary for action on behalf of human rights to be truly international and forthright.

## Human rights, religious and moral traditions

Were the problems of human rights implementation limited to forcing recalcitrant governments to take positive action, the problems would be relatively straightforward. However, as already mentioned, more complex difficulties arise from the fact that it is not only governments that violate human rights. As likely as not, violations will result from the actions of private individuals, families, and communities as well. What we call tradition or culture or religion may include types of behaviour and personal interaction that contravene the norms of human rights. In other words, safeguarding human rights may require changing the moral norms that underlie the law as well as the law itself.

Human rights such as gender and ethnic equality, or free choice of marriage partner, are by and large private matters. Their realisation and protection depend on personal interaction and community attitudes. For example, it is true that gender equality is strongly affected by numerous aspects of the law and government administration, from educational provision to inheritance and divorce regulations, and action by the state can be a powerful influence in changing attitudes. The role of the law in securing human rights in such spheres, however, will always be minor, if for no other reason than the difficulty of policing day-to-day interaction between men and women at home, in the workplace, or even in the public sphere. In such things education is more likely to be effective than legal enforcement, and where change is imposed regardless of community sentiments or values it is unlikely to work at all.

Human rights legislation, both domestic and international, is invaluable in reducing human rights violations by the state, where the problems arise from the misuse of state power and the context is a legal–administrative one. But where the individual's human rights are violated by private individuals, the family or the community, attempts to enforce legislation may create more difficulties than they solve. Where community norms have to be changed, legal decrees in themselves may do little more than demonstrate that the state treats these matters seriously. What we get back to here is the moral or normative basis of the law itself, the fact that obedience to the laws cannot be enforced where 'the rules' have not been internalised. Where rules are seen as alien—where governments tell people that the very concept of human rights is alien—their internalisation is that much less likely.

What must be avoided is the assumption that cultures should not change, and the idea that retaining one's 'own' culture is the most important principle of all. Paradoxically, those who adopt a cultural relativist position with respect to human rights turn out to be cultural absolutists, insisting as they do that nothing should be allowed to disturb the integrity of a society's culture. 'They argue not only that no one's sense of justice can transcend the boundaries of her own culture, they also argue that one ought not to transcend them.'[18] As well as saying that human rights are not part of their own tradition, in other words, they also assert that they *should* not become part of it. The second proposition is much harder to establish than the first. Cultural relativists tend to present cultures as static and monolithic, enormous stereotypes that embrace the whole of society. The stereotypes reflect ideals rather than social realities. They are idealisations, glorifications of tradition and communalism that appear all the more glorious because they are presumed to be unchanging. Such stereotypes are assertions of separateness and distinctiveness, the props of national identity, weapons for keeping others at a distance. Not surprisingly, they tend to reflect the elite versions of culture and legitimate the power and privilege of dominant social groups.

Indonesia's Minister for Foreign Affairs commented at the Vienna Conference on the irony of countries that insist on the need for democratic and free discussion *within* nations being so reluctant to make it the basis for interaction *between* nations. It could as easily be argued that the states that assert most strongly the need for free and equal discussion of human rights issues between nations are those that do most to inhibit free and open discussion of the issues among their own people. In any case, if, as is widely accepted, most cultures have concepts analogous to human rights, then human rights cannot pose a threat to those cultures.

Should governments impose change on society? It is tempting to reply, 'Yes of course, as long as the changes are desirable ones, that is, when they represent genuine reforms'. Many of those most critical of authoritarian states look to governments in Third World countries to overcome widespread ignorance and hostility there regarding human rights, since it is the government and the elite connected with it that may be the only part of the society familiar with international norms. Yet there is a serious problem if the attitudes of the state are in conflict with those of the general society, for in such situations the law lacks force. The state may be able to change behaviour by force, but it is much harder to change values or moral rules in this way. Further, the idea of imposing respect for universal human rights by state authority is fundamentally contradictory.

This problem has troubled the Sudanese jurist Abdullahi Ahmed An-Na'im when considering the lack of popular awareness of and support for human rights standards among the populations of Asian and African countries. He observes that 'Unless the majority or dominant segment of the population is persuaded to respect and promote the human rights of minorities and individuals, the whole society will drift into the politics of confrontation and subjugation rather than that of reconciliation and justice'. There has to be genuine popular consensus if respect and real protection for human rights are to be achieved there. Such consensus can only by established through wide participation by peoples from a broad range of cultural traditions in the ongoing development of international human rights standards. There are enormous problems involved, yet there is a ground for consensus in 'the principle of reciprocity' that forms the foundation of all the major moral and religious traditions of the world.[19]

I find myself in sympathy with this position. Respect for human rights cannot be firmly established by imposing on 'backward societies' a crash course in the principles of civilised behaviour. Rather, such peoples need informed discussion of the merits of the sometimes fairly abstract principles of human rights, how they relate to local customs and beliefs, and how they may be expressed in local laws and institutions. This includes frank discussion of the fact that it is not an adequate defence of a practice or attitude to say that it is traditional, and that there may be good grounds for changing customs that have long been authorised or praised on religious grounds. In relation to gender-based violence and exploitation this was stated clearly in the declaration of the 1993 Vienna Conference, which stressed the importance of working towards 'the eradication of any conflicts which may arise between the rights of women and the harmful effects of certain traditional or customary practices'.[20] Internationally there must be recognition too that declarations of human rights—no less than divine revelations—have to be expressed in the words and with the outlook of a given time and place, whatever their limitations, if humans are to comprehend them. This means that they will always have to be reinterpreted and reassessed. What is needed is firm commitment to principles, and also to understanding and tolerance in their implementation.

## Human rights in perspective

These considerations lead to the conclusion that while international human rights concepts and institutions may play an important role in establishing a fairer and more humane world, this goal will not be achieved unless their limitations are frankly acknowledged. The Universal Declaration was an attempt to formulate 'a common standard of achievement for all peoples and nations', spelling out the conditions necessary for a life of security, dignity and freedom. Few have been convinced that it is the final word on the subject, as is clear from the many declarations and conventions that have supplemented the Declaration since 1948. Many have reservations about particular human rights provisions or their absence. Yet there is overwhelming support around the world for the concept of human rights as one of the bases of an international moral and legal order. Globalisation in all its facets, at individual and national levels, has made such an order indispensable.

Human rights do not represent the totality of civilised or enlightened behaviour. There are many other ideals and institutions we would want to incorporate in our vision of the perfect society. But human rights articulate the minimum human needs of a society, spelling out in particular the role of the state in securing those needs.

It is possible to obtain universal support for this framework only by keeping it reasonably straightforward, and couched in terms of general principles, many of which will require interpretation and judgment in the context of specific cultures. It would be strange if this were otherwise.

It is impossible to draft human rights conventions that are entirely free of intellectual and cultural assumptions. Although it may be possible to reduce the influence of unquestioned assumptions in regard even to difficult areas such as family, and religious and cultural rights, assumptions about the nature of the state and its relation to society are harder to avoid. Human rights concepts assume that the state is secular and that its power over citizens must be limited. Much of the debate over 'Asian' and 'Western' values derives from this point. The dominant concept of the state in Western liberalism has been the largely negative one of an overzealous and not entirely trustworthy policeman, who limits individual liberty for the sake of social order, but whose role must be kept to a minimum if civil society is to flourish. This contrasts with the positive roles assigned to the state in Asian political traditions and in Marxism. If the state is seen as a positive force that works to secure basic human needs, there is less reason to limit its powers or to disobey it. While both positive and negative conceptions of the state may diverge from the reality experienced, they nevertheless lead to different perspectives on human rights issues.

## CHAPTER FOUR

# Ethnic Minorities

### How many ethnic minorities?

In Chapter 1 ethnic identity was defined in terms of linguistic and cultural distinctiveness and a shared history, usually involving association with a particular territory. In practice, it often happens that one commonly used criterion of ethnic distinctiveness contradicts another, such as when two groups share a common language yet have cultures that in many other respects are sufficiently different to be regarded as separate. Sometimes there may be dispute regarding whether differences in, say, religion are sufficient reason for regarding two groups in one society as having different cultures. Many analysts argue that minorities that are indigenous or 'native' to an area need to be considered differently from those that are not. It is not unusual for discussion to slide from minorities defined in one way (for example, on the basis of religion) to minorities defined in other ways (such as by social organisation or language). In this chapter the main focus is on indigenous minorities that differ from the dominant society in a number of major aspects of culture. However, especially when competing definitions of ethnicity are being used by minorities as political weapons, it is difficult to keep these separate.

On the basis of the number of languages spoken, it has been estimated that there are at present about six thousand distinct ethnic groups in the world, while the number of nation states stands at around two hundred. Roughly a third of all ethnic groups are located in Asian countries. How many there are in some countries is uncertain. States preoccupied with issues of national unity are inclined to play down ethnic distinctions and be reluctant to gather basic statistical information that may reinforce ethnic as distinct from national identities. Some states go so far as to deny that there are any ethnic minorities within their borders. Lack of accessible information on ethnic minorities is often an indication of the difficulties minorities experience in gaining recognition and consideration from the state. False or misleading information, however, is often no less of a problem.[1]

From the limited information that is available, it is clear that the number of ethnic minorities in Asian countries varies widely (see Table 4.1). North and South Korea

**Table 4.1** Ethnic minorities in selected Asian countries

| | *Number of distinct minorities* | *Estimated total population of minorities (millions, 1998)*[1] | *Minorities as % of national population* |
|---|---|---|---|
| Bangladesh | 29 | 1.4 | 1.1 |
| China | 55 | 100.5 | 8 |
| India | 200+ | 78.6 | 8 |
| Indonesia[2] | 300+ | 112.7 | 55 |
| Iran | 17 | 32.2 | 49 |
| Japan | 3 | 1.3 | 1 |
| Laos | 42 | 1.7 | 33 |
| Myanmar | 15 | 14.2 | 32 |
| Pakistan[3] | 8+ | 77.1 | 52 |
| Philippines | 50+ | 8.7 | 12 |
| Vietnam | 53 | 10.1 | 13 |

Notes:

1. Total population figures have been obtained by multiplying 1998 national population estimates by the recent and most reliable estimate of minority population as a percentage of the national population for each country. In some cases these measures are little more than educated guesses, while in others they are derived from recent census figures.
2. For Indonesia the figure for percentage of the national population consisting of minorities has been obtained by subtracting the estimated proportion of the population that is Javanese from the national total. Strictly speaking, of course, the Javanese are a minority too.
3. Figures for Pakistan are based on the 1981 census figures for speakers of all languages except Punjabi. These include an 'other languages' category, comprising 2.8 per cent of the population, for very small indigenous language groups. The exact number of distinct groups is uncertain, but the total number of minorities is understated accordingly.

have no indigenous minorities, though people of Chinese descent have long lived in both states and migrant workers from other Asian countries have moved there recently. Indonesia has well over three hundred different ethnic groups living within its boundaries, which makes its national motto, *Bhinnek tunggal ika*, or 'Unity in Diversity', appropriate—particularly if it is read as an aspiration rather than a description of reality. Many of the ethnic groups are very small, with populations counted in the hundreds or less. Some areas are particularly varied in terms of ethnic composition. This is true especially of West Papua and the eastern part of the archipelago. If the number of different languages spoken is used as an indicator of the number of ethnic groups, then there are more than two hundred in West Papua, the small Tanimbar Islands in the South Moluccas are home to six distinct groups, while the medium-size islands of Flores and Sumba further west together are inhabited by twenty ethnic groups speaking mutually unintelligible languages. The densely populated island of Java has three major indigenous groups speaking different languages: Javanese, Sundanese and Madurese. With a population of around 90 million in 2000, the Javanese are by far the largest ethnic group in Indonesia, but in the national population of 203 million are well short of being a majority, despite their political and economic dominance.

In this sort of situation, talking about *minorities* and their problems is apt to become confusing unless careful note is taken of how diverse the category has become. When identifying indigenous minorities the Indonesian government has come up with a total population figure of 1.5 million. It is a figure that has meaning only if the category of indigenous minorities is so narrowly defined as to exclude everything but communities whose culture and social structure diverge sharply from the norm as understood in Jakarta, and are seen as particularly backward or primitive. The Constitution of 1945 refers to tribal communities 'whose social life, economic performance and level of civilisation are below acceptable standards'. It is to these groups, mostly to be found in isolated parts of West Papua, Kalimantan, Sulawesi, and Sumatra, that the label 'indigenous minority' is being applied. This is a restrictive definition that ignores the fact that serious problems may also be encountered by larger groups whose cultures are much less divergent from what is regarded as the national norm.

The Acehnese (around 4 million) and the Minangkabau (around 10 million) of Sumatra are Muslims with a long history of agriculture centred on rice-growing, and in this regard they are not very different from, say, the Javanese. Yet the people of Aceh prize their cultural and political separateness, and have long fought to preserve it—first against the Dutch (1873–1903), and more recently against the Indonesian state. After decades of suppression by the Indonesian army, the Aceh Merdeka independence movement remains strong, and while a decree by Indonesian president Megawati Sukarnoputri in August 2001 conferred greater autonomy on the province, it may be too little and too late to satisfy the Acehnese. The cultural distinctiveness of the Minangkabau is most obvious in respect of their matrilineal social structure. This, like other Minangkabau traditions, has been subject to pressures resulting from national incorporation.[2]

In other Asian countries the ethnic situation is somewhat less complicated than in Indonesia because the number of distinct ethnic groups is smaller and, usually, the total population of minority groups is a relatively small proportion of the national figure. From the viewpoint of the dominant society, this is likely to result in greater national cohesion and make far simpler, for example, the provision of public services such as health and education. For the minorities, however, the problems may be greater because it is easier for the state to ignore their needs.

In 1950 the president of India officially declared there to be 212 'scheduled tribes' in his country. According to the 1981 census data India had 635 tribal communities, speaking 105 different languages with 225 dialects. On the basis of the 1991 census (which, unlike that of 1981, included Assam), it appears that there are around 450 tribes and sub-tribes, with a total population at the time of 67.8 million, amounting to 8 per cent of the national population. At much the same time the fifty-three minorities in Vietnam had a total population of 8.2 million, or 13 per cent of the national figure. In the Philippines more than fifty distinct ethnic groups are recognised, which in 1986 had a combined population in the vicinity of 6.5 million, some 12 per cent of the national total. In 2000, China's fifty-five minorities had a total population of 106.3 million, representing 8.4 per cent of the national population.

Elsewhere the number of distinct minorities may be smaller, while as a proportion of the national population they are more prominent. In Laos, the definition of ethnic identity primarily in terms of language spoken results in forty-eight distinct groups being identified in three broad linguistic categories. Of these, the Lao Lum (speakers of six different languages of the Tai family) form a majority of 67 per cent, while the Lao Theung (thirty-one distinct groups, speaking a variety of Mon–Khmer languages, who inhabited the area before the arrival of the Tai-language speakers) make up 23 per cent, and the Lao Sung (ten distinct groups, the most recent arrivals in the area, and mainly from China) make up the remaining 10 per cent of the population. In Myanmar the Burman people represent 68 per cent of the population, with the

Lisu girls in New Year costume, northern Thailand.

remaining population being made up of sixteen other indigenous groups. In countries where ethnic groups are relatively balanced in terms of population and political power, and there is a long history of ethnic conflict, national unity may prove fragile, as Myanmar's half-century of civil war testifies.

The situation of some ethnic groups is complicated by the fact that they live across the borders of a number of countries. Some groups in this situation have pursued unification in an independent state of their own. The Kurds of northern Iran and Iraq, and southern Turkey and Armenia, have attracted a lot of attention by their militant struggle for political independence. Others have shown little interest in secession and the redrawing of international boundaries. This is more likely when groups are largely tribal in structure, with local loyalties and identities. It applies, for example, to the Akha (also known as Hani), who live in the border regions of China, Laos, Thailand, Vietnam and Myanmar; the Lisu, who live in China, Myanmar, north-east India, and Thailand; and the Hmong (Miao or Meo), who live in China, Vietnam, Laos and Thailand.[3]

## The recent experience of minorities

The recent historical experience of ethnic minorities, in Asian countries as elsewhere, can be understood only in the context of globalisation, the development of a world system of nation states whose economic, political and cultural reach has been all-pervasive. The situation of ethnic minorities has been strongly influenced by the centralisation of state power, economic development, and the emergence of a world market. For indigenous minorities these trends have commonly resulted in political powerlessness, social marginalisation and economic deprivation. At the same time, for individuals able and willing to move, they have also brought new opportunities for personal advancement, which has led to mixing of ethnic groups within state borders and the formation of new ethnic minorities by those pursuing opportunities across state borders.

In general terms, the recent historical experience of indigenous minorities has been grim. One account sums it up in terms of militarisation, loss of land and resources, transmigration and population relocation, and cultural genocide.[4]

Loss of land and the control of its resources has surely been the most fundamental problem experienced by indigenous minorities. The rapid population growth that has been part of development has increased enormously the pressure on land. Numerically and politically weak minorities have not been able to resist the influx of settlers into their traditional territories, whether in central and north-eastern India, the Chittagong Hill Tracts of Bangladesh, or the northern and north-western provinces of China. Economic development has resulted in new demands for resources from the traditional lands of indigenous minorities. Massive deforestation, as in the Nepalese and Indian Himalaya, Sarawak and the Philippines, is commonplace. From the Binuan and Chico rivers of northern Luzon in the Philippines to the Bakun River in Sarawak, the Song Da basin in Vietnam, and the Narmada River in central India, once-isolated river valleys are being flooded for irrigation and hydroelectricity, displacing many thousands of indigenous people. Minerals on traditional minority lands are claimed by the state, and their extraction typically brings little but environmental destruction to the peoples in question.

Governments eager for more revenue encourage foreign multinationals to exploit the resources, with little concern over environmental impact, and a willingness to provide military enforcement of their operations if necessary against the wishes of the minorities affected. Governments in the Philippines and Indonesia have a bad record in this regard. The history of the Freeport gold mine in West Papua is a classic example.[5]

Frequently, loss of control of land and resources is the result of direct military action. The Chinese invasion of Tibet in 1950–51, the ongoing campaigns against the minorities of Myanmar and the north-eastern provinces of India, and the 1975 incorporation of East Timor by Indonesia are notorious. However, effective control and assimilation of indigenous minorities are often more efficiently achieved by means of enforced relocation of minorities coupled with state-organised transmigration of dominant groups to minority homelands. Both were important aspects of Indonesian policy under Suharto's 'New Order' (1965–98). In March 1994 the Indonesian Minister for Transmigration stated that the government planned to resettle all of Indonesia's indigenous peoples because that was the only way they would 'leave behind backwardness'.[6] Under its transmigration program, the government moved in the space of thirty years some seven million people from densely populated regions (especially Java) to outer islands largely inhabited by indigenous minorities—this despite strong evidence that much of the land being occupied was unsuitable for agriculture and unable to support large populations. In 2000, in the wake of Indonesia's economic crisis and in the face of evidence of massive corruption and increasing provincial resistance, the program came to a halt.[7]

China and Vietnam too have a history of population transfers to reinforce national unity and to speed up the development of 'backward' minorities, while at the same time bringing about a more even population distribution. In China migration of the Han majority has been strongly encouraged, with the result that in Xinjiang Province (Eastern Turkistan) between 1949 and 1990 the Han, as a proportion of the population, increased from 7 per cent to 37 per cent. It is widely claimed that Han migration to Tibet is being encouraged as part of a strategy to undermine Tibetan culture and autonomy, although this is not reflected by official population figures and unofficial estimates vary wildly. The aim of the Vietnamese Fixed Cultivation and Permanent Settlement Program has been to move indigenous minorities from the highlands and resettle them closer to government control, replacing their shifting agriculture with modern farming methods and their social traditions with the norms of Viet society. At the same time, the government has encouraged migration of Viet into the highlands to bring about more even development. The official target was the relocation of 10 million people by 2000.

The culture and autonomy of indigenous minorities are undermined in many ways in the context of nation-building and economic development. Population movement is perhaps the most irresistible method of doing away with the distance between minorities and the modern nation state, but there are others almost as effective. Many proceed from good intentions, if we accept as sincere the desire expressed by almost every Asian government to confer on members of 'primitive' groups the benefits of modern civilisation. Such strategies may include, for example, programs to end nomadic lifestyles by replacing swidden (shifting) agriculture, hunting and gathering with sedentary agriculture, and new industries. The provision of modern housing, health services, and compulsory schooling all weaken traditional culture and autonomy, as do the introduction of new political institutions and the construction of transport and communication links with the wider world.

Formal education is a powerful example of the way new services may both improve and worsen the situation of minorities. Education can empower by conferring new knowledge and skills, opening up new opportunities to participate in and benefit from economic development. Yet at the same time the new education system undermines local systems of knowledge and authority. Determined by a national agency, much of the content of education is strange to minorities and frequently includes discriminatory material. Doing well at school for the children of minorities often means alienation from their own traditions. Usually instruction is in the national language. This may seriously impair the academic performance of the children of minorities, undermine their sense of self-worth and reinforce negative stereotypes.

This is a particular problem in Pakistan, where the national language Urdu is the first language of less than 8 per cent of the population. However, except in the Sindhi-speaking region it is the language in which all schooling is provided. That the great majority of children receive their primary education in a second language is one factor behind Pakistan's relatively low levels of literacy and education participation.

In Vietnam education for minorities is in the national language, which the government sees as a force for national unity. A 1986 study revealed a school enrolment rate among minorities in Vietnam of only 16 per cent and a drop-out rate well in excess of 50 per cent. While human rights documents call for schooling to be made available in the child's first language, it is necessary to recognise the serious obstacles developing countries face in this regard. Where there are many different linguistic minorities, as in most Asian countries, the expertise and resources to provide schooling in each of the languages spoken may simply be unavailable, even when the goal is taken seriously.

A determination to face up to the suffering experienced by indigenous minorities as a result of globalisation should not be allowed to lead to the simplistic conclusion that only harm has come from interaction with the wider world. In reality, the experience of most groups has been neither unmitigated disaster nor unending bliss. Demographic data indicate that rapid population increase has been widespread among minorities over the past few decades, and that much of it is due to improved health and life expectancies. Population increase is not always evidence of improved living conditions since it may be the result of a breakdown of traditional mechanisms of fertility control, such as late marriage and extended periods of breastfeeding. (These matters are discussed further in Chapter 6.) Nevertheless, where reliable data are available they show that despite the health and social problems often resulting from severe cultural dislocation, population increase has been largely due to falling mortality rates associated with better health care, housing and nutrition. The population growth of minority groups themselves is one factor behind the greater pressure on land and resources experienced in many regions. Growing populations create ecological imbalance and reduce the viability of traditional patterns of economic activity, already threatened by external forces.

Secular education and compulsory schooling are not part of the traditional cultures of most minorities, and if provided without regard to linguistic and cultural differences may do harm. Yet there can be no doubt that literacy and formal education are essential if minorities are to be able to cope with the world impinging on them, and to have a measure of control over their own futures. While literacy and formal education may be largely irrelevant to their traditional culture, maintaining a traditional lifestyle in isolation is no longer a realistic option. Whatever hope minorities have for the future will depend on the acquisition of new knowledge and skills through literacy and formal education. The evidence of increasing educational participation and achievement among many groups must therefore be regarded as an encouraging trend, even if the type of educational provision is often inferior and inappropriate.

## Ethnicity and equality

Malaysia's Prime Minister Mahathir was expressing widely held sentiments regarding indigenous minorities when, responding to criticisms of deforestation destroying the traditional lifestyle of the Penan people of Sarawak, he said: 'We don't intend to turn [them] into human zoological specimens to be gawked at by tourists and studied by anthropologists while the rest of the world passes them by ... It is our policy to eventually bring all jungle dwellers into the mainstream ... There is nothing romantic about the helpless, half-starved and disease-ridden people.'[8]

Such sentiments are often regarded as part of the racist heritage of colonialism acquired by Westernised elites. Yet the situation of minorities in Asia cannot be understood just as a product of colonialism and the postcolonial world order. We cannot understand the present without recognising in it the presence of the past. Relations between ethnic groups or peoples in Asia, like those elsewhere, have tended to be characterised by inequality in power and status, by assertions of superiority, by prejudice, aggression, exploitation. Sedentary societies have looked down on nomadic societies, agricultural societies on hunters and gatherers, literate societies on illiterate ones, urban on rural ones. Usually the compliment has been returned.

In many cases social rules and moral principles were seen as applying only in dealings with members of one's own society. Members of other social groups were often seen as less human, as incapable of understanding or perversely refusing to follow the rules of civilised behaviour. These 'inferior' species were there to be exploited mercilessly or to have 'superior' customs and beliefs imposed on them.

These attitudes have no more vanished from Asian societies than they have from the West. While the idea of a mission to civilise may owe something to colonialism, the assumption of superiority on which it is based is certainly not confined to it. The belief that the values and institutions of one's own society are the only proper ones is well-nigh universal, among 'backward' no less than among 'advanced' peoples, though we tend to hear it always from the perspective of literate societies. It may be that a belief in the superiority of their own ways is crucial to the survival of a people, since without it cultural distinctiveness could soon disappear. The self-concept of the Chinese has long been expressed in terms of the centre of civilisation, surrounded by barbarians who may in effect become 'Chinese' by recognising the superiority of Chinese customs and institutions and adopting them. *Zhongguo*, China, means the state at the centre. Chineseness, at least until the nineteenth century, was understood in cultural terms. It involved embracing 'the way of the sages' (*sheng dao*), the values and traditions formalised and institutionalised by Confucianism.

The sinicised elite of what is now northern Vietnam adopted this view. The Vietnamese refer to themselves as *kinh* or 'cultured/central', in contrast to the minorities living in forested and mountainous regions who are *moi* or barbarians (those whom the Chinese called *man* and among whom the Viet were formerly included).

The people of the Khmer empire also saw themselves as civilised, in contrast to the savages (*phnong*) of the forests and mountains. The Lao, in common with other speakers of Tai languages, call the hill peoples *kha*, meaning slaves or servants. Several Tai groups have a myth that tells how their own ancestors acquired clean bodies and clear minds, and so became 'clever enough to rule the country', in contradistinction to the ancestors of mountain peoples such as the Wa, Lua and Laveue. In Indonesia, continuing Javanese political and economic dominance reinforces their traditional sense of cultural superiority to other ethnic groups: although peoples such as the Sundanese, Minangkabau, Bugis and Batak are regarded as being on a comparable cultural level, the Javanese see themselves as having little in common, for example, with the peoples of the Kalimantan hinterland or West Papua. Like the Han Chinese, the Javanese tend to regard themselves as being at, or *being* the centre: 'Since the establishment of Indonesia's nation-state, the Javanese concept of *pasisir* (periphery) has been enlarged to include the non-Javanese cultural sphere'.[9]

It is fair to say that the historical range of customs in the Indonesian archipelago is sufficient to test even the most extreme advocates of cultural relativism. It is not just a question of other groups lacking the elaborate codes of politeness and restraint characteristic of Javanese society. Some groups in West Papua have practised cannibalism and ritual necrophagia. Headhunting has been a feature of many groups on islands including Timor, Sumba, Sulawesi, the Moluccas, and Borneo. While such customs have always been badly misunderstood and condemned as quintessential savagery, even an informed interpretation requires acknowledgment of the gulf in understanding that has existed between such groups and the state-building groups of the region. Headhunters such as the Naga of north-east India and Myanmar, the Wa of southern China and the Golden Triangle, the Ilongot of the Philippines, and the Dayak peoples of Borneo have long symbolised primitive violence and savagery for those who see themselves as the bearers of civilisation.[10]

In the case of Vietnam and China, traditional assumptions of superiority by the Viet and the Han have been overlaid by the evolutionist assumptions of the Marxist theory of history. Communist leaders in China have warned at various times of the dangers of 'great Han chauvinism' and the common tendency of Han Chinese to look down on the minorities, while these same leaders never wavered in their belief that many aspects of minority culture reflected primitive attitudes and social institutions that had to be supplanted by communism, the most advanced form of socio-economic organisation. There is not necessarily a contradiction in this, if we recognise that respect for other cultures need not imply uncritical acceptance of all aspects of them. The Vietnamese leadership appears, if anything, to be even more confident than the Chinese of its duty to raise the minority peoples to a higher socio-economic plane, to help them discard their primitive lifestyles and step up to the level of the *kinh* majority.[11]

Assumptions of superiority and inferiority reflect inequalities in power and control, if nothing else, and the history of those inequalities is evident in the waves of settlement and conquest that have swept through most of the Asian region. The present distribution of ethnic minorities is the outcome of a historical process that is far from over, and that is unlikely to stop just because the world system is dominated by rich states intent on preserving existing borders. Ethnic conflict did not begin with Western colonialism and is unlikely to end with it. Globalisation and development have greatly intensified the problems faced by ethnic minorities, but in essence they have always amounted to the same thing: to survive within the limits set by the environment and the pressures of adjacent peoples.[12]

One historical constant appears to be the fanning out of peoples from Central Asia, to the south and to the east. To some extent this is no doubt an illusion, produced by the fact that Central Asia appears at the edge of everybody's map, one of those blanks early cartographers filled in with monsters, largely legendary. It may also be due to the fact that the limited number of negotiable mountain passes there are historical crossroads that just about everyone has had to use, no matter where they have been bound. Anyway, the evidence of waves of migration south and east from Central Asia is strong. Sometimes the Chinese were able to resist or absorb these migrants and sometimes not. The expansion of the Chinese people themselves has primarily been southward. This has resulted in the displacement of other ethnic groups from the area now known as southern China, and their migration to the countries of South-East Asia, where they in turn displaced other groups.

The Mon and Khmer were among the earliest-known ethnic groups to dominate large areas of mainland South-East Asia. They were displaced, to a large extent, by the Burman, Tai and Viet peoples, all of whom are thought to have migrated from China. About the origins of the Burman there is some debate, but it is likely that they came from western China and Tibet, before eventually making their way south from Yunnan. The Viet originated in south-eastern China, where during the Eastern Zhou period (771–256 BCE) there was the kingdom of Yue (Viet). When this was overthrown by the state of Chu in 334 BCE, some of the people moved to the north Vietnam region.

The Tai family of language-speakers includes the Dai (or Lü) minority of Yunnan, the Lao Lum of Laos, the Shan of Myanmar and the Ahom of Assam, as well as the distinct Thai groups of northern and central Thailand. They are thought to have originated in central China south of the Yangtze River, near the region now occupied by the Zhuang, contemporary China's largest ethnic minority, which belongs to the same family. The Tai peoples began moving south at around the beginning of the Common Era, but did not enter what is now Thailand until about the eleventh century.

This process of displacement has continued in more recent times. In the late seventeenth and eighteenth centuries the Manchu rulers of China used their military strength to extend control into Tibet, Burma, and Vietnam. The nature of the terrain and its inhabitants, however, made consolidation of power difficult. Even after international borders had reached more or less their present arrangement, rebellions continued to break out among the many mountain-dwelling minorities that felt little inclined to respect the claims of distant rulers. Repeated pacification campaigns by Chinese armies in the nineteenth century, and growing competition between minorities themselves, resulted in many thousands of minority peoples moving south into Laos, Vietnam, and Thailand. They included members of the Akha (Hani), Hmong (Miao), Lahu, Lisu, Mien (Yao), and Lolo (Yi) groups.

Of these it is the Hmong who have the longest history of resistance to Han Chinese domination. The origins of the Hmong are not clear; one scholar has argued from the appearance among them of Caucasian features such as fair skin and blue eyes that they must have originated far to the west. Be that as it may, for at least two thousand years they have resisted incorporation by the Han despite living in the Chinese heartland. Some Hmong still live there, in Hunan province, but over the centuries much of the population has been pushed to the south and scattered. Those who migrated to Laos and Vietnam were caught up in the bitter wars there of the 1960s and 1970s, with many of those who fought on the losing side subsequently emigrating to the United States, Canada, France, and Australia.[13]

A historical perspective helps us to understand that not all ethnic minorities are disadvantaged, exploited, oppressed. Some do their share of the exploiting and oppressing. This basic point may disappear from view if we think in terms of a dichotomy of, on the one hand, small indigenous minorities who are victims of nation-building, and, on the other, a social mainstream bent on modernisation and

Mien wedding couple, northern Thailand.

development that is ethnically anonymous. There is a continuum of both ethnic distinctiveness and the extent to which groups are the masters or the victims of change. What is more, the situation of a given minority may alter sharply over time.

The Manchu people of China provide a good illustration of this. In the sixteenth century the Manchu were a semi-nomadic people in the area north-east of China that came to be known as Manchuguo or Manchuria. In the seventeenth century they conquered China, overthrowing the indigenous Ming Dynasty and establishing themselves as the ruling elite. In many ways their situation was similar to that of European colonial elites in nineteenth-century Asia. They monopolised military and political power, took care to maintain distance from their Chinese subjects in terms of dress and customs, prohibited intermarriage, and forbade Chinese to live in the

Manchu homeland. Over time, however, distinctions blurred between rulers and ruled and, like the Mongols before them, the Manchu found themselves absorbed into the Chinese socio-cultural mainstream. By the time the Manchu (Qing) Dynasty was finally toppled in 1911, much of the distinctive Manchu identity had disappeared, and what had not disappeared was hidden because it had become a liability. During the first thirty years of the People's Republic it remained so. Only in recent years has Manchu ethnic identity become acceptable again. This helps to explain the fact that between 1982 and 1990 the number of people claiming Manchu identity in the Chinese national census increased by 128 per cent (from 4.3 million to 9.8 million), despite the fact that knowledge of Manchu culture is limited and few are able to speak the Manchu language, let alone read the Manchu script.[14]

The Hindu minority of Pakistan has a population of more than 2.5 million, around 2 per cent of the national total. The great majority of Hindus moved to India after Partition in 1947. Those who chose to remain live almost entirely in the urban centres of the province of Sind, where they are a strong presence in cultural and commercial life, and also in government administration. In terms of literacy and educational attainment they far exceed the national average, despite the fact that the number of higher education places available to them is limited under a quota system. Overall, their economic and social situation compares very favourably with that of the majority of the population, despite the fact that Pakistan is an Islamic republic, and despite the sectarian conflict that has been endemic there.[15]

The ethnic Chinese of Malaysia (comprising 30 per cent of the population) are another group for which being a numerical minority has not meant marginalisation and disadvantage. In terms of health, education and wealth they are better off than the Malay majority. Business and professional life in Malaysia has been dominated by them. The larger numbers of the Malays, however, has enabled them to retain control of government and introduce programs to improve their situation, for example, by giving Malays preferential access to higher education and business opportunities. Between 1971 and 1990, Bumiputra ownership of business rose from 2 per cent to 20 per cent, while over the same period the proportion of Malay families living in poverty fell from 49 per cent to 16 per cent. Life expectancy, literacy levels and educational participation rates for the Malay population also increased more than did those of the Chinese minority over the same period. Yet despite the fact that the gap in living standards between the two ethnic groups has narrowed, it remains considerable.[16]

These examples give an indication of how easy it is to overgeneralise about the situation of ethnic minorities. Although it is true that many ethnic minorities—especially indigenous minorities—have suffered greatly in the process of nation-building and globalisation, others have not. Most, it is fair to say, have gained in some ways from the process and lost in others.

The historical experience of each minority is determined by many factors. Population size is one such factor. A relatively large minority, such as the Sundanese of Java or the Pashtuns (Pathan) of Pakistan, will usually be able to safeguard its interests more easily than a very small minority. Peoples living in remote, hostile environments of little strategic significance have historically been subjected to fewer pressures than those living in agriculturally productive regions on paths of regular migration.

Unfortunately for small groups until recently able to live undisturbed in forests, mountains and deserts, the globalisation process has resulted in unprecedented demands for resources and new strategic considerations, which have left them no further retreat. Nothing illustrates this more vividly than the cold war conflicts that reached into the remote mountains of the Hmong in Laos, the arming of the Hmong by the American military to fight the communist Pathet Lao and, following the Pathet Lao victory, the dispersal of many thousands of Hmong refugees across the Western world.

More fundamentally, the experience of a people is determined by the nature of its relations with the peoples around it. Power relations are important, and not only in military terms: cultural power and influence are more significant in the longer term. No less basic, however, is the question of how much danger the other culture poses, how much damage it may do. The cultural disruption and dislocation likely to result from outside influences depend to a large extent on the degree of what may best be called cultural dissonance.

Cultural dissonance is the extent to which two cultures diverge in their basic structures, institutions and values. It is not a question of one culture being more advanced or backward than the other. Attributing relative merit to cultures as if they are entities that can be isolated from the historical circumstances in which they have evolved is absurd. Both cultures may be perfectly appropriate, given their historical and social context, yet when put together they clash, in much the same way that a Buddhist hymn and a Beethoven piano sonata are awful when played together, regardless of their separate merits. That is cultural dissonance.

Where there is little cultural dissonance, individuals may experience only limited stress and conflict if they have to move from one culture to the other, or have elements of the alien culture forced upon them. But as cultural dissonance increases, so does the pressure on individuals when they try to accommodate the two systems in their lives. If the influence of a dissonant culture is strong, the potential for social disintegration is great. This has been the experience of many indigenous minorities, such as the reindeer herding Ewenki of north-eastern China, the Asmat of West Papua, and the Wanniyalaeto ('forest-dwellers') of Sri Lanka. However, indigenous minorities differ widely in terms of social and economic organisation. Not all are small nomadic or semi-nomadic tribal societies living close to nature. Some minorities may in certain respects be hard to distinguish from the dominant society, either because their cultures have always been similar or because of enculturation over a long period. If the gap between the two cultures is not too great, the minority may be able to benefit strongly from the dominant society without suffering much harm.

The recent experience of indigenous minorities has overwhelmingly been one of deprivation and hardship, together with loss of independence and autonomy. In many cases they have been incorporated by states with little but contempt for their cultural distinctiveness, which has been equated with backwardness. Rapid assimilation, forced if necessary, has widely been regarded as the best and kindest course for them. Ironically, it is often those states most vocal about the evils of imperialism that are most prepared to force indigenous minorities to assimilate. As to the benefits of development, for minorities these have all too often proved illusory. Cultural dislocation and social disintegration have been commonplace, resulting in problems such as high rates of suicide, community violence, alcohol and drug abuse, which are taken by the state and dominant society as further evidence of the primitive and degenerate nature of the minorities in question. Impoverished, weakened, powerless, in many respects indigenous minorities recapitulate the experience of Third World nations in the global system.

While the present situation of indigenous minorities is largely the result of those trends that together have been labelled globalisation, the surge of interest in and concern for indigenous minorities, and the usefulness of ethnic identity as a tool for advancing group interests, are equally a part of globalisation. If peoples around the world are asserting their ethnic identities it is because international agencies and international law have established ethnic distinctiveness as a legitimate basis for claiming equality and fair treatment from one's own nation state and others. The same globalising process that has destroyed or undermined so many ethnic identities has also provided new mechanisms for protecting those that remain, and good reasons for nurturing new ones.

## Self-determination

Principles of ethnic equality and non-discrimination have become widely accepted and are enshrined in most national constitutions as well as in international human rights documents. The International Covenant on Civil and Political Rights, for example, declares the right of ethnic, religious and linguistic minorities 'to enjoy their own culture, to profess and practice their own religion, or to use their own language', in addition to proscribing discrimination on the basis of race, colour, sex, language, religion, political or other opinion, national or social origin, property, birth or other status (Articles 26 and 27). In December 1992, after fourteen years of preparatory work, the UN finally adopted its Declaration on the Rights of Persons Belonging to National or Ethnic, Religious and Linguistic Minorities, which calls on state parties to 'protect the existence and ... identity of minorities' and requires the interests of members of minorities to be given due regard in national policies and programs. Preparatory work on a convention on the rights of indigenous peoples has been in progress for some time. However, even those closely involved with the UN find themselves forced to admit that the organisation's record in this area is not impressive.

At the heart of the problem has been the issue of self-determination, the first right set out in both the International Covenant on Economic, Social and Cultural Rights and the International Covenant on Civil and Political Rights: 'All peoples have the right to self-determination'. The great reluctance on the part of the international community to deal with the situation of minorities has been due to a common fear of member states that rights for minorities would result in political dismemberment through secession. One semi-official overview of the UN's efforts up to the time of adoption of the new Declaration referred to the need to overcome the frequently negative stance of governments towards their minorities and the fear of secession. A close observer of the UN Working Group on Indigenous Populations has commented that states 'are not alone in assuming that the right to self-determination leads to a single predetermined end: secession. The Working Party generally joins them in this assumption'.[17]

When the principle of the self-determination of peoples was first articulated in President Wilson's draft covenant for the League of Nations in 1918, it was with the intention that all 'peoples' would be free to determine their own political allegiance. Peoples would decide state borders rather than states determining how peoples would be divided. The draft asserted that 'the peace of the world is superior in importance to every question of political jurisdiction or boundary', and that state parties would have to adjust their borders as required by acts of self-determination of peoples. The word 'peoples' was understood essentially to mean 'ethnic groups'. Wilson was subsequently persuaded of the dangers this idea posed for the international political order and it disappeared. When it resurfaced after the Second World War, during the period of decolonisation, it was with a different interpretation.

Acts of self-determination now were to take place only on the basis of existing political borders. It would be state borders that fixed the lines of distinction between peoples, rather than differences in ethnicity leading to borders being redrawn if necessary. The term 'peoples' would henceforth be applied only to the citizens of nation states. Members of ethnic minorities would have no right to self-determination over and above that which they had in common with all other citizens.[18]

The inter-ethnic violence that has erupted in recent years, in places like the former Yugoslavia and Sri Lanka, has led some to argue that the concept of self-determination has outlived its usefulness. Whereas in earlier times the fight for self-determination was an expression of democracy, now, it is claimed, it is often an attempt to destroy democracy.[19] It is true that secession, especially when achieved through violent means, does not necessarily help anyone, and that what are really needed are tolerance, understanding, and equality. But if intolerance, prejudice and inequality persist it becomes hard to accept that self-determination is anti-democratic.

Independence movements and rebellions against national governments notwithstanding, it is wrong to assume that self-determination on the part of ethnic minorities will invariably lead to secession and political independence. As minority representatives have argued on numerous occasions, it is a serious mistake for states to assume that minorities have no other purpose in mind, since other political arrangements may be much more realistic and attractive for them. A form of free association with the nation state, or genuine local autonomy, may well offer greater scope for a minority to control its own affairs and maintain its own identity than complete political independence and exposure to the full blast of international political and economic forces. Support for independence movements tends to arise from a sense of grievance, a belief that the group has been the victim of serious injustice and that existing political arrangements perpetuate or aggravate the problems. Where grievances are dealt with and the minority in question is given a measure of real autonomy in the handling of its affairs, political and social stability are much more likely to result than when unrest is crushed by force. Once the path of armed conflict has been taken, any vestiges of mutual trust disappear and it is difficult to turn back.

Illustrations of the classic pattern of ethnic disputes, in which a failure to reach agreement on modest demands is followed by adoption of increasingly extreme positions by both sides, and then spiralling violence, are depressingly easy to gather. The pattern is still in a relatively early phase in Xinjiang (East Turkistan) and Tibet, where some indigenous people have turned to violence because of Chinese government intransigence in the face of demands for greater local autonomy, intransigence on which non-violent action has had no effect. Some Tibetans, for example, have rejected the Dalai Lama's commitment to non-violent resistance and his acceptance of Tibetan autonomy under Chinese rule rather than full independence. They say that time is running out and that, without independence, Tibetan culture and identity will soon be extinct.

The people of East Timor and West Papua, experiencing similar intransigence on the part of the Indonesian government, also turned to armed confrontation. In East Timor's case, the unusual set of political circumstances that surrounded the resignation of Suharto and the installation of Habibie as president in Indonesia in 1999 enabled an act of political self-determination to take place under UN scrutiny. While the history of armed conflict undoubtedly was a factor that led to the act of self-determination, it was the latter that secured East Timor's independence. The political freedom East Timor won undoubtedly strengthened the drive for independence among the people of West Papua, yet East Timor's success may make the emergence of an independent West Papua less likely, given Indonesian army and government fears of national disintegration. In August 2001, the Indonesian authorities were hoping that greater regional autonomy of the sort just granted to Aceh would neutralise the Papuan push for independence.[20]

In Sri Lanka, civil strife has escalated steadily over time, as early Tamil attempts to gain fair treatment by political means were frustrated, moderates on both sides found themselves increasingly sidelined, and the government opted for a military 'solution' to separatist terrorism. Where armed conflict has continued over very long periods, and current clashes are modern variants of struggles going back to earlier centuries—as in Myanmar and the southern Philippines—violence has become so habitual and mutual mistrust so ingrained, that it is difficult to see relations between minorities and the state becoming established on another basis.[21]

## Being indigenous

The idea of 'indigenous peoples', in relation to much of Asia, is problematical, if 'indigenous' is understood literally to mean 'native' or 'in-born' of a particular region or territory. The many waves of settlers that have moved through a region, sometimes displacing earlier settlers, sometimes blending with them, often make it impossible to say who should be regarded as the first. The question may indeed be irrelevant. What can often be done, however, is to establish an approximate order of precedence in occupancy and 'ownership'. The question of what special consideration should be extended to prior inhabitants can then be addressed.

In its simplest form this issue is little more than a variant of the question as to who is a citizen of a nation state and who is an immigrant. Five of the six major hill tribes of northern Thailand—the Akha, Hmong, Lahu, Lisu and Mien—did not settle there until the late nineteenth and early twentieth centuries. Most of their people have arrived only since the 1960s, to escape conflicts in Laos, Vietnam, and Burma. By contrast, the Karen began to migrate into Thailand during the eighteenth century. Members of the other hill tribes are not regarded as Thai citizens by the Thai authorities, even if they were born in Thailand. They are seen as aliens bringing instability, opium and communism into the country, with no legitimate claim to the land they occupy. Their traditional shifting agriculture is effectively prohibited because it relies on fire to clear land, and they are under strong pressure to turn to other, sedentary and approved ways of making a living—in other words to become Thai.[22]

Frequently the designation 'indigenous' is not so straightforward, either because no one is quite sure when the relevant migrations occurred or because state borders have been vague or very different from what they are now. The UN Working Group on Indigenous Populations defines indigenous peoples as follows:

Karen mother and child, northern Thailand. Many Karen have crossed into Thailand to escape ethnic conflict in Myanmar.

> Indigenous populations are composed of the existing descendants of the peoples who inhabited the present territory of a country wholly or partially at the time when persons of a different culture or ethnic origin arrived there from other parts of the world, overcame them and, by conquest, settlement or other means, reduced them to a non-dominant or colonial situation; who today live more in conformity with their particular social, economic and cultural customs and traditions than with the institutions of the country of which they now form a part, under a State structure which incorporates mainly the national, social and cultural characteristics of other segments of the population which are predominant.[23]

This is qualified, *inter alia*, by the observation that a group need not have suffered conquest or colonisation in order to be regarded as indigenous.

This latter point sometimes gets overlooked. For example, according to another definition, for a group to be indigenous members must regard themselves as a distinct ethnic group; have experience of, or a real vulnerability to, severe disruption, dislocation or exploitation; have a longstanding connection with the region in question; and must wish to retain their distinct identity. They would also be expected to have a number of other characteristics, such as having a close cultural affinity with the land, being distinct in socio-economic and socio-cultural terms from the ambient population, and being regarded by the ambient population as indigenous.[24]

It is a definition that focuses on what have been the dominant aspects of the recent historical experience of indigenous peoples, namely, that despite long occupancy of their lands they have been pushed aside or colonised by other, more recent and more

Launching a Lahu/Thai program at a Lahu school in northern Thailand. The King's photograph is prominently displayed in the background.

powerful arrivals. To these newer arrivals they have lost control of not only their lands, but also their economic, social and political institutions. From the point of view of indigenous peoples it makes little difference whether these late arrivals come from the same nation state or from another. (It need not be, as the UN definition asserts, that the new arrivals come from another part of the world, except in the trivial sense that any new arrival must come from another point on the earth's surface.) What matters is the marginalisation, dislocation and exploitation that results from the loss of control.

A weakness of this second definition is that it takes aspects of the recent common experience of indigenous minorities and tries to make them true by definition. That an indigenous group has not experienced severe social dislocation or economic exploitation (due to physical isolation, say, or a history of exploiting other indigenous minorities) is no reason to refuse to classify it as indigenous. Nor should the fact that an indigenous people does not show a strong inclination to retain a distinct identity be seen as a reason for not regarding it as genuinely indigenous. This point deserves emphasis. Those who fight for the rights of indigenous peoples are naturally predisposed to see failure to maintain a distinct identity, or a lack of interest in doing so, as a sign of weakness, as evidence of decline or cultural and social disintegration. We have at least to recognise the possibility, however, that members of a given ethnic group (indigenous or otherwise) may well reach a considered conclusion, singly or communally, that their long-term interests and perhaps the survival of the valued aspects of their culture would best be served by integration with the social mainstream rather than trying to stand against it.

It could be argued that to regard indigenous groups *by definition* as vulnerable to dislocation and exploitation is in fact to take over the view, so common among nineteenth-century colonists and twentieth-century apostles of development, that indigenous peoples are invariably backward and weak, and able to progress only with help from more advanced peoples.

In South Asia, those who see themselves as indigenous peoples refer to themselves as *adivasi*, a Hindi equivalent of 'aborigine' coined in the 1930s by those campaigning for the rights of such people in India. Unfortunately the meaning of the term has become distorted by the socio-political history to which it was hitched. Brahmin prejudice and British racism shared a low opinion of 'tribal' peoples who appeared to live at the margins of well-ordered society, often leading a semi-nomadic existence and dependent for their livelihood on shifting agriculture or hunting and gathering. They were regarded as being at the very bottom of the social hierarchy, along with the untouchables or *dalits*. Primitive, ignorant and unclean, they needed special assistance from their social superiors to rise to a more civilised mode of life.

High-ranking Hindus and British alike chose to ignore the fact that some of the non-Hindu states of the Indian subcontinent were as powerful politically and economically as many of the Hindu kingdoms, and no less sophisticated in their culture; that those living tribal or semi-nomadic lives were frequently Hindus; and that those living under such circumstances, whether Hindu or not, had often been reduced to a poor and marginal existence by the socio-political upheavals resulting from British colonialism. When the British introduced the administrative category Scheduled Castes and Tribes it was prompted by the mixture of paternalism and cynical self-interest typical of colonial powers. Untouchables and tribals were deemed to need the special care of the Crown, and because they were unable to look after their own interests the imperial government had to control their affairs directly. This included control of land and all resources, as well as administration.

On independence the national government of India inherited this cluster of ideas and assumptions. The need to protect scheduled castes and tribes was written into the Constitution, Article 46 of which says that 'The State shall promote with special care the educational and economic interests of the weaker sections of the people, and in particular of the scheduled castes and scheduled tribes, and shall protect them from social injustice and all forms of exploitation'. Policies have been implemented to achieve this end, especially in the form of reservation of places in education and government. The national census continues to collect data on scheduled castes and tribes, so that 'tribal' continues to mean those who are not part of settled Indian society, who by definition are backward and in need of special assistance.[25]

Being labelled backward has not deterred families and communities from putting themselves in the scheduled tribes category if it brings the possibility of government assistance or other benefits. Between 1951 and 1981 the proportion of the total population of India classified as tribal increased from 5.3 per cent to 7.8 per cent, a rise difficult to account for in terms of natural increase. India is not alone in this. Rapid increases in the populations of indigenous peoples compared with those of the dominant society have been reported in many countries around the world in recent years, including Australia, Canada, China, and New Zealand. It is likely that some of this rapid growth can be accounted for by members of the dominant society assuming an indigenous identity in order to become eligible for whatever government assistance or preferential treatment is offered to indigenous groups. However, other factors will also be involved, including the likelihood that earlier population figures for indigenous minorities were understated because some individuals denied their ethnic origins for fear of discrimination.

The proportion of the Chinese population identified as belonging to 'minority nationalities' in 1953 was 6.1 per cent. In 1964 it fell to 5.8 per cent before rising to 6.7 per cent in 1982 and 8 per cent in 1990. According to the 2000 national census, the proportion had increased to 8.4 per cent. While figures for 1953 and 1964 are not very reliable, particularly for the remote regions where most of the minorities live, it is safe to conclude that between 1953 and 1964 the population of minorities overall grew more slowly than that of the Han majority, whereas since 1964 the opposite has been true (see Table 4.2). There can be little doubt that most of the difference—especially the dramatic growth recorded for some groups during the 1980s—must be attributed to changes in government policy and social attitudes.[26]

The biggest increase registered has been for the Gelao, a group from remote parts of Guizhou, Yunnan, and Guangxi provinces not identified as a separate minority until 1964. Between 1982 and 1990 it showed a population increase of 811 per cent, which is largely attributable to their late success in obtaining official recognition as an indigenous minority distinct from those who live in close proximity to them: the Hmong, Yi, Zhuang, and Buyi. Over the same period the population of the Manchu people rose by 128 per cent and that of the Tujia people by 101 per cent. Both of the

**Table 4.2** Populations of China's nationalities (thousands)

| *Nationality* | *1953 census* | *1964 census* | *1982 census* | *1990 census* |
|---|---|---|---|---|
| Han | 547 283 | 651 296 | 940 880 | 1 042 482 |
| Zhuang | 6 611 | 8 386 | 13 388 | 15 490 |
| Manchu | 2 419 | 2 696 | 4 304 | 9 821 |
| Hui | 3 559 | 4 473 | 7 227 | 8 603 |
| Miao | 2 511 | 2 782 | 5 036 | 7 398 |
| Uygur | 2 776 | 3 996 | 5 963 | 7 214 |
| Yi | 3 254 | 3 381 | 5 457 | 6 572 |
| Tujia | – | 525 | 2 835 | 5 704 |
| Mongol | 1 463 | 1 966 | 3 417 | 4 807 |
| Tibetan | 2 777 | 2 501 | 3 874 | 4 593 |
| Bouyei | 1 248 | 1 348 | 2 122 | 2 545 |
| Dong | 713 | 836 | 1 426 | 2 514 |
| Yao | 666 | 857 | 1 404 | 2 134 |
| Korean | 1 120 | 1 340 | 1 766 | 1 921 |
| Bai | 567 | 707 | 1 132 | 1 595 |
| Hani | 481 | 629 | 1 059 | 1 254 |
| Kazakh | 509 | 492 | 908 | 1 112 |
| Li | 361 | 439 | 818 | 1 111 |
| Dai | 470 | 535 | 841 | 1 025 |
| She | – | 234 | 369 | 630 |
| Lisu | 317 | 271 | 481 | 575 |
| Gelao | – | 27 | 54 | 438 |
| Lahu | 139 | 191 | 304 | 411 |
| Dongxiang | 156 | 147 | 279 | 374 |
| Wa | 286 | 200 | 295 | 351 |
| Shui | 134 | 156 | 286 | 346 |
| Naxi | 143 | 157 | 254 | 278 |
| Qiang | 36 | 49 | 103 | 198 |
| Tu | 53 | 77 | 159 | 192 |
| Xibe | 19 | 33 | 84 | 173 |
| Mulam | – | 53 | 90 | 159 |
| Kyrgiz | 71 | 70 | 114 | 142 |
| Daur | – | 63 | 94 | 121 |
| Jingpo | 102 | 58 | 93 | 119 |
| Salar | 31 | 35 | 69 | 88 |
| Blang | – | 39 | 58 | 82 |
| Maonan | – | 22 | 38 | 72 |
| Tajik | 14 | 16 | 27 | 34 |
| Primi | – | 14 | 24 | 30 |
| Achang | – | 12 | 20 | 28 |
| Nu | – | 15 | 23 | 27 |
| Ewenki | 5 | 10 | 19 | 26 |
| Gin | – | 4 | 12 | 19 |
| Jinuo | – | – | 12 | 18 |
| Benglong or Deang | – | 7 | 12 | 15 |
| Uzbek | 14 | 8 | 12 | 15 |
| Russian | 23 | 1 | 3 | 14 |
| Yugur | 4 | 6 | 11 | 12 |
| Bonan | 5 | 5 | 9 | 12 |
| Monba | – | 4 | 6 | 7 |
| Oroqen | 2 | 3 | 4 | 7 |
| Derung | – | 3 | 5 | 6 |

**Table 4.2** (continued)

| *Nationality* | *1953 census* | *1964 census* | *1982 census* | *1990 census* |
|---|---|---|---|---|
| Tatar | 7 | 2 | 4 | 5 |
| Hezhen | – | 0.7 | 1 | 4 |
| Gaoshan | 0.3 | 0.4 | 2 | 3 |
| Lhoba | – | – | 2 | 2 |
| Nongren | 196 | – | – | – |
| Sharen | 112 | – | – | – |
| Others | 1 073 | – | – | – |
| Others not yet identified | – | 32 | 882 | 749 |
| TOTAL | 582 603 | 691 220 | 1 003 937 | 1 133 683 |

Source: C. Mackerras, *China's Minorities: Integration and Modernisation in the Twentieth Century*, Oxford University Press, London, 1994, 238–40.

Note: Population figures for separate minority nationalities from the 2000 census were not yet publicly available in March 2002.

latter groups are physically similar to the Han Chinese, their cultures have been heavily sinicised, and both have had recent experience of strong prejudice and discrimination (the Manchu as the former alien ruling elite, the Tujia as a former regional elite in the west of Hunan province). In other words, these were groups whose members could hide their identity relatively easily when it was a liability and reclaim it when it could prove to their advantage.

That between 1982 and 1990 the minorities in China almost without exception registered higher population growth than the Han (the Korean minority was the only group that recorded lower growth rates) cannot be explained simply by reference to the fact that the one-child family policy was less strictly applied to minorities than it was to the Han: the timespan is so short and many of the increases so large that biological explanations are out of the question. It is much more likely, as many observers have pointed out, that exemption from the one-child family policy was one of the factors that made adoption of minority identity attractive to some who had formerly identified as Han Chinese, along with other aspects of government policy such as tax concessions and preferential access to education. These policies will have prompted many of those who had earlier kept their minority identity secret to reregister, and children of mixed marriages to adopt minority rather than Han identity.

This is dramatic evidence that individuals are prepared to change their ethnic identity in order to secure perceived advantages. But we have to be careful not to reduce concerns about ethnic identity just to issues of economic or political advantage.

## The creation of new ethnic identities

It is difficult to refute the argument by proponents of ethnic self-determination that there is nothing sacrosanct about present international boundaries. To assert that they cannot be changed is to attempt to stop history. Similarly, however, there is nothing sacrosanct or final about ethnic divisions. It is wrong to claim that boundaries of nation states should follow lines of ethnic division because the latter reflect natural differences in identity and affiliation. Ethnic identities can be created and revised in much the same way that national identities can be changed.

Ethnic minorities of China: Ge women, Kaili, Guizhou (top); Tibetan women, Zhongdian, Yunnan (above).

Another 'minority nationality': Uygur children, Kashgar, Xinjiang, China.

As already indicated, ethnic identities are neither fixed nor inevitable. What is true is that the time frame in which ethnic identities are created and modified tends to be larger than that needed to generate or modify national identities. But not always. One indication of the time required for new ethnic identities to develop comes from the experience of former British colonies such as Australia, Canada, New Zealand, and the United States. The peoples of those countries assert that despite their common language and (by and large) common cultural heritage, they each have a distinct cultural identity, different from each other's and different from that of the inhabitants of the United Kingdom. If we accept these claims, then about two hundred to three hundred years seems to be sufficient time for the generation of new ethnic identities.

An ethnic identity cannot be created *ex nihilo*. Nevertheless it may have a reasonably clear beginning. In the case of the Sikhs, that beginning was the teachings of Guru Nanak (1469–1538). Guru Nanak's point of departure in a religious sense was Hindu devotionalism (*bhakti*), from which he created a concept of universal love that expressed itself through action rather than words. He taught that what mattered was neither origin nor religious creed, but only the actions of the individual and the love they manifested. At first there was little concern among his followers for religious conformity, let alone a more broadly based cultural commonality. But over time religious teachings were standardised in the Sikh holy book, the Granth Sahib, and elements of a distinctive Sikh identity began to emerge. These included rejection of caste distinctions; a relatively low degree of gender inequality; an emphasis on martial virtues such as bravery and physical strength; prohibition of smoking, alcohol, and cutting bodily hair; and even adoption of a common family name, Singh (Lion).

Despite their broad geographical distribution, Sikhs early on identified the Punjab as their homeland. In post-independence India this led to Sikh separatism, culminating in the assassination by Sikh militants of India's Prime Minister Indira Gandhi in 1984. Economic as well as religious considerations were behind the push for secession. In 1969, in response to demand, Sikh-dominated areas of the Indian state of Haryana were detached from Hindu-dominated regions to create the state of Punjab. Sikh success in agriculture and trade made it the richest state of the Union, and a sense of having to carry other parts of India economically strengthened demands for full independence among some Sikhs. Sectarian violence following Mrs Gandhi's death also heightened the Sikh sense of difference. Yet since the 1980s demands for political separation have become weaker rather than stronger.[27]

In some ways similar to the history of the Sikhs is that of the Ahmadiyya sect of Pakistan, which also originated in the Punjab. It was founded by Mirza Ghirlan Ahmad (1839–1908), who saw himself as one in a line of prophets including Jesus, Krishna, and Muhammad, whose role it was to interpret the Koran for his contemporaries. While regarding himself as a true Muslim who recognised the one true God and Muhammad as his messenger, he did not believe that Muhammad was the last messenger. His followers, who amount to only 2 or 3 per cent of the national population, have had their claim to Muslim identity rejected by the Pakistani government on the grounds that they do not believe in 'the absolute and unqualified finality of the prophethood of Muhammad'. As a group, the Ahmadis do not possess the militancy that has been a feature of recent Sikh history. Their founder specifically rejected the principle of jihad or militant struggle on behalf of the true faith. Neither do they identify strongly with a particular homeland in the way the Sikhs do. Nevertheless they have a well-developed group identity, reinforced by relatively high levels of education and social standing, and a commitment to propagating their beliefs. Should they continue to find themselves excluded from participation in mainstream society it would not be surprising to see the Ahmadis developing more fully a distinct ethnic as opposed to a religious identity.[28]

Another type of ethnic identity is resulting from the pressures exerted by nation states on indigenous minorities to unite. Common problems and the need for united action if they are to survive are leading some groups to play down cultural and historical differences and develop a shared identity. Perhaps the clearest example is that of the Aboriginal Australians. Aboriginal Australians still speak some ninety different languages, even though about twice that number have already become extinct under the impact of colonisation. Despite enormous cultural variation between tribes from regions as different as Tasmania, the Western desert and tropical Arnhem Land, at least in the public domain Aboriginal identity tends to be presented as singular and unified, because that is the only way such a small and scattered minority can hope to assert itself against the dominant society. Similar forces are at work among the *adivasi* of the Indian subcontinent.[29]

The Chittagong Hill Tracts of Bangladesh, a small part of the long mountain chain running from the eastern Himalaya to southern Myanmar, contain twelve distinct ethnic groups that together make up the bulk of the nation's indigenous minority population. In response to the intense pressures these groups have been experiencing, especially as a result of Bengali migration into the hills, a common identity has begun to emerge where none existed before. Calling themselves Jumma, from an old Bengali term for swidden cultivators, the minorities are playing down their internal differences to highlight their linguistic, religious and cultural separateness from the Bengalis who dominate them politically and economically, and label them backward. Jumma identity, like Adivasi identity, is in part a reaction to or inversion of the dominant society's indiscriminate dismissal of tribal peoples as primitive 'junglis' or forest-dwellers.[30]

## The value of cultural distinctiveness

The widespread suffering and injustice arising from the subjugation of peoples and destruction of whole societies in the name of modernisation and development have led to the conclusion that the loss of ethnic identity is a tragedy. Not only does cultural genocide mean misery for the peoples whose ways of life are being destroyed, but for humanity as a whole it also means cultural impoverishment. An analogy is drawn between the extinction of cultures and the destruction of biodiversity. The forces of globalisation, through the operations of authoritarian governments, multinational corporations and international development agencies, are destroying cultural diversity as quickly as they are destroying the environment. As well as causing environmental degradation and impoverishment, it is argued, it is also diminishing the range of cultural alternatives available to the human race for solving its problems, precisely when the need for alternatives is quickly becoming more obvious.

While some equate Westernisation of the world with progress, others regard with acute alarm the possibility that current trends may lead inexorably to a global monoculture:

> The result [of Western-style development] has been a tremendous loss of diversity. The worldwide simplification of architecture, clothing, and daily objects assaults the eye; the accompanying eclipse of variegated languages, customs and gestures is already less visible; and the standardisation of desires and dreams occurs deep down in the subconscious of societies. Market, state, and science have been the great universalizing powers; admen, experts and educators have relentlessly expanded their reign ... The mental space in which people dream and act is largely occupied today by western imagery. The vast furrows of cultural monoculture left behind are, as in all monocultures, both barren and dangerous. They have eliminated the innumerable varieties of being human and have turned the world into a place deprived of adventure and surprise; the 'Other' has vanished with development. Moreover, the spreading monoculture has eroded viable alternatives to the industrial, growth-oriented society and dangerously crippled humankind's capacity to meet an increasingly different future with creative responses. The last forty years have considerably impoverished the potential for cultural evolution.[31]

This position is readily understandable as a reaction to uncritical assumptions about progress and cultural superiority, the sort of bigotry that leads colonial powers and political elites to claim a duty to impose their culture on others 'for their own good'. But how far should this reaction be taken? It easily leads to the view that indigenous groups losing their cultural distinctiveness are declining, that outside forces are imposing change and robbing them of their identity. Yet it may be that the groups in question are not concerned with maintaining a separate identity, that at least in some respects they want to change. If we accept the idea of cultures as adaptive systems that must evolve in response to a changing environment, then prima facie it could be argued that it is those groups that borrow strategically from those around them that will be best placed to survive in the long run. Those groups that attempt to remain isolated from change and do everything they can to retain their distinctiveness may find, when change proves irresistible, that they have left themselves with little room to manoeuvre.

This raises the question of the value of cultural distinctiveness. Can it come down to a choice between cultural distinctiveness and survival? What value does a culture have independently of the well-being of the people who bear it?

There is danger in caring more about cultures than about peoples. There is little point in mourning the passing of cultural traditions if those who upheld them are content to let them pass, if they have decided that this is the best way forward, and see the losses (which they may deeply regret) as being outweighed by the gains. The great majority of indigenous peoples welcome some of the changes they experience, whether they be Western medicine, canned food or television. Few choose to live in total isolation from the global system that is undermining their traditions. The fact that people from rich, industrialised countries find traditional cultures colourful, entertaining spectacles or regard them as attractive alternatives to their own unsatisfying lifestyle is surely an inadequate reason for maintaining those traditions. Sources of spectacle or ethnographic case study, tourist attraction or museum: not only are these insufficient reasons for keeping cultural traditions alive, but it is also absurd to think that traditions *could* be kept alive by these means. A culture only exists to the extent that it informs the life of a people. It *is* the life of a people, and has value only to the extent that it enables them to satisfy their needs and live with dignity.[32]

There are many examples, nevertheless, of minorities that maintain a distinct identity when to outsiders it appears to result in serious economic, social and political deprivation. Is this irrational or are things perhaps not what they seem?

The answer is not straightforward. The question implies that people are in a position to choose and change their ethnic identity at will. Sometimes there is a degree of choice, and many do opt for assimilation or choose to hide their ethnic origins. One of the attractions cities hold for rural people is that often the latter is easier there. However, where cultural distinctiveness coincides with physiological differences, changing ethnic identity is seldom an option. Where there are prejudice and discrimination people of Han Chinese descent are likely to be treated as Chinese because they look Chinese, no matter how many generations of their family have lived in Australia or Indonesia.

Even where there are no physiological markers of difference, in general individuals have relatively little control over the forces that shape their ethnic identity, just as they have little control over the social forces influencing their lives generally. Parents may be able to make some decisions on behalf of their children, such as whether they will learn the language of the dominant society as their first language, or which religion they will follow, but usually their ability to choose is also limited. Parents in a Nepalese mountain village are seldom in a position to choose the sort of formal education their child will receive, while employment opportunities are so restricted that the concept of occupation is largely irrelevant. In traditional societies that are strongly hierarchical and communal, the very idea of choice may barely apply.

The matter is further complicated by the fact that the choices relating to ethnic identity are themselves far from clear. To ask why people choose to maintain their cultural distinctiveness when they would be better off assimilating implies that there is agreement as to what 'better off' means in this context, which is not the case. Agreed criteria as to what is the better lifestyle are precisely what are lacking, and choice is made all the more difficult by the uncertainty of the future.

Nevertheless it still makes sense to ask why individuals and communities maintain their traditional lifestyles and identities when it involves hardship and discrimination that are to some extent avoidable. Some ethnic groups, such as the Hmong, the Karen and the Kurds, have through the centuries pursued separateness very vigorously, frequently at high human cost. It is not enough for them to argue that persecution and exploitation by the dominant groups around them, rather than their own traditions, have condemned them to misery. Given that unpleasant reality, why continue to try to remain apart? Would it not be better, as individuals, to enter the mainstream?

Maintaining cultural boundaries is closely bound up with autonomy and control. Well-being involves psychological as well as economic security, and a well-integrated cultural identity can help to provide it. Maintaining a distinct ethnic identity can offer a way of retaining some measure of control, as well as helping to develop a sense of belonging and self-worth. While remaining culturally outside or peripheral to the dominant society may carry costs, it is a way of staying beyond the reach of that society. A separate ethnic identity may be the psycho-social equivalent of being geographically remote from the centre of socio-political power. Even if a decision to remain apart limits one's domain of freedom in some respects, what remains is more truly one's own. It confers greater predictability and security at the cost of diminished opportunity.

Anxiety is more psychologically damaging than economic deprivation. This is evident from the fact that in most societies inequality is accepted as long as it provides a degree of security in return for acceptance of obligations towards the elite. Similar considerations frequently apply in relations between ethnic groups: in an ethnically mixed society, a group may accept a position of low status and relative deprivation provided that it offers a degree of predictability and security.

Being different, or making oneself different, is closely related to being autonomous. If being different can give rise to a wish for autonomy, so too can a wish for autonomy lead to the creation or accentuation of difference. Recent history provides examples of both tendencies. Being different, having different needs (or different ways of meeting them), can form the basis of a claim to political autonomy that in the current political climate is widely seen as legitimate.

What matters, in the end, is not cultural difference *per se*, but rather that peoples are able to control the important aspects of their lives. What is important is not that cultures remain pure or distinct, but that they enable needs to be met. The quest for cultural separateness is best seen as a means to this end. Where societies attempt to purify themselves by either ethnic or cultural cleansing, the results tend to be horrific or pathetic. Being in control of one's own affairs usually requires borrowing from one's neighbours, mixing with them, trading with them. The pursuit of cultural purity and uniqueness arises from the illusion that societies and cultures evolve in isolation from each other and that their traditions and achievements owe nothing to anyone else. Examples of such splendid isolation are hard to find.

## Ethnicity, identity, and control

Those who look to ethnicity to provide the solidity and certainty lacking in nation states and nationalism are likely to be disappointed. Ethnic identity may be less fluid than national identity, but it is more like a viscous sludge than social bedrock. Nor is this really surprising. Since ethnic distinctions are drawn largely in cultural terms, and cultures are themselves processes of change, it could hardly be otherwise.

Ethnic identities are created, modified, adapted, merged. Change is normal. A wish to maintain cultural continuity and identity rarely translates into determination to resist all change. Continuity does not equal changelessness. There are very few ethnic groups whose members do not see some benefit in interaction with the wider world. At the same time, there are also very few where members do not want to control, as far as possible, the social, economic, and cultural changes they undergo. What is resisted, often, is not so much change itself as the imposition of change by outsiders. It is the wish to be in control that leads to attempts to insulate the society from external forces, to emphasise and preserve cultural distinctiveness.

When change does come from outside it is difficult to control even where it is not imposed. Things good in themselves—such as improved nutrition, literacy, new medicines—may have far-reaching effects that are hard to predict, let alone to manage. A sense that life threatens to run out of control leads readily to a reassertion of the rules and values of tradition. Yet often it is the fittingness or desirability of those rules and values that are being called into question.

Is it permissible to force change on other peoples for their own good? The right, even the obligation, to do so is claimed by authoritarian states everywhere. Primitive, childlike 'natives' are ignorant of what is best for them, we are told, and need someone wiser to watch over their interests. It cannot be disputed that good may come from enforced change. Does the good then justify the compulsion, or is autonomy an absolute value that must never be compromised, despite the fact that the concept of personal freedom may be quite foreign to the cultures of those whose autonomy is being protected?

This way of posing the question is misleading. Freedom or autonomy is neither an undifferentiated concept nor an absolute value. If we ourselves value autonomy and treasure the ability to control our own affairs, there is no need to assume that others conceptualise freedom in exactly the same way in order to ascribe similar attitudes to them. The concept of basic human needs requires us to do so.

Enforced cultural change, while it may achieve specific short-term goals, is likely to have many negative side effects, if for no other reason than that it is enforced. Change initiated by a legitimate authority may be implemented willingly, but an external power is unlikely to be regarded as legitimate. Furthermore, the idea that values and attitudes can be altered by force is hardly convincing. If change is to go deep and endure, those involved have to be persuaded that it is in their interests, or that it is 'right'. This is more likely to be achieved through education and positive reinforcement than coercion, as was argued, for example, in relation to improved understanding and implementation of human rights concepts.

Ethnicity requires us to think about issues such as culture, tradition, change, and autonomy largely in terms of social organisation and social relations within the borders of nation states. Development, the subject of the next chapter, gives rise to similar issues mainly in the light of relations between nation states.

## CHAPTER FIVE

# Economic and Social Development

## The concept and agenda of development

The age of development is sometimes presented as having a precise beginning: at the hour on 20 January 1949 when the incoming US president Harry Truman announced a new agenda to bring peace and prosperity to the world. It was one in which the rich, 'advanced' nations of the Free World would share with poor 'backward' nations the benefits of modern science and technology, to help them generate wealth and a better standard of living for all. Truman declared:

> We must embark on a bold new program for making scientific advances and industrial progress available for the improvement and growth of underdeveloped areas ... The old imperialism—exploitation for foreign profit—has no place in our plans ... greater production is the key to prosperity and peace. And the key to greater production is a wider and more vigorous application of modern scientific and technical knowledge.[1]

Two points stand out in this declaration on behalf of world progress. One is that economic growth is presented as the key to peace and prosperity. The other is the emphasis on modern science and technology as the basis for economic development. Peace and prosperity go together, according to Truman. It is poverty that causes social and political unrest and attracts people to communism. The way to fight communism, therefore, is to share with poor nations the Western know-how that will enable them to generate wealth of their own. World peace is at risk, it is asserted, because not enough wealth is being generated. There is no suggestion that the problem may have something to do with the way the available wealth is distributed within and between nations.

Many commentators have emphasised that development as an ideal and as an agenda was strongly anti-communist in its origins. Looking back at the state of world politics in 1949, it is not hard to see why this would have been so. But its anti-communist origins do not do much to explain the almost universal enthusiasm with which the idea has been pursued by the international community, or the level of support it has managed to retain despite the often appalling results of development programs in countries around the world. Even a president of the United States would find it hard to be that persuasive. Likewise, the interpretation favoured by some, that development is a neo-imperialist plot to gain control of the world, is unlikely to account for its popularity. Somewhere we have to come to grips with the fact that a large part of the world's population sees something valuable in the idea of development, even if the ideological fog surrounding it hinders our ability to make out precisely what that is.

One point already fading from consciousness, with the cold war over, is that development and international aid have not been the concern solely of capitalist or self-declared free nations. The Soviet Union and China also provided financial and technical assistance to Third World countries that, like aid from the United States and other capitalist countries, was used to further their own interests. The motives behind development assistance are complex and often confused; national self-interest and genuine humanitarian concern are hard to separate.

Yet whether or not self-interest is actually advanced will largely depend on whether the recipient country or its leaders believe that genuine assistance has been provided. In other words, real benefits must be seen to accrue. This is no less true of, say, Soviet assistance to build Egypt's Aswan Dam (1953–60) and China's construction of the Tanzania–Zambia railway (completed 1975) than of Japanese assistance to China in the 1990s to address the latter's environmental problems. This point gets lost in critical discussion of development assistance provided by Western countries and Japan: so much energy is spent on criticising the serious problems it causes that little effort is made to reflect soberly on the benefits it brings.

Truman's announcement of the development agenda identified economic growth as its essence. That economic growth through industrialisation based on modern science and technology was the basis for greater well-being was the conventional wisdom of capitalists and communists alike. Economic growth for underdeveloped areas was an objective that had been aired during the 1940s and incorporated into the UN charter in 1947. It is fair to say that despite repeated attempts during the last years of the twentieth century to see development in broader and more sophisticated terms, it has, in practice, proved very resistant to change.

It is not just that governments and international agencies have continued overwhelmingly to pursue economic growth at the national level without paying much attention to how their activities affect particular communities or sections of the population. At a more fundamental level, attempts to deepen and refine the meaning of development have so expanded its scope and made it so amorphous that there is little it cannot cover. Often development is merely a synonym for everything seen as good or desirable in modern life, an idea that can neither be specified nor refuted. While such a vague expression of optimism or approval may seem harmless enough, as a basis for government policy and economic decision-making it has repeatedly proved disastrous.

Reading through the voluminous literature on the subject, it is impossible not to be struck by the many subtle refinements and strategies devised in the history of development. One after another they have failed to be implemented and in due course have been buried by the next wave of creative, but ultimately frustrated, thinking. So it is not as if there has been a lack of understanding of the shortcomings of development theory and practice. Dissatisfaction with the narrow economic interpretation led soon enough to an emphasis on what was called 'social development', though as the UN Research Institute for Social Development later found itself obliged to acknowledge, in the 1960s social development 'was seen partly as a precondition for economic growth and partly as a moral justification for it and the sacrifices it implied'. This was followed in the 1970s by a concern for integrated development and human-centred development, and advocacy of a basic needs approach that would ensure that everyone's lives would be improved by the sweeping social and economic changes they were experiencing. In the 1990s 'human development' was the label applied to this socially aware and responsive concept of development, which acquired currency at much the same time as 'sustainable development', designating development that was ecologically aware and responsible.

The most outspoken critics of development argue that the failure to implement any of these revisions of the concept is simple to understand. As well as encountering the entrenched interests of the rich and powerful who continue to control what is done under the label 'development', these conceptual refinements have failed to overcome the limitations of the underlying idea itself—in particular, the idea that there is but a single path of economic and social development along which all nations travel. The term 'development' permits only the expression of differences of degree, not of kind. To develop is to improve, to advance, to grow or mature, to increase in sophistication and complexity. Like 'evolution', the term was popular with biologists and philosophers of social improvement in the eighteenth and nineteenth centuries, and was used to articulate the idea that some species had developed further, were more highly evolved, than others. The rich and powerful nations of the West, critics of development argue, have succeeded in persuading the rest of the world that there is only their path to follow, that they represent the most highly evolved form of socio-economic life. Understood like this, the idea of development amounts to little more than a restatement of social Darwinism, the dogma of progress and nationalistic survival of the fittest that was influential in the early twentieth century among educated elites of countries such as China, Japan, and India as well as in Western countries.

It is noteworthy that the term 'progress', which seemed to have disappeared from the official vocabulary of development, was making a cautious reappearance at the beginning of the new century. The United Nations Development Program (UNDP), in its *Human Development Report 2000*, said that human development includes 'an abiding concern with progress', with progress to be understood as 'the progress of human lives and wellbeing', including the enjoyment of human rights.[2] If progress, however understood, is what development means, then it is good to be explicit about it.

## Development trends

Given the all-embracing nature of the concept of development, it is wise to focus discussion of trends on those aspects regarding whose meaning it is possible to reach some agreement, that is, aspects of economic development. On this front, in Asian countries, there have been far-reaching changes. Many modern industries have been established, and with them the support systems such industries presuppose, including transport and communications networks, energy supplies, finance and banking systems, and education and training institutions. Traditional industries, including agriculture, have been transformed by the application of new technology. In most cases, something approaching a national economy, as opposed to a number of discrete and independent regional economies, has been established for the first time. For the first time also, in most cases, those national industries find themselves competing in international markets. Advanced technologies and production systems are circulating internationally to an unprecedented extent, partly owing to the operations of multinational corporations, and partly owing to the determination of governments and indigenous firms to acquire as quickly as possible the technology essential for international competitiveness.

Yet, even in narrow economic terms, these changes have not proven as beneficial as was hoped. In global terms, the gap between developed and developing countries has widened rather than narrowed. Since 1960 the income disparity between the richest 20 per cent and poorest 20 per cent of the world's population has doubled. Developed countries, with less than 25 per cent of the world's population, consume 85 per cent of its resources. Between 1970 and 1985 world economic output rose by 40 per cent, yet the number of people living in poverty rose by 17 per cent. During 1980–93, per capita income fell for more than a billion people; between 1990 and 1998, the average per capita income fell in fifty countries.[3]

National debt, largely the result of borrowings to finance major development undertakings such as dams, harbours, and highway systems, has become a massive problem for many Third World countries. Between 1970 and 1992 the total foreign debt of Third World countries rose from $US100 billion to $US1500 billion, with service payments (interest) amounting to $US160 billion in 1992. Debt-servicing between 1983 and 1992 resulted in flows of capital away from developing countries, at an average of $US14.7 billion per year, rather than towards them.[4] While the indebtedness of developing countries in Asia is generally less of a problem than in Africa and Latin America, debt-servicing for some is a serious drain on funds (see Table 5.1). In 1999 Indonesia, Pakistan, and South Korea were among the worst cases. During the financial crisis of 1997–98, countries with significant external debt were badly affected. Indonesia's situation deteriorated seriously—as did that of Thailand, South Korea, and the Philippines, although not to the same degree.

To qualify for loans and, more particularly, to obtain approval for rescheduling of existing debt repayments, Third World countries are required by the World Bank and the IMF to agree to structural adjustment packages—measures that, according to neoclassical economic principles, will strengthen their economies and hence their capacity to continue servicing their debts, if not eventually to repay them. These measures, which include opening up domestic markets and industries to foreign competition, and cutting government spending on non-productive social services, may in fact weaken the capacity of developing countries to establish new industries and infrastructure, thereby undermining their long-term economic prospects, while at the same time impairing their capacity to care for the most vulnerable sections of the population.[5]

**Table 5.1** External debt of selected Asian countries

| | *External debt as % of GNP* | | *Debt servicing as % of exports of goods and services* | |
|---|---|---|---|---|
| | *1980* | *1999* | *1980* | *1999* |
| Bangladesh | 33.4 | 23 | 25.6 | 10.1 |
| China | 2.2 | 14 | 4.4 | 9.0 |
| India | 11.9 | 16 | 10.0 | 15.0 |
| Indonesia | 28.0 | 113 | 13.9 | 30.3 |
| Iran | 4.8 | 8 | 7.4 | 22.6 |
| Malaysia | 28.0 | 64 | 6.6 | 4.8 |
| Pakistan | 42.4 | 43 | 18.1 | 30.5 |
| Philippines | 53.7 | 65 | 13.9 | 14.3 |
| South Korea | 47.9 | 31 | 20.3 | 24.6 |
| Sri Lanka | 46.1 | 45 | 12.4 | 7.9 |
| Thailand | 25.9 | 78 | 20.4 | 22.0 |
| Vietnam | | 76 | | 9.8 |

Source: World Bank, *From Plan to Market: World Development Report 1996*, Oxford University Press, New York, 1996, 220–1, and *World Development Indicators 2001*, http://www.worldbank.org/data/wdi2001/pdfs, accessed 10 April 2002.

In terms of technological capacity, too, the gap between developed and developing countries has widened. Recent experience contradicts the widespread assumption, common in thinking about technological development until the early 1970s, that as a result of increased international links, technology transfer and trade, there would be a gradual international convergence in technological terms. Developed countries, it was believed, would acquire similar levels and types of technological expertise, and developing countries would in time move closer to them. This has not happened. Although, in general terms, there is some evidence of technological convergence between the United States, Japan, and members of the European Union, this group as a whole has moved further ahead of the Third World than ever. The rapid technological development of Hong Kong, Singapore, South Korea, and Taiwan indicates that it is still possible to bridge the gap. But if there has been evidence of global technological convergence anywhere, it has been in the consumption of technology rather than its production, as growing world trade and the operations of multinational corporations push mass-produced articles into all corners of the globe. While there is optimism in some quarters about the capacity of information and communications technology to promote technologically advanced industries in developing countries, and talk of innovative 'hotspots' spread around the world in a 'networked' global economy, the fact that the hotspots are so internationally oriented leaves their contribution to broader domestic development uncertain.[6]

Development has not brought about economic and technological equality within nations any more than it has done between them. In many cases, regional and class inequalities have been exacerbated rather than expunged, making an integrated national economy a wish rather than a reality. Economic segmentation is common, as uneven development results in the emergence of Westernised or modernised enclaves largely detached from the bulk of the population and the economy that sustains it. Modern industries are concentrated in the cities, where skilled workers and the necessary infrastructure are likely to be found, so that rural areas are often bypassed, especially if occupied by ethnic minorities. The rush to be up to date, together with the status attached to large-scale and high-tech ventures, often leads to uneven and inefficient allocation of resources. Minor innovations in traditional industries often have the potential to improve the livelihood of large numbers of people, yet are likely to be overlooked precisely because they are not radical enough. The benefits of both international aid and local credit are frequently monopolised by those already economically advantaged.

Economic development certainly has not done away with inequality. Some would argue that nobody ever said it would. Be that as it may, it cannot be denied that the broader development process has improved the human condition in a number of fundamental ways. In the second half of the twentieth century average human life expectancy has increased sharply. Between 1960 and 1992, for example, the average life expectancy at birth for those in the large countries of South and West Asia rose by fifteen years or more (seventeen years in Iran and Iraq, sixteen years in India, fifteen years in Pakistan, twelve years in Bangladesh). Infant mortality rates fell by between 75 per cent (Iran) and 30 per cent (Bangladesh), while the proportion of underweight children aged five years or under fell substantially in each case. Adult literacy rose over the same period by between 27 per cent (Iran) and 13 per cent (Bangladesh). These are substantial changes, which surely cannot be interpreted as anything other than gains for the populations in question. Over the same period those populations grew dramatically, as a result of falling mortality rates, better health care, and nutrition. Yet with the application of modern science and technology in agriculture, initially through international programs and institutions—what became known as the green revolution—these countries greatly enhanced their food production and capacity to sustain their populations.

Nevertheless the broader benefits of development, like those of economic growth, have been unevenly shared. Rural areas again have tended to benefit far less than urban centres. Much of the explanation lies in the concentration of new industries in the cities, where skilled workers are most readily found, energy supplies are more reliable, and transport and communication links relatively cheap and dependable. Where there are no obvious economic gains, governments with limited resources are much less likely to provide communities with road and rail links, connection to the national electricity grid, or education and health services comparable to those available in urban areas. The socio-economic gap between country and city then widens quickly.

The changes associated with the green revolution, while they increased agricultural productivity and enabled growing populations to be fed, also had negative effects. Social and economic inequalities in many country areas were aggravated, as those already relatively well off found they were able to benefit from the changes, while the poor found themselves pushed off the land and their work opportunities diminished. Peasants who earlier had been making a subsistence living were drawn into the cash economy. No longer able to use part of last year's harvest as seed, they now had to buy seed of the new high-yield varieties, and with it the chemical fertilisers and pesticides needed to obtain a satisfactory crop. Rural credit—and debt—became an issue in ways quite unprecedented. The new intensive agricultural methods and the technology on which they depended resulted in widespread environmental degradation and ecological damage, as marginal soils were overworked; irrigation led to rising water tables, soil waterlogging, and salination; monoculture increased the risk of plant disease and pest plagues; and heavy use of pesticides and fertilisers resulted in pollution.[7]

Sometimes, moreover, it may be government policy to use agriculture and other rural industries to underwrite industrial growth in the cities. This was done by the governments of Korea and Taiwan in the 1970s and 1980s, for example, when they controlled agriculture prices in order to control urban food costs and hence contain wages pressure from the urban workforce on which international competitiveness depended. The communist government in China has followed well-tried imperial precedents by buying grain from producers below market rates, for subsequent distribution and sale at prices carefully regulated to reduce the risk of social unrest. Thailand, Malaysia, and Indonesia have not hesitated to sell their forests to fund the acquisition of new industries and advanced technologies. Sometimes this sort of trade-off is more conspicuous than others. In July 1994, for example, the Indonesian government allocated funds obtained from logging concessions, supposedly for reafforestation projects, to its high-profile and enormously expensive aircraft industry, despite the fact that according to its own regulations the funds should have been directed to forest research, replanting and so on. What makes the case interesting is not that rainforests are being sacrificed for industrial development—that is commonplace—but rather the way in which the sacrifice is explicitly linked to the funding of a particular high-tech initiative.[8]

Rural dwellers are not the only population category to miss out on many of the benefits of development. Indigenous minorities, most of whom live in rural areas, are particularly likely to bear a disproportionate part of the cost of economic development while receiving less than their fair share of the benefits. They are likely to find their lands deforested and opened up for agriculture 'in the national interest', or be denied their traditional usage of forests on the grounds that they are a national resource that henceforth is to be managed scientifically. Mining activities on their lands are rarely under their control. When water conservation and hydroelectric power schemes submerge their most productive valleys, again in the national interest, they often receive little or nothing in compensation.

Women tend to obtain fewer benefits from development than men, unless gender issues are specifically addressed in the development process. Until recently this problem received only limited attention, and that primarily from non-government organisations. During the 1990s, however, it became a major focus of UN programs. The UN Development Program's 1995 report took gender as its theme, as did the UN Population Fund's 2000 report on the state of the world population.[9]

The problem is not only that on almost every conventional measure of economic and social development, from educational participation to nutrition, women fare poorly compared to men. It is more complicated than that. There is evidence from many Third World countries that the changes associated with development may aggravate gender inequality and make the position of women worse rather than better. The emergence of a cash economy results in a distinction being drawn between work in the sense of paid employment, and household tasks that attract no monetary reward. In some societies, from South Asia to Latin America, it has been noted all too frequently that when the men become involved in growing cash crops, they spend the money on themselves rather than on their families. The men acquire watches, radios, and bicycles while the women and children, deprived of their labour, have to support themselves as best they can.

Traditional women's tasks, such as gathering cooking fuel and fetching water, have become increasingly time-consuming and laborious as a result of the ecological pressures associated with development. In countries such as Bangladesh, India, and Nepal it is common for women and girls to have to walk for hours every day, carrying loads so heavy that they cause severe health problems including skeletal deformity. The distinction between paid work and household tasks is likely to result in a decline in the status and authority of women, especially if it coincides with cultural norms restricting the opportunities of women to work outside the home. In some parts of northern India these sorts of changes have led to higher mortality rates for young girls, as growing economic pressures and the falling status of women result in limited food and health care being directed to male family members at the expense of females.[10]

The more widely the word 'development' is interpreted, the harder it becomes to talk meaningfully about whether development is good or bad. As commonly understood, development entails much more than industrialisation, economic growth, and the technological and other changes on which those things directly depend. It frequently comes to mean something as broad and ill-defined as 'modernisation' or 'progress according to the Western model'. It includes the introduction of 'modern' systems of education and health care, whether directly linked to industrialisation or not. It includes demographic changes of the sort discussed in Chapter 6, which appear to have some connection with economic development and the widespread adoption of modern contraceptive technologies, though what sort of connection is far from clear. It includes the use of information technology and systems of telecommunications, for entertaining populations as well as directing and controlling them (see Chapter 10). It includes the high-speed, high-volume transport systems, tourism, and leisure activities that hold together regional, national, and international markets. It also includes the weapons industry and its products, ranging from intercontinental missiles to undetectable landmines. Such technological systems and industries, and their roles in contemporary society, defy global evaluation. At most we can judge individual examples and applications, resisting the temptation of easy generalisations.

## A single path of development

The analogy of adaptation and evolution could be used to argue against the assumption of a single path of development, by returning to the idea that cultures are adaptations to specific environments, that the environment in which each nation finds itself is shaped by its own history, and that each must therefore respond on its own terms to the situation in which it finds itself. (This approach was in fact advocated by Unesco in the late 1970s, under the label 'endogenous development'.) Once we reject the idea of a single path of development the concept of progress becomes much more diffuse: nations develop, true, but they head off in different directions, and it is no longer so

China's Great Wall attracts tourist hordes rather than repels them. Tourism is one of the most obvious manifestations of globalisation, presupposing sound transport, communication and business links, as well as disposable income.

easy to say that this one is the most advanced, that one particularly backward. At the very least it becomes necessary to specify the way in which the nations in question are said to be advanced or backward.

In practice, this is not what has happened. While it is easy to overstate the extent to which the idea of a single path of development has been pushed, there is no doubt that it has dominated much of the thinking of influential international agencies, as well as the governments of developed and developing countries alike.

For Third World countries, the path to developed status has been mapped out as follows. Since industrialisation based on modern science and technology is the foundation of peace and prosperity, Third World countries must establish the infrastructure and industrial base that will enable them to compete with advanced nations for world trade. For this they need capital, which they can borrow through specially established institutions such as the World Bank and the IMF. Investment and technological expertise will necessarily come from developed nations and their multinational corporations. Care must be taken that scarce resources are not diverted to non-productive areas such as welfare and social services, or to industries that are not internationally competitive. Industrial production must be export-oriented, and the temptation to protect weak or inefficient industries by tariffs and other restrictions on free trade must be resisted. The validity of these principles, it is claimed, has been demonstrated by the economic success of Japan, South Korea, Taiwan, Singapore, and Hong Kong, and the rapid progress towards developed status made by the second wave of developing Asian countries, including Malaysia, Thailand and China. If a country like South Korea can rise to developed status in the space of some thirty years, there is no reason why others cannot do likewise, as long as they follow the path outlined.

The governments of some Asian countries, and the elites that support them, have embraced this line enthusiastically. While they may perceive that the operation of a largely open world market advantages rich, technologically advanced nations, they are sufficiently impressed by the achievement of Japan and South Korea to want to emulate them. Others have had acquiescence forced upon them as a condition for loans, investment, and aid through international agencies, especially the World Bank and the IMF. What has to be addressed is not only the general question of whether there is only one path of development, but also the more particular one of whether what, until the financial crisis of 1997–98, was called the East Asian miracle can in fact be explained by the principles suggested. If the answer to the last question turns out to be negative, then this in turn calls into question the adequacy of standard accounts of how the West grew rich.

Many critics of development have been struck by the apparently indestructible nature of neoclassical thinking on development, which has ironically been labelled 'Western fundamentalism'. Why do economists continue to espouse so fervently the need for continual growth, capital, free markets and non-interference by governments when the outcomes have so often been the opposite of what was desired, when many Third World countries have been crippled by debt and much of their social and economic life is controlled by foreign powers? Not surprisingly, some have concluded that the whole development agenda is a massive fraud on the part of rich, powerful

Jute remains one of Bangladesh's biggest exports.

countries, with the aim of continuing domination and exploitation of weaker ones, a modern variety of colonialism that relies more on economic than military control.

These ideas fall under the headings of world system theory (associated above all with the work of Immanuel Wallerstein, beginning in 1974) and dependency theory (originally formulated on the basis of Latin American and African experience in the 1960s). They may be understood as the mirror opposite of neoclassical thinking. What one side sees as a program for world modernisation and equity, the other regards as a strategy for creating dependency and perpetuating exploitation. Where one side sees all nations freely pursuing their comparative advantage and trading with others in the global market, to the maximum benefit of all, the other finds a world system structured in terms of unequal relationships, in which strong nations impose their will on weaker ones and direct the system's operation to the satisfaction of their own needs.

What both views, or types of views, have in common is the inclination to operate with a single explanation, to interpret the experience of all countries as variations on a small set of universal axioms. Both fail to do justice to the range of experience that has to be squeezed under the heading of development. What is needed is an account that deals realistically with the fact that relations between nations are not equal, and that most of the rules are set by the strong. At the same time, however, even small and relatively powerless nations have some degree of freedom; their destiny is not entirely in the hands of others.

## The Human Development Index

It could be argued that the continuing hold the idea of a single path to development has on the thinking of those influential in international development is demonstrated by the human development reports of the UNDP, which began to appear in 1990. In particular, this idea seems evident in the construction of the Human Development Index (HDI), conceived as a composite measure of the level of economic and social development that makes it possible to give all countries a numerical score and rank them in terms of development. There is no suggestion here that the paths nations pursue may be, or should be, incommensurate with each other.

Yet the construction of the HDI was, in fact, an attempt to move thinking on development beyond a preoccupation with economic growth measured in terms of gross national product (GNP). The originator of the index, Mahbub ul Huq, believed that what was needed for this purpose was 'a measure of the same level of vulgarity as GNP—just one number—but a measure that is not blind to social aspects of human lives as GNP is'. So it is not as if there has been ignorance of the inherent limitations of the HDI. Moreover, since its first appearance in 1990 there have been continuing efforts to refine it.[11]

The HDI has three components, which together are regarded as giving an indication of the extent to which populations are able to lead secure and satisfying lives. The three components are: (1) longevity or life expectancy; (2) educational attainment, which is measured in terms of a combination of levels of adult literacy and participation in formal education (as indicated by the number of students enrolled in each level of education as a proportion of the population in the relevant age groups); and (3) average income per person, expressed in terms of 'parity purchasing power'. For each component a nation receives a score within a possible range from 0 to 1, then the three scores are added together and divided by three to produce the final human development score, also within a range of 0 to 1. In 1995 the method of measuring educational attainment was revised, while in 1999 the way income per capita was calculated was also amended. Unfortunately, these changes limit the comparability of HDI values and rankings over time. The 2001 results for selected nations are shown in Table 5.2.

Not surprisingly, the Index has come in for a lot of criticism, much of it well founded, yet it would be a mistake to dismiss it altogether. For one thing, it does represent a serious attempt to move away from the absurd position that equates development with economic growth and sees such growth as an end in itself. Further, as the HDI has been revised and made more sophisticated over time, it has managed to address some of the criticisms levelled against it. For example, the need to take into account gender difference in human development has been taken seriously, especially in the 1995 report. Another objection considered has been that dividing national economic output by total population tells us little about the actual circumstances of individuals because it does not consider the purposes to which wealth is put. If national wealth is not applied to improving the circumstances of the bulk of the population by meeting basic needs, then including it as part of a measure of human development is quite misleading. To address this concern, countries have been ranked by their gross domestic product (GDP) as well as by HDI, with the former ranking subtracted from the latter so that those with a relatively high level of human development for a given level of national resources end up with a positive score, while those not doing well in human development terms end up with a negative score (see the final column in Table 5.2).

On this measure, in 2001, Armenia had the highest score (44) and Botswana the lowest (–55) (see Table 5.2). Following Armenia, the best-performing Asian countries were the former Soviet Republics Tajikistan (36), Georgia (32), and Azerbaijan (27), with Myanmar (22), the Philippines (21), Sri Lanka (19), and Vietnam (19) also doing well. Asian countries with the lowest rankings were Oman (–33), Saudi Arabia (–26) and Qatar (–24). However, it is best to be rather sceptical about such rankings and, in many cases, the reliability of the data used to construct them: they are no more than approximations giving a rough idea of where countries stand. The limitations of the HDI are evident from the way revised methods of measuring educational attainment in 1995 and income per capita in 1999 altered the rankings. Even small revisions to the data for many countries may result in big shifts.

If there is reason for misgivings about the reliability of some of the data used to construct the HDI, so too are there grounds for uncertainty as to what the results mean. Life expectancy is an attractive indicator because increased life expectancy is linked to a range of measures for meeting basic needs such as improved nutrition, housing, water supply and sanitation, and health care. Implicit in the Index, however, is the assumption that development always increases life expectancy (i.e. development equals progress), when in some cases it may have the opposite effect. Indigenous

**Table 5.2** Human Development Index 2001

| *HDI rank* | *Country* | *Life expectancy at birth (years) 1999* | *Adult literacy rate (% age 15 and above) 1999* | *Combined primary, secondary and tertiary gross enrolment ratio (%) 1999* | *GDP per capita (PPP[1] US$) 1999* | *Human Development Index Value 1999* | *GNP per capita rank minus HDI rank* |
|---|---|---|---|---|---|---|---|
| 1 | Norway | 78.4 | 99.0 | 97 | 26 433 | 0.939 | 2 |
| 2 | Australia | 78.8 | 99.0 | 116 | 24 574 | 0.936 | 10 |
| 3 | Canada | 78.7 | 99.0 | 97 | 26 251 | 0.936 | 3 |
| 4 | Sweden | 79.6 | 99.0 | 101 | 22 636 | 0.936 | 13 |
| 5 | Belgium | 78.2 | 99.0 | 109 | 25 443 | 0.935 | 4 |
| 6 | USA | 76.8 | 99.0 | 95 | 31 872 | 0.934 | –4 |
| 7 | Iceland | 79.1 | 99.0 | 89 | 27 835 | 0.932 | –3 |
| 8 | Netherlands | 78.0 | 99.0 | 102 | 24 215 | 0.931 | 5 |
| 9 | Japan | 80.8 | 99.0 | 82 | 24 898 | 0.928 | 2 |
| 10 | Finland | 77.4 | 99.0 | 103 | 23 096 | 0.925 | 5 |
| 11 | Switzerland | 78.8 | 99.0 | 84 | 27 171 | 0.924 | –6 |
| 13 | France | 78.4 | 99.0 | 94 | 22 897 | 0.924 | 3 |
| 14 | UK | 77.5 | 99.0 | 106 | 22 093 | 0.923 | 5 |
| 17 | Germany | 77.6 | 99.0 | 94 | 23 742 | 0.916 | –3 |
| 19 | New Zealand | 77.4 | 99.0 | 99 | 19 104 | 0.913 | 3 |
| 20 | Italy | 78.4 | 98.4 | 84 | 22 172 | 0.909 | –2 |
| 24 | Hong Kong | 79.4 | 93.3 | 69 | 22 090 | 0.880 | –4 |
| 26 | Singapore | 77.4 | 92.1 | 75 | 20 767 | 0.876 | –5 |
| 27 | South Korea | 74.7 | 97.6 | 90 | 15 712 | 0.875 | 5 |
| 55 | Russian Federation | 66.1 | 99.5 | 78 | 7 473 | 0.775 | 0 |
| 56 | Malaysia | 72.2 | 87.0 | 66 | 8 209 | 0.774 | –4 |
| 66 | Thailand | 69.9 | 95.3 | 60 | 6 132 | 0.757 | –3 |
| 70 | Philippines | 69.0 | 95.1 | 82 | 3 805 | 0.749 | 21 |
| 72 | Armenia | 72.7 | 98.3 | 80 | 2 215 | 0.745 | 44 |
| 74 | Ukraine | 68.1 | 99.6 | 77 | 3 458 | 0.742 | 22 |
| 75 | Kazakhstan | 64.4 | 99.0 | 77 | 4 951 | 0.742 | 1 |
| 76 | Georgia | 73.0 | 99.6 | 70 | 2 431 | 0.742 | 32 |
| 79 | Azerbaijan | 71.3 | 97.0 | 71 | 2 850 | 0.738 | 27 |
| 81 | Sri Lanka | 71.9 | 91.4 | 70 | 3 279 | 0.735 | 19 |
| 83 | Turkmenistan | 65.9 | 98.0 | 81 | 3 347 | 0.730 | 16 |
| 87 | China | 70.2 | 83.5 | 72 | 3 617 | 0.718 | 7 |
| 90 | Iran | 68.5 | 75.7 | 73 | 5 531 | 0.714 | –2 |
| 92 | Kyrgyzstan | 67.4 | 97.0 | 68 | 2 573 | 0.707 | 15 |
| 94 | South Africa | 53.9 | 84.9 | 93 | 8 908 | 0.702 | –49 |
| 99 | Uzbekistan | 68.7 | 88.5 | 76 | 2 251 | 0.698 | 15 |
| 101 | Vietnam | 67.8 | 93.1 | 67 | 1 860 | 0.682 | 19 |
| 102 | Indonesia | 65.8 | 86.3 | 65 | 2 857 | 0.677 | 3 |
| 103 | Tajikistan | 67.4 | 99.1 | 67 | 1 031 | 0.660 | 36 |
| 114 | Botswana | 41.9 | 76.4 | 70 | 6 872 | 0.577 | –55 |
| 115 | India | 62.9 | 56.5 | 56 | 2 248 | 0.571 | 0 |
| 116 | Mongolia | 62.5 | 62.3 | 58 | 1 711 | 0.569 | 7 |
| 118 | Myanmar | 56.0 | 84.4 | 55 | 1 027 | 0.551 | 22 |
| 121 | Cambodia | 56.4 | 68.2 | 62 | 1 361 | 0.541 | 13 |
| 127 | Pakistan | 59.6 | 45.0 | 40 | 1 834 | 0.498 | –5 |
| 129 | Nepal | 58.1 | 40.4 | 60 | 1 237 | 0.480 | 7 |
| 131 | Laos | 53.1 | 47.3 | 58 | 1 471 | 0.476 | –2 |
| 132 | Bangladesh | 58.9 | 40.8 | 37 | 1 483 | 0.470 | –4 |

Source: United Nations Development Program, *Human Development Report 2001*, Oxford University Press, New York, 2001, 141–44.

1 Parity purchasing power.

minorities may experience social disintegration as a result of being forced from their traditional lands and lifestyles; a deterioration in housing and nutrition, widespread drug and alcohol abuse, endemic social violence and high suicide rates may follow. In many countries water pollution due to industrial effluents, pesticides, and fertilisers is a growing health hazard, as is air pollution caused by industry, power generation, and motor vehicles. Therefore populations may register an overall increase in life expectancy due to better nutrition, housing, and health care, yet have potential gains reduced by early deaths resulting from pollution.

The education component of the Index directly raises the question of the relevance of education in the form of schooling and tertiary study to non-literate societies. In most traditional societies personal opportunity and material security have not depended on literacy and formal education; it has been possible to live a full and satisfying life without them. This is germane to the situation of many indigenous minorities. International human rights legislation confers on minorities the right to enjoy their traditional lifestyles, yet literacy and schooling are not likely to be part of that way of life. Therefore, were a country with substantial indigenous minorities to interpret this human right literally, it would score poorly in terms of the human development of its indigenous peoples. This is an issue in developed countries such as Canada and Australia no less than in developing countries such as Indonesia and Vietnam.

The biggest difficulties raised by the HDI have to do with GDP per capita as a measure of income or economic activity. Gross domestic product is an estimate of all economic activity to which monetary value is attached, and so produces many anomalies. With regard to indigenous minorities again, GDP figures do not take into account economic activity that has value in terms of barter or self-sufficiency rather than monetary exchange. This means that a semi-nomadic herder from Iran or Mongolia, or a swidden farmer from Laos or West Papua, may have quite a comfortable, secure life based on subsistence agriculture and a bit of barter, yet appear impoverished in terms of the HDI because his or her economic activity is not seen as having cash value. For societies that do not have a cash economy, income figures of the sort used to calculate the Index may be particularly misleading.

A similar point applies to the unpaid work done by women. Because it carries no cash value, it is not counted within economic productivity and until recently was largely ignored as a focus for human development. In 1995 a global value of $US11 trillion a year was set on this unrecognised contribution by women. Surveys show that in almost every country in the world women do more work than men, with the difference being larger in developing than developed countries. In Indonesia, for example, women worked an average of 9 per cent longer than men; in Nepal the difference was 5 per cent. If rural areas alone are considered the differences are much greater: women tend to work much longer hours than men, doing everything from housekeeping to fetching fuel and water, tending animals and growing crops for family consumption. In rural Nepal and the Philippines it is on average around 20 per cent more, in Bangladesh 10 per cent. Some studies, however, have concluded that women carry an even larger share of the burden. In one village in northern India, for example, it was found that women frequently worked twice as many hours per day as men.[12]

Because GDP represents an estimate of all economic-related activity to which a cash value may be attributed, including production, goods, and services, major items that by any normal understanding should be regarded as a cost end up being counted as a contribution to economic productivity. For example, the costs of cleaning up major environmental disasters such as those at Minamata and Bhopal show up as contributions to the economic growth of Japan and India respectively. Further, GNP figures nowhere take into account the resource or environmental costs of economic activity, in terms of either depletion of natural resources or environmental degradation. Nor do they include any measure of national debt, which for many Third World countries has become the most pressing of all problems. GDP, in other words, is a crude estimate of economic productivity that fails to give any indication of the economic viability of the activities in question, let alone their social or environmental impact.[13]

The figures relating to change over time in HDI values certainly call for careful consideration of the sorts of limitations mentioned. However, they also indicate shifts of a scale that are difficult to dismiss as mere statistical illusions. For the period 1975–99, according to the revised HDI, the nations recording the largest gains in human development in the world were Indonesia, China, South Korea, and Nepal (see Table 5.3). Sceptics will note that Indonesia and China are both large countries in which, even with enormous effort, it is extremely difficult to obtain accurate national data, and that both have had governments not averse to 'cooking the books' in order to appear in a better light. Noteworthy too is the very uneven development of those countries, and also that of Nepal, with remote rural regions lagging a long way behind industrialised urban areas.[14] Nonetheless, the magnitude of the changes registered on the HDI cannot be totally spurious.

What do changes on this scale mean in terms of real gains for individuals? For example, during the period 1975–98, in the case of Indonesia, it meant an increase in average life expectancy of 15.8 years, and average individual income increasing by 259 per cent. For China, the corresponding increases were 6.6 years and 527 per cent,

**Table 5.3** Improvement in human development, selected Asian countries, 1975-99

| | *HDI value 1975* | *HDI value 1999* | *Increase 1975–99* |
|---|---|---|---|
| Indonesia | 0.467 | 0.677 | 0.210 |
| China | 0.522 | 0.718 | 0.196 |
| South Korea | 0.687 | 0.875 | 0.188 |
| Nepal | 0.292 | 0.480 | 0.188 |
| Saudi Arabia | 0.587 | 0.754 | 0.167 |
| India | 0.406 | 0.571 | 0.165 |
| Malaysia | 0.614 | 0.774 | 0.160 |
| Iran | 0.556 | 0.714 | 0.158 |
| Singapore | 0.719 | 0.876 | 0.157 |
| Pakistan | 0.343 | 0.498 | 0.155 |
| Thailand | 0.603 | 0.757 | 0.154 |
| Bangladesh | 0.332 | 0.470 | 0.138 |
| Hong Kong | 0.754 | 0.880 | 0.126 |
| Sri Lanka | 0.614 | 0.735 | 0.121 |
| Philippines | 0.649 | 0.749 | 0.100 |

Source: United Nations Development Program, *Human Development Report 2001*, Oxford University Press, New York, 2001, 145–8.

and for Nepal 14.0 years and 147 per cent respectively. Even average performers (in terms of improving human development over the period) such as India and Pakistan registered substantial gains.

In the face of such changes it is hard to accept arguments that development is a neocolonial plot to subordinate and exploit Third World countries in perpetuity. Modernisation may embrace a host of undesirable things, including forms of dependency and exploitation, and new forms of inequality. Yet it cannot be denied that without (largely) Western science and technology, life expectancy in China could not have increased by 75 per cent between 1950 and 1992; it would be impossible for India to feed its population, despite the fact that between 1950 and 1994 this grew by nearly 250 per cent; and diseases such as smallpox, malaria and bubonic plague would not have been eradicated or contained. These gains may have given rise to new problems, it is true. Increased life expectancy has led to rapid increases in population. The green revolution in many rural areas has aggravated social inequality at the same time as increasing food production. Those who equate development with imperialism and the imposition of Western values, and who call for the maintenance of traditional lifestyles, tend to overlook the low life expectancies and material insecurity that characterised those lifestyles. Although in pre-modern societies life was not nasty, brutish and short for everyone, on average it certainly was shorter than it is for those who have experienced the mixed blessings of development.

As for going back to those traditional lifestyles that sometimes appear so attractive when imagined in terms of small harmonious communities living in balance with nature: the fact is that it is too late. The ecological balance has been changed irrevocably. Whatever possibility traditional cultures offered in the past for a secure and satisfying life, the population increases of recent decades have largely destroyed it.

## Many paths

The problems resulting from grandiose and ill-conceived development plans in many Third World countries—crippling foreign debt, degraded environments, foreign control of key industries, uncontrolled urbanisation, cultural and social dislocation—must not be allowed to blind us to the fact that often the results of development have been good. Sometimes, for example, big undertakings backed by World Bank advice and funding have been timely and well targeted. Sometimes new industries have increased the wealth of whole regions, not just the social elite, and ordinary people have benefited from programs conceived by foreign experts and imposed from the top down. Furthermore, despite the enormous influence of bodies such as the World Bank and the IMF, and the development orthodoxy they have imposed on developing countries around the world, the reality of development has been, and certainly is becoming, far more varied than we are sometimes led to believe.

Some national and provincial governments have pursued development paths that have been anything but orthodox. This includes those of China, Sri Lanka, and the southern Indian state of Kerala, which are discussed further on in this chapter. But even those that have tended to follow a more conventional economic path have sometimes used quite varied strategies. The same is true of international agencies and non-government organisations.

The Asian Development Bank, as well as funding large projects in such areas as energy supply, transport and communications, has also supported technological development for small and medium-size enterprises. The International Labour Organisation has supported a program for the transfer, adoption and diffusion of technology for small and cottage industries, which has done valuable work in countries such as Bangladesh, India, Laos, Sri Lanka, and Thailand. The technological improvement of traditional small-scale industries can be an important counterweight to the preoccupation with large-scale and high-tech industries so common in developing countries, enabling productivity to be increased with minimal cost and minimal socio-economic upheaval. During the late 1980s, in South Asia, more than 80 per cent of those employed in manufacturing were working in small or cottage industries. Towards the end of the twentieth century, the World Bank, which has a history of preoccupation with top-down, large-scale development, seemed to be becoming more supportive of local initiatives, and appeared more sensitive to the social and environmental impacts of development. More generally, the idea of micro-credit was attracting a lot of attention. Particularly influential was the example of the Grameen Bank in Bangladesh, established by Muhammad Yunus to provide small loans to poor people, especially women, in order to set up small enterprises.[15]

The national government of India, which has certainly had its share of problems arising from ambitious, costly and socially insensitive development projects, has also encouraged the development and application of alternative or appropriate technologies. The Centre for the Application of Science and Technology to Rural Areas, established at the Indian Institute of Science, Bangalore, in 1974, has made a valuable contribution in this regard. In 1992 the Indian government established a Ministry for Non-Conventional Energy, to support work in fields such as wind and photo-voltaic power generation, though sceptics claim that it generates more tax breaks than electricity. The Thai government, which is certainly committed to the path of economic growth through large-scale industrialisation, has established its T-Bird Program (Thai Business Initiative in Rural Development), under which major corporations help to establish small-scale industries in the countryside.[16]

Growing concern over the environmental impact of industrialisation, much of it expressed in terms of the fashionable concept of sustainable development, has led to a resurgence of official interest in appropriate technology. There is also a growing awareness, however, of the need for development from below that offers scope for community input and decision-making if problems are to be addressed successfully at the village level. Blanket solutions imposed from the top often do not work, whether because local circumstances are not taken into account or because villagers feel alienated and refuse to cooperate. The realisation is spreading that those whose problems are ostensibly to be solved may in fact have insight into how it may best be done, that local traditional knowledge may be essential, and that if people have a sense of involvement in development projects they are much more likely to be enthusiastic about them. This may require difficult changes in attitude and behaviour on the part of 'experts' and officials, shifting to an approach that is consultative and democratic instead of directive and authoritarian. Non-government organisations have played a leading role in bringing about a greater emphasis on community-based, collaborative undertakings in which experts come to work with local people rather than trying to impose preconceived solutions on them.[17]

Much of the push for alternative technology in South Asia, where it has been stronger than elsewhere in Asia, comes from outside government circles and often in opposition to official policy. It may be that this owes something to the democratic political systems of the countries of the region, especially India and Sri Lanka. However, it also owes a lot to the strong alternative economic tradition that has flourished there and is associated above all with Gandhi. Gandhi was opposed to the large-scale industrialisation and modernisation advocated by Nehru, independent India's first prime minister, which have dominated national economic policy since 1947. Because of Gandhi's leading role in the struggle for independence, however, and his teaching that India must remain true to her own heritage, Gandhi's alternative outlook is as much part of modern Indian identity as is Nehru's vision.

Gandhi believed that modern life was distorted by the preoccupation with economic growth and wealth. While meeting material needs was essential, as he told a group of economists, there must also be higher goals:

> I hold that economic progress is antagonistic to real progress. Hence, the ancient ideal has been the limitation of activities promoting wealth. This does not put an end to all material ambition. We should still have, as we have always had in our midst, people who make the pursuit of wealth their aim in life. But we have always recognised that this is a fall from the ideal ... I have heard many of our countrymen say that we will gain American wealth but avoid its methods. I venture to suggest that such an attempt, if it were made, is foredoomed to failure.[18]

Gandhi's ideal was a life of concern for all living things, which found its social expression in cooperative, self-reliant communities that produced enough to satisfy their own simple needs. In such communities ordinary people would have control over their own lives and make the decisions directly affecting them, and all would be actively involved in production. Gandhi opposed large-scale industrialisation and centralised government that left large numbers of people idle and took away their responsibilities. He made the spinning wheel his symbol.

The data collected by the UNDP indicate that regardless of the orthodoxy concerning the achievement of development, or how widely it is assumed to be a unilinear process, the reality is far from uniform. When we look at what is done rather than what is said, it soon becomes clear that, despite some common scenery along the way, the paths nations follow vary considerably.

The Human Development Index shows, among other things, that some nations achieve relatively high levels of human development despite low GDP per capita, while some that by this measure are much wealthier have devoted much less effort to human development. This suggests that economic growth is less vital for human or social development than is commonly claimed, and that it is a matter, rather, of consciously directing national resources, however modest, to those ends. If the policies and resources of the state are directed to achieving economic growth, that growth may be achieved without any improvement in the situation of the bulk of the population. Three places where a relatively high level of human development has been reached despite low per capita incomes are Sri Lanka, the state of Kerala in southern India, and the People's Republic of China.

Traditional and modern development, Sri Lanka: rice paddies, Badulla District, and Victoria Dam, Mahaweli River.

Sri Lanka's unusual situation has been the subject of attention since the late 1970s, when it was observed that living standards there were much higher than those of other countries with a similar per capita income. When its per capita income was only $US130, the average life expectancy in Sri Lanka was 69 years, which was the norm for nations twenty times as wealthy. Since then, despite the terrible social and economic burden of the continuing armed conflict in the country's northeast, the people of Sri Lanka have continued to enjoy standards of health care, welfare and education usually associated with wealthier nations.

A notable feature is the relative equality enjoyed by women. Not only is adult literacy widespread (91 per cent in 1999), but also among females it is not much less than among males, being 94 per cent of the male rate. Women are more likely than men to be enrolled in tertiary educational institutions, while women's wages for non-agricultural work average 90 per cent of those of men, compared, for example, with about 70 per cent in the United Kingdom and 75 per cent in the United States (see Table 5.4). The emancipation of Sri Lankan women partly explains the low national fertility rate, which in the late 1990s had fallen to 2.1, compared with 3.2 in Malaysia, 3.6 in the Philippines and 1.7 in South Korea. It is widely accepted that Sri Lanka has completed the demographic transition regarded as characteristic of industrialised countries, moving from a high birth rate and high death rate to a low birth rate and low death rate.[19]

Kerala's achievements have been similar to those of Sri Lanka. Kerala has been relatively poor by Indian standards, in 1987 ranking eleventh out of seventeen states in terms of per capita income. Yet in terms of human development it has outperformed all the others, including the wealthy states of Punjab, Maharashtra, and Haryana. In the areas of life expectancy, adult literacy, infant mortality, and fertility rate, Kerala has more closely resembled the United States than the rest of India. It could be argued too

**Table 5.4** Average wage for women working in non-agricultural sectors as a percentage of that for men

| | % |
|---|---|
| Tanzania | 92.0 |
| Vietnam | 91.5 |
| Australia | 90.8 |
| Sri Lanka | 89.8 |
| Iceland | 89.6 |
| Sweden | 89.0 |
| New Zealand | 80.6 |
| USA | 75.0 |
| Singapore | 71.1 |
| UK | 69.7 |
| Thailand | 68.2 |
| Canada | 63.0 |
| Philippines | 60.8 |
| China | 59.4 |
| South Korea | 53.5 |
| Bangladesh | 42.0 |

Source: United Nations Development Program, *Human Development Report 1995*, Oxford University Press, New York, 1995, 36.

Note: Data is for the latest available year.

that Kerala's early investment in literacy and education is one of the reasons why between 1987 and 1997 it recorded the highest economic growth of all Indian states. The 'Kerala model' is controversial, but has been widely acclaimed as an alternative development path for Third World countries to follow.[20]

Coir (coconut fibre) workers, Cochin, Kerala, India.

China has also attracted a lot of attention as an alternative model, though since the late 1970s and its shift towards a market economy it has become unfashionable. In the Third World, as in the West, it is now seen largely as another example of the failure of communism, a candidate, along with the countries of Eastern Europe and the former Soviet Union, for redevelopment in accordance with neoclassical principles. Yet in terms of meeting the basic needs of its people, communist China was widely regarded in the 1960s and 1970s as having made more progress than other countries at a comparable stage of economic development, despite the political campaigns that brought continuing social and economic instability. The commune system had many shortcomings, particularly from an economic perspective, yet it made possible the delivery of services previously unexperienced in most of rural China. The health care system, for example, with its heavy emphasis on primary health care in a context of community education and development, its strong reliance on paraprofessionals (including the so-called 'bare-foot doctors'), and an eclectic approach to treatment involving both Western and indigenous methods, attracted worldwide attention in the late 1970s. Even rich developed countries such as the United States believed that some aspects of the Chinese approach might help them develop new health care systems. In 1979 it was enthusiastically acclaimed by the World Health Organisation (WHO) and held up as a model for other Third World countries anxious to solve their health problems.[21]

The achievements by Sri Lanka, Kerala, and China have in recent years attracted criticism, however. It is claimed that all three made the mistake of spending their limited resources on unproductive social services such as welfare and health care when they should have been investing more heavily in industry. As a result, it is alleged, they won short-term gains in their unusually high levels of human development, but in the longer term have suffered by lagging behind economically, and in recent years have found themselves unable to keep up with other countries in human development. To some extent their low levels of per capita income are a consequence of earlier tender-hearted profligacy. It is an argument that scarcely comes as a surprise, since it is an expression of the conventional wisdom on how development should be handled. The same view is contained, for example, in IMF conditionality agreements requiring Third World countries to curtail spending on social services in order to qualify for loans or have existing debts rescheduled.

Common sense tells us that excessive government spending, however well intentioned, will at some point become a problem if no attention is paid to productivity and revenue. However, it is impossible to specify the proportion of government resources that should be spent on services at a given stage of economic development, or to infer from its level of human development that a nation is spending too much on social services. This would assume what is being claimed: that there is only one path of development. It would also assume that a given level of resources will buy the same increase in living standards, regardless of the country or the way the resources are applied. But what makes the cases of Sri Lanka, Kerala, and China special is the way in which relatively few resources have been used to implement very effective programs. In other words, part of their success is attributable to the cost-effective way they have gone about providing services.

Neoclassical economists and libertarians who complain about the restrictive and parasitic role of the state have a pronounced tendency to take for granted the existence of all the things that a well-run state provides, such as an impartial and honest legal system, structures that ensure the integrity and functioning of financial markets, banks and commercial institutions, labour market regulation, the provision of educational and training institutions, transport and communication links and energy supplies. The governments of many developing countries would at best have a limited capacity to provide these, even if substantial funds were available. Sri Lanka, Kerala, and China have demonstrated determination and skill in developing programs that work in the villages where the great majority of the people live, and have seen to it that the necessary personnel were available to make the programs work.

There is no evidence that they have bought rapid human development at the cost of longer-term economic and social gains. A 1994 study of Sri Lanka's experience concluded that even a poor country can bring about rapid improvement in the living standards of its people by adopting a judiciously designed welfare strategy, and further that the pursuit of rapid gains in this manner need not involve conflict with growth and hence need not entail a loss of welfare in the long term.[22]

The study also concluded, however, that a reasonable rate of economic growth is necessary if provision of welfare and social services is to remain secure. If it is accepted that the way resources are applied, as well as their availability, is important, it becomes clear that the nature of government organisation may be a significant factor. For example, a centralised, top-down approach relying on large but reasonably effective bureaucracies may be essential for provision of nation-wide quality services in health, education, and welfare. If services are to be truly comprehensive and inclusive, and meet the needs of the great majority of people, efficient delivery mechanisms have to be in place. This may require an organisational capacity many poor and recently established nation states find difficult to achieve. Yet heavy reliance on centralised government structures may be much less effective for long-term economic development. This could help to explain a striking fact about the HDI: communist and ex-communist countries tend to rank higher than would be expected on the basis of per capita income. This has been true of the countries of Eastern Europe and the former Soviet Union as well as China and Vietnam.

The claim that China's economic growth before 1979 was retarded by overspending on social security and services is quite unconvincing.[23] The commune structure, coupled with a radical approach to services such as health care, made it possible to provide services cheaply and ensure that they extended to all parts of the country. While it is the convention to attribute China's rapid economic growth from 1979 to the introduction of the responsibility system in economic production and the dismantling of the communes, there is good reason to hold that the commune system played an indispensable role in laying the foundations for post-1979 growth. It made possible the low-cost provision of health care and education, child care and social security; enabled (indeed, compelled) people to take part in new forms of production and industrial organisation; gave vast numbers of peasants and workers the opportunity to acquire new skills ranging from tractor-driving to book-keeping; and broadened employment opportunities, particularly for women, in ways that before the 1960s were inconceivable.

Furthermore, the introduction of communes had ended private ownership of land, and leasing arrangements following their dismantling have made possible efficient land use to a degree out of the question in, say, India and the Philippines. In short, the commune system played a central role in producing a much healthier, better housed and fed, and much more skilled workforce, which could be more effectively utilised from 1979 when some of the constraints and disincentives of the commune system had been removed, and there was greater scope in the workplace for individual initiative and reward.

The assumption that investment in economic growth and human development is a zero-sum game is facile, especially when notions of capital have been expanded to include human as well as financial capital. The problem is that economic growth does not automatically lead to human development or vice versa; it has to be made to happen. It is now generally accepted that the state is not an adequate substitute for the private sector when it comes to economic production. What is not so well understood is that the private sector is not an adequate substitute for the state when it comes to provision of social services, infrastructure, and management of the legal–institutional framework that an efficient private sector presupposes.

## Democracy? Choices?

True believers in development assert that it is about increasing personal autonomy, the ability of the individual to do what he or she really wants and so achieve greater fulfilment. Development provides opportunities to make choices and the means of acting on them. 'Human development', according to the authors of the first human development report produced by the UNDP, 'is a process of enlarging people's choices. The most critical of these wide-ranging choices are to live a long and healthy life, to be educated and to have access to resources needed for a decent standard of living. Additional choices include political freedom, guaranteed human rights and personal self-respect.'

While the language is a bit peculiar, the ideas are straightforward enough. It is a theme elaborated in subsequent human development reports, gaining in sophistication over time. The 2000 report, for example, expresses the goal of development in human rights terms, as being 'to secure the freedom, well-being and dignity of all people everywhere'. Understood in this way, 'freedom' includes freedom from want, discrimination, injustice, and fear; and also freedom to develop and realise one's human potential, freedom of thought and speech, and freedom to obtain and perform decent work. A similar approach has been taken by Amartya Sen, who sees development as 'the process of expanding the real freedoms that people enjoy'. Moreover, Sen explicitly rejects any suggestion that there is a ready formula of neoliberalism that can maximise freedom. It is a characteristic of freedom, he says, that it 'cannot yield a view of development that translates readily into some simple "formula" of accumulation of capital, or opening up of markets, or having efficient economic planning ...'[24]

The data presented in the human development reports certainly indicate that the relationship between human development and political and economic liberalism is by no means free of ambiguities. Of the ten nations identified in the 1994 report as having achieved the most progress in human development between 1960 and 1992, none was conspicuous for its socio-political or economic liberalism; nor have these been dominant characteristics of the countries identified in the 2001 report as showing the most improvement in human development between 1975 and 1999 (see Table 5.3). So while personal freedoms may be necessary for the full enjoyment of human potential realised by development, some of the UNDP's own evidence could be interpreted as supporting the argument put by the governments of many developing countries, that individual freedoms may need to be limited in the short or medium term for the well-being of society as a whole to be maximised. If communism is equated with lack of personal freedoms, the data relating to communist and ex-communist countries point to the same conclusion. As mentioned earlier, these countries, including China and Vietnam, have tended to record levels of human development above those of other countries with comparable levels of per capita income.

Critics of development tend to argue that, far from increasing choices and opportunities, for most people development restricts the capacity to choose or find fulfilment. The majority of people in Third World countries have no choice about being caught up in the development process, and they have little influence on the way it shapes their social and economic life. Moreover the process of development, once commenced, is irreversible. There is no going back to traditional lifestyles once the forces of modernisation have gone to work. Cultural choices disappear before the onslaught of globalisation.

Development initiatives have tended to be imposed by governments and elites that scarcely consult those whose lives are directly affected. One of the strongest criticisms of development in practice has long been that it results in the concentration of power and authority in the hands of Westernised elites. Traditional forms of authority and institutions are undermined as new types of organisation and expertise are deemed essential for progress. Local knowledge is devalued; suddenly experts are needed to advise on matters that were formerly handled on the basis of generations of personal experience. Local knowledge and cultural traditions, once lost, are lost forever. Development cannot be undone. If it extends choice in some directions, it eliminates it in others.[25]

## When miracles become routine

Until the financial crisis of 1997–98, a whole rash of economic 'miracles' had been identified in East and South-East Asia: Japan, Korea, Taiwan, Singapore, Hong Kong, Malaysia, Thailand, China, Indonesia ... But there was disagreement as to how those miracles came about. Some saw them as a demonstration of what can be achieved when entrepreneurial energy and competition are freed from state control, while others saw them as the product of command capitalism, the result of vigorous government intervention and manipulation of the private sector and, more generally, as a triumph of 'Asian values'.

It is not entirely surprising that interpretation of the subsequent crisis involved a similar range of views regarding causes and remedies. On the one hand, many Western market-liberalism enthusiasts were inclined to say 'I told you so', in that what had been labelled miracles were never more than mirages. They claimed that the crisis was an inevitable consequence of state economic interference, coupled with the corruption and disregard for sound financial practice that are characteristic of nations that, quite simply, have never been able to get their act together. On the other hand, advocates of Asian values and the 'third way' tended to blame Western capitalists and to see evidence of Western conspiracies to undermine successful Asian competitors.

The reality, inevitably, was much more complex. The precipitating factor in the crisis was indeed the behaviour of international investors, whose panic resulted in an abrupt and massive outflow of capital from the region. That behaviour was in response—however disproportionate—to problems arising from the weaknesses of financial institutions in those countries. Although those weaknesses also help to explain the extent of the damage caused by the crisis, it is impossible to ignore other, more fundamental factors that made the countries in question so vulnerable. Above all, these were a heavy reliance on overseas borrowing and direct foreign investment, linked—in all Asian cases except for South Korea—with uneven, export-oriented development. The serious consequences were moreover further aggravated by the ill-considered, formulaic 'remedies' imposed by the IMF. The rapid recovery of the economies in 1999 and 2000 (leaving aside the problematic case of Indonesia) indicates that the crisis had little connection with Asian values, state economic strategies that defied conventional market wisdom, or even cronyism and corruption. What the financial crisis *did* highlight was the need for new forms of national and international market regulation, to at least keep pace with the technological and institutional change of recent decades.

In any case, even before the crisis there was a lot of evidence indicating that much of the success of the newly industrialised countries of East Asia has been due to the fact that they have not applied neoclassical economic principles. Far from leaving things to the market, the state has steered, coaxed, and bullied the private sector in the directions it has set. In Japan and Korea, for example, the state has used wide-ranging controls and incentives to direct the *keiretsu* or *chaebôl*, that is, the big industrial conglomerates that have played such a big part in establishing them as leading industrial nations. On the one hand, state intervention has included the selective provision of credit and foreign exchange for approved undertakings, preferential treatment in regard to government contracts, access to land and services at reduced rates or free of charge, and provision of industrial intelligence and support services, as well as more orthodox activities such as the development of infrastructure and human resources. On the other hand, it has included punitive action and withdrawal of support when the private sector has ignored government expectations or has failed to meet government targets.

The state has not hesitated to protect new industries from foreign competition and, far from embarking on export-oriented growth from the start, has used import-substitution and development of domestic markets as a way of building up industrial capacity. While doing so, however, it has insisted upon profitability and international competitiveness in the longer term. Where necessary, the state has not hesitated to establish key industries itself and, when they are fully established, sell them to the private sector. This was done by the Meiji government in late nineteenth-century Japan to develop a modern steel industry, and it was done by the Korean government in the 1960s, when, against the advice of the World Bank, it established the Pohang Iron and Steel Company (Posco), which twenty years later had become one of the world's leading steel manufacturers.[27]

The World Bank, in its 1993 report *The East Asian Miracle*, found itself obliged to admit that 'East Asia does not wholly conform to the neoclassical model', and, more recently, has accepted the idea that governments do, after all, have an important economic role to play. In its report to mark the beginning of the new century, the World Bank identified, as one of the elements of an 'emerging consensus' on future development policy, the principle that 'governments play a vital role in development, but there is no simple set of rules that tells them what to do'.[28]

South Korea's steel and shipbuilding industries are symbols of the nation's economic rise, as is the global reach of multinationals such as Hyundai.

The Asian Development Bank has been less inhibited about recognising the unconventional paths East Asian nations have followed in quest of economic growth. It has observed that Korea, Taiwan, and Singapore have all used a 'judicious combination' of state encouragement and control, and capitalist enterprise. Only Hong Kong, it claims, has relied purely on a 'free wheeling capitalist economy'.[29]

In regard to Hong Kong, however, the Asian Development Bank appears to have been mistaken. The Hong Kong economy too has benefited from far-reaching state intervention. As in Singapore, in Hong Kong the government has by its control of land played a crucial role in reducing housing and building costs. Whereas in Singapore the government has enforced acquisition of land at below market value to provide public housing, in Hong Kong all land is state-owned, which has enabled the government to obtain substantial revenue from the sale of leases while ensuring that cheap housing was available for most of the workforce. Together with the bulk food supplies being obtained from the People's Republic below market prices, this effectively provided working-class families with a 50 per cent subsidy of their household costs. The resulting cheap (but skilled) labour force was for many years Hong Kong's major comparative advantage, which together with low expenditure on social services and low taxation enabled the city state to compete well internationally. Yet it would not have been possible without shrewd state management and control of key economic factors.[30]

This is not to say that 'command capitalism' always works, or that it does not have its dangers. Government bureaucracies can get in the way, especially when different arms of them pull in different directions, and sometimes they make mistakes. This is true of any large organisation. Peculiar to the close interaction between government and industry that characterises command capitalism, perhaps, are the opportunities it presents for corruption and the use of state power to further private interests. Official corruption is one of the biggest concerns of many Asian nations, and much of it involves collusion between politicians and big business. As already mentioned, many observers saw large-scale corruption of this sort as one of the precipitating factors behind the Asian financial crisis.

That industry protection and the erection of barriers to international trade also carry dangers was generally accepted in negotiations for the General Agreement on Tariffs and Trade and creation of the World Trade Organisation. However, errors and occasional pointless meddling by states do not mean that they should do nothing. Erection of trade barriers is just one of a range of strategies a state can pursue to further its economic interests, and is perhaps the least imaginative of all. The transformation of a national economy and the creation of modern industries able to hold their own internationally require broad vision and long-term commitment, and resources on a scale not commonly found among private business corporations.

Even in the more orthodox types of economic activity, the governments of newly industrialised Asian countries stand out for their thoroughness and energy. Two key areas in which the 'four dragons' of East Asia (South Korea, Taiwan, Hong Kong, and Singapore), and to a lesser extent the second wave of newly developing countries, including Malaysia and Thailand, have outperformed other developing countries are human resource development and rapid acquisition of foreign technology by every means available to them.[31]

## Technological leapfrogging

The acquisition of knowledge, technical mastery, and technological hardware play a central role in rapid industrialisation, and this indicates the potentially misleading nature of the maxim that nations must build on their comparative advantage. Third World countries, especially if resource-poor, have little to compete on except cheap labour and an absence of government controls on such things as labour and environmental protection. Their comparative advantage, in short, tends to amount to the willingness of the state to tolerate labour exploitation and environmental degradation. However, countries content to rely on labour-intensive industries alone find that the gap between them and industrially advanced nations continues to widen, as technological advances continue to be incorporated into industrial production.

Unless developing nations acquire the technological mastery to compete internationally, they will be condemned forever to the role of proletariat in the international economy. The question is whether technological catch-up is a realistic proposition, or whether the only feasible response on the part of Third World countries is to delink themselves from the world system and aim, if not for self-sufficiency, then at least for semi-independent economic arrangements that will satisfy the basic needs of the population in the longer term.

Countries such as South Korea and Taiwan have not been content to continue in the role of cheap labour force for the international economy. Rather, they have made the most of labour-intensive industries while pushing as rapidly as possible into technologically advanced ones. Like Japan before them, they have demonstrated that, to a significant degree, technological and economic catch-up is feasible, that 'learning by doing' makes it possible to develop an advanced technological capacity if the state provides the right sort of leadership and support.

This lesson has not been lost on other developing Asian countries. In Indonesia during the last decade of the Suharto government there was competition for influence between two camps, known as the technocrats and the technologs, over the best way to develop the country. The technocrats, who were influential in the National Planning Agency (Bappenas) and the Ministry of Finance, advocated the conventional approach that had been dominant—namely, the development of labour-intensive and resource-based industries, with the help of foreign multinationals, leading to export-oriented manufacturing and the accumulation of the technological capacity to establish more advanced industries in the longer term. The technolog camp, centred on the Minister for Research and Technology (and later, President), Dr B. J. Habibie, argued that industrialisation based on Indonesia's comparative advantage as conventionally conceived—abundant cheap labour and natural resources—was not enough. The technologs advocated a more direct approach to the acquisition of leading-edge technical skills and development of an economy based on technological mastery. Habibie believed that, with careful preparation and planning, 'the capabilities of any country anywhere can be increased so that it can undertake a leap in its reasoning ability and the power of its imagination to master even the most sophisticated technology appropriate and useful for the solution of concrete questions which it faces in its daily life and to improve value-added processes'.

Neither side managed to become dominant, and while there was scepticism regarding Habibie's technological springboard strategy, his ideas were clearly attractive to many in the government. In May 1994 President Suharto stated, 'We do not want to continue to be mere consumers of foreign science and importers of technology from other countries. We wish to be self-reliant.'[32] The sixth national Five Year Plan (1995–99) gave priority to high-tech industries intended to enable Indonesia to take its place among the developed nations of the world.

One of the major thrusts of Indonesian government policy at that time was to identify a number of industries or sectors that, as well as having strategic importance in their own right, could serve as vehicles (*wahana*) for technological and economic development. They were industries that had a large potential domestic market, required high levels of technological expertise, would encourage the emergence of other advanced industries, and would help to spread technological mastery throughout the workforce. These industries included shipping, electronics and telecommunications, energy, and agricultural engineering. The best known and most controversial, however, was the aircraft manufacturing industry, in the development of which Habibie, himself an aeronautical engineer, was closely involved.

While few observers doubted the technological competence of the aircraft-manufacturing corporation Habibie managed to establish, many questioned the economic wisdom of such an enterprise and its capacity to play the sort of technological leadership role envisaged. Certainly the enterprise's opportunity cost was high. The huge amounts of government funds it soaked up were not available for other projects seen by many economists as more appropriate at that point in Indonesia's development. The matter came to a head during Indonesia's acute economic problems following the 1997–98 financial crisis, when the IMF demanded sharp cuts in government spending as a condition for the big loans the country needed in order to survive. This brought to an end the enormous subsidies the corporation had been enjoying, if not the corporation itself. To survive it will have to scale down its ambitions drastically, and consider the commercial viability of its operations no less than their contribution to national pride.

The appropriateness or otherwise of a particular undertaking depends to a large extent on the other initiatives to which it is linked. The problem with the Indonesian aircraft industry is not that it has been out of step with conventional development thinking, but rather that not enough has been done to ensure that the hoped-for technological and economic flow-ons will occur. On the contrary, the aircraft industry has been isolated from the rest of Indonesian industry as a privileged undertaking not required to feed into the wider economy. There has been no notable diffusion of skills and technologies, and little has happened in the way of developing support industries.

Not only has the Indonesian government paid too little attention to the linkages needed to obtain benefits from the good work that has been done, but it has also neglected the education and skill levels of the workforce as a whole.

On this last point, the contrast between South Korea and Indonesia is stark. South Korea has directed considerable resources to education and training, and as a result has quickly developed a well-educated and skilled workforce. Indonesia, starting from much further back and with much greater obstacles to overcome, has made progress, but levels of education remain so low that they will continue to be an impediment to economic development for some time to come. Between 1980 and 1997 the proportion of the relevant population age group enrolled in secondary education rose from 30 per cent to 49 per cent, while the proportion of the relevant age group enrolled in post-secondary education rose from 4 per cent to only 11 per cent. For a nation aspiring to self-reliance in science and technology and the development of advanced industries, this remains a huge obstacle.[33]

What the Indonesian case shows is that there are limits to the speed-up of technological development. This kind of development, it is good to remind ourselves, is not so much a question of the acquisition of hardware as the accumulation of know-how, the development of knowledge and skills, techniques, methods, systems. An increase in know-how can be accelerated only so far, because technical knowledge, like other sorts of knowledge, is cumulative and dependent on things previously learnt. This is one reason why the South Korean government, despite the country's rapid technological and economic growth, remains anxious that its workforce is not acquiring enough of the skills needed to be internationally competitive.[34]

Yet Indonesia's technologs identified a crucial issue. Third World countries have found that the technological and economic gap separating them from developed nations is growing rather than shrinking. Many experts in Third World development and technology transfer have reached the conclusion that, with a few exceptions, it will be impossible for developing nations ever to catch up. The reason is that Western science and technology, seen by all advocates of development as the basis of hope, are not things that can be easily or quickly transplanted. More and more it is being understood that technology transfer, which is central to economic and social development, has to entail must more than the acquisition of hardware. If the modes of understanding, techniques, know-how, organisational systems and so on that constitute Western science and technology are not mastered and internalised, then Third World development based upon science and technology is no more than a mirage. 'Technology transfer is first and foremost the transfer of culture.'[35]

Taken far enough this argument reduces to absurdity: if cultures had to be transferred in their entirety, technology transfer would be a historical impossibility. Recognition of the fact that technology transfer is much more complicated than has commonly been believed, that its success depends on extensive and subtle learning processes, should not be allowed to lead to the conclusion that it is impossible. The benefits of science and technology seem to be a mirage only to those looking for instant technological fixes. Technological shortcuts *are* possible, but even shortcuts take time. This is why Indonesia's technologs were correct in pushing ahead with sophisticated technologies even when the direct economic returns were uncertain. Building up an advanced technological capacity is an extended undertaking. While learning by doing can speed things up, as the Korean steel industry has shown, there is a limit to the rate at which knowledge can be absorbed and skills acquired. With scientific and technological understanding advancing as rapidly as they are, delaying entry into sophisticated technological fields is likely to reduce the possibility of future catch-up even further.

## The Confucian development model

Economic success always sparks the search for a general rule or formula that will enable it to be replicated elsewhere. Sometimes the formula identified is not easily transferable. The success of Japan and the 'four dragons' has led some to look for an explanation in the cultural characteristics they have in common—in particular, their shared Confucian heritage.

Most of these explanations focus on the group aspect or collectivist values of Confucianism. The active role played by the state in economic affairs is explained in the paternalistic terms characteristic of Confucian political thought: the supreme authority acts to secure the welfare of the people, who in turn offer loyalty and support to the state. There is an emphasis on order, discipline, respect for authority. It is argued, for example, that business organisations are efficient and effective in East Asia because their members are more responsive to the needs and demands of the group than are individualistic Westerners. The Confucian values of East Asian bosses are said to make them more alert to and considerate of the needs of their workers, while the workers are obedient and mindful of authority. In other words, the Confucian view of society as a system of hierarchical relationships entailing mutual obligations is particularly well suited to the needs of modern economic organisation and industrial production.

Other explanations focus on the capacity of East Asians for hard work. Chinese, Japanese, and Korean workers, we are told, have been toughened by history. They have been willing to work long hours for little reward. Moreover, success in achieving wealth and high status has always been regarded as bringing glory to one's ancestors, and therefore ancestor-worshipping Confucians have an additional motivation for industry and thrift not to be found among Westerners. What we get, in other words, is a Confucian version of Max Weber's thesis on Protestantism and the rise of capitalism.

To establish links between economic success in modern East Asian societies and something that may with some degree of historical accuracy be labelled Confucianism is by no means straightforward, especially since the impact of Confucian ideology and institutions in each of the countries in question has been far from uniform. Further, knowledge that the continuing influence of Confucianism in the late nineteenth and early twentieth centuries has been widely blamed for China's failure to compete with Western powers and with Japan does not make one enthusiastic about trying.[36]

Some of the aspects of the 'Confucian' tradition that may most plausibly be referred to when trying to account for the economic success of contemporary East Asian countries historically arose in opposition to Confucianism. State involvement in economic production, for example, was opposed by Confucian scholars from earliest times. In the so-called 'salt and iron debates' at the Chinese imperial court in 81 BCE, they argued strongly against the economic interventionist role espoused by the leading officials of the day. The latter were strongly influenced by principles and techniques of government espoused by the Legalist thinkers such as Shang Yang (died 338 BCE) and Han Fei (died 233 BCE), who dismissed Confucian ideas of rule by the influence of virtue as hopelessly idealistic. Instead, these thinkers advocated vigorous administration based on clear delineation and scrupulous fulfilment of government functions, in accordance with a rigorously applied code of laws. If ideas regarding the influence of Confucianism have any plausibility, it is in relation to China's long and sophisticated tradition of administration and institution-building. Confucianism may have provided the ideals in the name of which the system operated, but many of the institutions and organisational techniques that proved so durable and were exported to the other countries of East Asia owe more to other elements of the Chinese tradition. An important exception is the civil service examination system, which is undoubtedly a factor behind the value attached to formal education in post-Confucian societies, both by the state in terms of human resource development and by individuals as a path to wealth and status.

Arguments that locate the decisive influence of Confucianism in the family rather than the operations of the state may claim support from the fact that ethnic Chinese communities in South-East Asian countries are relatively successful in business even where there is no question of Confucian influence in government, as in Thailand, Malaysia, and Indonesia. This economic success of ethnic Chinese regardless of government direction strengthens the case of those who claim that it is the group orientation of Confucian values that is decisive, in particular their strong family focus. Two historical characteristics of the Confucian family have been the multiplicity of functions it has served and its highly institutionalised nature, which have enabled it to provide support and direction in times when political order has been largely non-existent. It is the resilience it has given the family as an institution that accounts for much of the strength of the Confucian tradition. The majority of firms even in Japan and Korea remain family enterprises that in their operation are able to draw on strong traditions of family-based economic production.[37]

In the end, however, we have to ask just how distinctive Confucianism can claim to be in this regard. Family-based economic production is a characteristic of most pre-modern societies. The Arabs, for example, may also claim a tradition of sophisticated economic techniques and institutions, as well as special motivation to succeed because, as in the case of Protestants, success is regarded as evidence of God's favour. Yet few claim that Arabs are destined by their commercial traditions for economic success in the modern world.

Explanations of the rash of economic miracles in East and South-East Asia must include factors other than Confucian influences. The wider context in which they have occurred—which we may or may not want to label a world system—cannot be ignored. The impact of cold war politics, for example, was strong. Given the preoccupation, especially of the United States, with the containment of communism, it is unlikely to be just coincidence that Japan and the 'four dragons' have been bastions of anti-communism.

Japan, South Korea, and Taiwan have benefited from close economic links with the United States. Japan's economy was boosted by the Korean War; Korea's economy was boosted by the Vietnam War. China's political and economic isolation until the 1970s left the way open for other East Asian countries to move ahead. Hong Kong's position as a colonial pimple on a communist pumpkin helped it to obtain cheap and industrious labour while making the most of the nascent capitalism across the border. We cannot overlook the fact that if some countries succeed it is because others fail or are prevented from competing. Nations are not necessarily free agents any more than individuals are; they can only make the most of the opportunities available. Those opportunities are determined to a large extent by the power relations between nations.

## Developing autonomy

Development is a conceptual swamp. This key word is so deceptive that when we think it offers solid ground to stand on we soon find ourselves in mud up to our necks. It owes much of its appeal to the way it is able to envelop any aspect of the modern world seen as desirable. In fact, it often seems no more than another way of saying 'modern and desirable', so it is little wonder that it becomes difficult to argue that development is not a good thing. There is the further complication that, as well as meaning something like 'progress' or 'evolution', in conventional usage the term also designates a state or threshold that, once attained, is there for good. 'Developed' countries are those that have achieved the state of bliss; 'developing' countries are still moving towards it. Because 'developed' sometimes means 'industrialised', the illusion can be created that once, say, Vietnam or India has achieved developed status, it will have caught up with other developed countries such as France or Japan. Of course there is no magic threshold, and by the time developing countries reach what may now appear to be one, the developed countries will have moved on again.

There are any number of economic and social development paths that nations may follow. Neoclassical economic principles, it is clear, are not the only plausible guide to the route. Frequently they have shown themselves to be downright dangerous, with some key directions having been omitted. East Asian countries have shown that for effective economic and social development the state must play a leading role. The state cannot be an adequate substitute for the private sector, but neither can the private sector be a substitute for the state. It is all too easy, in an orderly and stable socio-political system, to take for granted everything that the state does, and to take seriously claims that it makes no positive contribution to social and economic well-being. However, that would be totally to misconstrue history and the liberalist philosophy it is alleged to validate. Government support and control are indispensable for a flourishing private sector, and this has always been so:

> Neoliberal ideologues see the state as parasitic, as a non-productive sector that makes little or no positive contribution to society's well-being. They are wrong. As Adam Smith repeatedly stresses, government does add value to commercial affairs. Whatever the tenets of economic fundamentalism are, the best thing the state can do for the private sector is not always just to get out of the way. There are too many things that are easier to do collectively, such as maintaining a system of laws for economic exchange, providing new technology, building infrastructure, assuring mass education. These functions are essential to a well-run capitalist economy. For markets to thrive, sometimes the state must be reinforced, not dismantled.[38]

The same conclusion was driven home in relation to the global market by the 1997–98 Asian financial crisis, which showed graphically the economic and social costs of inadequate transparency and effective regulation of international currency trading and investment. There is no natural or inevitable flow-on from economic development to social or human development. The state has to *make* it happen. Moreover, the examples of Sri Lanka, Kerala, and China show that a state can make human development happen even without rapid industrialisation or strong economic growth. The negative concept of the state prominent in neoclassical economics is the same one that prevails in a lot of thinking on human rights. The state is seen essentially as something that sets limits, as a constraint on individual liberty. Human rights law, in turn, places constraints on the power of the state. The positives are taken for granted: morality, social order, civic institutions, religion. These things are regarded as the products of reason, custom and civil society, and not of the secular state. But those who do not regard the state as secular, or do not take morality and order as given, naturally find a negative concept of the state troubling. They are also less inhibited when it comes to reflecting on economic roles for the state.

There is a striking parallel between neoclassical advocates of economic development and spokesmen for authoritarian government (communist or post-Confucian) who claim that economic development must take priority over human rights. Both groups have a reductionist vision in which the single path to a better existence is paved by economics. Oddly enough, many of those concerned about human rights in Third World countries are also keen to speed up economic development there, and even to force it on people against their will because it is in their best interests. A US general observed in 1900, when suppressing anti-American resistance in the Philippines, that 'it may be necessary to kill half the Filipinos in order that the remaining half may be advanced to a higher plane of life than their present semi-barbarous state affords'. More recently, a senior official of a North African country reassured the UN National Assembly: 'If we have to we will drive our people to paradise with sticks, we will do so for their good and for the good of those who come after us'.[39]

In the second half of the twentieth century, peoples of the Third World were asked to make many sacrifices in the name of development. They continue to be told that those sacrifices are necessary if their long-term needs are to be met. Personal and political liberty often count among the things to be sacrificed. Yet the basic human needs development is supposed to satisfy include freedom. The way freedom is conceived and the value attached to it are subject to cultural influences. Yet people want to be in control of their own affairs, to make, or at least to be able to participate in, the decisions affecting their lives and the lives of those they care for. If human development means anything, it means enlarging the autonomy people have, not necessarily in an individualistic way, but in terms of acquiring the human resources, skills and knowledge that make it possible to live responsibly and with dignity. This is a point argued convincingly by Amartya Sen and the authors of the human development reports.

Choice, being in control, empowerment, autonomy: call it what you will, it has to be specifically identified as part of the development process rather than being seen as a goal to which development may or may not lead. Autonomy, or being in control, means that although governments, experts and international agencies may give essential leadership and advice, ordinary people must be able to participate in making decisions and carrying them out. We have to develop ourselves. No one else can do it for us.

CHAPTER SIX

# Patterns of Population Change

## The scale of change

Demographic movements since the nineteenth century can only be described as awesome. No matter how detached or objective we try to remain, it is hard not to respond emotively to the population changes taking place. They have massive implications, not just for humanity, but for all life on the planet. The phrase 'turning-point in history' is a terrible cliché, yet in this context it is unavoidable.

Undoubtedly the most dramatic aspect of demographic change is the rate at which the world's population is growing. It is estimated that in 1650 it was about 600 million, and that it did not reach 1 billion until around 1804. While it had taken all of human history to reach the 1 billion mark, it took only another 123 years to reach 2 billion, in 1927. The third billion was reached thirty-three years later, in 1960; the fourth billion fourteen years later, in 1974; and the fifth billion thirteen years after that, in 1987. In October 1999, the total world population was officially declared to have reached 6 billion.

At present the world population is increasing at a rate of around 9000 people per hour, or 78 million per year. Even if the total fertility rate of all females in the world were to fall immediately to replacement level, the population would still continue to rise for many years to come. This is because the rapid growth of recent decades has resulted in a greater proportion of young people in the population, and hence a sharp increase in the number of females who will be having children in the years to come. For example, although Japan achieved replacement fertility in 1957, its population will not stabilise until 2006. Present projections have the world population reaching between 7.3 billion and 10.7 billion around the year 2050, with a figure of around 8.9 billion considered the most likely. Longer-term projections put the total at about 12 billion by 2100, with a peak being reached some time later in that century.[1]

When we shift our attention from the global picture to what is happening in particular Asian countries, the figures are no less dramatic. However, their impact has to do with much more than just population growth. Some of the most important figures are set out in Table 6.1.

Six of the ten most populous countries in the world are in Asia. According to 1998 population estimates, China has 21 per cent of the world population, India has 16.6 per cent, and Indonesia has 3.5 per cent. (According to census figures, in November 2000 China had a population of 1.266 billion—or 1.295 billion including Hong Kong, Macau, and Taiwan. In February 2001 India had a population of 1.027 billion. Indonesia's population stood at 203 million people in July 2000). Pakistan, Bangladesh, and Japan each have more than 2 per cent of the world population; while Vietnam, the Philippines, Iran, and Thailand each have more than 1 per cent.

Bangladesh has by far the highest population density of any Asian country except the city state of Singapore and the Hong Kong Special Autonomous Region. At 963 people per square kilometre, it is roughly twice that of Taiwan and South Korea, about three times that of Japan and India, and around eight times that of China and Indonesia. These comparisons may be misleading, however, if we fail to take into account other factors, such as the proportion of national territory suitable for agriculture (arable land) and the proportion of the population living in urban areas. For example, while

**Table 6.1** Population of selected Asian countries

| | *Estimated population 1998 (millions)* | *Population density 1998 (per km²)* | *Arable land (%)* | *Annual population growth (%) 1975–98* | *Projected annual population growth (%) 1998–2015* | *Urban population as % of total* |
|---|---|---|---|---|---|---|
| Afghanistan | 21.4 | 34 | 12 | n.a. | n.a. | n.a. |
| Bangladesh | 124.8 | 960 | 70 | 2.1 | 1.5 | 20 |
| Brunei | 0.3 | 57 | 1 | 3.0 | 1.6 | |
| Cambodia | 10.7 | 60 | 14 | 1.8 | 1.8 | 22 |
| China | 1255.7 | 135 | 10 | 1.3 | 0.7 | 33 |
| Hong Kong | 6.7 | 6251 | 7 | 1.8 | 0.8 | 95 |
| India | 982.2 | 330 | 57 | 2.0 | 1.2 | 28 |
| Indonesia | 206.3 | 114 | 12 | 1.8 | 1.1 | 38 |
| Iran | 65.8 | 40 | 11 | 3.0 | 1.4 | 61 |
| Japan | 126.3 | 335 | 12 | 0.5 | 0.0 | 79 |
| Laos | 5.2 | 22 | 4 | 2.4 | 2.4 | 22 |
| Malaysia | 21.4 | 65 | 15 | 2.5 | 1.5 | 56 |
| Mongolia | 2.6 | 2 | 1 | 2.5 | 1.5 | 62 |
| Myanmar | 44.5 | 67 | 15 | 1.7 | 1.1 | 27 |
| Nepal | 22.9 | 168 | 17 | 2.6 | 2.1 | 11 |
| North Korea | 23.4 | 195 | 17 | n.a. | n.a. | n.a. |
| Pakistan | 148.2 | 192 | 27 | 3.0 | 2.4 | 36 |
| Philippines | 72.9 | 243 | 31 | 2.3 | 1.7 | 57 |
| Singapore | 3.5 | 5601 | 2 | 1.9 | 0.8 | 100 |
| South Korea | 46.1 | 465 | 21 | 1.2 | 0.6 | 84 |
| Sri Lanka | 18.5 | 285 | 30 | 1.3 | 1.0 | 23 |
| Thailand | 60.3 | 118 | 39 | 1.7 | 0.8 | 21 |
| Vietnam | 77.6 | 239 | 21 | 2.1 | 1.3 | 20 |

Source: Department of Economic and Social Affairs, United Nations Population Division, *Revision of the World Population Estimates and Projections (1998)*, http://www.popin.org/pop1998/; United Nations Development Program, *Human Development Report 2000*, Oxford University Press, New York, 2000, 224–6; World Bank, *Entering the 21st Century: World Development Report 1999/2000*, Oxford University Press, New York, 2000, 230–1.

Bangladesh has a population density more than seven times that of China, the proportion of arable land in Bangladesh is also almost seven times that in China. In effect, therefore, the two factors cancel each other out.

On the other hand, in Japan the proportion of arable land is nearly as low as it is in China, while the population density is much higher, indicating much more severe pressure on land. Japan's ability to cope with this pressure can be understood largely in terms of its higher degree of urbanisation (79 per cent) and industrialisation. South Korea's population density is even higher than that of Japan. Again, this can be accommodated thanks to a combination of a higher proportion of arable land and a higher level of urbanisation. In Indonesia, regional differences in population density are extreme. In 2000, 52 per cent of the national population was squeezed onto the island of Java, which constitutes only 7 per cent of the land area. By contrast, West Papua had 22 per cent of the land area but less than 1 per cent of the population.

In terms of actual population growth, India rather than China is registering the highest figures. For, while China has a larger population than India, its fertility rate has fallen sharply and is much lower than the Indian rate. On current trends, by 2035 India will have taken China's place as the most populous country on earth.

Although India is at present registering the greatest increases in population, some Asian countries are expected to continue to have higher population growth *rates* during the first decade of the twenty-first century. These include Pakistan, which is expected to overtake Brazil by the year 2020 to become the fifth-largest country of the world in terms of population; and Bangladesh, which is expected to displace Russia as the sixth-largest country in population terms. Other Asian countries that will continue to have relatively high rates of population increase are Cambodia, Laos, Nepal, and the Philippines. The lowest growth rates since 1975 have been in Japan, South Korea, China, and Sri Lanka. In these, as in almost all Asian countries, population growth rates are expected to continue to decrease during the next decade.[2]

Working the fertile soil of Bangladesh: rice-planting by women of the Santal minority.

## Population control and the state

In a world where population pressures are rising on an unprecedented scale, it is hardly surprising that the overriding concern of governments and international organisations is to reduce them, to slow population growth and, where necessary, to bring it to an end. Historically, however, the reduction of human fertility is not something in which the state has taken an interest. On the contrary, in most large-scale, hierarchical societies the state has regarded population growth as a good thing. More people meant greater strength in the form of soldiers and more wealth in the form of taxes. On the other hand, control of fertility appears always to have been a matter of concern for private individuals. The range of substances used to control fertility through the ages is testimony to both human ingenuity and the urgency with which the matter was regarded.[3]

However fascinating the history of contraception or strong the drive of modern states and agencies to control population growth through contraception, there is widespread disagreement regarding its contribution in this regard. Demographers emphasise that, throughout history, even high levels of fertility have fallen well short of what has been called 'unrestrained fertility', the rate of reproduction that is biologically possible in the absence of controlling mechanisms.

While the controls available appear generally to have included contraceptive measures, these cannot have been used as widely as was possible. It is argued that much more significant in reducing fertility has been the impact of social rules and practices relating to marriage, intercourse, and child-rearing. A high marriage age together with strict prohibition of premarital sex, for example, reduces the length of time during which a woman is likely to bear children. Similarly, the spacing of children is strongly influenced by breastfeeding customs, since lactation suppresses ovulation. Customs regarding frequency of intercourse, sexual abstinence, abortion, infanticide, remarriage of widows, and religious celibacy also affect birth rates. Whether social rules or customs have ever been framed with the conscious purpose of limiting fertility is debatable. There is evidence from many societies, however, that some rules, such as the age at which young people may marry, have tended to change quickly in response to shifting social and economic circumstances. Some analysts argue that if, until recently, populations have remained more or less stable, this has been because of the restraining effect of social rules and customs rather than high mortality rates. Societies have had mechanisms for limiting population growth because it has been a matter of ecological necessity to have them.

These sorts of considerations have led some to argue that the state has no role to play in controlling fertility. Especially when faced with state population control programs that involve, or have involved, coercion, such as those in China and India, many are inclined to adopt the position that intercourse, contraception and child-bearing are private matters in which decisions should be made only by the couple in question, guided by the relevant norms of their society. When fertility declined sharply in Western societies during the nineteenth and early twentieth centuries it did so without state intervention or fertility control programs. What then is the need for state action to limit population growth in developing countries? The position taken on this issue will be influenced by the way declines in fertility are explained.

## Explaining fertility decline

Fertility control as an area of government policy and international activity is part of the global political order that emerged after the Second World War. Under the leadership of the United States, the UN articulated the goal of global development, which would be achieved through international cooperation and the removal of obstacles to economic and social well-being through the application of modern science and technology. When framing the development agenda, experts persuaded Third World governments that one of the biggest obstacles to economic development was rapid population growth of the sort many of those countries were experiencing. Countries with rapidly growing populations, it was argued, would not be able to direct their resources to economic development because the resources would be consumed in meeting needs such as health care, housing, water and sewerage systems, education, and welfare. The World Bank and the IMF, the main funders of development projects in the Third World, included in their list of conditions for loan approval the implementation of fertility control programs by governments seeking funds.

The view of unchecked population growth as a cause of poverty and underdevelopment was the conventional wisdom of the time, widely believed to have been confirmed by the experience of Western countries. After all, it was surely no coincidence that the rich industrialised countries were also those that had greatly reduced their fertility rates. It was a view, what is more, that had been part of the mainstream of Western thought since the publication of Thomas Malthus' work, *An Essay on the Principle of Population*, in 1798. Malthus argued that unchecked population growth leads to scarcity because 'the power of population is infinitely greater than the power of the earth to produce sustenance for man'. Scarcity in turn leads to a fierce 'struggle for existence', an idea that helped to inspire Charles Darwin's theory of the origin of species through natural selection. In the second (1803) edition of his essay Malthus emphasised the power of human inventiveness to improve the lot of humanity, while arguing reasonably that there are definite limits to what the earth can sustain. However, he did not regard contraception as a morally acceptable form of innovation. As far as he was concerned, moral and legal constraints were the means by which natural checks on population growth should be reinforced.[4]

In itself, the argument that unchecked population growth puts strain on natural resources and thereby poses a threat to the well-being of the population is neither particularly modern nor particularly Western. There seems to be a tacit recognition of the problem underlying the apparently universal use of social rules and customs to keep fertility well below its natural limits. In Malthus' own lifetime similar views were being expressed in China. Whereas in Europe at the end of the eighteenth century population pressure was a largely theoretical issue, in China its strains had begun to affect the welfare of the people. Over the centuries, technological advances and territorial expansion at the expense of indigenous minorities had enabled the Chinese population to expand. But by the late eighteenth century territorial expansion had more or less stopped, technological innovation had stalled, and government administration had begun to decline. In 1793 the scholar Hong Liangji wrote that to protect the welfare of the people the population of the empire had to be limited. It was a view shared by Wang Shiduo, who advocated a range of measures to decrease fertility, including raising the marriage age, more nunneries, prohibiting the remarriage of widows, punitive taxation of families with more than two children, sterilisation of women, and female infanticide.[5]

According to the Malthusian interpretation, population growth is the outcome of a human sexual urge that carries with it only limited interest in the procreative consequences of the action. This leads easily to the view that all that is holding most couples back from having fewer children is a lack of reliable contraception, and that, if the means of preventing pregnancy are available, couples will use them. This is why priority must be placed on family planning programs: governments have to make sure that cheap and reliable contraceptives are widely available, and then, in theory, the problem will be solved. Unfortunately reality does not always accord with theory.

During the 1960s and 1970s the view of high fertility as a cause of poverty and underdevelopment was increasingly called into question, partly because of the perceived failure of the family planning programs that had been introduced in Third World countries to have much effect. Symptomatic of shifting opinion was the adoption at the United Nations Population Conference in Bucharest in 1974 of the slogan 'development is the best contraceptive'. The phrase expressed the conclusion reached by many, that the low fertility rates of Western countries and Japan were the result rather than the cause of the economic and social development those countries had undergone, and that the best way to reduce fertility in Third World countries would be to bring about similar levels of development. Only then would Third World couples have reason to be satisfied with fewer children.

The fertile earth, or just a hysterical pregnancy? On the occasion of the World Population Conference, Cairo, September 1994.

According to this interpretation, parents in pre-modern or underdeveloped societies are well aware that having fewer children means having fewer mouths to feed and smaller demands on family resources. The fact is that under the conditions that prevail for most people in such societies—where economic production is family-based, where children are the only source of care and support for the elderly, and child mortality rates are high—having a large number of children has traditionally been the only way of ensuring sufficient labour for the family's needs and security for the parents in their old age. In such a society there are good reasons for not reducing fertility even when the means of contraception are available.

In developed countries, the argument goes, the circumstances that encourage high fertility have been removed. Industrialisation reduces the role of the family in economic production and increases the need for formal education and training. Accordingly, the free and largely unskilled labour of children offers little economic advantage. Modern health care, housing, sanitation, and improved nutrition mean that child mortality rates are low. Compulsory schooling and formal education extend the period of dependence of children on the parents and increase the cost of bringing them up. The education of women and the availability of a wider range of skilled employment opportunities outside the home mean that there are potentially rewarding alternatives to the role of full-time mother and housewife. The existence of state-funded social security systems means that even those who have no children need not be dependent on charity in retirement. Under such circumstances there are good reasons for couples to make use of whatever contraceptive means are available and to have only a small number of children.

## Demographic transition theory

Support for the idea that low fertility is the result rather than the cause of economic well-being owes a lot to the influence of what is known as demographic transition theory. Demographic transition refers to the shift from a high death rate and high birth rate to a low death rate and a low birth rate. This has been seen as characteristic of societies undergoing industrialisation and urbanisation. The fall in death rates results in rising population levels until the birth rates fall too and demographic stability re-establishes itself. This pattern has been identified in the experience of the United States, Canada, Australia, New Zealand, and north-western Europe in the late nineteenth and early twentieth centuries, and not much later in the remainder of Europe and Japan.

To account for the fall in death rates is easy; it is much harder to explain the fall in birth rates. Those associated with the theory have tended to explain reduced fertility largely in terms of economic influences, while leaving some room for cultural factors as well. For example, the US demographer Kingsley Davis identifies 'household economic strain' as the most significant factor leading to efforts to reduce fertility through contraception and other means. It is the need to reduce economic strain or, positively, to take advantage of the opportunities resulting from the modernisation process to improve the household's economic situation, that motivates individuals or families to have fewer children. Davis rejects cultural explanations of demographic change because of what he regards as the circularity of the arguments: patterns of behaviour are 'explained' as the result of cultural preferences for those sorts of behaviour. This capacity of the concept of culture to serve up non-explanations is something we have encountered before. However, it is not a reason for disregarding the possible influence of the wide range of things that are put under that heading.

Later modifications of transition theory have given more weight to the place of cultural and structural factors in changing patterns of fertility. For example, economic and cultural factors are mixed in the Australian demographer Jack Caldwell's theory of intergenerational wealth flows. While the basic mechanism of the theory is still economic, its operation has to be understood in terms of broader cultural change. According to Caldwell, couples begin to have fewer children when wealth ceases to flow from children to their parents and starts to flow instead from the parents to the children, that is, when children become an economic burden rather than an asset. The shift away from family-based production to modern industrial organisation, according to Caldwell, is accompanied by the 'emotional nucleation' of family life. This includes greater importance being placed on the bond between husband and wife, and on the obligations of the parents towards their children. It is a trend that has spread to Asian countries and other parts of the world as an element of Western cultural influence generally, reinforced by the spread of innovations such as mass education.[6]

Since the 1970s the theory of demographic transition has come under strong criticism, partly because of a tendency on the part of those associated with it to want to have their cake and eat it too. For example, while Frank Notestein and Kingsley Davis reached the conclusion that demographic transition was an outcome of a complex process of economic and social modernisation, this did not stop them from advocating family planning programs in Third World countries in advance of the economic and social transformation supposed to be the precondition of changed fertility behaviour. The causal links between demographic change and socio-economic change came to be so flexibly interpreted that the theory became, according to one study of the history of demographic thought, 'empirically irrefutable'.[7]

A large number of studies in developed and in Third World countries have found that the links between certain sorts of socio-economic change and reduced fertility are in fact far from uniform. Detailed historical studies have shown that fertility began to decline at the same time in a number of European countries despite the fact that their social and economic circumstances varied widely. In some cases fertility began to fall in advance of any signs of decreasing mortality. Fluctuations in fertility in developed countries, such as the postwar baby boom, are difficult for the theory to accommodate. Similarly, historical studies and recent experience in developing countries have shown that in some cases fertility has fallen without any significant change in socio-economic circumstances, while in others fertility has remained high despite expectations on socio-economic grounds that it would fall. According to one widely held view, much of the variation in the timing and extent of fertility reduction may be attributed to the ways in which knowledge of contraceptive techniques has spread through populations. Sri Lanka and Bangladesh are good examples.

According to conventional economic measures Sri Lanka remains relatively poor, yet its birth rate and total fertility compare favourably with those of much wealthier developing countries. By the turn of the century Sri Lanka had achieved replacement fertility levels. The explanation appears to lie on the one hand with Sri Lanka's high level of human development relative to economic development, and on the other the relatively low degree of gender inequality there. Family planning did not become a national policy until 1965, but when introduced it was done in the context of a comprehensive maternal and child health care program, with a strong emphasis on information, education and communication to make it acceptable. Marriage postponement was encouraged, a variety of contraceptives were made widely available, and sterilisation was encouraged with cash incentives. At the same time, high levels of female literacy and educational attainment were achieved, along with wider participation by women in formal and informal economic activities.

Like Sri Lanka, Bangladesh has experienced only limited economic growth, industrialisation and urbanisation, and further has the problems of relatively low status for women, low female literacy and educational attainment, and limited economic participation by women. Yet here too birth rate and total fertility rate have dropped substantially since the mid-1970s. It has been suggested that falling living standards for most of the 1970s and 1980s may be part of the explanation, together with lower child mortality leading to extended overall breastfeeding and amenorrhoea (suppressed ovulation). Recent analyses leave little doubt, however, that the biggest factor has been wide acceptance of family planning through a national program integrated with primary health care services and rural poverty alleviation programs.[8]

The experience of neither Sri Lanka nor Bangladesh can be explained easily in terms of demographic transition theory. The same is true of the evidence collected by Virginia Abernethy in her survey of population trends around the world. Abernethy concludes that fertility rises and falls in response to levels of 'perceived opportunity' for reproduction. Historically, lower child mortality has prompted higher birth rates, not lower ones. Essentially, human beings are like other animals. The signals they receive from their environment influences their reproductive behaviour. Where they differ is in the fact that the environment to which they respond is cultural as well as 'natural'. When circumstances are promising, human fertility rises; when circumstances are poor or deteriorating, fertility falls. According to this interpretation humans are rather like kangaroos: in times of plenty they give birth to one young after another, but in times of drought the process is suspended and reproduction waits until better times return.[9]

Such a pattern is at odds with classic formulations of demographic transition theory. Improved circumstances lead to higher rather than lower fertility. Optimism about the future, a sense of living in fortunate times, material satisfaction and political security—these things produce a 'euphoria effect' and encourage people to have more rather than fewer children. (For this reason, as the eighteenth-century scholar Hong Liangji observed, the consequences of long periods of peace and security are to be feared no less than times of violence and instability.) The political and social implications of such a pattern could be grim. It implies that efforts to improve the circumstances under which populations live will be counterproductive unless steps are also taken to limit population growth by new or traditional means. In Third World countries, international aid and development programs will only make things worse, argues Abernethy, if 'they get in the way of people's correctly interpreting negative signals from the environment'. In other words, international aid frees Third World peoples from the ecological consequences of copulation. This could be a basis for savage politics.

The fact that improved socio-economic circumstances or environments have been found to both increase and decrease fertility suggests, at the very least, that while material or economic circumstances certainly affect fertility, how they affect it is influenced by other factors peculiar to the case in question, that is, cultural and structural factors, as well as diffusion of contraceptive techniques. Therefore the environment in which fertility changes has to be understood broadly enough to include such factors. It cannot be assumed that they can be reduced to other, more basic considerations, such as economic factors. What count as 'perceived opportunities' and 'negative signals' need to be understood in culture-specific ways.

If demographic transition theory is so beset by contradictory evidence and interpretations, why has it been so influential? Part of the explanation is that it seemed to offer a straightforward explanation of a wide range of social phenomena, which is what social scientists look for in a theory, and in many cases—at least at first—the explanation looked convincing. Moreover there was no attractive alternative theory to challenge it. This remains the situation, which helps to explain why there has been such reluctance to jettison it. However, part of the theory's attractiveness for social scientists in developed countries also lies in the fact that it translates into demographic terms assumptions about the advanced nature of Western societies *vis-à-vis* the rest of the world. Having led the way to industrialisation and modernity, according to the theory, Western nations were the first to achieve stable populations based on low mortality and low fertility. Demographic transition provided another reason why other nations could only follow where the West had led. Part and parcel of development theory, in other words, was a demonstration of Western superiority.

This sort of predilection is present in a lot of demographic writing.[10] Even those well informed and sensitive to cultural differences find it hard to avoid. Caldwell, for example, suggests that a Western-style nuclear family will become the norm as the Third World develops, with emphasis on a close, affectionate bond between husband and wife, and the obligation of parents to meet the material and emotional needs of their children. Such predictions ignore that, in statistical terms, the nuclear family or simple household appears in recent history to have been the dominant domestic arrangement in most Asian societies, particularly among the poor who could be expected most keenly to pursue the economic benefits large families are supposed to bring.

There is in fact evidence that a convergence of family structure is not occurring, that despite industrialisation, urbanisation and widespread Western cultural influences, in many societies distinctive types of family structure persist basically unchanged. (These issues are discussed further in Chapter 8.) Further, demographic transition theory and responses to it such as Caldwell's can lead all too easily to the conclusion that it is only well-to-do parents in developed countries who really love and care for their children. Only they have children because they want them, not because they need them. In Third World countries, we are told, children are regarded primarily as a source of labour and old-age security. Because of high infant and child mortality they need to be looked upon as a renewable resource rather than as individuals to be cherished in their own right.

There is evidence that poor parents in Third World countries do not necessarily regard children in this way. Some studies have found that high child mortality does not encourage women to have more babies. If anything, it has the opposite effect: women who have lost children are less likely to try again than those who have not. That children may bring economic advantages to the family unit does not mean that the emotional bonds between them and their parents are less strong, or that the parents learn to love their children by becoming Westernised. Even if parents mention labour needs or old-age security as reasons for wanting children, it does not mean that bonds of affection will not develop when they actually have them.[11]

## Cultural factors

The links between cultural, economic, and other sorts of factors in fertility change need further consideration. In particular, the idea of culture needs clarifying if it is to be useful in this context. The term 'socio-economic' tends to move around too in explanations of demographic change. Sometimes it is hard to know where the cultural, social and economic categories end and what degree of overlap there is between them. The following statement illustrates some of the problems that occur in writing on demography:

> In recent years, in the absence of a clear association between socio-economic development and the time of fertility decline, several different causal mechanisms have been proposed to explain the initiation of fertility decline. These mechanisms include modern ideas and aspirations, cultural factors, women's rights, transport and communications networks, modern systems of mass education, and the adoption and diffusion of contraception.[12]

Presumably here 'culture' excludes modern ideas and aspirations, women's rights and mass education; it also appears to exclude social and economic change. It seems to mean something like 'fundamental beliefs and values shared by members of a society that are traditional and unchanging' or 'religious and moral verities'.

As argued in Chapter 2, there are problems with a concept of culture that leaves out a large segment of human experience, such as economics, because it is regarded as the domain of a particular discipline, or, more particularly, because its laws and principles are claimed to exist outside cultural influences. But if the anonymous rational actor of universal economic theory fails to offer a convincing way of understanding behaviour, so too do the cultural relativists in their splendidly varied folk costumes.

Explaining India's population growth by reference to Hindu and Muslim values, for example, loses much of its initial plausibility once regional differences within India are considered. In 1991 India's total fertility rate (that is, the estimated average number of births a woman has, according to current birth rates) was 3.6. In the southern state of Kerala, however, it was 1.8, well below replacement level, compared with 5.2 and 3.1 respectively in the northern states of Uttar Pradesh and Punjab. In Tamil Nadu, another southern state, total fertility was also relatively low at 2.2. Some scholars point out that women in southern India generally have higher status and more autonomy than those in northern India, which they relate to the continuation of ancient Dravidian cultural values there, undisturbed by the periodic foreign invasions of the north.[13] While regional differences in culture certainly are a factor, there is more to it than this.

In Kerala as in Sri Lanka, reduction in fertility has coincided with a high level of human development despite low economic development. Compared with other parts of India, until recently Kerala had little industry and low income levels, yet it has the best public health, education, and welfare of any of the Indian states. Life expectancies are the highest in India and compare favourably with those of developed countries. The ratio of females to males in the population, unlike that in other parts of India, is similar to that of countries with relatively little gender inequality. The marriage age is high and infant mortality is low. Female literacy and school participation rates are the highest in India, and customary constraints on women's education have all but disappeared. The same applies to involvement by women in public life. Where Kerala has not scored particularly well is in relation to university education and workforce participation, which has reflected the state's relatively low level of economic development. In general, therefore, Kerala appears to provide strong support for the UN Population Fund's conclusion that women's education and health care are crucial for limiting the size of families.[14] The regional differences in demographic behaviour in India demonstrate the need to consider regional and local social, political and economic circumstances, in addition to underlying cultural influences.

Another useful illustration of the inadequacy of broad cultural explanations of fertility change is that of the Malay populations of Indonesia, Malaysia, and Singapore. Since the 1960s all three populations have experienced a decline in fertility, along with economic and social development. In Singapore, however, Malay fertility fell extremely sharply, while among the Malay population of peninsular Malaysia it has remained high in comparison with both Indonesian Malays and Malaysian Chinese. Yet economically Malaysia is much better off than Indonesia.

To understand this, political and social factors have to be considered as well as economic and cultural ones. Central to understanding fertility change in Malaysia are the tensions between the politically dominant Malays and the economically dominant Chinese and Indians. Government policies since the early 1970s have favoured Malays over ethnic Chinese and Indians in terms of education, employment, and business, resulting in restricted opportunities for children of Chinese and Indian background. Families of Malay descent have also benefited from government education subsidies and the greater availability of cheap child care in Malay communities. These factors together suggest that Malay families will have been encouraged by perceived opportunities and subsidised costs to continue having more children than their counterparts in Indonesia and Singapore.[15]

## More than a hundred million missing women

An unanticipated consequence of state pressure to reduce fertility, which illustrates the strength and pervasiveness of some cultural influences, has been a decrease in some countries in the proportion of births that are female or, as commonly expressed, an increase in the male–female sex ratio at birth. In societies where importance is attached to having sons, couples are taking steps to ensure that they have at least one son while still responding to government pressure to reduce total fertility. What has made this possible is the availability of methods of foetal sex determination. Early in pregnancy, the sex of the foetus a woman is carrying can be identified (using techniques such as amniocentesis, ultrasound scanning and chorionic biopsy) and, if it is female, abortion can follow. While this problem has been most widely discussed in relation to India and China, it is not restricted to those countries and cannot be attributed to societies being poor and 'backward'. The phenomenon occurs also, for example, in South Korea and Taiwan. It has been estimated that by 1990 some 100 million females were 'missing' worldwide as a result of these practices.[16]

For India there are no statistics available relating to sex ratio at birth. Nonetheless, throughout the twentieth century, Indian demographers have noted a rising sex ratio for the population as a whole, with the proportion of the population that is male steadily increasing. Whereas in 1901 there were 972 females for every 1000 males, by 1991 the ratio had fallen to 927. Only in the 2001 census did the trend go in the opposite direction, with the figure rising again to 933. Until recently India was one of the few countries in the world where the life expectancy for women was shorter than that for men. It appears that 1992 was the historical turning point when, for the first time, females being born could, on average, expect to outlive males. What is worrying is that this increase in the proportion of women in the population as a whole coincided with a sharp fall in the proportion of the 0–6-years age group that is female. This occurred in all states except Kerala, Sikkim, Tripura, and Mizoram, and was particularly pronounced in Punjab, Harayana, and other northern states. There is strong evidence that the two trends are directly linked in a straightforward way: if unwanted females can be prevented from entering the world in the first place, those who are born are less likely to die early from neglect, mistreatment and discrimination. Since the early 1980s, foetal sex-determination technologies have been widely available in India, with ultrasound overtaking amniocentesis as the most popular method. Private clinics and mobile units, advertising their services in newspapers and magazines, have spread throughout the country. Costs have been low enough to ensure that it is not only the well-off who make use of such services, while the volume of trade means that, in the words of a WHO report, *Women's Health*, 'sex determination has become a lucrative business'. Malpractice has been widespread. Some clinics perform ultrasound tests too early in pregnancy to be reliable, while some of those offering amniocentesis do not perform the tests at all: they simply report all cases as female, confident that the clients will abort and not contest the 'analysis'.[17]

In China the male–female sex ratio at birth during the 1960s and 1970s was close to the norm of 106. In 1981 it was 108.5 and in 1989 was 113.8. In 1995 the ratio had increased to 116.5, with figures at the provincial level ranging from 131.6 in Hubei to 98.8 in Tibet. (The figure in Tibet suggests that there could be 'missing boys' to account for.) The fact that the sharpest rise coincided with the implementation of the one-child family policy led some analysts to see a causal connection.

It has been estimated that by 1989 some 30 million Chinese females were 'missing'. However, it appears that a number of factors are involved. One of these is the under-reporting of female births: couples who already have one or two children and want to avoid the penalties associated with exceeding their quota may not report the birth to the authorities. It has been estimated that about half of the missing cases can be accounted for by the Chinese capacity for ignoring or circumventing rules. Some analysts claim that female infanticide continues to be practised, as it was in earlier times, and therefore is a second factor. But while female infanticide may continue to occur in remote regions, given the severe sanctions against it and the fact that easier options are now available, it is unlikely that it has brought about a worsening of the sex ratio at birth.

Examination of the changes that have occurred indicate that the remainder of the missing Chinese females can be accounted for by prenatal sex determination and selective abortion. A study of hospital births in twenty-nine provinces between 1988 and 1991 found that male–female sex ratios at birth were highest in the most economically advanced provinces, and for births to women from urban areas and those with most education. On the other hand, data obtained from the 1990 national census, rather than hospital records, indicate that the sex ratio at birth was higher in townships and rural districts than in the cities. Moreover, figures from the 1995 One Percent National Population Survey do not reveal any evidence of the socio-economic pattern apparent earlier at the provincial level. This may be explained in part by the fact that by 1995 ultrasound examinations had become a standard procedure in IUD check-ups. The technology was widely available in clinics even at the township and village level. Foetal sex determination therefore commonly did not require a special medical examination.[18] It appears then that some of the rising sex

Sisters, Chengdu, Sichuan, China. Since 1980, the female proportion of Chinese new-born has fallen.

imbalance is attributable to economic factors, including the benefits seen to flow from sons in the move towards a market economy (especially in agriculture). More significant, however, is that the availability of foetal diagnostic techniques has made it possible, in a situation where the number of children is limited either by preference or pressure, to act in accordance with a cultural preference for a male child.

This is confirmed by trends in Taiwan, Hong Kong, and South Korea. As in China, natal male–female sex ratios in these places began to rise sharply during the 1980s, first and most noticeably in the cities, but in due course also in country areas. In Korea, the trend was most conspicuous in an urban region noted for its social conservatism. When sex ratio according to birth order (first born, second born and so on) is examined, Taiwan, Korea, and China also show a common pattern. In each case the higher the birth number, the greater the sex ratio; or, putting the same point differently, the more children a couple had already, the more likely that the next one would be a boy. The only explanation that fits all cases is the growing use of sex determination and selective abortion as a way of ensuring that smaller families would still include at least one son. In Taiwan, Hong Kong, and South Korea there has been no reason to under-report female births, and infanticide is out of the question. Neither has there been particularly heavy government pressure on couples to limit the number of children they have, which suggests that in this regard the impact of strict population control policies in China since 1979 may not have been as great as some have suggested.[19]

In 1990, concern over the growing sex imbalance led the South Korean government to introduce legislation providing for cancellation of the licences of medical practitioners performing sex determinations. The national government of India as well as a number of Indian state governments have also passed legislation prohibiting prenatal sex determination. Even among women's groups, however, this step has led to a lot of dispute. It is recognised that enforcing the laws will be difficult and the most likely result will be to send the testing and abortion underground, putting the lives of more women at risk. The only effective solution, it is argued, is changing the social position and status of women. But that will not be easily or quickly achieved.

In China too the national government and some provincial governments moved in 1994 to outlaw prenatal sex determination. There the situation is complicated by the fact that reforms of the national health system have put intense pressure on public hospitals to find additional sources of revenue. Ultrasound machines have proved handy income-earners for the establishments that have them. Even health practitioners and administrators who find foetal sex determination and selective abortion ethically offensive may find it difficult to suspend practices that fund the provision of other, more urgently needed health services.

## Is population growth really a problem?

Demographic transition theory encouraged a shift in thinking, from regarding low fertility as a cause of economic development to regarding it as a consequence. While it did not stop governments from continuing to place priority on fertility control programs, it was welcomed by those who found government activity in this area distasteful. If lower fertility really is a consequence of development, then population growth can be checked in Third World countries by raising living standards and providing more social services. Consequently, in countries such as China and India there is no justification for state intervention in fertility control, let alone state coercion.

This is a comfortable position for those who believe in the invisible hand of the market and the power of economic forces to bring about the best of all possible worlds. It is a view that appealed to cold war champions of Western democracy, reconfirming as it did that Western social and political norms were the goal towards which world history was leading. It is also a view that has appealed to Third World elites convinced that Western-style modernisation is the only solution to the problems facing them. What is intriguing is that a similar position was taken up by opponents of Westernisation, those who see development as badly disguised neocolonialism. Many of these critics find in family planning programs a conspiracy by Western bureaucrats and capitalists to control developing countries and continue to live at their expense. They point out, quite plausibly, that if declining fertility is a result of better socio-economic circumstances, then what is needed is not family planning programs supported by international agencies, Westernising governments and multinational drug companies, but rather direct efforts to improve the conditions under which the mass of the people in developing countries live.

Some of these critics argue that there is no population problem in developing countries, that if there is a problem it is one of economic or distributive justice. Thanks to modern technology and the globalisation of trade, production of food and other essentials has increased faster than population. Despite the fact that the world's population has increased fourfold since Malthus' day, it is better fed and more secure than ever. What is more, there is no reason why the world will not be able to accommodate large population increases in the future, so long as technological advances are shared and markets are able to operate without government interference. A typical statement of these views in the lead-up to the UN Population Conference in Cairo in 1994 came from the *Far Eastern Economic Review*:

> In fact things are getting better, for everyone, not just for those in the richer nations. By almost every measure of human welfare, the world has shown a steady improvement since Malthus' day. As for the population explosion, fertility rates have been declining for years, dramatically in most places. If we have more of us around today, it's because fewer of us die at birth and on average we live longer. Surely that should be a cause for celebration, not despair.[20]

Those who do not believe in the ability of the market to bring about the best of all possible worlds see the problem as one of distributive justice. It is not the large populations of Asian and other developing countries that threaten ecological catastrophe, but rather it is the high levels of consumption in developed countries, and the denying of developing countries their fair share of the resources available. An Indian critic of Malthusianism and neo-Malthusianism, for example, points out that since per capita energy consumption in the United States is fifty times that in India, one birth in the United States has fifty times the ecological impact of one in India.

Yet it is about Indian births that population controllers worry. The same argument has been used by the Chinese government to rebut or ignore demands for China to reduce its greenhouse gas emissions. Since China only produces a quarter of the gas emissions per capita produced by developed countries, the government's view is that those countries have no business demanding that China or other developing countries reduce their emissions.[21]

According to such critics the solution is not for all Third World countries to follow the development path of the West and copy its extravagant lifestyle. Rather, a just distribution of goods within and between countries is needed, and the pursuit by each of a mode of development that is culturally appropriate, building on indigenous forms of social and economic organisation. If Westernisation is rejected, the argument goes, and in particular the concept of development based on continuous economic growth, then ecological balance can be maintained just as it was in pre-colonial times.

These arguments have force, and highlight the fact that population issues cannot be considered in isolation. Patterns of consumption cannot be ignored, since environmental impact depends on how much people consume as well as how many of them there are. Questions of distributive justice and economic control are crucial. The ability of a population to meet its needs depends very much on the degree of control it has over its resources and means of production. It is also true that over the last fifty years the earth's capacity to sustain humanity has proved far more elastic than Malthus could ever have imagined. Nor can we see any limit to the ability of technology to expand that productive capacity still further.

Yet there can be no doubt that there *are* limits, both to technology and the earth's carrying capacity. Technology cannot be a substitute for resources on a global basis. A Japan or a Singapore may be able to rely on technology to overcome through trade a shortage of natural resources, but it is a strategy that works only if the resources are available elsewhere. It is not an option for the world as a whole. Earth is finite, and is likely to remain so.

As to the claim that population growth is a problem caused by Western interference, in a sense it is true, but it does not follow that the problem will go away if Western interference is stopped. It is too late for that. Largely as a result of such interference, population levels and life expectancy have shot up in many Third World countries. In South Asia between 1970 and 1998 life expectancy at birth for women increased from 49.0 to 63.6 years, while in China it increased from 64.0 to 72.3.[22] This alone represents a big rise in the potential total fertility of the population, even if we allow for the fact that much of the increase in life expectancy may go beyond the child-bearing age of women. Those who argue that developing countries would have no population problem if they followed their own cultural paths presumably do not mean there should be a return to the low life expectancies that were a common feature of them.

Massive population growth and associated trends such as urbanisation make reliance on tradition an unlikely solution. Even where there have been rules to limit fertility in traditional societies, it cannot be assumed the traditional mechanisms will continue to work when the societies in question have undergone radical change. Efforts may be made to limit trends such as industrialisation and large-scale urbanisation, but to roll them back and stop their impact is impossible.

If tradition is not the answer, neither is leaving everything to the market. We know that improved living conditions may result in greater rather than less fertility. This means that raising living standards in the hope that this will induce couples to have fewer children is uncertain at best, and could lead to absolute disaster. Besides, if the only way to save the planet from overpopulation is to provide everyone in it with a US or Japanese standard of living, then it is a futile exercise. The resource depletion and pollution this entails would finish off the earth even more quickly.

The statement that 'development is the best contraceptive' is clearly false if 'development' is taken to mean something like 'Western-style economic development and consumerism'. But there are other development paths that can be pursued, and some of these may be more helpful in addressing the population problems facing developing countries in Asia. Certainly economic needs must be addressed if solutions are to be found, and while the idea of reliance on tradition is unconvincing, there is no doubt that close attention to cultural factors is necessary if population growth is to be understood and controlled. Culture and economics are artificial categories if they are seen as being mutually exclusive. A society's economic practices are part of its culture. Specific areas of its culture, such as reproductive behaviour, in turn are influenced by economic factors. There is nothing mysterious about this.

As for the role of the state, there is a strong *prima facie* case for its involvement in family planning and fertility control: demographic transition is not an inevitable consequence of economic and social development. Traditional mechanisms for limiting fertility cannot always be relied upon in societies that have undergone extensive change. The spread of contraceptive techniques, which is a major factor in when and where reductions in fertility occur, can be encouraged by the state. The resources and authority of the state can also play a leading role in changing social norms pertaining to the number and spacing of children.

## Individual choice, persuasion, coercion

There is no provision in early international human rights instruments, such as the Universal Declaration of Human Rights and the International Covenant on Civil and Political Rights, that confers on couples a right to decide the number of children they will have. However, in the Convention on the Elimination of All Forms of Discrimination Against Women, which was adopted by the United Nations General Assembly in 1979 and came into force in 1981, such a right is articulated. Article 16.1(e) requires parties to the treaty to take measures to ensure that men and women enjoy equally 'the same rights to decide freely and responsibly on the number and spacing of their children and to have access to the information, education and means to enable them to exercise those rights'. The wording of this article, which was echoed in the resolution of national delegates of the 1984 United Nations Population Conference in Mexico City, indicates that it is not to be regarded as an unqualified right: it has to be exercised 'responsibly'. In this respect it is the same as some other human rights, which are to be exercised only to the extent that they do not conflict with the requirements of 'national security or of public order, or of public health or morals'.[23]

Historically, couples or individuals have rarely been able to make a completely 'free' decision as to the number and spacing of their children. This has not been because a lack of contraception has made the idea of choice irrelevant much of the time. Husband and wife remain members of extended families. (The idea of 'founding a family', articulated in human rights documents such as the Universal Declaration and the International Covenant on Civil and Political Rights, is badly misleading in this sense.) They are also part of a community. Family and community influences on the number of children couples have and when they have them have been strong in most societies. The pressures may sometimes be positive, rewarding those who do what others want them to, and sometimes they may be negative, punishing those who disregard the expectations of family and community. Usually they have been both at once.

Pressure to comply with the wishes or expectations of others is a matter of degree. It ranges across a continuum from encouragement, which involves strengthening someone's commitment to an agreed course of action, to persuasion, which entails using means other than force to change their mind and adopt another point of view or course of action, and finally to coercion, which is a matter of imposing a view or course of action on others regardless of whether they agree or not. In practice the distinctions are hard to draw, particularly in cross-cultural situations.

If we regard pressure from family and broader community as the historical norm, the role in fertility control of contemporary governments takes on a different appearance. To be sure, there is a difference between civil and state pressure, but from the couple's perspective the constraints on choice may be just as unpleasant in either case. Although this sort of historical precedent does not necessarily make government interference in birth control right, it does highlight the fact that the issues involved reach beyond the concerns of individuals or couples to matters in which the state may properly claim an interest. It may be a legitimate concern of the state, as of particular families and communities, either to encourage population growth or to discourage it.

Pronatalist policies have not been common in Asian countries in recent times, at least not if that is taken to refer to implementation of government programs specifically designed to encourage population growth. In the days of heady nationalistic fervour early in their reigns, Mao Zedong in China and Sukarno in Indonesia both identified their large populations as a source of strength rather than a problem. Both stated that their country could support two or even three times the population it then had (a view that to a large extent has been vindicated). However, neither Mao nor Sukarno did anything actively to encourage higher fertility, and subsequently both introduced birth control programs.

By contrast, Singapore pursued an antinatalist policy from 1973 before switching in 1984 to a more pronatalist position. In 1987 the Singapore government introduced the slogan 'Have three, or more if you can afford it' as part of a policy that has been described as selectively pronatalist. It was a response to below-replacement fertility, rapid ageing of the population, and the fact that highly educated people had fewer children than those lower down the social hierarchy. In Japan, concern over the rapidly ageing population led the government in 1991 to introduce policy initiatives aimed at 'creating an environment for rearing healthy children', in other words, to encourage couples to have more children. Measures included provision of more generous child allowances, wider availability of day care facilities, and the option of up to one year of child care leave (unpaid) for either parent. Experience with programs aimed at increasing fertility elsewhere in the world—mainly Europe—suggests that material incentives have little impact on total fertility. They may lead to closer spacing of births, but not more births overall.[24]

One aspect of pronatalist policies that may have considerable impact on fertility rates is the prohibition of abortion and all or some types of contraceptives. Of course the effectiveness of such measures depends on an ability to enforce the law, and religious or moral sanctions may be more effective in this regard than legal ones. However, religious influences are far from uniform. In India in 1989, only 29 per cent of Muslims used modern contraceptive methods, compared with 41 per cent of Hindus. In Iran in 1992, by contrast, 64 per cent of women reported using contraceptives, almost twice the proportion before the revolution of 1979. Despite a surge in fertility in the years immediately after the revolution, when family planning programs were wound back and population growth rose from 2.7 per cent in 1976 to 3.8 per cent in 1986, modern contraceptive techniques were not seen as irreligious. Ayatollah Khomeini issued a *fatwa* (directive) approving birth control as long as it was not harmful to mothers and children and excluded abortion. The Iranian High Judicial

Taking the television set for an outing? Kyoto, Japan. An increasing proportion of Japanese couples are choosing not to have children.

Council stated in 1988 that 'family planning does not have any Islamic barrier', and the strong family planning program launched the following year helped to reduce the population growth rate to 2.5 per cent by 1991. In Bangladesh, where the great majority of the people are Muslims, family planning is gaining wide acceptability. It is lowest in the Chittagong region, which some explain in terms of stronger and more conservative Islamic influences there.[25]

Antinatalist or fertility control programs now operate in most Asian countries, with a wide range of incentives, disincentives and degrees of compulsion. A characteristic of Indian programs, which began as early as 1952, has been an emphasis on sterilisation. Incentives have included one-off cash payments or rewards, such as transistor radios, to those agreeing to sterilisation. While higher incentives tended to improve acceptance rates, material considerations were not the only thing that influenced couples' decisions. Not surprisingly, those most likely to respond to incentives of this sort were poor couples who already had many children.[26]

Although wide provision of contraceptives has also been a dominant aim of Indian programs, it is sometimes argued that insufficient effort has been put into making them acceptable to all sections of the public, and that this, together with undue emphasis on terminal sterilisation, explains the very patchy achievements in fertility control in India. Nevertheless there are areas of high achievement. One measure that has been successful in reducing fertility is the simple strategy of raising the legal age for marriage. In 1961 the average age at marriage for Indian women was 16.1 years. By 1992, after the legal minimum age for women had been set in 1978 at eighteen years, it had risen to about twenty years.[27]

There is no doubt that government coercion during the national emergency of 1975–76 also set back fertility control in India. Thousands of men had vasectomies forced on them, in some places as a result of large-scale night-time raids on villages by police and family planning officials, but more often by means of harassment and heavy 'persuasion'. The state of Maharashtra tried to introduce a law making sterilisation compulsory after three children, only to have it blocked by the national president. Such events helped to bring about the downfall of Indira Gandhi's government in 1977, and in the years since has continued to breed suspicion of family planning programs and resistance to their implementation.[28]

The Thai family planning program is regarded as one of the great success stories of fertility control in Asia. From its beginnings in the 1960s, it has focused on presenting family planning in ways that will make it acceptable to ordinary villagers. Since 1974 much of the initiative has been taken by the Population and Community Development Association (PDA), a non-government organisation operating with strong Thai government support. PDA makes fertility control an integral part of community economic and social development, relying on community leadership and initiative to drive the program. Family planning is presented as one of a range of strategies for improving community life, along with such things as improved water supply and sanitation, health care, and projects for income generation. Influential individuals within the community, such as teachers, religious leaders, and shopkeepers, are drawn in to mobilise support, and objectives are decided on a community basis, according to needs identified by the villagers themselves. Village development funds are provided by PDA to finance small projects to improve quality of life in the community and reward fertility control. Villagers' religious doubts about contraceptive acceptance have been overcome by such steps as getting the abbot of Bangkok to bless contraceptive pills and condoms.[29]

While the Thai program has never involved coercion, it does rely to a large extent on community pressure. In light of the hands-off approach taken by the government, however, and the degree of local decision-making in the operation of the program, it may be argued that the community pressure for compliance is not so different from the sort of community pressure that has traditionally enforced customs governing fertility.

The Indonesian family planning program has many similarities to the Thai program, but has more direct government involvement. It too relies heavily on organisation at the village level, coopting opinion-moulders within the community, bringing community pressure to bear, and tying fertility control to other community development initiatives. In such a situation, accepting contraceptives generates a sense of participation and belonging, as well as material benefits. Under a village development program linked to family planning, those who accept contraceptives are able to borrow funds for income-generation projects. Nevertheless, fertility remains higher in Indonesia than in Thailand.[30]

## Fertility control in China

China's fertility control program has received more attention than that of any other country. Some regard it as an exemplary achievement, a model of what can be done with strong government commitment to limiting population growth; others see it as a grotesque misuse of power and abuse of human rights. There is no argument over what has happened: since the late 1960s, China's population growth rate has fallen sharply. Between 1965 and 1970 the population increased at an average of 2.8 per cent per year; between 1975 and 1980 the average was 1.4 per cent, while over the next five years the average was 1.3 per cent. There is a good deal of argument, however, over how this has been achieved, about the nature of the one-child family policy and its effectiveness, and whether the use of state coercion in fertility control can ever be justified. The Chinese government claims that coercion has never been part of official policy, while defending its vigorous approach to population as a matter of ecological necessity, an approach for which the rest of the world should be grateful. According to the government-controlled *Beijing Review*:

> The world's people have never been so eager for interdependence in economic development and environmental protection. We are in the same sailing boat, with one Chinese passenger out of five. Other passengers should rejoice at the fact that their Chinese traveling companions have made unusual and successful efforts for controlling population growth.[31]

During the 1950s and most of the 1960s Chinese efforts at fertility control were limited, and completely overshadowed by the political and social upheavals of the time. It was only in 1969 that the issue began to be faced seriously. Within a decade, average total fertility had fallen from just under 6 to 2.5; in urban areas it had gone down to 1.5, well below replacement level. Over the same period birth rates fell from over 35 to less than 20 per thousand. Yet at the end of the 1970s population policies became even more strict.

The one-child family policy was introduced in 1979, the year the Convention on the Elimination of All Forms of Discrimination Against Women, to which China is a party, was adopted by the UN. The policy has remained in force since then, with some major amendments. A wide range of incentives have been used to encourage couples to commit themselves to having only one child. These have included a small monthly allowance paid by the government until the child is fourteen years old; provision of a plot of farm land for the child from birth; subsidised medical care; preschool and school subsidies; and preferential treatment in terms of work opportunities. These advantages are lost if a second child is born, and for a third or subsequent pregnancy a couple faces further disincentives. Like incentives, disincentives have varied from province to province, but have included a fine and/or a reduction in wages; loss of paid maternity leave and the subsidy of medical costs associated with pregnancy and delivery; loss of the right to housing; and being subjected to heavy pressure to have an abortion or agree to sterilisation. Since 1984, however, it has been official policy to recognise a number of grounds for permitting a second child.

Attempts to enforce a rigid one-child policy met with strong resistance as many families began to take desperate steps to ensure that, one-child policy notwithstanding, they would have a son to carry on the patrilineal line of descent. The result was a considerable variation in provinces and regions in implementation. In the closing years of the twentieth century, in the province of Jiangsu and in the municipalities of Beijing, Tianjin, Shanghai, and Chongqing, few exceptions to the one-child policy were permitted. On the other hand, in the rural areas of eighteen provinces that account for some 70 per cent of the national population, couples were allowed to have a second child if the first was a girl. In the rural areas of five other provinces all couples were permitted to have two children as long as they were born four or more years apart, while in autonomous regions inhabited by ethnic minorities couples could have two or three children.[32]

It is clear that fertility control in China has commonly involved reliance on intensive community pressure and coercion by the state. In this it has not been very different from many other aspects of life in the People's Republic. Permits for pregnancy, workplace and community monitoring of menstrual cycles and contraceptive use, public criticism and severe financial punishment for breaking the rules—these sorts of measures are much the same as Chinese citizens have had to put up with in other aspects of life and, while they are unpleasantly bureaucratic and authoritarian, a plausible case could be constructed in support of them. However, this seems much more difficult in regard to actions such as enforced abortion, sterilisation, and the killing of babies as they are being born, all alleged to have been common. Yet for the women involved, the unremitting social pressure may be even more distressing, and is known to have resulted in the suicide of many.[33]

Critics of China's population policy tend to argue either that fertility control is not necessary (because economic development will fix it, now that China is moving to a market economy) or that coercive measures have in fact contributed little to reducing fertility—that the program would have worked just as well (or better) by being less heavy-handed. A problem with the latter argument is that it is difficult to isolate the effects of coercive aspects of the program from those of other elements and the socio-political context in which the program operates.

To reach any sort of conclusion we have to look at more than the one-child policy. As pointed out earlier, China's birth rate had already sharply reduced in the 1970s, before the one-child policy was introduced. There is little doubt that much of the reduction was due to a massive family planning campaign that made the full range of measures freely available throughout the country and imposed very strong pressure on couples to use them, measures including abortion and male and female sterilisation as well as modern contraceptives. According to J. S. Aird, the compulsory insertion of intra-uterine devices was widespread. But other steps were also taken. The slogan *wan xi shao* (later, longer, fewer) indicates this broader approach. Married couples were told to have fewer children. Young people were encouraged to postpone marriage until well beyond the legal minimum set down in the Marriage Law of 1950 (eighteen years for women and twenty years for men; in the revised Marriage Law of 1980 the minimum ages were raised to twenty and twenty-two years respectively). Wider spacing of children was encouraged, though longer breastfeeding did not feature much in the methods prescribed to achieve it.

The program was implemented when China's commune system was at full strength. It was a time when all aspects of social life and economic activity were closely regulated by the state. The commune system aided the regulation of fertility because through it state control reached right down to the family unit. But social control was not the only function of the communes. All social services were delivered through them, including health care, education and social welfare. The commune system brought unprecedented security into the lives of the great majority of Chinese. If there is any truth at all in economic and social security explanations of high fertility, then the commune system will have been a potent force in convincing couples that they did not need as many children as they would have in prerevolutionary circumstances. While the counter argument—that the unprecedented security would have had a euphoria effect and so led to higher birth rates—cannot be dismissed out of hand, the experience of other developing countries strongly suggests that China's sweeping social and economic reforms would have brought about a substantial drop in fertility quite independently of its population program. Amartya Sen, an authority on development and population issues in Asia, has commented:

> Many of China's longstanding social and economic programs have been valuable in reducing fertility, including those that have expanded education for women as well as men, made health care more generally available, provided more job opportunities for women, and stimulated rapid economic growth. These factors would themselves have reduced the birth rates, and it is not clear how much 'extra lowering' of fertility rates has been achieved in China through compulsion ...
>
> While China may get too much credit for its authoritarian measures, it gets far too little credit for the other, more collaborative and participatory, policies it has followed, which have themselves helped to cut down the birth rate.[34]

Kindergarten outing, Beijing, China.

There is much in what Sen says. However, two points must be made by way of qualification. First, the fact that coercive aspects of a fertility control program may not help to achieve its goals does not mean that the program itself is not essential. A government-directed family planning program can be a powerful force in changing social attitudes: the authority of the state can be used constructively no less than destructively. Second, we cannot dismiss the idea that coercion has contributed to the rapid decline in China's birth rate just because we find it distasteful. During the 1980s there were quick surges in the birth rate whenever implementation of the one-child policy became less stringent. It is hard to explain these surges except by the fact that a large proportion of the population still want more children than they are allowed under government policy. In other words, factors such as economic growth, education, and labour force participation by women have not resulted in a shift in attitude far enough or permanent enough for individual preferences to align completely with official targets. That is the point of coercion, after all: it aims to push changes in behaviour ahead of changes in attitude. By definition what is achieved by coercion will be unstable.

Economic and social reforms since 1979 have in fact contributed to the problem. The shift to the responsibility system and family-based production, together with the dismantling of the commune system and the winding back of state-funded social services and welfare, has undermined the very achievements identified as likely to result in a reduction of fertility. Whatever else the developing market economy may bring, for many people increased security is not part of it. It is particularly interesting, therefore, that some recent initiatives in fertility control in China resemble those that have been found to work in countries such as Thailand and Indonesia: presenting family planning as part of a package of measures for village-level social and economic development, with an emphasis on community participation and—it has to be said—community persuasion. In Sichuan, one of the most heavily populated provinces of China, local governments are giving priority to those practising family planning when allocating village development funds. They are also allocated more land and are given preferential opportunities for factory work, which offers higher and more stable incomes than farming.[35]

## The unnaturalness of choice

Having children is often presented as the outcome of a decision based on cost–benefit analysis. Reductionist versions present the costs and benefits as purely economic, while more sophisticated accounts expand the analysis to include other preferences: costs may include child-rearing expenses, loss of paid employment by the mother, increased household stress, financial insecurity, a bigger house, ecological impact and social burden; benefits may include emotional satisfaction, additional family labour, better old-age security, continuation of the line of descent, and enhanced social status for the parents.

Is this how it happens? Our answer will depend to some extent on how much we believe rational decision-making to be a feature of human behaviour generally. But nowhere does the claim that humans are rational seem less persuasive than in regard to sexual behaviour. The consequences of intercourse are usually remote from the sexual desire that leads to the act itself. However, we know that sexuality is never just purely instinctive behaviour, that even sexuality is subject to rules and customs that, among other things, may play an important part in determining fertility levels. Just as eating is a combination of physiological need, instinct, and cultural norms, so too is sexuality.

With the availability of cheap and reliable contraceptive technologies, having children can become a matter of conscious decision-making, whether or not the decisions are actually made in terms of cost–benefit analyses. However, the idea that it *can* be a subject of conscious decision-making, let alone the idea that it *should* (especially *individual* decision-making), may represent a massive cultural shift. The potential of such a shift for enhancing the autonomy and self-determination of women is enormous. Seeing decision-making regarding fertility as proper or legitimate presupposes change in many areas of society and culture other than sexuality.

Even where social and cultural change is minimal, women may welcome the enhanced power to choose that family planning brings. Child-bearing is, after all, something directly affecting the mental and physical well-being of women. But it is much easier for family planning to gain acceptance when it coincides with social and economic change that can point to new sorts of advantages to be gained by having fewer children. There is little doubt that economic considerations do play a central role for the great majority of people, though the actual weight they carry relative to other factors will vary.

One of the weaknesses of standard rational actor models of explanation is that they tend to assume that individuals have the complete information needed to make a well-informed or rational decision. This may be overcome to some extent by introducing the idea of *bounded* rationality. A more serious weakness is the assumption that each decision represents a discrete event, the outcome of a separate weighing up of wants or preferences. For a particular choice cannot be considered independently of all the other choices an individual has to make; the human condition requires us to bear in mind all our preferences when making choices, not just one. Economic gain, social standing, and moral propriety, for example, often need to be considered all at once. Shall I ask the market price for my rice or will I respect other people's right to subsist in this time of scarcity? The choices are economic, social, and moral all at once. It is this clustering of choices that makes it hard to change one aspect of behaviour in isolation. When a number of overlapping choices change it may be much easier.

Parents have aspirations for themselves and for their children. Ideal family size is one sort of aspiration. Aspirations require a sense that there are real alternatives. Real alternatives must be both available and legitimate. Individuals and families have at most a limited say regarding which alternatives are legitimate, but not so the state. The state can be a powerful force in determining what may be done and what not, in the area of fertility control as elsewhere. But the operation of societal forces may be equally strong, and may change what the state is prepared to legitimise. It is hard to discuss this sort of change in terms other than of culture.[36]

What do villagers from western Nepal or central Sulawesi think when asked by an obviously educated and well-dressed visitor why they want children? To laugh at a guest would be rude, but really! It is like asking why birds fly or the sun rises. Having children is what adults do. It is what being adult means. Having to think up reasons for it must seem a curious exercise. Nevertheless, they have to give reasons that will satisfy the inquisitor, and so they refer to the need for extra hands to work in the fields, or support them in their old age. No doubt they believe what they say. What they are less inclined to say, perhaps because it is so obvious that it is embarrassing that the distinguished visitor is unaware of it, is that a house without children is empty and forlorn. Fortunately, God willing, babies come, and while they bring anxieties they also bring great joy. Parents and children give each other affection as well as material support. For someone who thinks in these terms, the idea that having children can be a matter of personal choice takes some digesting.

# CHAPTER SEVEN

# Environmental Impact

## Global economy and shared environment

An image much used in publications on the environment is that of Earth from out in space, the blue of its oceans and the green and brown of its continents wreathed in a white pattern of weather systems. That picture expresses some of the strongest themes in environmental literature: the beauty and fragility of the planet, finite and unique, on which all living things are interdependent and for which we are all responsible. The trouble with all wide-angle pictures, however, is that some of the detail gets lost. It is rather churlish to point out that the view from space does not reveal political and socio-economic boundaries, or highlight the fact that some parts of the world are in greater environmental danger than others, and that some groups are doing more harm to the environment than others. Yet such distinctions are as essential to an understanding of environmental issues as ideas such as wholeness and interdependence. They may get in the way of our emotional response to the image, but they cannot be ignored in attempts to address the serious environmental problems being experienced in Asia and others parts of the world. Environmental problems cannot be solved unless social, economic, and political issues are also given due consideration.

Photographs of Earth from space do have this benefit: they give immediacy to the concept of globalisation, which must feature prominently in any account of what has been happening to the environment in recent decades. The two most significant general factors underlying environmental change are intimately bound up with the globalisation process and with each other: population growth, and increased consumption resulting from economic growth. However, population growth alone may have far-reaching ecological consequences even where levels of individual resource consumption remain unchanged. This is obvious in relation to the population dynamics of non-human species as well as humans. In densely populated areas, population growth alone may be sufficient to bring about ecological crisis. Where population growth coincides with increased per capita consumption, as is the case almost everywhere in the developing world, the resulting pressures are potentially catastrophic.

It is difficult to separate the impact of population growth from that of increased per capità consumption because, as is shown in Chapter 6, interaction between fertility trends and economic development is complicated. The evidence suggests that, like other animals, humans increase their reproductive rate when environmental conditions are favourable, unless specific cultural factors—including the availability of reliable contraceptive technology—intervene. To a large extent, what are conventionally labelled cultural and economic factors work independently of each other. While modernisation within the world economic system encourages a degree of cultural and technological convergence, it is not the case, as is widely asserted, that all nations are moving to economic, cultural, and demographic uniformity. Certainly there is insufficient evidence to support those congenital optimists who argue that population is not a problem, that the only problem is poverty, and that, once everyone enjoys the higher living standards to which economic development leads, the population issue will have disappeared. The planet will be saved, in other words, by raising per capita consumption in Third World countries to levels closer to those of the First World. The implausibility of the argument will become more evident from what follows.

Ecological pressure is often caused by factors other than local population growth or increased consumption. One important aspect of the relationship between population increase and development, central to the process of globalisation, is the way the population growth in some areas is made possible by the utilisation of natural resources in others, as a result of economic specialisation, increased production, systems of trade, new forms of energy supply, and improved transport and communication networks. What globalisation does, in effect, is to separate population growth from some of its local environmental impositions and consequences. This is most obvious in relation to big urban centres such as Tokyo, Shanghai, and Bangkok. These massive concentrations of population are viable to the extent that necessities such as food, water, and energy can be supplied from elsewhere. Similar considerations apply at the regional and national levels. Globalisation does not merely raise levels of individual consumption; it also lifts consumption out of its local environment. Globalisation makes it possible to consume other people's natural resources. Whether they get a fair return for those resources is not the issue here. What matters is that globalisation and the technological systems on which it depends make viable population levels for any given locality elastic.

This has implications for the concept of sustainability that has dominated discussion of economic development and environmental issues over the past decade. A certain population with a given level of resource consumption may appear sustainable in its present locality only because it manages to obtain its natural resources from somewhere else. As it becomes easier to obtain supplies from elsewhere, sustainable population and consumption levels will rise. Conversely, when essential supplies from distant sources become unavailable, sustainable population and consumption levels will fall. Much of the thinking about sustainable development assumes, first, that natural resources will always be available from somewhere else, and, second, that those who have control over them will be willing to sell them. Neither assumption is justified. The first leads to the fallacy of a 'resource-free world'; the second highlights the fact that sustainability is as much a question of political and social organisation as of natural resources.

The resources of the earth are finite. This does not worry those who dismiss neo-Malthusian arguments as alarmist nonsense, who point out that, despite steep population increases around the world, the limits to the earth's ability to support humanity are nowhere in sight. These optimists refer to human ingenuity, the capacity to create new technology that continues to extend the bounty of nature. However, it has been pointed out that technology can be a substitute for natural resources to only a limited extent. Technology needs resources to work on: even the most sophisticated of industrial processes need material input. A nation like Japan or Singapore may rely on obtaining the resources it needs from other countries in exchange for manufactures, but the sources are limited and may one day dry up. Offsetting resource deficiencies by technological innovation is a solution only to the extent that other nations have natural resources they are prepared to trade.[1]

Nations poor in technology and manufactured goods to trade with run up against the limits of sustainability sooner than rich and densely populated nations such as Japan and the Netherlands, which are able to support their people thanks to the natural resources they secure from overseas as a result of their human resources and manufacturing capacity. Both Japan and the Netherlands were helped along the way by being able to rely on their colonies for natural resources while building up their industrial capacity. A large proportion of their food needs, as well as energy and industrial inputs, comes from foreign sources. The situation in poor and densely populated nations such as India, Bangladesh, and Indonesia is very different. They do not have the means to obtain essential natural resources through foreign trade, and have begun to encounter limits to growth. Less of a shortage is being experienced in minerals and energy, since demand for such things remains limited in the absence of

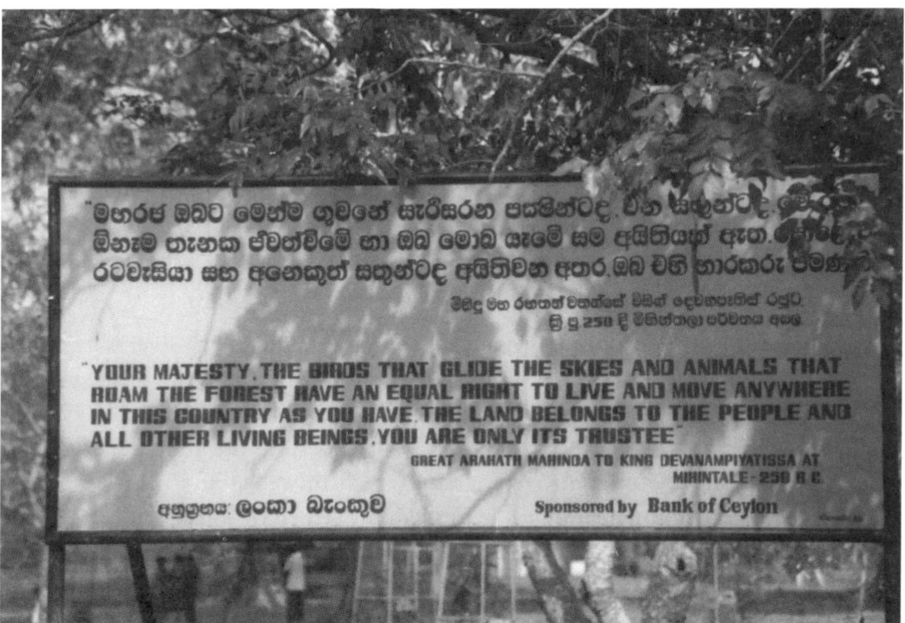


Ancient environmental wisdom, modern sponsor: Sri Maha Bodhi, Anuradhapura, Sri Lanka.

large-scale industrialisation, than in water and soil, the basic prerequisites for life, which are difficult and expensive to produce by technological means.

The political and social factors that determine sustainable population and consumption levels cannot escape the limits set by the existence or non-existence of natural resources. Natural resources cannot satisfy the needs of populations unless those populations have the technological capacity to use them effectively. It is now fashionable to trace the decline of numerous civilisations in world history to ecologically unsustainable activity, to excessive population growth and consumption. It tends to be overlooked that political decline and social instability may be a key factor in this. When public administration, trade, transport, and communications break down, it becomes impossible for vital resources to circulate widely enough. Famines, it is now understood, are more likely to be caused by failure to get adequate food supplies to the population in need than by inability to produce sufficient food.[2] Productive technology is useless unless it is backed by the expertise required to keep administrative and economic systems functioning at regional, national and, where appropriate, international levels.

Meeting the needs of large population concentrations, then, particularly those with high levels of consumption, presupposes an ability to ensure supply of natural resources over considerable distances. Colonial powers can enforce supply. Industrialised and developed regions within nations can exchange goods for them. In all cases it requires highly developed organisational and administrative capacities. Increasing those, therefore, may help to raise the levels of population and consumption that can be sustained. Of course such skills may also be invaluable in devising quite different sorts of responses. One type of strategy is to relocate factors that limit population and consumption. Moving environmentally harmful industries off-shore is a strategy used by many developed countries, with Japan and South Korea being the major Asian exponents. Relocation of such industries preserves the local environment and its capacity to support the local population while shifting the environmental burden of production elsewhere. These are problems commonly experienced by indigenous minorities in developing countries as well as by the developing countries themselves in relation to industrialised ones.

## Java's prospects

The island of Java illustrates many of the environmental problems experienced in contemporary Asia, and the urgency that attends them. Java, quite simply, can no longer support its population, which census figures from 2000 put at 120.4 million, and which continues to grow steadily. This is despite the Indonesian government's long-running transmigration program, which moved millions of Javanese and the associated environmental strains to more thinly settled regions of Sumatra, Kalimantan, and West Papua. The rich volcanic soils and reliable tropical rain that have enabled Java to sustain its historically high population levels are no longer enough. Food production has fallen in recent years, as more and more of the most productive farmland is taken over by urban development and industry.

In 1984 Indonesia became self-sufficient in rice production, with Java making by far the largest contribution. Self-sufficiency had been a major government objective and its achievement was an occasion of national pride. Since then the rate of increase in production has been outstripped by population growth. In 1995 Indonesia began to import rice again.[3] In terms of quantity it represented only a small proportion of national consumption, but was seen as having symbolic significance. In Java, as elsewhere, the green revolution that enabled food production to be increased dramatically has brought environmental problems with it. Water usage has sharply increased in agriculture, and, in combination with rising demand for urban water supplies and limited storage, this means that in some locations there is no longer enough. In one respect Java's plentiful rainfall has become a problem: deforestation of uplands has increased erosion and sedimentation, making it harder to control the monsoonal run-off. The heavy use of chemical fertilisers and pesticides used to grow the high-yield variety crops of the green revolution also harms the environment and, in conjunction with industrial pollution of water and air, is reducing productivity over the longer term.

In urban centres overuse of groundwater is causing acute problems. One is salinisation of groundwater supplies. Beneath Jakarta, salt water has penetrated about 15 kilometres inland from the sea, rendering wells in a large part of the city unfit for human consumption. There is surface subsidence resulting from the fall in groundwater levels, which heightens flood dangers as the multiplication of roads and buildings makes it harder for rainwater to penetrate underlying rock strata and replenish badly needed supplies. It has been argued that by the year 2015, by which time (if not before) Java's population will have reached 130 million, there will not be enough water to sustain it. No wonder then that in 1995 the Minister of Public Works identified water supply as the greatest priority.

Water shortages are aggravated by widespread pollution. A World Bank report concluded that most of Java's rivers are seriously polluted by raw sewage, rubbish and industrial effluents, posing acute risks to public health and welfare. The water is unfit for human consumption and unable to sustain aquatic life, meaning that a traditionally important food source has disappeared. The river that flows through Surabaya, Indonesia's second-largest city, has been found to contain the highest levels of mercury of any body of water in the world. While the local fishing industry has largely been destroyed, consumption of the fish and shellfish that do remain is causing serious health problems. Illnesses identified are said to include 'Minamata'—mercury poisoning similar to that which devastated the coastal community of Minamata in Japan in the 1950s.[4]

Energy needs in Java are acute. In rural areas a large proportion of the population continues to burn as fuel the crop residues and manure badly needed to fertilise the soil. Forests are subject to such intense population pressure that government attempts to manage them along Western lines, barring all but authorised personnel from entry, have caused widespread resistance and even violence. Only where local people are given an economic interest in the forests, and hence reason to protect them, are commercially important species such as teak likely to reach maturity. While progress has been made with rural electrification, the huge population means that potential demand far exceeds the available supply. To meet the needs of industry and big urban centres such as Jakarta and Surabaya, electric power already has to be obtained from other islands, especially Sumatra. Government plans for a nuclear power system, beginning with a facility on a dormant volcano at Mount Muria on the northern Java coast, have also caused concern, although Indonesia's economic and political problems appear to have halted these plans, at least temporarily.[5]

The impact of population and consumption is as strong on the sea as on the land. Coral reefs are being blown up and the rubble brought to shore to produce the materials needed for urban construction. The shortage of farmland and the oversupply of labour have forced many peasants to turn to the sea in the hope of making a living. However, the coastal shelves have been fished out and little remains to be caught by large numbers of poor fishermen with simple nets. Deep ocean fishing offers a livelihood, but requires expensive vessels and sophisticated equipment, which puts it beyond the means of ordinary fishermen. The scale of the operation and the investment required encourage those involved to sell their catch to lucrative overseas markets rather than locally, with the result that supplies for local consumption are severely curtailed.[6]

Jakarta exemplifies the environmental problems experienced in most of the big cities of Asia. Urban growth continues to be rapid, as people from rural Java and other parts of Indonesia come in search of work and the hope of a better life. In the large shanty towns created, housing is insecure and unhealthy, water and sewerage provision largely non-existent. Social services such as health care and education cannot keep pace with demand. Air pollution from traffic and industrial gas emissions is severe throughout the urban region.

This summary of environmental conditions in Java is given largely in human terms. It does not raise issues such as loss of biodiversity, deforestation, or harm to species other than humans. From a perspective restricted to human interests, it might be argued that few, if any, of the problems mentioned are insoluble. There are technological solutions for many, such as those arising from industrial pollution, while concerns relating to shortages of soil and water for food production disappear once we free ourselves from the obsession with local sustainability. Whereas in 1965 only 12 per cent of Indonesia's gross domestic product (GDP) derived from industrial output, in 1992 it was 42 per cent, with agriculture registering most of the offsetting fall. This may be seen as a reason for joy rather than alarm. Industrialisation will enable Java to buy food elsewhere, and so support a population substantially larger than the present one. After all, the Netherlands and Japan are able to sustain population densities of 454 and 335 per square kilometre respectively, and provide their people with a high standard of living. There is no reason to suppose that Indonesia, once developed, would not be able to do the same.

However, the situation of Indonesia, and Java in particular, differs from that of the Netherlands and Japan at a comparable level of economic development. The difficulties faced are much greater. Although the national population density of Indonesia, at 113 per square kilometre, is only a quarter that of the Netherlands and a third that of Japan, there are 882 people per square kilometre in Java. Industrialisation may make it easier in some respects to accommodate Java's enormous population, but any reduction in its role as the main food producer of the archipelago places much heavier demands on the other, less productive islands, and on the international market. Were heavy demand on the international food market to coincide with demand from other large nations, particularly China and India, which are also shifting from agricultural production to manufacturing, it would be difficult to satisfy.

When the Netherlands and Japan were industrialising they were relatively affluent, and could obtain food and natural resources cheaply from their colonies (in the Dutch case, of course, chiefly Indonesia). Indonesia, by contrast, is relatively poor, which makes it difficult to import large amounts of food while also investing heavily in new industries and the infrastructure necessary for a modern nation state. Like other late-developing countries, Indonesia faces the dilemma of having both to compete with developed nations (such as the Netherlands and Japan) and to address urgent social issues that may threaten national stability.

Indonesia's experience during 1997 and 1998 highlighted the nation's vulnerability within the global economy, and it was in Java, the main focus of industrialisation and foreign investment, that the problems were most acute. Rapid inflation and widespread unemployment made circumstances even grimmer for the large proportion of the population that had already been close to the poverty line. Many of those who had moved to the cities in search of better opportunities returned to the villages, only to find that they were not welcomed by people already struggling to cope with problems of their own. Java's heavy reliance on labour-intensive, export-oriented industry, and the limited technological capacity and low educational levels of its workforce, coupled with a history of extreme disparities in income, left it open to serious economic and social dislocation. Some senior government figures voiced the opinion that Indonesia should turn its attention away from export-oriented (and foreign-funded) industrialisation and direct more effort towards agriculture and food production. 'Agriculture should be the backbone for future growth', said the Minister for Co-ordination of Economy and Finance in 1998. 'We need to draw up a new strategy ... In the past we paid too much attention to manufacturing.'[7]

The growing ecological strains outlined, exacerbated as they have been by recent economic and political turmoil, indicate that Java faces a difficult future. Certainly in the intermediate term and probably in the long term, industrialisation is unlikely to enable the population of Java to sidestep its ecological predicament. Environmental, demographic, economic, and social problems must be solved together if they are to be solved at all.

## Japan, Malaysia, and globalisation

The problems arising from the industrialisation of Asia within the world economy, and the ways in which the environmental circumstances of nations affect each other, are well illustrated by Japan. In addition to having longer experience than other Asian nations of industrialisation and the environmental problems associated with it, Japan has a history of exporting ecological strain.

The eagerness and energy with which the Japanese elite turned to modernisation and Western-style industrialisation in the late nineteenth and early twentieth centuries left them little time to consider the environmental impact of the changes being introduced. Serious cases of industrial pollution soon emerged.[8] However, Japan managed to avoid much of the environmental cost of rapid industrialisation and the population growth that accompanied it by shifting the burden to the colonies it acquired: Taiwan, Korea, southern Sakhalin and, later, Manchuria. While there has been a tendency in Japan, as in other former colonial powers, to discount the benefits obtained from its colonies, and assert that what the colonies gained in terms of civilisation was greater than what was taken away, for their supply of natural resources the colonies were crucial. Between 1885 and 1920 Japan's population increased by 56 per cent, which meant that, despite improved agricultural productivity, by 1920 it was no longer able to feed its population. It was Korea and Taiwan that had to supply most of the shortfall. In the 1920s they provided 80 per cent of the rice and 65 per cent of the sugar imported by Japan, as well as other foodstuffs. Korea and Sakhalin supplied most of the timber needed for construction and paper production.

In other words, at the time when Japan was industrialising, her colonies were a cheap and reliable source of food and industrial resources, making it possible to fund modern industries and infrastructure at the same time as feeding a rapidly growing population. When in 1945 Japan lost its colonies, it had little option but to develop an export-oriented economy if it was to feed its people. Fortunately by then its industrial capacity, infrastructure and human capital were well established.[9]

The Minamata industrial pollution case in Japan is one of the worst in contemporary Asian experience. Only the Bhopal tragedy in northern India, following a gas leak at a Union Carbide chemical plant in December 1984, is its equal in sheer awfulness.[10] Unlike the Bhopal disaster, the Minamata case was the result not of an industrial accident but of a production process continued over many years, even long after its environmental consequences were known. As early as 1926 fishermen from the village of Minamata, on the west coast of the island of Kyushu, protested that effluent from a chemical factory established by the Nippon Chisso Corporation was polluting the bay in which they fished, diminishing their catch. However, thanks to its close links with government and the military, the corporation thrived, and Minamata grew into a city thanks to its economic strength. In the postwar years, Chisso played a leading role in Japan's reindustrialisation, establishing new production processes that entailed extensive use of organic mercury compounds as reaction catalysts. By 1956 local people were dying after severe convulsions, crazed mental states and comas. Pregnant women began to experience miscarriages; babies were stillborn or born with terrible deformities and brain damage. By the 1970s, hundreds of people had died, while the total number of victims in the early 1990s was estimated at more than ten thousand.

Although it had been established as early as 1959 that the mercury compounds discharged into Minamata Bay by the Chisso Corporation were the probable cause, it was a long time before the causal link was officially accepted. It was not until 1968 that production involving the mercury compounds was stopped, and it is alleged that it stopped then because it had ceased to be profitable rather than because of the environmental devastation it caused. For more than forty years the victims had to fight for social and legal justice, during which time they were ignored, deceived, criticised, bullied, ostracised and obstructed by the corporation, the national government, local authorities, and a substantial part of the community in which they lived. On all sides they were seen as troublemakers threatening community prosperity and the national interest. Not until September 1995 did the resulting litigation come to some sort of a conclusion, when the Japanese government, which hitherto had denied any liability and had tried to impose a very narrow definition of 'victim' in order to minimise compensation payouts, finally admitted that it and the local government had been negligent, along with the Chisso Corporation. Chisso, which had earlier been bankrupted by compensation payouts to victims but was propped up financially by the government, received further funds to settle with the victims, while the government was required as part of the settlement to give a formal apology.[11]

Some commentators have argued that Minamata disease, as the mercury poisoning with its excruciating symptoms has come to be known in Japan, is better seen as a social condition than as a medical one. The *real* Minamata disease is a socio-political sickness whose symptoms are a willingness to sacrifice anything for the sake of economic growth and profit; collusion between government and industry that leaves ordinary citizens powerless; and a rotting of the social fabric that is as destructive and terrible as the disintegration of the minds and bodies of mercury-poisoning victims. Understood in this way, Minamata disease is not a peculiarly Japanese condition, though some Japanese commentators believe that the climate created by Japanese cultural norms and socio-political institutions encouraged it to flourish. It could be seen as the sickness of our time, the pathological consequence of growth economics experienced by developed and developing nations alike.

Catastrophes such as Minamata increased environmental awareness in Japan. During the 1970s, new environmental laws and controls were introduced, leading to big improvements in some areas. For example, in relation to control of air pollution by industry, Japan quite rightly claims to be a world leader. The development of technology to minimise air pollution, and indeed the development of environmentally friendly industrial technology generally, has been a major focus of government policy in Japan. Although this has attracted Japanese corporations because of its international market potential, corporate and government attitudes regarding environmental protection have not changed as much as might have been hoped. With the introduction of tighter environmental safeguards at home, many Japanese companies moved their dirty industries to developing Asian countries that were more accommodating. This was done with the encouragement and support of the Japanese government. As the Ministry of International Trade and Industry explained in its White Paper for 1976, Japan's environment had to be conserved for the well-being of the Japanese people.

More recently, the government has moved to improve Japan's standing with its neighbours, to be seen to take a leading role on environment issues. However, efforts by Japanese industry to improve its environmental image internationally have been half-hearted at best. Typical is the Global Environment Charter launched in April 1991 by the Japanese Federation of Economic Organisations (Keidanren), supposedly to provide Japanese corporations with guidelines for environmentally friendly operations overseas. The charter's requirement that companies 'shall strictly observe all national and local laws and regulations for environmental protection' is rather meaningless, since many operations are located where they are precisely because of the absence of such laws and regulations, while the further call on companies to set additional standards of their own 'where necessary' adds nothing of substance.[12] Not surprisingly, a recommendation by the Japanese Bar Association that the overseas operations of Japanese corporations be made subject to Japanese environmental controls has been largely ignored.

One of the industries moved off-shore in response to the tightening of environmental controls at home was Mitsubishi's processing of the elements known as rare earths. This was moved to the state of Perak in Malaysia, where in 1982 it commenced production through Asian Rare Earth, a joint venture between Mitsubishi and Malaysian private and government organisations. The company extracts yttrium from the mineral monazite, which occurs in conjunction with tin deposits, also producing radioactive waste with a high concentration of thorium.

The Malaysian government saw the thorium, over 300 tonnes of which were being produced each year, as a potential source of nuclear energy and so decided to stockpile it. Protests by the villagers of Bukit Merah, where the plant was located, and Papan, where the thorium waste was stored, began almost immediately. They were assured by the Prime Minister and Minister for Science, Technology, and Environment that every precaution had been taken to ensure public safety and that the radioactive storage facility met the most stringent safety standards, and they were told that the production process was essential for the national interest. Despite the reassurances, serious health problems began to emerge in the district, with abnormally high rates of cancer, impaired immune systems, miscarriages, and birth defects being recorded.

What unfolded resembled the Minamata case, though on a smaller scale. A drawn-out legal battle developed between local people who wanted the operation closed down, and the company and the Malaysian government, which were determined to continue it. Protests and civil disobedience resulted in some local leaders being imprisoned under Malaysia's Internal Security Act. In 1992, after seven years of legal dispute, the local people won a victory when the High Court ordered the plant to be shut down within fourteen days. Before the period had expired, Asian Rare Earth, with government backing, had appealed against the court ruling, which was suspended indefinitely, pending the outcome of an independent evaluation of the radiation issue by the Supreme Court. In 1997, the report of a UN Special Rapporteur on 'the adverse effects of the illicit movement and dumping of toxic and dangerous products and wastes on the enjoyment of human rights' commented, 'It is unclear when the [Supreme Court's final] decision will be made.' It noted, however, that in 1994, because of 'widespread public protest', Mitsubishi had decided not to resume operations through Asia Rare Earth. This prompted the response from the Japanese government that Mitsubishi's decision had not been the result of 'environmental reasons and ... posing health threats to villagers at Bukit Merah' or the alleged 'widespread public protest'. It was simply a business decision based on the company's assessment of the prospects of the rare earth industry in Malaysia.

Questions of liability and damages remain undecided. Further, the whole case is complicated by a dimension that has scarcely been broached in public: the villages affected were ethnic Chinese villages, which raises potentially explosive issues such as whether ethnic considerations influenced decisions regarding location of the processing plant and radioactive dump in the first place, or whether they influenced the Malay-dominated government's attitude towards the protests and legal proceedings undertaken by the villagers.

The Bukit Merah case is a good illustration of the way environmental problems arise from industrialisation and economic globalisation. It exhibits all the major symptoms of the Minamata socio-political disease. What it also illustrates is the internationalisation of environmentalism, the way in which community and non-government organisations establish links across national borders, and in their work are able to draw on the expertise and financial support of like-minded individuals and organisations elsewhere. The people of Bukit Merah have been helped by Japanese environmental organisations that have condemned Mitsubishi's role, petitioned the Malaysian Prime Minister to shut down Asian Rare Earth, and have provided financial support and expert advice for legal proceedings. Other international support has ranged from technical reports by European and American authorities on radioactivity and public health, to visits from Japanese parliamentarians expressing shame over the actions of Mitsubishi and showing solidarity with the victims. While globalisation brings new problems, it may also introduce new resources and strategies for coping with them.[13]

## Major environmental issues

These illustrations of the environmental consequences of globalisation primarily have to do with industrial pollution. It is necessary now to give an overview of other environmental issues facing Asian nations, which means returning to some of the problems already mentioned briefly in relation to Java against the background of population increase and rising levels of consumption.

### Water

One of the most serious problems that will face the world in the twenty-first century is scarcity of fresh water. The United Nations Food and Agricultural Organisation, in its November 1996 report to the World Food Summit in Rome, concluded that the global demand for fresh water already exceeded sustainable supply. At the same time, the Independent Commission on Population and Quality of Life warned of the 'impending water crisis'. An international survey of environmental experts that was conducted in preparation for the United Nations Environment Program's Global Environment Outlook 2000 study found that fresh-water scarcity was more likely to be identified as a major issue than anything except climate change.[14]

A global study undertaken by the International Water Management Institute (IWMI), based in Colombo, Sri Lanka, concluded that, by the year 2025, nearly 1.4 billion people, or just fewer than one-quarter of the world population, will experience severe water scarcity. Some countries will experience 'absolute water scarcity'—that is, on current projections they will not have enough water to meet 'reasonable population requirements'. In Asia these countries include Iran, Afghanistan, Pakistan, and Singapore. (Singapore already gets most of its water from Malaysia and Indonesia.) The authors of the IWMI study argue that countries faced with this predicament will have little choice but to stop using water for irrigation, and to industrialise and import most of their food requirements. However, it is difficult to see Afghanistan or Pakistan industrialising by 2025.

In large countries such as India and China, there is great variability in fresh water availability. Parts of north-east India have some of the heaviest rainfall on earth, yet about one-third of the Indian population, or more than 300 million people, lives in areas that will experience absolute water scarcity by 2025. One-third of the Chinese population, or around 400 million people, will face a similar predicament by that time. Much of northern China, including the densely populated North China Plain, routinely experiences water shortages. This applies to both cities and farmland. In Beijing, water consumption increased almost one-hundredfold between 1950 and 1990. Like most developing countries, India and China have responded to the surging demand for water by constructing numerous dams. Many have been massive undertakings designed to meet energy as well as water needs, the appropriateness of which has been questioned on practical, social, and environmental grounds. Chinese authorities have plans for a gargantuan engineering project that would enable large quantities of water to be transferred from the water-rich south to the parched north. It is a scheme whose rationale, like that of the Three Gorges Dam and India's Narmada Valley project, is widely questioned.[15]

Increasing demand for water in urban and rural locations has resulted in greater reliance on subterranean sources as well as greater exploitation of surface water. As in the case of surface water, present rates of consumption are unsustainable. Groundwater levels have fallen dramatically in many regions. In India, where groundwater is used to meet about half of all water needs, the National Environmental Engineering Research Institute found that water tables in crucial areas were falling 'at an alarming rate'. In China, due to overpumping, the water table below the North China Plain is falling at a rate of between 1 and 1.5 metres a year. Groundwater levels in Beijing have fallen by more than 40 metres, and in Shijiazhuang by 30 metres. This in turn has led

Water pollution is not enough to stop Bangkok children from swimming in the canals.

to deterioration of water quality by salination, and to widespread surface subsidence. Parts of Shanghai and other eastern cities in China have sunk by more than 2 metres since 1965. The experience of other Asian cities has been similar. In Bangkok, groundwater levels have fallen by more than 50 metres since 1955, causing subsidence, salination, and heightened flood risk. In Jakarta, Manila, and Chennai, groundwater quality has seriously deteriorated through overuse.[16]

Although the difficulties of satisfying the growing demand for water are particularly obvious in big urban centres, it has been increased agricultural production—especially the intensive production characteristic of the green revolution—that has been the biggest factor in overuse of surface water and groundwater supplies. Many experts argue that most, if not all, problems of water scarcity in the foreseeable future could be overcome by ending inefficient and marginal irrigation.

It was excessive diversion of water for irrigation purposes that produced one of the worst of all modern ecological disasters: the destruction of the Aral Sea, formerly in the Soviet Union and now half in Kazakhstan, half in Uzbekistan. Once biologically rich and able to support a big fishing industry, it is now shrinking at an alarming rate and is almost biologically dead. Uncontrolled exploitation of the rivers that fed it prevented any water entering it after 1980. In 2000, the once enormous lake had been reduced to a sixth its former size. The salt content of what remains has steadily increased and, as the water continues to evaporate, the salt is blown onto the surrounding land, rendering the land sterile. The livelihoods of the 50 million or so people living in the Aral Sea's basin are at risk.[17]

Another disaster story concerning excessive use of water for agriculture comes from the Ganges basin in West Bengal, India, and nearby districts in Bangladesh. In order to irrigate new high-yield rice strains in the late 1960s, thousands of tube wells were sunk to depths of 150 metres or more. Where farmers had traditionally grown one crop a year, they were able to grow three or even four crops. But, as in many parts of the world, the rock strata from which the groundwater was tapped contained arsenic, which dissolved in the water and became more concentrated as groundwater levels fell with overuse. Now, in some villages, not a single well is free of arsenic, while the arsenic content of the water drawn at one village amounts to 147 kilograms per year. The result is that more than 200 000 people have suffered death and disfigurement from cumulative arsenic poisoning. Not only do the victims suffer physically: they are also ostracised because the terrible skin lesions symptomatic of the poisoning are mistaken for leprosy or thought to be contagious. The name given to the water when the wells were first sunk has proved prophetic: 'the devil's water'. Similar problems have emerged in Bangladesh; in Taiwan, where 20 000 people have been affected; and in Inner Mongolia, where 50 000 people have been affected.[18]

Almost everywhere, the problem of water scarcity has been compounded by degradation and pollution of the water that is available. Deforestation has badly harmed watersheds by reducing the soil's capacity to hold and retain moisture, resulting in erosion, siltation, and flooding. Industrial pollution and inadequate sewage treatment render much surface water unfit for use. At the end of the twentieth century, levels of suspended solids in Asian rivers were typically four times the world average and twenty times those in developed countries. Levels of coliform bacteria (which is caused by sewage pollution) were in Asian rivers at three times the world average, with median levels at fifty times the acceptable level set by the WHO. Groundwater supplies, too, are at risk—not only from 'natural' pollutants such as heavy metals in rock substrata, but also from man-made pollutants ranging from petrochemicals and radioactive waste to pesticides and chemical fertilisers. Use of chemical fertilisers in northern China, for example, has resulted, at numerous locations, in groundwater nitrate levels that measure five times the WHO maximum. In Sri Lanka nearly 80 per cent of groundwater samples exceed the WHO limits.[19]

Political and social conflict over the control of water has also been a serious problem, one widely expected to get worse as needs grow and untapped resources diminish. Irrigation needs in the Punjab have resulted in water disputes between villages and provinces, and have been a source of tension between India and Pakistan. Deforestation in Nepal aggravated flooding problems in the Ganges basin in India and Bangladesh, and those countries in turn had a lengthy dispute regarding use of Ganges water. It was only in December 1996 that they were able to reach agreement on the issue. Along the Mekong, tensions have also risen over water utilisation. China's work on a major hydroelectric scheme on the Lancang (as the Mekong is called in China) has upset Cambodia, Laos, Thailand, and Vietnam, all of which have plans of their own. These plans, which include the construction of eleven dams, were the subject of the Agreement on Cooperation for the Sustainable Development of the Mekong River Basin, signed in April 1995.[20]

## Air

Like water pollution, air pollution is most conspicuous in the big cities of Asia. Rapid urbanisation and industrialisation, coupled with few effective environmental controls, mean that except in a few of the richer countries such as Japan and Singapore it is quickly getting worse. Energy generation, motor vehicles, and heavy industry—all three strongly associated with urban growth—are the major causes. But it is air pollution, more than anything else, that demonstrates that environmental problems are global. The acid rain that falls on Taiwan, Japan, and Korea is partly caused by the sulphur dioxide emitted by China's coal-fired power stations. Mongolia receives acid rain from Asian Russia. Singapore shares the consequences of industrial pollution and forest fires in Malaysia and Indonesia. Climate change resulting from greenhouse gas emission and deforestation affects all countries, from the Maldive Islands to eastern Siberia.

Air pollution is not a modern invention. The pollution resulting from the burning of biomass such as wood, straw, and dung for domestic energy needs has always been a factor in the high incidence of respiratory diseases in peasant and other pre-modern societies, and continues to be one in rural areas of all developing countries. To this extent it could be argued that thermal generation of electricity has merely moved air pollution from the home into the market place, along with the rest of the economy. But the scale and intensity of contemporary air pollution are unprecedented.

International studies indicate that the situation in Asian cities is particularly bad. In the late 1980s, twelve of the fifteen cities in the world with the highest levels of pollution in the form of airborne particles were in Asia, as were six of the fifteen with the highest levels of sulphur dioxide. In terms of overall air pollution, five out of seven of the worst cities in the world were in Asia (see Table 7.1). Conspicuously absent from the list were the big Japanese urban centres such as Tokyo and Osaka, which like most Japanese cities had experienced serious air pollution in the preceding decades. Since the late 1960s the development of cleaner technologies, together with legal measures to enforce their adoption, has made it possible to bring about a strong improvement, and also for the Japanese authorities to claim a world leadership role in this field. Air pollution control mechanisms featured prominently in Japan's environment-related development aid to China during the 1990s.[21]

**Table 7.1** Air pollution in Asian cities, late 1980s

| *Highest levels of particulate matter* | *Highest levels of sulphur dioxide* | *Worst overall ranking* |
|---|---|---|
| Shenyang | Shenyang | Calcutta |
| Xi'an | Seoul | Jakarta |
| New Delhi | Xi'an | New Delhi |
| Beijing | Beijing | Beijing |
| Calcutta | Manila | Shenyang |
| Jakarta | Guangzhou | |
| Shanghai | | |
| Guangzhou | | |
| Illigan City | | |
| Bangkok | | |
| Bombay | | |
| Kuala Lumpur | | |

Source: C. Brandon and R. Ramankutty, *Toward an Environmental Strategy for Asia*, World Bank Discussion Paper no. 224, World Bank, Washington, DC, 1993, 22.

A summer morning on Chang'an Avenue in Beijing. The haze of air pollution is unmistakable.

## Soil

Soil loss and soil degradation are also major problems that limit the capacity of Asian countries to sustain their growing populations. As mentioned in relation to Java, urbanisation is resulting in large tracts of the most productive land being lost for agriculture. The large dams being constructed to provide electric power in most countries have a similar effect. Soil erosion resulting from practices such as deforestation, clearing of marginal land, overgrazing and other forms of poor land management affect much larger areas. Dry regions are particularly vulnerable. In the mid-1990s, nearly 180 million hectares of China's grasslands were found to be degraded, as were 110 million hectares in India and 62 million hectares in Pakistan. This amounted to 56, 57, and 86 per cent respectively of the vulnerable dry lands of those countries. Between them, China, India, and Pakistan also accounted for about half of the world's irrigated land damaged by salination, which together with waterlogging is another major factor in soil degradation. The heavy reliance on chemical pesticides and fertilisers associated

The forest strikes back, Angkor Wat, Cambodia.

with monoculture production of up to three or four crops a year also results in ground poisoning and water pollution, and depletes soils of organic nutrients.[22]

## Forests

Deforestation is perhaps the most visible evidence of the rate of environmental change occurring in Asian countries. Not that it is a new problem. In some regions it has been many hundreds of years since primary forests were cleared. For example northern China, with its dense population, big urban centres and, above all, highly developed iron industry to support, was largely deforested by the end of the twelfth century. The fertile and heavily populated plains of the Indus and the Ganges experienced the same fate early in their history.

Deforestation is still occurring in China, Pakistan, India, and Bangladesh, but now it is in the remote regions that contain most of the remaining areas of forest cover: Heilongjiang in north-eastern China, and Yunnan, Sichuan, and Guangxi in the south-west; the foothills of the Karakoram in Pakistan; the Himalaya and Andaman and Nicobar Islands in India; and the Chittagong Hill Tracts in Bangladesh. Colonialism enforced deforestation in some regions during the nineteenth and early twentieth centuries, including northern and southern India, Myanmar, the Malaysian peninsula, western Indonesia, and parts of the Philippines. But this was mild compared with what has occurred since the 1950s in the context of postcolonial nation-building, population growth, and increased world demand for timber. Nepal, Thailand, and the Philippines have only a small proportion of their original forest cover remaining, while in Myanmar, Cambodia, Laos, Vietnam, the Malaysian states of Sabah and Sarawak, the outer islands of Indonesia, and also eastern Siberia, deforestation is occurring at alarming rates (see Table 7.2). Between 1990 and 1995 the rates of deforestation in the Mekong

**Table 7.2** Rate of deforestation in Asian countries

| | *Average annual rate of deforestation 1980–90 (%)* | *Average annual rate of deforestation 1990–95 (%)* |
|---|---|---|
| Bangladesh | 1.8 | 0.9 |
| Cambodia | 2.4 | 1.6 |
| China | -0.6 | 0.1 |
| India | -1.1 | 0.0 |
| Indonesia | 0.8 | 1.0 |
| Iran | 1.8 | 1.8 |
| Japan | - | 0.1 |
| Laos | - | 1.2 |
| Malaysia | 2.1 | 2.4 |
| Myanmar | 1.2 | 1.4 |
| Nepal | 0.9 | 1.1 |
| Pakistan | 3.1 | 2.9 |
| Philippines | 3.3 | 3.5 |
| South Korea | -2.0 | 0.2 |
| Sri Lanka | 1.0 | 1.1 |
| Thailand | 3.1 | 2.6 |
| Vietnam | 0.9 | 1.4 |

Source: United Nations Development Program, *Human Development Report 2000*, Oxford University Press, New York, 2000, 231–4.

basin (1.6 per cent a year) and South-East Asia (1.3 per cent a year) exceeded those in any other region of the world.

The causes of deforestation are many. Advocates of development often blame traditional swidden agriculturalists and their unscientific forest management, while opponents of development blame the greed of commercial loggers and shortsighted governments. The evidence overwhelmingly supports the latter argument. However, the former argument cannot be lightly dismissed either. While slash and burn agriculture traditionally appears to have had little environmental impact, the population increase experienced in recent decades by some of its practitioners has made it much more difficult, if not impossible, to maintain ecological balance. Moreover, where hill tribes have been persuaded to replace traditional cash crops such as opium with other, more socially acceptable crops such as vegetables and fruit, land-use patterns have changed, and now often involve the use of chemical fertilisers and pesticides, as well as greater quantities of water.

Forest-clearing for sedentary agriculture continues to deprive indigenous minorities of their customary lands. In Kalimantan and West Papua in Indonesia, in north-eastern India and Bangladesh, this has led to violence and armed clashes, and louder calls for self-determination for indigenous minorities. However, fuel needs account for the bulk of wood consumption. These needs become ever harder to meet as population pressures increase. Fires associated with the movement of more people into forested areas also wreak havoc. In 1982–83 fire destroyed some 25 per cent of the rainforest in eastern Kalimantan, while in Heilongjiang in 1987 more than 1 million hectares of conifer forest were destroyed by a single fire. In Mongolia in 1996, fire destroyed 3 million hectares. In Vietnam, Laos, and Cambodia, vast tracts of forest were destroyed during the protracted warfare of the 1960s and 1970s.

The extensive fires in drought-stricken Kalimantan during 1997 destroyed large tracts of peat soil along with the forests, and created smog that disrupted life and threatened public health in neighbouring countries as well as other parts of Indonesia. The scale of destruction and pollution, together with the political tensions generated, demonstrated vividly that environmental problems often transcend political boundaries and cannot be regarded simply as domestic issues.[23]

## Biodiversity

Loss of biodiversity is one of the most serious consequences of deforestation, through both clearfelling of primary forest and its replacement with monoculture plantations. The forests of South-East Asia and the Indian subcontinent are particularly rich in biodiversity. It is estimated that the South-East Asian forests alone contain between 20 and 25 per cent of the earth's plant species. Their destruction represents the irretrievable loss of a rich variety of fauna as well as flora. Continued hunting, often illegal, of rare and endangered animals that fetch a high price as culinary exotica or in traditional medicines, places them further at risk. Water pollution and siltation of rivers and lakes seriously threaten the survival of many aquatic species of animals and plants, in both fresh and estuarine waters. The threat to sealife is more difficult to assess, but depletion of fish stocks in continental waters, pollution, and destruction of habitats such as coral reefs, give serious grounds for concern.[24]

## Wastes

Water and air pollution is largely the result of industrial and household wastes such as factory effluent, smoke and exhaust gases, and sewage. Increasing production of solid and toxic wastes is best treated as a problem distinct from water and air pollution, despite the connections so terribly obvious in places such as Minamata and Surabaya. Especially in the big urban centres, safe disposal of solid and toxic wastes is becoming an urgent matter. Solid waste is particularly a problem in the more affluent countries such as Japan, Korea, and Taiwan. Over the decade 1982–92, the amount of garbage produced by Japan's urban population increased by more than a third. Per capita production of garbage in Seoul far exceeds that of any city in Asia except those in Japan. It has been estimated that in China, where in 1996 the average person produced 440 kilograms of garbage each year, by 2020 per capita garbage production will have increased fourfold, largely as a result of higher living standards. In Taiwan in 1993, 'garbage wars' broke out when communities refused to permit further dumping of rubbish (whether legal or illegal) in their locales, an indication of the levels of frustration and anger aroused by the waste issue.[25]

While toxic waste problems have already been mentioned, special reference must be made here to nuclear waste. Japan, Korea, and Taiwan rely heavily on nuclear energy for electric power. Other countries, including China and India, have also embarked on nuclear energy programs. The problem of long-term storage of spent fuel rods remains unsolved, just as the nuclear energy generation process itself remains susceptible to errors and accidents. For the Japanese, who have committed themselves to the development of fast breeder reactors using recycled fuel, the problems of waste storage are serious, particularly in view of the difficulties of finding in Japan, located as it is at the junction of four tectonic plates and subject to frequent earthquakes, a site sufficiently stable geologically to ensure the long-term security of the waste stored. A serious accident at a nuclear power station in December 1999 increased public opposition to further expansion of Japan's nuclear energy program.[26]

For many years the South Korean government has encountered strong community opposition wherever it has proposed to establish a permanent nuclear waste dump, despite the fact that more than 40 per cent of the nation's energy comes from nuclear generators, and temporary storage facilities have only a limited capacity. With plans to increase the number of reactors from 14 to 28 by the year 2015, a decision could not be further delayed and the government chose a site on a small island 80 kilometres west of the city of Inchon. Early in 1997, the South Korean government itself vented its fury against Taiwan for obtaining agreement from the North Korean government to store low-level radioactive waste there. The South Korean authorities labelled the scheme a plan to turn the Korean peninsula into 'a death zone' and succeeded in stopping it after intense diplomatic lobbying.[27]

## Responses to environmental problems

The environment is the setting for human action and so bears the consequences of all that humans do: procreate, eat, defecate, produce, despoil, die. Some would argue that it is thinking in environmental terms—seeing the natural world merely as a place for humans to feed, fight and fornicate—that is a large part of the problem. However, it does imply that environmental problems can be solved only by changing all that humans do. This is just another way of saying that environmental problems are actually human problems. Environmental problems require us to solve political, social, and economic ones.

There are those who scoff at technological solutions, the claim that there is a technological solution for everything from air pollution to loss of biodiversity or inadequate

Rethinking the urban environment: the Step Garden of Acros Fukuoka, Fukuoka, Japan, has thirteen levels. The building's interior is designed around an atrium fourteen storeys high.

food supply. While they may be inclined to see technology as an evil and overlook the fact that alternative societies are just as technologically dependent, they are right in saying that technological innovation alone can achieve little. The forces that lead to environmental destruction are often the same ones that inhibit the sorts of technological innovation needed to develop viable alternatives. The recent history of family planning shows that even efficient and reliable technology can fail to have an impact if it runs up against countervailing social and political forces. Sophisticated water purification and supply systems, sewage treatment plants, and environmentally friendly industrial production technologies are of little use to Third World countries that cannot afford to buy them. Capital-intensive agriculture may produce more food in the short and intermediate term, yet cause huge social and economic dislocation in rural areas, prompting mass migration to the cities and widespread political unrest. The argument that water-poor developing countries such as Pakistan can solve their urgent water needs by halting irrigated agriculture, industrialising, and then importing their food requirements, is hardly realistic.

Legal responses to environmental problems are like technological ones. In conjunction with other measures they may make an impact, but on their own they are unlikely to have much effect at all. Environmental law has in recent decades become one of the fastest-growing areas of legal activity, both internationally and within the jurisdiction of individual states.

At the national level, most constitutions include provisions on the rights and duties of citizens in regard to the environment. For example, the Constitution of India declares that 'The State shall endeavour to protect and improve the environment and to safeguard the forests and wildlife of the country' (Part 4, Article 48A), and that 'It shall be the duty of every citizen of India to … protect and improve the natural environment including forests, lakes, rivers and wild life, and to have compassion for living creatures' (Part 4A, Article 51A).

The reciprocal obligations of state and citizens are also set out in the Constitution of the Republic of Korea: 'All citizens shall have the right to a healthy and pleasant environment. The State and all citizens shall endeavour to protect the environment' (Chapter 2, Article 35). The Iranian Constitution declares that 'The preservation of the environment, in which the present as well as future generations have a right to flourishing social existence, is regarded as a public duty in the Islamic Republic. Economic and other activities that inevitably involve pollution of the environment or cause irreparable damage to it are therefore forbidden.'[28]

Specific environmental laws have also been widely introduced. These range from overarching legislation such as Japan's Environmental Basic Law (1993), which sets out the principles and administrative mechanisms to guide environmental regulation and the nation's obligations regarding international protection of the environment, to laws addressing particular issues such as deforestation or industrial pollution. Like other legal measures, these face the problems of implementation. As with human rights, it is much easier to introduce laws to protect the environment than to make those laws work. The authorities may not have the resources or the expertise to enforce the legislation, or may choose not to try to enforce it, because of indifference, for personal gain, or on compassionate grounds.

Especially in densely populated and relatively poor nations such as India, Bangladesh, and China, local officials often have to choose between enforcing environmental laws and allowing families they know personally to obtain food, fuel, or other essentials. The people themselves often ignore the laws, despite the risk of police harassment and extortion, because for them it is quite literally a matter of life and death. It may come down to a decision to cut down the last tree, to turn the last Javanese rhinoceros into tomorrow's dinner. The words of a village headman from north-east Thailand sum up the predicament of many of the rural people of Asia: 'The forest is diminishing. The droughts are getting longer, and food is harder to find. Hunger is the enemy we still cannot beat.'[29]

The law, like technology, will be largely ineffective in protecting the environment unless it is supported by far-reaching political and economic change. One sort of change widely touted as a solution to environmental problems—indeed, to all problems—is of course more development. Economic development, we are told, will put an end to population growth, leading to more environmentally friendly industries, and better educated and environmentally conscious citizens. It will also lead to more democratic systems of government, which will enable citizens to compel their representatives to

Wholesale fish market, Dhaka, Bangladesh.

act on behalf of the environment. 'Promoting economic development', in the words of a former chief economist of the World Bank, 'is the best way to protect the environment'. Market forces will encourage responsible attitudes towards use of natural resources. Problems of water supply, it is widely believed, will be solved when water comes to be regarded as an economic good that must be paid for rather than a natural right. Such an approach would curb waste and, by introducing the profit motive, encourage private investment in water supply and treatment services. Predictably, this view is strongly advocated by the World Bank and the Asian Development Bank. According to the latter, for example, 'scarcity of water is largely an economic issue. This idea, that water has an economic value in all its competing uses and should be recognised as an economic good, must underlie all efforts for rational water resource management.'[30]

There are those who react with dismay and disbelief to the suggestion that growth-oriented development and market forces are the answer to environmental problems. They argue that political and economic change must go in the opposite direction if either the human race or the natural world is to survive. Many pin their hopes on what they see as going back to tradition, to small, largely self-sufficient communities living in harmony with their surroundings, with natural resources owned and worked in common. This stream of thought is particularly strong in India and Sri Lanka, partly due to the influence of Gandhi and his ideal of village republics devoted to cooperative labour in cottage industries and handicrafts. Gandhi believed that large-scale industrialisation and consumption along Western lines was not an option for India. 'God forbid', he commented in 1928, 'that India should ever take to industrialisation after the manner of the west. The economic imperialism of a single tiny island kingdom [England] is today keeping the world in chains. If an entire nation of 300 million took to similar economic exploitation, it would strip the world bare like locusts.' Those influenced by him point to the strength of grassroots environmentalism in the Indian countryside, whether in preservation forests or the establishment of green villages and rehabilitation of communal lands.[31]

Both lines of thinking reduce themselves to absurdity if pushed far enough. The economic libertarian position is perhaps the more intellectually and emotionally distasteful of the two, in view of the fervour with which it is preached in government and business circles, and hence its greater capacity to do harm when, inevitably, it fails to deliver what its advocates promise. They have been prudent enough to build into their theory a mechanism to safeguard it from falsification, in the form of the concept of market failure: when things do not work out as predicted, it is because reality rather than the theory has failed. Were the market to function perfectly, and all costs and benefits were properly considered, events would unfold as the theory requires.

Contrary to the common perception, we are told, there is no trade-off between environmental protection and economic growth. Rational policies will factor in long-term environmental and social costs as well as shorter-term financial gains, and so maximise economic efficiency and social return on investment.[32] Unfortunately, the majority of economic actors are sufficiently rational to recognise that no one has ever been required to meet the full environmental and social costs of production and innovation, and that market and government alike are too preoccupied with current issues to give serious consideration to the problems that will face later generations. Hence they cheerfully continue to transfer the costs incurred by their private gain to society in general and to future generations.

Attempts to reckon up the economic and social costs of natural resource usage and environmental damage may be seen as a move to make the market more rational. The cost of acid rain, desertification, deforestation, water pollution, and other types of environmental damage cannot be omitted from national balance sheets if they are in any way to approximate reality. A 1996 study of China, for example, concluded that the cost of environmental degradation and pollution was around 10 per cent of GDP, 'a burden clearly justifying much higher investment in environmental protection and management'.[33] Exhaustion of non-renewable natural resources must also be factored into the equation. Yet resources such as minerals, fossil fuels, and rainforest timbers continue to be regarded as free, with the only costs to the producer being those of production. Once a nation's oil or iron ore deposits are exhausted, however, those things have to be purchased elsewhere. It is normal accounting practice to subtract depreciation of plant and equipment from the output of goods and services used to calculate GDP, but not to subtract the costs of resource depletion and environmental damage. What this means, it has been argued, is that 'Every country is practising the environmental equivalent of deficit financing in one form or another'.[34]

It is easy to become hypnotised by the language of economics, to be seduced into agreeing that all our problems would be over if only we could develop a suitably precise system of accounting. The fact remains that there are many aspects of human interaction with the natural world that cannot be measured in economic terms. The value of biodiversity, for example, or the wish to save animal and plant species from extinction, defies monetary calculation. The same is true of the value attached to different lifestyles.

The opposing intellectual trend, which I have linked to the name of Gandhi and which for simplicity's sake may be labelled traditionalism, also degenerates quickly into self-parody. This occurs when middle-class urban intellectuals become afflicted with nostalgia for community and tradition, and look for social justice and environmental balance in villages sustained by spiritual values and freed from the imperative of development. An idealised past replaces the economically rational future. Convinced that the great majority gain no benefit from development, they argue that it is in traditional social forms and bodies of knowledge that hope lies. But the majority of peasants, it appears, remain unconvinced and continue to aspire to the benefits of development, and while many are forced to leave their village by economic dislocation, others are glad to leave behind the constraints of village life.

In 1928 Gandhi wrote that Western-style industrialisation was not an option for India, and the combined population of what is now India, Bangladesh, and Pakistan was 300 million. A vision of society based on village communities engaged in traditional agriculture and handicraft production had little of nostalgia about it; rather, it was a perception of things more or less as they were. More than seventy years of industrialisation and urbanisation and an additional 1 billion people later, the suggestion that tradition alone could give the people of India, Bangladesh, and Pakistan a secure and satisfying life that development could not provide is hardly credible. Fortunately the argument is rarely expressed in such black and white terms.

## Grassroots environmentalism

At the heart of traditionalist thinking is the conviction that development has made many people worse off while reducing the control they have over their lives, most conspicuously their control over the physical setting in which they live. Reversion to village communities largely self-sufficient in production is a local form of insulation, a regional equivalent of delinking from the global economy, and similarly intended to bring greater autonomy and control. Economically and environmentally, it is seen as an expression of popular opposition to the developmentalist state, in much the same way as Gandhi's *satyagraha* movement expressed opposition to the colonial state, using similar means. Whatever doubts one might have concerning the capacity of tradition alone to provide solutions to the environmental problems facing Asian societies, it is hard to disagree with the view that there must be more opportunity for grassroots input to environmental management and protection, and political participation generally. The environmental dangers arising from economic globalisation are particularly acute when they coincide with centralisation of decision-making and control at the national level, so that communities lose control over their environment and over the political processes that would allow them to respond to their predicament.

The emergence of grassroots environmental protest across Asia in recent decades has been a striking development. It has occurred not only in countries such as India and the Philippines, which have relatively strong traditions of political protest and alternative socio-economic organisation, but also in countries without such traditions: Indonesia, Malaysia, Taiwan, South Korea and, more recently, the People's Republic of China. That protest occurs even under repressive governments is evidence of the strength of the concerns being expressed, in which environmental, social, and economic issues may be indistinguishable from each other. Particularly in cases involving indigenous minorities, protests against environmental destruction tend to be protests also against the destruction of the economic and social life of the peoples in question.

The Chipko Movement of the Indian Himalaya began with mountain people whose economic and cultural survival was threatened by commercial exploitation of the forest. The public protest and civil disobedience of the Penan of Sarawak was prompted by similar fears of environmental and socio-cultural destruction. Such activism may appear very different from some of the most conspicuous varieties of environmentalism in Western societies, which frequently equate any economic activity with environmental destruction. However, much environmental protest in Asia is indistinguishable from that in the West, for example protest in response to pollution problems such as Minamata in Japan and Bukit Merah in Malaysia, or on behalf of plant and animal species threatened by extinction, such as Yunnan's golden monkey and the Siberian tiger.[35]

Grassroots environmentalism, whether analogous to dominant forms of environmentalism in the West or not, matters because it brings out into the open problems that might otherwise be ignored or suppressed in the name of the 'national interest'. Environmental concerns, particularly when linked to issues of personal survival or well-being, easily become explosive if suppressed, a threat to what governments like to call public order. But grassroots environmentalism must not be regarded merely in negative terms, as protest or grievance against the state. Popular environmentalism matters above all because it can contribute to the solution of environmental problems. Blanket responses imposed from above often fail because they do not adequately take account of local circumstances, while communities and local organisations can frequently take initiatives that would be risky or impossible as national policy.

What we must not do, however, is allow enthusiasm for grassroots activities and despair of developmentalist governments to lead to the conclusion that local action can be a substitute for environmental action on a national scale. Many environmental problems, such as acid rain, ozone depletion, and global warming, are beyond the reach of local action. Even disputes over water usage and pollution of international rivers such as the Mekong and the Ganges have to be settled at the national level. Local knowledge and initiative may be effective in preventing environmental degradation and undertaking rehabilitation, especially in the face of government indifference or incapacity. But where governments and communities work together the results are likely to be more impressive still.[36]

## Innovation within tradition

When in 1928 Gandhi declared that Western-style industrialisation was not a realistic option for India, he did not have access to much of the information we now possess. Yet his conclusion was basically correct.

In relation to China, it has been demonstrated that even with population growth kept to moderate levels through strict fertility control programs, the state's ambitious economic modernisation plans coupled with the rising socio-economic expectations of the people imply increasing strain on local ecosystems already severely damaged, and very heavy demands on other parts of the natural world. The author of the study in question is too cautious to say outright that China's needs and aspirations cannot be satisfied, but sees little reason for optimism even in the intermediate term:

> the environmental foundations of China's national existence are alarmingly weak, and they continue to deteriorate at high rates. This state of affairs, worrisome in itself, must give rise to even greater concerns when one considers the enormous resource needs implied in the country's continuing high absolute population growth and in its ambitious plans for economic modernization.[37]

While much may be achieved by technological innovation and environmental regulation energetically pursued, basic limits to growth such as availability of soil and water leave very little room to manoeuvre. Because of its population size and relatively low income levels, China cannot escape its predicament by building up an advanced industrial economy and satisfying its growing food and natural resource needs through foreign trade.

The same is true of India, which in terms of economic development lags behind China while its population is growing faster, and by the year 2035 will be the largest in the world. When the situations of India, China, Indonesia, Pakistan, and Bangladesh are considered together, it becomes plain that Western-style industrialisation, coupled with importation of a large proportion of their food and natural resource requirements, is not a realistic option for any one of them. They *must* do things differently, ordering their economies in such a way as to continue producing the bulk of their food requirements and other natural resource needs. This implies, in turn, that the powerful trend of urbanisation must be slowed, perhaps stopped, and the larger part of the workforce encouraged to remain in agriculture and primary production.

It was some time before 1920 that Gandhi adopted the spinning wheel as a symbol of his quest for a mode of production different from the large-scale industrialisation encouraged in India by the British colonial authorities. For him the spinning wheel represented production through human effort, application of that human energy with which India was generously endowed and which Western technology threatened to make redundant. Yet even then spinning wheels had already fallen into disuse.[38] In a sense, Gandhi's program represented a return to the past, a past shaped by indigenous traditions and technologies rather than the demands of a foreign power.

Today it is clear that the search for modes of economic production other than those based on continuous growth and free market principles need not imply a rejection of advanced technologies from abroad. Indeed, adoption of such a position looks very silly. While traditional skills and bodies of knowledge may prove invaluable in developing alternative, ecologically appropriate economic strategies, the contribution of modern scientific knowledge and technology is likely to prove no less so. The search for alternatives must not be reduced to xenophobic antiquarianism. Some of the most impressive achievements in intermediate or alternative technology have come from the blending of the traditional and modern, while others have been the result of the most advanced scientific and technological know-how being used to solve prosaic, commonplace Third World problems.

Nor is the quest for alternative modes of production in some areas, such as agriculture, necessarily incompatible with the development of large-scale, high-tech industries, such as renewable energy supply, in others. In the global economy, nations cannot afford to turn their backs on modern, technologically advanced production, but neither can they afford to ignore the need for mixed economies fitted to their ecological and economic circumstances. Once we have rejected the assumption of universal solutions to the environmental and economic predicaments in which nations find themselves, it becomes clear that providing opportunity for grassroots input is not an indulgence or a pre-emptive political strategy, but rather an environmental, economic, and social necessity. It is a matter of enabling people to find their own solutions instead of having them imposed.[39]

## Social justice

If the solution of environmental problems requires democratic participation, so too does it require social justice.[40] Social justice demands that everyone should be able to satisfy their basic human needs. It also demands that no particular social groups or nations should bear a disproportionate part of the burden of socio-economic change and its environmental impact, while receiving less than a fair share of the benefits of change. In a global economic system that impinges on a global ecosystem, social justice is a matter of relations between nations as well as within them.

Those struggling to survive have little time or inclination to reflect on the ecological soundness of their actions or the situation of future generations. The need to secure food and fuel in an overcrowded, degraded landscape does not encourage cooperation to achieve environmental goals unless it is clear that those goals and basic human needs may best be fulfilled together. Nowhere is this more evident than in relation to forests. Where forests are declared government property and closed to local communities for traditional usage, both the law and the government's forestry objectives are likely to be ignored. Afforestation projects are doomed to failure. But where local communities are able to derive economic and other traditional benefits from the forests, they are likely to be much more vigilant than any government authority in caring for them. This has been demonstrated in virtually every Asian country. 'Social forestry' may have its problems, but these are minor compared with its long-term benefits.[41]

Social justice requires that ethnic minorities and rural people not be deprived of their land and natural resources in the name of national development; or, where they are deprived, that they receive adequate compensation. Often environmental protests are not directed against the development project itself so much as failure of the authorities to provide adequate compensation for those displaced or otherwise affected, and the fact that those at whose cost the project is undertaken will receive little benefit from it. There is a tendency for protests of this sort to be dismissed as insular selfishness and failure to identify with the nation and its purpose. Western investors and consultants are particularly inclined to dismiss protests as a NIMBY (Not In My

Trees provide shelter from the summer heat in Xi'an, Shaanxi, China.

Backyard) reflex, as if the protests were middle-class expressions of concern about lifestyle, as sometimes happens in affluent countries. When those affected by a development project are on the brink, it is life rather than lifestyle that is at stake, and where an indigenous minority is denied the advantages of political and economic participation, there is little reason for its members to identify with a national purpose.

A social system in which elites and foreign investors grow rich from industries that are environmentally destructive, while imposing on the general society the costs of that destruction, is neither just nor environmentally sound. Justice demands that those who profit from water and air pollution, deforestation and resource depletion must contribute to the cost of remedial action. Such concerns have led to a range of taxation measures—including so-called 'carbon taxes'—in many countries to ensure that those who inflict environmental damage in pursuit of private gain pay some of the cost.[42] Internationally, it is unjust as well as environmentally unsound for wealthy, technologically advanced nations to profit by selling environment-friendly technologies to nations whose environments they have helped to destroy in their hunger for natural resources. In this regard, Japan's development aid to China in the form of technology to prevent acid rain is a welcome departure.

In some cases there may be grounds for compensation as well as technological assistance. There are precedents for this. In 1992, for example, the International Court of Justice ruled that Australia had a case to answer in a claim for damages by the Pacific island nation of Nauru, relating to phosphate mining carried out before independence. An out-of-court settlement in 1993 saw Australia pay $A107 million in compensation.

A developing nation with a large foreign debt to service cannot be expected to devote much of its resources to protection and regeneration of the environment. It was this consideration that led to the concept of Debt for Nature Swaps, an arrangement under which an environmental agency or government of a developed country offers to pay out part of a developing country's debt, at a discounted rate agreed with its creditors, if the developing country is willing to spend the discounted amount on an agreed environmental project. Between 1987 and 1992 there were nineteen such swaps worldwide. The only one involving an Asian nation was in the Philippines. Concern over possible infringement of national sovereignty has led some governments, including Indonesia, to break off negotiations.[43]

Although Debt for Nature Swaps have proved useful in achieving specific and limited environmental objectives, they do little to reduce the debt burden of the nations in question, and do even less to alter the economic, social, and political pressures that generated the debt and the environmental problems in the first place. This latter point applies even to larger-scale initiatives to reduce debt burdens, such as those undertaken in 2000–01 by the G-8 group of countries and (in a preparatory way only) by the World Bank and the IMF. In any case, these initiatives have only been directed towards so-called 'heavily indebted poor countries' (HIPCs), of which none is Asian, though Laos and Myanmar have been considered for inclusion.[44] One can still imagine a situation arising in which the government of other nations with serious debt burdens, such as Indonesia, Pakistan, or the Philippines, might declare that it owes it to the world to repudiate its debts and use some of the funds that would otherwise have gone towards paying interest to play its part in protecting the global environment.

## One world

The image of Earth from out in space drives home the interdependence of living things and everything they do. As far as understanding environmental issues is concerned, and formulating solutions to problems, nothing can be left out. The effects of rising population and consumption levels are felt globally, but not equally. Economic globalisation and technological development have made it possible for powerful societies and groups to transfer ecological strain to others. Sustainability is elastic at the local level, if not in global terms. But technology cannot do away with the need for resources altogether, and it is in regard to basic requirements such as water and soil that the finite nature of resources is most evident. Responding to the serious environmental problems facing Asian societies requires social and technological innovation as well as traditional knowledge and strategies. Innovation and tradition cannot be seen as mutually exclusive alternatives. While opportunities for grassroots involvement are essential for harnessing local knowledge and support, both national and international action is necessary to address issues that transcend local concerns. Collaboration at all levels is required if social justice is to be achieved.

It might be asked, at this point, whether ecological balance and environmental harmony may not be achieved more readily under the influence of some cultural traditions than others. It is often claimed that systems that place human beings firmly within the natural order—such as Buddhism, Daoism, and Shinto—are much to be preferred in this regard to systems such as Christianity and Islam, which put human beings in a special position, declaring that the natural world exists for their benefit. Some argue that a dualism of soul and body, fundamental to Christianity and Islam, leads to a split between humans and nature, which in turn leads Western conservationists to become obsessed with wilderness, nature untouched or undisturbed by human hands, while regarding all human activity as a threat to nature. A Buddhist or Daoist, by contrast, sees humans as part of nature and subject to its laws, and therefore will be mindful of the need to live in harmony with the natural world, rather than attempting to dominate it. The counter argument is that while God gave humans dominion over the natural world, he also made them responsible for it. Moreover, it is only when we have left behind human interests and 'speciesist' assumptions that we can become genuinely concerned about the well-being of other species, gain adequate scientific understanding of them, and act effectively for their protection.[45]

Both views have their strong points, and both positions may be used to argue for environmental responsibility. It would be rash to insist that one is superior to the other, because in practice it appears to make much less difference than might be expected. Evidence of greater environmental wisdom and care in any one of the 'great traditions' is difficult to detect. For lots of reasons, it seems more appropriate to locate humans within the natural order rather than above it. But at the same time it is necessary to recognise that humans are different from other living things, even if the difference is one of degree rather than kind. Humans have a power to destroy and to protect that sets them apart. It does not matter particularly which arguments are used to persuade them to protect rather than to destroy, so long as they are persuaded.

CHAPTER EIGHT

# Family Matters

## The question of convergence

It is in the family, we are told, that society reproduces itself. It is no less true, of course, that it is through the family that society changes.

One question about the family that has dominated recent research in Asian countries is whether there is convergence towards a single family pattern that is an outcome of the development process. Are all societies becoming alike in terms of family structure and functions, with people everywhere moving towards the small, 'simple' (nuclear or conjugal) family, shorn of most of its traditional functions, and widely believed to be the norm in the West?[1] To many the answer seems so obvious that this sort of trend in family arrangements is considered proof or part of development itself, and as such becomes an occasion for either hope or despair. There is a parallel with demographic transition, a phenomenon that holds many implications for the family. As discussed in Chapter 6, demographic transition has variously been identified as a result of economic development; as a cause; and as part of development or the all-encompassing process of change labelled 'modernisation'.

The question of convergence is not easy to deal with, requiring as it does a knowledge of the range of family structures and functions in Eastern and Western societies, as well as of current trends and what is driving them. There is a good deal of evidence, however, that contradicts the assumptions underlying much conventional thinking about the evolution of the family. Contrary to what has been commonly thought, the nuclear or conjugal household is not the invention of Western industrialised and urbanised societies, and has in fact been common in many Asian societies for hundreds of years. While the size of households has decreased in recent decades, the proportion of complex households among them has not necessarily diminished in all societies. There is no evidence of a uniform trend towards nuclear families in the context of economic development, and while industrialisation, urbanisation, formal education, and other aspects of development certainly have a strong impact on the family, the precise impact depends on cultural and local factors as much as global ones. So while the family in Asian societies is undoubtedly undergoing rapid change, the changes are not converging on 'the Western model', if there is such a thing.

## Families and households

It is useful at the outset to distinguish between families and households. Simply put, 'family' has to do with kinship, while 'household' has to do with co-residence. To some social scientists in recent years, focusing attention on the household has appeared attractive as a way of avoiding many of the problems those preoccupied with kinship theory have created for themselves.

Unlike kinship systems, households are social units that are easily observed; they are activity-based groups whose behaviour can be examined and compared fairly readily across cultures. Much of what is written about the family as a social unit is better understood as being about households.[2] But equating family with household can be seriously misleading, especially if it results in inferences regarding kinship attitudes and values being made on the basis of housing arrangements. For example, a trend towards nuclear households is often taken as evidence of greater individualism or selfishness on the part of a population, without any evidence beyond the conviction that people in large multi-generational households are inclined to be more group-oriented, more sensitive to the welfare and interests of others. The fact is that there is no neat correlation to be found between type of household structure and particular sets of family and social values, and a change in one cannot always be read as evidence of a change in the other.

Not all of those who live together are necessarily kin. A group of single workers or students sharing a house is not a family, even though it may be more cohesive than many families. An upper-class or middle-class household in most Asian societies would traditionally have included a number of dependants, such as servants, retainers and protégés of various sorts, who were not kin but had entitlements in some ways not very different from those of family members. Conversely, households that do consist of kin do not always function as a unit either economically or socially. Husbands or married sons, for example, may refuse to contribute to a common purse; daughters may refuse to provide the sort of care for young or old that tradition prescribes.

Nevertheless, any attempt to draw too sharp a distinction between family and household soon leads to problems. The fact is that without considering the kinship links on which most households are based it would be impossible to understand why they function as they do. Understanding the ways in which members of a household interact, the obligations and entitlements each has in respect of the others, requires a knowledge of their kinship links that depends on more than just observation. Therefore it is easy to overstate the methodological advantages of making the household rather than the kin group the focus of research.

That a household is a socio-economic unit need not mean that it functions independently of other households with which it has kinship links. This is most obvious in respect of corporate families, where a number of households may have an interest in the corporate family property, and relationships between households are formalised by appointment of a family head and other positions. Similarly, in a village where most or all the households have kinship links, as is often the case in rural areas, the affairs of individual households may be particularly difficult to distinguish from those of others. Responsibilities, interests, and bonds are likely to extend beyond the front door. This is true of Western societies as well as Asian ones.

Classifications of household structure may mask the variety of arrangements that exist and the ingenuity social groups show in adapting to the changing environment in which families function. There is reason to think that social scientists have attached too much significance to household structures, in much the same way that natural scientists used to pay too much attention to the skins and feathers of unfamiliar species of wildlife: they are visible, often spectacular, but do not necessarily tell us much and may distract attention from the more interesting bits inside. We need to get beyond a taxidermist approach to the study of family life.

## What family units do

To understand why families have certain sorts of living arrangements or household structures, we have to consider what it is those families do. Whether we refer to what families do as activities or functions does not really matter. What is important is to recognise that to endure as entities, family units or households have to satisfy the needs of household members and the demands of the wider society.

In the most general terms, households may be seen as having seven sorts of functions; or, to put it another way, what households do may best be understood from seven vantage points: *reproduction*; *care*; *affection*; *economic production* and *consumption*; *transmission*; *religious functions*; and *socio-political functions*. While these categories or perspectives overlap, each is sufficiently important to warrant separate identification.[3]

### Reproduction

Having children is usually a straightforward type of activity. It may or may not be linked to the regulation of sexuality in society, which is sometimes identified as another function of families or households. As is clear from Chapter 6, reproduction is an activity much less prominent in households now than at other points in recorded history, which leaves more opportunity for other activities, especially economic production and consumption. Actually, reproduction is a rather narrow term, since it does not allow for the strategies many families have to resort to when natural reproduction fails, especially that of adoption.

### Care

'Care' is a broad term referring to the role households play in providing their members with psychological and emotional support, and opportunity for development, as well as taking care of their material needs. Socialisation of the young, often identified as a function of households, is but one aspect of care, which is no less essential for adults. Care includes looking after the needs of the elderly and those who are unable to look after themselves, such as the sick, the disabled, and the unemployed. In other words, care includes roles that are sometimes placed under the separate heading of social security functions. Unfortunately the term 'social security' often means no more than meeting minimum material needs, and is therefore quite misleading as a description of what most households do for their vulnerable members. Besides, the obligation of care between household members does not cover only young, elderly or vulnerable individuals. Mutual obligations of care extend to everyone. Of course, obligations of care may also extend beyond the household.

## Affection

As a function of households, affection is closely related to care. But it is so fundamental and so badly neglected in studies of the family, that it must be mentioned separately. Moreover, affection differs from care in this important way: whereas mutual care is usually seen as an obligation, mutual affection is not. While family members may be exhorted to love each other and show mutual affection, emotions cannot be forced. Nevertheless love and affection are basic human needs that households, above all, are expected to satisfy. Cultures may vary as to which relationships are likely to be most intimate and affectionate and which will be formal and constrained. In some, the conjugal relationship may be regarded as particularly important for its affection and emotional bonds; in others the relationship between siblings, or the relationship between mother and children, may be more significance. Most have an ideal in which all family bonds contribute to a household atmosphere of mutual affection, respect, concern, and harmony. Particularly in situations where the reproductive and economic production roles of households diminish, it might be expected that a greater preoccupation with mutual affection and companionship would result. However, affection and companionship are not an afterthought or optional extra as far as the effective functioning of households is concerned. Without them, the family unit disintegrates just as surely as when material needs are not met.

## Economic production and consumption

Economic production and consumption provide a focus for much of the study of kinship systems and households. There is no denying the importance of the topic. Yet, as pointed out elsewhere, there is a danger in reducing everything to a function of economics. Whether the household is the unit of production or individual members take part in industrial production, a household's capacity to fulfil its other functions will to a large extent depend on its ability to be economically productive. A household's economic consumption obviously depends on having something to consume, but also on social and family rules regarding distribution, involving concepts of needs and entitlements. While households typically pool their resources, allocation and individual consumption of them is frequently quite unegalitarian, with criteria such as age, generation, and gender playing a big part in determining who gets what.

## Transmission

Transmission may be thought of as a particular type of economic function or form of economic distribution, since it usually brings to mind patterns of inheritance, widely regarded as one of the keys to understanding household structures. But this would be a narrow interpretation. There are occasions other than inheritance after death when property is transmitted from generation to generation, just as there are things besides land, housing, and other durables that are transmitted. Dowry and bride wealth, by means of which property is passed on to members of the younger generation at the time of marriage, are also significant forms of transmission, which often complement inheritance norms. Leaving aside the genetic transmission of looks, intelligence, and congenital defects, in most cultures more than property is passed on. It may include, for example, community status, noble rank, or official positions and privileges owned by kin groups rather than individuals. Among Hindus, caste status is transmitted. In societies where ancestor worship prevails, the ancestors are seen as conferring their blessings and afflictions on descendants.

## Religious functions

The religious functions of the household are closely related to line of descent. In some cultures it is the family or kin group itself (that is, every family) that is the focus or object of religious activity. In the range of practices labelled ancestor worship, associated above all with Confucian influences in East Asia, previous generations of the family itself are an object of veneration, prayer, and sacrifice. In other cultures, particular families are regarded as having a religious leadership role and a responsibility to perform religious functions on behalf of the wider community. In Hinduism, for example, members of the Brahmin caste see themselves as having religious responsibilities on behalf of Hindu society generally. It is not the Brahmin family as an entity that has this religious function, but the family does pass on Brahmin status from generation to generation, and with it the function. Elsewhere, religious functions may appear to be hereditary in this way yet be little more than a traditional family occupation. In Japan there has been a tradition of Buddhist temples remaining under the control of particular families, with some members of each consecutive generation working there.

## Socio-political functions

The seemingly vague residual category of socio-political functions has to do with the obligations or duties of the household towards the wider socio-political order. These may vary considerably from society to society. Many pre-modern societies, including those of the Chinese empire, Indian (and Indianised) states, and Islamic states, counted their populations on a household basis, and often it was the household rather than the individual that had obligations towards the state. In many societies it was (and sometimes still is) the household unit that paid taxes, provided army conscripts, voted in community affairs, and contributed labour for state and community construction projects. Households often had a policing function, since state control rarely reached to the community level. They had a responsibility to ensure that their members kept the peace and obeyed the law, and could be held to account if they failed to do so. An example of the use of households to police themselves and their neighbours is the Chinese *baojia* (mutual guarantee) system, used in various forms from the fourth century BCE to the twentieth century. Traditionally the population was divided up into groups of ten households, with each household held responsible for wrongdoing by members of any other family in the group. Not surprisingly, it encouraged people to take a close interest in what their neighbours were doing and was a powerful mechanism for state control.

## Household structures

The variety of living arrangements established by kinship groups are classified under two broad headings: simple (nuclear, conjugal) households and complex (extended) households. Simple households are composed of one married couple and their unmarried children, while complex households consist of two or more related married couples and their unmarried children. A further distinction is drawn between *stem* households and *joint* households. In stem households the married couples belong to different generations, as when a married son lives with his wife and children in the paternal home. In a joint family the married couples belong to the same generation, as when two married brothers with their wives and children have a common household.

Kinship systems have a strong influence on family living arrangements. They are a key factor in determining who lives with whom, where they live, the extent to which households are nuclear or complex, and the forms they take. The majority of societies are patrilineal, that is, they trace family descent on the male side while attributing less significance to kinship ties on the female side. Family name, social position, and property inheritance tend to follow the male line, and males typically command higher status and authority in the household. Patrilineal kinship systems are characteristic of the societies of East and West Asia and the Indian subcontinent. The major religious traditions of the Asian region—Hinduism, Buddhism, Confucianism and Islam—are all patrilineal and patriarchical in their assumptions. The traditional legal codes of countries such as China, Japan and Korea enshrined and protected patriliny.

Although in global terms matrilineal societies are much less common than patrilineal ones, many are to be found in Asia. In the context of the world system of nation states, however, none could be considered a dominant society. Best known are the Nayar caste of southern India (who actually are no longer formally matrilineal) and the Minangkabau of West Sumatra and Negeri Sembilan on the Malay peninsula. Less familiar are groups such as the Garo, Jaintia, and Khasi of Meghalaya in north-east India, the Mosuo of China, the Karen of Myanmar and neighbouring countries, and minorities of Vietnam such as the Ede, Coho, Mnông, Cham, and Churu.

Bilateral kinship systems, which formally trace descent on both the male and the female side, are common in South-East Asia. The Javanese reckon kinship bilaterally, as do Filipinos and *bumiputra* of Malaysia. Many of the indigenous minorities in the region do likewise. Much of Sri Lankan society operates in terms of bilateral kinship, while in Korea and Vietnam indigenous bilateral kinship systems were largely displaced in pre-modern times by patrilineal Confucian influences from China.[4]

Depending on the dominant kinship system, then, complex households may be structured on the basis of male kinship links, female ones, or bilateral connections. Big patrilineal complex households feature prominently in writing about Confucian families. The most famous of all is that portrayed in Cao Xueqin's (?1715–63) great novel *Hong lou meng* (*Dream of Red Mansions*, or *The Story of the Stone*). In this very large and wealthy household (modelled on Cao's own) four generations and numerous branches of the Jia lineage, with a huge number of servants and dependants, live, love, and squabble together inside the family compound in Beijing. The fluid structure of the household is vividly demonstrated, and so too are its many functions: bearing children and continuing the family line; performing religious rites of ancestor worship; advancing the household's economic interests through business ventures and strategic marriage alliances; consuming the household's resources, sometimes to excess; nurturing the young; respecting and caring for the elderly; providing material security for poor relations and household dependants; provision of schooling for the younger generation; and regulation (often ineffective) of the behaviour of all.[5]

Matrilineal equivalents are not hard to find. In 1901, in Kochi in southern India, the census revealed Nayar *taravad* or matrilineal households consisting of up to a hundred people living and eating together. A. K. Gopalan (1905–77), one of Kerala's early communist leaders, who grew up in such a household, described it as living in 'something like a community hostel'. It is a view echoed by a Minangkabau writer giving his account of the matrilineal household into which he was born in 1913: 'it was like being born in a barracks, since there were more than forty people living in that house at the time', all of them contributing to the noise and confusion that resulted from 'individual needs, dispositions, and behaviors colliding'. No less like a hostel or barracks are the lineage longhouses of the Ede in Vietnam. Early in the twentieth century one measured 215 metres long and was occupied by an appropriately large kin group. In 1980 longhouses were less common, but were still found to contain as many as 115 people.[6]

As well as stem and joint complex households, there are polygamous households. These occur in many Asian countries, though much less commonly now than formerly. Polygyny, or having more than one wife, was permitted by all the four major religious traditions of Asia and was widespread from the Confucian societies in the east to the Muslim societies in the west. Polyandry, having two or more husbands, was practised by some Hindu and Buddhist groups. While some contemporary nation states have prohibited polygamous marriages, others continue to regard them as a legitimate aspect of their social and religious traditions. In 1967 some Hindu castes in the Jaunsar Bawar region of Uttar Pradesh in northern India were declared to be a scheduled tribe—largely on the ground that polyandry is widespread among them. This led to an outcry because tribal status conferred rights to preferential government treatment, yet the people in question were predominantly from the land-owning and largely well-off Brahmin and Rajput castes.[7]

The corporate families of East and South-East Asia are widely seen as a form of family organisation that in pre-modern societies was particularly effective. Corporate families are kinship groups with property that is owned by the group as a whole and cannot be alienated. The benefits derived from the property are shared among the kin group, membership of which is recorded and monitored to ensure that only those with a genuine claim belong. For example, the female members of a Minangkabau lineage live together in the lineage longhouse and hold their hereditary fields in common, rotating particular landholdings between members on a regular basis to equalise returns. However, not all corporate families live in extended households. Arrangements have always been more flexible than that, and in many cases it appears that corporate family arrangements serve as an alternative or supplement to complex households. Where kin groups become very large or dispersed, corporate ownership of property may offer a way of protecting the economic interests of the extended family even when its members live in nuclear households. In China during the Song dynasty (960–1279), for example, many people lived in nuclear households 'embedded' in the corporate structures of their lineage or clan.[8]

Complex households feature prominently in the ideals of family life in many Asian cultural traditions. They have widely been seen as providing the best opportunity for kin to fully discharge their mutual obligations, and the most effective arrangement for doing all that households should do. Traditionally they have been presented as having a capacity to be largely self-sustaining and self-governing, able in normal circumstances to safeguard their interests without state intervention. By pooling its resources, it has been held, an extended family group can achieve greater economic strength and flexibility, find it easier to provide care and support for all members, regardless of age or situation, and discharge its responsibilities towards the community or state.

What is striking is that despite all the changes that contemporary Asian societies have undergone, or perhaps because of them, ideals of the complex household continue to receive widespread support.[9]

## Complex households in pre-modern Asian societies

It is hard to determine how prevalent multigeneration complex households were in pre-modern Asian societies. This is partly because historical records are limited, especially in relation to the lower social strata, and partly because the information we do have tends to be couched in terms of how things should be rather than how they actually were. Often, as just mentioned, complex households were seen as representing social ideals, and recent work indicates that scholars have been inclined to mistake the ideal for the reality. This is not to say that ideal and reality are unrelated. Status and influence could result from achieving social ideals pertaining to the family, so there were good practical reasons for trying to do so. The example of influential families could in turn reinforce or modify the ideal.

But demographic constraints made it impossible for most people to live in multigeneration households. Because life expectancy was much lower than now, by the time a man and a woman married and had children, their own parents often did not have much longer to live, which meant that three-generation households, never mind four- or five-generation households, were at best intermittent. If we assume, say, that on average males became fathers at the age of eighteen (with females becoming mothers at a slightly earlier age), then for households to contain three generations on a continuing basis, males would had to have a lifespan of at least fifty-four years. In most pre-modern societies, however, the average life expectancy was much lower. This demographic constraint on household formation has led scholars to pay close attention to the concept of the life cycle of families: any given household is likely to be nuclear at one time and complex at another, as new generations appear, old ones die out, and household members leave to marry and start households of their own. This means that even in a society that places great value on complex households, the proportion of such households at any given point in time may be quite small.

No less significant is the fact that in many pre-modern societies it was possible to maintain close kinship bonds and discharge intergenerational obligations without living under one roof. Living in proximity to close kin rather than sharing a house with them often brings most of the advantages of co-residence while avoiding some of the more serious problems it can create. Villages in Asian societies today, from Iran to the Philippines, still often consist of members of a small number of kin groups, so that an individual may be related to a very large proportion of the inhabitants of his or her village and be part of a network of mutual obligations that links most of the households. The sort of social isolation often regarded as an inevitable feature of life in nuclear households becomes an issue only when the predominance of nuclear households coincides with high population mobility. In pre-modern Asian societies population mobility was limited, and even in the cities the members of households belonging to one kin group were likely to live close to each other.

Ideals are ideals precisely because reality does not match up with them. So it is not surprising to learn that despite Confucian glorification of the extended family, what evidence there is suggests that in East Asia multigeneration complex households were far from universal. Surviving household registers from the Tang Dynasty (618–907), for example, show that most Chinese households consisted of a married couple and their children, with perhaps retired parents or single relatives living with them. Over the two thousand years of Chinese imperial history, the size of the average household appears to have fluctuated between five and six persons, with the proportion of nuclear households invariably high. Early social science research, undertaken in China in the 1920s and 1930s, also showed that the typical Chinese household was not large, and that only a small proportion of the population lived in multigeneration complex households. The typical household in a Jiangsu village in the late 1930s, as described by the pioneering Chinese anthropologist Fei Hsiao-t'ung, closely resembled that revealed by Tang Dynasty household registers more than one thousand years earlier. It included a married couple and their unmarried children, with a parent or other single relative living with them.[10]

These findings have been confirmed by computer simulations of Chinese patterns of household formation based on all that is known about historical life expectancies, marriage and fertility data, and norms of household formation. The simulations indicated that although most individuals will have lived in a household with three or more generations at some stage of their lives, the great majority will at some point also have lived in a household with only one or two generations. On average, those living to age 20 or more would have spent about half of their lives in the latter type of household.[11]

Historically, the situation in Japan has been much the same. A number of studies have concluded that during the Tokugawa period (1603–1867) some 70 per cent of households were nuclear, or nuclear with a small number of additional single relatives. Complex stem or joint households made up only some 20 per cent of the total, though the proportion was considerably higher for upper-class families.[12]

In Korea the nuclear household was predominant throughout the Chosun period (1392–1910). It was not until the seventeenth century that Confucian influences became strong enough to establish the patrilineal stem household as the ideal for the population generally. But, as in China and Japan, it remained an ideal only. This was reflected in the size of households, which in the seventeenth century averaged just over four people, compared with 5.5 in 1966. In the 1950s, before industrialisation and modernisation got seriously under way, complex households of the stem type still accounted for less than one-third of the total.[13]

For South Asia reliable historical information on household structures is limited. What there is, however, agrees with that from East Asian countries: complex households were in the minority. Analysis of results of the 1820–30 Indian census, which covered what is now Bangladesh and Pakistan as well as India, indicates that the average household contained between four and five people, which does not suggest a preponderance of complex households. Data from subsequent censuses show that the average size of households remained largely unchanged until 1951. Reliable data for one village in western India indicate that in 1967 there were at least as many extended households, and probably more, than in 1819, despite the sweeping socio-economic changes over that period.[14]

In Thailand and the Philippines it is also evident that households have long been predominantly nuclear in structure, if not in operation. The dominant cultures of both countries have attached importance to extended kinship networks, as have most of the numerous cultures of South-East Asia, but usually this has not translated into extended kin groups living together. In rural Thailand around the mid-twentieth century, before development had made much of an impact, nuclear households were widely seen as ideal. Traditional patterns of household formation involved a married daughter living in the parental home until either her first child was born or a younger sister married, and then establishing a separate household with her husband. Normally only the youngest daughter continued to live with her parents after marriage, caring for them in their old age and eventually inheriting their house and land. However, there have been regional variations. Uxorilocal residence (that is, living near the wife's parents) has been stronger in the rural north-east and north-west, while elsewhere virilocal residence (near the husband's parents) has predominated, partly as a result of an ethnic Chinese presence.[15]

## A modern shift?

Historically, all countries, but especially large and ethnically mixed ones, have had regional variations in household structure. In contemporary Asian societies such variations continue to be strong, and may even have become more pronounced as a result of divergent regional experience of development and modernisation. Appreciation of the immense diversity of Chinese family arrangements, for example, especially since 1979, has led one Chinese expert on these issues to comment that discussion in terms of such sweeping generalities as 'the Chinese family' and 'the situation of Chinese women' reduces her to embarrassed silence.[16] India too provides a good example of the difficulties of interpreting trends without knowledge of local factors.

Analysis of rural Indian census data for 1961 (that is, when development was only beginning to make an impact) by Pauline Kolenda has shown that there was wide variation from district to district in the proportion of complex households. It has also shown that explanations of change in household structure sometimes regarded almost as self-evident are not supported by the data, and that one trend may have quite dissimilar explanations in relation to different social groups. For example, there was no evidence to support the idea that complex households were particularly common among farming families, even those with relatively large landholdings they might not want to divide. Nor were they particularly common in districts with a large proportion of high-caste families.[17]

While Kolenda's work provides information regarding the prevalence of complex households in 1961, where they occurred and the various factors associated with them, it does not tell us much about the sorts of complex households involved. Other studies indicate that there are at least ten different sorts of complex households common in India. They also show that there is no uniform trend of complex households breaking down into nuclear households. To be sure, there are factors associated with development that tend to correlate with low incidence of complex households. But sometimes they work both ways. For example, while migration from villages to the city causes division of complex households in rural areas, it often results in new ones being established in the urban areas, as kin and acquaintances turn to each other for help in the unfamiliar environment. A cash economy removes some of the constraints on division of households, by making it easier for individuals to control their earnings and families to convert their assets, but it also makes it easier for family members to support each other from a distance, as often happens when individuals look for work in the city or overseas. To equate a cash economy with destruction of family values is absurd. There is no doubt, however, that a cash economy enables and indeed requires families to function in new ways.[18]

It is not only India and China, the giants of Asia, that exhibit such variability and complexity in household structure. Nor is it only there that it is difficult to discern a uniform trend. In Malaysia, widely seen in the mid-1990s as nudging 'developed' status, studies from the 1960s to the late 1980s have given such wildly divergent results that, even allowing for inconsistencies of classification, it would take more persistence than is healthy to find evidence of the nuclearisation trend we are told is a concomitant of development. In seventeen different studies, estimates of the proportion of nuclear households in urban areas varied from 22 per cent to 98 per cent and in rural areas from 31 per cent to 76 per cent, without any discernible chronological sequence.[19]

One of the most venerable of clichés in studies of the family is that urbanisation results in family fragmentation and a trend towards nuclear households. Yet this is not always the case. *Dalit* (untouchable) families in rural India live predominantly in nuclear households, but in the cities those with education tend to form complex households. In the Philippines, complex households are more common in urban than in rural areas. This is explained in terms of the fact that, although residentially the Filipino family has tended historically to be nuclear, functionally it is extended. Even if they do not share a common household, kinsmen 'identify with and assist one another, participate in joint activities, pool resources, share responsibilities, and maintain expressive and emotional relations'. Therefore when families migrate to the city, housing shortages and the need for support encourage them to turn to relatives already living there.

There is evidence of a similar trend in the context of urbanisation in Malaysia. In Bangladesh, too, urban households are on average larger than rural ones. In Thailand, on the other hand, which in many ways is in a similar socio-economic position to Malaysia, people moving from the country to the city are not inclined to move in with relations to form complex households.[20] Korea and Japan likewise show the more familiar pattern of nuclearisation occurring with urbanisation.

Housing shortages and lack of living space, widely associated with urbanisation, are seen as having different effects in different countries. In Japanese cities pressures on housing are cited as a reason for young couples living neolocally (that is, separate from parents) after marriage, rather than living in the parental household in accordance with a widely professed wish. In Chinese cities, however, housing shortages are seen as a partial explanation of a surprisingly high level of complex households.

Like urbanisation, industrialisation in the West has been seen as a force for nuclearisation of the family, largely because of a shift from household-based agricultural production to factory-based production, and increased worker geographic mobility connected with this shift. The economic miracles of East and South-East Asia, however, are understood by many at least partly in terms of strength of kinship organisation and the continuing dominance of family-based production and commercial activity. Even in developed countries such as Japan and Korea a high proportion of workers continue to be employed in family enterprises. Some areas of modern industry, such as electronic component assembly, provide new opportunities for cottage or family-based production. China's rapid moves since 1979 towards a market economy have led to a resurgence of family-based production. In the Chittagong region of Bangladesh, where in 1963 there was evidence of a trend towards nuclear families, some twenty years later there was a strong trend the other way. Unemployment (resulting from the nationalisation of industries in the city following Bangladeshi independence) and land shortages were forcing extended families to work and live together as single units.

A number of Indian studies have found that industrialisation encourages maintenance of kinship ties. Extended-family living arrangements are relatively common in urban business communities, often in the form of joint (fraternal) households. Even where brothers and the nuclear families live in separate households, frequently they operate as a single unit for business purposes, come together on ritual and festive occasions, and provide mutual support.[21] It is possible that similar arrangements may be encouraged in the countryside by the industrialisation of agriculture, since it encourages rationalisation of landholdings and rewards the operation of bigger units of production.

Modern education, particularly education of women, is another factor widely seen as encouraging nuclearisation of the family. Here too the outcomes are far from uniform. In India, for example, educated middle-class women tend to favour nuclear households because they see them as holding the possibility of greater personal autonomy and a better, more equal relationship with their husband. Yet those wanting a career outside the home—in India still a minority of women—recognise that living with a mother-in-law or sister-in-law may offer flexibility in child care and other household tasks not available in nuclear households.

In this they are no different from the countless urban working women, in India and in other countries such as China and the Philippines, who seek paid employment in order to survive rather than for personal fulfilment, and rely on elderly in-laws or other live-in relatives for help with household tasks. If incompatibility of tasks or purposes has historically led to formation of complex households in agricultural societies,[22] there is every reason to expect families in industrialised societies to adopt similar strategies where other options are limited. Even a woman who values personal autonomy may find, when that objective is to be reconciled with other obligations and aspirations, that living in some sort of extended family arrangement is best.

## Households, development, and demographic change

If a trend towards nuclear households is a natural (perhaps inevitable) part of industrialisation, urbanisation, and the associated changes that make up what is known as development, we would expect to see it furthest advanced in the most developed Asian countries: Japan, South Korea, Taiwan, Hong Kong, and Singapore. It is not as straightforward as that, however. While they all show a decline in the proportion of complex households and an increase in the proportion of nuclear ones, they also reveal a remarkable resilience in the types of family organisation and values associated with traditional complex households.

Between 1920 (the date of the first Japanese census) and 1991, the proportion of complex (stem) households in Japan fell from an estimated 40 per cent to 14 per cent. In the same period the proportion of nuclear households increased from 54 per cent in 1920 to a high of 61 per cent in 1988, then fell again to 60 in 1991. Most of the increase, however, was in one-person households, which as a proportion of the total rose from 6 per cent to 21 per cent. In urban areas the trend towards nuclearisation has been stronger than in rural areas. Much of the increase in the proportion of one-person households, and also of nuclear households consisting of only one couple, is due to the rapid ageing of the Japanese population. Whereas in 1960 only 6 per cent of one-person households consisted of a person sixty-five years or older, in 1991 it was 16 per cent; and the proportion of elderly married-couple-only households rose from 8 per cent to 22 per cent. In other words, being elderly is no less 'modern' than is living alone.

An increase in the proportion of households consisting of elderly individuals or couples should not be taken to represent a shift in values, away from filial piety and intergenerational obligations to selfish unconcern on the part of adult children. Despite the unambiguous evidence of greater nuclearisation of households in Japan, the proportion of elderly people living with their children continues to be much higher than in the developed countries of the West: around 60 per cent, nearly twice the proportion in the West. While most of the population has rejected the traditional model of the family (known as *ie*), elements of the traditional pattern—particularly those relating to co-residence with elderly parents—continue to be valued, and not just in a hypothetical way.

The persistence of co-residence in Japan and the high value attached to it has led some analysts to describe the Japanese household structure of recent years as a *modified* stem family. Similar arrangements are common in South Korea and Taiwan, where co-residence with elderly parents also remains high, despite showing some decrease over time. The typical family arrangement in Hong Kong has been characterised as both 'modified extended family' and 'modified nuclear family'.[23] The latter phrase, which emphasises mutual care and support through 'networking' rather than co-residence, is also appropriate for arrangements common in cities in the People's Republic of China. Families there exhibit a similar flexibility and fluidity in responding to the pressures and changing conditions of contemporary life. Research on urban families in the 1980s and 1990s highlights the fact that 'residence in separate households does not necessarily mean functionally separate families. Cooking, childcare, care of the elderly and disabled, and monetary transfers all frequently take place among geographically divided branches of "networked" families.'[24]

But, for all that, living together where possible remains important for extended families. Analysis of 1982 and 1990 Chinese census data show that the proportion of complex households has remained stable at between 18 and 19 per cent, despite a continuing fall in fertility. Some of this persistence is the result of housing shortages. While these have generally been more severe in urban than in rural areas, in most locations they have made starting new households difficult and have forced young couples to live with parents (usually those of the husband) after marriage. Restrictions on internal migration have also been a constraint on establishing new households, in urban and rural areas alike. Positive incentives for pooling resources and living together in extended family groups have resulted in rural areas from the reversion in the late 1970s to family-based production, though the impact of these changes in economic policy has varied from region to region, even village to village.[25]

Undoubtedly the biggest factor of all behind the persistence of complex households in the People's Republic, however, in the face of all the intense pressures family life there has been subjected to, is the rapid increase in the average life expectancy of the Chinese people. While Chinese are now having far fewer children than they were even forty or fifty years ago, increased life expectancies make it much more likely that grandparents will still be alive when their grandchildren are born and, therefore, all other things being equal, are more likely to be members of the same household. This demographic trend, coupled with a continuing strong sense of intergenerational obligation on the part of the majority of Chinese, has resulted in the Chinese family showing 'a marked tendency towards the stem-family or the quasi-stem-family model'. While the bulk of the population lives in nuclear households, the majority of elderly Chinese live with their families, often in multigeneration complex households. This apparently contradictory state of affairs is possible because the elderly are a small (though rapidly growing) proportion of the national population.[26]

Together, the factors mentioned have counteracted whatever forces for nuclearisation of the family may be associated with industrialisation and modernisation. When at the beginning of the 1980s Fei Hsiao-t'ung returned to the Jiangsu village where he had undertaken his pioneering study in 1936, there were *more* complex households than before, not fewer. A survey in 1981 showed that the proportion was 21 per cent, compared with less than 10 per cent forty-five years earlier.[27]

## Families do not just live together

Family life in all societies is hemmed in by ideals and prescriptions. 'Family values' and their resurrection are a favourite concern of religious and state authorities everywhere. How families compose and comport themselves is widely regarded as a measure of civilised life and the well-being of society. Those who take a scholarly interest in the subject of the family are as likely to be caught up in this as anyone. So if there is evidence of a trend towards nuclear households, some look upon it as a sign that Asian societies are indeed converging to the norms of 'advanced' nations. Others lament it as proof of the decline of Asian societies, a weakening of the customs that have been the basis of their claim to superiority over the West, a loss of cultural distinctiveness. What these responses have in common is a tendency to see the family as emblematic of something beyond itself, an embodiment of civilisation, a revelation of the workings of the spirit of society.

We need to resist this tendency. What matters is not whether the family approximates to some idealised arrangement or other, but whether it works, that is, satisfies the needs of its members. This means doing the sorts of things listed earlier in this chapter, as appropriate in the prevailing circumstances. If demographic circumstances change, for example, and there are more elderly people to care for, then arrangements have to be adapted accordingly. The same applies to the changing work opportunities resulting from industrialisation and increased worker mobility.

The evidence suggests that adaptation is precisely what families are good at: it comes down to a question of doing what is likely to work best for family members in the circumstances. Hence the existence of 'modified extended families', 'modified nuclear families', 'networked families', families that may be nuclear in terms of household definition but complex in their living arrangements. We should not make out living under one roof to be more important than it really is. Supporting one another, caring for one another, may require close kin to live apart, perhaps even in different countries. Family bonds and affections do not expire at the door.

These points are nicely illustrated by a Muslim lineage in the southern Indian city of Chennai, studied by Sylvia Vatuk in the 1980s. Some members of this large family group slept in one household and ate in another. Some dwellings housed only one commensual group (that is, people who eat together), while others housed two or three. Many of the men and a few of the women maintained two residences, one near their place of employment and one with close kin. Some men lived and worked in the Middle East and returned home only once or twice a year, while others had commuter marriages. Complex households, where they occurred, arose as a practical response to the needs of elderly and other family members rather than the wish to approach an ideal family structure. 'Living together', Vatuk observes, 'is only one thing that family members do with one another.'[28]

## Marriage and convergence

As far as household structure is concerned, then, the argument of convergence to a common pattern is difficult to sustain, not least because it soon becomes unclear just which pattern we are supposed to identify. In neither the East nor the West is the nuclear household a recent innovation. The majority of households have long been nuclear, and so cannot be understood as a response to, or partial explanation of, industrialisation and urbanisation. Nor can a shift away from complex households be assumed to reveal a transformation of fundamental social and family values. Family members care for and support each other in ways that defy simple categorisation, forcing us to resort to such labels as modified extended families, modified nuclear families, and networked families. The variations of form are as numerous as the needs that give rise to them. Whatever else may be asserted, the changes taking place cannot be described as traditional complex family structures being superseded by a modern, more highly evolved simple or nuclear structure.

Ideas of progress and convergence are also applied to other aspects of family life, in particular to marriage. Pre-modern or primitive marriages, the argument goes, typically resemble a business transaction between two families. There is little or no choice for the two principals and no interest in love or affection. The marriage is arranged by parents or elders with a view to advancing the economic or social position of the families involved rather than the happiness of the couple. The utilitarian nature of the transaction is clear from such practices as dowry and bride wealth (bride price), which fix a market price for the spouse in much the same way as a cow or a horse is purchased. The modern marriage, in contrast, is the result of free choice by the partners based on mutual affection. In international human rights conventions and the marriage laws of many modern nation states, it is this concept of marriage, or at least its voluntary nature, that is articulated and protected.

The reality of marriage and the changes taking place in the institution of marriage are far more complicated than stereotypes such as these imply. In pre-modern and Third World societies the variety of marriage arrangements has been extensive, entailing a wide range of degrees of individual choice and freedom, and it would require remarkable audacity to claim that conjugal love was invented by the West, along with individualism and capitalism. As to the idea of convergence, while there is undoubtedly a strong trend towards individual choice in marriage in Asian societies, backed by the authority of capitalist and communist governments alike, this does not mean that families have no say or that all individuals are choosing on the basis of affections real or imagined.

To keep the discussion manageable I will restrict it to monogamous marriage, noting only that polygyny and (less frequently) polyandry still occur in many Asian societies. However, in regard to both monogamous and polygamous marriages, it is certainly true that the norms of some social groups have approximated rather well to the stereotype of pre-modern marriage sketched above. In societies where family descent has religious significance, as in Hindu or Confucian societies, it is to be expected that marriage would be seen as a family responsibility and decision, and too important to be determined by the hormones of the younger generation. In all societies, however, marriage has been more carefully controlled in families from the upper levels of society than those near the bottom. The obvious reason is that there is more at stake. Where there is aristocratic rank, land, wealth, or social status to be handed on from one generation to the next, family control of marriage makes good sense. (Marriage norms and inheritance rules, it may be observed, are usually closely linked.)

In Japan until the late nineteenth century, marriage among commoners was largely a matter of formalising a relationship initiated by the man and the woman on the basis of mutual attraction. Even the formalisation process tended to be minimal. Although marriage was carefully controlled among members of the samurai class, this was not the case for those with no rank and little property. Commoners in Korean society had similar freedom to choose their marriage partner, at least until the beginning of the Chosun period (1392–1910), when social life became more closely regulated under the influence of Neo-Confucianism. In China, too, marriage arrangements were freer and more open early in the imperial period rather than in later times. Among Thais, marriage has traditionally been the result of a free decision by man and woman based on mutual regard. As elsewhere, however, freedom to choose has not necessarily excluded advice and help from family, friends, or a professional matchmaker. Many Thai marriages have been, and continue to be, consensual marriages; that is, de facto relationships arising simply from a decision to live together, without having been formalised or registered. There is in fact no formal wedding ceremony prescribed by Thai Buddhism. The ceremonies most widely performed in Thailand to formalise marriage derive from Hindu culture.[29]

It is possible to find examples of greater 'freedom' in marriage customs in Asian societies. Famous, or notorious, in this regard are the customs of some of the matrilineal societies. Among the Jaintia of north-east India, marriage is essentially a sexual relationship and does not result in a new household being established. The man remains a member of his mother's household, visiting his wife in the house of her matriliny to procreate and to sleep. The Nayar caste of southern India encouraged their daughters to take lovers rather than entering into a permanent marriage relationship, for among them too kinship and inheritance were reckoned matrilineally. The Mosuo (referred to also as the Yongning Naxi) of the Yunnan province in China have a similar system. Women and men both remain in their respective matrilineal households and form only *azhu* (friend or partner) relationships, which may be terminated by either party at will. The men visit the women at night, but children born from the union remain with the mother. All three marriage systems have come under strong pressure from the surrounding dominant society to 'normalise': Hindu and Christian pressures in Meghalaya and Kerala in India, Confucian and communist pressures in China.[30]

In such societies, types of behaviour elsewhere construed as freedom or promiscuity mean something quite different. This suggests that ideas about 'freedom' relating to marriage may be quite difficult to isolate from particular cultural contexts. More generally, the examples given warn against looking for a tidy historical trend from compulsion to individual choice, and from material considerations to mutual affection as the basis for marriage. What has to be considered is the purposes marriage is intended to serve. Contrary to what might be assumed, these have not been the same in all societies.

For many, the widespread custom of child marriage sums up the evils of many traditional or pre-modern marriage systems. It is seen as evidence of disregard of the child's interests and wishes, prompted by the desire to improve the family's economic or social position, for example by obtaining a dowry or bride wealth, having one less mouth to feed, or augmenting the family's labour force.

Yet child marriage may serve a wide range of purposes, and certainly cannot be assumed to imply a lack of concern for the welfare of the child. In many social contexts it has been one of the few options available to parents wanting to safeguard

Mosuo women, Yunnan, China.

the interests of their child. For the poor, child marriage has often been an alternative to infanticide, or selling a child they cannot afford to keep. Marrying off a daughter at an early age, to a family known to the parents, was a way of trying to ensure that the child would be fed and cared for in an uncertain world. Where stem households were the norm—the newly married couple living with the older couple—early marriage could help minimise mother-in-law/daughter-in-law conflict (one of the most common problems associated with stem households), while giving the young couple the opportunity to mature under the tutorship of the older couple before gaining control of the household in their turn.[31]

The regulation of sexuality has been one of the primary purposes of early marriage. Both Hinduism and Islam, for example, have encouraged it largely for this reason. When Islam spread to the Malay world, this produced outcomes that again complicate argument regarding the convergence and modernisation of marriage systems. The need to reconcile traditionally liberal Malay sexuality and marriage customs with the stricter requirements of Islam prompted a similar response in Java, southern Thailand, and Trengganu and Kelantan in the Malayan peninsula. Daughters were married at around puberty by their parents, but without expectation that the marriage would last. Approximately half of all marriages ended in divorce, frequently at the wife's initiative, an arrangement that allowed the women to regain a measure of their traditional freedom. Early arranged marriage, in this context, was in effect a way of preserving individual autonomy and choice rather than curtailing it.

As this pattern of marriage has given way in recent decades—in the face of 'modernising' influences that emphasise personal choice and romantic love—it has produced a trend running in the opposite direction to that usually associated with convergence to Western norms: divorce rates have fallen sharply. It is a trend reinforced by government moves in both Malaysia and Indonesia to make divorce laws more restrictive, but which can be understood only by reference to the fact that young women are increasingly able to exercise their autonomy directly rather than circuitously through divorce. Is the freedom they are enjoying modern Western or traditional Malay freedom? It does not appear to be a useful question to ask.[32] Nor are these Malay societies the only ones in which modernisation has coincided with a fall in divorce rates. In Japan the postwar divorce rate rose to 1.51 per thousand in 1983, then fell again before staring to rise once more in the early 1990s. The rate in 1999 was 2.00 per thousand—higher than at any other time since the Second World War, yet still much lower than the 1883 rate of 3.39 per thousand.[33]

However sceptically we may regard the concept of convergence, there is no denying that in all the dominant Asian societies for which data are available, there is an increasing say by young people about the person they will marry. Even in societies, and among social categories, where parents traditionally arranged marriages for their children, the children now frequently choose their marriage partner alone or play a leading role in the decision-making, in consultation with parents or other relatives. As already mentioned, this is a trend backed by legal mechanisms in most nation states. At varying speeds and to varying degrees, this is happening in Iran, Pakistan, India, and Bangladesh. It is also happening in Indonesia, the Philippines, Malaysia, and all the countries of East Asia.

In some cases, attitudes are changing quickly. A survey of parental attitudes in South Korea in 1959 showed that 79 per cent believed their own opinion mattered more than that of their son in arranging his marriage, while 89 per cent held the same attitude towards their daughter's marriage. In 1990 the proportions were 21 per cent and 12 per cent respectively. During the war years in Japan, some 70 per cent of marriages were arranged, whereas by 1999 the figure had fallen to 10 per cent.

A few of the problems of interpreting such figures, however, are revealed in the case of Japan. There it has become conventional, among researchers as well as the public, to contrast *miai* (arranged marriages) with *renai* (love matches). Hence the sharp drop in the proportion of arranged marriages just mentioned correlates with a reported rise in the proportion of love matches, from 30 per cent to 87 per cent in 1991. Yet arranged marriages and love marriages are asymmetrical categories that are not mutually exclusive. Nor do they exhaust the possibilities. While ideas of romantic love have certainly influenced the aspirations and decisions of many Japanese regarding marriage, it is seriously misleading to assume that all marriages not arranged by parents are decided on the basis of love. Young men and women able to choose their own marriage partner may base their decision on a range of factors; mutual affection or love, however it is conceived, is likely to be one of them. But it is not self-evident that every act of free choice will make love the primary consideration, or even that it should.

A study in the early 1990s of the criteria for choosing a spouse regarded by Japanese as important found that women were becoming much less concerned about the family background (lineage) of their partner in life, and more concerned about his personal characteristics. This could be claimed as support for the love match interpretation, were it not for the fact that the characteristics identified by most women as important were occupation and income. Romantic sentiment, it appears, is still mixed with more prosaic concerns. (Unfortunately, physical attractiveness was not among the criteria that survey respondents were asked to rank.) Other ways of exercising choice regarding marriage also deserve mention here: one is to delay marriage, another is choosing not to get married at all. The latter is an option being pursued by a numerically small but rapidly increasing proportion of Japanese. The national marriage rate, which reached a postwar high of 10.0 per thousand in 1970, fell in 1987 to 5.7 per thousand, before recovering somewhat in the 1990s to reach 6.1 per thousand in 1999. Nonetheless, in a society with a history of almost universal marriage, this is a big shift.[34]

The considerations we have already discussed, except for the decision not to marry, apply even more strongly to marriage in the People's Republic of China, where again there has been a trend away from arranged marriages, but a slower one than in Korea and Japan. The right of all to choose their marriage partner was declared in the Marriage Law of 1950 and its revision of 1980. A 1990 Chinese replication of a Japanese study of marriage trends revealed a similar shift from 'arranged marriages' to 'love matches'. In Chinese cities, photographic studios make romantic wedding photos their stock in trade, with softly lit decorous poses by the bride a speciality. Yet convergence of marriage patterns still seems a long way off within China, never mind internationally. If many Chinese men and women yearn for romance, the majority still appear to adopt a down-to-earth attitude to marriage. Freedom of choice cannot be equated with either a love match or a unilateral decision. Most parents still play a part in the decision-making but, where once they controlled and compelled, now they influence, introduce, and advise. The circumstances of daily life—which often require the newlyweds to live with their parents, to interact closely with them if unable to establish their own nuclear household, but which in any case require mutual support and cooperation to achieve individual and family purposes—make intergenerational compatibility a consideration of continuing importance. Usually parental involvement in what for many young people is a difficult process, complicated as it is by a lack of opportunities and private settings for courtship, is welcomed rather than resented. What matters, after all, is that the marriage process works for those directly involved, that it meets their needs. This may require something more than preconceived ideas of personal choice or love.[35]

The Pretty Bride Photographic Studio, Xi'an, China, will take pictures of 'the most precious, most loved person in the world'.

White wedding, Urumqi, Xinjiang, China.

## Contemporary ideals, contemporary reality

Other aspects of family life are also identified as candidates for convergence. The most significant, in terms of its implications, is gender relations or, more specifically, gender equality. The principle of gender equality is incorporated in the major international human rights conventions and, like freedom of choice in marriage, is a goal officially supported by most governments. Gender equality clearly is not just a family issue but, as has frequently been argued, if gender equality is going to be established anywhere it will have to be established within the family. Yet even the specific issue of equality within marriage, as opposed to gender equality generally, is much more diffuse and complicated than the matter of choice of marriage partner, and consequently it is less widely supported. While choice of marriage partner may be a step towards equality within marriage, it certainly does not make it inevitable, as the general experience in Western societies demonstrates. Thai women have traditionally had a substantial amount of say in the choosing of a husband. But most, like the majority of Thai men, believe that it is right for men to have greater say in family matters. In Muslim societies many educated women campaign vigorously for greater gender equality, but are just as vigorous in their rejection of typical manifestations of gender equality in Western societies.[36] In other words, the ideal of gender equality is not only less widely supported, but there is also strong disagreement over what it should mean in practice. Convergence in this area will not be swift.

Historically, families in Eastern and Western societies have been much more alike than their divergent ideals about the family would have us believe. On the Indian subcontinent in the mid-nineteenth century, the average household consisted of between four and five people. It was the same in Korea and Japan, while in China the figure tended to be a bit more than five. In England throughout the nineteenth century, the size of the average household remained, as it had during the seventeenth and eighteenth centuries, constant at 4.75.[37] The majority of the households in each country were nuclear in structure. The functions of the households were much the same, and could be described in terms of the categories listed near the beginning of this chapter.

If it is possible to compile a reasonably coherent list of what families in general do for their members, how useful is the idea of convergence? In providing the list, are we not asserting that, at one level at least, families or households are the same everywhere, even though the detail of how they go about their tasks may vary? But 'the detail' matters. We have seen that although the majority of households in Asian countries are nuclear in structure, they are often described as extended, or complex, in function. This is another way of saying that the members of those households continue to take *ideals* of the extended family seriously, that their behaviour is guided by traditional conceptions of what kin should do for each other. In other words, research on the way households work in contemporary Asian societies gives some precise meaning to the often-made assertion that Asian cultures place greater emphasis than do Western societies on group values.

It could be argued that the resilience of extended family ideals and values will prove to be only temporary. Industrialisation, urbanisation, increased life expectancy, and declining fertility are relatively recent in Asian societies. Perhaps ideals and values are just lagging behind changing social and economic realities. That is possible. But it is at least as likely that Asian societies will continue to draw on traditional ideals and values while adjusting to change, and that family life in the future will be no more uniform than it has been in the past.

CHAPTER NINE

# The World of Work

## The working individual

It is in the work that individuals do that the combined effects of family, social, ecological, and economic influences are most visible. The constraints under which they live and the opportunities open to them are revealed in the sorts of things they do for a living. Opportunities in this context include those for material gain, naturally, but there is also room for personal development through work and the participation in social life that it usually entails. If individuals may be seen as developing to adulthood within the family, it is particularly through work that maturation is completed and given expression. It is also in the work individuals do that abstractions such as 'economic development', 'industrialisation', and 'social change' acquire their clearest meaning.

In Chapter 8 we saw that one of the historical functions of the family or household unit has been economic production. With industrialisation, that function has diminished. Increased economic specialisation associated with industrialisation and globalisation has encouraged a scale of production larger than that normally associated with cottage industry and craft. Agricultural production has also tended to become larger in scale, partly as a result of the changes arising from the green revolution.

However, pre-modern economies were not simply composed of household production units, even where those economies were largely agricultural in nature. While family-based production was dominant, many individuals worked for families other than their own. The links between households and larger units of economic production were numerous, and to that extent the emergence of modern industries does not necessarily involve anything dramatically new. The revolutionary change has been in terms of industrial organisation, technology, production skills and techniques, and the effects of these factors on individual work opportunities.

## Sectoral change

The rapid industrialisation and urbanisation experienced by many Asian nations is reflected in a shrinking agricultural employment sector (see Table 9.1). The most rapidly industrialising Asian nations have registered the sharpest declines in the proportion of their workforce in agricultural production. In South Korea, between 1965 and 1990, agricultural employment shrank by 38 percentage points; in Malaysia it shrank by 32 percentage points; and in Taiwan by 31 points. Only in a small number of countries did the proportion of workers employed in industry fall during this period. Myanmar was the only nation in which a fall in industry employment coincided with an increase in the proportion of workers in agriculture. This reflects the military government's decision in 1962 to set off down the 'Burmese road to socialism', a road that has been largely isolated from the economic and social changes that have swept the rest of the world.

Taiwan, Japan, and Hong Kong recorded the biggest fall in the relative size of the industrial sector of their workforce, with the proportion of workers falling by 27, 24, and 19 percentage points respectively. However, labour force statistics alone are not a reliable indicator of the economic importance of the various sectors. Shifts in employment away from the industrial sector to the services sector are usually seen as evidence of a maturing economy. As industrial production becomes technologically advanced it turns away from labour-intensive systems. At the same time, improved living standards at home and full incorporation into the global economy are likely to lead to greater demand for service industries of all kinds. Taiwan, Japan, and Hong Kong certainly fit this pattern, with the proportion of workers in the service sector rising by 31, 43, and 21 percentage points during the period. Korea, Singapore, and Bangladesh also recorded strong growth in the services sector. Iran recorded a big shift towards service sector employment, but without a corresponding decrease in the industrial sector.

A decrease in the relative size of a labour force sector need not mean, of course, that fewer workers are employed in it. The strong population growth experienced by most Asian countries since the 1950s has meant, in the great majority of cases, a sharp rise in the number of individuals employed in *all* sectors. Where population growth has coincided with falling job opportunities as a result of new technologies and increased mechanisation of production, as in many rural areas, workforce numbers, productivity and unemployment may all increase simultaneously.

## Unemployment

One peculiarity of the human development reports published by the UN is that, while unemployment statistics are provided for developed countries, comparable figures for developing countries are not included. Unfortunately this could be taken to imply that unemployment is a peculiarly modern phenomenon, the result of industrialisation and technological development. But unemployment and underemployment were widespread in pre-modern Asian economies. Since those economies were overwhelmingly agricultural in terms of production, labour demand was largely seasonal and subject to the whims of nature. Periods of intense activity and high labour demand were followed by slack periods when there was little work available for any but those with special skills. For landless labourers, casual work was usually intermittent and uncertain, and in times of drought, for example, was likely to dry up

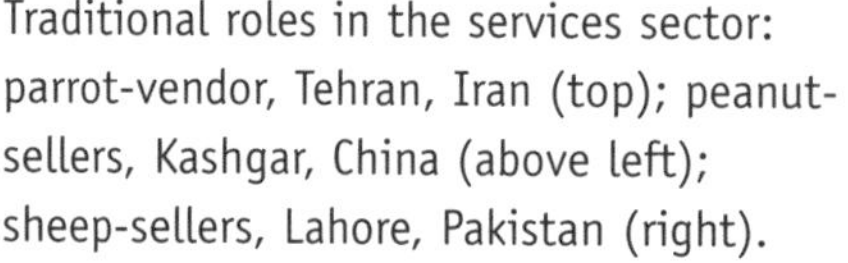

Traditional roles in the services sector: parrot-vendor, Tehran, Iran (top); peanut-sellers, Kashgar, China (above left); sheep-sellers, Lahore, Pakistan (right).

with the soil. Lack of transport greatly restricted the range of options available even in the best of times.

The difficulty and uncertainty of making a living in pre-modern societies explain the many social security mechanisms of those societies. These included the *jajmani* system of rural India, which imposed on landlords an obligation to look after their bonded labourers in hard times, including periods when, for whatever reason, economic production was impossible. According to the traditional *bawon* system in Java, anyone who comes to help harvest the rice crop must be given a share of the harvest, and the landowner cannot restrict the number of harvesters. In recent times this social security mechanism has come under strain, as the rural population has increased and become more mobile, thereby increasing the number of potential harvesters. Landowners have used technological change as a reason for restricting access to their crops and avoiding customary obligations. The traditional *ani-ani* knife used to cut the rice panicles one by one has been largely replaced by sickles and mechanical harvesters that, landowners argue, require skills few workers possess. Even at this level, therefore, technological change is affecting the availability of work.[1]

The term 'unemployment', like 'employment', has modern industrial and labour market overtones, but is no less applicable to situations in pre-modern rural societies where, because of land shortages, natural disasters, or socio-political disturbances, large sections of the population were without a secure livelihood. Nor were the problems restricted to landless or unskilled labourers. Complete specialisation was a realistic option for only a small number of workers. The great majority had to turn their hand to whatever was available, and so combined agricultural work with a range of crafts or cottage industries of varying sophistication, as well as labour on community and state projects. Home-based textile production, for example, was common in most Asian countries until large-scale mechanisation began to make its impact in the late nineteenth century.

Trekking guide, Nepal. Tourism remains the country's only big industry.

A rickshaw boy ekes out a living in Chengdu, Sichuan, China.

Do technological development and industrialisation reduce employment opportunities or create them? Many of those concerned at the socio-economic impact of new technologies and new production methods argue the former, while advocates of economic growth and development argue the latter. Gandhi contended that industrialisation along Western lines would be disastrous for India because it would do away with the economic resource with which India was so richly endowed—cheap labour—while depriving millions of the opportunity to participate in society through meaningful work.[2] In his view of modern technology as labour-saving, Gandhi was following the standard Western interpretations of industrialisation of his time.

But saving physical and mental effort is only one function of technology; at least as significant, in the longer term, is enabling labour or effort to be used in new ways. Technology has created more types of jobs than it has abolished. Unfortunately, most of those new kinds of work require extensive education and training, effectively putting them beyond the reach of many people, particularly in developing countries. If economic security has traditionally been understood primarily in terms of access to land, now it is in terms of human capital—the skills required to participate in a technologically and organisationally complex economy. The impact of industrialisation and technological change on opportunities for work therefore varies widely from individual to individual, depending on their capacity to take advantage of such new openings as do arise.

## Changing opportunities

Nowhere is the varied impact of economic and technological development on work opportunities clearer than in relation to gender. In many parts of the Third World it has been observed that industrialisation and the shift from subsistence to a market economy encourages a distinction between housework, which is unpaid, and productive labour, which receives direct material reward. The problems flowing from this are likely to be particularly pronounced in societies that attach value to female seclusion. As subsistence economic production becomes less important and work increasingly belongs to the public domain, effective opportunities for women to contribute visibly to the economic well-being of their families may be seriously diminished.

In parts of northern India, for example, the industrialisation of agriculture has reduced the opportunities for women to engage in farm work together with close male relatives. The resulting inability to contribute directly to family income appears to have further lowered the status of women, which in conjunction with the escalating demands made by prospective husbands for dowries is having deleterious effects. Neglect of daughters is becoming more common as some families adopt it as a semi-conscious strategy for reducing the number of female, and therefore financially burdensome, family members. Economic development, in this case, is reducing rather than increasing both the work opportunities and the life expectancy of women.[3]

Elsewhere the trend has been different. In Java, a society with a tradition of greater gender equality, it has been argued that rural women have been better placed than men to seize the work opportunities that have come with industrialisation and modernisation. Whereas men traditionally worked in agricultural production only, women were widely involved in commerce and handicraft production. This meant they had a wider range of skills to offer industrial employers. However, such an advantage is likely to be short-term, associated with labour-intensive industries in the early stages of industrialisation rather than mature industries. That opportunities to acquire the formal education and skills needed for success in an industrial workforce are more likely to go to Indonesian men than women is clear from national education statistics (see Table 11.1, p. 291). A similar pattern may be observed in Japan and Korea, where in the early phases of industrialisation large numbers of young women from country areas came to the cities to find employment in the new factories. Their skills and adaptability may have been factors in their favour, but so too were their perceived docility and willingness to accept lower wages than men. In occupations requiring high levels of education and training, men were clearly dominant.[4]

In China, Laos, North Korea, and Vietnam, communist ideology helped to expand employment opportunities for women in the context of industrialisation, a trend also encouraged by commune systems while they operated. All have relatively high proportions of female workers in the labour force: between 47 and 43 per cent. The proportions are similar to those of the former communist countries of Eastern Europe and the richest countries of the OECD. Of developing Asian countries, only Thailand is comparable, with 45 per cent (see Table 9.1).

However, even where women's participation in the workforce is high, it may follow a different pattern from that of men. In Japan, where 41 per cent of the workforce is female, the working lives of women follow the so-called M-curve. Entry into the workforce rises quickly from school-leaving age to the early twenties, then falls sharply as women marry and have children. The pattern is then repeated as women re-enter the workforce when child-bearing and child-rearing have been completed, and continue working until retirement. This M-shaped pattern also holds for Korean women, but not those from Taiwan, Hong Kong, or Singapore, where there is little re-entry into the workforce after child-rearing. Whatever the M-curve describes, it is not the lifelong employment with one firm so much discussed by Western observers of the Japanese economy, which pertains to no more than 30 or 40 per cent of male employees. Although the pattern has become less pronounced in recent years, many large Japanese firms still expect women to resign on marriage, and when women eventually do rejoin the workforce they find many options closed to them. Women returning to work are outsiders in an organisation culture in which the distinction between outsiders and insiders is extremely important.[5]

Not surprisingly, Japanese women and Korean women who do re-enter the workforce tend to end up in part-time or casual work, or they become self-employed,

**Table 9.1** Labour force, by gender (1994–98) and sector (1965 and 1990–92)

| | | *Percentage of labour force in* | | | | | |
|---|---|---|---|---|---|---|---|
| | *Women as % of LF 1994–98* | *Agriculture 1965* | *Agriculture 1990–92* | *Industry 1965* | *Industry 1990–92* | *Services 1965* | *Services 1990–92* |
| Bangladesh | 38 | 84 | 59 | 5 | 13 | 11 | 28 |
| Cambodia | 41 | 80 | 74 | 4 | 7 | 16 | 10 |
| China | 43 | 81 | 73 | 8 | 14 | 11 | 13 |
| Hong Kong | 40 | 6 | 1 | 53 | 35 | 41 | 64 |
| India | 38 | 85 | 81 | 4 | 6 | 11 | 13 |
| Indonesia | 38 | 70 | 56 | 9 | 14 | 21 | 30 |
| Iran | 19 | 49 | 30 | 26 | 26 | 25 | 44 |
| Japan | 41 | 26 | 7 | 58 | 34 | 16 | 59 |
| Laos | 45 | 80 | 76 | 5 | 7 | 15 | 17 |
| Malaysia | 33 | 58 | 26 | 13 | 28 | 29 | 46 |
| Myanmar | 36 | 63 | 70 | 14 | 9 | 23 | 21 |
| Nepal | 32 | 94 | 93 | 2 | 1 | 4 | 6 |
| North Korea | 46 | 57 | 43 | 23 | 30 | 20 | 27 |
| Pakistan | 13 | 60 | 47 | 18 | 20 | 22 | 33 |
| Philippines | 38 | 58 | 45 | 16 | 16 | 26 | 39 |
| Singapore | 42 | 6 | 0 | 27 | 35 | 67 | 65 |
| South Korea | 40 | 55 | 17 | 15 | 36 | 30 | 47 |
| Sri Lanka | 35 | 56 | 49 | 14 | 21 | 30 | 30 |
| Taiwan | | 44 | 13 | 41 | 14 | 15 | 46 |
| Thailand | 45 | 82 | 67 | 5 | 11 | 13 | 22 |
| Vietnam | 47 | 79 | 67 | 6 | 12 | 15 | 21 |

Source: World Bank, *From Plan to Market: World Development Report 1996*, Oxford University Press, 1996, 176–7, 201; International Labour Office, *Year Book of Labour Statistics 1998*, Geneva, 1998.

Note: Figures are for the latest year in the period specified. More recent figures are available through the ILO Labour Statistics website at <http://laborsta.ilo.org>, but not for all the countries in the table. Revision of labour force classification categories limits the validity of comparisons over time and among countries.

or work for relatives. The high percentage of Japanese and Korean women self-employed or working in a family business marks them off from those in Taiwan, Hong Kong, and Singapore.

Gender is not the only sphere where the changes resulting from industrialisation and technological development vary widely. The same applies to ethnic, caste, and class distinctions. As pointed out in Chapter 4, indigenous minorities commonly suffer serious economic and social hardship as a result of economic globalisation. Nevertheless individuals from those minorities are often able to benefit, especially if they move to urban areas beyond the reach of traditional prejudices and barriers. The relative anonymity of urban life can be liberating as well as alienating. Work relations in a modern factory located in the neutral territory of a big city may be relatively free and open, detached to some extent from traditional prejudices.

Caste identities in South Asia have traditionally been constructed around occupation. Members of a given *jati* or subcaste have tended to have the same kind of work, which fixed the group's religious and social position. The explosion of new occupations and the increased occupational mobility that accompany industrialisation have increased the difficulties of maintaining caste distinctions. A classical Hindu text such as the *Laws of Manu* may have plenty to say about preserving distinctions between traditional occupational groups, but offers little clarification regarding the religious and social standing of biotechnologists, computer analysts, or bus drivers. This point has been well expressed by one Indian worker: 'When I put on my shirt to go to my factory, I take off my caste.'[6]

## Human capital

The conventional wisdom of economic development, as we have seen, is that nations must exploit their comparative advantage, which for newly developing countries means cheap labour, while gradually building up their human capital by investment in skill development. Labour-intensive industries provide the starting point. This was certainly true of Japan's route to advanced industrial status, and has been the experience of Korea, Taiwan, and Hong Kong. But for what may be called later-developing countries it is at best only partially correct. Heavy demand for cheap industrial labour, if it occurs at all, tends to be brief, while some industries that have traditionally been leaders in industrialisation are no longer labour-intensive. The result is that opportunities for participation by large numbers of poorly skilled workers in modern industries are limited. Mass education and heavy state investment to raise the skill levels of the workforce are essential if development is to benefit more than social elites.

Industrialisation is very different now from what it was 200 years ago, when there were no powerful industrialised countries setting the rules, no global financial markets competing for foreign investment, or multinational corporations able to relocate operations from one country to another in response to changing labour costs, resource availability, and market opportunities. Therefore it is hardly surprising that its effects on individual employment opportunities are extremely variable.

The textile industry has long been regarded as a major vehicle of industrialisation, often serving as a bridge from 'pre-industrial' skills and forms of organisation to those characteristic of large-scale industry. This was true of the cotton mills of northern England in the eighteenth century, when they began to mass-produce the cheap fabrics that undermined the Indian textile industry, and true of the Japanese silk industry in the late nineteenth and early twentieth century, whose expansion hastened the industry's decline in China. In Japan in the 1920s and 1930s, and Korea in the 1960s and 1970s, textile factories were large employers giving many employees their first experience of modern industrial working conditions. But the integrated textile mills established in Indonesia during the 1980s and 1990s have depended on advanced technology rather than large numbers of employees for their productivity. The workers now employed have to be more highly skilled than those who found work in the industry thirty or forty years ago.[7]

It is a lack of skills that prevents a large part of the workforce in developing Asian countries from benefiting from industrialisation, and also limits the extent to which genuine industrialisation, as opposed to the establishment of industrial enclaves, can occur. In almost all the miracle economies of East and South-East Asia, skilled workers are in short supply, and there is concern whether they have the technical competence and creativity to sustain the ambitious modernisation programs on which those countries have embarked.

In Japan the problem is demographic rather than one of education and training: the main concern is the projected shortage of workers of any kind in a rapidly ageing society. However, for most other Asian nations this demographic complication is still some way off. Nor is the skills shortage they face the sort often complained of in Japan and Western industrialised countries—that is, a shortage of engineers and researchers to expand the technological frontier and create the next wave of products needed to ensure international competitiveness. Rather, it is a skills shortage at all levels of the workforce, including technicians, process and construction workers, tradesmen, and paraprofessionals.[8]

An educated and skilled workforce has been one of the characteristics of the late-development success stories of East Asia: Singapore, Hong Kong, Taiwan, and Korea. On the other hand, education alone is not enough to drive industrialisation and expansion of job opportunities. In 1992 the Indian state of Karnataka alone, with a population of 45 million, had more than eighteen thousand unemployed engineering graduates. Despite Karnataka's relatively strong economic position, exemplified by the capital Bangalore and its thriving information technology industry, they were unable to contribute to national development or to obtain personal economic advantage from their education. In 1999 alone, the United States issued more than 30 000 work visas to skilled professionals from India, the bulk of whom had expertise in information technology. The state of Kerala has the highest literacy levels and school attainment of all the Indian states, yet has lagged behind other parts of the country in terms of industrialisation. It has had difficulty attracting industry and investment largely because of a lack of infrastructure and the reputation of its 'restive' workforce. The result was extensive emigration of workers to places such as Mumbai and the Persian Gulf.[9]

There is widespread concern that the late and rapid economic development being pursued by Asian countries may not be associated with the emergence of an educated and technically skilled workforce, and that modernisation will therefore remain superficial, benefiting only a small proportion of the population. Late development, it is feared, may turn out to be a mobile sweatshop, driven by foreign investors looking for cheap labour and tax breaks, who move on when those things dry up, without leaving anything in the way of increased skill or productive capacity behind them.

Boatman, Kochi, Kerala, India.

Sustainable sand mining, Kochi, Kerala, India.

Some of the dominant strategies for acquiring advanced industrial technology and skills from overseas offer only limited opportunities for expanding the skills of the local workforce. Direct foreign investment, the kind of arrangement frequently entered into by multinational corporations, typically involves foreign construction of the plant as well as foreign management, technical control and supervision of production. Local workers tend to fill only lower-level positions and carry out routine tasks.

Outright purchase of production technologies in the form of 'turnkey' plants likewise brings only limited scope for skills development. The result, it is feared, will be that late-developing countries may become locked into the role of proletariat of the global economy, doing the international equivalent of piece work for foreign capitalists. Some analysts concluded that the 'technology-less industrialisation' that is the outcome of this trend was one of the factors that made some Asian countries so vulnerable during the financial crisis of 1997–98. It is an interpretation that is more persuasive in relation to, say, Indonesia and Thailand than to Korea, which now can hardly be described as technology-less. However, there is no doubt that raising education and skill levels in the workforce takes much longer than building modern factories with foreign capital. Even with full government backing, the process cannot be rushed. In the short to intermediate term this can leave developing countries vulnerable to rapid departure of foreign technology and expertise as well as capital.[10] Table 9.2 shows that, as a proportion of GNP, developed countries tend to spend much more than developing countries on education and training. For example, during 1995–97 Sweden spent 8.3 per cent, New Zealand 7.3 per cent, and the United States 5.4 per cent, compared with 1.4 per cent in Indonesia, 2.3 per cent in China, and 3.2 per cent in India. Education expenditure in Japan and South Korea, at 3.6 per cent and 3.7 per cent respectively, was low compared with most other developed countries, while expenditure in Thailand at 4.8 per cent, and Malaysia at 4.9 per cent, was high for developing countries.

The pattern is different, however, for government spending only, with governments of some developing Asian countries directing a higher proportion of public resources to education than do their counterparts in developed countries. Singapore and Thailand spent more than 23 per cent of public funds on education; Iran, Hong Kong, and South Korea more than 17 per cent; and Malaysia and the Philippines more than 15 per cent. This reflects the importance those governments attach to education—for economic-development purposes, of course, but also for other reasons. Certainly Iran's public expenditure on education cannot be understood simply in terms of pursuit of economic development.

## Job mobility

As economic change accelerates it becomes increasingly likely that individuals will have to change their occupation a number of times during the course of their working lives. OECD forecasts of economic change in developed countries indicate that the occupations in which the majority of workers will be employed several decades from now have yet to be invented. In other words, most of the jobs in which people now

**Table 9.2** Government expenditure on education, 1995–97

| | *Education as percentage of GNP* | *Education as percentage of all government expenditure* | *Secondary as percentage of all government education expenditure* | *Higher education as percentage of government education expenditure* |
|---|---|---|---|---|
| Sweden | 8.3 | 12.2 | 38.7 | 27.2 |
| New Zealand | 7.3 | 17.1 | 40.3 | 29.1 |
| Canada | 6.9 | 12.9 | | 35.3 |
| France | 6.0 | 10.9 | 49.5 | 17.9 |
| Australia | 5.5 | 13.5 | 38.9 | 30.5 |
| US | 5.4 | 14.4 | 36.1 | 25.2 |
| UK | 5.3 | 11.6 | 44.0 | 23.7 |
| Malaysia | 4.9 | 15.4 | 30.6 | 25.5 |
| Italy | 4.9 | 9.1 | 49.2 | 15.1 |
| Thailand | 4.8 | 20.1 | 20.0 | 16.4 |
| Germany | 4.8 | 9.6 | | 22.5 |
| Iran | 4.0 | 17.8 | 33.9 | 22.9 |
| South Korea | 3.7 | 17.5 | 36.6 | 8.0 |
| Japan | 3.6 | 9.9 | 41.8 | 12.1 |
| Philippines | 3.4 | 15.7 | 23.3 | 18.0 |
| Sri Lanka | 3.4 | 8.9 | 74.8 | 9.3 |
| India | 3.2 | 11.6 | 26.5 | 13.7 |
| Nepal | 3.2 | 13.5 | 19.0 | 19.0 |
| Vietnam | 3.0 | 7.4 | 26.0 | 22.0 |
| Singapore | 3.0 | 23.3 | 34.6 | 34.8 |
| Hong Kong | 2.9 | 17.0 | 35.0 | 37.1 |
| Pakistan | 2.7 | 7.1 | 27.9 | 13.0 |
| China | 2.3 | 12.2 | 32.2 | 15.6 |
| Bangladesh | 2.2 | 13.8 | 43.8 | 7.9 |
| Laos | 2.1 | 8.7 | 30.7 | 7.4 |
| Myanmar | 1.9 | 14.4 | 40.3 | 11.7 |
| Indonesia | 1.4 | 7.9 | | 24.4 |

Source: United Nations Development Program, *Human Development Report 2001*, Oxford University Press, New York, 2001, 170–3.
Note: Data is for the latest year available in the period shown.

work will have disappeared by then or been radically altered. As the ever-changing industrial and technological environment makes career changes more necessary, retraining and continuing education will become essential. Entry-level training, whether a university degree or an apprenticeship, will no longer be adequate. Workers will need to return periodically to study, to update skills and acquire new ones.

To some extent, the idea that greater job mobility is a consequence of accelerating economic change is an illusion. In part, it is a consequence of predominant Western patterns of work demarcation, certification, and systems of education. In earlier times, methods of economic production and work tasks changed too, but because there was little concern about formal qualifications and learning was largely done on the job, it was easier for individual workers to adapt to changing circumstances while continuing in what was nominally the same occupation.

Where there is a strong emphasis on workplace training rather than formal certification—as in Japan—it is possible for workers to cope with industrial change without having to take up a new career. In fact, in this regard a number of aspects of what has come to be regarded as 'the Japanese system' are mutually reinforcing. The principle of lifelong employment, which has guided the treatment by corporations of their core employees and has demanded reciprocal loyalty from them, has encouraged employers to invest heavily in workplace training. It has been observed that Japanese firms attach relatively little importance to the formal educational qualifications of those they hire because they themselves ensure that workers acquire the necessary skills. If we add to this the practice of requiring job mobility within the firm from core workers, a relatively low level of occupational mobility or career change is not surprising. While such workplace practices have never extended throughout Japanese industry, and were adversely affected by the stagnation and economic recession that began in the 1990s, they underline the fact that appropriate industrial practices may greatly reduce the cost to individual workers of rapid industrial and technological change.[11]

Nevertheless, where changes to particular production technologies or the organisation of entire industries run deep, it may be impossible for employers or employees to cope within existing structures. Then widespread occupational shifts become unavoidable. Deep-seated changes of this kind are common in the context of economic globalisation. Unskilled and semi-skilled workers are particularly vulnerable because many of the changes result from the introduction of labour-saving technologies. Yet for skilled workers industrial and technological change may present more difficulties than for unskilled workers. The reason has already been suggested. For a labourer used to doing dirty or heavy manual work it makes little difference, for example, whether he is working on a landowner's farm or on a city construction site. As long as he is able to find a job, the tasks involved will not differ greatly. But for a worker with advanced skills that were time-consuming and costly to acquire, having those skills made obsolescent by technological change or industrial restructuring may be disastrous. Acquiring a new set of skills able to yield comparable income and status will often be out of the question. Unless the worker is lucky enough to find an employer willing to provide or finance the acquisition of new skills, the economic burden may be too great.

Families in many Asian societies are prepared to spend a large proportion of their resources on education for one or more family members, to enable them to obtain a professional qualification that will help to advance the economic and social standing of the family as a whole. This is not the sort of strategy that can be repeated a number of times in the working life of a single generation.

The high human cost of skills obsolescence is not an argument for resisting economic change. However, there is a case for those benefiting from technological and industrial change to bear much of the cost of reskilling the workers adversely affected by it. Long-term interest as well as considerations of equity demand that the state and private employers provide education and retraining: unless continuing education and retraining are widely available at minimal cost to individual workers, the workforce and the economy as a whole will lack the flexibility necessary to thrive in a time of rapid change.

These considerations become particularly important in the light of the demographic changes taking place in Asian countries. Again, it is in Japan that the issue is most conspicuous. Because of the rapid ageing of the Japanese population, the number of new entrants to the workforce is shrinking and the Japanese economy is facing a labour shortage. The combination of a labour shortage and technological and industrial change makes the task of minimising skills obsolescence particularly urgent. Even in terms of economic self-interest, therefore, there will be good reason for firms to invest more rather than less in workplace training. It was during an earlier time of labour shortage, the 1920s and 1930s, that the Japanese institution of lifelong employment emerged. Firms did their best to keep the employees they had trained. Hence in the coming years in Japan it would not be surprising to see an increasing polarisation of labour market experience: a skilled core, largely in lifetime employment, with opportunities for retraining in response to changing company and economic needs, and a periphery of largely unskilled and technically obsolete workers drifting from employer to employer, with little hope of job continuity, let alone permanency.

In countries with very young populations and economies still in the early phases of industrialisation, motivation either to train or to retrain workers is much weaker. There is an ample supply of cheap labour, and the skill requirements of operations established through direct foreign investment are often met by importing personnel as well as production processes. Because few firms provide much workplace training, there is a fear of losing skilled workers on the part of those who do. The *laissez-faire* mentality that in many countries accompanies industrialisation does not encourage loyalty on the part of either employees or firms.

## Going in search of work

Some workers are able to cope with changing labour market demands and conditions by moving from job to job within a single organisation or location. Others do not have that option, or prefer to look for better opportunities elsewhere. Not everyone feels regret at leaving his or her native village or town, with its predictable pattern of employment, even when it offers a degree of security. People have diverse reasons for moving away. Many go to escape the constraints of rural life, its institutionalised inequalities, rigidity, predictability, boredom. If some move to the city in desperation, others make the change with eager anticipation. Nevertheless it is undoubtedly true that if the city did not hold, or was not seen to hold, greater economic opportunities, its attractions on other fronts would be less compelling.

Economic data suggest that for many workers the decision to look for better opportunities in the city is well founded. Economic growth is concentrated in urban regions to such a degree that urban/rural differences are widely regarded as a threat to national cohesion and stability. This is particularly so in large countries such as China, India, and Indonesia. A sharp increase in economic inequality was one of the consequences of China's shift to a market economy from 1979. During the mid-1990s, urban incomes were estimated to be two and a half times as high as rural incomes. In human development terms, the metropolitan areas of Beijing, Tianjin, and Shanghai scored nearly twice as high as undeveloped inland provinces such as Qinghai, Guizhou, and Tibet.

In Thailand, too, the income gap between urban and rural areas is seen as a serious problem. In the early 1990s, agricultural workers, on average, earned only one-twelfth of what non-agricultural workers earned; in the 1960s it had been one-sixth. With around 15 per cent of the nation's population, Bangkok is producing more than 40 per cent of its wealth. Under such circumstances, moving to the city is likely to make good sense, just as it does in the Philippines, where the average per capita income in

Qingdao, Shandong, China. Architecture of the late twentieth-century boom mingles with evidence of Qingdao's history as a German treaty port.

Finding personal space in the megacity: Tokyo, Japan.

Manila is more than twice the national average and its contribution to GDP is some three times what may be expected on a population basis.[12] Although such figures mask the huge disparities in income and lifestyle characteristic of city life, and give no indication of its stresses or the social and environmental problems it generates, they do confer some plausibility on the dreams of those who make the move. For those with education, workplace skills, or money, the opportunities are there. For those with little more than determination the struggle to survive is intense, yet may still offer more choices than are available at home.

In the first three decades of the twenty-first century, the proportion of the population in Asian countries that is urban is expected to increase from 37 per cent to 53 per cent (compared with a rise from 47 per cent to 60 per cent for the world population overall). The entire population increase in Asia during that period—projected at just under 1.3 billion—is expected to occur in urban areas, with the rural population to fall slightly. While some of the increase will occur in 'megacities', with cities such as Mumbai, Dhaka, Jakarta, and Manila continuing to grow at more than 2 per cent a year (see Table 9.3), most of it will be accounted for by urban centres with less than 5 million inhabitants.[13] A fascination with megacities may be as dangerous for those trying to understand internal migration as for the participants. Urbanisation is transforming all regions, not only national capitals and world-oriented megacities. Landless

**Table 9.3** Population (in millions) and projected growth rates of cities with 10 million inhabitants, 2000–15.

| | *2000* | | | | *2015* | |
|---|---|---|---|---|---|---|
| | *City* | *Population* | *Growth rate 2000–2015 (%)* | | *City* | *Population* |
| 1 | Tokyo | 26.4 | 0.0 | 1 | Tokyo | 26.4 |
| 2 | Mexico City | 18.1 | 0.4 | 2 | Mumbai | 26.1 |
| 3 | Mumbai | 18.1 | 2.4 | 3 | Lagos | 23.2 |
| 4 | Sao Paulo | 17.8 | 0.9 | 4 | Dhaka | 21.1 |
| 5 | New York | 16.6 | 0.3 | 5 | São Paulo | 20.4 |
| 6 | Lagos | 13.4 | 3.7 | 6 | Karachi | 19.2 |
| 7 | Los Angeles | 13.1 | 0.5 | 7 | Mexico City | 19.2 |
| 8 | Kolkata | 12.9 | 1.9 | 8 | New York | 17.4 |
| 9 | Shanghai | 12.9 | 0.8 | 9 | Jakarta | 17.3 |
| 10 | Buenos Aires | 12.6 | 0.7 | 10 | Kolkata | 17.3 |
| 11 | Dhaka | 12.3 | 3.6 | 11 | Delhi | 16.8 |
| 12 | Karachi | 11.8 | 3.2 | 12 | Metro Manila | 14.8 |
| 13 | Delhi | 11.7 | 2.4 | 13 | Shanghai | 14.6 |
| 14 | Jakarta | 11.0 | 3.0 | 14 | Los Angeles | 14.1 |
| 15 | Osaka | 11.0 | 0.0 | 15 | Buenos Aires | 14.1 |
| 16 | Metro Manila | 10.9 | 2.1 | 16 | Cairo | 13.8 |
| 17 | Beijing | 10.8 | 0.9 | 17 | Istanbul | 12.5 |
| 18 | Rio de Janeiro | 10.6 | 0.8 | 18 | Beijing | 12.3 |
| 19 | Cairo | 10.6 | 1.7 | 19 | Rio de Janeiro | 11.9 |
| | | | | 20 | Osaka | 11.0 |
| | | | | 21 | Tianjin | 10.7 |
| | | | | 22 | Hyderabad | 10.5 |
| | | | | 23 | Bangkok | 10.1 |

Source: UN Population Division, *World Urbanization Prospects: The 1999 Revision*, http://www.un.org/esa/population/urbanization.htm, accessed 19 July 2001.

Some corners of Bangkok have been little affected by its modern transformation: temples in the Royal Palace Precinct (left) and canal-side houses (above).

peasants looking for employment may prefer to go to the local town or district capital rather than to a distant megacity, particularly if they have no relatives or village connections on whom they can rely to ease the transition. Those who venture to the megacities often have some experience of city life at the district or provincial level.

Just as a preoccupation with the international metropolis may result in insufficient attention being paid to what is happening at the district and provincial levels, so too a preoccupation with urbanisation may mean that population movement in the countryside is being overlooked. For country areas also are being affected by fundamental economic and social changes, and the search for better opportunities often results in rural relocation rather than a decision to try city life. China offers a good illustration of the complexity and variability of the population movements taking place in Asian countries.

In China, population flow from rural to urban areas is certainly strong. The 1990 census found that around 27 per cent of the population was urban. Should the annual urban growth rate in coming years be similar to that of the 1980s and 1990s, at around 4 or 5 per cent, then by the year 2010 about half of China's population would be urban. The population of cities and towns would grow, but so too would the number of population centres classified as cities and towns. Between 1984 and 1990, for example, the number of officially designated urban centres in China nearly doubled, increasing from 6506 to 12 391. Villages grow into towns and towns into cities. While there are big regional variations and some contrary patterns, the One Percent National Population Survey in 1995 found that the main migrant flow was from the poorer, less-developed western and central regions to the wealthier, developed eastern provinces. Moreover the migrants, who were predominantly male, tended to be literate and educated to above the national average.[14]

The aspirations of individuals and families are not the only factor influencing where they move in search of work and economic security. Government policy is another. While few governments match the attempts of the Chinese state to control the movement of its people, all have policies that influence movement. The most obvious example is state sponsored or directed internal migration to encourage population redistribution or growth in particular areas. This has been a major aspect of government policy in Indonesia and Vietnam as well as China, as discussed in Chapter 4. But other sorts of policy may be no less significant, including the establishment of cities and regions to act as centres for technological or economic development.

Perhaps the most elaborate example of this sort of policy is Japan's technopolis program, introduced in 1980 with the aim of establishing a 'technostate' of research and development cities dispersed across the country. In all, twenty-six locations have been identified under the program, all close to substantial regional cities, as required by the program guidelines. Significantly, the program was prompted originally by concern over social and economic inequalities in country areas, rather than the aim of promoting technological innovation and the development of knowledge-based industries. It soon became apparent, however, that the social and economic regeneration of the countryside, and creation of new industries able to drive the national economy, could to some extent be achieved together. The distribution of technopoles throughout the country would stop the brain drain from rural to major urban areas, and ease accommodation and infrastructure pressures in the major cities, while helping to spread more evenly the economic benefits of advanced industrialisation.

Other initiatives, such as the development of Tsukuba Science City and Kansai Science City, are closely related to the technopolis program, but have addressed the goal of scientific and technological innovation more directly. Nonetheless they are alike in concentrating highly skilled workers in knowledge-intensive industries at strategic locations.

Similar initiatives, though less grandiose, have been taken in other Asian countries. They include Korea, with its Taedok Science Town and strategic 'technobelts'; India, with its concentration of high-tech industries in Bangalore; and Taiwan, Singapore, and Malaysia, all competing to establish concentrations of information technology and microelectronic industry. Many governments share the dream of creating, by bureaucratic action, another Silicon Valley, and so bring together inventive and highly skilled workers in the hope of engendering the creativity and synergy that in the Californian case resulted in dramatic industrial breakthroughs. While the goal of generating new knowledge-intensive industries is far from assured, the effects of such policies on the employment opportunities and migration patterns of research and development personnel and other skilled workers are clear.[15]

The strategies used by nations in earlier phases of industrialisation also involve steering or manipulating the movement of particular sorts of workers towards selected destinations. Often these destinations are close enough to existing population centres to benefit from existing infrastructure and services, yet sufficiently distinct to amount to new developments. In China, thirty years ago, Shenzhen was just an insignificant village near the Hong Kong border. At the beginning of the new century it had 4 million inhabitants and was the centre of a special economic zone that has played a leading role in the transformation of South China's economy, with a concentration of hi-tech and service industries, and the second-largest port in the country. Border police joke with workers trying to cross illegally into Hong Kong that the city lies in the opposite direction.

Like China, Indonesia has established special economic zones in an attempt to speed up industrialisation and direct it from labour-intensive towards skill-based production. One of these zones is the SIJORI development triangle, a joint initiative with the Malaysian and Singapore governments. The Indonesian corner of the triangle is Batam, a small island (416 square kilometres) at the eastern end of the Malacca Straits, only 20 kilometres from Singapore. Between 1973 and 1998 the population increased from 6000 to 400 000, and was sufficiently skilled to make the island a centre of modern industry and international trade. In 1997, Batam attracted more than $US5 billion in foreign investment, mainly from Japan and Singapore. It is regarded both as a development success story and an exemplar of the cronyism and corruption characteristic of the Suharto period.[16]

## International labour migration

If multinational corporations are the organisational embodiment of economic globalisation, international labour migration is its personal expression. The age of globalisation has also been dubbed the age of migration.[17] In migration we see its inequity and mercilessness as well as its opportunities and rewards. Most current discussion of labour migration in Asia focuses on unskilled and semi-skilled workers, in contrast with the earlier preoccupation with 'brain drain' or the exodus of highly qualified workers to Western countries. Economic development across the Asian region as a whole has transformed opportunities, creating better career prospects for professionals at home and demand for semi-skilled and cheap labour in rapidly developing economies abroad. Greater ease of movement coupled with massive economic disparities between countries in the region has encouraged a considerable international movement of workers.

Since the majority of all but migrant professionals tend to be illegal, the number of individuals involved can only be estimated indirectly. Reasonable estimates put the total number of migrant workers in East and South-East Asia in the mid-1990s at around 5 million. The main host nations were Malaysia, Thailand, Japan, Hong Kong, Taiwan, and Singapore (see Table 9.4). South Asia has tended to export rather than import labour, with much of it in the 1980s going to the wealthy oil-producing nations of the Persian Gulf. However, that destination lost much of its appeal with the outbreak of the Gulf War in January 1991, when nearly 1.5 million workers returned to their homelands in a space of four months. The Asian financial crisis of 1997–98 had a similar but less severe effect in South Korea, Thailand, and Malaysia, as local unemployment rates soared, prompting authorities to block entry to new foreign workers and to expel those in the country illegally. In Malaysia in February 1998, government officials were reported as appealing to the public to make citizens' arrests of illegal migrants.

Of the estimated 2 million migrant workers in Malaysia in 1997—almost a quarter of the labour force—less than half were registered foreign workers. The great majority of Malaysia's migrant workers came from Indonesia, a common language making the move easier than most of the alternatives. In Thailand most foreign workers were

**Table 9.4** Estimated number of migrant workers in selected Asian countries

| | *Year* | *Number (thousands)* | *Number as % of labour force* |
|---|---|---|---|
| Japan | 1986 | 119 | 0.2 |
| | 1992 | 601 | 0.9 |
| South Korea | 1992 | 66 | 0.7 |
| | 1994 | 200 | 1.0 |
| Taiwan | 1989 | 100 | 0.8 |
| | 1995 | 220 | 2.0 |
| Hong Kong | 1981 | 140 | 8.1 |
| | 1995 | 405 | 13.6 |
| Singapore | 1970 | 14 | 2.0 |
| | 1980 | 125 | 8.8 |
| | 1996 | 370 | 20.5 |
| Malaysia | 1984 | 500 | 10.0 |
| | 1997 | 2000 | 24.0 |
| Thailand | 1988 | 165 | 0.7 |
| | 1994 | 725 | 3.0 |
| | 1997 | 1700 | 6.0 |

Source: P. Athukorala and C. Manning, *Structural Change and International Migration in East Asia: Adjusting to Labour Scarcity*, Oxford University Press, Melbourne, 1999, 2.

Burmese escaping the economic stagnation of their own country, many of them from the Tai-speaking Shan minority.

The standard explanation of labour migration is that rapid and sustained economic growth creates labour shortages. As locals take advantage of the situation to move into the better-paying and more attractive jobs, migrant workers, unless they have skills in particular demand, come in at the bottom of the labour market, to do the jobs that are dirty, dangerous and difficult. It is argued that countries such as Malaysia have little choice but to import labour. In the words of one expert: 'It's not a gradual process where you can reconfigure your domestic labour supply. Speed is the key feature—the speed of investment and the need for an instantaneous labour force.'[18]

Although there may be areas of acute labour and skills shortage at times of fast growth—for example, in building and construction—this explanation is easily overstated. South Korea has experienced more rapid industrialisation and economic growth than any other Asian nation, and has become an inspiration for newly industrialising South-East Asian countries. Yet from the mid-1960s to the late 1980s, when GNP per capita was increasing at around 8 per cent a year, Korea did not find it necessary to import labour. Rigid state control of wages ensured that labour remained cheap and production costs low. Moreover, by heavy investment in education and training, it was able to meet most of the skill needs generated by rapid industrialisation.

Even in the mid-1990s, after huge wage rises that severely impaired the country's economic competitiveness, and a demographic shift resulting in fewer young people entering the workforce, the number of foreign workers in Korea was estimated at only 200 000. During its period of high economic growth, Korea in fact exported a substantial amount of labour, reaching a maximum of just under 200 000 workers in 1983. Therefore if countries such as Malaysia and Thailand import skilled and unskilled labour, it is not only because economic growth increases the total demand for labour. Much of the growth, after all, results from mechanisation and automation of production rather than the creation of new jobs. Unskilled labour is imported because it is cheap and easy to control if legal, easy to exploit if illegal. Migrant workers, whether male or female, tend to be young and single. Because they are rarely in a position to bring their families with them, they make few demands on the housing, utilities and services of already overcrowded cities. They provide their labour while expecting little from the host society in return. Importing labour is analogous to relocating production off-shore: it is a way of keeping down costs, for not only is the foreign labour cheap, but it also helps to suppress local wage demands. Where skilled labour has to be imported because government and industry have failed to invest adequately in education and training, the need to limit unskilled and semi-skilled labour costs will be all the greater.

Labour migration is a response to the opportunities presented by economic globalisation, but those opportunities necessarily arise from inequalities, or 'market differentials', to use a more neutral phrase. A nation such as Thailand or Malaysia has no labour shortage, in absolute terms, since in many rural areas people often have difficulty finding gainful employment of any sort. The problem is rather one of uneven and limited development, with industrialisation concentrated in a few areas around the major cities, and education and skill development limited to a small proportion of the population. When international boundaries are kept open, 'leaving it to the market' is likely to seem a convenient minimalist response.

International migration of labour, like internal migration, is strongly influenced by government policies as well as individual aspirations. Some governments have encouraged workers to go abroad, as a way of reducing unemployment, reducing national balance of payments problems, and acquiring skills. Nations troubled by high levels of foreign debt have been particularly attracted to this strategy. Pakistan, the Philippines, and South Korea have all used it; since 1997, so has China. Pakistan in the early 1980s had around 2 million nationals working overseas, and during the 1982–83 financial year their remittances had a value 10 per cent higher than that of Pakistan's exports (see Table 9.5). While since then the proportion of overseas earnings represented by migrant worker remittances has fallen to well below 50 per cent, in the early 1990s around 10 per cent of the Pakistani labour force was still working abroad. South Korea too relied heavily on overseas remittances to weather its foreign debt crisis in the early 1980s, and for the national economies of the Philippines and Bangladesh they have also been important. In Bangladesh in 1985, remittances amounted to a third of national overseas earnings; in 1993 the proportion was only slightly less. The Philippines government estimated that in the mid-1990s more than 4.2 million Filipinos, or 15 per cent of the nation's labour force, were working in 120 foreign countries. Since 1980 their contribution to the national economy has risen steadily.

In such circumstances it is no exaggeration to say that migrant workers play a critical role in the economic survival of their countries as well as that of their families.[19]

**Table 9.5** Migrant worker remittances in relation to GDP and value of merchandise exports (%)

| | *Year* | *GDP* | *Merchandise exports* |
|---|---|---|---|
| Philippines | 1980 | 1.9 | 10.6 |
| | 1985 | 2.6 | 17.4 |
| | 1990 | 3.3 | 17.8 |
| | 1993 | 4.7 | 22.3 |
| Bangladesh | 1980 | 2.2 | 36.1 |
| | 1985 | 4.0 | 50.1 |
| | 1990 | 3.7 | 46.6 |
| | 1993 | 4.2 | 44.1 |
| India | 1980 | 1.6 | 32.7 |
| | 1985 | 1.0 | 25.6 |
| | 1990 | 0.7 | 12.4 |
| Pakistan | 1980 | 8.9 | 82.1 |
| | 1985 | 8.7 | 97.2 |
| | 1990 | 5.5 | 40.4 |
| | 1993 | 3.3 | 23.7 |
| Sri Lanka | 1980 | 3.5 | 13.1 |
| | 1985 | 3.9 | 17.7 |
| | 1990 | 4.6 | 19.9 |
| | 1993 | 5.4 | 19.8 |

Source: Asian Development Bank, *Asian Development Outlook 1996 and 1997*, Oxford University Press, Hong Kong, 1996, 207.

## Labour rights and conditions

Establishment of the World Trade Organisation, with the aim of promoting the outcomes of the General Agreement on Tariffs and Trade, was followed by debate over whether its role should include implementation of universal labour laws and enforcement of minimum working conditions. The United States and many European countries have argued that it should; Asian countries, including Japan, have argued that it should not, and so have Australia and New Zealand.

Those pushing for promotion of universal labour rights and standards argue that there is a need to protect the human rights and well-being of workers in the developing Asian economies. They are able to point to many serious violations of the labour rights set out in international human rights legislation and International Labour Organisation (ILO) conventions, as well as widespread failure to enforce domestic labour laws and conditions. Critics of labour practices in developing Asian countries have coined the phrase 'social dumping'. This refers to what is claimed to be a strategy of refusing to ensure that workers receive the fair pay and reasonable working conditions employers in developed countries are obliged to provide. This enables developing countries to compete unfairly, at the expense of their workers, with those committed to fair treatment of their labour force.

Those taking the opposite view dismiss this as moralistic window-dressing of an attempt to undermine the competitiveness of developing countries. When a country has little to compete on but its cheap labour, they retort, it should not have imposed on it the rules and conditions of rich nations, standards that tend to be far in excess of what is appropriate or looked for by workers in developing countries. Besides, developed countries have taken two hundred years or more to reach their present position, and during that time their workers have experienced conditions similar to those being criticised now in newly industrialising Asian countries. Therefore it is unreasonable to expect developing Asian countries to adopt such standards, all the more so since it would effectively prevent them from ever improving their economic position. Free trade means allowing each nation to compete according to its comparative advantage. If the workers of Malaysia or Indonesia are prepared to labour long and hard for wages low by international standards, they should not be prevented from doing so.[20]

Both sides in this debate have been somewhat disingenuous. There is no doubt that thinly disguised self-interest frequently underlies the positions of Western governments on these issues. The line adopted by the United States towards labour conditions in Indonesia in the 1990s, for example, was rather different from the one it followed in South Korea in the 1960s and 1970s. In Korea, unionism and demands for workers' rights were interpreted as intimations of communism, threats to the stability of the military regime the United States supported, and were therefore to be suppressed. In the case of Indonesia, however, these things were said to be legitimate demands for economic and social justice that should be met by any government genuinely concerned for the welfare of its people. Naturally this led Indonesians to suspect that Americans, consistent in their self-interest, were now seeking to protect those interests by undermining the competitiveness of Indonesian manufacturers.

On the other hand, during the Suharto period there were plenty of reasons for concern over labour conditions in Indonesia, concern being expressed by Indonesian non-government organisations and international organisations such as the ILO as well as the United States and other Western governments. The causes for concern included a prohibition on all but government-sponsored unions; intervention by police and the military in labour disputes; and failure to enforce minimum wages and conditions, the prohibition of child labour and forced labour, or workplace health and safety standards. For many observers, labour conditions in Indonesia under the New Order were summed up in 1993 by the savage beating, rape, and murder of labour activist Marsinah. Strikes and protests by workers became more and more frequent in the 1990s, despite government suppression, as worker dissatisfaction and resentment over their treatment increased. It remains to be seen what priority the new Indonesian government will give to labour reform. Faced with acute economic difficulties as it is, it may argue that such reform should be delayed 'in the national interest'.[21]

Labour conditions in Indonesia have been typical of industrialising Asian countries where limited labour organisation has coincided with low levels of state protection. However, it is necessary to examine the claim that this *laissez-faire* approach is necessary on economic grounds, and is in the long-term interests of the workforce and the society generally. It is related to the arguments used by the governments of developing countries in relation to observance of international human rights standards, that unless and until their nations achieve a certain level of economic development, it is unrealistic to expect those standards to be achieved. The objections that can be raised against it are similar. It may be agreed that in a time of rapid population growth, economic growth and development alone can guarantee the minimal economic security needed for anyone to be able to enjoy their civil, political, social, and cultural rights. But mechanisms guaranteeing some degree of equitable distribution of resources and opportunities also have to be in place. Civil and political rights—such as the right to form trade unions—in fact may be crucial for securing minimal economic rights, such as a minimum wage or safe working conditions.

The direct cost to employers of some key workplace reforms is small, and accordingly the claim that they impair the international competitiveness of developing countries is weak. No one is arguing that developing Asian countries should be required to establish Scandinavian-style welfare systems. As was pointed out in Chapter 5, a number of countries have shown that providing a reasonable standard of living for all is possible without strong economic growth or frittering away resources needed for future development. If industrialisation and development cannot offer workers a better and more secure livelihood, it is difficult to see what they are meant to achieve. As to the claim that the efficacy of market forces must not be put at risk by government intervention, even when it is clear that a large proportion of the population is being harmed by those forces, this prompts the basic question, what then is the purpose of government?

Be that as it may, changes in labour laws and conditions do carry costs, and their introduction, whether forced or voluntary, may have far-reaching economic as well as social consequences. Some of the dilemmas involved are illustrated by the operations of multinational corporations in developing Asian economies. On the one hand, multinationals are accused of ruthless exploitation of developing countries, using cheap labour, cheap natural resources, and lax environmental standards to extract maximum profit while leaving nothing, not even high skill levels, in return. Often critics add the charge that workers are forced to submit to workplace practices and treatment that may be regarded as acceptable in the corporation's home country, but are culturally inappropriate in the country in question. Korean and Taiwanese managers, for example, are accused of imposing iron discipline on Chinese, Vietnamese, Thai, and Indonesian workers, forcing them to march and stand to attention in the workplace, and inflicting corporal punishment.

Early in 1997, the shoe manufacturer Nike was accused of underpaying and sexually harassing female workers in Vietnam, as well as humiliating workers and forcing them to kneel in the hot sun. A Taiwanese subcontracting firm is alleged to have punished workers by forcing them to run around its plant in the sun, until many passed out and had to be hospitalised. This followed earlier reports of poor treatment by Nike of its workers in Indonesia, and ran counter to the corporation's adoption in 1993 of a Memorandum of Understanding under which all its suppliers and contractors agreed to abide by all local labour market legislation and conditions, non-discrimination principles, and environmental requirements.[22]

On the other hand, multinational corporations that try to introduce better working conditions and regulations than are required locally are often accused of clumsy social engineering that may make the situation worse rather than better. Clothing manufacturer Levi Strauss, for example, shut down operations in China and Myanmar in the 1990s in response to continuing human rights violations there, and adopted a policy of 'ethical sourcing' to protect the values and reputation of the corporation. But not only is such a principled approach difficult to enforce, it can also have perverse effects. The discovery that child workers were employed in its Bangladesh factories prompted management to insist that corporate guidelines be observed. When it was pointed out that sacking them would deprive some of their families of their only means of support, compliance with the rule was waived.[23] A generalised version of this argument is that if a plant closes down, either because of moral scruples or excessive generosity on the part of its management, it benefits no one. 'The misery of being exploited by capitalists', it has been observed, 'is nothing compared to the misery of not being exploited at all'.[24]

## Child labour

The problem of child labour encapsulates many of the difficulties involved in labour reform in developing countries. Despite the economic and social 'progress' made over the last forty years it remains extremely widespread, especially in South Asia. The ILO estimates that at least 15 per cent of children aged ten to fourteen years work. Because most work informally, in occupations that are unlikely to be regulated or monitored by officials, estimates vary greatly. Almost everywhere, however, unofficial estimates are more than double official figures. In India in the mid 1990s, for example, the government put the number of child workers at 17.5 million, while unofficial estimates ranged from 50 to 100 million. Government figures from Pakistan and

Bangladesh were 7.5 million and 6.2 million, while the unofficial estimates were 19 million and 15 million respectively (see Table 9.6).

Condemnation of continuing use of child labour in developing countries, often aroused by television documentaries showing children working long hours in dangerous and unhealthy conditions, or engaged in repetitious and degrading tasks for extremely low wages, has prompted moves for trade sanctions and boycotts against employers and governments not doing enough to stamp out the practice. Observers note that well-meaning actions such as those in the Levi Strauss case mentioned earlier may make the situation of child workers and their families worse. The children work because it is necessary for family survival and, if they are sacked from a factory because of pressure from Western activists or politicians, their only option may be to retreat further into the informal sector, taking work that is more exploitative and degrading.

It is necessary to identify precisely what makes child labour objectionable. That someone under the legal employment age has to work may be regrettable, but in itself is not as morally objectionable as the fact that he or she is likely to be exploited, degraded and mistreated. This point was made eloquently in 1997 at a conference on child labour in Amsterdam when representatives of child worker organisations themselves declared that the right of children to work should be respected, and that it is freedom from exploitation, ill-treatment, abuse, and social exclusion, not from work, that they seek.[25] Because use of child labour is illegal almost everywhere, it tends to occur where there is least surveillance or most corruption. Children are hired because they are cheap and docile and, because illegally employed, have little legal recourse in the eventuality of mistreatment. In this regard their situation is like that of illegal migrant labour. Where the situation of child workers differs is that young children are judged to be more vulnerable than adults and regarded as needing care, education, and the sorts of opportunities for personal development set out, for example, in the United Nations Convention on the Rights of the Child. Workplace exploitation and mistreatment of children is one issue; missing out on education and the opportunity to develop in a secure and supportive family environment is another. It was the need to steer a middle path through these difficulties that finally led to the adoption by the international community in 1999 of the International Labour Organisation's Worst Forms of Child Labour Convention (No. 182). The convention aims to eliminate child slavery and similar practices, including the recruitment of children in armed conflict; child prostitution and pornography; child involvement in illicit activities such as drug trafficking; and work likely to harm the safety and morals of children.

**Table 9.6** Child workers in Asian countries, 1995 (millions)

| | *Government estimate* | *Unofficial estimate* | *Population under 16 yrs* |
|---|---|---|---|
| India | 17.5 | 50–100 | 340 |
| Pakistan | 7.5 | 19 | 62 |
| Bangladesh | 6.2 | 15 | 49 |
| China | NA | 12 | 340 |
| Philippines | 0.8 | 5 | 29 |
| Thailand | 1.6 | 4 | 20 |
| Indonesia | 2.2 | 3.3 | 69 |

Source: Derived from ILO, UNICEF, and NGO reports.

It cannot be assumed that a family that sends one or more of its children out to work does not care for its young. Although there are families that sell their children into bondage, or to work in the sex trade, they are only a minority. Most give their children the care and support their circumstances permit; if, for example, the parents do not send their children to school, it is either because they cannot afford it or because schooling seems irrelevant to their situation.

The argument that child labour is due to poverty and will be eradicated by economic growth guided by the invisible hand of market forces, provided that do-gooders from developed countries do not attempt to inhibit the free operation of those forces, is hardly convincing. Neither is the argument that because the evils of child labour are the result of its illegality it should be legalised. Child labour is the result of market forces and is not going to be eradicated by them. Legal sanctions and their enforcement are necessary to prevent the exploitation and mistreatment of children in the workforce, but eradicating child labour will require government spending of the sort governments of some developing Asian countries often dismiss as unaffordable, and welfare programs that are seen as a reason for the decline of the

Brick kiln workers at school, Peshawar, Pakistan. A brickyard established near a refugee camp benefits from child labour, but allows young workers to attend an on-site school. In an area where employment is scarce, refugee families are thankful if any of their members can work.

West. Trade sanctions by developed countries tend to be either ineffectual or counter-productive. The solution can only be based on government action that makes adult labour more profitable than child labour, makes schooling more attractive and available to poor families, and relieves those families of some of the direct economic burden that results from not sending their children to work.

The greater the extent to which skills are needed for economic production, the less feasible is reliance on child labour and the more essential does education become for earning a living. Therefore as industrialisation moves beyond labour-intensive production, child labour becomes less attractive from the point of view of both employers and parents. While some forms of modern industrial technology, such as assembly of electronic appliances and components, may encourage the use of child labour, others have greatly reduced demand. If adult work opportunities are to be expanded and the economic value of education to be increased, some economic growth through technological development seems necessary. Making education free and more relevant should not be an impossible task. Assefa Bequele of the ILO, who has long experience relating to child labour, has observed that 'With very, very few exceptions, no nation in the world today is too poor to provide free primary education for its children'.[26]

Directing resources towards education is in any case the only way that skill levels in the workforce generally are going to be lifted, and this is the only way that developing

Young street vendor, Vientiane, Laos.

countries can hope to become something other than the sweatshops of the global economy. Where education is provided together with direct support for children, such as school meals, the impact can be considerable. Family planning may also be important, but will not be an attractive option for parents unless they have some assurance of greater economic security, especially when they are no longer able to work. Welfare and social security mechanisms are essential for this. In many cases communities will be best placed to provide these, for reasons of utility as well as cost, but governments will still have to provide leadership by giving priority to the abolition of child labour and the socio-economic circumstances that nurture it.[27]

The experience of Sri Lanka in this area is revealing. Of South Asian countries, Sri Lanka is the only one that has come close to eradicating child labour. A 1999 survey found that while 21 per cent of the 5–17-years age group of the Sri Lankan population took part in economic production, two-thirds of the children in question combined it with schooling or housekeeping duties, and worked only for short periods. Of those working and not attending school, 79 per cent were aged 15–17 years, and 77 per cent were involved in family-based economic activity, the bulk of it agricultural. An earlier (1993) study attributed Sri Lanka's success in addressing the problem 'primarily to education and child welfare policies, the availability of cheap and often skilled female labour, and the impact of labour legislation and trade union policy'. The education and labour force participation of women encouraged mothers to send their children to school and enabled them to benefit from welfare programs, while legal prohibitions and union activism changed public attitudes.[28]

What the example of child labour illustrates, among other things, is the futility of trying to distinguish 'market forces' from social factors. It is futile not because all social phenomena are economic in origin, but rather because economic phenomena have mixed causes, as does everything human. The operation of the market (including the labour market) depends on myriad political, social, and cultural factors, and successful intervention depends on identifying the relevant factors and influencing them directly, rather than hoping that injections of money may work miraculous cures.

This suggests that the concept of free trade, on which so much faith is pinned for future prosperity, is ultimately an illusion. Were all trade tariffs and imposts on imports abolished, international trade would in one sense be free. However, governments would still be able to manipulate the price of exports in countless ways, including the use of cross-subsidies, tax relief, selective provision and non-provision of social services. A government might, for example, reduce the cost of basic foodstuffs to keep down wage costs in industry, decline to provide social welfare at public expense, direct funds to building up higher education and research institutions, or subsidise rural transport and communication links. All such decisions redistribute costs and benefits among the population and are legitimate issues for consideration by the state.

In the end, everything connects. It is easy to imagine the World Trade Organisation, or a similar body, becoming caught up in endless disputes between states over what is or is not a legitimate method of underwriting export costs. What is certain is that the views of the citizens of the nations in question, regarding the legitimacy of the costs they have to bear in order to secure advantageous terms of trade, will often diverge from those of their government.

CHAPTER TEN

# Media, Communication, Censorship

## Control through information

The study of mass media was one of the first areas to give rise to ideas of globalisation. Enthusiasts said that electronic mass media did away with distance and isolation. As mass media shrank the world to village dimensions, people everywhere would acquire the same access to information, and with it enhanced possibilities for mutual understanding and cooperation.

Those of a more critical turn of mind said that mass media did away with difference and autonomy as well as distance, and saw the potential for new modes of domination. This led to the concept of cultural imperialism, the imposition of ways of understanding and values by the rich and powerful nations that control world media. Some argue that cultural imperialism is a more sophisticated version of the gunboat and Bible imperialism of the nineteenth century and that it has the same purpose of enforcing subservience and dependence. In any event, control by media is regarded as an efficient and cost-effective substitute for military control. It is a concept that can be applied not only between nation states, but also between ethnic groups or social classes within them.

A concept such as cultural imperialism highlights the fact that communication, whether via mass media or not, is subject to power relations, and that there is much at stake in controlling the flow of information, and of misinformation. All governments exercise some degree of control over communication within and across national boundaries, though the reasons they give vary. A common concern among the governments of Third World countries is the use of mass media for 'nation-building', that is, creating a national consciousness while minimising what are seen as harmful external influences. Concern over the harmful effects of government control of information, in developed as well as developing countries, has resulted in freedom to receive and to give information being identified as a human right. The human rights perspective on the control and manipulation of information relates to many of the issues considered elsewhere in this study, particularly those in Chapter 3. It also relates closely to the general issue of knowledge and society, which is examined in the final chapter.

## Technological change and communication

The importance of efficient and reliable communication systems for political cohesion and control has long been realised. The empires of ancient Rome and China owed much of their durability to reliable and rapid government communication with all parts of the realm. The Romans relied largely on a network of roads and the postal service that travelled it. The Chinese had a system of waterways as well as roads, and on special occasions also used fire beacons and drums to convey intelligence. However, like the Roman system, Chinese communications depended essentially on efficient transport that allowed messengers to travel as quickly as possible.

It was not until the invention of the telegraph in the nineteenth century that an effective means was found of separating the message from the messenger, thereby doing away with the need for the latter. Around 1870, when the first Suez–Bombay marine telegraph cable was being laid, the fastest ship from London to Sydney or Melbourne took fifty-four days to reach its destination. In 1872, when those cities were linked by telegraph, messages travelled the distance in fewer than twenty-four hours. In Asia the telegraph quickly became a 'weapon of empire' that enabled first Western powers and later Japan to control their far-flung colonies. By the end of the Sino-Japanese war in 1895 a well-developed telegraph network linked all parts of the Japanese empire, including Taiwan, Korea, Sakhalin, and Japanese interests in China.[1]

If the telegraph freed communication from its historical dependence on transport, radio opened the way for mass communication that did not rely on the printed word. Printing had been used to circulate information widely in China, Korea, and Japan as early as the eighth century, with the desire to spread Buddhist teachings apparently providing much of the motivation for technological innovation. A forerunner of modern newspapers, a government gazette, was circulated among Chinese officials during the eighth century.[2] But the printed word has two major drawbacks: it still relies on transport and it assumes the ability to read. Radio circumvents both these difficulties, which is why it has been particularly influential in Third World countries with poor infrastructure and low literacy levels. When in the 1960s the transistor radio became widely available and radio receivers no longer had to be hooked up to an electricity grid, radio's impact became even more far-reaching. The predominantly rural populations of countries such as India, China, Indonesia, and the Philippines rapidly gained access to information inconceivable only a short time before.

In its early days radio, like the telegraph, was a tool of empire, and was used to good effect by the Western imperial powers and Japan. Superior radio technology has been identified as a factor in Japan's victory over Russia in the war of 1904–05. The French found radio useful in controlling Vietnam, as did the Dutch in ruling Indonesia. At an international conference in 1921–22, when China demanded the closure or surrender of 'all electrical means of communication, including wireless stations maintained in China by foreign countries, the imperialist powers refused to relinquish the control their communications media gave them.[3]

But if radio could be used to break a nation, it could also be used to make one. The Indonesian nationalists learned from the Dutch and the Japanese the power of radio for communication and control across the thousands of islands that make up the

Indonesian archipelago. It has been argued that 'without its broadcasters Indonesia as we know it might never have come into existence'. Using the thirty-nine radio stations left behind in 1945 by the Dutch and Japanese occupiers, the Indonesian revolutionary forces were able to transmit their message instantaneously to the largely illiterate peoples of the region.[4] Ever since, the Indonesian government has remained alert to the potential role of electronic mass media in strengthening national unity and its own control.

In 1976 Indonesia became the third nation in the world, after the United States and Canada, to acquire a satellite communication system, and so was able to establish telephone, radio, and television links across the archipelago. The system has proved invaluable for accelerating national development and integration, bringing social as well as economic benefits to many parts of the country. The government television service, for example, has helped to spread the use of the national language, promote public health and family planning, and provide access to university education, while at the same time widening the information and cultural horizons of the population generally. It has also contributed to greater government efficiency and more effective military control. Further, ownership of the Palapa 1 satellite gave Indonesia new power to influence communication in neighbouring nations, by leasing some of its transmission capacity first to the governments of Malaysia, Thailand, and the Philippines, and later to Western information services such as the US-owned Cable News Network (CNN).[5]

The increasing power and sophistication of communications technology has encouraged governments to try to control it, both in order to strengthen their own nation and to interfere in the affairs of others. However, recent technological innovations have made it much more difficult than in the past for governments to control either domestic or international information flows. When communications technology manufacturers began to direct their efforts away from producing systems for military or state use, to equipment that could be owned and operated by private individuals, government control over information was greatly impaired. Consumer products such as shortwave transistor radios, audio-cassette recorders, video-cassette recorders, facsimile machines, and personal computers have altered the balance of power between the state and the individual, at least in terms of information control.

In the late 1970s, when Ayatollah Khomeini was living in exile in Iraq and France, audio-cassettes of his sermons against the Pahlavi regime were smuggled back to Iran and widely distributed, establishing a focal point for widespread resistance and laying the foundation for Khomeini's eventual rise to political power.

During the popular protests in Bangkok in May 1992 against the military government, video-cassette recordings played a key role. When news of the protests was heavily censored on state-controlled radio and television, uncensored videotapes showing the army's brutal suppression of the demonstrations were sold at roadside stalls. Many Bangkok residents said they became involved in the protests because the video footage they saw showed how far from the truth official coverage was. Residents with satellite television receivers were able to obtain full coverage of the events from foreign news services. Princess Sirindhord, in Paris at the time, was so shocked by the violent scenes shown on French television that she rang her father

King Bhumibol of Thailand interviews Prime Minister Suchinda, May 1992.

King Bhumibol to express her concern. This in turn prompted a request from the Thai palace to the British Broadcasting Corporation for uncensored coverage, and precipitated the king's decision to intervene in the events. Soon the world was to see more startling footage, recorded by the palace itself, showing the prime minister, Suchinda Kraprayoon, and the leader of the opposition on their knees before the king. Suchinda's resignation and this shrewdly publicised demonstration of royal influence increased King Bhumibol's popularity even further.[6]

Video coverage of anti-government protests in Jakarta in August 1996 showed what has become common under repressive governments everywhere: official news media providing one sort of coverage and sympathetic amateurs another, while secret police and military personnel record for their own purposes the identities and actions of participants.

International radio broadcasting has been used for many years to influence political and social events abroad. The cold war superpowers worked hard to counter each other's influence in this way. More recently, the US government has continued activity on this front by establishing Radio Free Asia. Its purpose is clear from the languages in which it broadcasts: Korean, Mandarin, Cantonese, Uygur, Tibetan, Vietnamese, Lao, and Khmer.[7] Nevertheless the reach of international radio, powerful though it is, has become less significant with the development of satellite television. The 'footprint' or possible reception area of a single communications satellite such as AsiaSat or Apsat can cover most of the Asian region, giving it the power to project foreign images, with all their immediacy and power, to even the most isolated communities.

In the desert regions of Chinese Central Asia, for example, the few trees able to survive the harsh climate are adorned with bits of wire to receive these foreign

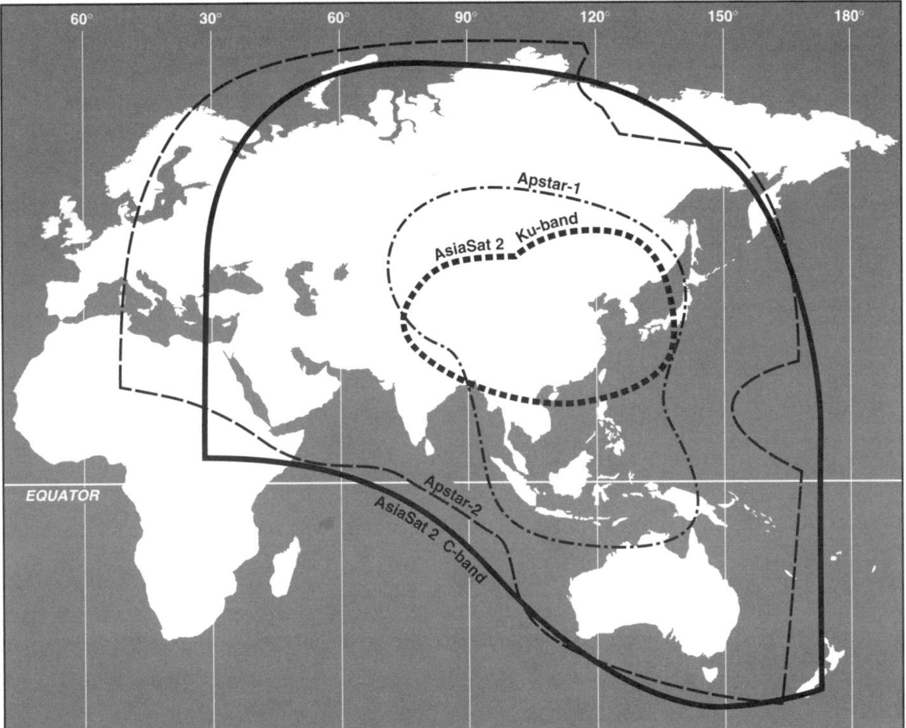


**Figure 10.1** Satellite footprints over Asia

messages. Governments concerned with such external influences, for whatever reason, have tried to control access to satellite television. In October 1993 the Chinese government banned privately owned satellite dishes (parabolic antennae). In April 1995 the Iranian government requested citizens owning satellite dishes to demonstrate their respect for Islamic culture by removing them.[8] As the technology needed to receive international television signals becomes less conspicuous, however, television, like radio, will become increasingly difficult for governments to control.

If electronic communications media affect the nature and fate of nations, they play no less significant a role in the lives of business organisations. It is no coincidence that the first multinational corporations emerged during the late nineteenth and early twentieth centuries, when the international telegraph networks were established. While some of the firms had been in business well before this, it was only when rapid and reliable international communication developed that they found it possible to operate efficiently in a number of countries simultaneously. Commercial expansion across borders thereby became much more attractive and international trade expanded accordingly. In the 1990s a large number of the companies ranked in the world's top five hundred established their own very small aperture transmission systems (VSATS), then regarded as the cutting edge of telecommunications technology. The emergence of a global financial system, able to respond quickly to market signals from any part of the world, would have been impossible without the innovations in communication of the past few decades. The completely automated National Stock Exchange of

India, which began operating in July 1994, was a symbol of the times. Without satellite technology and the Internet it could not function.[9] However, as the financial crisis of 1997–98 showed, technology now enables the instantaneous global communication of panic as well as financial facts and figures.

The centrality of effective communication for trade and economic activity, especially at the international level, helps to explain a problem encountered by governments that do manage to block information flows they consider undesirable: they often find that access to information they need, such as information necessary for economic development or military intelligence, is also closed off. This is because it is easier to shut down whole institutions or channels of communication than to screen out the particular types of information found objectionable. As Deng Xiaoping observed when introducing the post-Mao reforms in China, 'When you open the window to let in some fresh air, you can't stop the germs coming in too.' The Chinese authorities since Deng have continued to argue over how wide the window should be opened.

International computer links are another headache in this regard. The benefits of allowing Chinese researchers, businesses, and government agencies to hook up to the Internet are obvious, but access to up-to-date world information comes at the cost of diminished government control. This includes loss of control over such things as pornography and online gambling as well as politically sensitive material and unauthorised political activity. While many commentators dismiss the idea that it is possible to censor the Internet effectively, in the case of the Chinese government it will not be for want of trying. In December 1997 it issued Regulations on the Security and Management of Computer Information Networks and the Internet, outlawing subversive and anti-social material, and requiring Internet service providers to submit to surveillance of their activities. Revised regulations issued in October 2000 require Internet content providers to record for sixty days and submit for inspection on demand everything that appears on their sites, as well as details of users. They are also responsible for censoring any offensive or subversive material.

Nor is the concern about regulation limited to communist countries. In 1996, the Singapore Broadcasting Authority, for example, introduced a licensing system and Internet Code of Practice (revised in 1997) that relies largely on self-regulation by Internet service providers and Internet content providers to block out material that is 'objectionable on the grounds of public interest, public morality, public order, public security, national harmony, or otherwise prohibited by applicable Singapore laws'. There is awareness of the technological difficulties of close censorship of the Internet and of the damage that attempts to enforce it would do to Singapore's ambition to become an international communications and information technology hub. Similar dilemmas face the Malaysian government, which like its Singapore counterpart is finding it difficult to reconcile its authoritarian tendencies with its high-tech ambitions. While a Malaysian government minister warned citizens in September 2000 that 'even the Sedition Act could be applied' to censor the Internet, if necessary, such a strategy for control would generate big technical and economic as well as political problems.[10]

To trade with the rest of the world one has to be prepared to communicate with it. To overcome public health problems one has to be prepared to discuss them in public. Here too the role of electronic communication media may be crucial. In Asia, the largest numbers of AIDS sufferers are to be found in India, Myanmar, and Thailand. The predominant strain is the type E virus, which unlike the type B virus common in Europe, North America, and Australia is transmitted through heterosexual activity as well as homosexual activity and intravenous drug use. Until recently Myanmar was largely closed to foreigners, but the problem there is worse than anywhere else in Asia, especially in rural districts close to the opium-growing region. However, drug use is not the only cause. Large numbers of Burmese women, willingly or unwillingly, work in the Thai sex trade, where they contract the disease and then return home. (The same problem has also become common in southern China and Laos.)

Significantly, very high rates of infection occur in conjunction with widespread ignorance of the disease. In one mining town in northern Myanmar, for example, more than nine out of ten drug-users tested HIV positive, yet more than two-thirds said they had never heard of AIDS. While infection rates are high in the Thai provinces adjoining Myanmar, it appears that some progress is being made there in controlling the disease, with television playing an important role in spreading knowledge of the problem. One study of AIDS education and prevention in north-east Thailand found that 92 per cent of survey respondents had gleaned some knowledge of the disease from television, while only 57 per cent had obtained information from the medical profession.[11]

## Censorship and propaganda

It is easy to adopt a simplistic attitude towards state control of information, and to measure socio-political progress in terms of degrees of freedom of information. Yet all states exercise some control over it, though its forms and the rationales vary. Nor is state control of information a recent innovation.

A distinction may be drawn between suppressing information and generating information, or misinformation, to counteract other influences. The former is generally called censorship, the latter ideology or propaganda. In practice the distinction is hard to maintain because some actions involve both. In the day-to-day functioning of societies and governments little distinction is made between the way things are and the way they should be. Norms, social expectations, and dominant values are perceived as part of reality; the primary function of much political and religious ideology is to render them natural and inevitable.

All governments censor information and generate their own, and not always in the blatant manner associated with repressive regimes. At one end of the spectrum there are populations kept uneducated and ignorant, with newspapers banned and radio broadcasts jammed, while official media spread propaganda seldom taken seriously by either the people or those who rule over them. At the other end are societies where lying is often called marketing or public relations, where governments produce self-serving media releases that highlight successes but make no mention of failures, and encourage 'self-regulation' of private media to protect what is labelled as public order or the national interest. The distance from the one to the other is not as great as is commonly supposed. In 1994, results of an international survey showed that Australia's news media were among the world's 'most free'. A year later it was revealed that they are subject to a system of self-censorship, intended to protect the national interest, that they are not permitted to discuss in public.[12]

There is a tendency for those from Western societies to regard censorship and propaganda simply as tools of power, the means by which authoritarian rulers maintain their hold over a rebellious populace. Maintaining political control is certainly one of their main functions, though the manner in which this is done varies between political systems and is often conceived in terms of maintaining political legitimacy, public confidence, or trust. It appears that very large sections of the population of most countries hold the view that some control must be exercised over the information permitted to circulate in society, even though there is wide disagreement about what control is appropriate. Some want certain political ideologies suppressed, others want to restrict heterodox religious teachings, while others again are concerned about the circulation of material relating to sexuality, pornography, violence, racism, or criticism of specific government policies and programs. Disrespect for the king in Thailand is prohibited in much the same way that criticism of the Communist Party is banned in Vietnam. Concern over sexual permissiveness is strong among Indians, just as concern over violence is common among Americans.

In human rights law the right to receive and give information is not regarded as absolute. The International Covenant on Civil and Political Rights does declare that 'Everyone shall have the right to freedom of expression; that right shall include freedom to seek, receive and impart information and ideas of all kinds, regardless of frontiers ...' (Article 19[2]). However, the right is subject to such restrictions as are necessary to preserve the rights and reputations of others and 'the protection of national security or of public order, or of public health or morals'. These qualifications leave a lot of scope for interpretation and for this reason are much used by authoritarian governments everywhere. Yet it is hard to see how they could be avoided.

As well as the maintenance of political power, censorship and propaganda have to do with enhancement of social cohesion and identity, autonomy and control. Political power or authority impinges on these things, but they are concerns of the general society as well. It is not only governments that fear heterodoxy and foreign influence: they are widely seen as dangerous by individuals and communities too, a threat to social stability and personal well-being. Communities may be as brutal in their enforcement of conformity as the most savage of dictatorships, and impose their own forms of control over information in order to achieve it.

To interpret censorship and propaganda merely as issues of state control is grossly to oversimplify. Often, state-owned channels of information are seen as more trustworthy than commercial operations. In much of the English-speaking world—and other parts of the globe as well—the British Broadcasting Corporation (BBC) is highly regarded as a truthful and reliable news source. In Australia, many well-informed people rely on the Australian Broadcasting Corporation rather than privately owned news media. Therefore there is nothing remarkable or particularly 'Asian' about the confidence felt by Singaporeans or Malaysians in the state-owned media of their countries.

Media baron Rupert Murdoch has celebrated the power of new communications technology to put information beyond state control:

> Advances in the technology of telecommunications have proved an unambiguous threat to totalitarian regimes everywhere. Fax machines enable dissidents to bypass state-controlled print media; direct dial telephony makes it difficult for a state to control interpersonal voice communications. Satellite broadcasting makes is possible for information-hungry residents of many closed societies to bypass state-controlled television.[13]

These remarks were made when Murdoch's News Corporation was acquiring the Star TV network, which is transmitted via AsiaSat 1, whose footprint covers most of Asia, including China (see Figure 10.1). Soon after this, in October 1993, the Chinese government prohibited private households from owning satellite transmission receivers. This prompted News Corporation to attempt to ingratiate itself with the Chinese authorities by removing BBC World Service Television, a twenty-four-hour news and information channel that had become the target of Chinese government displeasure, from that part of AsiaSat 1's footprint covering China. Chinese government support was important for News Corporation not only because of its ambition to gain a large share of the potentially huge Chinese television market, but also because the Chinese government, paradoxically, is a major shareholder of the satellite on which Star TV's entire operation in Asia depends. (AsiaSat 2 went into orbit in November 1995. Also partly owned by the Chinese government, it has customers including government agencies from China, Hong Kong, Malaysia, and Vietnam, as well as commercial operators such as Star TV and a number of European organisations.)[14]

Anyone who has watched Star TV, in China or elsewhere in Asia, must have serious doubts about the likelihood of it contributing to the emancipation of any society. Like the lowest common dominator of commercial television elsewhere, it appears more likely to reduce the capacity for critical or independent thought than to develop it. Much of the programming epitomises the vulgarity, materialism, and self-indulgence many members of Asian societies associate with Western or, more specifically, US culture. Western intellectuals frequently share the view that commercially dispensed 'information' of this sort may be just as harmful to society as control of information by the state. The pursuit of market advantage can clearly be as much of an obstacle to freedom of expression and access to information as the pursuit of political advantage. This points to the need for a multiplicity of sources of information that the market alone cannot guarantee.

Such criticisms of commercial mass media, familiar enough to Westerners, are often accompanied in Asian countries by further charges of insensitivity and irresponsibility, in regard both to the way issues are presented and their social impact. A willingness to say or show anything likely to return a profit is rendered all the more offensive, it is argued, by a lack of consideration of the likely effect of the material in diverse social or cultural settings. Such criticisms relate to more than complaints about sexual permissiveness and violence.

On 6 December 1992 the attention of world media focused on Ayodhya in India, where destruction of the Babri Mosque led to serious and widespread rioting. When international television services such as BBC World Service Television and CNN showed footage of the violence, Indian authorities tried to restrict circulation of the material, which at the time certainly did pose a risk to public order and national security. They cut cable television transmission to Muslim districts and protested, to no avail, against the coverage they regarded as ill-considered and dangerous. No consideration was given, one Indian commentator has observed, to the fact that in India public portrayal of the events might lead to 'more violence resulting in more deaths'.[15]

The same point was made by a Singapore senior official, who saw the incident as having universal significance:

> The recent Ayodhya incident demonstrated one important dimension for societies all around the globe. The Indian media tried to control emotional reactions by restricting the broadcasting and distribution of video scenes of the destruction of the mosque. But by now many Indian homes can see video clips (transmitted through satellites and tapes) from foreign news agencies which felt no reason to exercise social, political or moral restraint. Those who happily transmitted the video clips never had to bear the consequences themselves. They were sitting comfortably in Atlanta, Georgia or in Hong Kong, the riots that followed in India as a result of their TV transmissions never reached their homes. Unfortunately, these media personnel did not stop to consider whether they could have saved other human lives, not their own, by exercising restraint.[16]

## Nation-building and the media

In developed countries there is an inclination to look upon lack of freedom of expression as evidence of political and social underdevelopment, which can be overcome by more democratic government and opening the media up to market forces. Such interpretations appear to be confirmed when governments of developing countries use a similar argument to justify their control of the media. Nation-building, they argue, cannot be effective if the media adopt a critical or anti-government approach that encourages dissent, dissatisfaction, social unrest, or division. The media must be positive and supportive of the government, helping to spread nationalism, civic consciousness, and idealism among the people.

This view is associated with what has become known as development journalism, a term that during its relatively short span has experienced a rapid shift in meaning. As originally articulated during the 1960s by bodies such as the Press Foundation of Asia, the Philippines Press Institute and the Press Institute of India, it referred to a perceived need for journalists with sufficient economic expertise to be able to report in an informed and objective way on the complex issues confronting developing nations. As taken up by governments in Third World countries, however, it came to mean 'good news' journalism that supported the government, showing its policies and programs in a favourable light appropriate to the noble task of nation-building. Any limits to freedom of expression, from this perspective, would be the result of self-regulation, those that would inevitably follow from a proper weighing of the national interest.[17]

This is the view that has dominated official thinking about the media in Indonesia. Former president Suharto stated in 1989, for example, on the occasion of Indonesia's

National Press Day, that 'one area of activity which needs follow-up by the national press is the wider dissemination of information about progress, the creation of new values and the formation of public opinion, all of which will help us be a strong nation. The press should be a partner in the process of nation building'.[18] The first article of the code of ethics of the Indonesian Journalists Association, until June 1998 the only such organisation permitted by the government, declared that Indonesian journalists shall be 'faithful to Pancasila', the national creed first articulated in 1945. However, self-regulation for the sake of the national interest can prove a tricky business, since there are likely to be occasions when even the most nationalistic and circumspect of editors concludes that the national interest would be better served by frank criticism than by silence, and even members of the government may disagree over what should be left unsaid.

After the banning in June 1994 of three leading periodicals following their criticism of a government decision, attributed to the then Minister for Research and Technology, B. J. Habibie, to buy thirty-nine former East German warships, even some members of the government became openly critical. In retrospect, this appears to have been a turning point for freedom of information and expression in Indonesia.

The May 1995 ruling by the State Administrative Court, that the ban was authoritarian and unlawful, was welcomed by many as evidence of the growing independence of the judiciary and tolerance of dissent, despite the fact that an appeal by the government to the Supreme Court resulted in the decision being overturned. The Alliance of Independent Journalists was established by journalists who refused any longer to be the mouthpiece of the state, its members declaring that they rejected 'all kinds of interference, intimidation, censorship and media bans which deny freedom of speech and open access to information'. Since President Suharto's resignation in May 1998 there has been a general easing of controls over both domestic and foreign media, but the harsh economic circumstances that have prevailed since then have posed new difficulties for the survival of independent and socially responsible channels of information and expression.[19]

Implicit in much of the talk of nation-building and development journalism is the idea that government control of the media is a temporary necessity, which will end when the development process is complete and the nation has been fully established. The paternalism this expresses closely resembles that of the colonialism of which it is an heir. But such a position is easily transformed into one that has greater permanency. Perhaps the most provocative way of doing so is by adopting the position articulated by Prime Minister Mahathir of Malaysia. After reiterating the argument that freedom of expression is more dangerous in developing countries than developed ones, and hence that laws to curb the media are essential there, he took the matter further by saying that freedom of expression could exist only in a mature society capable of distinguishing right from wrong. He then went on to observe that 'there is no such ideal society in the world'.[20] What is not explained is how governments and those responsible for imposing censorship manage to leave behind the childishness to which the rest of society is forever condemned.

Another way of arguing for continuing government control of the media and limits to the right of freedom of expression is to claim that acceptance of them is evidence of distinctive Asian values that place social harmony and political stability ahead of Western-style individualism and political confrontation. It is a position that is hard to refute, unless we are prepared to insist that freedom of expression is an absolute value admitting of no qualification, and that judgments regarding the priority to be given to harmony and stability cannot vary from one social context to another. However, it is a view expressed more by governments than ordinary citizens, and since the latter are often denied the opportunity to express opinions critical of government it is difficult to know how many of them really share it.

In South-East Asian countries such as Indonesia, Malaysia, and Singapore, experience of ethnic tensions spilling over into violence has resulted in government preoccupation with the issues of social harmony and political stability, and effectively a prohibition on public discussion of ethnic or racial issues. Prime Minister Mahathir has commented, for example: 'One of the problems [for stability] is the threat of racial conflict. If you allow extremists to instigate people and say it's all right, it's only a little thing, you don't know how fast it can develop into a major thing ... there is one thing we don't allow: confrontation, racial intolerance.'[21]

Some find supporting evidence for the need to restrict public discussion of ethnic or racial issues in the increased ethnic and religious conflict in areas such as Kalimantan and the Maluku Islands, which has coincided with diminishing government control over the media in Indonesia since the early 1990s. It is claimed that if the cohesion of Indonesia as a nation state appears under threat in places such as Aceh and West Papua (leaving aside what has already happened in East Timor), perhaps it is due to the greater publicity that ethnic and separatist issues are receiving from unthinking and unscrupulous journalists. However, it may be argued in response that less control over the media coincided with less control over many things—not least the army and the economy—and that ethnic conflict and separatism are symptoms of problems much deeper than journalistic irresponsibility. It is more plausible to regard them as the result of the government's long-term refusal to discuss ethnic issues constructively and to take seriously the problems caused by the transmigration program, economic inequality, and the lack of local autonomy. In any case, it is difficult to accept that enforced silence is the best way to resolve ethnic or religious conflict.

It may be that there are times when restraint, or silence, is the sensible and responsible option for the media, as in relation to the Ayodhya incident. But as a general policy, ignorance on the part of the people and paternalism on the part of the government are not good options. The development mentality may encourage the view that this is only a temporary measure, that when the nation is fully mature the problem will have solved itself, but as the advocates of development themselves argue, development entails leaving ignorance and dependence behind. If development means anything, in social terms, it means maturity, acquiring the skills and understanding necessary to act in a capable and responsible manner, showing due respect for the needs and rights of others while securing one's own. It is impossible for individuals or societies to mature in this way if they are routinely denied the opportunity to make informed and well-considered judgments. Sound judgment and responsible action presuppose access to the relevant information. Nor does the need for critical and independent consideration of it imply a dangerous individualism. It is not as if by providing access to information states or communities surrender the opportunity to influence how individuals think. It just means that their influence needs to be exercised more energetically than before.

The content of a medium such as television is open to many different interpretations. Visual immediacy brings impact, but also the need to interpret, for in the media such immediacy is fabricated: 'the facts' do not speak for themselves. As noted by a commentator on video reporting of the public demonstrations in Bangkok in May 1992, 'video, like other media, is a reporting of events through a crafting of available information ... There are always metres of truth left on the cutting room floor'.[22] The meaning the audience extracts depends on previous experience as well as what it is directed to see. The famous image from the Tian'anmen incident of June 1989, of a solitary individual with a shopping bag facing a line of tanks, was presented in the West as a symbol of the free individual standing up against the power of the authoritarian state. Chinese television, on the other hand, presented it as testimony to the restraint shown by the military in controlling a threat to public order and stability. Suppression of the material might have helped to limit the impact of the Tian'anmen incident and minimise the perceived harm it would do, but it also would have made it impossible to draw good from the material, that is, to use the information to construct knowledge seen as socially desirable.[23]

Video clips of the Ayodhya disturbances could have been used to reinforce policies of tolerance, coexistence, and equality. That they were not could be interpreted as a manifestation of the Hindu chauvinism in government that many regarded as a cause of the troubles. Governments and the media alike have great power to do good or evil. It is commitment to social service and integrity that is needed, not what is euphemistically called restraint. Social harmony and stability ultimately depend on mutual trust, and trust is more likely to be established by open and constructive exchange of information than by censorship and the circulation of misinformation. History shows us that where the people are denied opportunity to express their concerns and grievances, the only alternative to passive acceptance is revolt.

## Cultural imperialism

There is a disposition in Western political and intellectual circles to equate efforts by Asian governments to control information with authoritarianism—evidence of the 'Asian despotism' once treated as a defining characteristic of the region. This is despite the fact that all societies place some limits on freedom of expression and that the need for limitation is articulated, for example, in international human rights legislation. The need to protect public order and national interest may be conceived in a variety of ways, and though it is entirely proper to debate the content of these concepts, it cannot be denied that in dissimilar social and historical circumstances it may be appropriate to reach different conclusions about how such goals are best pursued.

In developing countries, on the other hand, there is a tendency to interpret arguments for freedom of information and expression as manifestations of cultural imperialism. The meaning of the term 'cultural imperialism', like that of expressions such as 'globalisation' and 'modernisation', tends to move around according to context. However, at the heart of it lie the elements carried forward from the earlier concept of imperialism: domination of weaker nations by the forces of capitalism for the purpose of economic exploitation. Only instead of domination being achieved by armed force or colonisation, it is now achieved by cultural means. The cultural means in question are identified in a variety of ways. Some focus on the consumer products of multinational corporations, which may include anything from food and drink to toys for adults and children. The Iranian government became so anxious about the

Tian'anmen, Beijing, June 1989. (Reuters)

influence on young girls of the immensely popular American Barbie dolls that it designed and manufactured an Iranian equivalent to combat it. The Iranian Sara doll has darker skin, black hair and eyes, and wears either a chador (veil) or the traditional costumes of Iran's ethnic minorities. The Iranian government is also producing its own non-violent video games to counteract the harmful effects of imported games.[24]

Others focus on the impact of international (mainly Western) mass media on aspirations and values, while others again are more concerned with the importation of (mainly Western) know-how, institutions, and systems. The basic idea of cultural imperialism, it may be said, is colonisation of the mind, implanting in the consciousness of populations an alien way of thinking and understanding, values, and aspirations that are not part of their own traditions or cultural identity, and which, many argue, are intended to seduce the populations in question to perpetual exploitation and dependence on capitalist powers.

The concept of cultural imperialism throws up some difficult questions. Who is dominating whom? Whose culture is being undermined or impaired? Is it possible to speak meaningfully of imposing a culture? Are the issues at stake peculiar to relations between developed and developing nations, or are they also relevant to relations between and within developed nations? Is there ever such a thing as individual choice in relation to culture? Doesn't the concept of cultural imperialism move argument beyond the reach of empirical evidence that could prove or disprove it, since it asserts that if people act in the foreign way they do it is not because this is what, if left to themselves, they would want to do, but because their desires have been tampered with? Since it is assumed that the desires must have been implanted in them by an external agent, the claim of cultural imperialism becomes self-validating.

Some of these problems are illustrated, for example, by a 1993 study of the impact of Western (read 'US') mass media on Chinese culture. The study examined the effect on 'traditional' values—such as strong family orientation, educational achievement, and social responsibility—of exposure to Western news and Western popular culture through radio, television, and the cinema. It showed a strong correlation between this type of exposure to Western culture and the relatively low value being placed on serving or protecting the public interest. Those who tended to watch Western television and movies or listen to Western radio were found to be relatively detached from society and inclined to be concerned about their personal well-being and interests, more concerned to enjoy life than to work hard and contribute to society. The authors' dominant interpretation is evident from their study's title: *The Great Wall in Ruins*. Modern communications technology has breached the barriers that have long protected Chinese culture, which is now being undermined by Western individualism, hedonism and materialism.[25]

To the authors' credit, they recognise that it is difficult to say which way causality is running. It is unclear whether exposure to Western culture makes Chinese more individualistic and socially detached or whether having those characteristics leads some Chinese to prefer Western media. Probably, they observe, causality is operating in both directions at once. Moreover, while they present Western influence largely in negative terms, they do emphasise that it can have positive elements, such as encouraging personal qualities of adventuresomeness and initiative. What is striking, however, is their equation of 'Western' with individualism, egocentrism, consumerism, and the influence of mass media. It appears that Karl Marx has been declared an honorary Chinese and Chinese Marxism just a reworking of Confucianism. Yet as far as Western influence is concerned, there is reason to think that nearly fifty years of state-orchestrated Marxism and the veneration of Western science and technology so integral to it may have had a bigger impact than a relatively brief exposure to third-rate Hollywood movies and television shows.

The interpretation offered appears to reflect the ethnic Chinese authors' views of the US society in which they live as much as those of their Chinese respondents. It is a useful reminder that the criticisms of what they equate with 'Western culture' have been voiced by many Westerners as well. In other words, at least some of the problems subsumed under the label of cultural imperialism also occur in rich and powerful capitalist countries, and criticism of them is no less a part of Western culture than the problems themselves.

In the rich nations of Western Europe, in Japan, Canada, Australia, and New Zealand, it is common to hear expressions of anxiety over traditional cultures being undermined, national identity destroyed, and social cohesion threatened. The culprit is identified variously as the United States, multinationals, immigrants (Asian or African), or government policies of multiculturalism. Similar anxieties are expressed in the United States. Indigenous minorities everywhere fear that they are losing their distinctive identity as a result of having the culture of the dominant society imposed upon them. One of the problems faced by those who regard the role of mass media as crucial in this context, who see 'electronic colonialism' as a threat to autonomy and social integrity, is the need to acknowledge that individuals do in fact retain a lot of control of the media. No one makes Third World peasants buy television sets, while those who do generally are able to choose what to watch or whether to watch at all.

Some of the difficulties encountered by cultural imperialism arguments are illustrated in an article by an Indian intellectual published in 1994. In the course of an eloquent critique of the situation in India, the author refers to an invasion of cable television networks that have penetrated all parts of the country. 'Invasion' is the only adequate way to describe a phenomenon, he observes, that has been so swiftly engineered, monitored, and legislated for, and brings international television, blue movies, and Doordashan (the Indian government television network) to 'villages which continue to be denied the bare necessities of life'. What makes the implications of this invasion so enormous, he says, is 'the grotesque disparity between the consumerist representation of "development" on television (what is *desirable*) as opposed to the abject economic conditions of its viewers (which determine what is *available*)'.[26]

The term 'invasion' resonates with the meanings of cultural imperialism. There is no doubt that it is the rich capitalist countries, with their high-tech communications media and apparently endless supply of lewd and materialistic entertainment, that are the primary target of the author's anger. Yet the national and state governments of India, and Indian intellectuals committed to development, are also implicated, since presumably they have done most of the engineering, monitoring, and legislating that has made the invasion possible. Furthermore, if the disparities in Indian villages between what is available and what is desired make the intrusion of foreign broadcasts particularly grotesque, this is partly because the presence in a village of satellite television on the one hand, and houses denied basic necessities on the other, highlights socio-economic inequalities that need to be addressed by the government and people of India.

Even the most silver-tongued cultural imperialist would find it hard to sell television sets to peasants who lack basic necessities, much less tell them what to watch. While it is possible that watching foreign television (and for uneducated villagers we must include most of what issues from Mumbai or Delhi under this heading) may help to raise aspirations to unrealistic levels, it is far from clear that watching happy endings from Hollywood or Bollywood leads villagers to believe their own lives could end that way, any more than listening to Hindu epics leads them to conclude that they may mix with the gods. It is more likely that the desperately poor will aspire to be like the owner of the television set in the village than the US and Indian movie stars who appear on it. In other words, they will aspire to what they know to be possible because it has been achieved by someone they know.[27]

The influence of television, even the television purveyed by capitalists, need not be as damaging or as negative as is often alleged. It could be argued that, if there is damage, it has already been done before the television set is turned on. The poison of consumerism has already taken hold when a villager buys the set or aspires to higher status within the community by becoming a television owner; it has been spread downward from the social elite rather than communicated directly by foreign imperialists and their satellites.

But blaming materialism on development and Westernised elites is not very helpful either. Most pre-modern societies have used conspicuous consumption and the scarcity value of commodities as mechanisms for acquiring or demonstrating social status. Besides, cable television and direct satellite transmission provide access to more than trashy adult fantasies. There are opportunities to acquire useful knowledge as well as indulge in fantasy or escapism, and it is difficult to generalise about the effects a particular program is likely to have on members of a community. Those most attracted by the alternatives—possible or fantastic—are likely to be those most dissatisfied with their present situation and the local culture that shapes it.

Arguments about cultural imperialism are quickly bogged down in the treacherous terminology in which they are conducted, particularly the concept of culture itself. Once we start asking whose culture is being subverted and whose culture it is that is being imposed on others, it becomes clear that much of what is said makes sense only if it is assumed that cultures are homogeneous, static entities that change abruptly when we move from one side of an international border to another, in much the same way as territory changes colour in an atlas. When we consider that national cultures are fluid and variable, it becomes easier to understand what is at stake.

National identity has to be constructed and culture provides the content of identity. Some social groups are more influential than others when it comes to fixing the rules and values according to which society operates, especially its political, religious, and intellectual elites. To a poor peasant in Bangladesh or a tribesman from the Kalimantan interior, the culture of the wealthy elite of Dhaka or Jakarta may appear as foreign as anything a television screen might reveal of New York or Tokyo. In present-day

China, 'the directors of transnational corporations and the peasants of mountainous border villages inhabit two separate worlds, and are like citizens of two different countries'.[28] The Indian culture that a Mumbai intellectual wants to preserve, or the Thai culture a Bangkok artist believes should be strengthened, may embody values and ways of thinking with which a poor and illiterate compatriot feels little in common. For these reasons it is better to regard the issue underlying critiques of cultural imperialism as the *creation* of national culture rather than its preservation. Culture, whether national or local, is a never-ending process. Even the past, or tradition, is continually being reconstructed. For those involved it is a ceaseless competition for influence.

The patterns by which everyday life is understood and given direction are constantly being revised, and if one party does not wield its influence another will. Censorship and propaganda are the two main strategies used in efforts to direct and manipulate information flows in society. While governments are the groups best placed to exercise this control, they are not the only ones. Multinational communication corporations have emerged as another powerful group. But attempts to control information flows occur at all levels of society. What is labelled 'cultural imperialism' does not necessarily differ significantly from other attempts to control communication; it is just that the groups in question have been identified, largely on the basis of nationality, as having no business wielding the sort of influence they do, as having stepped beyond their legitimate sphere of influence.

The communication or cultural influences identified as illegitimate will depend on circumstances. Many Asian countries point to the United States because of its political and economic power, and the cultural influence associated with it. In Korea it is the influence of the former colonial power Japan that arouses the most hostility. While South Korea initiated its own direct satellite broadcasting in 1995, Japanese satellite television attracts a large audience. Those who watch Japanese television are also more likely than other Koreans to use other Japanese media, such as radio, magazines, videos, and CDs. There is a concern that young Koreans in particular are being unduly influenced by Japanese culture. 'From pop songs to fashion and hairstyles, it is direct satellite broadcasting that aggravates the situation in a society infiltrated by Japanese culture ... brutal Samurai and erotic dramas have the tendency to not only destroy Korea's unique culture but also spread violence and wrong ideas to youth.'[29]

It was anxiety over the perceived threat posed by foreign media that lay behind the South Korean government's reversal in 1995 of its earlier policy of excluding the *chaebôl*, or industrial conglomerates, from media ownership. Faced with strong competition from Japanese and other foreign direct-broadcasting satellite networks such as Star-TV, the Korean authorities became less concerned with the issue of state versus private control than with the issue of Korean versus foreign control. It was felt that the *chaebôl* were the only Korean organisations with the resources and expertise required to compete in the global market.[30]

Anxieties over the undue influence of outsiders are as much the result of historical memory as of contemporary reality. It is not only rich capitalist countries whose influence is feared. Just as Indian intellectuals express concern at Western influences, so too do those of other South and South-East Asian countries regard with misgivings the exposure of local populations to aspects of Indian popular culture, especially the wide circulation of Indian movie videos. The strong involvement of Chinese corporations and the Chinese government in the launch of the Apstar 1 and Apstar 2 satellites during 1994–95 opened the way for China to pursue its own varieties of cultural imperialism, should it choose to do so.[31]

In the end, however, the impact of foreign media, whether carried by satellites or by more prosaic means, is far from clear. If it is difficult to describe accurately a phenomenon as broad as cultural imperialism, because of the generality and ambiguity of the concepts involved, so too is it difficult to say precisely what the results of exposure to foreign media actually are. Little research has been done and, as already mentioned in relation to the Chinese study, where research has been done it has been difficult to determine what is cause and what is effect.

Surveys conducted in the 1990s—albeit on a relatively small scale—in a number of countries ranging from Japan to Malaysia and India, indicate that while most Asian television viewers tend to prefer local programs to foreign ones, they welcome the

China's space program has enabled it to play a leading role in the development of satellite communications in Asia.

opportunity to watch programs produced in other countries. They do not believe that they are being exposed to foreign influences against their will; nor do they believe that foreign television poses a threat either to national culture or to their personal values. Most significantly, the great majority reject the view of paternalistic intellectuals and political leaders that access to foreign television should be carefully controlled.[32] Where viewers tune in to foreign television it appears to be less because they have been seduced by foreign values and ways of thinking than because local programs are found to have little to offer in terms of either entertainment or information. Heavy-handed censorship may be less successful in capturing audience attention than improving the quality of local programs. If people want a bit more entertainment and a bit less propaganda, it may be better to supply it than to force them to turn to foreign providers. It is when people have learnt not to trust the local media that they are most likely to opt for others.

## Communication and being in control

The rationales for state control of information have an initial plausibility and attraction. For those convinced that they have the Truth—whether obtained from God, Karl Marx, Adam Smith, or their own perspicacity—or those who merely want to monopolise power, it makes sense to communicate their message as widely and as frequently as possible while censoring sources of alternative information. It makes sense also for those who see foreign influences, political or cultural, as a threat to their national identity and sovereignty. And it makes sense for those who see the need to limit the circulation of particular sorts of information within their own society, such as those believed to threaten national security or public morality. However, attempts to achieve total state control of information are not only futile but also counter-productive.

Modern communications technology has made it impossible—it is tempting to say more impossible—for governments to control and monopolise information. Because it is impossible, governments that persist in attempts to do so, in ways inimical to the interests of the majority of the population, are likely to find their authority quickly eroded. It appears that few people have ever believed completely what their rulers have told them, but a lack of alternative sources of information has made it difficult for them to judge the extent to which they have been deceived. Whatever else the gadgets of consumer technology may have done, they have changed that. Where censorship has become impossible, it makes good sense for governments to put their energies into propaganda—that is, to try to talk the alternative sources of information down rather than shut them up, to use the technologies of mass communication instead of trying to prohibit them.

But control of communication cannot be understood in terms of a crudely conceived conflict of interest between state and people. All societies recognise the need for some limits to freedom of expression and, while governments sometimes pay lip service to the public interest and use it as a pretext for neutralising threats to their power, on other occasions they act out of genuine concern for the good of society.

The recognition that freedom of expression is not absolute, and that various social groups and political authorities may want to set the limits differently, makes it difficult to accept the claim that any removal of constraints on expression or communication represents progress. Nor does it seem feasible that Asian countries trying to restrict communication either within or across their boundaries are simply revealing their socio-political immaturity. Acceptance of the principle that rational and well-informed people may disagree regarding limits to freedom of expression suggests in turn that there should be popular input into setting those limits, if for no other reason than that it will be impossible to enforce them without a degree of social agreement and support.

Secure societies do not feel a need to insulate themselves from foreign influences. This is obvious but important. If we see benefits in mixing with others, we do so; if not, we try to keep our distance. For a nation state, ethnic minority, or community to want to interact with its neighbours, it has to be convinced that its members will not be disadvantaged thereby. Communication between social groups and between individuals is alike to this extent: the weaker party will rarely be in a position to set the conditions under which communication takes place. In the process of globalisation weaker nations may find that shutting communication down is one of the few options open to them for maintaining a degree of control over their own affairs. Nations concerned about the restrictions on freedom and human rights that this entails may achieve more by promoting the economic and political security of their neighbours than trying to force change on them. The same applies to ethnic groups within nations.

Assertions of the need to protect cultural uniqueness or to prevent the decay of tradition are best understood as expressions of anxiety or a sense of vulnerability. It is not that those making the assertion are trying to insist either that their culture must be quarantined from outside influences or that cultural innovation spells disaster. Rather, they are saying that they want to have control over their own affairs and choose the terms on which they will interact with the wider world. The idea of cultural imperialism is another way of expressing these anxieties and aspirations.

Communication between nations and ethnic groups also resembles communication between individuals in this respect: interaction with others can benefit us, culturally and intellectually as well as materially. Communication is to intellectual and artistic culture what trade is to material production. Our products have value only to the extent that they are in circulation, and if there is fair exchange we are all likely to be the richer for it. The wise listen to those around them, to benefit from what they have learnt. They appreciate the advantages of obtaining information from many sources. Effective communication, they understand, depends on the opportunity to listen as well as the ability to speak.

CHAPTER ELEVEN

# Using and Creating Knowledge

## Knowledge is everything

Issues relating to knowledge pervade everything discussed so far. They include how knowledge is conceptualised, who is regarded as possessing it, and how it is institutionalised, transmitted, and controlled. Development, for example, is largely seen in terms of the application of Western or 'modern' science and technology to economic production and raising living standards. Access to contraceptive knowledge and techniques is a key factor in demographic change, which in turn affects family structures and functions. Discussion of the mass media raises important questions about the ways in which information shapes both individual and society, and whether information flows should be controlled.

It is time to address the subject of knowledge directly. This must be done in two ways. First, it must be considered as a key area of activity in the context of globalisation and insulation, with particular emphasis on the internationalisation of science and technology, and how this is affecting Asian societies. Second, it must be considered in terms of what it means for the present study, the ways in which participation in the knowledge-generating enterprise is subject to the processes of change described here, and how the concepts of knowledge used in turn influence the way change is understood.

## Internationalisation of science and technology

As pointed out in Chapter 1, the globalisation or internationalisation of science and technology as a policy agenda is a relatively recent phenomenon. It has arisen primarily in developed countries and has been articulated above all in documents from the OECD. The rationale underlying it has been twofold. On the one hand there has been a growing awareness of the increasing dependence of economic and social well-being on advanced knowledge, while on the other there has been a realisation that even the richest nations in the world—the United States, Japan, and Germany—cannot afford to undertake all the research and development that could be advantageous. The ever-increasing scope of research and development, coupled with its sharply rising costs, makes greater international specialisation and collaboration a logical response.

The essential idea, as the phrase 'internationalisation of science and technology' implies, is that of a collaborative exercise in which all nations participate and from which all alike receive benefit. As so often is the case, the wording conveys a spirit of egalitarianism and free cooperation, the idea of an enterprise in which the participants are equals. Third World countries, it is claimed, will be able to contribute more and more as their research capacity increases with the development of universities, government research institutes, and private sector research and development activities, the latter being aided especially by the transfer of advanced technologies from overseas and the operations of multinational corporations. In reality, the internationalisation of science and technology—to the extent that it is occurring—is anything but an egalitarian enterprise. It is characterised by the same inequalities and power relations that can be observed in other aspects of globalisation.[1]

While there *has* been increased international collaboration in science and technology in recent years, overwhelmingly it has been between developed countries, that is, the members of the OECD, including Japan and Korea. To be able to collaborate and compete in this international research effort—and both are important—researchers have to remain within a reasonable distance of the leaders, those at the cutting edge. This presupposes quality of training, state-of-the-art equipment and facilities, communication links, and other sorts of infrastructure provisions that are difficult for Third World countries to provide. Moreover there is a limit to which the acquisition of scientific and technological mastery can be accelerated, which makes the business of catching and keeping up with the leading edge uncertain

In its 2001 Report, the United Nations Development Program focused on the role of technology in development. In a generally positive discussion, it argued that while knowledge production is dominated by wealthy, developed countries, there are grounds for optimism—for example, in the emergence of high-tech hubs in developing countries. Such hubs are concentrations of scientific and technological expertise integrated within the 'networked' global economy, thanks largely to the information and communications technology around which much of the hubs' activity revolves. Asian hubs identified include Bangalore in India, Singapore, Kuala Lumpur, Hong Kong, Taipei and Hsinchu in Taiwan, and Inchon in South Korea. The Report's authors also found reason for hope in the fact that some research is being done, in both developing and developed countries, that does address directly some of the big problems faced in the Third World, despite the fact that research and development agendas overwhelmingly reflect the priorities of rich nations and multinational corporations.[2]

That developing countries find it difficult to influence R & D agendas dominated by rich and powerful nations is a serious matter. Even more serious, however, is the fact that they have little influence over the knowledge system that supports those agendas. Nations at the periphery of the global economic system, it must be observed, are just as distant from the knowledge system that sustains it. While it is easy to exaggerate the extent to which there is a global knowledge system that is unified and homogeneous—this is often presented as the ideal to which we must aspire, if not the present reality—there is no denying the dominance and power of the major claimant to global status: the essentially Western scientific knowledge system. The dominance of that system becomes problematic when it leads to the assertion that only knowledge generated by its procedures and institutions is truly knowledge, when other knowledge systems are devalued and debased, and when different bodies of knowledge and alternative ways of conceptualising reality are summarily dismissed as 'unscientific'. The claim that only the knowledge generated by 'scientific' procedures and institutions is truly objective and universal is made routinely, yet in practice (for example, in the experience of development), it has frequently been shown to be unfounded. 'Local knowledge' derived from traditional sources has had to be called upon to supplement or correct 'universal knowledge'. All too often, objective reality as conceived within the confines of the laboratory and the library turns out to be a simplistic, feeble counterfeit when it ventures out into the harsh light, dirt, and complexity of the world of experience. It is then that we need the correction of other ways of seeing, other modes of understanding, and this is why the atrophy of alternative knowledge systems is so dangerous—not only for the social groups whose traditions are threatened, but for the entire world community.

## Technological convergence and divergence

It is useful to approach the subject of knowledge from the direction of technology, for the study of technology is not characterised by the intense theoretical and ideological battles that surround the idea of scientific knowledge.

Technology is not just hardware such as machines and tools, though as conventionally understood it includes those things. Technology is also knowledge of how to use those machines and tools, practical knowledge including methods of organisation, procedures, management techniques, strategies, skills. The best short definition of technology is *know-how*. It would sound a bit strange to say that technology is something that people carry around in their heads, but not to say that there is technology *only* because of what people carry around in their heads.[3]

As mentioned in Chapter 5, it was widely assumed in the 1960s and 1970s that, as a result of international cooperation, technology transfer, and trade, there would be a gradual international convergence in technological terms. Developed countries would acquire similar levels and types of expertise, and those of developing countries would not be very different. But by the early 1990s there was evidence that convergence was not occurring. In the most general terms, there had been a degree of technological convergence between the United States, Japan, and members of the European Union, as a result of greater collaboration in research and development, and relocation of the R & D activities of multinational corporations. Yet to some extent this convergence was more apparent than real, a result of the fact that these countries as a group had moved further away from the rest of the world.

Within the developed Triad, as it is called, individual countries and large corporations have moved in different directions. For example Japan, Sweden, Germany, and Switzerland have improved their R & D performance, while that of the United States and Britain has deteriorated. Areas of strength or relative advantage in technology, as might be expected, continue to vary widely. Only the rapid technological development of countries such as South Korea, Taiwan, and Singapore inspires any confidence that the growing gap between technologically advanced countries and the rest of the world can be bridged. Despite their new paradigm of a 'networked age', the authors of the *Human Development Report 2001* did not see any prospect of closing the 'yawning gap' that has resulted from 'the long-standing concentration of scientific research and technological innovation in developed countries'.[4]

If technological convergence is to occur, it is less likely to come about as a result of international R & D collaboration than through the operation of global markets. Though multinational corporations may prefer to locate their R & D operations close to established centres of technological innovation, they will manufacture and sell their products throughout the Third World. As far as the technology of production is concerned, therefore, and technological consumption, it is safe to predict continuing convergence. People throughout Asia and other parts of the world will buy the same motorbikes, radios, refrigerators, and sports shoes. They will also operate similar sorts of production technology, since disparities in living and production costs will continue to encourage multinational corporations to relocate off-shore.

But in regard to this sort of technology, relations of inequality and dependence are likely to become stronger rather than weaker. While developing countries will continue to receive advanced technology, it is unlikely to be the *most* advanced technology. As commercial advantage becomes increasingly dependent on technological edge, corporations will become increasingly reluctant to surrender any technological advantage they possess, and will accordingly reinforce dependence on the innovative centre.

## Know-how is always local

It is conventional to distinguish between technological innovation and technology transfer. The first involves creating a new technology of one's own; the second involves acquiring technology from another and incorporating it into the existing technological system or way of doing things. The first is seen as inventive and dynamic, the second as derivative and passive. As far as national identity and prestige are concerned, much is made of the former while the latter counts for little. Yet the huge literature on the subject of technology transfer between nations demonstrates clearly that if technology transfer is to work at all it cannot be passive. This is because it is rarely a matter of simply moving technological hardware in the form of machines or gadgets. Effective technology transfer means having the expertise to use the hardware in question, being able to adapt the new technology and existing systems to make them fit each other, and rethinking methods of organisation, skills development, and operation.

In other words, technology transfer does not do away with the need for technological mastery. The need to absorb new knowledge and incorporate it into local frameworks of understanding remains. This is why, as we have seen, technological and economic development cannot be accelerated beyond a certain point.

The realisation that technology transfer is primarily concerned with moving know-how, and may best be regarded as transferring a piece of culture from one country to another rather than just a machine or a factory, is hardly new. Throughout history it has been understood that the best way to transfer a given technology from one country to another is to move people with the relevant skills. This is why, when in 751 BCE Arab armies captured Chinese paper-makers, they took them to Baghdad to establish the technology among their own people. It is also the reason the Japanese warlord Hideyoshi took Korean potters back to Japan following his attempted conquest of the peninsula in 1592. The one resulted in the diffusion of paper-making techniques throughout Muslim and subsequently Christian lands; the other established the foundations of a pottery industry that came in time to be regarded as quintessentially Japanese in its artistry.[5]

Similar sorts of understanding may be observed in the debates in nineteenth-century China, Korea, and Japan over the adoption of Western technology. In each of these countries it was strongly debated by intellectuals and government figures. Few disputed the usefulness of Western technologies such as guns, railways, the telegraph, and steelmaking, especially when it came to resisting Western encroachment. What worried many of the more conservative thinkers was the realisation that wholesale adoption of Western technology would result in sweeping social and cultural change of a sort they opposed. They saw clearly that it was not just a question of using foreign machines or implements. Using those things would require new ways of thinking, new values and methods of organisation, and would introduce sources of power at odds with the indigenous system. In all three countries a workable formula was looked for in terms of a traditional distinction (from Chinese philosophy) between substance and application, *ti* and *yong* in Chinese. It was argued that while the substance or goals of society should be defined in terms of traditional values, the world in which those goals are achieved could be understood in Western terms. In other words, the proposed solution was one of indigenous ends, Western means.

Despite its superficial attractiveness, however, this approach did not work, as was realised by most of those taking part in the debates. By the 1880s, in Japan, those favouring full Westernisation wielded political and military power. Japanese influence in Korea triggered far-reaching reforms there during 1894–96, at the same time that Japan was demonstrating the success of her modernisation tactics by defeating China in the war of 1894–95. In China attempts at reform according to the *ti* and *yong* formula persisted until 1898. But these were ineffectual, for both political reasons and the reasons pertinent to the discussion here: foreign technology cannot be adopted without taking over the know-how and values it incorporates, and the social systems it presupposes.[6] Unfortunately the lessons of East Asia in the late nineteenth century had to be relearnt throughout the Third World in the second half of the twentieth century.

Since technology is essentially knowledge—knowledge of how to do things—it cannot be quarantined from other areas of knowledge. Technological understanding must influence social and moral understanding, for example, and vice versa. Nothing is more misleading than the assertion that there are different *kinds* of knowledge or understanding that somehow operate independently of each other, like radio stations operating on different frequencies and unable to listen in on each other.

In the last two or three decades, some of the most insightful work on technology has focused on its characteristics as knowledge, looking there for understanding of technological trends. It has been emphasised, for example, that technological mastery or know-how is not the sort of knowledge that is easily codified or put into words and acquired by reading; rather, it is the sort of knowledge that is embodied in people and institutions, is acquired by doing, and is transmitted by means of apprenticeship and collaboration. Like other sorts of knowledge, technology is cumulative: mastery of skills and techniques occurs over time, with each extension of expertise being built onto what is already in place. This cumulative aspect of technology helps us to understand that it is always localised, that is, shaped by local circumstances and technological traditions. Whether it is on the part of an individual, a firm, or a community, technological development will be shaped by the sorts of mastery already achieved, and mastery will to a large extent be reckoned in terms of ability to succeed in local circumstances.

The cumulative and localised nature of technology also explains another important aspect: what is called path dependency or technological trajectory. The type of technological development that is likely is to a large extent determined by the technology already in place. Established ways of doing things, skills already mastered, effort and resources already invested, all encourage further movement down the path chosen. To set off in a new direction may not just require more effort and expense; it may even be impossible.[7]

Consideration of the tacit nature of know-how, its cumulative and localised nature, and path dependency, helps us better to understand social and economic change. As well as explaining why technological catch-up is so difficult, for example, it points to some of the reasons why technological advantage can be retained even during political and economic catastrophe. After the Second World War, Japan did not have to rebuild from scratch because the technological skills of its workforce had not been destroyed. Major corporations such as Mitsubishi and Toyota were able to play a leading role in Japan's economic recovery by drawing on their organisational memory and technological mastery.[8] It also helps to explain why economic development based on foreign technology is likely to result in economic segmentation and enclavement, with new industries being isolated from an undeveloped hinterland both geographically and structurally. Above all, it helps to explain why education and training—or human resource development, to give it an economic flavour—is crucial to the fate of communities and nations.

## Local knowledge, universal knowledge

The aspects of technology considered here call into question easy assumptions about the universality of knowledge. At least as far as practice is concerned, the localised nature of learning and knowing cannot be ignored. In relation to economic and social development, the need for local knowledge and understanding has begun to be widely recognised. As well as growing awareness of the need for community-based development that takes into account the views of those directly involved and utilises local knowledge when framing strategies, there is a tendency to argue that bodies of local or indigenous knowledge are valuable in themselves, that where their survival is under threat they must be preserved.[9]

Attempts to distinguish between Western or scientific knowledge and indigenous knowledge encounter huge problems. Since knowledge has always moved across cultural and political boundaries, it is often just as difficult to say where a particular body of knowledge originated as it is to determine which peoples are truly indigenous to a given region. In the latter case one can usually say which groups have a longer history of settlement than others in a region, while in regard to knowledge we can distinguish traditional or long-established ways of understanding and doing things from those of recent origin. Much of the present interest in indigenous knowledge comes from appreciation of the fact that other cultures often include knowledge systems based on careful observation and close interaction with their environment over very long periods of time, which despite being organised in ways different from scientific or international knowledge, and being based on different premises, do *work*. This is likely to include environmental and agricultural knowledge, for example, and knowledge of the medicinal properties of local plants and substances. A spectacular example of the latter, known because much of it has been written down, is the traditional Chinese pharmacopoeia.[10]

The crucial question is whether modern, 'scientific' knowledge is fundamentally different from either modern technology or indigenous knowledge systems, and can manage to liberate itself from the constraints of provincialism. Is scientific knowledge, can scientific knowledge, be truly universal? It is often claimed that what makes scientific knowledge different is that it consists of theories, which are essentially patterns read into the generality of experience and which can be confirmed or invalidated by particular observations. Technology, in contrast, is held to be the *application* of science, and since applications must always be localised in time and space they inevitably lack the claim to universality that legitimately belongs to science itself. So not only is science different from other knowledge systems—often dismissed as backward or the creation of primitive mentalities—it is also said to be different from itself when put to work in the real world. There is reason to be suspicious of these claims.

A distinction between science and technology is difficult to draw. Two hundred years ago, when the Industrial Revolution was gathering momentum, it seemed much easier. Scientists were regarded primarily as theorisers who aimed to discover laws of nature, while invention of the machines that seemed to drive progress was being done by mechanical tinkerers without much formal knowledge of science. Whatever value this distinction may have once had, during the twentieth century it became increasingly suspect: 'doing science' now requires mastery of a wide range of advanced technologies, while technological innovation requires familiarity with current scientific understanding. Technological advances are just as likely to expand scientific understanding as the other way around. Both are 'knowledge', and to say they are different kinds of knowledge, one theoretical and the other practical, is misleading if it is taken to imply that the correctness of theoretical knowledge is determined in anything other than practical ways or that theory is somehow more valuable than practice.[11]

In regard to technology, as already mentioned, it is argued that knowledge is tacit; it entails the acquisition of skills, learning by doing. Technological knowledge may be difficult to put into words, and understanding the words will be no guarantee that the skills have been acquired in any case.

It is unfortunate that it has become conventional to talk as if knowledge can exist independently of the minds of individuals, as if scientific knowledge can accumulate in texts, computer programs, libraries, and all that is needed to acquire such knowledge is to read the texts or programs in question. The advancement of knowledge is conceived rather like a glacier: snowstorms of facts fall anonymously on the upper slopes, where their accumulated weight forms a mass of knowledge that grinds its way remorselessly down the valley. The fact is that scientific knowledge no less than technology adheres in individuals and organisations, it entails a good deal of learning by doing, and its accumulation too is likely to be local in character.

More and more it is being understood that science has to be seen as a social undertaking.[12] The idea that scientific knowledge is generated by sceptical individuals who accept only the evidence of their own experience is giving way to the recognition that even the most sceptical and clinically detached of individuals obtain almost everything they know from others. Our reliance on what we have been told is a point that was appreciated long ago by Indian philosophers. Early Buddhist thinkers and those of the Hindu Nyaya school recognised as sources of knowledge not only reason and the evidence of our senses, as has been commonly done by Western philosophers, but also *testimony*, that is, knowledge obtained secondhand from a trustworthy person. We can rightly claim to *know* when our own experience and reflection are confirmed by the testimony of those who are honest and reliable.[13]

The fact that most of our knowledge is dependent upon testimony gives rise to two fundamental questions: where our information comes from and why we should believe it; or, rephrasing in social terms, with whom do we *communicate* and whom can we *trust*? These questions are relevant to all systems of knowledge regardless of their cultural context. They draw attention to the fact that any knowledge system, in order to become established, requires a system of communication and a system of accreditation.

What makes modern science distinctive is the particular way it has institutionalised both communication and accreditation. The institutions and conventions on which scientific communication and trust are based are the product of a long evolutionary process.[14] Essentially, we are told we can trust anyone who has been formally trained and certified by an appropriate institution, an institution that itself has been accredited, usually a university. Communication is through specially established media and institutions, such as academic journals and learned academies, controlled by practitioners of high standing within the scientific *community*. These two aspects of modern scientific knowledge, and their implications for contemporary Asian societies, need to be considered further.

## Communication and knowledge

For knowledge to be accumulated, to become systematic, there has to be effective communication. This is no less true for farmers sharing their experience in remote villages in Pakistan or Laos than for information engineers in Singapore or Bangalore.

The limits of communication, the blanks and distortions within it, define the limits of our knowledge. In view of its claim to universality, this is particularly important for science, which many prefer to call international science rather than Western science, in recognition of the contributions made by researchers in places such as Delhi, Seoul, and Tokyo, as well as in order to reassert its claim to universality. But even in Western countries seen as having a common culture, and despite specialist journals, international information technology, telecommunications, and patent registration systems, the generation of scientific knowledge is far from being a unified and universal exercise. Communication is faulty or non-existent across discipline boundaries and across national and institutional horizons and traditions, often resulting in a localisation of knowledge similar to that found in technology.[15]

Where communication is faulty, for whatever reason, or intentionally restricted or distorted, the localised quality of knowledge becomes stronger, perhaps to the point where the claim that it is knowledge becomes spurious. Where communication is controlled by the state through censorship and regulation of communications media, as described in Chapter 10, the local limits of knowledge soon reveal themselves. However, even where a state does its best to provide open access to international information, there may be formidable obstacles. The most obvious of these is language.

The dominant language of international scholarship or science is English. Anyone who wants access to the bulk of the world's information or who wants to advance scientific knowledge has little choice but to use that language, at least some of the time. This sort of linguistic inequality is by no means unprecedented in the world of learning. For much of European history Latin was the international language of learning. Arabic played a similar role in West Asia and other Muslim areas, while classical Chinese was used by intellectual elites throughout East Asia until the twentieth century. The utility and status of those languages inevitably widened the influence of the bodies of knowledge recorded in them, the less desirable as well as the highly esteemed. It is the same with English.

The dominance of one language makes it easy for its speakers to ignore the contributions to knowledge made by speakers of other languages, which in turn reinforces whatever biases or provincialisms happen to afflict them. Work written in a major language such as Chinese or Hindi thus tends to remain out of sight, beyond the communication horizon. In the world knowledge system, China and India, for example, remain 'gigantic peripheries'.[16]

From the perspective of communication, the distinction between science and local knowledge could be seen as having some substance. Ideally, at least, science aims to be universal, and has communications structures in place designed to realise this aspiration—structures made ever more effective by technological progress. But is there any knowledge system that does not carry with it the assumption of universality?

In most societies it has seemed natural to regard the earth or one's place on it as the centre of the universe, or even to equate it with the universe. Over time we have learnt that the earth revolves around the sun, and that the sun is just one very ordinary star among many millions located in the arms trailed through space by the spiral galaxy we call the Milky Way, a galaxy that is but one of a cluster of galaxies with no claim to special significance among the countless other clusters except for the fact that we call it home. It has all been rather humbling. It would seem to require a degree of perversity to continue claiming that our situation is somehow special, and a remarkable leap of faith to assume that it all exists for our benefit.

In much the same way we have discovered that beyond the boundaries of our native village or cultural region there exist many other societies, the members of which organise their affairs differently and often hold values and beliefs at odds with those of home. Many of these societies have recorded histories of achievement no less impressive than our own and function every bit as effectively. Expanding our sphere of communication, and with it our body of knowledge, requires us to rethink ways of understanding previously taken for granted, and to acquire a certain amount of humility with the realisation that the rest of the world is under no compulsion to conduct itself according to the rules our village sees as immutable and obligatory. The wider our knowledge the more adequate our understanding.

The extension of our knowledge does not mean that we attach value only to generalisations of ever-increasing scale or that local concerns are no longer seen as fit subjects of enquiry. In some areas of study, particular importance may attach to local and time-specific elements of knowledge. Many social scientists and historians, for example, are acutely aware that much of their knowledge is based on unique examples, and loses a good deal of its value if that uniqueness is ignored. What it does mean is that what is local or ephemeral must be recognised for what it is. Knowledge is a matter of recognising patterns or continuities in change, making it possible to anticipate and, to some extent, control the future; it is also a matter of being able to draw precise distinctions between particulars. Perceiving patterns and seeing differences are different aspects of a single process. It is in terms of patterns that we think about or respond to the particulars of the world we inhabit. To emphasise the local or the ephemeral, to refer to things as unique or distinctive, is to say that for the purpose at hand their differences matter more than their similarities. But this is not to deny that what in this context are differences may on other occasions be described in terms of patterns not relevant now. The real test of knowledge is not leaving all that is local or particular behind, but recognising the ways in which it is local or particular, how it may fit into patterns not visible to a parochial observer. These considerations apply to all knowledge, scientific and non-scientific, Eastern and Western.

## Making scientists trustworthy

It is claimed that what makes Western scientific knowledge different from other knowledge is its systematic, objective, and analytical nature, the openness of scientific practice and the validity of its conclusions independent of social or cultural context, and its strong institutional basis. It has been observed, however, that these characteristics as well as others such as reliance on experimentation and critical assessment by peers, may be regarded as features of anything that may legitimately be called knowledge, whether 'Western science' or non-Western 'local knowledge'.[17] Is there then nothing that makes science different; are there no characteristics that would help to explain, for example, the unprecedented rate of technological innovation of the last two hundred years that has transformed the face of the earth and all aspects of human experience? I think there are.

One characteristic of science is maintenance of the distinction, in theory if not always in reality, between the way things are and the way they should be, that is, between empirical knowledge and moral principles. The more informal and socially pressing contexts in which everyday knowledge has to operate make this distinction hard to uphold. It lay at the heart of Enlightenment thinking, and is the source of both the strength and the weakness of science: strength because it allows knowledge to develop independently of moral or religious dispute, and weakness, because the division once made is difficult if not impossible to overcome—we cannot argue from the way the world is to how it should be without underlying moral values or principles to help us bridge the gap.

Another distinctive feature of science is what may be called its mathematical bias: a historical tendency to regard mathematics as the condition to which all knowledge aspires, and a methodological preference for what can be measured or mathematically expressed. Again, this is both a strength and a weakness. One outcome of this bias is the popular hierarchy of disciplines, which puts mathematics, physics and other 'hard' sciences at the top and the 'soft' social sciences at the bottom. This in turn has led to many misguided attempts to introduce the methods of the hard sciences into areas of social study where they are unhelpful, often resulting in little more than mathematical verification of social clichés. In cross-cultural contexts the mathematical bias can be particularly damaging. Yet that same bias is invaluable in its contribution to developing standardised and systemic methodologies, qualities that are essential if the creation of knowledge is to be a collaborative and cumulative undertaking.

It is above all in its emphasis on methodology, or how to generate knowledge, that the distinctiveness of modern or international science is to be found. One of the most intriguing aspects of its development is the way virtues such as disinterestedness, truthfulness, and integrity, originally personal qualities regarded as essential to the functioning of the scientific community, were over time transferred to what is often called 'the scientific method'. As the scientific community expanded and personal knowledge of other practitioners became impossible, trustworthiness increasingly was seen as a matter of having been trained to use the right methodology. As early as the eighteenth century, the twin requirements of standardised communication and standardised method began to impose themselves. The subject of study, whether 'nature' or 'society', began to contract to what could be communicated in a standardised way. In the words of one historian, 'It would be an exaggeration, but not a distortion, to claim that it was scientific communication that was the precondition for the uniformity of nature rather than the reverse.'[18] It is an observation particularly applicable to the social sciences.

It appears to be this standardisation of communication and methodology that has provided much of the basis for the claim that the foundation of the West's greatness (or degeneracy, depending on one's point of view) is its distinctive mentality or way of thinking. Other peoples or cultures think differently from those of 'the West', we are told, which alone have achieved rationality. Other peoples have different logics. They have failed to progress beyond superstition and primitive thinking. Yet the claim that Western culture is the product of distinctive mental processes or logic, that the ability to think rationally is peculiar to, or most highly developed in, the West is quite without foundation, as is the claim that the concept of rationality (in the West or anywhere else) may be reduced to an abstraction known as the scientific method, which is universally applicable and is the test of trustworthiness.[19]

Being accredited, or made trustworthy, in science is best understood in terms of being inducted into a scientific culture and demonstrating ability and willingness to abide by its norms. But *the* scientific method is an ideal rather than a reality, and is not seen by everyone as undifferentiated. Like other cultures, the scientific culture prescribes a range of possible roles, ideals and acceptable procedures, and contains within it many subcultures, which vary according to discipline, institution, and geographic location. Conceiving science as a culture makes it possible to avoid the trap of regarding it as the embodiment of a particular mental capacity, while still recognising that it does encourage specific intellectual habits and qualities. Emphasis on the scientific community rather than the scientific method makes it easier to see that, in essence, the social construction of scientific knowledge is not so very different from the social construction of knowledge in any locality.

What makes scientific knowledge distinctive from other bodies of knowledge is not its institutionalisation, but rather the nature of the institutions in which training and accreditation take place. In all societies dominant knowledge systems are institutionalised. Religious knowledge systems have tended to rely on priestly and monastic orders. Confucian education was institutionalised through the imperial examination system, local academies, and the educational activities of family units. Science depends above all on the activities of universities, research institutes, and scholarly and professional organisations. It is these institutions and the communication systems that support them that are largely responsible for training, certification, and self-regulation, as well as the actual generation of scientific knowledge. They therefore have a dual function of maintaining a capacity for scientific research and ensuring that the operation of the scientific enterprise is beyond suspicion—that it may be seen by the public as trustworthy and authoritative.

The institutionalisation of knowledge systems and their accreditation systems helps to explain the intensity of the conflicts that arise when one knowledge system is being replaced by another. There is a lot at stake. It is not merely one set of ideas being replaced by another, but also one group of experts being replaced by another. The competition for power and status can be bitter. This is what happened in East Asian countries in the late nineteenth and early twentieth centuries, when the Confucian knowledge system was largely supplanted by Western learning. It is a process still occurring among indigenous minorities in developing countries, as traditional ways of knowing and doing lose their influence. It is still occurring also in the dominant societies of many of those countries, as the impact of globalisation intensifies.

## Education

Universities, the main institutional base for the communication and accreditation on which scientific knowledge depends, were established in Asian countries using Western models. In the Philippines they date back to the seventeenth century, but elsewhere, including India and Japan, they did not appear before the nineteenth century. Although some countries, such as China, did have traditional institutions of 'higher learning', these did not significantly influence the nature of the new institutions.

Some of the universities took up the role of preserving indigenous literary and artistic traditions at the same time as establishing new competencies in Western science and technology. However, these sometimes conflicting roles did not prompt any serious attempts to evolve a distinctive new type of institution. In view of the role universities have played in providing an institutional base for participation in the dominant international knowledge system, this is not entirely surprising. At the beginning of the twenty-first century there is much preoccupation with the changing role of universities and their need to re-create themselves in response to the impact of information technology and a 'new knowledge production system' that requires greater collaboration with other types of institutions and organisations. However, there remains little suggestion that nations will need to develop new and distinctive institutions of their own to meet these challenges. It tends to be assumed that everyone faces similar problems and will solve them in similar ways.[20] As far as introducing foreign influences is concerned, it should be noted that this international orientation of the upper level of educational systems in developing countries is likely to be a much stronger influence than the mass media, especially since universities have a habit of imposing their demands and aspirations on the school systems below them.

Some of the practical implications of the very difficult issues discussed here become clearer when we consider the general question of educational provision. Much of the thinking about Asian educational issues can only be described as bizarre. It is bizarre not because what is said is not reasonable, but because the assumptions behind it are so enormous that even the most sensible conclusions are likely to be reduced to nonsense. It is widely assumed that education can be discussed meaningfully without reference to its content. Frequently, education is equated with what is referred to as modern Western education, that is, education incorporating dominant Western conceptions of knowledge, with a strong emphasis on literacy, mathematics, and science, and delivered through educational institutions based largely on Western models, in particular, state-funded mass schooling systems and universities. It is often assumed that in discussions of education everyone agrees that it amounts to what may comfortably be labelled 'human resource development' and will lead to modernisation or development along Western lines.

As long as we ignore the content of education, how the content is to be taught and who is to do the teaching, it is easy to agree on the value and desirability of education. Saying that education is important is rather like saying that morality is important. The question is, what sort of education or morality, what type of understanding and behaviour are we trying to instil? Education can be made to serve just about any social, economic, moral, or political purpose we care to mention. This is what we find in contemporary Asian societies: education is called upon to further all kinds of objectives, from communist revolution to Islamic morality, from maintaining traditional social hierarchies to developing advanced technological capacities in industry, from providing avenues for individual social mobility to preventing AIDS.

As in Western countries, education in Asia has come to be regarded as a universal panacea; the objectives and functions attributed to it have multiplied over time, and sometimes are quite contradictory. Even in the most development-oriented nations, the human resource development perspective cannot dominate educational policy completely, if for no other reason than the fact that education cannot be equated with scientific and technological training. The various parts of the educational system are likely to be nudging society in different directions, according to the range of purposes attributed to education and the influence of the various pressure groups in society. Education is particularly likely to reflect the competing forces at work in society and the various aspirations they have for the future, the sorts of changes they hope to bring about.

One function of education that has received rather less official attention in Asian countries than in the West has been that of aiding individual social mobility. The preoccupation with this topic in the West, it must be observed, arises largely from its implications for ideals of equality: the belief that everyone is equal, that all individuals have an equal say and equal control over their own lives and society's affairs, and that all receive from society what they deserve. The idea of social mobility through education gives plausibility to these ideals. If educational achievement largely determines capacity

Education is one of the few grounds of hope for these Afghan refugee children, Peshawar, Pakistan.

to participate in social and political affairs, and social position and rewards, and universal education is provided by the state, then it may be claimed that the individual's position in terms of income, status, and power is based on personal merit. Human rights documents proclaim the individual's right to education not only because education is regarded as good in itself, but also because it is necessary for social equality.

At the family level, in Asian societies, great importance is attached to education as an avenue for the upward mobility of children, and through them for the family as a whole. Parents in the most impoverished circumstances and isolated locations, from the steppes of Central Asia to the remotest islands of the Philippines and Indonesia, see in education whatever hope they have of a better future for their children. But Asian governments have shown only limited interest in achieving social equality through education. This is evident from the nature and extent of educational provision, which—even allowing for the complex educational problems facing the countries in question and the limited resources available for dealing with them—have rarely amounted to serious attempts to grapple with the issue. The result is that educational participation and achievements, particularly at post-compulsory levels, remain strongly skewed towards members of social elites, males, dominant ethnic groups, and city-dwellers. The less well off, females, members of indigenous minorities, and those living in rural areas—that is, those most in need of the benefits that education can bring—are least likely to participate in it and most likely to drop out early.

In relation to gender, for example, glaring inequalities appear at both the lower and the upper levels of educational systems (see Table 11.1). In most Asian countries, literacy levels are much lower for females than they are for males. Girls are less likely than boys to go to school, and more likely to leave school earlier.

The lower schooling attainment of girls is naturally one of the factors behind their low rates of participation in post-school education, but at this level traditional gender attitudes continue to operate. Parents impose traditional expectations and choices on their daughters, in the context of which higher education frequently represents little more than a mechanism for making daughters more eligible brides.

Employers have similar attitudes. In India the proportion of university graduates who are women is low, at around 30 per cent, yet the proportion of female graduates unable to find work is much higher than for male graduates. This pattern is common in East Asia as well as the countries of South and West Asia. In China in 1996 a survey by an official student newspaper, *21st Century*, revealed widespread prejudice against hiring female graduates, who made up 34 per cent of the graduate pool. Of forty-two government organisations, twenty-seven refused to hire women. Japanese parents have much lower educational aspirations for their daughters than for their sons, so that only 15 per cent of women complete a university education compared with 33 per cent of men. Women who do make it into higher education are likely to be concentrated in low-status liberal arts colleges studying subjects considered appropriately 'feminine', while employment opportunities on graduation are limited by employer bias in favour of men. The use of educational systems as a mechanism for achieving gender equality has clearly not been pursued by Asian governments with much energy or enthusiasm. The same applies to other sorts of social equality. Different functions of education have been given greater priority.[21]

China provides an interesting example in this context, for there are reasonable grounds for saying that the Chinese communist government has seriously tried to bring about greater social equality through education. Under Mao's leadership in the 1960s and early 1970s, there were attempts to remove traditional biases in favour of urban elites. Strong emphasis was placed on rural education and through the commune system schooling was made available to large parts of the population, both male and female, which had never had access to education before. The quality of the education provided, which was poor to begin with, deteriorated further as political indoctrination became more dominant, while during the chaotic Cultural Revolution the education system closed down altogether.

Since the late 1970s there has been a reaction against the revolutionary excesses of the Maoist period. Education has been made to serve economic development and Chinese nationalism, without too much intrusion of communist ideology. In response to the dilemma 'Red or expert?', which generated so much conflict in the Mao years, Deng Xiaoping declared that it was possible to be 'Red *and* expert': knowledge or expertise, if put at the service of the socialist society, does not need to be subordinated to ideological correctness. Yet the public educational system that emerged during the

**Table 11.1** Educational participation by women

| | *Female adult literacy rate* | | *Primary education* | | *Secondary education* | | *Tertiary education* | |
|---|---|---|---|---|---|---|---|---|
| | *As % of population age 15+ 1998* | *As % of male participation rate 1998* | *As % of female primary age population 1997* | *As % of male participation rate 1997* | *As % of female secondary age population 1997* | *As % of male participation rate 1997* | *Female tertiary students per 100 000 women 1994–97* | *Female participation rate as % male rate 1994–97* |
| Bangladesh | 28.6 | 56 | 69.6 | 87 | 15.6 | 58 | 129 | 20 |
| Cambodia | 19.9 | 35 | 99.9 | 100 | 30.9 | 66 | 32 | 23 |
| China | 74.6 | 82 | 99.9 | 100 | 65.1 | 88 | 327 | 54 |
| Hong Kong | 89.1 | 93 | 93.2 | 104 | 71.5 | 107 | 1437 | 79 |
| India | 43.5 | 65 | 71.0 | 86 | 48.0 | 68 | 479 | 61 |
| Indonesia | 80.5 | 88 | 98.6 | 99 | 53.4 | 91 | 812 | 53 |
| Iran | 67.4 | 82 | 89.2 | 98 | 75.8 | 88 | 1311 | 60 |
| Iraq | 43.2 | 68 | 69.6 | 88 | 33.8 | 66 | | |
| Japan | 99.0 | 100 | 99.9 | 100 | 99.9 | 100 | 2706 | 76 |
| Laos | 30.2 | 49 | 69.2 | 90 | 52.9 | 72 | 158 | 44 |
| Malaysia | 82.0 | 90 | 99.9 | 100 | 68.5 | 115 | 646 | 91 |
| Mongolia | 51.0 | 71 | 87.5 | 106 | 63.7 | 132 | 2742 | 216 |
| Myanmar | 79.5 | 90 | 98.5 | 99 | 53.0 | 96 | 717 | 156 |
| Nepal | 38.4 | 53 | 70.2 | 74 | 40.0 | 52 | 108 | 21 |
| Pakistan | 28.9 | 50 | | | | | 220 | 59 |
| Philippines | 94.6 | 100 | 99.9 | 100 | 78.5 | 102 | 3383 | 113 |
| Singapore | 87.6 | 91 | 90.5 | 98 | 74.8 | 98 | 3256 | 89 |
| South Korea | 95.9 | 97 | 99.9 | 100 | 99.9 | 100 | 4629 | 61 |
| Sri Lanka | 88.3 | 94 | 99.9 | 100 | 79.3 | 109 | 388 | 69 |
| Thailand | 93.2 | 96 | 89.2 | 103 | 46.9 | 97 | 2138 | 111 |
| Vietnam | 90.6 | 95 | 99.9 | 100 | 54.2 | 97 | | |

Source: United Nations Development Program, *Human Development Report 2000*, Oxford University Press, New York, 2000, 255–8.

1980s and 1990s has failed to meet the needs of the Chinese economy as well as proving socially regressive in many respects. Numerous schools in rural areas have been closed, and in some regions educational participation and literacy rates have fallen. By the mid-1980s the educational system was showing striking similarities to the system of the 1930s: a reversion to elitist traditions of schooling and learning unresponsive to the needs of the mass of the population; inadequate and inefficient teaching; preferential access to the best schools from the primary level upwards for the children of well-connected parents; educational streaming at the primary level, with brighter students going to elite schools; a sharp distinction at the secondary level between higher-education-oriented and work-oriented schools; and a higher-education system too small either to offer advanced study to more than a select few or to meet the human resource needs of a rapidly developing nation. Many families with high educational aspirations are sending their children to private schools and colleges, despite the substantial costs involved.[22]

China's failure to build an educational system adequate for the needs of its population and economy cannot be blamed just on continuing fallout from the Maoist period, its limited resources, or its massive population and the organisational difficulties this generates, though these problems are very real. In the end it is hard to avoid the conclusion that the government has simply failed to appreciate the crucial role played by good-quality mass education in modern economic and social development.

It is tempting to identify the problems as a cultural hangover from the imperial period, when it was considered appropriate to provide education only for a small ruling elite. But this explanation appears less adequate when we remember that China's failure needs to be compared with the success of Japan, Korea, Taiwan, Hong Kong, and Singapore, each of which can claim to be heir to a Confucian elitist view of education. The priority they have given to education and training has been identified as a key factor in their rapid development since the Second World War. Some argue that it was the opposing attitudes of China and Japan to mass education in the second half of the nineteenth century that determined the paths taken by each country thereafter: Japan moved quickly after 1868 to provide mass education and so was soon able to compete with Western nations; China did not and is still paying the price.[23]

Where China differs from Japan and the other East Asian countries mentioned is in its strongly rural and agrarian population. Because the bulk of the population is engaged in agricultural production, many attach little value to formal education. This is why, for example, when the responsibility system was introduced and there was a resurgence of family-based production, many rural families took their children out of school. They believed it was better for children to contribute to the family economy than to acquire an education judged largely irrelevant to their needs. Such attitudes still occur in some government circles. But lack of education and training is more conspicuous in the major urban centres than among country people, if for no other reason than that the demands of industrialisation are stronger there. Some would argue that, in terms of education, the communist government has got what it long wanted: a population that has basic literacy and skills, is submissive to authority, appreciates the value of national cohesion and strength, and sees the importance of serving the nation, educated up to a point but without the resources or inclination for critical and independent reflection, able to follow orders but unable to question them. If more recently the government has realised that modernisation requires more or different sorts of education, it has yet to appreciate fully the time and resources needed to turn things around.

We do not have to accept the negative interpretation to see that Chinese educational policy is a product of competing objectives and priorities as well as resource constraints. Education for industrialisation and modernisation, education as a basic human need and right, moral education, political education, education for creativity and innovation—all have to be weighed in relation to each other. This is true everywhere. What complicates the process in many Asian countries is that some kinds of education (or educational objectives) are associated with foreign influences.

Any temptation to assume that education inevitably leads down the highway of modernisation or Westernisation is blown away by the example of post-1979 Iran. For some fifty years prior to 1979 Iran's rulers had regarded education as an instrument for modernising the nation. In the 1920s a centralised educational bureaucracy was established that developed a secular school system for both girls and boys. Where traditionally education had been provided largely through religious institutions, now the influence of Islam on education was minimised. This trend continued into the 1960s and 1970s, when increased oil revenues enabled the government to expand provision of schooling and develop a modern system of higher education. Yet at the time of the Islamic revolution of 1979 the impact of this secular educational activity remained concentrated largely among the relatively small urban population.

The Islamic government that came to power with the revolution saw secularism and Westernisation as evidence of decadence and enslavement rather than enlightenment and progress, and turned to education to counteract the trend. In March 1980 its leaders called for an end to Iran's cultural dependence on the West and moved to cleanse the educational system of the disease of Westernisation. Curricula and textbooks from primary to tertiary level were rewritten to reflect Shi'ite Islamic teachings. Co-educational schooling was prohibited. All university students were required to take courses in Islamic knowledge.[24]

Support for the Islamisation of society came from not only the conservative, rural, and less-educated sections of the population. Many of the supporters of the revolution were beneficiaries of the Western, secular educational system developed by the Pahlavi regime. University students played a major role in the overthrow of the monarchy. It may be that many students did not expect the process of Islamisation to go as far as it did, but clearly there was widespread hostility to the Shah's regime among the educated middle class as well as among the common people. That hostility had a number of different targets: while the more conservative sections of the population resented the enforced secularisation of Iranian society and the weakening of Islamic customs and institutions, others equated Westernisation with Western imperialism and the loss of Iranian sovereignty, while others again reacted primarily against the oppressive nature of the regime, its reliance on secret police (SAVAK) to silence critics, and the large gap between the privileged elite and the situation of the bulk of the people. Islamic ideals presented plausible alternatives for those educated to a greater sense of nationalism and political awareness as well as concern for social justice. In this, educated Iranians were no different from many people in other Muslim countries attracted to Islamic radicalism as a response to the political, economic, and social problems to which their education—obtained in Western or Western-style institutions of learning—had opened their eyes.[25]

The situation of Iran before 1979 shows that the impact of modern Western education is not always the same, and may in fact be contrary to what is looked for. Iran since 1979, like communist China, demonstrates that education can be made to serve objectives other than modernisation or Western-style development. More generally, it shows that the purposes education is made to serve depend on who has influence or power over the education system. This is true regardless of whether the society in question is a strongly polarised revolutionary society or a more pluralistic open one. In the latter case the goals of education are likely to be more varied, perhaps even contradictory, with little agreement as to which goals should have priority. In all cases, however, the goals are certain to be numerous.

When in 1965 Singapore separated from Malaysia to become an independent state, it had a history as a regional trading centre, a British colonial heritage, and a multi-ethnic population (75 per cent Chinese, 15 per cent Malay and 7 per cent Indian). It became independent at a time when Malay–Chinese tensions were running high in Malaysia, Indonesia was experiencing a violent anti-communist (and often anti-Chinese) movement, and the People's Republic of China was looming very large and revolutionary. This all helps to explain why from the beginning the Singapore government has emphasised three broad purposes of education: economic development, national unity, and social stability.

With no other resources to draw upon, the Singapore authorities were attracted strongly to a human resource development approach to education, stating as early as 1966 that 'Singapore's national wealth lies in our human resources, and our human potential must therefore be developed to the fullest possible extent. An educated and enlightened population is our guarantee for a prosperous future.' This approach, which has been maintained into the twenty-first century, led to provision of universal free primary education, rapid expansion of secondary- and tertiary-education opportunities, and an emphasis on mathematics, science, and technical education. International surveys in 1996 indicated that for their age Singapore students had the highest levels of mathematical and scientific achievement in the world.

Concern with national unity is evident in the government's policy on language education. Under the policy of compulsory bilingualism introduced in 1966, all students, whether they spoke Chinese, Malay, or Tamil, had to learn English in addition to their mother tongue. This policy was reconfirmed by the Minister of Education in 1986, when he explained that 'children must learn English so that they will have a window to the knowledge, technology and expertise of the modern world. They must learn their mother tongues to enable them to know what makes us what we are.'

It appears that most Singapore families have been less concerned that their children 'know who they are', in the minister's phrase, than to maximise their employment opportunities. This has resulted in a massive movement of students away from Chinese-language schools to those where English is the primary language of instruction. Between 1959 and 1979, the proportion of students in English-language

Schoolboys, Bam, Iran (top); schoolgirls, Esfahan, Iran (above).

schools rose from 47 per cent to 90 per cent, while that in Chinese-language schools fell from 46 per cent to 10 per cent. More recently, with the growing economic influence of the People's Republic of China, Taiwan, and Chinese communities in other South-East Asian countries, Mandarin has begun to attract more attention as a language with career potential, in Singapore and elsewhere.

Social stability as a goal of education in Singapore includes an emphasis on social harmony, order, and respect for authority, the sorts of values frequently articulated by the government. The Ministry of Education in 2001 saw its mission as being 'to mould the future of the nation, by moulding the people who will determine the future of the nation. The [Education] Service will provide our children with a balanced and well-rounded education, develop them to their full potential, and nurture them into good citizens, conscious of their responsibilities to their family, society and country.' It identified as a cornerstone of education policy 'the inculcation of sound moral values to serve as a cultural ballast in the face of rapid progress and change'. As might be expected, such concerns led to the introduction of moral education as a specific subject. The chairman of the committee responsible regarded the new moral-education program as a cultural bulwark against 'extraneous influences ... which have perverted the character of [Singapore's] people', and as a way of ensuring that the society remains 'cohesive under stress'. Nationalism and morality coincide, in other words, in more ways than one.[26]

For a city state like Singapore it is relatively easy to find agreement on priorities for education, despite its multi-ethnic population; for a large and ethnically diverse nation like Indonesia it is much more difficult. The economic and social situation of the population is more varied, the range of ideas of what education should do is much wider, and the coexistence of a number of different school systems means that there is considerable variation in educational practice as well.

The dominant educational force is certainly the secular government school system, which in 1997 had 95 per cent of primary school enrolments, 71 per cent of junior secondary and 47 per cent of senior secondary enrolments. Under the Suharto government it aimed to provide education based on the national philosophy of Pancasila and was directed towards economic and social development. Education embodying its principles was seen as encouraging national unity and well-being, mutual respect and social harmony, discipline and orderliness, science and technology, creativity, and intellectual independence. These were all desirable attributes, yet in practice they often clashed, forcing the state, parents, teachers, and individual students to pursue one rather than another. The state showed a preference for nationalism, discipline, and orderliness over creativity, intellectual independence, and even science and technology.

In the post-Suharto period of political and economic liberalisation there is support in some quarters for a move away from the centralised education system of the past, and towards a decentralised system offering autonomy and control at the regional and even local community level. Although such a move could help to ensure that education provision reflects local needs, it could also prove disastrous unless adequate resources and expertise are provided to support the educational choices communities make.

In the past, some educational choice has been available through Taman Siswa, a private school system influenced by the educational philosophy of Montessori and patronised by middle-class families with high educational aspirations for their children. Different sorts of aspirations are provided for by Islamic schools, run by a variety of local and regional religious bodies rather than a nationwide authority and therefore embodying a range of educational approaches and ideals. Those that in the government's eyes emphasise Islamic ideals at the expense of national ones are regarded with suspicion, as potentially divisive and destabilising. In education as in society, the role of Islam is strongly contested.[27]

## Knowledge and change

Education systems embody judgments about the sorts of knowledge and competencies useful for society. They reflect the influence of those with power and authority in society, and the agreements and compromises they reach regarding the directions in which society should be steered. The value attached to particular bodies of knowledge and types of skill is always changing, as individuals and groups change their minds about what they need, what will work, and whose claims to expertise they can trust.

In relation to technology a concept commonly used is obsolescence: a given skill, technique, or machine is obsolete when it has lost its purpose, when it has been replaced by better or more useful alternatives. When this happens the masters of the skills and techniques or the proprietors of the machines lose social status and influence as well as their capacity to make a living. For example, in traditional Malay societies metal-working was a highly skilled profession, and making the *keris* or sword was seen as requiring spiritual as well as manual competencies. Social and economic change means that there is no longer any demand for the largely ceremonial *keris*, with the result that the very sophisticated knowledge its manufacture entails is close to extinction.[28] In this case the skills have not been replaced with anything better or technically superior; it is just that the product itself has lost its purpose, other than the attraction it holds for collectors or tourists.

Traditional systems of medical knowledge also experience obsolescence, losing out to Western or scientific medicine in terms of perceived efficacy or reliability. In this context, however, one system of knowledge often does not so much replace the other as complement it, despite apparent conflicts between them in theory and practice. In health matters, people like to hedge their bets: if one system does not work, they will try another. Traditional knowledge may be used in some contexts, scientific medicine in others. Even individual practitioners may combine methods of treatment.[29]

The idea of obsolescence can be extended beyond the sphere of technology. We may use the term 'epistemic obsolescence' to refer to judgments that bodies of knowledge, ways of understanding, complete knowledge systems have lost their value. Whether in fact revolutions in knowing and understanding are ever as sweeping as all that is in a sense neither here nor there. What matters is that judgments or assertions to this effect are very common. They are made continually in cross-cultural contexts, where one culture claims to be more advanced or civilised than another. But they are also common within cultures, as when a group claims new religious insight or access to new methods of acquiring knowledge.

In Western scientific and scholarly circles they are an everyday feature of the argument and rhetoric of the advancement of knowledge. In the sciences and the humanities, theories are rendered obsolete by competing theories that are sometimes more high-powered, sometimes are only more fashionably expressed, or derive from a source with higher status. Schools of interpretation vie with each other. Academic disciplines compete for influence and prestige. Whether the differences are substantial or ephemeral, the aspiration for dominance will be just as strong.

In the humanities and the social sciences genuine obsolescence may be far less common than is supposed. While the knowledge they yield is cumulative, it does not mean that what lies near the bottom of the heap can be ignored. It is more useful to see the expansion of knowledge as occurring horizontally rather than vertically. When we adopt a new perspective on experience—whether cultural, historical, theoretical, or disciplinary—the perspective has value because it complements other perspectives and forces us to reconsider them. It does not render them obsolete. Rather, it reminds us that all seeing is seeing in perspective, and that seeing something in its entirety requires us to fit perspectives together. It is impossible to achieve a 'view from nowhere'.[30] One of the benefits of studying the many cultures and long history of the Asian region is that it forces us to come to terms with the narrowness of our horizons, to acknowledge that our own understanding of the world is the product of a particular location in time and culture, a sandbank formed from the sediment of the river, soon to be eroded and deposited elsewhere.

One of the characteristics of our particular sandbank seems to be a growing fascination with the river itself, that is, with the process of change and what change implies for knowledge, the need to understand knowledge formation in the same dynamic terms as reality itself. This is forcing the realisation that the idea of bridge-building is overly ambitious and inappropriate, that what we really need is a good raft that will enable us to reach other sandbanks without resisting the current, and from time to time to tie up with other rafts.

Preoccupation with understanding change is not new, as the ancient Greek and Chinese philosophers Herakleitos and Zhuangzi would point out. In an era of globalisation and accelerating change, however, it is essential. In the simplest terms, we have to understand that the patterns we see in experience are the ones we have been taught to see, and that the protocols of knowledge are like other customs of the tribe: they are maintained by social agreement, and we ignore them at our peril. Yet the patterns we are taught to see change over time, and as we stand further back they may appear differently because of what we see around them. As a result of our own experience of change and greater familiarity with the experiences of others, we begin to look for new patterns. That is part of what this study has tried to do.

# Conclusion

What conclusion can one come to about contemporary Asia? Is it possible to offer more than a few platitudes about cultural difference, globalisation, and change, while hoping that the value of the exercise has been in the detail of the description? Certainly appreciating the rich variety of the Asian region and the scale and complexity of the changes taking place there is valuable in itself and requires no further justification. Nonetheless there are some other important lessons to be learnt from it, if we can remain open to them.

Focusing on change and describing it in detail is useful enough. But it becomes much more useful if we alert ourselves to the assumptions contained in the terminology used to describe it. One of the most pervasive assumptions is the idea that change is only temporary, an aberration, a brief lapse as we pass from one state to another. A quick search of the library catalogue shows that there are literally thousands of books with the phrase 'in transition' in the title, all apparently reassuring us that the particular changes they describe will soon be over, and therefore are not a cause for alarm. Perhaps this is a modern expression of the traditional philosophical prejudice that only what is changeless is real.

We think in terms of dichotomies such as *tradition* and *modernity*, as if they represent stable states with little in between. Of the many difficulties surrounding the terms 'developed' and 'developing', as applied to nations and economies, perhaps the greatest is the belief or expectation generated that development is a brief transition from an undeveloped state to a developed one, and that the developed state, once attained, is forever. But if we conceive development as a continuing process rather than a passing phase, we start to adopt a different attitude towards, for example, the sorts of sacrifices commonly demanded and made for its sake. The implicit idea that once societies have achieved modernity—become developed—they will all somehow be the same and equal, seems rather silly when it is brought out into the open.

Expressions such as 'development', 'globalisation', and 'modernisation' draw attention to the fact that similar forces are at work in many countries, which is useful. Unfortunately, all too often they do little more than restate nineteenth-century ideas of evolution and progress, without openly admitting it. They are testimony to the remarkable resilience and pervasiveness of assumptions about the superiority of the

West. To be sure, these things are now expressed more subtly than formerly. Nevertheless they persist, in intellectual understanding as well as in popular culture.

The concept of convergence, we have seen, has been used explicitly in relation to a number of spheres, such as law, the family, and technology. In practice, it too is a euphemism for Westernisation. Anyway, no one seems to be suggesting that European countries are revising their legal codes to make them more like Chinese codes, or that US families are adopting stem and joint household structures like those of Japan and India.

I wonder whether within convergence theory somewhere there lurks the ultimate ethnocentric illusion. It starts with the assumption that societies initially are a long way apart. Some are incapable of rational thought, technological innovation, or economic organisation. Fortunately, however, with the help and guidance of the West, they are able to develop, to acquire civilised ways of thinking and behaving. The West is twice exalted: first for being the most advanced, then again for raising others to its own level. 'Really, these Asiatics, Africans, and what have you. They're quite like us now. Quite enlightened and capable.' But could it not be, in fact, that 'they' have been like 'us' all along, only it has taken us a long time to realise it? Convergence has been a perspectival illusion, a trick of the light: we thought we were raising them up, yet they were actually standing beside us all the time.[1] It brings to mind a passage from *Don Quixote* in which the absurd knight-errant comments to his long-suffering squire Sancho Panza that he, Sancho, is becoming less stupid and more sensible. To this Sancho replies, with his usual shrewdness, that it must be the result of his association with Don Quixote: 'I am like a piece of land that of itself is dry and barren, but if you scatter manure over it and cultivate it, it will bear good fruit. By this I mean that your Grace's conversation is the manure that has been cast upon the barren land of my dry wit.'[2] This would be an apt comment on theories of convergence and development.

To some this may seem far too negative. After all, have not many good things been achieved through development? Are not many aspects of modernity highly desirable? Surely the idea of progress is not just an illusion.

Of course many things *have* been achieved, though their cost is often underestimated. As long as the discussion relates to specific changes, terms such as 'modernisation' and 'development' may make perfectly good sense. Clean water, better health, opportunities for personal development through meaningful work or education: these things make sense however they are expressed. I agree, too, that it is possible to talk sensibly about progress, in relation to the satisfaction of particular human needs and purposes. But often it is easier to talk nonsense, particularly when development is turned into a generalised state largely emptied of content, when whole societies and cultures (rather than specific practices and institutions), are labelled 'primitive' or 'advanced'. Nor do I mean to imply that only those from Western societies are guilty of crude and unreflecting ethnocentrism. Indeed, this is yet another proof of the underlying sameness and equality of humanity: we all share a marvellous capacity for bigotry.

There is one other sphere in which the idea of convergence is widely used, and it is here that the concept becomes most potent: in relation to knowledge.[3] It is claimed that, as knowledge becomes truly objective or value-free, people everywhere will learn to see the world from the same point of view, that which is, in effect, 'the view from nowhere'. All knowledge systems will converge and become one. Here too convergence is seen as tending towards Western norms, this time the dominant

Western concept of scientific knowledge and the proper methods and criteria for advancing it. In due course, science will yield a unified understanding of reality that will be accessible to and shared by all ... well, all those who understand the standardised methodologies and are able to speak English, anyway.

In many respects knowledge is cumulative, though in branches of learning such as the social sciences and humanities its cumulative aspect is much less distinct or certain than in others. It would seem perverse to deny that progress in understanding is possible. To realise that our particular view of things is but one view, and that there are others that cast them in a different light, must amount to progress if it leads to some attempt to reconcile or integrate the various views in question.

However, there is a difference between identifying commonalities and insisting on the reduction of other perspectives to one's own. To argue that a particular cultural perspective offers the only proper understanding, while disregarding others, is chauvinistic. To claim that one particular branch of learning, such as economics or mathematics, forms the foundation on which all other knowledge rests and to which it may be reduced, is obtuse. To insist that all bodies of knowledge must be fully translatable, and if truly knowledge they must be convertible to Western or international science, is woefully dogmatic. Generation of knowledge is a social undertaking. It requires, among other things, some basic social skills, including the ability and willingness to listen to others, to treat what they have to say seriously, with respect. Reciprocity is as essential in epistemological dealings as in social ones.

My starting point was the assumption that people are much the same everywhere, with the same basic human needs and aspirations. It is a difficult proposition to prove, but useful as a working hypothesis. Of course it does not mean that differences do not matter. At this point I can draw on the religious authority of the Dalai Lama: 'if we consider humanity as a whole we can of course find numerous factors that divide us, such as religious faith, customs, language, and culture. Although such diversity is also a source of enrichment for all of us we must not overemphasise it to the detriment of the whole of humanity, or we risk encountering numerous useless problems.'[4]

Paradoxically, recognition of similarity at one level makes it easier to perceive differences at another, to see them clearly and sharply, in a non-judgmental way.

Studying the societies of contemporary Asia forces us to reconsider the assumptions underlying the way we think about society and the forces underlying social change. It does this whether we come from a Western intellectual tradition or an Eastern one. Grand generalisations about the East and the West; whole societies characterised and evaluated by reference to a few core values; cultures and traditions conceived as fixed entities; lofty assertions about progress and the development of nations ... The region we call Asia cannot be understood in such terms, and neither can the West. It is necessary to reorient ourselves: to accept change as the only reality; to recognise that a variety of ways of conceptualising change may enhance rather than undermine our understanding of it; to appreciate that, although societies all face much the same issues and problems, it may be appropriate to respond in different ways. These things require us to reorient ourselves, not once but continuously. In this sense, the book's title may be read as an exhortation as well as a statement of its contents. And if we are going to continue reorienting ourselves, it may be best not to sink too many theoretical piles. In any case, reorienting is easier to do on a raft than on a bridge.

# NOTES

**Introduction**

1 R. Murphey, *A History of Asia*, HarperCollins, New York, 1992, 5.

2 On historical interaction, see, for example, D. F. Lach, *Asia in the Making of Europe*, 3 vols, University of Chicago Press, Chicago, 1965–93; K. N. Chaudhuri, *Asia Before Europe: Economy and Civilisation of the Indian Ocean From the Rise of Islam to 1750*, Cambridge University Press, Cambridge, 1990; A. Pacey, *Technology in World Civilization*, Blackwell, Oxford, 1990; J. H. Bentley, *Old World Encounters: Cross-Cultural Exchanges in Pre-Modern Times*, Oxford University Press, Oxford, 1993; and F. Fernández-Armesto, *Millenium: A History of the Last Thousand Years*, Bantam Press, London, 1995.

3 In regard to the changing concept of Europe see J. van der Dussen and K. Wilson, eds, *The History of the Idea of Europe*, Routledge, London, 1995. Changing ideas of territories and boundaries in Europe and Asia are discussed in C. Grundy-Warr, *Eurasia: World Boundaries Volume 3*, Routledge, London, 1994.

4 For a useful discussion of academic disciplines and how they affect the dynamics of knowledge generation see T. Becher, *Academic Tribes and Territories: Intellectual Enquiry and the Cultures of Disciplines*, The Society for Research into Higher Education and Open University Press, Bristol, Pennsylvania, and Milton Keynes, 1989; E. Messer-Davidow, D. Shumway and D. Sylval, *Knowledges: Historical and Critical Perspectives on Disciplinarity*, University Press of Virginia, Charlottesville, 1993; and A. D. Abbott, *Chaos of Disciplines*, University of Chicago Press, Chicago, 2001.

5 On 'foundationalism', see S. C. Hetherington, *Knowledge Puzzles: An Introduction to Epistemology*, Westview Press, Boulder, Colorado, 1996; S. Crook, *Modern Radicalism and Its Aftermath: Foundationalism and Anti-Foundationalism in Radical Social Theory*, Routledge, London, 1991; and S. Seidman, *Contested Knowledge: Social Theory in the Postmodern Era*, Blackwell, Oxford, 1994.

6 P. Davies, *Superforce: The Search for a Grand Unified Theory of Nature*, Penguin, Ringwood, Victoria, 1995; Q. Skinner, ed., *The Return of the Grand Theory in the Human Sciences*, Cambridge University Press, Cambridge, 1985; T. E. Cook, *The Rise and Fall of Regimes: Toward a Grand Theory of Politics*, P. Lang, New York, 2000.

7 G. S. Snooks, *The Dynamic Society: Exploring the Sources of Global Change*, Routledge, London, 1996, 13.

8 See, for example, M. Max-Neef et al., *Human-Scale Development*, Apex Press, London, 1991; L. Doyal and I. Gough, *A Theory of Need*, Macmillan, London, 1991; M. Nussbaum and A. Sen, *The Quality of Life*, Clarendon Press, Oxford, 1993; and A. Sen, *Development as Freedom*, Oxford University Press, New York, 1999.

9 S. C. Dube, *Modernization and Development: The Search For Alternative Paradigms*, United Nations University and Zed Books, Tokyo and London, 1988, 53–61.

10 B. Moore Jnr, *Injustice: The Social Bases of Obedience and Revolt*, M. E. Sharpe, White Plains, New York, 1978, ch. 1.

11 A. Heller, 'A Theory of Needs Revisited', *Thesis Eleven*, no. 35, 1993, 18–35.

## Chapter 1 Globalisation and Insulation in Asia

1 The catalogue of the National Library of Australia lists 260 books published between 1989 and 2001 with the word 'globalisation' in the title. Probably no fewer treat the topic but do not include the word in their title. The latter include, for example, critical and polemical works such as J. Brecher and T. Costello, *Global Village or Global Pillage: Economic Reconstruction from the Bottom Up*, South End Press, Boston, 1994; W. Greider, *One World, Ready or Not: The Manic Logic of Global Capitalism*, Simon and Schuster, New York, 1997; J. Gray, *False Dawn: The Delusions of Global Capitalism*, Free Press, New York, 1998; T. L. Friedman, *The Lexus and the Olive*, 2nd edn, HarperCollins, London, 2000; and N. Hertz, *The Silent Takeover: Global Capitalism and the Death of Democracy*, William Heineman, London, 2001. Journal articles on globalisation run to the thousands.

2 R. Murphey, *A History of Asia*, provides more detail in an easily digestible form.

3 P. Sieghart, *The International Law of Human Rights*, Oxford University Press, Oxford, 1983, 11–17, comments on the centrality of ideas of limited national sovereignty for human rights law, as does Inoue Tatsuo, 'Liberal Democracy and Asian Orientalism', in J. Bauer and D. Bell, eds, *The East Asian Challenge for Human Rights*, Cambridge University Press, Cambridge, 1999, 27–59. Useful material on the topic is assembled by H. Steiner and P. Alston, eds, *International Human Rights in Context: Law, Politics, Morals*, Oxford University Press, New York, 1996, 148–65. For extended discussion, see J. A. Camelleri and J. Falk, *End of Sovereignty? The Politics of a Shrinking and Fragmenting World*, Edward Elgar, Aldershot, 1992.

4 L. W. Beer, 'Introduction', in L. W. Beer, ed., *Constitutional Systems in Late Twentieth Century Asia*, University of Washington Press, Seattle, 1992, 1, identifies as one of the outstanding aspects of postwar change the 'convergence in the world towards relatively few living traditions of modern law, and the beginnings of mutual comprehension among legal scholars and practitioners of these different traditions'. For general discussion of legal issues arising from globalisation, see W. Twining, *Globalisation and Legal Theory*, Butterworths, London, 2000.

5 United Nations, Office of the High Commissioner for Human Rights, *International Human Rights Instruments*, http://www.unhchr.ch/html/intlist.htm, accessed 7 September 2001.

6 Critical study of the world economic system is associated above all with the work of Immanuel Wallerstein. See, for example, I. Wallerstein, *The Modern World-System*, Academic Press, New York, 1974; T. K. Hopkins and I. Wallerstein, *World-System Analysis: Theory and Methodology*, Sage Publications, Beverly Hills, California, 1982; and T. K. Hopkins and I. Wallerstein, *The Age of Transition: Trajectory of the World-System 1945–2025*, Atlantic Highlands, London, 1996. On dependency theory see R. A. Packenham, *The Dependency Movement: Scholarship and Politics in Development Studies*, Harvard University Press, Cambridge, Massachusetts, 1992.

7 The World Bank, International Monetary Fund and Asian Development Bank publish numerous reports and papers on their policies and activities. Their websites are a useful starting point for information. See the World Bank at http://www.worldbank.org/; the International Monetary Fund at http://www.imf.org/; and the Asian Development Bank at http://www.adb.org/.

8 Information on population figures and trends is provided in regular United Nations publications such as the *Demographic Yearbook*, *State of the World Population* and *World Population Prospects*, all available through the United Nations website at http://www.un.org/.

9 The expression 'global village' comes from M. McLuhan, *Understanding Media: The Extensions of Man*, Routledge & Kegan Paul, London, 1964, rpt. ARK Paperbacks, London, 1987. On electronic colonialism, see T. L. McPhail, *Electronic Colonialism: The Future of International Broadcasting and Communication*, 2nd edn, Sage Publications, Newbury Park, California, 1987. On cultural imperialism, see J. Tomlinson, *Cultural Imperialism: A Critical Introduction*, Pinter,

London, 1991; and P. Toynbee, 'Who's Afraid of Global Culture?', in W. Hutton and A. Giddens, eds, *Global Capitalism*, The New Press, New York, 2000.

10 In 1997 the Organisation for Economic Cooperation and Development (OECD) Committee for Scientific and Technological Policy developed the concept of a 'global research village', as well as making globalisation of industrial technological development a dominant concern. In collaboration with the Korean government it convened a major conference on internationalisation of science and technology in Seoul in October 1997, and another in Amsterdam in December 2000. See also OECD, *Science, Technology and Industry Outlook 2000*, OECD, Paris, 2000. The OECD website, at http://www.oecd.org/, is also a handy source of information.

11 On delinking, see S. Amin, *Delinking: Towards a Polycentric World*, Zed Books, London, 1990; on localisation see the World Bank, 'World Bank Sees "Localization" As Major New Trend In 21st Century', http://www.worldbank.org/html/extdr/extme/032.htm (accessed 7 September 2000).

12 Useful yearly overviews of issues relating to indigenous minorities are provided by the International Work Group on Indigenous Affairs, *The Indigenous World*. Also useful are the reports of the Minority Rights Group, London.

13 Lively essays along these lines are gathered together in W. Sachs, ed., *The Development Dictionary: A Guide to Knowledge as Power*, Zed Books, London, 1992.

14 L. Kenadi, *Revival of Buddhism in Modern India: The Role of B. R. Ambedkar and the Dalai Lama XIV*, Ashish Publishing House, New Delhi, 1995.

15 E. Hobsbawm, 'Introduction: The Invention of Tradition', in E. Hobsbawm and T. Ranger, eds, *The Invention of Tradition*, Cambridge University Press, Cambridge, 1983; 'Cambodia Looks at Becoming Giant Theme Park', *Canberra Times*, 7 August 1995.

16 Lu Xun, 'Random Thoughts, 35', in *Selected Works of Lu Hsun*, 5 vols, trans. Yang Hsien-yi and G. Yang, Foreign Languages Press, Beijing, 1956, vol. 2, 28–9.

17 A. Agrawal, 'Dismantling the Divide Between Indigenous and Scientific Knowledge', *Development and Change*, vol. 26, no. 3, July 1995, 413–39.

18 V. Shiva, *Monocultures of the Mind: Perspectives on Biodiversity and Biotechnology*, Zed Books and Third World Network, London and Penang, 1993, 60.

## Chapter 2 State, Society, Individual

1 E. Gellner, *Thought and Change*, Weidenfeld and Nicolson, London, 1964, 169; *Nations and Nationalism*, Blackwell, Oxford, 1983, 7; B. Anderson, *Imagined Communities: Reflections on the Origin and Spread of Nationalism*, Verso, London, 1983, 6.

2 See L. K. Fee and A. Rajah, 'The Ethnic Mosaic', in G. Evans, ed., *Asia's Cultural Mosaic*, Prentice-Hall, New York, 1993, 245–7.

3 On Ibn Battuta see R. E. Dunn, *The Adventures of Ibn Battuta: A Muslim Traveler of the 14th Century*, University of California Press, Berkeley, 1986.

4 C. Geertz, 'The Impact of the Concept of Culture on the Concept of Man', *The Interpretation of Cultures*, Basic Books, New York, 1973.

5 On anthropological interpretations of the concept of culture see R. M. Keesing, 'Theories of Culture', *Annual Review of Anthropology*, vol. 3, 1974, 73–94.

6 C. A. Moore, ed., *The Indian Mind: Essentials of Indian Philosophy and Culture*, *The Chinese Mind: Essentials of Chinese Philosophy and Culture*, and *The Japanese Mind: Essentials of Japanese Philosophy and Culture*, University of Hawaii Press, Honolulu, 1967.

7 W. Goodenough, *Culture, Language and Society*, Addison-Wesley, Reading, Massachusetts, 1972.

8 Nietzsche's epigram comes from *Dawn* (1881), trans. W. Kaufmann, *The Portable Nietzsche*, Viking, New York, 1954, 76. On the links between rules, reciprocity, social inequality and justice, see especially Moore, *Injustice*, ch. 1; F. de Waal, *Good Natured: The Origins of Right and Wrong in Humans and Other Animals*, Harvard University Press, Cambridge, Massachusetts, 1996; and J. S. Scott, *The Moral Economy of the Peasant*, Yale University Press, New Haven, 1976, *Weapons of the Weak*, Yale University Press, New Haven, 1985, and 'The Moral Economy as an Argument and a Fight', *Kajian Malaysia*, vol. 10, no. 1, June 1992, 1–19.

9 M. Gittinger, *Splendid Symbols: Textiles and Tradition in Indonesia*, The Textile Museum, Washington DC, 1979, quotes an observation by anthropologist James Fox: 'Designs often say what their owners can't'.

10 F. Nietzsche, *The Genealogy of Morals*, trans. F. Golffing, Doubleday, Garden City, New York, 1956, 160–2; Confucius, *The Analects*, trans. D. C. Lau, Penguin, Harmondsworth, 1979. Lau discusses the term *junzi* in his introduction, 13–17.

11 On footbinding see H. S. Levy, *Chinese Footbinding: The History of a Curious Erotic Custom*, W. Rawls, New York, 1966; Wang Ping, *Aching for Beauty: Footbinding in China*, University of Minnesota Press, Minneapolis, 2000.

12 N. Abercrombie, S. Hill and B. S. Turner, *The Dominant Ideology Thesis*, Allen & Unwin, London, 1980.

13 Murphey, *A History of Asia*, provides a useful introduction to the major religious traditions and their historical contexts.

14 See, for example, T. P. Day, *Great and Little Tradition in Theravada Buddhist Studies*, Edwin Mellen Press, Lewiston, New York, 1988.

15 On religion and state authority in Asia, see C. F. Keyes, H. Hardacre and L. Kendall, 'Contested Visions of Community in East and Southeast Asia', in C. F. Keyes, L. Kendall and H. Hardacre, *Asian Visions of Authority: Religion and the Modern States of East and Southeast Asia*, University of Hawaii Press, Honolulu, 1994, 1–16.

16 On the 1997 Java riots, see J. McBeth and M. Cohen, 'Tinderbox', *Far Eastern Economic Review*, 9 January 1997, 14–15; L. Williams, 'Muslim Rampage Tears Indonesia Apart', *Sydney Morning Herald*, 1 February 1997; and G. van Klinken, 'Tinder-box or Conspiracy?', *Inside Indonesia*, no. 50, April–June 1997, 6–8. A powerful personal account of caste violence in India is provided by Phoolan Devi, with M-T. Cuny and P. Rambali, *I, Phoolan Devi: The Autobiography of India's Bandit Queen*, Little, Brown & Co., London, 1996; see also V. Kannibiran and K. Kannibiran, 'Caste and Gender: Understanding the Dynamics of Power and Violence', *Economic and Political Weekly*, 14 September 1991, 2130–3; and L. Stone and C. James, 'Dowry, Brideburning, and Female Power in India', *Women's Studies International Forum*, vol. 18, no. 2, March–April 1995. On Taslima Nasreen, see S. Kamaluddin, 'Fundamental Problem: Religious Right Pushes for Blasphemy Law', *Far Eastern Economic Review*, 18 August 1994, 23; and M. Rashiduzzaman, 'The Liberals and the Religious Right in Bangladesh', *Asian Survey*, vol. 34, no. 11, November 1994, 974–90.

17 K. Rafferty, 'Quake Hits Myth of Classless Japan', *Sydney Morning Herald*, 28 January 1995.

18 This position was argued, for example, by Gandhi, who compared the social role of the outcaste bhangi (sweeper), with that of the brahmin: 'The Brahman's duty is to look after the sanitation of the soul, the bhangi's that of the body of society'. See V. Prashad, 'The Untouchable Question', *Economic and Political Weekly*, 2 March 1996, 557. It has been argued that the caste system became increasingly rigid over time, partly as a result of British colonialism, and that in earlier times there was opportunity for caste mobility on a group basis through a process known as Sanskritisation. This involved groups taking on, on their own initiative, the social and political roles, and ritual observances, of a higher caste. See M. N. Srinivas, *The Cohesive Role of Sanskritization and Other Essays*, Oxford University Press, Delhi, 1989.

19 A. C. Graham, *Yin–Yang and the Nature of Correlative Thinking* (IEAP Occasional Paper and Monograph Series no. 6), Institute of East Asian Philosophies, National University of Singapore, Singapore, 1986.

20 See M. Kishwar and R. Virata, eds, *In Search of Answers: Indian Women's Voices from Manushi*, Zed Books, London, 1984; papers from International Symposium on the Girl Child in Asia: A Neglected Minority, Kathmandu, 13 December 1990, in *Asia-Pacific Journal of Public Health*, vol. 14, no. 4, 1990; L. Devasia and V. V. Devasia, eds, *Girl Child in India*, Ashish, New Delhi, 1991; and B. D. Miller, *The Endangered Sex: Neglect of Female Children in Rural North India*, Cornell University Press, Ithaca, New York, 1991.

21 C. B. Park and N-H. Cho, 'Consequences of Son Preference in a Low-Fertility Society: Imbalance of the Sex Ratio at Birth in Korea', *Population and Development Review*, vol. 21, no. 1, March 1995, 59–84.

22 O. Yasuaki, 'Interplay Between Human Rights Activities and Legal Standards of Human Rights: a Case Study of the Korean Minority in Japan', *Cornell International Law Journal*, vol. 25, no. 3, Symposium 1992, 515–40.

23 United Nations Development Program, *Human Development Report 1996*, Oxford University Press, New York, 1996, 60.

24 This definition of civil disobedience follows P. Harris, *Civil Disobedience*, University Press of America, Lanham MD, 1989, 14.

25 An account of a Vietnamese case of self-immolation is provided by Sister Chan Khong (personal name Cao Ngoc Phuong), *Learning True Love*, Parallax Press, Berkeley, 1993, and a recent Tibetan case is discussed by Jamyang Norbu, 'Rite of Freedom: The Life and Sacrifice of Thupten Ngodup', *Tibetan Review*, vol. 33 no. 8, August 1998, 15–19. For general discussion, see K. Goldstein-Kyaga, ed., *Nonviolence in Asia: The Art of Dying or the Road to Change?*, Center of Pacific Asia Studies, Stockholm University, Stockholm, 1999.

26 M. K. Gandhi, *An Autobiography: The Story of My Experiments With Truth*, Beacon Press, Boston, 1957, 414.

27 On the Mandate of Heaven, see T'ang Chün-I, 'The T'ien Ming [Heavenly Ordinance] in Pre-Ch'in China', *Philosophy East and West*, vol. 11, no. 4, January 1962, 195–218.

28 For example, the philosopher Han Fei (died 233 BCE) advised rulers that 'one should use laws to govern the state, disposing of all matters on their basis alone'. See *Basic Works of Han Fei Tzu*, trans. B. Watson, Columbia University Press, New York, 1964, 28.

29 Beer, 'Introduction'; A. P. Blaustein and G. H. Flanz, eds, *Constitutions of the Countries of the World*, 17 vols, Oceana Publications, Dobbs Ferry, New York, permanent edn.

30 On the origin of the term 'West-stricken' or 'Westoxicated' (*gharbzadegi*), see V. M. Moghadam, 'Rhetorics and Rights of Identity in Islamic Movements', *Journal of World History*, vol. 4, no. 2, 1993, 245–6; and S. Farman Farmaian, *Daughter of Persia*, Corgi, London, 1993, 357.

31 Some of Weber's writings on bureaucracy and modern society are gathered together in S. Andreski, ed., *Max Weber on Capitalism, Bureaucracy, and Religion: A Selection of Texts*, Allen & Unwin, London, 1983.

32 Li Yinke, 'Village Culture', *Social Sciences in China*, vol. 15, no. 4, Winter 1994, 56–64; P. Guinness, 'Local Culture and Society', in H. Hill, ed., *Indonesia's New Order*, Allen & Unwin, St Leonards, NSW, 1994, 267–304.

33 *Daode jing*, traditionally attributed to Laozi (?sixth century BCE). See D. C. Lau, trans. *Lao Tzu: Tao Te Ching*, Penguin, Harmondsworth, 1963, ch. 17.

34 J. Gray, 'From Post-Communism to Civil Society: the Re-emergence of History and the Decline of the Western Model', *Social Philosophy and Policy*, vol. 10, no. 2, Summer 1993, 26–50.

## Chapter 3 Human Rights

1 For the text of the Proclamation of Tehran and the Declaration on the Right to Development, see W. E. Langley, *Human Rights: Sixty Major Global Instruments Introduced, Reprinted and Indexed*, McFarland & Co., Jefferson, North Carolina, 1992; and I. Brownlie, ed., *Basic Documents on Human Rights*, 3rd edn, Oxford University Press, New York, 1992. The links between human rights and development are discussed at length by A. Sen, *Development as Freedom*, Oxford University Press, Oxford, 1999; and in United Nations Development Program, *Human Development Report 2000*, Oxford University Press, New York, 2000. On changing attitudes towards group rights and their relation to individual rights, see, for example, W. F. Felice, *Taking Suffering Seriously: The Importance of Collective Human Rights*, State University of New York Press, Albany, New York, 1996; and D. A. Bell, 'The East Asian Challenge to Human Rights: Reflections on an East West Dialogue', *Human Rights Quarterly*, vol. 18, no. 3, 1996, 641–67.

2 For recent overviews of human rights violations, see Amnesty International, *Report 2001*, http://web.amnesty.org/web/ar2001.nsf/; and Human Rights Watch, *World Report 2001*, http://www.hrw.org/wr2k1/ (both accessed 10 August 2001). The construction of a Human Rights Index that gave all countries a score and rank order was attempted by C. Humana, *Human Rights World Guide*, Oxford University Press, New York, 1992.

3 Democracy campaigner Aung San Suu Kyi emphasises the army's role in establishing an independent Burma, while quoting her father Aung San's comment that 'the armed forces are meant for this nation and this people' and must retain the people's honour and respect. See Aung San Suu Kyi, 'Speech to a Mass Rally at the Shwedagon Pagoda', *Freedom From Fear and Other Writings*, 2nd edn, Penguin, Harmondsworth, 1995, 201. On the militarisation of Burmese society see F. K. Lehman, ed., *Military Rule in Burma Since 1962: A Kaleidoscope of Views*, Maruzen, Singapore, 1981; M. Smith, *Burma: Insurgency and the Politics of Ethnicity*, Zed Books, London, 1991; and B. Lintner, *Burma in Revolt: Opium and Insurgency Since 1948*, Westview Press, Boulder, Colorado, 1994.

4 On labour rights issues in Indonesia, see B. Waters, 'The Tragedy of Marsinah: Industrialisation and Workers' Rights', *Inside Indonesia*, no. 36, September 1993, 12–13; J. McBeth, 'Lost labour, lost reform', *Far Eastern Review*, 15 March 2001, 22–25; D. Djalal, 'Showdown at the Factory', *Far Eastern Economic Review*, 10 January 2002, 24–25; C. Manning, *Indonesian Labour in Transition: An East Asian Success Story?*, Cambridge University Press, Cambridge, 1998, and 'Labour Market Adjustment to Indonesia's Economic Crisis: Context, Trends and Implications', *Bulletin of Indonesian Economic Studies*, vol. 36 no. 1, April 2000, 105–36; S. Dhanini and I. Islam, 'Labour Market Adjustment to Indonesia's Economic Crisis: A Comment', *Bulletin of Indonesian Economic Studies*, vol. 37 no. 1, April 2001, 113–16.

5 United Nations, *Teaching Human Rights*, UN Publication, sales no. 63 I, 34, 1958, 1. On the particular problems arising from the private sphere see A. Clapham, *Human Rights in the Private Sphere*, Clarendon Press, Oxford, 1993.

6 Further information on the human rights treaties ratified by Asian nations, and also on human-rights-related provisions in their constitutions, is provided by F. de Varennes, ed., *Asia-Pacific Human Rights Documents and Resources*, Volume 2, Kluwer Law International, The Hague, 2000.

7 Material relating to the Bangkok and Vienna conferences of 1993 is included in appendices to J. T. H. Tang, ed., *Human Rights and International Relations in the Asia Pacific Region*, Pinter, London, 1995. The articles in Tang's book have influenced the ideas developed in this chapter.

8 S. Lukes, 'Five Fables About Human Rights', *Dissent*, Fall 1993, 427–37; J. Donnelly, *Universal Human Rights in Theory and Practice*, Cornell University Press, Ithaca, New York, 1989, 26; E. Kamenka, 'Human Rights, Peoples' Rights', in J. Crawford, ed., *The Rights of Peoples*, Oxford University Press, New York, 1988, 127.

9 Cited by Moore, *Injustice*, 28–9. On this issue, see particularly A. A. An-Na'im, 'Towards a Cross-Cultural Approach to Defining International Standards of Human Rights: The Meaning of Cruel, Inhuman or Degrading Treatment or Punishment', in A. A. An-Na'im, ed., *Human Rights in Cross-Cultural Perspective*, University of Pennsylvania Press, Philadelphia, 1992, 19–43.

10 On Michael Fay's case see 'Singapore and the Culture of Caning', editorial, *Sydney Morning Herald*, 7 May 1994; and F. Ching, 'Fay Case: Collision of Values', *Far Eastern Economic Review*, 5 May 1994, 38.

11 See, for example, D. J. Sullivan, 'Gender Equality and Religious Freedom: Towards a Framework for Conflict Resolution', *New York University Journal of International Law and Politics*, vol. 24, no. 2, 1992, 795–856; and I. Bloom, J. P. Martin and W. L. Proudfoot, eds, *Religious Diversity and Human Rights*, Columbia University Press, New York, 1996.

12 Aung San Suu Kyi, 'In Quest of Democracy', *Freedom From Fear and Other Writings*, 175.

13 Tran Quang Co, 'Rights and Values', *Far Eastern Economic Review*, 4 August 1994, 17.

14 His Holiness the Dalai Lama XIV, *Beyond Dogma: Dialogues and Discourses*, trans. A. Anderson, North Atlantic Books, Berkeley, 1996, 82–90; Aung San Suu Kyi, 'In Quest of Democracy', 169–73.

15 Abul A'la Mawdudi, *Human Rights in Islam*, 2nd edn, The Islamic Foundation, Leicester, 1980, 10.

16 Du Gangjian and Song Gang, 'Relating Human Rights to Chinese Culture: The Four Paths of the Confucian Analects and the Four Principles of a New Theory of Benevolence', in M. C. Davis, ed., *Human Rights and Chinese Values: Legal, Philosophical and Political Perspectives*, Oxford University Press, Hong Kong, 1995, 35–56; W. T. de Bary and Tu Weiming, eds, *Confucianism and Human Rights*, Columbia University Press, New York, 1998; J. Chan, 'A Confucian Perspective

on Human Rights for Contemporary China', in J. Bauer and D. Bell, eds, *The East Asian Challenge for Human Rights*, Cambridge University Press, Cambridge, 1999, 212–37. For a critical study of the Singapore government's claim that its position regarding rights is based on Confucian values, see N. Englehart, 'Rights and Culture in the Asian Values Argument: The Rise and Fall of Confucian Ethics in Singapore', *Human Rights Quarterly*, vol. 22, no. 2, May 2000, 548–68.

17 J. Donnelly, 'Human Rights and Human Dignity: An Analytic Critique of Non-Western Conceptions of Human Rights', *American Political Science Review*, vol. 26, 1982, 301–16.

18 R. Howard, 'Cultural Absolutism and the Nostalgia for Community', *Human Rights Quarterly*, vol. 15, 1993, 337. The tendency to present Asian cultures as homogeneous and unchanging is criticised by Y. Ghai, 'Human Rights and Governance: The Asia Debate', *Australian Yearbook of International Law*, vol. 15, 1994, 1–34.

19 A. A. An-Na'im, 'Islam, Islamic Law and the Dilemma of Cultural Legitimacy for Universal Human Rights', in C. E. Welch and V. Leary, eds, *Asian Perspectives on Human Rights*, Westview Press, Boulder, Colorado, 1990; also An-Na'im, 'The Cultural Mediation of Human Rights: The Al-Arqam Case in Malaysia', in J. Bauer and D. Bell, eds, *The East Asian Challenge for Human Rights*, Cambridge University Press, Cambridge, 1999, 147–68.

20 United Nations, World Conference on Human Rights, Vienna, 14–25 June 1993, *Vienna Declaration and Programme of Action*, section 2, paragraph 38, http://www.unhchr.ch/huridocda.huridoca.nsf/(Symbol)/A.CONF.157.23.En?OpenDocument (accessed 10 August 2001).

## Chapter 4 Ethnic Minorities

1 On the number and location of ethnic minorities, see G. Ashworth, ed., *World Minorities*, and *World Minorities in the Eighties*, Quartermaine House, London, 1977 and 1978; J. Burger, *Report From the Frontier: The State of the World's Indigenous Peoples*, Zed Books, London, 1987; W. Clay, 'Looking Back to Go Forward: Predicting and Preventing Human Rights Violations', in S. Miller et al., *State of the Peoples: A Global Human Rights Report on Societies in Danger*, Beacon Press, Boston, 1993, 65–71; C. Nicholas and R. Singh, eds, *Indigenous Peoples of Asia: Many Peoples, One Struggle*, Asia Indigenous Peoples Pact, Bangkok, 1996; and D. Levinson, *Ethnic Groups Worldwide: A Ready Reference Handbook*, Oryx Press, Phoenix, Arizona, 1998. An interesting illustration of the different ways in which minorities may be defined is provided by R. Tapper, 'Ethnic Identities and Social Categories in Iran and Afghanistan', in E. Tonkin, M. McDonald and M. Chapman, eds, *History and Ethnicity*, Routledge, London, 1989.

2 R. M. Koentjaraningrat, *Introduction to the Peoples and Cultures of Indonesia and Malaysia*, Cummings, Menlo Park, California, 1975; H. Geertz, 'Indonesian Cultures and Communities', in R. T. McVey, ed., *Indonesia*, Southeast Asian Studies, Yale University, New Haven, 1963; K. Brogan, 'The Forgotten Cost of Counter-Insurgency in Aceh', *Inside Indonesia*, no. 49, January–March 1997, 2–4; L. Jones, 'Aceh's Year of Living Dangerously', *Inside Indonesia*, no. 49, January–March 1997, 5–7; P. Sulistiyanto, 'Whither Aceh?', *Third World Quarterly*, vol. 22, no. 3, 2001, 437–52; 'Megawati Grants Aceh Special Autonomy', *Canberra Times*, 14 August 2001; T. Kato, *Matriliny and Migration: Evolving Minangkabau Traditions in Indonesia*, Cornell University Press, Ithaca, New York, 1982.

3 G. Wijeyewardene, ed., *Ethnic Groups Across National Boundaries in Mainland Southeast Asia*, Institute of Southeast Asian Studies, Singapore, 1990; Y. Hayashi and Yang Guangyuan, eds, *Dynamics of Ethnic Cultures Across National Boundaries in Southwestern China and Mainland Southeast Asia: Relations, Societies and Languages*, Lanna Cultural Center, Rajabhat Institute, Chiang Mai, and Center for Southeast Asian Studies, Kyoto University, Kyoto, 2000.

4 A. Gray, 'The Indigenous Movement in Asia', in R. H. Barnes et al., eds, *Indigenous Peoples of Asia*, Association for Asian Studies, Ann Arbor, Michigan, 1995, 35–58. Details regarding the situation of particular minorities are provided by the International Work Group on Indigenous Affairs (IWGIA), *The Indigenous World* (annual), and reports of the Minority Rights Group. By the latter, see also *World Directory of Minorities*, Minority Rights Group International, London, 1997. On South-East Asia, a recent overview is provided by G. Clarke, 'From Ethnocide to Ethnodevelopment? Ethnic Minorities and Indigenous Peoples', *Third World Quarterly*, vol. 22, no. 3, 2001, 413–36.

5 On the Freeport mine, see J. McBeth, 'Company Under Siege: Mining Firm Freeport Indonesia Hits Back at Critics', *Far Eastern Economic Review*, 25 January 1996, 50–2; Elizabeth Pinckard, 'Indonesian Tribe Loses in its Latest Battle Against Freeport-McMoRan, Operator of the World's Largest Gold and Copper Mine', *Colorado Journal of International Environmental Law and Policy*, vol. 9, 1998, 141–45; A. Abrash, 'The Amungme, Kamoro and Freeport: How Indigenous Papuans have Resisted the World's Largest Copper and Gold Mine', *Cultural Survival Quarterly*, vol. 25 no. 1, 2001, 38–43.

6 *Jakarta Post*, 7 March 1994, cited by IWGIA, *The Indigenous World 1993–1994*, 107. This report is also the source for the details of Vietnam's transmigration program that follow.

7 'Seen as Nation-Builder, Indonesian Resettlement Program Scrapped', http://www.cnn.com/2000/ASIANOW/southeast/12/10/settlers...nightmare.ap/ (accessed 14 December 2000).

8 Quoted by H. Thompson, 'Malaysian Forest Policy in Borneo', *Journal of Contemporary Asia*, vol. 23, no. 4, 1993, 512.

9 B. D. Magenda, 'Ethnicity and State-Building in Indonesia', in R. Guidieri, F. Pellizzi and S. J. Tambiah, eds, *Ethnicity and Nations: Processes of Interethnic Relations in Latin America, Southeast Asia and the Pacific*, Rothko Chapel, Houston, Texas, 1988, 345–61. For the Tai myth, see S. Cholthira, 'A Comparative Study of Structure and Contradiction in the Austro-Asiatic System of the Thai–Yunnan Periphery', in Wijeyewardene, *Ethnic Groups Across National Boundaries in Mainland Southeast Asia*, 74–101.

10 On headhunting in South-East Asia, see J. Hoskins, ed., *Headhunting and the Social Imagination in Southeast Asia*, Stanford University Press, Stanford, California, 1996. On cannibalism, see W. Arens, *The Man-Eating Myth: Anthropology and Anthropophagy*, Oxford University Press, New York, 1979; and P. R. Sanday, *Divine Hunger: Cannibalism as a Cultural System*, Cambridge University Press, Cambridge, 1986.

11 G. Evans, 'Central Highlanders of Vietnam', in Barnes et al., *Indigenous Peoples of Asia*, 247–72.

12 On the movement of peoples in world history, see W. H. McNeill and R. S. Adams, eds, *Human Migration: Patterns and Policy*, Indiana University Press, Bloomington, 1978.

13 K. Quincey, *Hmong: History of a People*, Eastern Washington University Press, Cheney, Washington, 1988; S. Chan, *Hmong Means Free: Life in Laos and America*, Temple University Press, Philadelphia, 1994; N. Tapp, *The Hmong of China: Context, Agency, and the Imaginary*, Brill, Leiden, 2001.

14 C. Mackerras, *China's Minorities: Integration and Modernisation in the Twentieth Century*, Oxford University Press, Oxford, 1994.

15 Ashworth, *World Minorities*, 120–2; Pakistan Information.com, 'Pakistan Statistics', http://www.pakistaninformation.com/pakistanstats.html, accessed 10 April 2002. The figure is based on the proportion of Hindi speakers in the national population (2 per cent).

16 United Nations Development Program, *Human Development Report 1994*, Oxford University Press, New York, 1994, 44.

17 G. Alfredsson and A. de Zayas, 'Minority Rights: Protection by the United Nations', *Human Rights Law Journal*, vol. 14, nos 1–2, 26 February 1993, 1–9; M. C. Lâm, 'Making Room for Peoples at the United Nations: Thoughts Provoked by Indigenous Claims to Self-Determination', *Cornell International Law Journal*, vol. 25, no. 3, Symposium 1992, 602–22.

18 K. Partach, 'Fundamental Principles of Human Rights: Self Determination, Equality and Non-Discrimination', in K. Vasak, ed., *The International Dimension of Human Rights*, vol. 2, Greenwood Press and Unesco, Westport, Connecticut, and Paris, 1982, 61–86.

19 A. Etzioni, 'The Evils of Self-Determination', *Foreign Policy*, Winter 1993, 21–35.

20 On events leading to an independent East Timor, see D. Kingsbury, *South-East Asia: A Political Profile*, Oxford University Press, Melbourne, 2001, 391–413; and J. Martinkus, *A Dirty Little War*, Random House, Sydney, 2001. On recent trends in West Papua, see 'West Papua: Towards a New Papua', Special Edition, *Inside Indonesia*, no. 67, July–September 2001. Historical background is provided by J. Saltford, 'United Nations Involvement with the Act of Self-Determination in West Irian (Indonesian West New Guinea)', *Indonesia*, no. 69, April 2000, 71–92.

21 Useful background on these conflicts is provided by S. J. Tambiah, *Sri Lanka, Ethnic Fraticide and the Dismantling of Democracy*, University of Chicago Press, Chicago, 1986; S. Bose, *States, Nations, Sovereignty: Sri Lanka, India, and the Tamil Eelam Movement*, Sage Publications, New

Delhi, 1994; B. R. Rodil and Minority Rights Group, *The Lumad and Moro of Mindanao*, Minority Rights Group, London, 1993; R. Tiglao, 'The Fire Next Time', and 'Commissar of the Faithful', *Far Eastern Economic Review*, 28 March 1996, 26–30; M. Forney, 'Under Fire', *Far Eastern Economic Review*, 27 February 1997, 17–20; and R. Tiglao, 'Return to Arms: Insurgent Group Drags Mindanao Back to Mayhem', *Far Eastern Economic Review*, 24 July 1997, 32.

22 J. McKinnon and Wanat Bhruksasri, eds, *Highlanders of Thailand*, Oxford University Press, Kuala Lumpur, 1983; P. Lewis and E. Lewis, *Peoples of the Golden Triangle*, Thames & Hudson, London, 1984.

23 Quoted by Burger, *Report From the Frontier*, 6–7.

24 B. Kingsbury, '"Indigenous Peoples" as an International Legal Concept', in Barnes et al., *Indigenous Peoples of Asia*, 13–34. See also Gray, 'The Indigenous Movement in Asia', *Indigenous Peoples of Asia*, 35–58.

25 C. Bates, '"Lost Innocents and the Loss of Innocence": Interpreting the Adivasi Movements in South Asia', in Barnes, et al., *Indigenous Peoples of Asia*, 103–20.

26 Colin Mackerras, *China's Minorities: Integration and Modernization in the Twentieth Century*, Oxford University Press, Melbourne, 1994, 233–45; China Population Information and Research Centre, *Major Figures of the 2000 Population Census* (no. 1), http://www.cpirc.org.cn/e5cendata1.htm (accessed 11 August 2001).

27 H. Oberoi, *The Construction of Religious Boundaries: Culture, Identity and Diversity in the Sikh Tradition*, University of Chicago Press, Chicago, 1994; D. Gupta, *The Context of Ethnicity: Sikh Identity in a Comparative Perspective*, Oxford University Press, Delhi, 1996.

28 Ashworth, *World Minorities*, 7–9. There are a number of Ahmadiyya websites on the Internet that provide up-to-date information on the religion in various countries.

29 A. Schmidt, *The Loss of Australia's Aboriginal Language Heritage*, Aboriginal Studies Press, Canberra, 1993.

30 W. van Schendel, 'The Invention of the "Jummas": State Formation and Ethnicity in Southeastern Bangladesh', in Barnes et al., *Indigenous Peoples of Asia*, 121–44.

31 Sachs, 'Introduction', *The Development Dictionary*, 4.

32 These issues are considered in relation to indigenous peoples of North America in G. P. Castile and G. Kushner, eds, *Persistent Peoples: Cultural Enclaves in Perspective*, University of Arizona Press, Tuscon, Arizona, 1981.

## Chapter 5 Economic and Social Development

1 Quoted by G. Esteva, 'Development', in W. Sachs, *The Development Dictionary: A Guide to Knowledge as Power*, Zed Books, London, 1992, 13. My comments on the history of the concept draw heavily on Esteva's discussion.

2 United Nations Development Program, *Human Development Report 2000*, Oxford University Press, New York, 2000, 19–26, and on-line at http://www.undp.org/hdr2000 (accessed 23 September 2001).

3 United Nations Development Program, *Human Development Report 1996*, Oxford University Press, New York, 1996, 2; United Nations Development Program, *Human Development Report 2000*, Oxford University Press, New York, 2000, 6.

4 United Nations Development Program, *Human Development Report 1994*, Oxford University Press, New York, 1994, 63–4.

5 On foreign debt see particularly C. Payer, *Lent and Lost: Foreign Credit and Third World Development*, Zed Books, London, 1991; S. George, *A Fate Worse Than Debt*, Grove Weidenfeld, New York, 1987; and F. Stewart, *Adjustment and Poverty: Options and Choices*, Routledge, London, 1995.

6 C. Freeman and J. Hagendoorn, 'Convergence and Divergence in the Internationalisation of Technology', in J. Hagendoorn, ed., *Technological Change in the World Economy: Convergence and Divergence in Technological Strategies*, Edward Elgar, Aldershot, 1995. On innovation hotspots and the networked economy, see J. Hillner, 'Venture Capitals', *Wired*, vol. 8, no. 7, July 2000, 258–71; United Nations Development Program, *Human Development Report 2001*, Oxford University Press, New York, 2001, 37–45, and on-line at http://www.undp.org/hdr2001/ (accessed 23 September 2001).

7 On the problems of the green revolution, see V. Shiva, *The Violence of the Green Revolution: Third World Agriculture, Ecology and Politics*, Third World Network, Penang, 1991; B. H. Joshi and H. K. Trivedi, *The Impact of the Green Revolution on Indian Farmers*, Deep and Deep Publishing, Delhi, 1986; M. Alauddin and C. Tisdell, *The Green Revolution and Economic Development: The Process and Its Impact in Bangladesh*, St Martin's Press, New York, 1991; B. Glaeser, ed., *The Green Revolution Revisited: Critique and Alternatives*, Unwin Hyman, London, 1987; and D. K. Freebairn, 'Did the Green Revolution Concentrate Incomes? A Quantitive Study of Research Reports', *World Development*, vol. 23, no. 2, 1995, 265–79.

8 W. Bello and S. Rosenfeld, *Dragons in Distress: Asia's Economic Miracles in Crisis*, Penguin, Harmondsworth, 1992; chs 4 and 11. On China, see J. Unger, 'Rich Man, Poor Man: The Making of New Classes in the Countryside', in D. S. G. Goodman and B. Hooper, eds, *China's Quiet Revolution*, Longman Cheshire, Melbourne, 1994. The Indonesian funding issue was reported in *Weekend Australian*, 30–31 July 1994, 20.

9 United Nations Development Program, *Human Development Report 1995*, Oxford University Press, New York, 1995; United Nations Population Fund, *The State of the World Population 2000: Lives Together, Worlds Apart*, http://www.unfpa.org/swp/swpmain.htm (accessed 13 September 2001).

10 I. Tinker, ed., *Persistent Inequalities: Women and World Development*, Oxford University Press, New York, 1990; Task Forces on Bangladesh Development Strategies for the 1990s, *Policies for Development vol. 1, Women In Development*, University Press, Dhaka, 1991; National Planning Commission of Nepal and UNICEF, Children and Women of Nepal: A Situation Analysis 1992, NPC and UNICEF, Kathmandu, 1992; S. Wadley, 'Family Composition Strategies in Rural Northern India', *Social Science and Medicine*, vol. 37, no. 11, 1993, 1367–76; United Nations Development Program, *Human Development Report 1995*, Oxford University Press, New York, 1995, 29–71; M. Seth, *Women and Development: The Indian Experience*, Sage, New Delhi, 2001. See also the references in A. Sen, *Development as Freedom*, Oxford University Press, Oxford, 1999, chapter 8.

11 Mahbub ul Huq is quoted by A. Sen, 'Assessing Human Rights', in United Nations Development Program, *Human Development Report 2000*, Oxford University Press, New York, 2000, 23. The description of the Human Development Index in the following paragraphs draws particularly on the Human Development Reports of 1990, 1995 and 1999.

12 UNDP, *Human Development Report 1995*, 87–88; M. Mies, *Indian Women in Subsistence Agricultural Labour*, International Labour Organization, Geneva, 1986; S. Raju and D. Bagchi, eds, *Women and Work in South Asia: Regional Patterns and Perspectives*, Routledge, London, 1994.

13 To be fair, it must be acknowledged that the authors of the human development reports have shown that they are aware of the limitations of their methodology. See UNDP, *Human Development Report 1996*, 57.

14 See, for example, United Nations Development Program, *China Human Development Report*, Oxford University Press, New York, 1999; S. Thapa, 'The Human Development Index: A Portrait of the 75 Districts in Nepal', *Asia-Pacific Population Journal*, vol. 10, no. 2, June 1995.

15 See, for example, World Bank, 'World Bank Sees "Localization" as Major New Trend in 21st Century', www.worldbank.org/html/extdr/extme/032.htm (accessed 7 September 2001); Global Development Research Centre, The Virtual Library on Microcredit, http://www.gdrc.org/icm/(accessed 7 September 2001); Muhammad Yunus, *Banker to the Poor: The Autobiography of Muhammad Yunus*, Aurum Press, London, 1998.

16 Asian Development Bank, *Technology Transfer and Development: Implications for Developing Asia*, Asian Development Bank, n.p., May 1995, 77–81; R. Islam, ed., *Transfer, Adoption and Diffusion of Technology for the Small and Cottage Industries*, Asia Regional Team for Employment Promotion, International Labour Organization, New Delhi, 1992; D. Raina, 'Technological Determinism Embodied in an Appro-Tech Programme: Small Science in a High-Tech Environment', *Journal of Scientific and Industrial Research*, vol. 52, 1993, 471–82; N. Jayaraman, 'Turn, Turn, Turn: Making Energy is a Breeze in Southern India', *Far Eastern Economic Review*, 30 March 1995, 62; R. Tasker, 'Hometown Jobs', *Far Eastern Economic Review*, 14 April 1994, 24, 28.

17 On the role of non-government organisations, see R. Holloway, ed., *Doing Development: Governments, NGOs, and the Rural Poor in Asia*, Earthscan, London, 1989; J. Clark, *Democratising Development: The Role of Voluntary Organisations*, Earthscan, London, 1991; D. Ghai and J. Vivian, eds, *Grassroots Environmental Action: People's Participation in Sustainable Development*, UNRISD and Routledge, Geneva and London, 1992; and J. Farrington and D. J. Lewis, eds, *Non-Government Organizations and the State in Asia*, Routledge, London, 1993.

18 Quoted by K. Chowdhry, 'Poverty, Environment, Development', *Daedalus*, vol. 118, no. 1, Winter 1989, 146.

19 P. Isengard, 'Basic Needs: The Case of Sri Lanka', *World Development*, vol. 8, no. 3, 1980, 237–58; A. T. P. L. Abeykoon, 'Sex Preference in South Asia: Sri Lanka an Outlier', *Asia-Pacific Population Journal*, vol. 10, no. 3, September 1995, 5–16.

20 R. Frank and B. Chasin, *Kerala: Radical Reform as Development in an Indian State*, Institute for Food and Development Policy, San Francisco, 1989, and 'Development Without Growth: The Kerala Experiment', *Technology Review*, vol. 93, no. 3, April 1993, 42–51; R. Jeffrey, *Politics, Women, and Well-Being: How Kerala Became 'a Model'*, Macmillan, London, 1992; G. Parayil, 'The "Kerala Model" of Development: Development and Sustainability in the Third World', *Third World Quarterly*, vol. 17, no. 5, 1996, 941–57; V. K. Ramachandran, 'Kerala's Development Achievements: A Review', in J. Dreze and A. Sen, eds, *Indian Development: Selected Perspectives*, Oxford University Press, Delhi, 1997; J. Tharamangalam, 'The Perils of Social Development Without Economic Growth: The Development Debacle of Kerala, India', *Bulletin of Concerned Asian Scholars*, vol. 30, no. 1, January 1998, 23–34, and 'A Rejoinder', *Bulletin of Concerned Asian Scholars*, vol. 30, no. 4, October–December 1998, 47–52; K. T. Rammohan, 'Assessing Reassessment of the Kerala Model', *Economic and Political Weekly*, 8 April 2000, 1234–6; 'Editorial', *Economic and Political Weekly*, 20 January 2001, 169–70; R. Veron, 'The "New" Kerala Model: Lessons for Sustainable Development', *World Development*, vol. 29, no. 4, 2001, 601–17.

21 World Health Organization, *Primary Health Care, The Chinese Experience: Reports of an Inter-Regional Seminar*, World Health Organization, Geneva, 1983; J. Purcal, 'Development of Health Care Services in Rural China: Lessons for Southeast Asia', in P. Cohen and J. Purcal, eds, *The Political Economy of Primary Health Care in Southeast Asia*, Australian Development Studies Network and ASEAN Training Centre for Primary Health Care Development, Canberra, 1989, 34–42; D. V. McQueen, 'China's Impact on American Medicine in the Seventies: A Limited and Preliminary Inquiry', *Social Science and Medicine*, vol. 21, no. 8, 1985, 931–6.

22 S. R. Osmani, 'Is There a Conflict Between Growth and Welfarism? The Significance of the Sri Lanka Debate', *Development and Change*, vol. 25, no. 2, April 1994, 387–421. A more critical assessment of Sri Lanka's post-independence development is provided by S. Kelegama, 'Development in Independent Sri Lanka: What Went Wrong?', *Economic and Political Weekly*, 22 April 2000, 1477–80.

23 For example, R. Pomfret, *Diverse Paths of Economic Development*, Harvester Wheatsheaf, New York, 1992, 218.

24 United Nations Development Program, *Human Development Report 2000*, Oxford University Press, New York, 2000, p. 1–6; A. Sen, *Development as Freedom*, Oxford University Press, Oxford, 1999, pp. 3, 297.

25 S. A. Marglin, 'Towards the Decolonization of the Mind', in F. Apffel Marglin and S. A. Marglin, eds, *Dominating Knowledge: Development, Culture and Resistance*, Clarendon Press, Oxford, 1990, 6.

26 Particularly useful on varying interpretations of the financial crisis (still misleadingly called 'Asian', despite the fact that countries as un-Asian as Russia and Brazil experienced the same problems), is Pasuk Phongpaichit and C. Baker, *Thailand's Crisis*, Silkwork Books, Chiang Mai, 2000. Useful treatments, offering a range of views, include W. Bello, 'The Rise and Fall of South-east Asia's Economy', *The Ecologist*, vol. 28, no. 1, January–February 1998, 9–17; and 'The Asian Economic Implosion: Causes, Dynamics, Prospects', *Race and Class*, vol. 40, nos. 2/3, 1998, 133–44; W. Bello, ed., 'The Asian Economic Crisis. East Asia: On the Eve of the Great Transformation?', Special Issue, *Ampo: Japan–Asia Quarterly Review*, vol. 28, no. 3, 1999; A. Singh and B. Weisse, 'The Asian Model: A Crisis Foretold?', *International Social Science Journal*, vol. 51, no. 2, 1999, 203–15; W. T. Woo, J. D. Sachs, and K. Schwab, eds, *The Asian Financial Crisis: Lessons*

*from a Resilient Asia*, MIT Press, Cambridge, Massachusetts, 2000; K. Jayasuriya and A. Rosser, 'Economic Orthodoxy and the East Asian Crisis', *Third World Quarterly*, vol. 22, no. 3, 2001, 381–96; and P. A. Volker, 'The Sea of Global Finance', and G. Soros, 'The New Global Finance Architecture', in W. Hutton and A. Giddens, *Global Capitalism*, The New Press, New York, 2000.

27 On the development of steel industries, see T. Morris-Suzuki, *The Technological Transformation of Japan: From the Seventeenth to the Twenty-first Century*, Cambridge University Press, Cambridge, 1994; L. H. Lynn, *How Japan Innovates: A Comparison With the US in the Case of Oxygen Steelmaking*, Westview Press, Boulder, Colorado, 1982; and A. H. Amsden, *Asia's Next Giant: South Korea and Late Industrialization*, Oxford University Press, New York, 1989, 219–318.

28 World Bank, *The East Asian Miracle: Economic Growth and Public Policy*, Oxford University Press, New York, 1993, 9; World Bank, *Entering the 21st Century: World Development Report 1999/2000*, Oxford University Press, New York, 2000, 13–14.

29 Asian Development Bank, *Technology Transfer and Development*, 8.

30 On Hong Kong, see J. Schiffler, 'State Policy and Economic Growth: A Note on the Hong Kong Model', *International Journal of Urban and Regional Research*, vol. 15, no. 2, 1991, 180–96; and M. Castells et al., *The Shek Kip Mei Syndrome: Economic Development and Public Housing in Hong Kong and Singapore*, Pion, London, 1990. On the economic unorthodoxy of East Asia generally, see Amsden, *Asia's Next Giant*; Bello and Rosenfeld, *Dragons in Distress*; R. Wade, *Governing the Market: Economic Theory and the Role of the Government in East Asian Industrialisation*, Princeton University Press, Princeton, 1990; R. P. Appelbaum and J. Henderson, eds, *States and Development in the Asia Pacific Rim*, Sage, Newbury Park, 1992; J. Henderson, 'Against the Economic Orthodoxy: On the Making of the East Asian Miracle', *Economy and Society*, vol. 22, no. 2, May 1993, 200–17; and T. Ozawa, 'Miracle: Politics, Economics, Society, Culture and History—A Review Article', *Journal of Asian Studies*, vol. 53, no. 1, 1993, 124–32.

31 C. Dahlman, 'Technology Strategy in East Asian Developing Economies', *Journal of Asian Economics*, vol. 5, no. 4, 1994, 541–72.

32 B. J. Habibie, 'Sophisticated Technologies: Taking Root in Developing Countries', *International Journal of Technology Management*, vol. 5, no. 5, 1990, 489–97. President Suharto is quoted from the Embassy of the Republic of Indonesia, *Newsletter*, Canberra, May 1994.

33 On the Indonesian aircraft industry and related technology issues, see D. McKendrick, 'Obstacles to "Catchup": The Case of the Indonesian Aircraft Industry', *Bulletin of Indonesian Economic Studies*, vol. 28, no. 1, April 1992, 39–66; H. Hill, 'Indonesia's Great Leap Foward? Technology Development and Policy Issues', *Bulletin of Indonesian Economic Studies*, vol. 31, no. 2, August 1995, 83–123; and M. Cohen, 'New Flight Plan', *Far Eastern Economic Review*, 2 March 2000, 45–6. Education statistics are from World Bank, *World Development Indicators 2001*, http://www.worldbank.org/data/wdi2001/pdfs, accessed 10 April 2002.

34 Science and Technology Policy Institute (Korea), *Review of Science and Technology Policy for Industrial Competitiveness*, Ministry of Foreign Affairs, Seoul, 1995; C. S. Lee, 'Innovation Deficit', *Far Eastern Economic Review*, 24 July 1997, 72–3; Y. S. Kim, 'Some Reflections on Science and Technology in Contemporary Korean Society', *Korea Journal*, vol. 28, no. 8, August 1988, 4–15.

35 J. J. Salomon and A. Lebeau, *Mirages of Development: Science and Technology for the Third World*, Lynne Rienner Publishers, London, 1993, 152.

36 A range of views on this issue is provided by P. Berger and M. H. H. Hsiao, *In Search of an East Asian Development Model*, Berger and Hsiao, New Brunswick, 1988; H. Tai, ed., *Confucianism and Economic Development: An Oriental Alternative?* Washington Institute Press, Washington DC, 1989; E. Vogel, *The Four Little Dragons: The Spread of Industrialization in East Asia*, Harvard University Press, Cambridge, Massachusetts, 1991; and Tu Wei-Ming, *Confucian Traditions in East Asian Modernity: Moral Education and Economic Culture in Japan and the Four Mini-Dragons*, Harvard University Press, Cambridge, Massachusetts, 1996.

37 The record of the 'salt and iron' debates of 81 BCE has been partially translated by E. M. Gale, *Discussions on Salt and Iron, 1931–34*, rpt Ch'eng-wen Publishers, Taipei, 1967. On non-Confucian influences in the history of Chinese political thought and institutions, see Hsiao Kung-Ch'üan, *A History of Chinese Political Thought*, Volume 1, trans. F. W. Mote, Princeton University Press, Princeton, 1978. On Chinese commercial success outside China, see S.

Seagrave, *Lords of the Rim: The Invisible Empire of the Overseas Chinese*, Putman, New York, 1995; and R. A. Brown, *Chinese Business Enterprise in Asia*, Routledge, London, 1995.

38 A. A. Goldsmith, 'The State, the Market and Economic Development: A Second Look at Adam Smith in Theory and Practice', *Development and Change*, vol. 26, no. 4, October 1995, 648.

39 Quoted by Murphey, *A History of Asia*, 337; and C. Alvares, 'Science', in Sachs, *The Development Dictionary*, 226.

## Chapter 6 Patterns of Population Change

1 In 1994, world population estimates for the year 2100 were: United Nations 11.2 billion, World Bank 11.7 billion, and International Institute of Applied Systems Analysis 12.6 billion. For discussion see W. Lutz, 'The Future of the World Population', *Population Bulletin*, vol. 49, no. 1, June 1994, 26–9.

2 This overview is based on E. Jamison and F. Hobbs, *World Population Profile: 1994*, US Department of Commerce and US Bureau of the Census, Washington DC, 1994; United Nations Population Division, *Revision of the World Population Estimates and Projections (1998)*, http://www.popin.org/pop1998/ (accessed 13 September 2001); and UNDP, *Human Development Report 2000*.

3 See, for example, A. McLaren, *A History of Contraception: From Antiquity to the Present*, Blackwell, Oxford, 1991.

4 V. Smil, *China's Environmental Crisis: An Inquiry Into the Limits of National Development*, M. E. Sharpe, Armonk, New York, 1993, 7–8, draws attention to the second edition of Malthus' essay and the need to avoid simplistic interpretations of his position.

5 L. Silberman, 'Hung Liang-Chi: a Chinese Malthus', *Population Studies*, vol. 13, no. 3, March 1960, 257–65. On Chinese ideas on population up to 1949 see G. T. Wang, *China's Population: Problems, Thoughts and Policies*, Ashgate, Aldershot, 1999, chapter 1.

6 Useful overviews of recent demographic theory are provided by G. McNicoll, 'Changing Fertility Patterns and Policies in the Third World', *Annual Review of Sociology*, vol. 18, 1992, 85–108; and by C. Hirschman, 'Why Fertility Changes', *Annual Review of Sociology*, vol. 20, 1994, 203–33. For Caldwell's views on fertility decline, see J. C. Caldwell, *Theory of Fertility Decline*, Academic Publishers, London, 1982.

7 S. Szreter, 'The Idea of Demographic Transition and the Study of Fertility Change: a Critical History', *Population and Development Review*, vol. 19, no. 4, December 1993, 659–701.

8 W. de Silva, 'Ahead of Target: Achievement of Replacement Level Fertility in Sri Lanka Before the Year 2000', *Asia-Pacific Population Journal*, vol. 9, no. 4, December 1994, 3–22; Abeykoon, 'Sex Preference in South Asia: Sri Lanka an Outlier', 5–16; R. Amin et al., 'Reproductive Change in Bangladesh: Evidence from Recent Data', *Asia-Pacific Population Journal*, vol. 8, no. 4, December 1993, 39–58.

9 V. D. Abernethy, *Population Politics: The Choices that Shape Our Future*, Plenum Press, New York, 1993.

10 This point has been made by others, including M. Rao, 'An Imagined Reality: Malthusianism, Neo-Malthusianism and the Population Myth', *Economic and Political Weekly*, 29 January 1994, PE–40–PE–52.

11 Abernethy, *Population Politics*, 38–9. Contrary evidence is discussed by G. D. Moffett, *Critical Masses: The Global Population Challenge*, Viking, New York, 1994, 219–20.

12 Amin et al., 'Reproductive Change in Bangladesh', 39–40.

13 T. Dyson and M. Moore, 'On Kinship Structure, Female Autonomy, and Demographic Behavior in India', *Population and Development Review*, vol. 9, no. 1, March 1983, 35–60.

14 K. Saradamoni, 'Women, Kerala and Some Development Issues', *Economic and Political Weekly*, vol. 29, no. 9, 26 February 1994, 501–9; United Nations Population Fund, *The State of the World Population 2000*, http://www.unfpa.org/swp/swpmain.htm (accessed 21 September 2001); J. Dreze and M. Murthi, 'Fertility, Education and Development: Evidence from India', *Population and Development Review*, vol. 27, no. 1, March 2001, 33–63. On comparisons between Kerala and other Indian states in terms of fertility and related factors, see also A Shariff, *India: Human Development Report: A Profile of Indian States in the 1990s*, Oxford University Press, Oxford, 1999.

15 G. W. Jones, 'Fertility Transitions Among Malay Populations of Southeast Asia: Puzzles of Interpretation', *Population and Development Review*, vol. 16, no. 3, September 1990, 507–37.

16 A. Sen, 'More Than 100 Million Women Are Missing', *New York Review of Books*, 20 December 1990; A. J. Coale, 'Excess Female Mortality and the Balance of the Sexes: an Estimate of the Number of "Missing Females"', *Population and Development Review*, vol. 17, no. 3, September 1991, 517–23; and M. K. Premi, *India's Population: Heading Towards a Billion*, B. R. Publishing, Delhi, 1991, 37–48. Sen provides further discussion in *Development as Freedom*, Oxford University Press, Oxford, 1999, 195–202, 221–3, as well as some useful references.

17 V. Patel, 'Sex-Determination and Sex Pre-Selection Tests in India: Modern Techniques of Femicide', *Bulletin of Concerned Asian Scholars*, vol. 21, no. 1, January–March 1989, 2–10; R. Chabra and S. C. Nuna, *Abortion in India: An Overview*, New Delhi, 1993; P. Oldenburg, 'Sex Ratio, Son Preference and Violence in India: A Research Note', *Economic and Political Weekly*, 5–12 December 1998. My discussion focuses on selective abortion. On neglect of girls and high female child mortality, see M. Das Gupta, 'Selective Discrimination Against Female Children in India', *Population and Development Review*, vol. 13 no. 1, 1987, 77–100. The link between falling female births and falling female child mortality rates is examined by S. B. Agnihotri, *Sex Ratio Patterns in the Indian Population: A Fresh Exploration*, Sage, New Delhi, 2000; and in 'Declining Infant and Child Mortality in India: How do Girl Children Fare?', *Economic and Political Weekly*, 20 January 2000, 228–33. See also A. Bose, 'Census of India 2001 and After', *Economic and Political Weekly*, 19 May 2001, 1685–7.

18 Zeng Yi et al., 'Causes and Implications of the Recent Increase in the Reported Sex Rate at Birth in China', *Population and Development Review*, vol. 19, no. 2, June 1993, 283–302; and Li Yongping and Peng Xizhe, 'Age and Sex Structures', in Peng Xizhe and Guo Zhigang, eds, *The Changing Population of China*, Blackwell, Oxford, 2000, 68–74.

19 Park and Cho, 'Consequences of Son Preference in a Low-Fertility Society'.

20 'The Good Earth: Life is Getting Better, But Malthus Reigns in Cairo', editorial, *Far Eastern Economic Review*, 8 September 1994, 5.

21 Rao, 'An Imagined Reality', *PE*–50.

22 UNDP, *Human Development Report, 1995*, 25–8.

23 United Nations World Conference on Population, Mexico City, August 1984, Report of the Main Committee. Quoted by H. P. David, 'Population, Policy and Reproductive Behaviour: Incentives and Disincentives', in L. G. Severy, ed., *Advances in Population: Psychosocial Perspectives*, vol. 1, Jessica Kingsley, London, 1993, 25.

24 M. T. Yap, 'Singapore's "Three or More" Policy: The First Five Years', *Asia-Pacific Population Journal*, vol. 10, no. 4, December 1995, 39–52; N. Ogawa and R. D. Retherford, 'The Resumption of Fertility Decline in Japan: 1973–92', *Population and Development Review*, vol. 19, no. 4, December 1993, 703–41.

25 A. Aghajanian, 'A New Direction in Population Policy and Family Planning in the Islamic Republic of Iran', *Asia-Pacific Population Journal*, vol. 10, no. 1, March 1995, 3–20; Amin et al., 'Reproductive Change in Bangladesh'.

26 J. K. Satia and R. M. Maru, 'Incentives and Disincentives in the Indian Family Welfare Program', *Studies in Family Planning*, vol. 17, 1986, 136–45; David, 'Population Policy and Reproductive Behaviour', 12–13.

27 L. Visaria and P. Visaria, 'India's Population in Transition', *Population Bulletin*, vol. 50, no. 3, October 1995.

28 On compulsion in the Indian fertility control program, see D. R. Gwatkin, 'Political Will and Family Planning: The Implications of India's Emergency Experience', *Population and Development Review*, vol. 5, 1979, 29–59; and D. Banerji, 'The Political Economy of Population Control in India', in L. Bondestam and S. Berstroem, eds, *Poverty and Population Control*, Academic Press, London, 1980, 83–102.

29 Mechai Viravaidya, Discussion at Ministerial Seminar on Population and Development, Australian Academy of Science, Canberra, 3 November 1993.

30 See, for example, T. H. Hull, *An Investigation of Reports of Coercion in the Indonesian Vasectomy Program*, Development Paper 1991 No. 1, Appraisals, Evaluation and Sectoral Studies Branch, Australian International Development Assistance Bureau, Canberra, 1991.

31 Naitao Wu, 'China Contributes to Reducing Global Population Pressure', *Beijing Review*, 29 January–4 February 1996, 4. The figures for China's population growth rate during the 1960s, 1970s and 1980s are from H.Y. Tien, *China's Strategic Demographic Initiative*, Praeger, New York, 1991, 16.

32 On the evolution of Chinese population policy see also A. Golstein and F. Wang eds, *China: The Many Facets of Demographic Change*, Westview Press, Boulder, Colorado, 1996; P. Kane, 'Population and Family Policies', in R. Benewick and P. Wingrove, eds, *China in the 1990s*, 2nd edn, UBC Press, Vancouver, 1999; G. T. Wang, *China's Population: Problems, Thoughts and Policies*, Ashgate, Aldershot, 1999, Chapter 3; and Xie Zhenming, 'Population Policy and the Family-Planning Programme', in Peng Xizhe and Guo Zhigang, eds, *The Changing Population of China*, Blackwell, Oxford, 2000.

33 On coercion see especially J. S. Aird, *Slaughter of the Innocents: Coercive Birth Control in China*, American Enterprise Institution Press, Washington DC, 1990; and S. Mosher, *A Mother's Ordeal: One Woman's Fight Against China's One-Child Policy*, Brace Harcourt, New York, 1994.

34 A. Sen, 'Population: Delusion and Reality', *New York Review of Books*, 22 September 1994, 62–71; also A. Sen, *Development as Freedom*, Oxford University Press, Oxford, 1999.

35 *Beijing Review*, 29 January–4 February 1996, p. 15.

36 See E. A. Hammel, 'A Theory of Culture for Demographers', *Population and Development Review*, vol. 16, no. 3, September 1990, 455–85; and R. A. Pollak and S. C. Watkins, 'Cultural and Economic Approaches to Fertility: Proper Marriage or Mésalliance?', *Population and Development Review*, vol. 19, no. 3, September 1993, 467–95.

## Chapter 7 Environmental Impact

1 R. Goodland et al., eds, *Environmentally Sustainable Development: Building on Brundtland*, Unesco, Paris, 1991.

2 See A. Sen, *Poverty and Famines: An Essay on Entitlement and Deprivation*, Clarendon Press, Oxford, 1981; J. Dreze and A. Sen, *Hunger and Public Action*, Clarendon Press, Oxford, 1989.

3 J. McBeth, 'Grain Games; Grain Pains: Indonesia's Self-Sufficiency in Rice Comes Under Threat', *Far Eastern Economic Review*, 29 June 1995, 63–4.

4 J. Hardjono, 'Resource Utilisation and the Environment', in Hill, *Indonesia's New Order*, 179–215; L. Williams, 'Villagers' Lives Eaten Away By the River of Death', *Sydney Morning Herald*, 7 December 1996; A. Lucas with A. Djati, *The Dog is Dead so Throw it in the River: Environmental Politics and Water Pollution in Indonesia*, Monash Asia Institute, Clayton, Vic., 2000.

5 Ooi Jin Bee, 'The Dimensions of the Rural Energy Problem in Indonesia', *Applied Geography*, vol. 6, 1986, 123–47; N. Peluso, *Rich Forests, Poor People: Resource Control and Resistance in Java*, University of California Press, Berkeley, 1991; A. Schlapfer and D. Marinova, 'Entering the Nuclear Debate in Indonesia', *Search*, vol. 26, no. 1, January–February 1995, 18–21; Directorate of Foreign Information, Indonesia, 'The Development of Nuclear Power Plants in Indonesia' http://www.dfa-deplu.go.id/english/nuklir.htm (accessed 27 November 2000).

6 F. Betke, Modernization and Socioeconomic Change in the Coastal Marine Fisheries of Java: Some Hypotheses, Working Paper No. 72, Sociology of Development Research Centre, University of Bielefeld, Bielefeld, 1985; also J-P. Platteau, 'The Dynamics of Fisheries Development in Developing Countries: A Global Overview', *Development and Change*, vol. 20, no. 4, October 1989, 565–98; T. Saywell, 'Fishing for Trouble', *Far Eastern Economic Review*, 13 March 1997, 50–4.

7 J. McBeth, 'Return to Roots', *Far Eastern Economic Review*, 4 June 1998, 64–5.

8 For examples, see Jun Ui, ed., *Industrial Pollution in Japan*, United Nations University Press, Tokyo, 1992. On the Japanese failure to consider social and cultural implications of many of the changes introduced in the Meiji period, see N. Oka, 'What Japan Has Left Behind in the Course of Her Modernization', *Proceedings of the Symposium on Social Perspectives of Technology Development in the Process of Modernization*, Jakarta, February 1986.

9 M. Peattie, 'The Japanese Colonial Empire 1895-1945', in *The Cambridge History of Japan, Volume 6: The Twentieth Century*, ed. P. Duus, Cambridge University Press, Cambridge, 1988.

10 On Bhopal, see U. Baxi and T. Paul, *Mass Disasters and Multinational Liability: The Bhopal Case*, N. M. Tripathi, Bombay, 1986; P. Shrivastava, *Bhopal: Anatomy of a Crisis*, 2nd edn, P. Chapman, London, 1992; and W. Morehouse, 'Ethics of Industrial Disasters in a Transnational World: Elusive Quest for Justice and Accountability in Bhopal', *Alternatives*, vol. 18, no. 4, Fall 1993, 475–504.

11 On Minamata see Jun Ui, 'Minamata Disease', in Ui, *Industrial Pollution in Japan*, 103–32; W. E. Smith and A. M. Smith, *Minamata: Words and Photos*, Holt, Rinehart, and Winston, New York, 1975; H. Masazumi, 'Minamata Disease as a Social and Medical Problem', *Japan Quarterly*, vol. 25, no. 1, January–March 1978, 20–34; A. Mishima, *Bitter Sea: The Human Cost of Minamata Disease*, trans. R. R. Gage and S. B. Murata, Kosei Publishers, Tokyo, 1992; B. Hills, 'Japan's Mercury Agony Nears End', *Sydney Morning Herald*, 30 September 1995; and R. Garran, 'Final Payout Made to Minamata Victims', *Australian*, 1 November 1995; Jun Ui, ed., 'Minamata', Special Issue, *Ampo: Japan–Asia Quarterly Review*, vol. 27, no. 3, 1997.

12 'Keidanren Global Environment Charter', *Keidanren Review*, no. 129, June 1991, 4–6.

13 Consumers' Association of Penang, *Wasted Lives: Radioactive Poisoning in Bukit Merah*, Consumers' Association of Penang, Penang, 1993; United Nations, Economic and Social Council, Commission on Human Rights, *Adverse Effects of the Illicit Movement and Dumping of Toxic and Dangerous Products and Wastes on the Enjoyment of Human Rights*, E/CN.4/1997/19, http://www.unhchr.ch/Huridocda/Huridoca.nsf/Test frame/7740a5eb74ab0c728025666a...; Human Rights Institute, 'Japan: Thematic Reports', *For the Record 1998*, http://www.hri.ca/fortherecord1998/vol3/japantr.htm

14 V. Haller, 'Water Works: Why Our Planet is Running Dry', *Sydney Morning Herald*, 9 November 1996; Independent Commission on Population and Quality of Life, *Caring for the Future: Making the Next Decades Provide a Life Worth Living*, Oxford University Press, Oxford, 1996, 103, 293; United Nations Environment Program, *Global Environment Outlook 2000*, http://www.unep.org/geo2000/english/0224.htm (accessed 29 August 2001).

15 D. Seckler et al., 'Water Scarcity in the Twenty-first Century', *Water Resources Development*, vol. 15, nos. 1/2, 1999, 29–42; Asian Development Bank, 'Water in the 21st Century', http://www.adb.org/Documents/Reports/Water (accessed 28 August 2001); United Nations Environment Program, *Global Environment Outlook 2000*, http://www.unep.org/geo2000/english/0224.htm, 67 (accessed 29 August 2001); J. E. Nickum, 'Is China Living on the Water Margin?', *The China Quarterly*, no. 156, December 1998, 880-98; Liu Changming, 'Environmental Issues and the South-North Water Transfer Scheme', *The China Quarterly*, no. 156, December 1998, 899–910; G. McCormack, 'Water Margins: Competing Paradigms in China', *Critical Asian Studies*, vol. 33, no. 1, 2000, 5–30; World Commission on Dams, *Dams and Development: A New Framework for Decision-Making*, Earthscan, London, 2000; R. R. Iyer, 'Water: Charting a Course for the Future', parts 1 and 2, *Economic and Political Weekly*, 31 March 2001, 1115–22, and 14 April 2001, 1235–47.

16 S. Postel, 'Groundwater Depletion Widespread', in L. Starke, ed., *Vital Signs 2000/2001: The Environmental Trends that are Shaping Our Future*, Earthscan, London, 2000, 122–3.

17 P. P. Micklin and W. D. Williams, eds, *The Aral Sea Basin*, Springer, Berlin, 1996; I. Kobori and M. H. Glantz, *Central Eurasian Water Crisis: Caspian, Aral, and Dead Seas*, United Nations University Press, Tokyo, 1998.

18 F. Pearce, 'Death and the Devil's Water', *New Scientist*, 16 September 1995, 14-15; R. Nickson et al., 'Arsenic Poisoning of Bangladesh Groundwater', *Nature*, 24 September 1998, 338. Ministry of Health and Family Welfare, Bangladesh, 'Arsenic Contamination Project', Ministry of Health and Family Welfare, Dhaka, 1998.

19 United Nations Environment Program, *Global Environment Outlook 2000*, http://www.unep.org/geo2000/english/0224.htm, 67 (accessed 29 August 2001); P. Sampat, 'Groundwater Quality', in L. Starke, ed., *Vital Signs 2000/2001: The Environmental Trends that are Shaping Our Future*, Earthscan, London, 2000, 124-5; C. Datta, 'Yamuna River Turned Sewer', *Economic and Political Weekly*, 5 December 1992, 2633–6.

20 See V. Shiva, *The Violence of the Green Revolution: Third World Agriculture, Ecology and Politics*, Third World Network, Penang, 1991, 121–70; L. Ohlsson, *Hydropolitics*, Zed Books, London, 1995. A

useful overview of problems in the Mekong Basin is provided by M. Osborne, *The Mekong*, Atlantic Monthly Press, New York, 2000. More detailed discussion is in P. Hirsch, 'Dams, Resources and the Politics of the Environment in Mainland Southeast Asia'; and M. Mitchell, 'The Political Economy of Mekong Basin Development', in P. Hirsch and C. Warren, *The Politics of the Environment in Southeast Asia*, Routledge, London, 1998. See also the journal *Watershed*, published by Towards Ecological Recovery and Regional Alliance (TERRA), Bangkok.

21 A. Markham, *A Brief History of Pollution*, St. Martin's Press, New York, 1994; W. Foells, et al., eds, *RAINS-Asia: An Assessment Model for Air Pollution in Asia*, World Bank, Washington DC, 1995; V. Bashkin and S. Park, eds, *Acid Deposition and Ecosystem Sensitivity in East Asia*, Nova Science Publishers, Commack, New York, 1998; H. Nishimura, ed., *How to Conquer Air Pollution*, Elsevier, Amsterdam, 1989; P. Evans, 'Japan's Green Aid', *China Business Review*, July–August 1994, 39–43; United Nations Environment Program, *Global Environment Outlook 2000*, http://www.unep.org/geo2000/english/0224.htm, 69 (accessed 29 August 2001); E. B. Vermeer, 'Industrial Pollution in China and Remedial Policies', *The China Quarterly*, no. 156, December 1998, 952–85.

22 United Nations Environment Program, *Global Environment Outlook 2000*, http://www.unep.org/geo2000/english/0224.htm, 64 (accessed 29 August 2001); P. Ho, 'China's Rangelands Under Stress', *Development and Change*, vol. 31, no. 2, March 2000, 385–412.

23 On deforestation, see United Nations Environment Program, *Global Environment Outlook 2000*, http://www.unep.org/geo2000/english/0224.htm, 65 (accessed 29 August 2001); M. Doornbos, A. Saith and B. White, eds, 'Forests, Nature, People, Power', Special Issue, *Development and Change*, vol. 31, no. 1, January 2000; R. L. Bryant, 'The Politics of Forestry in Burma', and M. D. Vitug, 'The Politics of Logging in the Philippines', in P. Hirsch and C. Warren, *The Politics of Environment in Southeast Asia*, Routledge, London, 1998; J. Harkness, 'Recent Trends in Forestry and Conservation of Biodiversity in China', *The China Quarterly*, no. 156, December 1998, 911–34; F. M. Cooke, *The Challenge of Sustainable Forests: Forest Resource Policy in Malaysia, 1970–1995*, Asian Studies Association of Australia, with Allen & Unwin and University of Hawaii Press, 1999; and L. E. Sonsel, T. N. Headland, and R. C. Bailey, eds, *Tropical Deforestation: The Human Dimension*, Columbia UP, New York, 1996.

24 On biodiversity, see United Nations Environment Program, *Global Biodiversity Assessment*, Cambridge University Press, Cambridge, 1995; United Nations Economic and Social Commission for Asia and the Pacific, and the Asian Development Bank, *State of the Environment in Asia and the Pacific 1995*, UNESCAP, Bangkok, 1995; United Nations Environment Program, *Global Environment Outlook 2000*, http://www.unep.org/geo2000/english/0224.htm, 66 (accessed 29 August 2001); S. Braatz, *Conserving Biological Diversity: A Strategy for Protected Areas in the Asia-Pacific Region*, World Bank Technical Paper no. 193, World Bank, Washington DC, 1992; C. A. Perrings et al., eds, *Biodiversity Conservation: Problems and Policies*, Kluwer Academic, Dordrecht, 1994; and M. J. Valencia, J. M. van Dyke and N. A. Ludwig, *Sharing the Resources of the South China Sea*, Martinus Nijhoff, The Hague, 1997.

25 On Taiwan, see L. G. Arrigo, 'The Environmental Nightmare of the Economic Miracle: Land Abuse and Land Struggles in Taiwan', *Bulletin of Concerned Asian Scholars*, vol. 26, nos 1–2, 1994, 33. Other examples come from Brandon and Ramankutty, 'Toward an Environmental Strategy For Asia', 24, 26; M. C. Howard, 'Introduction', in M. C. Howard, ed., *Asia's Environmental Crisis*, Westview Press, Boulder, Colorado, 1993, 8; and Dai Xingyi and Peng Xizhe, 'China's Environment and Environment Protection', in Peng Xizhe and Guo Zhigang, eds, *The Changing Population of China*, Blackwell, Oxford, 2000, 244.

26 'Japan's New Long-Term Plan for R&D on Nuclear Power', *Science and Technology in Japan*, no. 53, 1995, 4–12.

27 S. J. Hoon, 'Not on My Island', *Far Eastern Economic Review*, 20 July 1995, 68; C. S. Lee and J. Baum, 'Radioactive Ruckus', *Far Eastern Economic Review*, 6 February 1997, 16; 'Northeast Asia', *Asian Defence Journal*, 1998, 41; N. Lenssen, 'Nuclear Power Rises Slightly', in L. Starke, ed., *Vital Signs 2000/2001: The Environmental Trends that are Shaping Our Future*, Earthscan, London, 2000, 54–5.

28 For the constitutions of Asian countries, see A. P. Blaustein and G. H. Flanz, eds, *Constitutions of the Countries of the World*, 17 vols, Oceana Publications, Dobbs Ferry, New Jersey, permanent

edn. An overview of legislative responses to environmental problems is provided by United Nations Environment Program, *Global Environment Outlook 2000*, http://www.unep.org/geo2000/english/0224.htm, 159–60 (accessed 29 August 2001).

29 Quoted by S. Ekachai, *Behind the Smile: Voices of Thailand*, Thai Development Support Committee, Bangkok, 1990, 45.

30 The World Bank spokesman is quoted by S. George and F. Sabelli, *Faith and Credit: The World Bank's Secular Empire*, Penguin, Harmondsworth, 1994, 170. The Asian Development Bank quote is from the Asian Development Bank, 'Water in the 21st Century', http://www.adb.org/Documents/Reports/Water, 11 (accessed 28 August 2001). See also J. Karp, 'Water, Water, Everywhere', *Far Eastern Economic Review*, 1 June 1995, 56; and W. Stottman, 'The Role of the Private Sector in the Provision of Water and Wastewater Services in Urban Areas', in J. I. Uitlo and A. K. Biswas, eds, *Water for Urban Areas*, United Nations University Press, Tokyo, 2000.

31 See J. Seabrook, *Victims of Development: Resistance and Alternatives*, Verso, London, 1994, 109-23; S. Kothari and P. Parajuli, 'No Nature Without Social Justice: A Plea For Cultural and Ecological Pluralism in India', in W. Sachs, ed., *Global Ecology: A New Arena of Political Conflict*, Zed Books, London, 1993, 224–41; A. Agrawal and S. Narain, 'Towards Green Villages', in Sachs, *Global Ecology*, 242–56; M. Gadgil and R. Guha, *Ecology and Equity: The Use and Abuse of Nature in Contemporary India*, Routledge, London, 1995; and M. K. Gandhi, quoted from *Young India*, 20 December 1928, 422, by V. K. Akula, 'Grassroots Environmental Resistance in India', in B. T. Taylor, ed., *Ecological Resistance Movements: The Global Emergence of Radical and Popular Environmentalism*, State University of New York Press, Albany, New York, 1995, 131.

32 Brandon and Ramankutty, *Toward an Environmental Strategy for Asia*, 27.

33 Smil, *Environmental Problems in China*, 57.

34 L. Brown, 'A New Era Unfolds', in Worldwatch Institute, *State of the World 1993*, Earthscan, London, 1993, 5–11.

35 On grassroots environmentalism see INSAN (Institute of Social Analysis), *Logging Against the Natives of Sarawak*, INSAN, Petaling Jaya, 1989; J. Reardon-Anderson, *Pollution, Politics, and Foreign Investment in Taiwan: The Lukang Rebellion*, M. E. Sharpe, Armonk, New York, 1992; Howard, *Asia's Environmental Crisis*; Gadgil and Guha, *Ecology and Equity*; G. Wehfritz, 'Green Heat', *Newsweek*, 8 October 1996, 75–9; P. J. Brosius, 'Prior Transcripts, Divergent Paths: Resistance and Acquiescence to Logging in Sarawak, East Malaysia', *Comparative Studies in Society and History*, vol. 39, no. 3, 1997, 468–510; A. Kalland and G. Persoon, *Environmental Movements in Asia*, Curzon, Richmond, Surrey, 1998; J. Broadbent, *Environmental Politics in Japan: Networks of Power and Protest*, Cambridge University Press, Cambridge, 1998; and Y. F. Lee and A. Y. So, eds, *Asia's Environmental Movements: Comparative Perspectives*, M. E. Sharpe, Armonk, New York, 1999.

36 On the need for both local and national action, see especially the comments by J. Tendler on Chowdhry, 'Poverty, Environment, Development', 131–58.

37 Smil, *China's Environmental Crisis*, 66. See also Dai Xingyi and Peng Xizhi, 'China's Environment and Environment Protection', in Peng Xizhi and Guo Zhigang, eds, *The Changing Population of China*, Blackwell, Oxford, 2000.

38 Shiva, *The Violence of the Green Revolution*, 238–9.

39 On alternative technologies, see, for example, A. Bhalla and D. James, eds, *New Technologies and Development: Experiences in Technology Blending*, L. Rienner, Boulder, Colorado, 1988; F. Stewart, *Macro-Policies For Appropriate Technology in Developing Countries*, Westview Press, Boulder, Colorado, 1987; I. Smillie, *Mastering the Machine: Poverty, Aid and Technology*, Intermediate Technology Publications, London, 1991; and J. James, 'Pro-poor Modes of Technical Integration into the Global Economy', *Development and Change*, vol. 31, no. 4, September 2000, 765–83.

40 Kothari and Parajuli, 'No Nature Without Social Justice', 224–41.

41 D. Arora, 'From State Regulation to People's Participation: Case of Forest Management in India', *Economic and Political Weekly*, vol. 29, no. 12, 19 March 1994, 691–8; T. Banuri and F. Apffel Marglin, eds, *Who Will Save the Forests?*, Atlantic Highlands, London, 1993; Peluso, *Rich Forests, Poor People*; Wang Hongchang, 'Afforestation Problems in China's Ecological Economics', *Social Sciences in China*, Spring 1993, 165–77; M. Poffenberger, ed., *Keepers of the Forest: Land Management*

*Alternatives in Southeast Asia*, Kumarian Press, West Hartford, Conn., 1990; M. J. G. Parnwell and R. L. Bryant, eds, *Environmental Change in South-East Asia: People, Politics and Sustainable Development*, Routledge, London, 1996; M. Doornbos, A. Saith and B. White, eds, 'Forests, Nature, People, Power', Special Issue, *Development and Change*, vol. 31, no. 1, January 2000.

42 On taxation and other economic measures to protect the environment, see L. Bovenberg and S. Cnossen, eds, *Public Economics and the Environment in an Imperfect World*, Kluwer Academic, Boston 1995; United Nations Environment Program, *Global Environment Outlook 2000*, http://www.unep.org/geo2000/english/0224.htm, 161 (accessed 29 August 2001); and D. M. Roodman, 'Tax Shifts Multiplying', in L. Starke, ed., *Vital Signs 2000/2001: The Environmental Trends that are Shaping Our Future*, Earthscan, London, 2000, 138–9.

43 E. Webb, 'Debt For Nature Swaps', *Environmental and Planning Law Journal*, vol. 11, no. 3, June 1994, 222–44; A. Lewis, 'The Evolving Process of Swapping Debt for Nature', *Colorado Journal of International Environmental Law and Policy*, vol. 10, no. 2, 1999, 431–65; D. Didia, 'Debt-For-Nature Swaps, Market Imperfections, and Policy Failures as Determinants of Sustainable Development and Environmental Quality', *Journal of Economic Issues*, vol. 35, no. 2, 2001, 477–86.

44 J. Cavanagh, D. Wysham, and M. Arruda, *Beyond Bretton Woods: Alternatives to the Global Economic Order*, Pluto Press, London, 1994; G. Bird and A. Milne, 'Debt Relief for Poor Countries', *New Economy*, vol. 7, no. 4, 2000, 199–204; D. Froning, 'Will Debt Relief Really Help?', *Washington Quarterly*, vol. 24, no. 3, Summer 2001, 199–211. See also the World Bank, HIPC Initiative, www.worldbank.org/hipc/ (accessed 7 September 2001).

45 On concepts of nature in Asian cultural traditions, see J. B. Callicott and R. T. Ames, eds, *Nature in Asian Traditions of Thought: Essays in Environmental Philosophy*, State University of New York, Albany, New York, 1989; and M. G. Barnhart, 'Ideas of Nature in an Asian Context', *Philosophy East and West*, vol. 47, no. 3, July 1997, 417–32.

## Chapter 8 Family Matters

1 W. Goode, *World Revolution and Family Patterns*, Free Press, New York, 1963.

2 P. Laslett, 'Introduction: The History of the Family', in P. Laslett and R. Wall, eds, *Household and Family in Past Time*, Cambridge University Press, Cambridge, 1972; R. R. Wilk and R. M. Netting, 'Households: Changing Forms and Functions', in R. M. Netting, R. R. Wilk and E. J. Arnould, eds, *Households: Comparative and Historical Studies of the Domestic Group*, University of California Press, Berkeley, 1984, 1–28; K. Saradamoni, 'Introduction', in K. Saradamoni, ed., *Finding the Household: Conceptual and Methodological Issues*, Sage Publications, New Delhi, 1992, 17–30.

3 The categories identified here have been influenced by M. Mitterauer and R. Sieder, *The European Family*, trans. K. Oosterveen and M. Hörzinger, Blackwell, Oxford, 1982, 73–84; and Wilk and Netting, 'Households'. However, they diverge sharply at a number of points.

4 Useful chapters on kinship in Asian societies are provided in G. Evans, ed., *Asia's Cultural Mosaic*, Prentice-Hall, New York, 1993.

5 Cao Xueqin, *The Story of the Stone*, trans. D. Hawkes and J. Minford, 5 vols, Penguin, Harmondsworth, 1973–87.

6 A. K. Gopalan, *In the Cause of the People*, Orient Longman, Madras, 1973, 1, cited by Jeffrey, *Politics, Women, and Well-Being*, 36; Muhamad Radjab, *Semasa Kecil di Kampung*, trans. S. Rogers as 'Village Childhood', in S. Rogers, ed., *Telling Lives, Telling History: Autobiographical and Historical Imagination in Modern Indonesia*, University of California Press, Berkeley, 1995, 151; Nguyen Duy Thieu, 'Family Relationships of Some Ethnic Peoples in Tay Nguyen', in R. Liljestrom and Tuong Lai, eds, *Sociological Studies on the Vietnamese Family*, Social Sciences Publishing House, Hanoi, 1981, 85-102. Nguyen refers to the work of Henri Maitre.

7 G. S. Bhatt, 'Constraints of being polyandrous-tribal: the case of Jaunsar Bawar', in S. M. Dubey, P. K. Bordoloi and B. N. Borthakur, eds, *Family, Marriage and Social Change on the Indian Fringe*, Cosmo Publications, New Delhi, 1980, 59–82.

8 P. Ebrey, *Family and Property in Sung China*, Princeton University Press, Princeton, 1984.

9 For example R. Sriram, 'Family Studies in India: Appraisal and New Directions', in T. S. Saraswathi and B. Kaur, eds, *Human Development and Family Studies in India: An Agenda for*

*Research and Policy*, Sage Publications, New Delhi, 1993, 125, concludes that the ideology of the complex household 'governs the attitudes, values and preferences' of most Indians. Similar conclusions are reached in relation to Japan by F. Kumagai, 'Families in Japan: Beliefs and Realities', *Journal of Comparative Family Studies*, vol. 26, no. 1, Spring 1995, 158, and China by D. Davis and S. Harrell, 'Introduction: The Impact of Post-Mao Reforms on Family Life', in D. Davis and S. Harrell, eds, *Chinese Families in the Post-Mao Era*, University of California Press, Berkeley, 1993, 1–22.

10 Fei Hsiao-t'ung, *Peasant Life in China*, Routledge, London, 1939; O. Lang, *Chinese Family and Society*, Yale University Press, New Haven, 1946; R. L. Buck, *Chinese Farm Economy*, University of Chicago Press, Chicago, 1930; I. Taeuber, 'The Families of Chinese Farmers', in M. Freedman, ed., *Family and Kinship in Chinese Society*, Stanford University Press, Stanford, 1970; Zang Xiaowei, 'Household Structure and Marriage in Urban China: 1900–1982', *Journal of Comparative Family Studies*, vol. 24, no. 1, Spring 1993, 35–44.

11 Z. Zhao, 'Coresidential Patterns in Historical China: A Simulation Study', *Population and Development Review*, vol. 26, no. 2, June 2000, 263–93.

12 E. A. Hammel and P. Laslett, 'Comparing Household Structure Over Time and Across Cultures', *Comparative Studies in Society and History*, vol. 16, 1974, 73–109; C. Nakane, 'An Interpretation of the Size and Structure of the Household in Japan Over Three Centuries', in Laslett and Wall, *Household and Family in Past Time*, 517–43; F. Kinoshita, 'Household Size, Household Structure, and Developmental Cycle of a Japanese Village: Eighteenth to Nineteenth Centuries', *Journal of Family History*, vol. 20, no. 3, 1995, 239–60; O. Saito, 'Marriage, Family Labour and the Stem Family Household: Traditional Japan in a Comparative Perspective', *Continuity and Change*, vol. 15, no. 1, May 2000, 17–45.

13 Insook Han Park and Lee-Jay Cho, 'Confucianism and the Korean Family', *Journal of Comparative Family Studies*, vol. 26, no. 1, Spring 1995, 117–34.

14 H. Orenstein, 'The Recent History of the Extended Family in India', *Social Problems*, vol. 8, 1961, 341–50; A. M. Shah, *The Household Dimension of the Family in India: A Field Study of a Gujarat Village and a Review of Other Studies*, University of California Press, Berkeley, 1974; P. Kolenda, *Regional Differences in Family Structure in India*, Rawat, Jaipur, 1987, 177; L. Mullatti, 'Families in India: Beliefs and Realities', *Journal of Comparative Family Studies*, vol. 26, no. 1, Spring 1995, 11–26; A. M. Shah, *The Family in India: Critical Essays*, Orient Longman, Delhi, 1998, especially chapters 3 and 4.

15 H. E. Smith, 'The Thai Rural Family', in M. S. Das and P. D. Bardis, eds, *The Family in Asia*, Allen & Unwin, London, 1979, 16–46; Bhassorn Limanonda, 'Families in Thailand: Beliefs and Realities', *Journal of Comparative Family Studies*, vol. 26, no. 1, Spring 1995, 67–82.

16 Chen Yiyun, 'Out of the Traditional Halls of Academe: Exploring New Avenues for Research on Women', in C. K. Gilmartin et al., eds, *Engendering China: Women, Culture, and the State*, Harvard University Press, Cambridge, Massachusetts, 1994, 69–79.

17 P. Kolenda, 'The Joint Family Household in Rural Rajasthan: Ecological, Cultural and Demographic Conditions for Its Occurrence', in J. D. Gray and D. J. Mearns, eds, *Society From the Inside Out: Anthropological Perspectives on the South Asian Household*, Sage Publications, New Delhi, 1989, 55–106.

18 D. A. Chekki, 'Recent Directions in Family Research: India and North America', *Journal of Comparative Family Studies*, vol. 19, no. 2, 1988, 171–86; L. Mullatti, 'Changing Profile of the Indian Family', in Unesco, *The Changing Family in Asia*, Unesco Principal Regional Office for Asia and the Pacific, Bangkok, 1992, 84–5; Sriram, 'Family Studies in India', 124.

19 Zainal Kling, 'The Malay Family: Beliefs and Realities', *Journal of Comparative Family Studies*, vol. 26, no. 1, Spring 1995, 61, table 7.

20 Mullatti, 'Families in India', 17; B. T. G. Medina, *The Filipino Family*, University of the Philippines Press, Quezon City, 1991, 33; S. P. Go, 'The Filipino family in the Eighties', in Unesco Principal Regional Office for Asia and the Pacific, *The Changing Family in Asia*; Zainal Kling, 'The Malay Family', 62; A. Chowdhry, 'Families in Bangladesh', *Journal of Comparative Family Studies*, vol. 26, no. 1, Spring 1995, 32; Bhassorn Limanonda, 'Families in Thailand', 72.

21 T. Hara, *Studies in Socio-Cultural Change in Rural Villages in Bangladesh*, No. 1, Institute for the Study of Languages and Cultures of Asia and Africa, Tokyo, 1985; Mullatti, 'Families in India', 17.

22 B. Pasternak, C. R. Ember and M. Ember, 'On the Conditions Favoring Extended Family Households', *Journal of Anthropological Research*, vol. 32, 1976, 109–23.

23 The Japanese modified stem family is discussed by Kumagai, 'Families in Japan', 152–4, 158. My discussion of trends in Japan also draws on S. O. Long, *Family Change and Life Course in Japan*, East Asia Program, Cornell University, Ithaca, New York, 1987. The Hong Kong situation is described by H. Chan and R. P. L. Lee, 'Hong Kong Families: At the Crossroads of Modernism and Traditionalism', *Journal of Comparative Family Studies*, vol. 26, no. 1, Spring 1995, 91. See also M. Weinstein et al., 'Household Composition, Extended Kinship, and Reproduction in Taiwan, 1965–1985', *Population Studies*, vol. 44, no. 2, 1990, 217–39; N. Kim, S. Choi, and I. H. Park, 'Rural Family and Community Life in South Korea: Changes in Family Attitudes and Living Arrangements for the Elderly', in L. Cho and M. Yada, eds, *Tradition and Change in the Asian Family*, East West Center and University Research Center, Nihon University, Honolulu and Tokyo, 1994; T. Sun and Y. H. Liu, 'Changes in Intergenerational Relations in the Chinese Family: Taiwan's Experience', in Cho and Yada, *Tradition and Change in the Asian Family*, 319–62; M. Lee and T. Sun, 'The Family and Demography in Contemporary Taiwan', *Journal of Comparative Family Studies*, vol. 26, no. 1, Spring 1995, 101–16; and S. Kweon, 'The Extended Family in Contemporary Korea: Changing Patterns of Co-Residence', *Korea Journal*, 38, no. 3, Autumn 1998, 178–209.

24 Davis and Harrell, 'Introduction', 8.

25 See, for example, S. Harrell, 'Geography, Demography, and Family Composition in Three Southwestern Villages', in Davis and Harrell, *Chinese Families in the Post-Mao Era*, 77–102.

26 M. Cartier, 'Nuclear Versus Quasi-Stem Families: the New Chinese Family Model', *Journal of Family History*, vol. 20, no. 3, 1995, 307–27. The negative impact of aspects of communist policy on complex household formation are examined by D. Wu, 'Complex Households, a Fading Glory: Household Formation During the Collective Period in the People's Republic of China', *Journal of Family History*, vol. 25, no. 4, October 2000, 527–44.

27 Fei Hsiao-t'ung, *Chinese Village Close-Up*, New World Press, Beijing, 1983, 25, 259.

28 S. Vatuk, 'Household Form and Formation: Variability and Social Change Among South Indian Muslims', in Gray and Mearns, *Society From the Inside Out*, 110.

29 I. H. Park and L-J. Cho, 'Confucianism and the Korean Family', 127; J. L. Dull, 'Marriage and Divorce in Han China: A Glimpse at Pre-Confucian Society', in D. C. Buxbaum, ed., *Chinese Family Law and Change*, University of Washington Press, Seattle, 1978, 23–74; A. J. Cherlin and Aphichat Chamsatrithirong, *Variations in Marriage Patterns in Central Thailand*, Institute for Population and Social Research, Mahidol University, Bangkok, 1987; Bhassorn Limanonda, 'Families in Thailand', 74.

30 D. N. Majumdar, 'Household in the Matrilineal Societies of North East India', in Saradamoni, *Finding the Household*, 120; Zhan Chengxu, 'Matriarchal/Patriarchal Families of the Naxi Nationality in Yongning, Yunnan Province', *Social Sciences in China*, March 1982, 140–55; and 'Yongning Naxi Azhu Marriage and Matrilineal Household', *Chinese Sociology and Anthropology*, vol. 25, no. 4, Summer 1993, 25–38.

31 This pattern was described for Rajasthan in northern India in 1961 by P. Kolenda, 'The Joint Family Household in Rural Rajasthan', in Gray and Mearns, *Society From the Inside Out*, 55–106.

32 A. Malhotra, 'Gender and Changing Generational Relations: Spouse Choice in Indonesia', *Demography*, vol. 28, 1991, 549–70; G. W. Jones, *Marriage and Divorce in Islamic South-East Asia*, Oxford University Press, Oxford, 1994.

33 Kumagai, 'Families in Japan', 146–7; Japan Information Network, 'Divorces (1983–1999)' http://jin.jcic.or.jp (accessed 13 August 2001).

34 Kim, Choi and Park, 'Rural Family and Community Life in South Korea', 285; I. H. Park and L-J. Cho, 'Confucianism and the Korean Family', 128–9; Kumagai, 'Families in Japan', 144–6; Y. Natsukari, 'A Structural Study of Spouse Selection in Japan', in Cho and Yada, *Tradition and Change in the Asian Family*, 135–52; N. O. Tsuya, 'Changing Attitudes Towards Marriage and

the Family in Japan', in Cho and Yada, *Tradition and Change in the Asian Family*, 95–7; Japan Information Network, 'Marriages (1983–1999)' and 'Tying the Knot: The Changing Face of Marriage in Japan', http://jin.jcic.or.jp (accessed 13 August 2001); G. Hugo, 'Women's Empowerment, Marriage Postponement, and Gender Relations in Japan', in H. Presser and G. Sen, eds, *Women's Empowerment and Demographic Processes*, Oxford University Press, New York, 2000; R. Retherford, N. Ogawa and R. Matsukura, 'Late Marriage and Less Marriage in Japan', *Population and Development Review*, vol. 27, no. 1, March 2001, 65–102.

35 B. Pasternak, *Marriage and Fertility in Tianjin, China: Fifty Years of Transition*, Paper No. 99, East West Population Institute, Honolulu, 1986; M. K. Whyte, 'Changes in Mate Choice in Chengdu', in D. Davis and E. Vogel, eds, *Chinese Society on the Eve of Tiananmen*, Council on East Asia Publications, Harvard, 1990, 181–214; Xiaohe Xu and M. K. Whyte, 'Love Matches and Arranged Marriage: A Chinese Replication', *Journal of Marriage and the Family*, vol. 52, 1990, 709–22; N. E. Riley, 'Interwoven Lives: Parents, Marriage, and Guanxi in China', *Journal of Marriage and the Family*, vol. 56, 1994, 791–803; also the chapters by M. Seldon, H. Siu and M. K. Whyte in Davis and Harrell, *Chinese Families in the Post-Mao Era*.

36 Malinee Wongsith, 'Attitudes Toward Family Values in Rural Thailand', in Cho and Yada, *Tradition and Change in the Asian Family*, 401–18; N. Saadawi, 'Women and Islam', *Women's Studies International Forum*, vol. 5, no. 2, 1982, 193–206; W. Walther, *Women in Islam*, trans. C. S. V. Salt, Marcus Wiener, New York, 1993 (contains F. Zarinebaf-Shahr, 'Recent English-Language Bibliography on Women in the Middle East'); Moghadam, 'Rhetorics and Rights of Identity in Islamic Movements', 243–64; also see J. Hoffman-Ladd, 'Polemics on the Modesty and Segregation of Women in Contemporary Egypt', *International Journal of Middle East Studies*, vol. 19, 1987, 23–50.

37 The family in England is discussed by Mitterauer and Sieder, *The European Family*, 27–8.

## Chapter 9 The World of Work

1 Y. Hayami and M. Kikuchi, *Asian Village Economy at the Crossroads: An Economic Approach to Institutional Change*, University of Tokyo Press, Tokyo, 1982, 156; J-P. Platteau, 'Traditional Systems of Social Security and Hunger Insurance: Past achievements and Modern Challenges', and B. Agarwal, 'Social Security and the Family: Coping with Seasonality and Calamity in Rural India', both in E. Ahmad et al., *Social Security in Developing Countries*, Clarendon Press, Oxford, 1991.

2 Gandhi's ideas on work are discussed by Chowdhury, 'Poverty, Environment, Development', 131–58.

3 Wadley, 'Family Composition Strategies in Rural Northern India', 1367–76.

4 See R. Joseph, *Worker, Middlewomen, Entrepreneur: Women in the Indonesian Batik Industry*, Population Council, Regional Office for South and East Asia, Bangkok, 1987; Amsden, *Asia's Next Giant*; E. P. Tsurumi, *Factory Girls: Women in the Thread Mills of Meiji Japan*, Princeton University Press, Princeton, 1990; F. A. Rothstein and M. L. Blim, eds, *Anthropology and the Global Factory: Studies of the New Industrialization in the Late Twentieth Century*, Bergin and Garvey, New York, 1992; and R. Saptari, 'Rural Women to the Factories: Continuity and Change in East Java's Kretek Cigarette Industry', unpublished PhD thesis, University of Amsterdam, 1995.

5 M. C. Brinton, *Women and the Economic Miracle*, University of California Press, Berkeley, 1993, 223; see also J. Hunter, ed., *Japanese Working Women*, Routledge, London, 1995.

6 Quoted by Murphey, *A History of Asia*, 432.

7 Y. Park and K. Anderson, 'The Rise and Demise of Textiles and Clothing in Economic Development', *Economic Development and Cultural Change*, vol. 38, no. 3, April 1991, 531–48; H. Hill, 'The Emperor's New Clothes Can Now Be Made in Indonesia', *Bulletin of Indonesian Economic Studies*, vol. 27, no. 3, December 1991, 89–127; A. H. Amsden, 'The Textile Industry in Asian Industrialization: A Leading Sector Institutionally?', *Journal of Asian Economics*, vol. 5, no. 4, 1994, 573–84.

8 G. Fairclough et al., 'Failing Grades', *Far Eastern Economic Review*, 29 September 1994, 62–9; W. Bello, S. Cunningham and L. K. Poh, *A Siamese Tragedy: Development and Disintegration in Modern*

*Thailand*, Zed Books, London, 1998, 56–7; I. Gill and F. Fluitman, eds, *Vocational Education and Training Reform: Matching Skills to Markets and Budgets*, Oxford University Press, New York, 2000. Country summaries from the Gill and Fluitman work are available through the World Bank website, http://wbln0018.worldbank.org/HDNet/HDdocs.nsf/ (accessed 21 August 2001).

9 Jeffrey, *Politics, Women, and Well-Being*, 217–24; Prakash, *Kerala's Economy*; Ramachandran, 'Kerala's Development Achievements'; K. C. Zachariah, E. T. Mathews and S. I. Rajan, 'Social, Economic and Demographic Consequences of Migration on Kerala', *International Migration*, vol. 39, no. 2, June 2001, 43–71; United Nations Development Program, *Human Development Report 2001*, Oxford University Press, New York, 2001, 38.

10 On mechanisms of international technology transfer, see P. Shukla and S. R. Chowdhry, eds, *Multinational Corporations, Technology and Development*, Akashdeep, New Delhi, 1992; and S. Lall, 'Technological Capabilities and Industrialization', *World Development*, vol. 20, no. 2, 1992, 165–86, and 'Promoting Technology Development: the Role of Technology Transfer and Indigenous Effort', *Third World Quarterly*, vol. 14, no. 1, 1993, 95–186. The expression 'technology-less industrialisation' was coined by Yoshihara Kunio, *Ersatz Development in Southeast Asia* (in Japanese only), and used by R. Steven, *Japan's New Imperialism*, Macmillan, London, 1990. On this topic in relation to the Asian financial crisis, see W. Bello, ed., 'The Asian Economic Crisis', Special Issue, *Ampo: Japan–Asia Quarterly Review*, vol. 28, no. 3, 1998; and Bello at al., *A Siamese Tragedy*, 1998, 55–73.

11 J. R. Lincoln and K. McBride, 'Japanese Industrial Organization in Comparative Perspective', *Annual Review of Sociology*, vol. 13, 1987, 289–312; M. Nomura, 'Excerpts from Shushin Koyo [Lifetime Employment]', *Japanese Economic Studies*, vol. 24, no. 1, January–February 1996 (complete issue); S. Watanabe, 'The Japanese Model and the Future of Employment and Wage Systems', *International Labour Review*, vol. 139, no. 3, 2000, 307–33.

12 United Nations Development Program, *The China Human Development Report*, Oxford University Press, New York, 1999, 54–62; Bello et al., *A Siamese Tragedy*, 134–5, 160–1; W. McGurn, 'City Limits', *Far Eastern Economic Review*, 6 February 1997, 34–7; G. Fairclough and R. Tasker, 'Separate and Unequal', *Far Eastern Economic Review*, 14 April 1994, 22–3.

13 United Nations Population Division, *World Urbanization Prospects: The 1999 Revision*, http://www.un.org/esa/population/urbanization.htm (accessed 19 July 2001).

14 Kam Wing Chan, 'Urbanisation and Rural–Urban Migration in China Since 1982', *Modern China*, vol. 20, no. 3, July 1994, 243–81; Zhong Fenggan, 'Urbanization', in Peng Xizhe and Guo Zhi Gang, eds, *The Changing Population of China*, Blackwell, Oxford, 2000, 167–78; United Nations Development Program, *The China Human Development Report*, 66–8.

15 R. Smilor, G. Kosmetsky and D. V. Gibson, *Creating the Technopolis: Linking Technology, Commercialisation and Economic Development*, Ballinger, Cambridge, Massachusetts, 1988; M. Castells and P. Hall, *Technopoles of the World: The Making of Twenty-First-Century Industrial Complexes*, Routledge, London, 1994; J. W. Dearing, *Growing a Japanese Science City: Communication in Scientific Research*, Routledge, London, 1995; M. Hiebert, 'Future Shock', *Far Eastern Economic Review*, 27 February 1997, 44–9; S. Jayasankaran, 'Field of Dreams', *Far Eastern Economic Review*, 27 February 1997, 49–50; S. Elegant and M. Hiebert, 'Tech mecca', *Far Eastern Economic Review*, 16 March 2000, 48–50.

16 Li Rongxia, 'Shenzhen: 20 Years of Brilliant Achievements', *Beijing Review*, vol. 43, no. 39, 25 September 2000, 12–17; D. Anwar, 'Sijori: ASEAN's Southern Growth Triangle, Problems and Prospects', *Indonesian Quarterly*, vol. 22, no. 1, 1994, 22–33; J. M. Tesoro, 'En Route to Jakarta', *Asiaweek*, vol. 24, no. 35, 4 September 1998, 26–7; S. L. Smith, *Indonesian Political Economy: Developing Batam*, Institute of Southeast Asian Studies, Singapore, 2000.

17 S. Castles and M. J. Miller, *The Age of Migration: International Population Movements in the Modern World*, Macmillan, London, 1993.

18 Quoted by G. Silverman, 'Vital and Vulnerable', *Far Eastern Economic Review*, 23 May 1996, 61. A similar view underlies the detailed study by P. Athukorala and C. Manning, *Structural Change and International Migration in East Asia: Adjusting to Labour Scarcity*, Oxford University Press, Melbourne, 1999. On citizens' arrests in Malaysia, see 'Public enlisted to halt rise in illegal immigrants', *Sydney Morning Herald*, 28 February 1998.

19 Asian Development Bank, *Asian Development Outlook 1996 and 1997*, Oxford University Press, Hong Kong, 1996, 202-8; P. J. Lloyd and L. Williams, eds, *International Trade and Migration in the Asia-Pacific Region*, Oxford University Press, Oxford, 1996; T. Saywell, 'Workers' Offensive', *Far Eastern Economic Review*, 29 May 1997, 50–2; N. Harris, 'Chinese Workers in Israel: A Bizarre Tale', *Economic and Political Weekly*, 19 May 2001, 1688; S. Puri and T. Ritzema, 'Migrant Worker Remittances, Micro-Finance and the Informal Economy: Prospects and Issues', International Labour Organization Working Paper no. 21, 1999, http://www.ilo.org/public/english/employment/ent/papers/wpap21.htm (accessed 21 August 2001); Hiroshi Komai, *Migrant Workers in Japan*, trans. J. Wilkinson, Kegan Paul International, London, 1995, chapter 4. Note that the figures on the contribution of remittances to national economies used by Komai appear to be higher than those in Table 9.5.

20 See, for example, the editorial 'Labouring Under Delusions: Workers Rights Rules Strike at Free Trade', *Far Eastern Economic Review*, 21 April 1994, 5; and S. Santoso, 'Asia's New Little Dragon—the Real Reason for US Concern About Indonesian Workers' Rights', *Inside Indonesia*, no. 33, December 1992, 18–19.

21 On labour issues in Indonesia, see C. Manning, 'Labour Market Adjustment to Indonesia's Economic Crisis', *Bulletin of Indonesian Economic Studies*, vol. 36 no. 1, 2000, 105–66; J. McBeth, 'Lost Labour, Lost Reform', *Far Eastern Economic Review*, 15 March 2001, 22–5; D. Djalal, 'Showdown at the Factory' *Far Eastern Economic Review*, 10 January 2002, 24–5; Waters, 'The Tragedy of Marsinah'; M. Lane and J. Balowski, 'Striking Out at Great River—Labour Unrest Continues', *Inside Indonesia*, no. 44, September 1995, 26–7; F. Abdullah, 'Labourers Won't Bow to Repression', *Inside Indonesia*, no. 47, July–September 1996, 14–15; Cohen, 'Still Hard Labour'; and McBeth, 'Open Wound'.

22 For example A. Chan, 'The Industrial Unrest Behind the "Made In China" Tag', *Canberra Times*, 2 July 1994; 'Nike Accused of Exploitation', *Canberra Times*, 29 March 1997; and P. Hancock, 'The Walking Ghosts of West Java', *Inside Indonesia*, no. 51, July–September 1997, 16–19. More generally on this aspect of multinational operations, see J. Brecher and T. Costello, *Global Village or Global Pillage: Economic Reconstruction from the Bottom Up*, South End Press, Boston, 1994; and Essential Information, Inc., *Multinational Monitor*, available on-line at http://www.essential.org/monitor.monitor.html (accessed 24 August 2001).

23 M. Clifford, 'Social Engineers', *Far Eastern Economic Review*, 14 April 1994, 56–60

24 J. Robinson, quoted by W. Hout, *Capitalism and the Third World*, Edward Elgar, Aldershot, 1993, 174.

25 A. Swift, 'Let Us Work!', *New Internationalist*, July 1997, 21–3.

26 Quoted by G. Fairclough, 'It Isn't Black and White', *Far Eastern Economic Review*, 7 March 1996, 57.

27 On child labour, see especially A. Bequele and J. Boyden, eds, *Combating Child Labour*, International Labour Organization, Geneva, 1988; International Labour Organization, International Programme on the Elimination of Child Labour, http://www.ilo.org/public/english/standards/ipec/index.htm; R. Anker, 'The Economics of Child Labour: A Framework for Measurement', *International Labour Review*, vol. 139, no. 3, 2000, 257–80; Fairclough, 'It Isn't Black and White', 54–7; J. Karp, 'Caste-Iron Servitude', *Far Eastern Economic Review*, 7 March 1996, 57–8; B. Gilley, 'Following the Money', *Far Eastern Economic Review*, 7 March 1996, 58; S. Bessell, 'Children at Work', *Inside Indonesia*, no. 56, March 1996, 18–21; S. W. E. Goonesekere, *Child Labour in Sri Lanka: Learning From the Past*, International Labour Organization, Geneva, 1993; and Sri Lanka Department of Census and Statistics, *Summary of Findings of Child Labour Survey in Sri Lanka, 1999*, http://www.ilo.org/public/english/standards/ipec/simpoc/srilanka/report/srilan99/index.htm (accessed 24 August 2001).

28 Goonesekere, *Child Labour in Sri Lanka*, 67.

## Chapter 10 Media, Communication, Censorship

1 D. R. Headrick, *The Invisible Weapon: Telecommunications and International Politics, 1851–1945*, Oxford University Press, 1991.

2 On the development of printing in China and Korea, see Tsien Tsuen-Hsuin, 'Paper and Printing', Pt 1 in *Science and Civilisation in China*, vol. 5, ed. J. Needham, Cambridge University

Press, Cambridge, 1985; and S. Jeon, *Science and Technology in Korea: Traditional Instruments and Techniques*, MIT Press, Cambridge, Massachusetts, 1974, 167–83.

3 Headrick, *The Invisible Weapon*, 187–8.

4 C. Wild, 'The Radio Midwife: Some Thoughts on the Role of Broadcasting During the Indonesian Struggle for Independence', *Indonesia Circle*, no. 55, 1991, 34–42.

5 G. C. Chu, Alfian Schramm and W. Schramm, *Social Impact of Satellite Television in Rural Indonesia*, Asian Mass Communication Research and Information Centre, Singapore, 1991; J. L. Parapak, 'The Role of Satellite Communications in National Development: Future Trends', *Media Asia*, vol. 20, no. 1, 1993, 24–32; W. Atkins, *Satellite Television and State Power in Southeast Asia: New Issues in Discourse and Control*, Centre for Asian Communication, Media and Cultural Studies, Edith Cowan University, Perth, 1995, 2.

6 P. Handley, 'Press and Pirates', *Far Eastern Economic Review*, 11 June 1992, 10–11; Atkins, *Satellite Television and State Power in Southeast Asia*, 50–9; W. A. Callahan, *Imagining Democracy: Reading 'The Events of May' in Thailand*, Institute of Southeast Asian Studies, Singapore, 1998, 18–19.

7 M. Hopkins, 'A Babel of Broadcasts', *Columbia Journalism Review*, vol. 38, no. 2, 1999, 44–7; 'China: America's Radio Free Asia Draws Beijing's Ire', *Far Eastern Economic Review*, vol. 161, no. 27, 1998, 34–5. See also the Radio Free Asia website http://www.rfa.org/ (accessed 20 September 2001).

8 Details of the Chinese government's ruling are given in 'The Detailed Regulations of the Government Rules for Satellite TV Receivers—Ministry of Radio, Film and Television', *People's Daily*, 27 February 1994. On Iran, see 'Iran: Satellite Crack-Down', *Middle East International*, no. 539, 6 December 1996, 10.

9 P. M. Kennedy, *Preparing for the Twentyfirst Century*, HarperCollins, London, 1993, 49–50; S. Bell, 'VSATS in Transition', *Asian Communications*, June 1996, 48–50; Ravi Narain, 'A Floorless Exchange', *Asian Communications*, June 1996, 50–1.

10 P. S. Triolo and P. Lovelock, 'Up, Up, and Away—With Strings Attached', *China Business Review*, November–December 1996, 18–29; and G. Meaher, 'The Internet's Impact', *Asian Communications*, March 1996, 28–32; D. Lynch, *After the Propaganda State: Media, Politics and 'Thought Work' in Reformed China*, Stanford University Press, Stanford, 1999, 106–10, 208–15; 'China Enacts Sweeping Rules on Internet Firms', *Agence France Presse*, 2 October 2000; 'Reporters Without Borders Slam China's New Internet Rules', *Agence France Presse*, 5 October 2000; L. S. Malakoff, 'Are You My Mommy, or My Big Brother? Comparing Internet Censorship in Singapore and the United States', *Pacific Rim Law and Policy Journal*, vol. 8, no. 2, 1999, 423–52; S. B. Hogan, 'To Net or Not to Net: Singapore's Regulation of the Internet', *Federal Communications Law Journal*, vol. 51, no. 2, 1999, 429–47; M. K. Anuar, 'Malaysian Media and Democracy', *Media Asia*, vol. 27, no. 4, 2000, 183–93. See also T. S. Auh, 'Regulation of the Internet: Is it Desirable or Even Possible?', *Media Asia*, vol. 27, no. 2, 2000, 111–15; J. P. Abbott, 'Democracy@internet.asia? The Challenges to the Emancipatory Potential of the Net: Lessons from China and Malaysia', *Third World Quarterly*, vol. 22, no. 1, 2001, 99–114.

11 C. Lyttleton, 'Knowledge and Meaning: The AIDS Education Campaign in Rural Northeast Thailand', *Social Science and Medicine*, vol. 38, no. 1, 1994, 135–46; Bello et al., *A Siamese Tragedy*, 221–42.

12 'Australian Media is "Most Free"', and 'Ugly Dimensions of New Censorship', editorial, *Canberra Times*, 4 May 1994 and 29 May 1995.

13 Quoted in editorial, *Far Eastern Economic Review*, 19 May 1994.

14 Atkins, *Satellite Television and State Power in Southeast Asia*, 2–3, 62; 'Successful Launch of AsiaSat 2', *Asian Communications*, January 1996, 5.

15 R. Bharucha, 'Somebody's Other: Disorientations in the Cultural Politics of Our Times', *Economic and Political Weekly*, 15 January 1994, 108.

16 K. Mahbubani, 'An Asian Perspective on Human Rights and Freedom of the Press', *Media Asia*, vol. 20, no. 3, 1993, 161.

17 J. A. Lent, *Topics in Third World Mass Communications*, Asia Research Service, Hong Kong, 1979, and 'Mass Communication in Asia and the Pacific: Recent Trends and Development', *Media*

*Asia*, vol. 16, no. 1, 1989, 17; A. J. Jeffery, 'Free Speech and Press: An Absolute Right?', *Human Rights Quarterly*, vol. 8, no. 2, May 1986, 197–226.

18 President Suharto, 'Role of the Press in National Development', adapted from a speech on National Press Day, 9 February 1989, trans. S. Ramanathan and L. Y. Kam, in A. Mehra, ed., *Press Systems in Asean States*, Asia Mass Communication Research and Information Centre, Singapore, 1989, 131–4; Atkins, *Satellite Television and State Power in Southeast Asia*, 14–15, 22–6.

19 A. Romano, 'The Press in Indonesia: A Brief History', *Media International Australia*, no. 79, February 1996, 64–6, and 'The Open Wound: Keterbukaan and Press Freedom in Indonesia', *Australian Journal of International Affairs*, vol. 50, no. 2, July 1996, 157–69; K. Sen and D. T. Hill, *Media, Culture and Politics in Indonesia*, Oxford University Press, Melbourne, 2000, 54–6; A. Harsono, 'Indonesia: Dancing in the Dark', in L. Williams and R. Rich, eds, *Losing Control: Freedom of the Press in Asia*, Asia Pacific Press, Asia Pacific School of Economics and Management, Australian National University, Canberra, 2000, 74–92.

20 'Laws to Curb Media Necessary: Mahathir', *Canberra Times*, 23 October 1996 (report of a speech at Malaysian Press Institute, October 1996).

21 V. G. Kulkarni, M. Hiebert and S. Jayasankaran, 'Tough Talk: Premier Mahathir Thrives on No-Nonsense Policies', *Far Eastern Economic Review*, 24 October 1996, 23.

22 Callahan, *Imagining Democracy*, 19. See also B. MacGregor, *Live, Direct, and Biased? Making Television News in the Satellite Age*, Arnold, London, 1997.

23 J. Lull, *China Turned On: Television, Reform, and Resistance*, Routledge, London, 1991, 215–16.

24 M. Balali, 'Iran Gets Its Own Barbie Doll', *Canberra Times*, 22 October 1996.

25 G. C. Chu and Y. Ju, *The Great Wall in Ruins: Communication and Cultural Change in China*, State University of New York Press, Albany, New York, 1993.

26 Bharucha, 'Somebody's Other', 108.

27 On the issue of the influence of television in India, see also R. B. Crabtree and S. Malhotra, 'A Case Study of Commercial Television in India: Assessing the Organizational Mechanisms of Cultural Imperialism', *Journal of Broadcasting and Electronic Media*, vol. 44, no. 3, 2000, 364–85; and K. Johnson, *Television and Social Change in Rural India*, Sage, Delhi, 2000.

28 Chen Yiyun, 'Out of the Traditional Halls of Academe', 75.

29 W. Won, 'The Social and Cultural Impact of Satellite Broadcasting in Korea', *Media Asia*, vol. 21, no. 1, 1993, 17.

30 S. D. Kim, 'Wrongfully Intervened: Introducing Cable and Satellite Television in Korea, 1987–1996', *Korean Social Science Journal*, vol. 26, no. 1, 1999, 33–66.

31 J. Karp, 'High Anxiety', and 'Out of Space', *Far Eastern Economic Review*, 18 August 1994, 46–50.

32 Studies conducted in 1992 in Hong Kong, Indonesia, Malaysia, the Philippines, Singapore, South Korea, and Thailand are discussed by G. Wang, 'Satellite Television and the Future of Broadcast Television in the Asia-Pacific', *Media Asia*, vol. 20, no. 3, 1993, 147; later studies in Hong Kong, India, Japan, Malaysia, and the Philippines are reported in A. Goonasekera and P. Lee, eds, *TV Without Borders: Asia Speaks Out*, Asian Media Information and Communication Centre, Singapore, 1998.

## Chapter 11 Using and Creating Knowledge

1 Relevant OECD reports include: *Technology and the Economy: The Key Relationships*, OECD, Paris, 1992; *Managing National Innovation Systems*, OECD, Paris, 1999; *A New Economy: The Changing Role of Innovation and Information Technology in Growth*, OECD, Paris, 2000; and *Science, Technology and Industry Outlook 2000*, OECD, Paris, 2000. See also United Nations Development Program, *Human Development Report 2001*, Oxford University Press, New York, 2001, 27–117.

2 UNDP, *Human Development Report 2001*, 37–45. At this point the authors of the report rely heavily, and somewhat uncritically, on J. Hillner, 'Venture Capitals', *Wired*, vol. 8, no. 7, July 2000, 258–71.

3 N. J. Vig, 'Technology, Philosophy, and the State: An Overview', in M. E. Kraft and N. J. Vig, eds, *Technology and Politics*, Duke University, Durham, NC, 1988, 10.

4 United Nations Development Program, *Human Development Report 2001*, 96. On technological divergence see especially P. Patel and K. Pavitt, 'Divergence in Technological Development Among Countries and Firms', and Freeman and Hagendoorn, 'Convergence and Divergence in the Internationalisation of Technology', in J. Hagendoorn, ed., *Technological Change in the World Economy*.

5 A.Y. al-Hassan and D. R. Hill, *Islamic Technology: An Illustrated History*, Cambridge University Press and Unesco, Cambridge and Paris, 1986, 191.

6 The Chinese scholar and official Feng Guifen (1809–74) provided an influential early statement of the strategy of using indigenous knowledge as the substance or foundation, and Western knowledge as the application or means. For a translation see W. T. de Bary et al., *Sources of Chinese Tradition*, vol. 2, Columbia University Press, New York, 1964, 48–9.

7 K. Pavitt, 'International Patterns of Technological Accumulation', in N. Hood and J-E. Vahle, eds, *Strategies in Global Competition*, Croom Helm, Beckenham, 1988; M. Sharp and K. Pavitt, 'Technology Policy in the 1990s: Old Trends and New Realities', *Journal of Common Market Studies*, vol. 31, no. 2, June 1993, 130–1; J. Mokyr, *The Lever of Riches: Technological Creativity and Economic Progress*, Oxford University Press, Oxford, 1990, 162–5.

8 Y. Fukasaku, *Technology and Industrial Growth in Pre-War Japan: The Mitsubishi-Nagasaki Shipyard 1884-1934*, Routledge, London, 1992; Morris-Suzuki, *The Technological Transformation of Japan*, ch. 7.

9 The journal *Indigenous Knowledge and Development Monitor* (The Hague) provides useful information on this topic. See also Agrawal, 'Dismantling the Divide Between Indigenous and Scientific Knowledge'; C. Antweiler, 'Local Knowledge and Local Knowing: An Anthropological Analysis of Contested "Cultural Products" in the Context of Development', *Anthropos*, vol. 93, 1998, 469–94; P. Sillitoe, 'The Development of Indigenous Knowledge: A New Applied Anthropology', *Current Anthropology*, vol. 39, no. 2, April 1998, 223–52.

10 The most famous text is *Bencao gangmu* (1602), by Li Shizhen. P. Unschuld, *Medicine in China: A History of Pharmaceutics*, University of California Press, Berkeley, 1986, provides a general account of the field.

11 On the merging of science and technology, see B. Barnes and D. Edge, eds, *Science in Context*, Open University Press, Milton Keynes, 1982; R. Laudan, ed., *The Nature of Technological Knowledge: Are Models of Scientific Change Relevant?*, D. Reidel, Dordrecht, 1984; F. Narin and D. Olivastro, 'Status Report: Linkage Between Technology and Science', *Research Policy*, vol. 21, 1992, 237–49; and M. Gibbons, et al., *The New Production of Knowledge: The Dynamics of Science and Research in Contemporary Societies*, Sage, London, 1994.

12 Increasingly this basic position is being adopted not in order to make tedious assertions about the impossibility of 'real' knowledge, but rather as a first step towards understanding how knowledge is possible. The variety of approaches taken is exemplified by L. Nader, ed., *Naked Science: Anthropological Inquiry into Boundaries, Power, and Knowledge*, Routledge, New York, 1996; J. Golinski, *Making Natural Knowledge: Constructivism and the History of Science*, Cambridge University Press, Cambridge, 1998; S. Harding, *Is Science Multicultural? Postcolonialisms, Feminisms, and Epistemologies*, Indiana University Press, Bloomington, 1998; J. Ziman, *Real Science: What it is, and What it Means*, Cambridge University Press, Cambridge, 2000; B. Flyvbjerg, *Making Social Science Matter: Why Social Inquiry Fails and How it Can Succeed Again*, Cambridge University Press, Cambridge, 2001.

13 D. Kalupahana, *Buddhist Philosophy*, University of Hawaii Press, Honolulu, 1976, 17–20; S. Radhakrishnan and C.A. Moore, eds, *A Source Book in Indian Philosophy*, Princeton University Press, Princeton, 1957, 359; M. Hiriyanna, *Outlines of Indian Philosophy*, Allen & Unwin, London, 1932, 177-9, 257-8.

14 S. Shapin, *A Social History of Truth: Civility and Science in Seventeenth-Century England*, University of Chicago Press, Chicago, 1994.

15 See, for example, P. Galison and D. J. Stump, eds, *The Disunity of Science: Boundaries, Contexts, and Power*, Stanford University Press, Stanford, Calif., 1996; M. Carrier, G. Massey and L. Ruetsche, eds, *Science at Century's End: Philosophical Questions on the Progress and Limits of Science*, University of Pittsburgh Press, Pittsburgh, 2000; and D. Turnbull, *Masons, Tricksters and Cartographers:*

*Comparative Studies in the Sociology of Scientific and Indigenous Knowledge*, Harwood Academic, Amsterdam, 2000.

16 P. G. Altbach, 'Gigantic Peripheries: India and China in the World Knowledge System', *Economic and Political Weekly*, 12 June 1993, 1220–5; also Altbach's study, *The Knowledge Context: Comparative Perspectives on the Distribution of Knowledge*, State University of New York Press, Albany, New York, 1987. On the international role of English see D. Crystal, *English as a Global Language*, Cambridge University Press, Cambridge, 1997.

17 Agrawal, 'Dismantling the Divide Between Indigenous and Scientific Knowledge', 422–7.

18 L. Daston, 'Objectivity and the Escape from Perspective', *Social Studies of Science*, vol. 22, 1992, 597–618.

19 On rationality, see J. Goody, *The East in the West*, Cambridge University Press, Cambridge, 1996, chs 1 and 2.

20 See, for example, Gibbons et al., *The New Production of Knowledge*; P. Altbach, *Comparative Higher Education*, Ablex, Greenwich, Conn., 1998; P. Baggen, A. Tellings and W. van Haaften, eds, *The University and the Knowledge Society*, Concorde Publishing House, Bemmel, 1998; D. Smith and A. K. Langslow, eds, *The Idea of a University*, J. Kingsley, London, 1999; and S. Inayatullah and J. Gidley, eds, *The University Transformations: Global Perspectives on the Futures of the University*, Bergin and Garvey, Westport, Conn., 2000.

21 On gender and education generally, see E. M. King and M. A. Hill, eds, *Women's Education in Developing Countries: Barriers, Benefits, and Policies*, Johns Hopkins University Press, Baltimore, 1993; and M. Nussbaum and J. Glover, eds, *Women, Culture and Development: A Study of Human Capabilities*, Clarendon Press, Oxford, 1995. Statistical information is available from the Unesco website at http://www.unesco.org/ (accessed 8 August 2001). On the problems faced by Indian women, see D. R. Evans, 'The Challenge of Education for All in India', *Comparative Education Review*, vol. 44, no. 1, 2000, 81–7; and P. G. Pillai, 'Higher Education in India in the 21st Century', *Social Action*, vol. 50, no. 4, 2000, 390–403. On Chinese female graduates, see especially J. Kwong, ed., 'Women's Education and Employment', Special Issue, *Chinese Education and Society*, vol. 33, no. 2, March/April 2000.

22 S. Pepper, *China's Education Reform in the 1980s: Policies, Issues, and Historical Perspectives*, Institute of East Asian Studies, University of California at Berkeley, Berkeley, 1990, 182–3; and J. Lin, *Social Transformation and Private Education in China*, Praeger, Westport, Conn., 1999.

23 W. T. de Bary, *Dialogues on East Asian Civilization: A Dialogue in Five Stages*, Harvard University Press, Cambridge, Mass., 1988, 110–13, identifies the traditional Confucian elitist approach to education as an obstacle to modernisation, while arguing that the high value attached to education in Confucian culture has been a major factor in East Asia's spectacular postwar rise. See also R. Hayhoe, *China's Universities 1895–1995*, Hong Kong University Press, Hong Kong, 1999. On the economic and social benefits of developing education generally, see G. Psacharopolous, 'Returns to Investment in Education: A Global Update', *World Development*, vol. 22, no. 9, 1994, 1325–43; T. P. Schultz, ed., *Investing in Women's Human Capital*, University of Chicago Press, Chicago, 1996; and OECD, *Investing in Education: Analysis of the 1999 World Education Indicators*, OECD, Paris, 2000.

24 R. E. Rucker, 'Trends in Post-Revolutionary Iranian Education', *Journal of Contemporary Asia*, vol. 21, no. 4, 1991, 455–68; D. Menashri, *Education and the Making of Modern Iran*, Cornell University Press, Ithaca, New York, 1992, 307–28.

25 E. Sivan, *Radical Islam: Medieval Theology and Modern Politics*, Yale University Press, New Haven, 1990.

26 J. S. K. Yip and S. W. Kooi, *Evolution of Educational Excellence: 25 Years of Education in the Republic of Singapore*, Longman, Singapore, 1990; J. C. Oon Ai, 'Civics and Moral Education in Singapore: Lessons for Citizenship Education?', *Journal of Moral Education*, vol. 27, no. 4, December 1998, 505–24; J. Spring, *Education and the Rise of the Global Economy*, Lawrence Erlbaum, Mahwah, New York, 1998, 70–91.

27 On recent education trends in Indonesia, see G. W. Jones and P. Hagul, 'Schooling in Indonesia: Crisis-Related and Longer-Term Issues', *Bulletin of Indonesian Economic Studies*, vol. 37 no. 2, August 2001, 207–31; M. Oey-Gardiner, 'Schooling in a Decentralised Indonesia: New

Approaches to Access and Decision Making', *Bulletin of Indonesian Economic Studies*, vol, 36, no. 3, December 2000, 127–34; and Indonesia, Ministry of National Education, *Indonesian Education Statistics 1999–2000*, at http://www.pdk.go.id (accessed 10 August 2001).

28 S. J. O'Connor, 'Iron Working as Spiritual Inquiry in the Indonesian Archipelago', *History of Religions*, vol. 14, 1974, 173–90; G. Solyom and B. Solyom, *The World of the Javanese Keris*, East-West Center, Honolulu, 1978.

29 For example, see M. Lock, *East Asian Medicine in Urban Japan*, University of California Press, Berkeley, 1980; A. Nandy and S. Visvanathan, 'Modern medicine and Its Non-Modern Critics: A Study in Discourse', in F. Apffel Marglin and S. A. Marglin, eds, *Dominating Knowledge: Development, Culture and Resistance*, Clarendon Press, Oxford, 1990, 145–84; C. Chi, 'Integrating Traditional Medicine into Modern Health Care Systems', *Social Science and Medicine*, vol. 39, no. 3, 1994, 307–21; and J. Farquhar, *Knowing Practice: The Clinical Encounter of Chinese Medicine*, Westview Press, Boulder, Colorado, 1994.

30 T. Nagel, *The View from Nowhere*, Oxford University Press, Oxford, 1986.

## Conclusion

1 A similar argument is put by Goody, *The East in the West*, 226–49.

2 Miguel de Cervantes Saavedra, *The Ingenious Gentleman Don Quixote de la Mancha*, trans. S. Putnam, Viking, New York, 1949, vol. 2, pt 2, ch. 12, 580.

3 See S. C. Brown, ed., *Objectivity and Cultural Convergence*, Cambridge University Press, Cambridge, 1984; B. Williams, *Ethics and the Limits of Philosophy*, Harvard University Press, Cambridge, Mass., 1985; and R. Proctor, *Value-Free Science?*, Harvard University Press, Cambridge, Mass., 1992. Williams's work is discussed by Marglin, 'Towards the Decolonization of the Mind', in Apffel Marglin and Marglin, *Dominating Knowledge*, 12–13.

4 Dalai Lama, *Beyond Dogma*, 3.

# BIBLIOGRAPHY


Abbott, A., *Chaos of Disciplines*, University of Chicago Press, Chicago, 2001.

Abbott, J. P., 'Democracy@internet.asia? The Challenges to the Emancipatory Potential of the Net: Lessons from China and Malaysia', *Third World Quarterly*, vol. 22, no. 1, 2001, 99–114.

Abdullah, F., 'Labourers Won't Bow to Repression', *Inside Indonesia*, no. 47, July–September 1996, 14–15.

Abercrombie, N., Hill, S. and Turner, B. S., *The Dominant Ideology Thesis*, Allen & Unwin, London, 1980.

Abernethy, V. D., *Population Politics: The Choices that Shape Our Future*, Plenum Press, New York, 1993.

Abeykoon, A. T. P. L., 'Sex Preference in South Asia: Sri Lanka an Outlier', *Asia-Pacific Population Journal*, vol. 10, no. 3, September 1995, 5-16.

Abrash, A., 'The Amungme, Kamoro and Freeport: How Indigenous Papuans have Resisted the World's Largest Copper and Gold Mine'. *Cultural Survival Quarterly*, vol. 25 no. 1, 2001, 38–43.

Agarwal, B., 'Social Security and the Family: Coping with Seasonality and Calamity in Rural India', in E. Ahmad et al., *Social Security in Developing Countries*, Clarendon Press, Oxford, 1991.

Aghajanian, A., 'A New Direction in Population Policy and Family Planning in the Islamic Republic of Iran', *Asia-Pacific Population Journal*, vol. 10 no. 1, March 1995, 3–20.

Agnihotri, S. B., 'Declining Infant and Child Mortality in India: How do Girl Children Fare?', *Economic and Political Weekly*, 20 January 2000, 228–33.

——*Sex Ratio Patterns in the Indian Population: A Fresh Exploration*, Sage, New Delhi, 2000.

Agrawal, A., 'Dismantling the Divide Between Indigenous and Scientific Knowledge', *Development and Change*, vol. 26, no. 3, July 1995, 413–39.

Agrawal, A. and Narain, S., 'Towards Green Villages', in W. Sachs, ed., *Global Ecology: A New Arena of Political Conflict*, Zed Books, London, 1993.

Aird, J. S., *Slaughter of the Innocents: Coercive Birth Control in China*, American Enterprise Institution Press, Washington DC, 1990.

Akula, V. K., 'Grassroots Environmental Resistance in India', in B. T. Taylor, ed., *Ecological Resistance Movements: The Global Emergence of Radical and Popular Environmentalism*, State University of New York, Albany, NY, 1995.

al-Hassan, A. Y. and Hill, D. R., *Islamic Technology: An Illustrated History*, Cambridge University Press and Unesco, Cambridge and Paris, 1986.

Alauddin, M. and Tisdell, C., *The Green Revolution and Economic Development: The Process and Its Impact in Bangladesh*, St Martin's Press, NY, 1991.

Alfredsson, G. and de Zayas, A., 'Minority Rights: Protection by the United Nations', *Human Rights Law Journal*, vol. 14, nos. 1–2, 26 February 1993, 1–9.

Altbach, P. G., *Comparative Higher Education*, Ablex, Greenwich, Conn., 1998.

——*The Knowledge Context: Comparative Perspectives on the Distribution of Knowledge*, State University of New York Press, Albany, NY, 1987.

Alvares, C., 'Science', in W. Sachs, ed., *The Development Dictionary: A Guide to Knowledge as Power*, Zed Books, London, 1992.

Amin, R. et al., 'Reproductive Change in Bangladesh: Evidence From Recent Data', *Asia-Pacific Population Journal*, vol. 8, no. 4, December 1993, 39–58.

Amin, S., *Delinking: Towards a Polycentric World*, Zed Books, London, 1990.

Amnesty International, *Report 2001*, http://web.amnesty.org/web/ar2001.nsf/, accessed 10 August 2001.

Amsden, A. H., 'The Textile Industry in Asian Industrialization: A Leading Sector Institutionally?', *Journal of Asian Economics*, vol. 5, no. 4, 1994, 573–84.

——*Asia's Next Giant: South Korea and Late Industrialization*, Oxford University Press, New York, 1989.

An-Na'im, A. A., 'Islam, Islamic Law and the Dilemma of Cultural Legitimacy for Universal Human Rights', in C. E. Welch and V. Leary, eds, *Asian Perspectives on Human Rights*, Westview Press, Boulder, Colo., 1990.

——'The Cultural Mediation of Human Rights: The Al-Argam Case in Malaysia', in J. Bauer and D. Bell, eds, *The East Asian Challenge for Human Rights*, Cambridge University Press, Cambridge, 1999.

——'Towards a Cross-Cultural Approach to Defining International Standards of Human Rights: The Meaning of Cruel, Inhuman or Degrading Treatment or Punishment', in An-Na'im, ed., *Human Rights in Cross-Cultural Perspective*, University of Pennsylvania Press, Philadelphia, 1992.

Anderson, B., *Imagined Communities: Reflections on the Origin and Spread of Nationalism*, Verso, London, 1983.

Andreski, S., ed., *Max Weber on Capitalism, Bureaucracy, and Religion: A Selection of Texts*, Allen & Unwin, London, 1983.

Agnihotri, S. B., 'Declining Infant and Child Mortality in India: How do Girl Children Fare?', *Economic and Political Weekly*, 20 January 2000, 228–33.

——*Sex Ration Patterns in the Indian Population: A Fresh Exploration*, Sage, New Delhi, 2000.

Anker, R., 'The Economics of Child Labour: A Framework for Measurement', *International Labour Review*, vol. 139, no. 3, 2000, 257–80.

Antweiler, C., 'Local Knowledge and Local Knowing: An Anthropological Analysis of Contested "Cultural Products" in the Context of Development', *Anthropos*, vol. 93, 1998, 469–94.

Anuar, M. K., 'Malaysian Media and Democracy', *Media Asia*, vol. 27, no. 4, 2000, 183–93.

Anwar, D., 'Sijori: ASEAN's Southern Growth Triangle, Problems and Prospects', *Indonesian Quarterly*, vol. 22, no. 1, 1994, 22–33.

Appelbaum, R. P. and Henderson, J., eds, *States and Development in the Asia Pacific Rim*, Sage, Newbury Park, 1992.

Arens, W., *The Man-Eating Myth: Anthropology and Anthropophagy*, Oxford University Press, New York, 1979.

Arora, D., 'From State Regulation to People's Participation: Case of Forest Management in India', *Economic and Political Weekly*, vol. 29, no. 12, 19 March 1994, 691–8.

Arrigo, L. G., 'The Environmental Nightmare of the Economic Miracle: Land Abuse and Land Struggles in Taiwan', *Bulletin of Concerned Asian Scholars*, vol. 26, nos 1–2, 1994, 21–44.

Ashworth, G., ed., *World Minorities*, Quartermaine House, London, 1977.

——*World Minorities in the Eighties*, Quartermaine House, London, 1978.

Asian Development Bank, *Asian Development Outlook 1996 and 1997*, Oxford University Press, Hong Kong, 1996.

——*Technology Transfer and Development: Implications for Developing Asia*, Asian Development Bank, n.p., May 1995.

——'Water in the 21st Century', http://www.adb.org/Documents/Reports/Water, accessed 28 August 2001.

Athukorala, P., and Manning, C., *Structural Change and International Migration in East Asia: Adjusting to Labour Scarcity*, Oxford University Press, Melbourne, 1999.

Atkins, W., *Satellite Television and State Power in Southeast Asia: New Issues in Discourse and Control*, Centre for Asian Communication, Media and Cultural Studies, Edith Cowan University, Perth, 1995.

Auh, T. S., 'Regulation of the Internet: Is It Possible or Even Desirable?', *Media Asia*, vol. 27, no. 2, 2000, 111–15.

Aung San Suu Kyi, *Freedom From Fear and Other Writings*, 2nd edn, Penguin, Harmondsworth, 1995.

Australian Council for Overseas Aid, *Trouble at Freeport: Eyewitness Accounts of West Papuan Resistance to the Freeport-McMoRan Mine in Irian Jaya, Indonesia, and Indonesian Military Repression*: June 1994–February 1995, Canberra, 5 April 1995.

'Australian Media is "Most Free"', *Canberra Times*, 4 May 1994.

Baggen, P., Tellings, A., and van Haaften, W., eds, *The University and the Knowledge Society*, Concorde Publishing House, Bemmel, 1998.

Balali, M., 'Iran Gets Its Own Barbie Doll', *Canberra Times*, 22 October 1996.

Ballard, C. and Banks, G., 'Freeport Indonesia: 25 Years Up and 100 to Go', paper presented at Mining in Melanesia Series Seminar, Research School of Pacific and Asian Studies, Australian National University, Canberra, 15 March 1995.

Banerji, D., 'The Political Economy of Population Control in India', in L. Bondestam and S. Berstroem, eds, *Poverty and Population Control*, Academic Press, London, 1980.

Bangladesh: Ministry of Health and Family Welfare, *Arsenic Contamination Project*, Ministry of Health and Family Welfare, Dhaka, 1998.

Bangladesh: Task Forces on Bangladesh Development Strategies for the 1990s, *Policies for Development vol. 1, Women In Development*, University Press, Dhaka, 1991.

Banuri, T. and Marglin Apffel, F., eds, *Who Will Save the Forests?*, Atlantic Highlands, London, 1993.

Barnes, B. and Edge, D., eds, *Science in Context*, Open University Press, Milton Keynes, 1982.

Barnhart, M. G., 'Ideas of Nature in an Asian Context', *Philosophy East and West*, vol. 47, no. 3, July 1997, 417-32.

Bary, W. T. de, et al., *Sources of Chinese Tradition*, 2 vols, Columbia University Press, New York, 1964.

——*Dialogues on East Asian Civilization: A Dialogue in Five Stages*, Harvard University Press, Cambridge, Mass., 1988.

——and Tu Weiming, eds, *Confucianism and Human Rights*, Columbia University Press, New York, 1998.

Bashkin, V., and Park, S., eds, *Acid Deposition and Ecosystem Sensitivity in East Asia*, Nova Science Publishers, Commack, New York, 1998.

Bates, C., '"Lost Innocents and the Loss of Innocence": Interpreting the Adivasi Movements in South Asia', in R. H. Barnes et al., eds, *Indigenous Peoples of Asia*, Association for Asian Studies, Ann Arbor, Mich., 1995.

Baxi, U., and Paul, T., *Mass Disasters and Multinational Liability: The Bhopal Case*, N. M. Tripathi, Bombay, 1986.

Becher, T., *Academic Tribes and Territories: Intellectual Enquiry and the Cultures of Disciplines*, The Society for Research into Higher Education and Open University Press, Bristol, Pennsylvania, and Milton Keynes, 1989.

Beer, L. W., ed., *Constitutional Systems in Late Twentieth Century Asia*, University of Washington Press, Seattle, 1992.

Bell, D. A., 'The East Asian Challenge to Human Rights: Reflections on an East West Dialogue', *Human Rights Quarterly*, vol. 18, no. 3, 1996.

Bell, S., 'VSATS in Transition', *Asian Communications*, June 1996, 48–50.

Bello, W., *Perils and Possibilities: The Pacific in the Post-Cold War Era*, Evatt Foundation of Australia and Freedom from Hunger Campaign, Sydney, 1992.

——'The Asian Economic Implosion: Causes, Dynamics, Prospects', *Race and Class*, vol. 40, nos. 2/3, 1998, 133–44.

——'The Rise and Fall of South-East Asia's Economy', *The Ecologist*, vol. 28, no. 1, January/February 1998, 9–17.

——ed., 'The Asian Economic Crisis. East Asia: On the Eve of the Great Transformation?', Special Issue, *Ampo*, vol. 28, no. 3, 1998.

Bello, W., Cunningham, S., and Li Kheng Poh, *A Siamese Tragedy: Development and Disintegration in Modern Thailand*, Zed Books, London, 1998.

Bello, W. and Rosenfeld, S., *Dragons in Distress: Asia's Economic Miracles in Crisis*, Penguin, Harmondsworth, 1992.

Benewick, R., and Wingrove, P., eds, *China in the 1990s*, 2nd edn, UBC Press, Vancouver, 1999.

Bentley, J. H., *Old World Encounters: Cross-Cultural Exchanges in Pre-Modern Times*, Oxford University Press, Oxford, 1993.

Bequele, A. and Boyden, J., eds, *Combating Child Labour*, International Labour Organization, Geneva, 1988.

Berger, P. and Hsiao, M. H. H., *In Search of an East Asian Development Model*, Berger and Hsiao, New Brunswick, 1988.

Bessell, S., 'Children at Work', *Inside Indonesia*, no. 56, March 1996, 18–21.

Betke, F., *Modernization and Socioeconomic Change in the Coastal Marine Fisheries of Java: Some Hypotheses*, Working Paper No. 72, Sociology of Development Research Centre, University of Bielefeld, Bielefeld, 1985.

Bhalla, A. and James, D., eds, *New Technologies and Development: Experiences in Technology Blending*, L. Rienner, Boulder, Colo., 1988.

Bharucha, R., 'Somebody's Other: Disorientations in the Cultural Politics of Our Times', *Economic and Political Weekly*, 15 January 1994, 105–10.

Bhassorn Limanonda, 'Families in Thailand: Beliefs and Realities', *Journal of Comparative Family Studies*, vol. 26, no. 1, Spring 1995, 67–82.

Bhatt, G. S., 'Constraints of being polyandrous-tribal: The Case of Jaunsar Bawar', in S. M. Dubey, Bordoloi, P. K. and Borthakur, B. N., eds, *Family, Marriage and Social Change on the Indian Fringe*, Cosmo Publications, New Delhi, 1980, 59–82.

Bird, G., and Milne, A., 'Debt Relief for Poor Countries', *New Economy*, vol. 7, no. 4, 2000, 199–204.

Blaustein, A. P. and Flanz, G. H., eds, *Constitutions of the Countries of the World*, 17 vols, Oceana Publications, Dobbs Ferry, New York, permanent edn.

Bloom, I., Martin, J. P. and Proudfoot, W. L., eds, *Religious Diversity and Human Rights*, Columbia University Press, New York, 1996.

Bose, A., 'Census of India 2001 and After', *Economic and Political Weekly*, 19 May 2001, 1685–87.

Bose, S., *States, Nations, Sovereignty: Sri Lanka, India, and the Tamil Eelam Movement*, Sage Publications, New Delhi, 1994.

Bovenberg, L., and Cnossen, S., eds, *Public Economics and the Environment in an Imperfect World*, Kluwer Academic, Boston, 1995.

Braatz, S., *Conserving Biological Diversity: A Strategy for Protected Areas in the Asia-Pacific Region*, World Bank Technical Paper no. 193, World Bank, Washington DC, 1992.

Brandon, C. and Ramankutty, R., *Toward an Environmental Strategy for Asia*, World Bank Discussion Paper No. 224, World Bank, Washington DC, 1993.

Brecher, J., and Costello, T., *Global Village or Global Pillage: Economic Reconstruction from the Bottom Up*, South End Press, Boston, 1994.

Brinton, M. C., *Women and the Economic Miracle*, University of California Press, Berkeley, 1993.

Broadbent, J., *Environmental Politics in Japan: Networks of Power and Protest*, Cambridge University Press, Cambridge, 1998.

Brogan, K., 'The Forgotten Cost of Counter-Insurgency in Aceh', *Inside Indonesia*, no. 49, January–March 1997, 2–4.

Brosius, P. J., 'Prior Transcripts, Divergent Paths: Resistance and Acquiescence to Logging in Sarawak, East Malaysia', *Comparative Studies in Society and History*, vol. 39, no. 3, 1997, 468–510.

Brown, L., 'A New Era Unfolds', in Worldwatch Institute, *State of the World 1993*, Earthscan, London, 1993.

Brown, R. A., *Chinese Business Enterprise in Asia*, Routledge, London, 1995.

Brown, S. C., ed., *Objectivity and Cultural Convergence*, Cambridge University Press, Cambridge, 1984.

Brownlie, I., ed., *Basic Documents on Human Rights*, 3rd edn, Oxford University Press, 1992.

Bryant, R. L., 'The Politics of Logging in Burma', in P. Hirsch and C. Warren, eds, *The Politics of the Environment in Southeast Asia*, Routledge, London, 1998.

Buck, R. L., *Chinese Farm Economy*, University of Chicago Press, Chicago, 1930.

Burger, J., *Report From the Frontier: The State of the World's Indigenous Peoples*, Zed Books, London, 1987.

Caldwell, J. C., *Theory of Fertility Decline*, Academic Publishers, London, 1982.

Callahan, A., *Imagining Democracy: Reading 'The Events of May' in Thailand*, Institute of Southeast Asian Studies, Singapore, 1998.

Callicott, J. B. and Ames, R. T., eds, *Nature in Asian Traditions of Thought: Essays in Environmental Philosophy*, State University of New York, Albany, NY, 1989.

'Cambodia Looks at Becoming Giant Theme Park', *Canberra Times*, 7 August 1995.

Camelleri, J. A. and Falk, J., *End of Sovereignty? The Politics of a Shrinking and Fragmenting World*, Edward Elgar, Aldershot, 1992.

Cao Xueqin, *The Story of the Stone*, trans. D. Hawkes and J. Minford, 5 vols, Penguin, Harmondsworth, 1973–87.

Carrier, M., Massey, G., and Ruetsche, L., eds, *Science at Century's End: Philosophical Questions on the Progress and Limits of Science*, University of Pittsburgh Press, Pittsburgh, 2000.

Cartier, M., 'Nuclear Versus Quasi-Stem Families: the New Chinese Family Model', *Journal of Family History*, vol. 20 no. 3, 1995, 307–27.

Castells, M. and Hall, P., *Technopoles of the World: The Making of Twenty-First-Century Industrial Complexes*, Routledge, London, 1994.

Castells, M. et al., *The Shek Kip Mei Syndrome: Economic Development and Public Housing in Hong Kong and Singapore*, Pion, London, 1990.

Castile, G. P. and Kushner, G., eds, *Persistent Peoples: Cultural Enclaves in Perspective*, University of Arizona Press, Tuscon, Ariz., 1981.

Castles, S. and Miller, M. J., *The Age of Migration: International Population Movements in the Modern World*, Macmillan, London, 1993.

Cavanagh, J., Wysham, D., and Arruda, M., *Beyond Bretton Woods: Alternatives to the Global Economic Order*, Pluto Press, London, 1994.

Cervantes Saavedra, Miguel de, *The Ingenious Gentleman Don Quixote de la Mancha*, trans. S. Putnam, Viking, New York, 1949.

Chabra, R. and Nuna, S. C., *Abortion in India: An Overview*, New Delhi, 1993.

Chan, A., 'The Industrial Unrest Behind the "Made In China" Tag', *Canberra Times*, 2 July 1994.

Chan, H. and Lee, R. P. L., 'Hong Kong Families: At the Crossroads of Modernism and Traditionalism', *Journal of Comparative Family Studies*, vol. 26, no. 1, Spring 1995, 83–100.

Chan, J., 'A Confucian Perspective on Human Rights for Contemporary China', in J. Bauer and D. Bell, eds, *The East Asian Challenge for Human Rights*, Cambridge University Press, Cambridge, 1999.

Chan, Kam Wing, 'Urbanisation and Rural-Urban Migration in China Since 1982', *Modern China*, vol. 20, no. 3, July 1994, 243–81.

Chan, S., *Hmong Means Free: Life in Laos and America*, Temple University Press, Philadelphia, 1994.

Chan Khong, Sister (personal name Cao Ngoc Phuong), *Learning True Love*, Parallax Press, Berkeley, 1993.

Chaudhuri, K. N., *Asia Before Europe: Economy and Civilisation of the Indian Ocean From the Rise of Islam to 1750*, Cambridge University Press, Cambridge, 1990.

Chekki, D. A., 'Recent Directions in Family Research: India and North America', *Journal of Comparative Family Studies*, vol. 19, no. 2, 1988, 171–86.

Chen Yiyun, 'Out of the Traditional Halls of Academe: Exploring New Avenues for Research on Women', in C. K. Gilmartin et al., eds, *Engendering China: Women, Culture, and the State*, Harvard University Press, Cambridge, Mass., 1994, 69–79.

Cherlin, A. J. and Chamsatrithirong, Aphichat, *Variations in Marriage Patterns in Central Thailand*, Institute for Population and Social Research, Mahidol University, Bangkok, 1987.

Chi, C., 'Integrating Traditional Medicine into Modern Health Care Systems', *Social Science and Medicine*, vol. 39, no. 3, 1994, 307–21.

'China Enacts Sweeping Rules on Internet Firms', *Agence France Presse*, 2 October 2000.
China Population Information and Research Centre, *Major Figures of the 2000 Population Census* (No. 1), http://www.cpirc.org.cn/e5cendata1.htm, accessed 11 August 2001.
Ching, F., 'Fay Case: Collision of Values', *Far Eastern Economic Review*, 5 May 1994, 38.
Cholthira, S., 'A Comparative Study of Structure and Contradiction in the Austro-Asiatic System of the Thai-Yunnan Periphery', in G. Wijeyewardene, ed., *Ethnic Groups Across National Boundaries in Mainland Southeast Asia*, Institute of Southeast Asian Studies, Singapore, 1990.
Chowdhry, A., 'Families in Bangladesh', *Journal of Comparative Family Studies*, vol. 26, no. 1, Spring 1995.
Chowdhry, K., 'Poverty, Environment, Development' *Daedalus*, vol. 118, no. 1, Winter 1989, 131–58.
Chu, G. C. and Ju, Y., *The Great Wall in Ruins: Communication and Cultural Change in China*, State University of New York Press, Albany, NY, 1993.
Chu, G. C., Schramm, Alfian, and Schramm, W., *Social Impact of Satellite Television in Rural Indonesia,* Asian Mass Communication Research and Information Centre, Singapore, 1991.
Clapham, A., *Human Rights in the Private Sphere*, Clarendon Press, Oxford, 1993.
Clark, J., *Democratising Development: The Role of Voluntary Organisations*, Earthscan, London, 1991.
Clarke, G., 'From Ethnocide to Ethnodevelopment? Ethnic Minorities and Indigenous Peoples', *Third World Quarterly*, vol. 22, no. 3, 2001, 413–36.
Clay, W., 'Looking Back to Go Forward: Predicting and Preventing Human Rights Violations', in S. Miller et al., *State of the Peoples: A Global Human Rights Report on Societies in Danger*, Beacon Press, Boston, 1993.
Clifford, M., 'Social Engineers', *Far Eastern Economic Review*, 14 April 1994, 56–60.
Coale, A. J., 'Excess Female Mortality and the Balance of the Sexes: an Estimate of the Number of "Missing Females"', *Population and Development Review*, vol. 17, no. 3, September 1991, 517–23.
——'Still Hard Labour', *Far Eastern Economic Review*, 27 October 1994, 20–1.
Cohen, M., 'New Flight Plan', *Far Eastern Economic Review*, 2 March 2000, 45–6.
Confucius, *The Analects*, trans. D. C. Lau, Penguin, Harmondsworth, 1979.
Consumers' Association of Penang, *Wasted Lives: Radioactive Poisoning in Bukit Merah*, Consumers' Association of Penang, Penang, 1993.
Cook, T. E., *The Rise and Fall of Regimes: Toward a Grand Theory of Politics*, P. Lang, New York, 2000.
Cooke, F. M., *The Challenge of Sustainable Forests: Forest Resource Policy in Malaysia, 1970–1995*, Asian Studies Association of Australia, with Allen & Unwin and University of Hawaii Press, 1999.
Crabtree, R. B., and Malhotra, S., 'A Case Study of Commercial Television in India: Assessing the Organizational Mechanisms of Cultural Imperialism', *Journal of Broadcasting and Electronic Media*, vol. 44, no. 3, 2000, 364–85.
Crook, S., *Modern Radicalism and Its Aftermath: Foundationalism and Anti-Foundationalism in Radical Social Theory*, Routledge, London, 1991.
Crystal, D., *English as a Global Language*, Cambridge University Press, Cambridge, 1997.
Dahlman, C., 'Technology Strategy in East Asian Developing Economies', *Journal of Asian Economics*, vol. 5, no. 4, 1994, 541–72.
Dai Xingyi and Peng Xizhe, 'China's Environment and Environment Protection', in Peng Xizhe and Guo Zhi Gang, eds, *The Changing Population of China*, Blackwell, Oxford, 2000.
Dalai Lama XIV, His Holiness the, *Beyond Dogma: Dialogues and Discourses*, trans. A. Anderson, North Atlantic Books, Berkeley, 1996.
Das Gupta, M., 'Selective Discrimination Against Female Children in India', *Population and Development Review*, vol. 13, no. 1, March 1987, 77–100.
Daston, L., 'Objectivity and the Escape from Perspective', *Social Studies of Science*, vol. 22, 1992, 597–618.
Datta, C., 'Yamuna River Turned Sewer', *Economic and Political Weekly*, 5 December 1992, 2633–6.
David, H. P., 'Population, Policy and Reproductive Behaviour: Incentives and Disincentives', in L. G. Severy, ed., *Advances in Population: Psychosocial Perspectives*, vol. 1, Jessica Kingsley, London, 1993.
Davies, P., *Superforce: The Search for a Grand Unified Theory of Nature*, Penguin, Ringwood, Vic., 1995.
Davis, D. and Harrell, S., eds, *Chinese Families in the Post-Mao Era*, University of California Press, Berkeley, 1993.

Day, T. P., *Great and Little Tradition in Theravada Buddhist Studies*, Edwin Mellen Press, Lewiston, New York, 1988.

Dearing, J. W., *Growing a Japanese Science City: Communication in Scientific Research*, Routledge, London, 1995.

'The Detailed Regulations of the Government Rules for Satellite TV Receivers-Ministry of Radio, Film and Television', *People's Daily*, 27 February 1994.

Devasia, L. and Devasia, V.V., eds, *Girl Child in India*, Ashish, New Delhi, 1991.

Dhanini, S., and Islam, I., 'Labour Market Adjustment to Indonesia's Economic Crisis: A Comment', *Bulletin of Indonesian Economic Studies*, vol. 37, no. 1, April 2001, 113–16

Didia, D., 'Debt-For-Nature Swaps, Market Imperfections, and Policy Failures as Determinants of Sustainable Development and Environmental Quality', *Journal of Economic Issues*, vol. 35, no. 2, 2001, 477–86.

Djalal, D., 'Showdown at the Factory', *Far Eastern Economic Review*, 10 January 2002, 24–25.

Donnelly, J., 'Human Rights and Human Dignity: An Analytic Critique of Non-Western Conceptions of Human Rights', *American Political Science Review*, vol. 26, 1982, 301–16.

——*Universal Human Rights in Theory and Practice*, Cornell University Press, Ithaca, New York, 1989.

Doornbos, M., Saith, A., and White, B., eds, 'Forests, Nature, People, Power', Special Issue, *Development and Change*, vol. 31, no. 1, January 2000.

Doyal, L. and Gough, I., *A Theory of Need*, Macmillan, London, 1991.

Dreze, J., and Murthi, M., 'Fertility, Education and Development: Evidence From India', *Population and Development Review*, vol. 27, no. 1, March 2001, 33–63.

Dreze, J. and Sen, A., *Hunger and Public Action*, Clarendon Press, Oxford, 1989.

Du Gangjian and Song Gang, 'Relating Human Rights to Chinese Culture: The Four Paths of the Confucian Analects and the Four Principles of a New Theory of Benevolence', in M. C. Davis, ed., *Human Rights and Chinese Values: Legal, Philosophical and Political Perspectives*, Oxford University Press, Hong Kong, 1995.

Dube, S. C., *Modernization and Development: The Search For Alternative Paradigms*, United Nations University and Zed Books, Tokyo and London, 1988.

Dull, J. L., 'Marriage and Divorce in Han China: A Glimpse at Pre-Confucian Society', in D. C. Buxbaum, ed., *Chinese Family Law and Change*, University of Washington Press, Seattle, 1978.

Dunn, R. E., *The Adventures of Ibn Battuta: A Muslim Traveler of the 14th Century*, University of California Press, Berkeley, 1986.

Dussen, J. van der and Wilson, K., eds, *The History of the Idea of Europe*, Routledge, London, 1995.

Dyson, T. and Moore, M., 'On Kinship Structure, Female Autonomy, and Demographic Behavior in India', *Population and Development Review*, vol. 9, no. 1, March 1983, 35–60.

Ebrey, P., *Family and Property in Sung China*, Princeton University Press, Princeton, 1984.

'Editorial', *Economic and Political Weekly*, 20 January 2001, 169–70.

Ekachai, S., *Behind the Smile: Voices of Thailand*, Thai Development Support Committee, Bangkok, 1990.

Elegant, S., and Hiebert, M., 'Tech Mecca', *Far Eastern Economic Review*, 16 March 2000, 48–50.

Englehart, N., 'Rights and Culture in the Asian Values Argument: The Rise and Fall of Confucian Ethics in Singapore', *Human Rights Quarterly*, vol. 22, no. 2, May 2000, 548–68.

Essential Information, Inc., *Multinational Monitor*, http://www.essential.org/monitor.monitor.htm, accessed 24 August 2001.

Esteva, G., 'Development', in W. Sachs, ed., *The Development Dictionary: A Guide to Knowledge as Power*, Zed Books, London, 1992.

Etzioni, A., 'The Evils of Self-Determination', *Foreign Policy*, Winter 1993, 21–35.

Evans, D. R., 'The Challenge of Education for All in India', *Comparative Education Review*, vol. 44, no. 1, 2000, 81–7.

Evans, G., 'Central Highlanders of Vietnam', in R. H. Barnes et al., eds, *Indigenous Peoples of Asia*, Association for Asian Studies, Ann Arbor, Mich., 1995.

Evans, G., ed., *Asia's Cultural Mosaic*, Prentice-Hall, New York, 1993.

Evans, P., 'Japan's Green Aid', *China Business Review*, July–August 1994, 39–43.

Fairclough, G., 'It Isn't Black and White', *Far Eastern Economic Review*, 7 March 1996, 54–7.

Fairclough, G. and Tasker, R., 'Separate and Unequal', *Far Eastern Economic Review*, 14 April 1994, 22–5.

Fairclough, G., et al., 'Failing Grades', *Far Eastern Economic Review*, 29 September 1994, 62–9.

Farman Farmaian, S., *Daughter of Persia*, Corgi, London, 1993.

Farquhar, J., *Knowing Practice: The Clinical Encounter of Chinese Medicine*, Westview Press, Boulder, Colo., 1994.

Farrington, J. and Lewis, D. J., eds, *Non-Government Organizations and the State in Asia*, Routledge, London, 1993.

Fee, L. K., and Rajah, A., 'The Ethnic Mosaic', in G. Evans, ed., *Asia's Cultural Mosaic*, Prentice-Hall, New York, 1993.

Fei Hsiao-t'ung, *Chinese Village Close-Up*, New World Press, Beijing, 1983.

——*Peasant Life in China*, Routledge, London, 1939.

Felice, W. F., *Taking Suffering Seriously: The Importance of Collective Human Rights*, State University of New York Press, Albany, NY, 1996.

Fernández-Armesto, F., *Millenium: A History of the Last Thousand Years*, Bantam Press, London, 1995.

Flyvbjerg, B., *Making Social Science Matter: Why Social Inquiry Fails and How it Can Succeed Again*, Cambridge University Press, Cambridge, 2001.

Foells, W., et al., *RAINS-Asia: An Assessment Model for Air Pollution in Asia*, World Bank, Washington DC, 1995.

Forney, M., 'Under Fire', *Far Eastern Economic Review*, 27 February 1997, 17–20.

Frank, R., and Chasin, B., 'Development Without Growth: The Kerala Experiment', *Technology Review*, vol. 93, no. 3, April 1993, 42–51.

——*Kerala: Radical Reform as Development in an Indian State*, Institute for Food and Development Policy, San Francisco, 1989.

Freebairn, D. K., 'Did the Green Revolution Concentrate Incomes? A Quantitive Study of Research Reports', *World Development*, vol. 23, no. 2, 1995, 265–79.

Freeman, C. and Hagendoorn, J., 'Convergence and Divergence in the Internationalisation of Technology', in J. Hagendoorn, ed., *Technological Change in the World Economy: Convergence and Divergence in Technological Strategies*, Edward Elgar, Aldershot, 1995.

Friedman, T. L., *The Lexus and the Olive Grove*, 2nd edn, HarperCollins, London, 2000.

Froning, D., 'Will Debt Relief Really Help?', *Washington Quarterly*, vol. 24, no. 3, Summer 2001, 199–211.

Fukasaku, Y., T*echnology and Industrial Growth in Pre-War Japan: The Mitsubishi-Nagasaki Shipyard 1884–1934*, Routledge, London, 1992.

Gadgil, M. and Guha, R., *Ecology and Equity: The Use and Abuse of Nature in Contemporary India*, Routledge, London, 1995.

Gale, E. M., *Discussions on Salt and Iron, 1931–34*, rpt Ch'eng-wen Publishers, Taipei, 1967.

Galison, P. and Stump, D. J., eds, *The Disunity of Science: Boundaries, Contexts, and Power*, Stanford University Press, Stanford, 1996.

Gandhi, M. K., *An Autobiography: The Story of My Experiments With Truth*, Beacon Press, Boston, 1957.

Garran, R., 'Final Payout Made to Minamata Victims', *Australian*, 1 November 1995.

Geertz, C., *The Interpretation of Cultures*, Basic Books, New York, 1973.

Geertz, H., 'Indonesian Cultures and Communities', in R. T. McVey, ed., *Indonesia, Southeast Asian Studies*, Yale University, New Haven, Conn., 1963.

Gellner, E., *Nations and Nationalism*, Blackwell, Oxford, 1983.

——*Thought and Change*, Weidenfeld & Nicolson, London, 1964.

George, S., *A Fate Worse Than Debt*, Grove Weidenfeld, New York, 1987.

George, S. and Sabelli, F., *Faith and Credit: The World Bank's Secular Empire*, Penguin, Harmondsworth, 1994.

Ghai, D. and Vivian, J., eds, *Grassroots Environmental Action: People's Participation in Sustainable Development*, UNRISD and Routledge, Geneva and London, 1992.

Ghai, Y., 'Human Rights and Governance: The Asia Debate', *Australian Yearbook of International Law*, vol. 15, 1994, 1–34.

Gill, I., and Fluitman, F., eds, *Vocational Education and Training Reform: Matching Skills to Markets and Budgets*, Oxford University Press, New York, 2000.

Gilley, B., 'Following the Money', *Far Eastern Economic Review*, 7 March 1996, 58.

Gittinger, M., *Splendid Symbols: Textiles and Tradition in Indonesia*, The Textile Museum, Washington DC, 1979.

Glaeser, B., ed., *The Green Revolution Revisited: Critique and Alternatives*, Unwin Hyman, London, 1987.

Global Development Research Centre, *The Virtual Library on Microcredit*, http://www.gdrc.org/icm/.

Go, S. P., 'The Filipino Family in the Eighties', in Unesco, *The Changing Family in Asia*, Unesco Principal Regional Office for Asia and the Pacific, Bangkok, 1992.

Goldsmith, A. A., 'The State, the Market and Economic Development: A Second Look at Adam Smith in Theory and Practice', *Development and Change*, vol. 26, no. 4, October 1995, 633–50.

Goldstein, A., and Wang, F., eds, *China: The Many Facets of Demographic Change*, Westview, Boulder, Colorado, 1996.

Goldstein-Kyaga, ed., *Nonviolence in Asia: The Art of Dying or the Road to Change?*, Center of Pacific Asia Studies, Stockholm University, Stockholm, 1999.

Golinski, J., *Making Natural Knowledge: Constructivism and the History of Science*, Cambridge University Press, Cambridge, 1998.

'The Good Earth: Life is Getting Better, But Malthus Reigns in Cairo', editorial, *Far Eastern Economic Review*, 8 September 1994, 5.

Goode, W., *World Revolution and Family Patterns*, Free Press, New York, 1963.

Goodenough, W., Culture, *Language and Society*, Addison-Wesley, Reading, Mass., 1972.

Goodland, R. et al., eds, *Environmentally Sustainable Development: Building on Brundtland*, Unesco, Paris, 1991.

Goody, J., *The East in the West*, Cambridge University Press, Cambridge, 1996.

Goonesekere, S. W. E., *Child Labour in Sri Lanka: Learning From the Past*, International Labour Organization, Geneva, 1993.

Goonasekera, A., and Lee, P., eds, *TV Without Borders: Asia Speaks Out*, Asian Media and Information Centre, Singapore, 1998.

Gopalan, A. K., *In the Cause of the People*, Orient Longman, Madras, 1973.

Graham, A. C., *Yin-Yang and the Nature of Correlative Thinking* (IEAP Occasional Paper and Monograph Series no. 6), Institute of East Asian Philosophies, National University of Singapore, Singapore, 1986.

Gray, A., 'The Indigenous Movement in Asia', in R. H. Barnes et al., eds, *Indigenous Peoples of Asia*, Association for Asian Studies, Ann Arbor, Michigan, 1995.

Gray, J., 'From Post-Communism to Civil Society: The Reemergence of History and the Decline of the Western Model', *Social Philosophy and Policy*, vol. 10, no. 2, Summer 1993, 26–50.

——*False Dawn: The Delusions of Global Capitalism*, Free Press, New York, 1998.

Greider, W., *One World, Ready or Not: The Manic Logic of Global Capitalism*, Simon and Schuster, New York, 1997.

Grundy-Warr, C., *Eurasia: World Boundaries*, vol. 3, Routledge, London, 1994.

Guinness, P., 'Local Culture and Society', in H. Hill ed., *Indonesia's New Order*, Allen & Unwin, St Leonards, NSW, 1994.

Gupta, D., *The Context of Ethnicity: Sikh Identity in a Comparative Perspective*, Oxford University Press, Delhi, 1996.

Gwatkin, D. R., 'Political Will and Family Planning: The Implications of India's Emergency Experience', *Population and Development Review*, vol. 5, 1979, 29–59.

Habibie, B. J., 'Sophisticated Technologies: Taking Root in Developing Countries', *International Journal of Technology Management*, vol. 5, no. 5, 1990, 489–97.

Hagendoorn, J., ed., *Technological Change in the World Economy*, Edward Elgar, Aldershot, 1995.

Haller, V., 'Water Works: Why Our Planet is Running Dry', *Sydney Morning Herald*, 9 November 1996.

Hammel, E. A., 'A Theory of Culture for Demographers', *Population and Development Review*, no. 16, no. 3, September 1990, 455–85.

Hammel, E. A. and Laslett, P., 'Comparing Household Structure Over Time and Across Cultures', *Comparative Studies in Society and History*, vol. 16, 1974, 73–109.

Han Fei, *Basic Works of Han Fei Tzu*, trans. B. Watson, Columbia University Press, New York, 1964.

Hancock, P., 'The Walking Ghosts of West Java', *Inside Indonesia*, no. 51, July-September 1997, 16–19.

Handley, P., 'Press and Pirates', *Far Eastern Economic Review*, 11 June 1992, 10–11.

Hara, T., *Studies in Socio-Cultural Change in Rural Villages in Bangladesh*, No. 1, Institute for the Study of Languages and Cultures of Asia and Africa, Tokyo, 1985.

Harding, S., *Is Science Multicultural? Postcolonialisms, Feminisms, and Epistemologies*, Indiana University Press, Bloomington, 1998.

Hardjono, J., 'Resource Utilisation and the Environment', in H. Hill, ed., *Indonesia's New Order: The Dynamics of Socio-Economic Transformation*, Allen & Unwin, St Leonards, NSW, 1994.

Harkness, J., 'Recent Trends in Forestry and Conservation of Biodiversity in China', *The China Quarterly*, no. 156, December 1998, 911–34.

Harrell, S., 'Geography, Demography, and Family Composition in Three Southwestern Villages', in D. Davis and S. Harrell, eds, *Chinese Families in the Post-Mao Era*, University of California Press, Berkeley, 1993.

Harris, N., 'Chinese Workers in Israel: A Bizarre Tale', *Economic and Political Weekly*, 19 May 2001, 1688.

Harris, P., *Civil Disobedience*, University Press of America, Lanham MD, 1989.

Harsono, A., 'Indonesia: Dancing in the Dark', in L. Williams and R. Rich, eds, *Losing Control: Freedom of the Press in Asia*, Asia Pacific Press, Asia Pacific School of Economics and Management, Australian National University, Canberra, 2000.

Hayami, Y., and M. Kikuchi, *Asian Village Economy at the Crossroads: An Economic Approach to Institutional Change*, University of Tokyo Press, Tokyo, 1982.

Hayashi, Y., and Yang Guangyuan, eds, *Dynamics of Ethnic Cultures Across National Boundaries in Southwestern China and Mainland Southeast Asia: Relations, Societies and Languages*, Lanna Cultural Center, Rajabhat Institute, Chiang Mai, and Center for Southeast Asian Studies, Kyoto University, Kyoto, 2000.

Hayhoe, R., *China's Universities 1895–1995: A Century of Cultural Conflict*, Hong Kong University Press, 1999.

Headrick, D. R., *The Invisible Weapon: Telecommunications and International Politics, 1851–1945*, Oxford University Press, New York, 1991.

Heller, A., 'A Theory of Needs Revisited', *Thesis Eleven*, vol. 35, 1993.

Henderson, J., 'Against the Economic Orthodoxy: On the Making of the East Asian Miracle', *Economy and Society*, vol. 22, no. 2, May 1993, 200–17.

Hertz, N., *The Silent Takeover: Global Capitalism and the Death of Democracy*, William Heineman, London, 2001.

Hetherington, S. C., *Knowledge Puzzles: An Introduction to Epistemology*, Westview Press, Boulder, Colorado, 1996.

Hiebert, M., 'Future Shock', *Far Eastern Economic Review*, 27 February 1997, 44–9.

——Hill, H., 'The Emperor's New Clothes Can Now Be Made in Indonesia', *Bulletin of Indonesian Economic Studies*, vol. 27, no. 3, December 1991, 89–127.

——'Indonesia's Great Leap Foward? Technology Development and Policy Issues', *Bulletin of Indonesian Economic Studies*, vol. 31, no. 2, August 1995, 83–123.

Hillner, J., 'Venture Capitals', *Wired*, vol. 8, no. 7, July 2000, 37–45.

Hills, B., 'Japan's Mercury Agony Nears End', *Sydney Morning Herald*, 30 September 1995.

Hiriyanna, M., *Outlines of Indian Philosophy*, Allen & Unwin, London, 1932.

Hirsch, P., 'Dams, Resources and the Politics of the Environment in Mainland Southeast Asia', in P. Hirsch and C. Warren, eds, *The Politics of the Environment in Southeast Asia*, Routledge, London, 1998.

Hirschman, C., 'Why Fertility Changes', *Annual Review of Sociology*, vol. 20, 1994, 203–33.

Ho, P., 'China's Rangelands Under Stress', *Development and Change*, vol. 31, no. 2, March 2000, 385–412.

Hobsbawm, E. and Ranger, T., eds, *The Invention of Tradition*, Cambridge University Press, Cambridge, 1983.

Hoffman-Ladd, J., 'Polemics on the Modesty and Segregation of Women in Contemporary Egypt', *International Journal of Middle East Studies*, vol. 19, 1987, 23–50.

Hogan, S. B., 'To Net or Not to Net: Singapore's Regulation of the Internet', *Federal Communications Law Journal*, vol. 51, no. 2, 1999, 429–47.

Holloway, R., ed., *Doing Development: Governments, NGOs, and the Rural Poor in Asia*, Earthscan, London, 1989.

Hoon, S. J., 'Not on My Island', *Far Eastern Economic Review*, 20 July 1995.

Hopkins, M., 'A Babel of Broadcasts', *Columbia Journalism Review*, vol. 38, no. 2, 1999, 44–7.

Hopkins, T. K. and Wallerstein, I., *The Age of Transition: Trajectory of the World-System 1945–2025*, Atlantic Highlands, London, 1996.

——*World-System Analysis: Theory and Methodology*, Sage Publications, Beverly Hills, Calif., 1982.

Hoskins, J., ed., *Headhunting and the Social Imagination in Southeast Asia*, Stanford University Press, Stanford, Calif., 1996.

Hout, W., *Capitalism and the Third World*, Edward Elgar, Aldershot, 1993.

Howard, M. C., ed., *Asia's Environmental Crisis*, Westview Press, Boulder, Colo., 1993.

Howard, R., 'Cultural Absolutism and the Nostalgia for Community', *Human Rights Quarterly*, vol. 15, 1993.

Hsiao Kung-Ch'üan, *A History of Chinese Political Thought*, Volume 1, trans. F. W. Mote, Princeton University Press, Princeton, 1978.

Hugo, G., 'Women's Empowerment, Marriage Postponement, and Gender Relations in Japan', in H. Presser and G. Sen, eds, *Women's Empowerment and Demographic Processes*, Oxford University Press, New York, 2000.

Hull, T. H., *An Investigation of Reports of Coercion in the Indonesian Vasectomy Program*, Development Paper 1991 No. 1, Appraisals, Evaluation and Sectoral Studies Branch, Australian International Development Assistance Bureau, Canberra, 1991.

Human, C., *Human Rights World Guide*, Oxford University Press, New York, 1992.

Human Rights Institute, 'Japan: Thematic Reports', *For the Record 1998*, http://www.hri.ca/fortherecord1998/vol3/japantr.htm

Human Rights Watch, *World Report 2001*, http://www.hrw.org/wr2k1/, accessed 10 August 2001.

Hunter, J., ed., *Japanese Working Women*, Routledge, London, 1995.

Inayatullah, S., and Gidley, G., eds, *The University Transformations: Global Perspectives on the Futures of the University*, Bergin & Garvey, Westport, Conn., 2000.

Independent Commission on Population and Quality of Life, *Caring for the Future: Making the Next Decades Provide a Life Worth Living*, Oxford University Press, Oxford, 1996.

Indonesia: Directorate of Foreign Information, 'The Development of Nuclear Power Plants in Indonesia', http://www.dfa-deplu.go.id/english/nuklir.htm, accessed 27 November 2000.

Indonesia: Ministry of National Education, *Indonesian Education Statistics 1999–2000*, http://www.pdk.go.id, accessed 10 August 2001.

Ingli Labour Working Group, 'Labour Rights and Wrongs: Special Report' *Inside Indonesia*, no. 21, June 1991, 2–9.

Inoue, T., 'Liberal Democracy and Asian Orientalism', in J. Bauer and D. Bell, eds, *The East Asian Challenge for Human Rights*, Cambridge University Press, Cambridge, 1999.

INSAN (Institute of Social Analysis), *Logging Against the Natives of Sarawak*, INSAN, Petaling Jaya, 1989.

International Labour Organization, International Programme on the Elimination of Child Labour, http://www.ilo.org/public/english/standards/ipec/index.htm, accessed 24 August 2001.

'Iran: Satellite Crack-Down', *Middle East International*, no. 539, 6 December 1996, 10.

Isengard, P., 'Basic Needs: The Case of Sri Lanka', *World Development*, vol. 8, no. 3, 1980, 237–58.

Islam, R., ed., *Transfer, Adoption and Diffusion of Technology for the Small and Cottage Industries*, Asia Regional Team for Employment Promotion, International Labour Organization, New Delhi, 1992.

Iyer, R. R., 'Water: Charting a Course for the Future', parts 1 and 2, *Economic and Political Weekly*, 31 March 2001, 1115–22, and 14 April 2001, 1235–47.

James, J., 'Pro-Poor Modes of Technical Integration into the Global Economy', *Development and Change*, vol. 31, no. 4, 2000, 765–83.

Jamison, E. and Hobbs, F., *World Population Profile: 1994*, US Department of Commerce and US Bureau of the Census, Washington DC, 1994.

Jamyang Norbu, 'Rite of Freedom: The Life and Sacrifice of Thupten Ngodup', *Tibetan Review*, vol. 33, no. 8, August 1998, 15–19.

Japan Information Network, 'Divorces (1983–1999)', http://jin.jcic.or.jp, accessed 13 August 2001.

——'Marriages (1983–1999)', http://jin.jcic.or.jp, accessed 13 August 2001.

——'Tying the Knot: The Changing Face of Marriage in Japan', http://jin.jcic.or.jp, accessed 13 August 2001.

'Japan's New Long-Term Plan for R&D on Nuclear Power', *Science and Technology in Japan*, no. 53, 1995, 4–12.

Jayaraman, N., 'Turn, Turn, Turn: Making Energy is a Breeze in Southern India', *Far Eastern Economic Review*, 30 March 1995, 62.

Jayasankaran, S., 'Field of Dreams', *Far Eastern Economic Review*, 27 February 1997, 49–50.

Jayasuriya, K., and Rosser, A., 'Economic Orthodoxy and the East Asian Crisis', *Third World Quarterly*, vol. 22, no. 3, 2001, 381–96.

Jeffery, A. J., 'Free Speech and Press: An Absolute Right?', *Human Rights Quarterly*, vol. 8, no. 2, May 1986, 197–226.

Jeffrey, R., *Politics, Women, and Well-Being: How Kerala Became 'a Model'*, Macmillan, London, 1992.

Jeon, S., *Science and Technology in Korea: Traditional Instruments and Techniques*, MIT Press, Cambridge, Mass., 1974.

Jones, G. W., 'Fertility Transitions Among Malay Populations of Southeast Asia: Puzzles of Interpretation', *Population and Development Review*, vol. 16, no. 3, September 1990, 507–37.

——*Marriage and Divorce in Islamic South-East Asia*, Oxford University Press, Oxford, 1994.

Jones, G.W., and Hagul, P., 'Schooling in Indonesia: Crisis-Related and Longer-Term Issues', *Bulletin of Indonesian Economic Studies*, vol. 37, no. 2, August 2001, 207–31.

Jones, L., 'Aceh's Year of Living Dangerously', *Inside Indonesia*, no. 49, January–March 1997, 5–7.

Johnson, K., *Television and Social Change in Rural India*, Sage, Delhi, 2000.

Joseph, R., Worker, *Middlewomen, Entrepreneur: Women in the Indonesian Batik Industry*, Population Council, Regional Office for South and East Asia, Bangkok, 1987.

Joshi, B. H. and Trivedi, H. K., *The Impact of the Green Revolution on Indian Farmers*, Deep and Deep Publishing, Delhi, 1986.

Jun Ui, ed., *Industrial Pollution in Japan*, United Nations University Press, Tokyo, 1992.

——ed., 'Minamata', Special Issue, *Ampo: Japan–Asia Quarterly Review*, vol. 27, no. 3, 1997.

Kalland, A., and Persoon, G., *Environmental Movements in Asia*, Curzon, Richmond, Surrey, 1998.

Kalupahana, D., *Buddhist Philosophy*, University of Hawaii Press, Honolulu, 1976.

Kamaluddin, S., 'Fundamental Problem: Religious Right Pushes for Blasphemy Law', *Far Eastern Economic Review*, 18 August 1994, 23.

Kamenka, E., 'Human Rights, Peoples' Rights', in J. Crawford, ed., *The Rights of Peoples*, Oxford University Press, New York, 1988.

Kannibiran, V. and Kannibiran, K., 'Caste and Gender: Understanding the Dynamics of Power and Violence', *Economic and Political Weekly*, 14 September, 1991, 2130–3.

Karp, J. 'Caste-Iron Servitude', *Far Eastern Economic Review*, 7 March 1996, 57–8.

——'High Anxiety', and 'Out of Space', *Far Eastern Economic Review*, 18 August 1994, 46–50.

——'Water, Water, Everywhere', *Far Eastern Economic Review*, 1 June 1995, 54–8.

Kato, T., *Matriliny and Migration: Evolving Minangkabau Traditions in Indonesia*, Cornell University Press, Ithaca, New York, 1982.

Kaye, L., 'Coming Crisis', *Far Eastern Economic Review*, 10 July 1997, 64–8.

Keesing, R. M., 'Theories of Culture', *Annual Review of Anthropology*, vol. 3, 1974, 73–94.

'Keidanren Global Environment Charter', *Keidanren Review*, no. 129, June 1991, 4–6.

Kelegama, S., 'Development in Independent Sri Lanka: What Went Wrong?', *Economic and Political Weekly*, 22 April 2000, 1477–80.

Kenadi, L., *Revival of Buddhism in Modern India: The Role of B. R. Ambedkar and the Dalai Lama XIV*, Ashish Publishing House, New Delhi, 1995.

Kennedy, P. M., *Preparing for the Twenty-first Century*, HarperCollins, London, 1993.

Keyes, C. F., Kendall, L. and Hardacre, H., *Asian Visions of Authority: Religion and the Modern States of East and Southeast Asia*, University of Hawaii Press, Honolulu, 1994.

Kim, N., Choi, S. and Park, I. H., 'Rural Family and Community Life in South Korea: Changes in Family Attitudes and Living Arrangements for the Elderly', in L. Cho and M. Yada, eds, *Tradition and Change in the Asian Family*, East West Center and University Research Center, Nihon University, Honolulu and Tokyo, 1994.

Kim, S. D., 'Wrongfully Intervened: Introducing Cable and Satellite Television to Korea, 1987–1996', *Korean Social Science Journal*, vol. 26, no. 1, 1999, 33–66.

Kim, Y. S., 'Some Reflections on Science and Technology in Contemporary Korean Society', *Korea Journal*, vol. 28, no. 8, August 1988, 4–15.

King, E. M. and Hill, M. A., eds, *Women's Education in Developing Countries: Barriers, Benefits, and Policies*, John Hopkins University Press, Baltimore, 1993.

Kingsbury, B., '"Indigenous Peoples" as an International Legal Concept', in R. H. Barnes et al., eds, *Indigenous Peoples of Asia*, Association for Asian Studies, Ann Arbor, Mich., 1995.

Kingsbury, D., *South-East Asia: A Political Profile*, Oxford University Press, Melbourne, 2001.

Kinoshita, F., 'Household Size, Household Structure, and Developmental Cycle of a Japanese Village: Eighteenth to Nineteenth Centuries', *Journal of Family History*, vol. 20, no. 3, 1995, 239–60.

Kishwar, M. and Virata, R., eds, *In Search of Answers: Indian Women's Voices from Manushi*, Zed Books, London, 1984.

Klinken, G. van, 'Tinder-box or Conspiracy?', *Inside Indonesia*, no. 50, April–June 1997, 6–8.

Kobori, I., and Glantz, M. H., *Central Eurasian Water Crisis: Caspian, Aral, and Dead Seas*, United Nations University Press, Tokyo, 1998.

Koentjaraningrat, R. M., *Introduction to the Peoples and Cultures of Indonesia and Malaysia*, Cummings, Menlo Park, California, 1975.

Kolenda, P., 'The Joint Family Household in Rural Rajasthan: Ecological, Cultural and Demographic Conditions for Its Occurrence', in J. D. Gray and D. J. Mearns, eds, *Society From the Inside Out: Anthropological Perspectives on the South Asian Household*, Sage Publications, New Delhi, 1989.

——*Regional Differences in Family Structure in India*, Rawat, Jaipur, 1987.

Komai, Hiroshi, *Migrant Workers in Japan*, trans. J. Wilkinson, Kegan Paul International, London, 1995.

Korea: Science and Technology Policy Institute, *Review of Science and Technology Policy for Industrial Competitiveness*, Ministry of Foreign Affairs, Seoul, 1995.

Kothari, S. and Parajuli, P., 'No Nature Without Social Justice: A Plea For Cultural and Ecological Pluralism in India', in W. Sachs, ed., *Global Ecology: A New Arena of Political Conflict*, Zed Books, London, 1993.

Kulkarni, V. G., Hiebert, M. and Jayasankaran, S., 'Tough Talk: Premier Mahathir Thrives on No-Nonsense Policies', *Far Eastern Economic Review*, 24 October 1996, 23–7.

Kumagai, F., 'Families in Japan: Beliefs and Realities', *Journal of Comparative Family Studies*, vol. 26, no. 1, Spring 1995, 135–63.

Kweon, S., 'The Extended Family in Contemporary Korea: Changing Patterns of Co-Residence', *Korea Journal*, vol. 38, no. 3, Autumn 1998, 178–209.

Kwong, J., ed., 'Women's Education and Employment', Special Issue, *Chinese Education and Society*, vol. 33, no. 2, March/April 2000.

'Labouring Under Delusions: Workers' Rights Rules Strike at Free Trade', editorial, *Far Eastern Economic Review*, 21 April 1994, 5.

Lach, D. F., *Asia in the Making of Europe*, 3 vols, University of Chicago Press, Chicago.

Lall, S., 'Promoting Technology Development: the Role of Technology Transfer and Indigenous Effort', *Third World Quarterly*, vol. 14, no. 1, 1993, 95–186.

——'Technological Capabilities and Industrialization', *World Development*, vol. 20, no. 2, 1992, 165-86.

Lâm, M. C., 'Making Room for Peoples at the United Nations: Thoughts Provoked by Indigenous Claims to Self-Determination', *Cornell International Law Journal*, vol. 25, no. 3, Symposium 1992, 602–22.

Lane, M. and Balowski, J., 'Striking Out at Great River-Labour Unrest Continues', *Inside Indonesia*, no. 44, September 1995.

Lang, O., *Chinese Family and Society*, Yale University Press, New Haven, 1946.

Langley, W. E., *Human Rights: Sixty Major Global Instruments Introduced, Reprinted and Indexed*, McFarland and Co., Jefferson, NC, 1992.

Laslett, P. and Wall, R., eds, *Household and Family in Past Time*, Cambridge University Press, Cambridge, 1972.

Lau, D. C., trans. *Lao Tzu: Tao Te Ching*, Penguin, Harmondsworth, 1963.

Laudan, R., ed., *The Nature of Technological Knowledge: Are Models of Scientific Change Relevant?*, D. Reidel, Dordrecht, 1984.

'Laws to Curb Media Necessary: Mahathir', *Canberra Times*, 23 October 1996.

Lee, C. S., 'Innovation Deficit', *Far Eastern Economic Review*, 24 July 1997, 72–3.

Lee, C. S. and Baum, J., 'Radioactive Ruckus', *Far Eastern Economic Review*, 6 February 1997, 16.

Lee, M. and Sun, T., 'The Family and Demography in Contemporary Taiwan', *Journal of Comparative Family Studies*, vol. 26, no. 1, Spring 1995, 101–16.

Lee, Y. F., and So, A. Y., eds, *Asia's Environmental Movements: Comparative Perspectives*, M. E. Sharpe, Armonk, New York, 1999.

Lehman, F. K., ed., *Military Rule in Burma Since 1962: A Kaleidoscope of Views*, Maruzen, Singapore, 1981.

Lenssen, N., 'Nuclear Power Rises Slightly', in L. Starke, ed., *Vital Signs 2000/2001: The Environmental Trends that are Shaping Our Future*, Earthscan, London, 2000.

Lent, J. A., 'Mass Communication in Asia and the Pacific: Recent Trends and Development', *Media Asia*, vol. 16, no. 1, 1989.

Levinson, D., *Ethnic Groups Worldwide: A Ready Reference Handbook*, Oryx Press, Phoenix, Ariz., 1998.

Levy, H. S., *Chinese Footbinding: The History of a Curious Erotic Custom*, W. Rawls, New York, 1966.

Lewis, A., 'The Evolving Process of Swapping Debt for Nature', *Colorado Journal of Environmental Law and Policy*, vol. 10, no. 2, 1999, 431–65.

Lewis, P. and Lewis, E., *Peoples of the Golden Triangle*, Thames & Hudson, London, 1984.

Li Rongxia, 'Shenzhen: 20 Years of Brilliant Achievements', *Beijing Review*, vol. 43, no. 39, 25 September 2000, 12–17.

Li Yinke, 'Village Culture', *Social Sciences in China*, vol. 15, no. 4, Winter 1994, 56–64.

Li Yongping and Peng Xizhe, 'Age and Sex Structures', in Peng Xizhe and Guo Zhigang, eds, *The Changing Population of China*, Blackwell, Oxford, 2000.

Lin, J., *Social Transformation and Private Education in China*, Praeger, Westport, Conn., 1999.

Lincoln, J. R. and McBride, K., 'Japanese Industrial Organization in Comparative Perspective', *Annual Review of Sociology*, vol. 13, 1987, 289–312.

Lintner, B., *Burma in Revolt: Opium and Insurgency Since 1948*, Westview Press, Boulder, Colorado, 1994.

Liu Changming, 'Environmental Issues and the South-North Water Transfer Scheme', *The China Quarterly*, no. 156, December 1998, 899–910.

Lloyd, P. J. and Williams, L., eds, *International Trade and Migration in the Asia-Pacific Region*, Oxford University Press, Oxford, 1996.

Lock, M., *East Asian Medicine in Urban Japan*, University of California Press, Berkeley, 1980.

Long, S. O., *Family Change and Life Course in Japan*, East Asia Program, Cornell University, Ithaca, New York, 1987.

Lu Xun, *Selected Works of Lu Hsun*, 5 vols, trans. Yang Hsien-yi and G. Yang, Foreign Languages Press, Beijing, 1956.

Lucas, A., with Djati, A., *The Dog is Dead so Throw it in the River: Environmental Politics and Water Pollution in Indonesia*, Monash Asia Institute, Clayton, Vic., 2000.

Lukes, S., 'Five Fables About Human Rights', *Dissent*, Fall 1993, 427–37.

Lull, J., *China Turned On: Television, Reform, and Resistance*, Routledge, London, 1991.

Lutz, W., 'The Future of the World Population', *Population Bulletin*, vol. 49, no. 1, June 1994.

Lynch, D., *After the Propaganda State: Media, Politics and 'Thought Work' in Reformed China*, Stanford University Press, Stanford, 1999.

Lynn, L. H., *How Japan Innovates: A Comparison With the US in the Case of Oxygen Steelmaking*, Westview Press, Boulder, Colorado, 1982.

Lyttleton, C., 'Knowledge and Meaning: The AIDS Education Campaign in Rural Northeast Thailand', *Social Science and Medicine*, vol. 38, no. 1, 1994, 135–46.

McBeth, J., 'Company Under Siege: Mining Firm Freeport Indonesia Hits Back at Critics', *Far Eastern Economic Review*, 25 January 1996.

——'Grain Games; Grain Pains: Indonesia's Self-Sufficiency in Rice Comes Under Threat', *Far Eastern Economic Review*, 29 June 1995, 63–4.

——'Lost Labour, Lost Reform', *Far Eastern Economic Review*, 15 March 2001, 22–25.

——'Return to Roots', *Far Eastern Economic Review*, 4 June 1998, 64–5.

McBeth, J. and Cohen, M., 'Tinderbox', *Far Eastern Economic Review*, 9 January 1997, 14–15.

McCormack, G., 'Water Margins: Competing Paradigms in China', *Critical Asian Studies*, vol. 33, no. 1, 2000, 5–30.

MacGregor, B., *Live, Direct, and Biased? Making Television News in the Satellite Age*, Arnold, London, 1997.

McGurn, W., 'City Limits' *Far Eastern Economic Review*, 6 February 1997, 34–7.

McKendrick, D., 'Obstacles to "Catchup": The Case of the Indonesian Aircraft Industry', *Bulletin of Indonesian Economic Studies*, vol. 28, no. 1, April 1992, 39–66.

Mackerras, C., *China's Minorities: Integration and Modernisation in the Twentieth Century*, Oxford University Press, Oxford, 1994.

McKinnon, J., and Wanat Bhruksasri, eds, *Highlanders of Thailand*, Oxford University Press, Kuala Lumpur, 1983.

McLaren, A., *A History of Contraception: From Antiquity to the Present*, Blackwell, Oxford, 1991.

McLuhan, M., *Understanding Media: The Extensions of Man*, Routledge & Kegan Paul, London, 1964, rpt ARK Paperbacks, London, 1987.

McNeill, W. H. and Adams, R. S., eds, *Human Migration: Patterns and Policy*, Indiana University Press, Bloomington, 1978.

McNicoll, G., 'Changing Fertility Patterns and Policies in the Third World', *Annual Review of Sociology*, vol. 18, 1992, 85–108.

McPhail, T. L., *Electronic Colonialism: The Future of International Broadcasting and Communication*, 2nd edn, Sage Publications, Newbury Park, Calif., 1987.

McQueen, D.V., 'China's Impact on American Medicine in the Seventies: A Limited and Preliminary Inquiry', *Social Science and Medicine*, vol. 21, no. 8, 1985, 931–6.

Magenda, B. D., 'Ethnicity and State-Building in Indonesia', in R. Guidieri, F. Pellizzi and S. J. Tambiah, eds, *Ethnicity and Nations: Processes of Interethnic Relations in Latin America, Southeast Asia and the Pacific*, Rothko Chapel, Houston, Tex., 1988.

Mahbubani, K., 'An Asian Perspective on Human Rights and Freedom of the Press', *Media Asia*, vol. 20, no. 3, 1993, 159–66.

Majumdar, D. N., 'Household in the Matrilineal Societies of North East India', in K. Saradamoni, ed., *Finding the Household: Conceptual and Methodological Issues*, Sage Publications, New Delhi, 1992.

Malakoff, L. S., 'Are You My Mommy, or My Big Brother? Comparing Internet Censorship in Singapore and the United States', *Pacific Rim Law and Policy Journal*, vol. 8, no. 2, 1999, 423–52.

Malhotra, A., 'Gender and Changing Generational Relations: Spouse Choice in Indonesia', *Demography*, vol. 28, 1991, 549–70.

Malinee Wongsith, 'Attitudes Toward Family Values in Rural Thailand', in L. Cho and M. Yada, eds, *Tradition and Change in the Asian Family*, East West Center and University Research Center, Nihon University, Honolulu and Tokyo, 1994.

Manning, C., *Indonesian Labour in Transition: An East Asian Success Story?*, Cambridge University Press, Cambridge, 1998.

——'Labour Market Adjustment to Indonesia's Economic Crisis: Contexts, Trends, and Implications', *Bulletin of Indonesian Economic Studies*, vol. 36, no. 1, April 2001, 105–36.

Marglin, S. A., 'Towards the Decolonization of the Mind', in F. Apffel Marglin and S. A. Marglin, eds, *Dominating Knowledge: Development, Culture and Resistance*, Clarendon Press, Oxford, 1990.
Markham, A., *A Brief History of Pollution*, St Martin's Press, New York, 1994.
Martinkus, J., *A Dirty Little War*, Random House, Sydney, 2001.
Masazumi, H., 'Minamata Disease as a Social and Medical Problem', *Japan Quarterly*, vol. 25, no. 1, January–March 1978, 20–34.
Mawdudi, Abul A'la, *Human Rights in Islam*, 2nd edn, The Islamic Foundation, Leicester, 1980.
Max-Neef, M. et al., *Human-Scale Development*, Apex Press, London, 1991.
Meaher, G., 'The Internet's Impact', *Asian Communications*, March 1996, 28–32.
'Measuring the Limits of US Tolerance' and 'What Does America Demand of Indonesia?', *Economic and Business Review Indonesia*, no. 72, 28 August 1993, 6–14.
Mechai Viravaidya, Discussion at Ministerial Seminar on Population and Development, Australian Academy of Science, Canberra, 3 November 1993.
Medina, B. T. G., *The Filipino Family*, University of the Philippines Press, Quezon City, 1991.
'Megawati Grants Aceh Special Autonomy', *Canberra Times*, 14 August 2001.
Menashri, D., *Education and the Making of Modern Iran*, Cornell University Press, Ithaca, New York, 1992.
Messer-Davidow, E., Shumway, D., and Sylval, D., *Knowledges: Historical and Critical Perspectives on Disciplinarity*, University Press of Virginia, Charlottesville, 1993.
Micklin, P. P., and Williams, W. D., eds, *The Aral Sea Basin*, Springer, Berlin, 1996.
Mies, M., *Indian Women in Subsistence Agricultural Labour*, International Labour Organization, Geneva, 1986.
Miller, B. D., *The Endangered Sex: Neglect of Female Children in Rural North India*, Cornell University Press, Ithaca, New York, 1991.
Minority Rights Group, *World Directory of Minorities*, Minority Rights Group International, London, 1997.
Mishima, A., *Bitter Sea: The Human Cost of Minamata Disease*, trans. R. R. Gage and S. B. Murata, Kosei Publishers, Tokyo, 1992.
Mitchell, M., 'The Political Economy of Mekong Basin Development', in P. Hirsch and C. Warren, eds, *The Politics of the Environment in Southeast Asia*, Routledge, London, 1998.
Mitterauer, M. and Sieder, R., *The European Family*, trans. K. Oosterveen and M. Hörzinger, Blackwell, Oxford, 1982.
Moffett, G. D., *Critical Masses: The Global Population Challenge*, Viking, New York, 1994.
Moghadam, V. M., 'Rhetorics and Rights of Identity in Islamic Movements', *Journal of World History*, vol. 4, no. 2, 1993, 243–64.
Mokyr, J., *The Lever of Riches: Technological Creativity and Economic Progress*, Oxford University Press, Oxford, 1990.
Moore, C. A., ed., *The Chinese Mind: Essentials of Chinese Philosophy and Culture*, University of Hawaii Press, Honolulu, 1967.
——*The Indian Mind: Essentials of Indian Philosophy and Culture*, University of Hawaii Press, 1967.
——*The Japanese Mind: Essentials of Japanese Philosophy and Culture*, University of Hawaii Press, Honolulu, 1967.
Moore Jnr, B., *Injustice: The Social Bases of Obedience and Revolt*, M. E. Sharpe, White Plains, New York, 1978.
Morehouse, W., 'Ethics of Industrial Disasters in a Transnational World: Elusive Quest for Justice and Accountability in Bhopal', *Alternatives*, vol. 18, no. 4, Fall 1993, 475–504.
Morris-Suzuki, T., *The Technological Transformation of Japan: From the Seventeenth to the Twenty-first Century*, Cambridge University Press, Cambridge, 1994.
Mosher, S., *A Mother's Ordeal: One Woman's Fight Against China's One-Child Policy*, Brace Harcourt, New York, 1994.
Mullatti, L., 'Changing Profile of the Indian Family', in Unesco, *The Changing Family in Asia*, Unesco Principal Regional Office for Asia and the Pacific, Bangkok, 1992.
——'Families in India: Beliefs and Realities', *Journal of Comparative Family Studies*, vol. 26, no. 1, Spring 1995, 11–26.

Murphey, R., *A History of Asia*, HarperCollins, New York, 1992.

Nader, L., ed., *Naked Science: Anthropological Inquiry into Boundaries, Power, and Knowledge*, Routledge, New York, 1996.

Nagel, T., *The View From Nowhere*, Oxford University Press, Oxford, 1986.

Nakane, C., 'An Interpretation of the Size and Structure of the Household in Japan Over Three Centuries', in P. Laslett and R. Wall, eds, *Household and Family in Past Time*, Cambridge University Press, Cambridge, 1972.

Nandy, A., and Visvanathan, S., 'Modern Medicine and Its Non-Modern Critics: A Study in Discourse', in F. Apffel Marglin and S. A. Marglin, eds, *Dominating Knowledge: Development, Culture and Resistance*, Clarendon Press, Oxford, 1990.

Narain, R., 'A Floorless Exchange', *Asian Communications*, June 1996, 50–1.

Narin, F. and Olivastro, D., 'Status Report: Linkage Between Technology and Science', *Research Policy*, vol. 21, 1992, 237–49.

Natsukari, Y., 'A Structural Study of Spouse Selection in Japan', in L. Cho and M. Yada, eds, *Tradition and Change in the Asian Family*, East West Center and University Research Center, Nihon University, Honolulu and Tokyo, 1994.

Nepal: National Planning Commission, and UNICEF, *Children and Women of Nepal: A Situation Analysis 1992*, NPC and UNICEF, Kathmandu, 1992.

Nguyen Duy Thieu, 'Family Relationships of Some Ethnic Peoples in Tay Nguyen', in R. Liljestrom and Tuong Lai, eds, *Sociological Studies on the Vietnamese Family*, Social Sciences Publishing House, Hanoi, 1981.

Nicholas, C., and Singh, R., eds, *Indigenous Peoples of Asia: Many Peoples, One Struggle*, Asia Indigenous Peoples Pact, Bangkok, 1996.

Nickson, R., et al., 'Arsenic Poisoning of Bangladesh Groundwater', *Nature*, 24 September 1998, 338.

Nickum, J. E., 'Is China Living on the Water Margin?', *China Quarterly*, no. 156, December 1998, 880–98.

Nietzsche, F., *The Genealogy of Morals*, trans. F. Golffing, Doubleday, Garden City, New York, 1956.

——*The Portable Nietzsche*, trans. W. Kaufmann, Viking, New York, 1954.

'Nike Accused of Exploitation', *Canberra Times*, 29 March 1997.

Nishimura, H., ed., *How to Conquer Air Pollution*, Elsevier, Amsterdam, 1989.

Nomura, M., 'Excerpts from Shushin Koyo [Lifetime Employment]', *Japanese Economic Studies*, vol. 24, no. 1, January–February 1996 (complete issue).

'Northeast Asia', *Asian Defence Journal*, 1998, 41.

Nussbaum, M. and Glover, J., eds, *Women, Culture and Development: A Study of Human Capabilities*, Clarendon Press, Oxford, 1995.

Nussbaum, M. and Sen, A., *The Quality of Life*, Clarendon Press, Oxford, 1993.

Oberoi, H., *The Construction of Religious Boundaries: Culture, Identity and Diversity in the Sikh Tradition*, University of Chicago Press, Chicago, 1994.

O'Connor, S. J., 'Iron Working as Spiritual Inquiry in the Indonesian Archipelago', *History of Religions*, vol. 14, 1974, 173–90.

Oey-Gardiner, M., 'Schooling in a Decentralised Indonesia: New Approaches to Access and Decision Making', *Bulletin of Indonesian Economic Studies*, vol. 36, no. 3, December 2000, 127–34.

Ogawa, N. and Retherford, R. D., 'The Resumption of Fertility Decline in Japan: 1973–92', *Population and Development Review*, vol. 19, no. 4, December 1993, 703–41.

Ohlsson, L., *Hydropolitics*, Zed Books, London, 1995.

Oka, N., 'What Japan Has Left Behind in the Course of Her Modernization', *Proceedings of the Symposium on Social Perspectives of Technology Development in the Process of Modernization*, Jakarta, February 1986.

Oldenburg, P., 'Sex Ratio, Son Preference and Violence in India: A Research Note', *Economic and Political Weekly*, 5 December 1998,

Ooi Jin Bee, 'The Dimensions of the Rural Energy Problem in Indonesia', *Applied Geography*, vol. 6, 1986, 123–47.

Oon Ai, J. C., 'Civics and Moral Education in Singapore: Lessons for Citizenship Education?', *Journal of Moral Education*, vol. 27, no. 4, December 1998, 505–24.

Orenstein, H., 'The Recent History of the Extended Family in India', *Social Problems*, vol. 8, 1961, 341–50.

Organization for Economic Co-operation and Development, A *New Economy: The Changing Role of Innovation and Information Technology in Growth*, OECD, Paris, 2000.

——*Investing in Education: Analysis of the 1999 World Education Indicators*, OECD, Paris, 2000.

——*Managing National Innovation Systems*, OECD, Paris, 1999.

——*Science, Technology and Industry Outlook 2000*, OECD, Paris, 2000.

——*Technology and the Economy: The Key Relationships*, OECD, Paris, 1992.

Osborne, M., *The Mekong*, Atlantic Monthly Press, New York, 2000.

Osmani, S. R., 'Is There a Conflict Between Growth and Welfarism? The Significance of the Sri Lanka Debate', *Development and Change*, vol. 25, no. 2, April 1994, 387–421.

Ozawa, T., 'Miracle: Politics, Economics, Society, Culture and History—A Review Article', *Journal of Asian Studies*, vol. 53, no. 1, 1993, 124-32.

Packenham, R. A., *The Dependency Movement: Scholarship and Politics in Development Studies*, Harvard University Press, Cambridge, Mass., 1992.

Pakistan Information.com, 'Pakistan Statistics', http://www.pakistaninformation.com/pakistanstats.html, accessed 10 April 2002

Parapak, J. L., 'The Role of Satellite Communications in National Development: Future Trends', *Media Asia*, vol. 20, no. 1, 1993, 24–32.

Parayil, G., 'The "Kerala Model" of Development: Development and Sustainability in the Third World', *Third World Quarterly*, vol. 17, no. 5, 1996, 941–57.

Park, C. B. and Cho, N-H., 'Consequences of Son Preference in a Low-Fertility Society: Imbalance of the Sex Ratio at Birth in Korea', *Population and Development Review*, vol. 21, no. 1, March 1995, 59–84.

Park, Insook Han and Cho, Lee-Jay, 'Confucianism and the Korean Family', *Journal of Comparative Family Studies*, vol. 26, no. 1, Spring 1995, 117–34.

Park, Y. and Anderson, K., 'The Rise and Demise of Textiles and Clothing in Economic Development', *Economic Development and Cultural Change*, vol. 38, no. 3, April 1991, 531–48.

Parnwell, M. J. G. and Bryant, R. L., eds, *Environmental Change in South-East Asia: People, Politics and Sustainable Development*, Routledge, London, 1996.

Partach, K., 'Fundamental Principles of Human Rights: Self Determination, Equality and Non-Discrimination', in K. Vasak, ed., *The International Dimension of Human Rights*, vol. 2, Greenwood Press and UNESCO, Westport, Conn., and Paris, 1982.

Pasternak, B., *Marriage and Fertility in Tianjin, China: Fifty Years of Transition*, Paper No. 99, East West Population Institute, Honolulu, 1986.

Pasternak, B., Ember, C. R. and Ember, M., 'On the Conditions Favoring Extended Family Households', *Journal of Anthropological Research*, vol. 32, 1976, 109–23.

Pasuk Phongpaichit and Baker, C., *Thailand's Crisis*, Silkworm Books, Chiang Mai, 2000.

Patel, P. and Pavitt, K., 'Divergence in Technological Development Among Countries and Firms', in J. Hagendoorn, ed., *Technological Change and the World Economy*, Edward Elgar, Aldershot, 1995.

Patel, V., 'Sex-Determination and Sex Pre-Selection Tests in India: Modern Techniques of Femicide', *Bulletin of Concerned Asian Scholars*, vol. 21, no. 1, January–March 1989, 2–10.

Pavitt, K., 'International Patterns of Technological Accumulation', in N. Hood and J-E. Vahle, eds, *Strategies in Global Competition*, Croom Helm, Beckenham, 1988.

Payer, C., *Lent and Lost: Foreign Credit and Third World Development*, Zed Books, London, 1991.

Pearce, F., 'Death and the Devil's Water', *New Scientist*, 16 September 1995, 14–15.

Peattie, M., 'The Japanese Colonial Empire 1895–1945', in *The Cambridge History of Japan*, Vol. 6: *The Twentieth Century*, ed. P. Duus, Cambridge University Press, Cambridge, 1988.

Peluso, N., *Rich Forests, Poor People: Resource Control and Resistance in Java*, University of California Press, Berkeley, 1991.

Pepper, S., *China's Education Reform in the 1980s: Policies, Issues, and Historical Perspectives*, Institute of East Asian Studies, University of California at Berkeley, Berkeley, 1990.

Perrings, C. A., et al., eds, *Biodiversity Conservation: Problems and Policies*, Kluwer Academic, Dordrecht, 1994.

Phoolan Devi, with M-T. Cuny and P. Rambali, *I, Phoolan Devi: The Autobiography of India's Bandit Queen*, Little, Brown & Co., London, 1996.

Pillai, P. G., 'Higher Education in India in the 21st Century', *Social Action*, vol. 50, no. 4, 2000, 390–403.

Pinckard, E., 'Indonesian Tribe Loses in its Latest Battle Against Freeport-McMoRan, Operator of the World's Largest Gold and Copper Mine', *Colorado Journal of International Environmental Law and Policy*, vol. 9, 1998, 141–45.

Platteau, J-P., 'The Dynamics of Fisheries Development in Developing Countries: A Global Overview', *Development and Change*, vol. 20, no. 4, October 1989, 565–98.

——'Traditional Systems of Social Security and Hunger Insurance: Past Achievements and Modern Challenges', in E. Ahmad et al., *Social Security in Developing Countries*, Clarendon Press, Oxford, 1991.

Poffenberger, M., ed., *Keepers of the Forest: Land Management Alternatives in Southeast Asia*, Kumarian Press, West Hartford, Conn., 1990.

Pollak, R. A. and Watkins, S. C., 'Cultural and Economic Approaches to Fertility: Proper Marriage or Mésalliance?', *Population and Development Review*, vol. 19, no. 3, September 1993, 467–95.

Pomfret, R., *Diverse Paths of Economic Development*, Harvester Wheatsheaf, New York, 1992.

Postel, S., 'Groundwater Depletion Widespread', in L. Starke, ed., *Vital Signs 2000/2001: The Environmental Trends that are Shaping Our Future*, Earthscan, London, 2000.

Prashad, V., 'The Untouchable Question', *Economic and Political Weekly*, 2 March 1996, 551–9.

Premi, M. K., *India's Population: Heading Towards a Billion*, B. R. Publishing, Delhi, 1991.

Proctor, R., *Value-Free Science?*, Harvard University Press, Cambridge, Mass., 1992.

Psacharopolous, G., 'Returns to Investment in Education: A Global Update', *World Development*, vol. 22, no. 9, 1994, 1325–43.

'Public Enlisted to Halt Rise in Illegal Immigrants', *Sydney Morning Herald*, 28 February 1998.

Purcal, J., 'Development of Health Care Services in Rural China: Lessons for Southeast Asia', in P. Cohen and J. Purcal, eds, *The Political Economy of Primary Health Care in Southeast Asia*, Australian Development Studies Network and ASEAN Training Centre for Primary Health Care Development, Canberra, 1989.

Puri, S., and Ritzema, T., *Migrant Worker Remittances, Micro-Finance and the Informal Economy: Prospects and Issues*, International Labour Organization Working Paper no. 21, Geneva, 1999, http://www.ilo.org/public/english/employment/ent/papers/wpap21.htm, accessed 21 August 2001.

Quincey, K., *Hmong: History of a People*, Eastern Washington University Press, Cheney, Washington, 1988.

Radhakrishnan, S. and Moore, C. A., eds, *A Source Book in Indian Philosophy*, Princeton University Press, Princeton, 1957.

Radjab, Muhamad, Semasa Kecil di Kampung, trans. S. Rogers as 'Village Childhood', in S. Rogers, ed., *Telling Lives, Telling History: Autobiographical and Historical Imagination in Modern Indonesia*, University of California Press, Berkeley, 1995.

Rafferty, K., 'Quake Hits Myth of Classless Japan', *Sydney Morning Herald*, 28 January 1995.

Raina, D., 'Technological Determinism Embodied in an Appro-Tech Programme: Small Science in a High-Tech Environment', *Journal of Scientific and Industrial Research*, vol. 52, 1993, 471–82.

Raju, S. and Bagchi, D., eds, *Women and Work in South Asia: Regional Patterns and Perspectives*, Routledge, London, 1994.

Ramachandran, V. K., 'Kerala's Development Achievements: A Review', in J. Dreze and A. Sen, eds, *Indian Development: Selected Perspectives*, Oxford University Press, Delhi, 1997.

Rammohan, K. T., 'Assessing Reassessment of the Kerala Model', *Economic and Political Weekly*, 8 April 2000, 1234–6.

Rao, M., 'An Imagined Reality: Malthusianism, Neo-Malthusianism and the Population Myth', *Economic and Political Weekly*, 29 January 1994, PE-40-PE-52.

Rashiduzzaman, M., 'The Liberals and the Religious Right in Bangladesh', *Asian Survey*, vol. 34, no. 11, November 1994, 974–90.

Reardon-Anderson, J., *Pollution, Politics, and Foreign Investment in Taiwan: The Lukang Rebellion*, M. E. Sharpe, Armonk, New York, 1992.

'Reporters Without Borders Slam China's New Internet Rules', *Agence France Presse*, 5 October 2000.

Retherford, R., Ogawa, N., and Matskura, R., 'Late Marriage and Less Marriage in Japan', *Population and Development Review*, vol. 27, no. 1, March 2001, 65–102.

Riley, N. E., 'Interwoven Lives: Parents, Marriage, and Guanxi in China', *Journal of Marriage and the Family*, vol. 56, 1994, 791–803.

Rodil, B. R., and Minority Rights Group, *The Lumad and Moro of Mindanao*, Minority Rights Group, London, 1993.

Romano, A., 'The Open Wound: Keterbukaan and Press Freedom in Indonesia', *Australian Journal of International Affairs*, vol. 50, no. 2, July 1996, 157–69.

——'The Press in Indonesia: A Brief History', *Media International Australia*, no. 79, February 1996, 64-6.

Roodman, D. M., 'Tax Shifts Multiplying', in L. Starke, ed., *Vital Signs 2000/2001: The Environmental Trends that are Shaping Our Future*, Earthscan, London, 2000.

Rothstein, F. A. and Blim, M. L., eds, *Anthropology and the Global Factory: Studies of the New Industrialization in the Late Twentieth Century*, Bergin and Garvey, New York, 1992.

Rucker, R. E., 'Trends in Post-Revolutionary Iranian Education', *Journal of Contemporary Asia*, vol. 21, no. 4, 1991, 455–68.

Saadawi, N., 'Women and Islam', *Women's Studies International Forum*, vol. 5, no. 2, 1982, 193-206.

Sachs, W., ed., *The Development Dictionary: A Guide to Knowledge as Power*, Zed Books, London, 1992.

——*Global Ecology: A New Arena of Political Conflict*, Zed Books, London, 1993.

Saito, O., 'Marriage, Family Labour and the Stem Family Household: Traditional Japan in a Comparative Perspective', *Continuity and Change*, vol. 15, no. 1, May 2000, 17–45.

Salomon, J. J. and Lebeau, A., *Mirages of Development: Science and Technology for the Third Worlds*, Lynne Rienner Publishers, London, 1993.

Saltford, J., 'United Nations Involvement with the Act of Self-Determination in West Irian (Indonesian West New Guinea)', *Indonesia*, no. 69, April 2000, 71–92.

Sampat, P., 'Groundwater Quality', in L. Starke, ed., *Vital Signs 2000/2001: The Environmental Trends that are Shaping Our Future*, Earthscan, London, 2000.

Sanday, P. R., *Divine Hunger: Cannibalism as a Cultural System*, Cambridge University Press, Cambridge, 1986.

Santoso, S., 'Asia's New Little Dragon–The Real Reason for US Concern About Indonesian Workers' Rights', *Inside Indonesia*, no. 33, December 1992.

Saptari, R., 'Rural Women to the Factories: Continuity and Change in East Java's Kretek Cigarette Industry', unpublished PhD thesis, University of Amsterdam, 1995.

Saradamoni, K., 'Women, Kerala and Some Development Issues', *Economic and Political Weekly*, vol. 29, no. 9, 26 February 1994, 501–9.

——ed., *Finding the Household: Conceptual and Methodological Issues*, Sage Publications, New Delhi, 1992.

Satia, J. K. and Maru, R. M., 'Incentives and Disincentives in the Indian Family Welfare Program', *Studies in Family Planning*, vol. 17, 1986, 136–45.

Saywell, T., 'Fishing for Trouble', *Far Eastern Economic Review*, 13 March 1997, 50–4.

——'Workers' Offensive', *Far Eastern Economic Review*, 29 May 1997, 50–2.

Schendel, W. van, 'The Invention of the "Jummas": State Formation and Ethnicity in Southeastern Bangladesh' in R. H. Barnes et al., eds, *Indigenous Peoples of Asia*, Association for Asian Studies, Ann Arbor, Michigan, 1995.

Schiffler, J., 'State Policy and Economic Growth: A Note on the Hong Kong Model', *International Journal of Urban and Regional Research*, vol. 15, no. 2, 1991, 180–96.

Schlapfer, A. and Marinova, D., 'Entering the Nuclear Debate in Indonesia', *Search*, vol. 26, no. 1, January-February 1995, 18–21.

Schmidt, A., *The Loss of Australia's Aboriginal Language Heritage*, Aboriginal Studies Press, Canberra, 1993.

Schultz, T. P., ed., *Investing in Women's Human Capital*, University of Chicago Press, Chicago, 1996.

Scott, J. S., 'The Moral Economy as an Argument and a Fight', *Kajian Malaysia*, vol. 10, no. 1, June 1992, 1–19.

——*The Moral Economy of the Peasant*, Yale University Press, New Haven, 1976.

——*Weapons of the Weak*, Yale University Press, New Haven, 1985.

Seabrook, J., *Victims of Development: Resistance and Alternatives*, Verso, London, 1994.

Seagrave, S., *Lords of the Rim: The Invisible Empire of the Overseas Chinese*, Putman, New York, 1995.

Seckler, D., et al., 'Water Scarcity in the Twentyfirst Century', *Water Resources Development*, vol. 15, nos. 1–2, 1999, 29–42.

'Seen as Nation-Builder, Indonesian Resettlement Program Scrapped', http://www.cnn.com/2000/ASIANOW/southeast/12/10/settlers...nightmare.ap/, accessed 14 December 2000.

Seidman, S., *Contested Knowledge: Social Theory in the Postmodern Era*, Blackwell, Oxford, 1994.

Sen, A., *Poverty and Famines: An Essay on Entitlement and Deprivation*, Clarendon Press, Oxford, 1981.

——'More Than 100 Million Women Are Missing', *New York Review of Books*, 20 December 1990.

——'Population: Delusion and Reality', *New York Review of Books*, 22 September 1994, 62–71.

——*Development as Freedom*, Oxford University Press, New York, 1999.

——'Assessing Human Rights', in United Nations Development Program, *Human Development Report 2000*, Oxford University Press, New York, 2000.

Sen, K., and Hill, D. T., *Media, Culture and Politics in Indonesia*, Oxford University Press, Melbourne 2000.

Seth, M., *Women and Development: The Indian Experience*, Sage, New Delhi, 2001.

Shah, A. M., *The Household Dimension of the Family in India: A Field Study of a Gujarat Village and a Review of Other Studies*, University of California Press, Berkeley, 1974.

——*The Family in India: Critical Essays*, Orient Longman, Delhi, 1998.

Shapin, S., *A Social History of Truth: Civility and Science in Seventeenth-Century England*, University of Chicago Press, Chicago, 1994.

Shariff, A., *India: Human Development Report: A Profile of Indian States in the 1990s*, Oxford University Press, New York, 1999.

Sharp, M. and Pavitt, K., 'Technology Policy in the 1990s: Old Trends and New Realities', *Journal of Common Market Studies*, vol. 31, no. 2, June 1993, 129–51.

Shiva, V., *Monocultures of the Mind: Perspectives on Biodiversity and Biotechnology*, Zed Books and Third World Network, London and Penang, 1993.

——*The Violence of the Green Revolution: Third World Agriculture, Ecology and Politics*, Third World Network, Penang, 1991.

Shrivastava, P., *Bhopal: Anatomy of a Crisis*, 2nd edn, P. Chapman, London, 1992.

Shukla, P. and Chowdhry, S. R., eds, *Multinational Corporations, Technology and Development*, Akashdeep, New Delhi, 1992.

Sieghart, P., *The International Law of Human Rights*, Oxford University Press, Oxford, 1983.

Silberman, L., 'Hung Liang-Chi: a Chinese Malthus', *Population Studies*, vol. 13, no. 3, March 1960, 257–65.

Sillitoe, P., 'The Development of Indigenous Knowledge: A New Applied Anthropology', *Current Anthropology*, vol. 39, no. 2, April 1998, 223–52.

Silva, W. de, 'Ahead of Target: Achievement of Replacement Level Fertility in Sri Lanka Before the Year 2000', *Asia-Pacific Population Journal*, vol. 9, no. 4, December 1994, 3–22.

Silverman, G., 'Vital and Vulnerable', *Far Eastern Economic Review*, 23 May 1996, 61.

'Singapore and the Culture of Caning', editorial, *Sydney Morning Herald*, 7 May 1994.

Singh, A., and Weisse, B., 'The Asian Model: A Crisis Foretold?', *International Social Science Journal*, vol. 51, no. 2, 1999, 203–15.

Sivan, E., *Radical Islam: Medieval Theology and Modern Politics*, Yale University Press, New Haven, 1990.

Skinner, Q., ed., *The Return of the Grand Theory in the Human Sciences*, Cambridge University Press, Cambridge, 1985.

Smil, V., *China's Environmental Crisis: An Inquiry Into the Limits of National Development*, M. E. Sharpe, Armonk, New York, 1993.

——*Environmental Problems in China: Estimates of Economic Costs*, Special Report No. 5, East West Center, Honolulu, April 1996.

Smillie, I., *Mastering the Machine: Poverty, Aid and Technology*, Intermediate Technology Publications, London, 1991.

Smilor, R., Kosmetsky, G. and Gibson, D. V., *Creating the Technopolis: Linking Technology, Commercialisation and Economic Development*, Ballinger, Cambridge, Mass., 1988.

Smith, D., and Langslow, A. K., eds, *The Idea of a University*, J. Kingsley, London, 1999.

Smith, H. E., 'The Thai Rural Family', in M. S. Das and P. D. Bardis, eds, *The Family in Asia*, Allen & Unwin, London, 1979.

Smith, M., *Burma: Insurgency and the Politics of Ethnicity*, Zed Books, London, 1991.

Smith, S. L., *Indonesian Political Economy: Developing Batam*, Institute of Southeast Asian Studies, Singapore, 2000.

Smith, W. E. and Smith, A. M., *Minamata: Words and Photos*, Holt, Rinehart, and Winston, New York, 1975.

Snooks, G. S., *The Dynamic Society: Exploring the Sources of Global Change*, Routledge, London, 1996.

Solyom, G. and Solyom, B., *The World of the Javanese Keris*, East-West Center, Honolulu, 1978.

Sonsel, L. E., Headland, T. N., and Bailey, R. C., eds, *Tropical Deforestation: The Human Dimension*, Columbia University Press, New York, 1996.

Soros, G., 'The New Global Finance Architecture', in W. Hutton and A. Giddens, eds, *Global Capitalism*, The New Press, New York, 2000.

Spring, J., *Education and the Rise of the Global Economy*, Lawrence Erlbaum, Mahwah, New York, 1998.

Sri Lanka: Department of Census and Statistics, *Summary of Findings of Child Labour Survey in Sri Lanka, 1999*, http://www.ilo.org/public/english/standards/ipec/simpoc/srilanka/report/srilan99/index.htm, accessed 24 August 2001.

Srinivas, M. N., *The Cohesive Role of Sanskritization and Other Essays*, Oxford University Press, Delhi, 1989.

Sriram, R., 'Family Studies in India: Appraisal and New Directions', in T. S. Saraswathi and B. Kaur, eds, *Human Development and Family Studies in India: An Agenda for Research and Policy*, Sage Publications, New Delhi, 1993.

Steiner, H., and Alston, P., eds, *International Human Rights in Context: Law, Politics, Morals*, Oxford University Press, New York, 1996.

Steven, R., *Japan's New Imperialism*, Macmillan, London, 1990.

Stewart, F., *Adjustment and Poverty: Options and Choices*, Routledge, London, 1995.

——*Macro-Policies For Appropriate Technology in Developing Countries*, Westview Press, Boulder, Colo., 1987.

Stone, L. and James, C., 'Dowry, Brideburning, and Female Power in India', *Women's Studies International Forum*, vol. 18, no. 2, March–April 1995.

Stottman, W., 'The Role of the Private Sector in the Provision of Water and Wastewater Services in Urban Areas', in J. I. Uitlo and A. K. Biswas, eds, *Water for Urban Areas*, United Nations University Press, Tokyo, 2000.

'Successful Launch of AsiaSat 2', *Asian Communications*, January 1996, 5.

Suharto, President, 'Role of the Press in National Development', adapted from a speech on National Press Day, 9 February 1989, trans. S. Ramanathan and L.Y. Kam, in A. Mehra, ed., *Press Systems in Asean States*, Asia Mass Communication Research and Information Centre, Singapore, 1989, 131–4.

Sulistiyanto, P., 'Whither Aceh?', *Third World Quarterly*, vol. 22, no. 3, 2001, 437–52.

Sullivan, D. J., 'Gender Equality and Religious Freedom: Towards a Framework for Conflict Resolution', *New York University Journal of International Law and Politics*, vol. 24, no. 2, 1992, 795–856.

Sun, T. and Liu, Y. H., 'Changes in Intergenerational Relations in the Chinese Family: Taiwan's Experience', in L. Cho and M. Yada, eds, *Tradition and Change in the Asian Family*, East West Center and University Research Center, Nihon University, Honolulu and Tokyo, 1994.

Swift, A., 'Let Us Work!', *New Internationalist*, July 1997, 21–3.

Szreter, S., 'The Idea of Demographic Transition and the Study of Fertility Change: A Critical History', *Population and Development Review*, vol. 19, no. 4, December 1993, 659–701.

Taeuber, I., 'The Families of Chinese Farmers', in M. Freedman, ed., *Family and Kinship in Chinese Society*, Stanford University Press, Stanford, 1970.

Tai, H., ed., *Confucianism and Economic Development: An Oriental Alternative?* Washington Institute Press, Washington DC, 1989.

Tambiah, S. J., *Sri Lanka, Ethnic Fraticide and the Dismantling of Democracy*, University of Chicago Press, Chicago, 1986.

T'ang Chün-I, 'The T'ien Ming [Heavenly Ordinance] in Pre-Ch'in China', *Philosophy East and West*, vol. 11, no. 4, January 1962, 195–218.

Tang, J. T. H., ed., *Human Rights and International Relations in the Asia Pacific Region*, Pinter, London, 1995.

Tapp, N., *The Hmong of China: Context, Agency, and the Imaginary*, Brill, Leiden, 2001.

Tapper, R., 'Ethnic Identities and Social Categories in Iran and Afghanistan', in E. Tonkin, M. McDonald and M. Chapman, eds, *History and Ethnicity*, Routledge, London, 1989.

Tasker, R., 'Hometown Jobs', *Far Eastern Economic Review*, 14 April 1994, 24, 28.

Tendler, J., comments on K. Chowdhry, 'Poverty, Environment, Development', *Daedalus*, vol. 18, no. 1, Winter 1989.

Tesoro, J. M., 'En Route to Jakarta', *Asiaweek*, vol. 24, no. 35, 4 September 1998, 26–7.

Thapa, S., 'The Human Development Index: A Portrait of the 75 Districts in Nepal', *Asia-Pacific Population Journal*, vol. 10, no. 2, June 1995.

Tharamangalam, J., 'The Perils of Social Development Without Economic Growth: The Development Debacle of Kerala, India', *Bulletin of Concerned Asian Scholars*, vol. 30, no. 1, January 1998, 23–34.

——'A Rejoinder', *Bulletin of Concerned Asian Scholars*, vol. 30, no. 4, October–December 1998, 47–52.

Thompson, H., 'Malaysian Forest Policy in Borneo', *Journal of Contemporary Asia*, vol. 23, no. 4, 1993, 503–14.

Tien, H.Y., *China's Strategic Demographic Initiative*, Praeger, New York, 1991.

Tiglao, R., 'The Fire Next Time', and 'Commissar of the Faithful', *Far Eastern Economic Review*, 28 March 1996, 26–30.

——'Return to Arms: Insurgent Group Drags Mindanao Back to Mayhem', *Far Eastern Economic Review*, 24 July 1997, 32.

Tinker, I., ed., *Persistent Inequalities: Women and World Development*, Oxford University Press, New York, 1990.

Tomlinson, J., *Cultural Imperialism: A Critical Introduction*, Pinter, London, 1991.

Toynbee, P., 'Who's Afraid of Global Culture?', in W. Hutton and A. Giddens, eds, *Global Capitalism*, New Press, New York, 2000.

Tran Quang Co, 'Rights and Values', *Far Eastern Economic Review*, 4 August 1994.

Triolo, P. S. and Lovelock, P., 'Up, Up, and Away—With Strings Attached', *China Business Review*, November-December 1996, 18–29.

Tsien, Tsuen-Hsuin, *Paper and Printing*, pt 1, in *Science and Civilisation in China*, vol. 5, ed. J. Needham, Cambridge University Press, Cambridge, 1985.

Tsurumi, E. P., *Factory Girls: Women in the Thread Mills of Meiji Japan*, Princeton University Press, Princeton, 1990.

Tsuya, N. O., 'Changing Attitudes Towards Marriage and the Family in Japan', in L. Cho and M. Yada, *Tradition and Change in the Asian Family*, East West Center and University Research Center, Nihon University, Honolulu and Tokyo, 1994.

Tu Wei-Ming, *Confucian Traditions in East Asian Modernity: Moral Education and Economic Culture in Japan and the Four Mini-Dragons*, Harvard University Press, Cambridge, Massachusetts, 1996.

Turnbull, D., *Masons, Tricksters and Cartographers: Comparative Studies in the Sociology of Scientific and Indigenous Knowledge*, Harwood Academic, Amsterdam, 2000.

Twining, W., *Globalisation and Legal Theory*, Butterworths, London, 2000.

'Ugly Dimensions of New Censorship', editorial, *Canberra Times*, 29 May 1995.

Unger, J., 'Rich Man, Poor Man: The Making of New Classes in the Countryside', in D. S. G. Goodman and B. Hooper, eds, *China's Quiet Revolution*, Longman Cheshire, Melbourne, 1994.

United Nations, *Teaching Human Rights*, UN Publication, sales no. 63 I, 34, 1958.

United Nations Development Program, *China: Human Development Report*, Oxford University Press, New York, 1999.

——*Human Development Report 1994*, Oxford University Press, New York, 1994.

——*Human Development Report 1995*, Oxford University Press, New York, 1995.

——*Human Development Report 1996*, Oxford University Press, New York, 1996.

——*Human Development Report 2000*, Oxford University Press, New York, 2000.

——*Human Development Report 2001*, Oxford University Press, New York, 2001. Available on-line at http://www.undp.org/hdr2001/.

United Nations Economic and Social Commission for Asia and the Pacific, and the Asian Development Bank, *State of the Environment in Asia and the Pacific 1995*, UNESCAP, Bangkok, 1995.

United Nations, Economic and Social Council, Commission on Human Rights, *Adverse Effects of the Illicit Movement and Dumping of Toxic and Dangerous Products and Wastes on the Enjoyment of Human Rights*, http://www.unhchr.ch/Huridocda/Huridoca/nsf/TestFrame/7740a5eb74ab0c728025666a...

United Nations Environment Program, *Global Biodiversity Assessment*, Cambridge University Press, Cambridge, 1995.

——*Global Environment Outlook 2000*, http://www.unep.org/geo2000/english/, accessed 29 August 2001.

United Nations, Office of the High Commissioner for Human Rights, *International Human Rights Instruments*, http://www.unhchr.ch/html/intlist.htm.

United Nations Population Division, *Revision of the World Population Estimates and Projections (1998)*, http://www.popin.org/pop1998/, accessed 13 September 2001.

——*World Urbanization Prospects: The 1999 Revision*, http://www.un.org/esa/population/urbanization.htm, accessed 19 July 2001.

United Nations Population Fund, *The State of the World Population 2000: Lives Together, Worlds Apart*, http://www.unfpa.org/swp/swpmain.htm, accessed 13 September 2001.

United Nations World Conference on Human Rights, 14–25 June 1993, *Vienna Declaration and Program of Action*, section 2, paragraph 38, http://www.unchr.ch.huridocda.huridoca.nsf/(symbol)A.CONF.157.23.En?OpenDocument, accessed 10 August 2001.

Unschuld, P., *Medicine in China: A History of Pharmaceutics*, University of California Press, Berkeley, 1986.

'Upbeat Tempo', *The Economist*, 6 May 1995.

Valencia, M. J., van Dyke, J. M., and Ludwig, N. A., *Sharing the Resources of the South China Sea*, Martinus Nijhoff, The Hague, 1997.

Varennes, F. de, ed., *Asia-Pacific Human Rights Documents and Resources*, Vol. 2, Kluwer Law International, The Hague, 2000.

Vatuk, S., 'Household Form and Formation: Variability and Social Change Among South Indian Muslims', in J. D. Gray and D. J. Mearns, eds, *Society From the Inside Out: Anthropological Perspectives on the South Asian Household*, Sage Publications, New Delhi, 1989.

Vermeer, E. B., 'Industrial Pollution in China and Remedial Policies', *China Quarterly*, no. 156, December 1998, 952–85.

Veron, R., 'The "New" Kerala Model: Lessons for Sustainable Development', *World Development*, vol. 29, no. 4, 2001, 601–27.

Vig, N. J., 'Technology, Philosophy, and the State: An Overview', in M. E. Kraft and N. J. Vig, eds, *Technology and Politics*, Duke University, Durham, 1988.

Visaria, L. and Visaria, P., 'India's Population in Transition', *Population Bulletin*, vol. 50, no. 3, October 1995, complete issue.

Vitug, M. D., 'The Politics of Logging in the Philippines', in P. Hirsch and C. Warren, eds, *The Politics of the Environment in Southeast Asia*, Routledge, London, 1998.

Vogel, E., *The Four Little Dragons: The Spread of Industrialization in East Asia*, Harvard University Press, Cambridge, Mass., 1991.

Volker, A., 'The Sea of Global Finance', in W. Hutton and A. Giddens, eds, *Global Capitalism*, New Press, New York, 2000.

Waal, F. de, *Good Natured: The Origins of Right and Wrong in Humans and Other Animals*, Harvard University Press, Cambridge, Mass., 1996.

Wade, R., *Governing the Market: Economic Theory and the Role of the Government in East Asian Industrialisation*, Princeton University Press, Princeton, 1990.

Wadley, S., 'Family Composition Strategies in Rural Northern India', *Social Science and Medicine*, vol. 37, no. 11, 1993, 1367–76.

Wallerstein, I., *The Modern World-System*, Academic Press, New York, 1974.

Walther, W., *Women in Islam*, trans. C. S.V. Salt, Marcus Wiener, New York, 1993.

Wang, G., 'Satellite Television and the Future of Broadcast Television in the Asia-Pacific', *Media Asia*, vol. 20, no. 3, 1993, 140–8.

Wang, G. T., *China's Population: Problems, Thoughts and Policies*, Ashgate, Aldershot, 1999.

Wang Hongchang, 'Afforestation Problems in China's Ecological Economics', *Social Sciences in China*, Spring 1993, 165–77.

Wang Ping, *Aching for Beauty: Footbinding inChina*, University of Minnesota Press, Minneapolis, 2000.

Watanabe, S., 'The Japanese Model and the Future of Employment and Wage Systems', *International Labour Review*, vol. 139, no. 3, 2000, 307–33.

Waters, B., 'The Tragedy of Marsinah: Industrialisation and Workers' Rights', *Inside Indonesia*, no. 36, September 1993, 12–13.

*Watershed*, published by Towards Ecological Recovery and Regional Alliance (TERRA), Bangkok.

Webb, E., 'Debt For Nature Swaps', *Environmental and Planning Law Journal*, vol. 11, no. 3, June 1994, 222–4.

Wehfritz, G., 'Green Heat', *Newsweek*, 8 October 1996, 75–9.

Weinstein, M. et al., 'Household Composition, Extended Kinship, and Reproduction in Taiwan, 1965–1985', *Population Studies*, vol. 44, no. 2, 1990, 217–39.

'West Papua: Towards a New Papua', Special Issue, *Inside Indonesia*, no. 67, July–September 2001.

Whyte, M. K., 'Changes in Mate Choice in Chengdu', in D. Davis and E.Vogel, eds, *Chinese Society on the Eve of Tiananmen*, Council on East Asian Studies, Harvard University, 1990.

Wijeyewardene, G., ed., *Ethnic Groups Across National Boundaries in Mainland Southeast Asia*, Institute of Southeast Asian Studies, Singapore, 1990.

Wild, C., 'The Radio Midwife: Some Thoughts on the Role of Broadcasting During the Indonesian Struggle for Independence', *Indonesia Circle*, no. 55, 1991, 34–42.

Wilk, R. R. and Netting, R. M., 'Households: Changing Forms and Functions', in R. M. Netting, R. R. Wilk and E. J. Arnould, eds, *Households: Comparative and Historical Studies of the Domestic Group*, University of California Press, Berkeley, 1984.

Williams, B., *Ethics and the Limits of Philosophy*, Harvard University Press, Cambridge, Mass., 1985.

Williams, L., 'Muslim Rampage Tears Indonesia Apart', *Sydney Morning Herald*, 1 February 1997.

——'Villagers' Lives Eaten Away By the River of Death', *Sydney Morning Herald*, 7 December 1996.

Won, W., 'The Social and Cultural Impact of Satellite Broadcasting in Korea', *Media Asia*, vol. 21, no. 1, 1993, 15–20.

Woo, W. T., Sachs, J. D., and Schwab, K., eds, *The Asian Financial Crisis: Lessons from a Resilient Asia*, MIT Press, Cambridge, Mass., 2000.

World Bank, *The East Asian Miracle: Economic Growth and Public Policy*, Oxford University Press, New York, 1993.

——*Entering the 21st Century: World Development Report 1999/2000*, Oxford University Press, New York, 2000.

——'HIPC Initiative', http://www.worldbank.org/hipc/, accessed 7 September 2001.

——'World Bank Sees "Localization" As Major New Trend in 21st Century', http://www.worldbank.org/html/extdr/extme/032.htm, accessed 7 September 2001.

——*World Development Indicators 2001*, http://www.worldbank.org/data/wdi2001/pdfs, accessed 10 April 2002.

World Commission on Dams, *Dams and Development: A New Framework for Decision-Making*, Earthscan, London, 2000.

World Health Organization, *Primary Health Care, The Chinese Experience: Reports of an Inter-Regional Seminar*, World Health Organization, Geneva, 1983.

Wu, D., 'Complex Households, a Fading Glory: Household Formation During the Collective Period in the People's Republic of China', *Journal of Family History*, vol. 25, no. 4, October 2000, 527–44.

Wu Naitao, 'China Contributes to Reducing Global Population Pressure', *Beijing Review*, 29 January–4 February 1996, 4.

Xie Zhenming, 'Population Policy and the Family-Planning Programme', in Peng Xizhe and Guo Zhigang, eds, *The Changing Population of China*, Blackwell, Oxford, 2000.

Xu Xiaohe and Whyte, M. K., 'Love Matches and Arranged Marriage: A Chinese Replication', *Journal of Marriage and the Family*, vol. 52, 1990, 709–22.

Yap, M. T., 'Singapore's "Three or More" Policy: The First Five Years', *Asia-Pacific Population Journal*, vol. 10, no. 4, December 1995, 39–52.

Yasuaki, O., 'Interplay Between Human Rights Activities and Legal Standards of Human Rights: A Case Study of the Korean Minority in Japan', *Cornell International Law Journal*, vol. 25, no. 3, Symposium 1992, 515–40.

Yip, J. S. K. and Kooi, S. W., *Evolution of Educational Excellence: 25 Years of Education in the Republic of Singapore*, Longman, Singapore, 1990.

Yunus, M., *Banker to the Poor: The Autobiography of Muhammad Yunus*, Aurum Press, London, 1998.

Zachariah, K. C., Mathews, E. T., and Rajan, S. I., 'Social, Economic and Demographic Consequences of Migration on Kerala', *International Migration*, vol. 39, no. 2, June 2001, 43–71.

Zainal Kling, 'The Malay Family: Beliefs and Realities', *Journal of Comparative Family Studies*, vol. 26, no. 1, Spring 1995, 43–66.

Zang Xiaowei, 'Household Structure and Marriage in Urban China: 1900–1982', *Journal of Comparative Family Studies*, vol. 24, no. 1, Spring 1993, 35–44.

Zeng Yi et al., 'Causes and Implications of the Recent Increase in the Reported Sex Rate at Birth in China', *Population and Development Review*, vol. 19, no. 2, June 1993, 283–302.

Zhan Chengxu, 'Matriarchal/Patriarchal Families of the Naxi Nationality in Yongning, Yunnan Province', *Social Sciences in China*, March 1982, 140–55.

——'Yongning Naxi Azhu Marriage and Matrilineal Household', *Chinese Sociology and Anthropology*, vol. 25, no. 4, Summer 1993, 25–38.

Zhao, Z., 'Coresidential Patterns in Historical China: A Simulation Study', *Development and Population Review*, vol. 26, no. 2, June 2000, 263–93.

Zhong Fenggan, 'Urbanization', in Peng Xizhe and Guo Zhigang, eds, *The Changing Population of China*, Blackwell, Oxford, 2000.

Ziman, J., *Real Science: What it is, and What it Means*, Cambridge University Press, Cambridge, 2000.

# INDEX


Abernethy, Virginia 154
Aboriginal Australians 106
Abul A'la Mawdudi 77
air pollution 28, 178, 186–7
Ambedkar, Dr B.R. 33
Amnesty International 65
An-Na'im, Abdullahi Ahmed 79
Aral Sea 185
Asia:
  characteristics 1–5
  culture 1, 3–4, 5, 9–10, 28–9, 34, 40–2, 71–4, 107–9, 267–74
  financial crisis 114, 144
  geography 3–4
  and globalisation 24
  issues and disciplines 5–7
  maps 14–15
  'monsoon' 3, 4, 23
  pre-modern societies 1, 43, 210–12
  societies 1–2, 4–5, 12, 13, 30–1, 43, 57, 89, 109, 203, 210–12, 225, 276, 290
  values 3, 57, 74–8, 81, 89, 135, 136, 142–4, 225, 266
Asian Development Bank 127, 138, 194
Asia-Pacific region 76
Aung San 21
Aung San Suu Kyi 65, 74, 77
autonomy and development 144–5

Bangkok Declaration 69, 70, 72, 76
Bangladesh 23, 54, 86, 106, 127, 148, 154, 166, 194, 196, 212, 214, 227, 247
Bhutto, Zulfikar Ali 23
biodiversity, loss of 28, 35–6, 190–1
Buddhism 33, 40, 43, 47–8, 51, 55, 60, 74, 76–7, 202, 208
Burma *see* Myanmar (Burma)

Caldwell, Jack 153, 155
Cambodia 20
capitalism 32–3, 138, 142
care and family 205–6
censorship 261–4, 272
Chen Shui-bian 19
Chiang Kai-shek 19
China:
  agriculture 117
  communication 256, 259–60, 263, 273
  economy 32–3, 132, 133–4, 239, 244
  education 58, 290–3
  employment 231, 239, 243, 290–3
  environment 183–5, 189, 194, 195
  ethnic minorities 89, 90–3, 101–3
  families 212, 213, 214, 216, 219
  fertility control 167–71
  government 19, 38, 61, 62
  households 208, 210, 211
  human development 135, 145
  human rights 70
  innovation 198
  and knowledge 30
  life expectancy 27
  marriage 219, 222–3
  national identity 35
  political culture 57, 61
  population 27, 101, 147, 148, 150–1, 158–60, 162, 167–71, 198, 243, 244
  society 45, 47, 53, 54, 57, 62, 89
  women 45, 158–9

Christianity 33, 43, 47, 51, 55, 74, 202
civil disobedience 56
civil society 62–3
colonialism 24, 89, 100, 176
  electronic 28–9
communication 10
  and cultural imperialism 267–74
  and information technology 28–9
  and knowledge 283–5
  state control of 268–72, 274–5
communism 19–21, 111, 112
Confucianism 40, 41, 44, 47–8, 49, 51, 55, 62, 77, 89, 142–4, 208
constitutionalism 60–1
consumption 161–2, 174, 206
cross-cultural identities 40
cross-cultural influences 3
cross-cultural understanding 1, 10, 52, 73
cultural imperialism 267–74
culture:
  assumptions of human rights 71–4
  change 28–9, 41–2, 110
  defined 40–2
  distinctiveness 107–9
  globalisation 30
  insulation 34
  political and legal 57–60
  and population 156–7
  values 5, 9–10
  Western 74, 269–70

Dalai Lama 32, 76–7, 97, 301
Daoism 55, 62, 202
Darwin, Charles 8, 150
Davis, Kingsley 152, 153
decolonisation 24, 39
Debt for Nature Swaps 201
deforestation 28, 177, 185, 186, 189–90
demographic change 27, 28, 119, 215–17
demographic transition 27, 152–6, 203
  *see also* population
Deng Xiaoping 19
development 111–13
  paths 126–34
  single path 119–21
  social 113, 121–6, 144–5
  trends 113–19
  *see also* economic, development; human development
Donnelly, Jack 72

East Timor 32, 86, 97
economic(s)
  development 13, 27, 32–3, 58, 86, 113–21, 126–38, 174, 203, 231, 233, 245–6
  and globalisation 26–7, 32–3, 233, 244–5
  growth 32–3, 126–34, 239, 246, 249
  production and consumption 206
education 30, 54, 58, 87, 88, 124, 130, 152, 157, 214, 237, 238, 287–98
electronic colonialism 28–9
employment 226–7, 239–44
  and changing opportunities 231–3
  international migration 244–7
  mobility 236–9
  women 54, 118, 124, 152, 214–15, 231–3, 290–1
  *see also* labour
environment 35–6
  and global economy 173–6
  and globalisation 28
environmental impact of industrialisation 127, 177–8
environmental issues 28, 58–9, 176–9, 183–96, 201–2
environmentalism, grassroots 195, 197–8
equality and ethnicity 88–95
ethnic groups 37–40
ethnic identity 39–40, 82, 94–5, 103–6, 109–10
ethnic minorities 12, 32–4, 54–5, 82–8, 89, 90–5, 101–3, 231
  and self-determination 95–7
ethnic tensions 266
ethnicity and equality 88–95

families:
  and affection 206
  contemporary ideals 224–5
  and globalisation 28
  households 204–5, 208–12
  modern shift 212–13
  and reproduction 205
  socio-political function of 207–8
  structure and functions 3, 28, 73, 155–6, 203, 217
  and transmission 206–7
  units 3, 73, 205–12, 217
family planning programs 30, 59, 151, 171–2
fertility:
  change 156–7
  control 88, 149, 150–2, 161, 163–7
  control in China 167–71
  rates 152–6, 165
  trends 174
  *see also* women

forests *see* deforestation
Freud, Sigmund 8

Gandhi, Indira 22, 46, 105
Gandhi, Mohandas 23, 56, 62, 128, 195, 196, 198–9, 230
gender:
  equality 224
  inequalities 3, 53–4, 73–4, 118, 224, 290–1
General Agreement on Tariffs and Trade (GATT) 27, 138, 248
global economy 67, 173–6
globalisation 3, 12, 17, 36, 37
  aspects of 24–30
  and communications technology 28–9
  contexts of 18–24
  cultural 30
  and economics 26–7, 32–3, 233, 244–5
  and environment 28, 174
  and families 28
  and human rights 25–6
  and population trends 27
  reactions to 30–1
  science and technology 29–30, 276
Goodenough, Ward 42
gross domestic product (GDP) 121, 122, 124
Gulf War 24

Habibie, Dr B.J. 32, 97, 139–40, 265
Han Fei 142
health, public 58
Hegel, G.W.F. 62
Hinduism 22, 33, 41, 43, 47–8, 49, 51, 55, 60, 93, 100, 208, 221
Hong Kong 19, 115, 119, 138, 147, 160, 215, 216, 227
households:
  pre-modern Asian societies 210–12
  structures 3, 28, 73, 155–6, 203, 204–5, 208–10, 215–17
human capital 233–6
human development 113, 134–5, 145, 227
Human Development Index (HDI) 121–6, 128
human needs 10–12
human rights 12, 59–60, 255, 262
  complexity of 64–8
  defined 68–71
  and globalisation 25–6
  and labour 66–8, 248, 254, 262
  perspective 80–1
  religious and moral traditions 78–80
Human Rights Watch 65
Hussein, Saddam 24

India:
  caste system 52, 53–4, 72, 100–1
  economy 114, 124–5, 129, 239
  employment 124–5, 127
  environment 183–4, 185, 186, 189, 190, 193, 194, 195, 196
  ethnic identity 21–2, 40, 105–6
  ethnic minorities 84, 86, 100–1, 105–6
  families 209, 213, 214, 217, 219, 225
  government 38, 72
  industrialisation 128, 195, 196, 198–9, 230, 231
  marriage 219
  political culture 57
  population 147, 148, 156–7, 158, 160, 162, 165, 166, 196
  religion 21–2, 33, 40, 46, 105–6
  science and technology 30
  social security 229
  society 62, 124–5
  women 158, 214–15
indigenous peoples 55, 97–103, 233
Indonesia:
  communication 257
  and communism 20–1
  economy 139–41, 239, 244
  employment 66–7, 231, 243, 248–9
  environment 86, 117, 176–9, 190
  and ethnic groups 32, 38, 54, 62, 83–4, 89–90, 97, 266
  human development 125
  human rights 66–7
  politics 32
  population 83–4, 147, 148, 157, 167, 243, 244
  social security 59
  society 32, 38, 59, 62, 266
  technology 139–41
industrialisation 26, 33, 127, 177–83, 195, 196, 198, 203, 214, 226, 231, 233–4, 239, 244, 246
inequality 36, 52–5, 73–4, 106, 116, 118, 290
information technology 28–9
innovation 198–9, 202
insulation 12, 17, 31–6, 37
International Court of Justice 25
International Covenant on Civil and Political Rights 25, 69, 70, 71, 95, 163, 164, 262
International Covenant on Economic, Social and Cultural Rights 25, 69, 95

International Labour Organisation (ILO) 25, 66, 127, 248, 251
International Monetary Fund (IMF) 27, 114, 119–20, 126, 136–4, 150
Internet 28, 260
Iran 23–4, 33, 46, 57, 61, 85, 165, 294, 268–9
Iraq 23–4, 85
Irian Jaya (West Papua) 12, 32, 83, 90, 97, 148
Islam 33, 40, 41, 43, 47–8, 51, 55, 74, 77, 166, 202, 208, 221, 293–4

Japan:
- economy 18, 119, 120, 125, 143, 239, 243–4
- education 58
- employment 227, 231–2, 238, 239
- environment 58, 179–83, 191–2, 194
- ethnic minorities 54–5
- families 211, 215–16, 219, 221
- and globalisation 20–1, 30
- industrialisation 179–83
- marriage 219, 221, 222
- population 148, 243–4
- religion 33, 46, 47
- social security 59
- society 52–3
- technology 119–20
- women 231–2

Java 83, 89, 176–9, 229, 231
Jews 47

Kamenka, Eugene 72
Kant, Immanuel 62
Kerala (India) 33, 130–1, 132, 133–4, 145, 157
Khomeini, Ayatollah 23, 165, 257
knowledge:
- and change 297–8
- and communication 283–5
- defined 7, 276
- and globalisation 30, 276
- and society 255
- universal 281–3
- Western scientific 29–30, 35–6, 276, 285–7, 288

Kolenda, Pauline 213
Korea *see* North Korea; South Korea
Korean War 143
Kurds 85, 109
Kuwait 24

labour:
- child 250–4
- and human rights 66–8, 248, 254, 262
- migration, international 244–7
- rights and conditions 66–8, 248–50
- *see also* employment

language 42, 82, 83, 87–8, 91, 106
Laos 32, 84, 89, 91, 94, 97, 127, 148, 231
late-developing countries 67
law and morality 55–7
League of Nations 96
legal cultures 57–60
literacy 88, 130
Locke, John 74
Lu Xun 35
Lukes, Steven 72

Mahathir, Prime Minister 88, 265, 266
Malaysia:
- deforestation 117
- economy 58, 114, 157
- employment 227, 246
- environment 182–3
- ethnic minorities 55, 88, 93, 157, 266, 294
- families 213, 221
- globalisation 182–3
- human rights 70, 75–6
- population 157
- urbanisation 213–14

Malthus, Thomas 150–1, 161–2, 175
Mao Zedong 164
Marcos, Ferdinand 56
marriage 73, 78, 218–24
Marx, Karl 8, 45, 62, 270
Marxism 38, 62, 74, 90
media 264–7
- mass 28–9, 255

Mirza Ghirlan Ahmad 106
Mongolia 47
Moore, Barrington Jnr 10–11
morality and law 55–7
Muhammad Yunus 127
Murdoch, Rupert 263
Murphey, Rhoads 3, 5
Musharraf, General Pervez 23
Myanmar (Burma) 12, 21, 32, 38, 65–6, 84–5, 86, 97, 106, 227

Narak, Guru 105
Nasreen, Taslima 52
national identity 33–5, 271
nationalism 37–40
nation-building and the media 264
Nehru, Jawaharlal 46, 128
Nepal 54, 148
newly industrialised Asian countries 138
Nietzsche, Friedrich 8, 42, 44

North Korea 19, 32, 38, 82, 231
Notestein, Frank 153

Organisation for Economic Cooperation and Development (OECD) 29–30

Pakistan 22–3, 38, 87, 93, 106, 114, 148, 186, 188, 189, 196, 212, 247
Philippines 4, 38, 86, 114, 124, 148, 212, 241–2, 247
political culture 57–60
political order 24, 25, 60–1
population:
- and cultural factors 156–7
- control and the state 149
- growth 13, 88, 146–8, 160–3, 174
- scale of change 146–8
- transfer 87
- trends and globalisation 27
- *see also* demographic; fertility

propaganda 261–4, 272
Protestantism 142
punishment and society 72–3

religion 43
- functions and family 207
- India 21–2, 33, 40, 46, 105–6
- Japan 33, 46, 47
- and society 33–4, 46–52
- South Korea 33, 46, 47

reproduction *see* fertility
Reza Shah, Mohammed 23, 33, 46, 56
Reza Shah Pahlavi 33, 46
Roosevelt, Eleanor 68
Rousseau, Jean-Jacques 74

science and technology 29–30
- internationalisation of 35–6, 276–8

Sen, Amartya 134, 135
sexuality 221
Shang Yang 142
Shiva, Vandana 35–6
Sikhs 22, 40, 105–6
Singapore:
- communications 260
- economy 119, 138
- education 294, 296
- employment 227
- ethnic tension 266, 294
- households 215
- human rights 72, 75–6
- population 157, 164
- technology 115

social class 45, 53–4
social development 113, 121–6, 144–5
social justice 199–201
social marginalisation 86
social order 60–1
social rules 44–5, 55–7, 89
social security 59, 229
societies 42–4, 210–12, 224
society:
- Asian 1–2, 4–5, 12, 13, 30–1, 43, 57, 89, 109, 203, 210–12, 225, 276, 290
- civil 62–3
- difference and inequality 52–5
- and punishment 72–3
- and religion 33–4, 46–52
- Western 1, 63, 155, 203, 224

socio-political functions and family 207–8
soil degradation 188–9
South Korea:
- agriculture 117
- communication 272
- economy 58, 114–15, 119–20, 136–7, 138
- employment 139, 227, 246
- environment 192
- globalisation 19
- households 212, 215
- industrialisation 246
- marriage 219, 221
- nationalism 38
- politics 57
- population 148, 140–1, 158, 160
- religion 33, 46, 47
- technology 30
- women 54, 232

Sri Lanka 32, 96, 97, 127, 129–30, 132, 133–4, 145, 148, 153–4, 186, 195, 254
State, the 37–40, 61–2
Suharto, President 21, 140, 265
Sukarno, President 164
Sukarnoputri, Meagwati 84

Taiwan 19, 117, 138, 139, 147, 158, 160, 215
technoglobalism 29–30
technology 139–41
- change and communication 256–61
- communications 274–5
- convergence and divergence 278–9
- development 231, 175–6
- and globalisation 28–30, 276–8
- internationalisation of 35, 276–8
- and population redistribution 243–4
- in South Asia 128
- transfer 278, 279–81

Thailand 58, 59, 61, 91, 97–8, 114, 117, 127, 147, 166–7, 212, 213, 240, 246

Third World countries 12, 27, 33, 79, 112, 114–15, 118–19, 125, 126, 132, 145, 150, 151, 153–8, 193, 218, 277
Tibet 19, 32, 47, 86, 91, 97
trade barriers 26, 138
  *see also* General Agreement on Tariffs and Trade (GATT)
Truman, Harry 111–13

unemployment 227–30
United Nations (UN) 10, 18, 24–5, 27, 38, 65
United Nations Development Program (UNDP) 27, 113, 227
Universal Declaration and the Convention on the Elimination of All Forms of Discrimination Against Women 73
Universal Declaration of Human Rights (UDHR) 65, 68, 71, 72, 74, 76, 78, 80, 163
urbanisation 203, 213–14, 218, 225, 226, 241–3

values
  Asian 3, 5, 9–10, 57, 74–8, 81, 89, 135, 136, 142–4, 225, 266
  Western 71, 74–8, 81, 126
Vatuk, Sylvia 217
Vietnam 20, 32, 38, 54, 56, 87, 89, 90, 91, 97, 135, 147, 231, 243
Vietnam War 143

Wallerstein, Immanuel 121
Wang Shiduo 151
wastes 191
water pollution 177, 183–6
Weber, Max 61–2, 142
Western culture 74, 269–70
Western individualism 75
Western knowledge 30
Western scientific knowledge 29–30, 35–6, 276, 285–7, 288
Western societies 1, 63, 155, 203, 224
Western values 71, 74–8, 81, 126
Westernisation 1, 31, 33, 63, 107, 162, 198
West Papua *see* Irian Jaya
Wilson, President 96
women
  China 45, 158–9
  education 54, 130, 152, 214
  employment 54, 118, 124, 152, 214–15, 231–3, 290–1
  female infanticide 157–60
  human rights 157–60, 163
  India 158, 214–15
  inequality 3, 54, 118, 224, 290–1
  Japan 231–2
work *see* employment
World Bank 27, 114, 119–20, 126, 127, 137, 150, 194
World Health Organisation (WHO) 132
World Trade Organisation 27, 248, 254

Yugoslavia 96

Zia, General ul Haq 23